June 13–16, 2011
Pisa, Italy

Association for
Computing Machinery

Advancing Computing as a Science & Profession

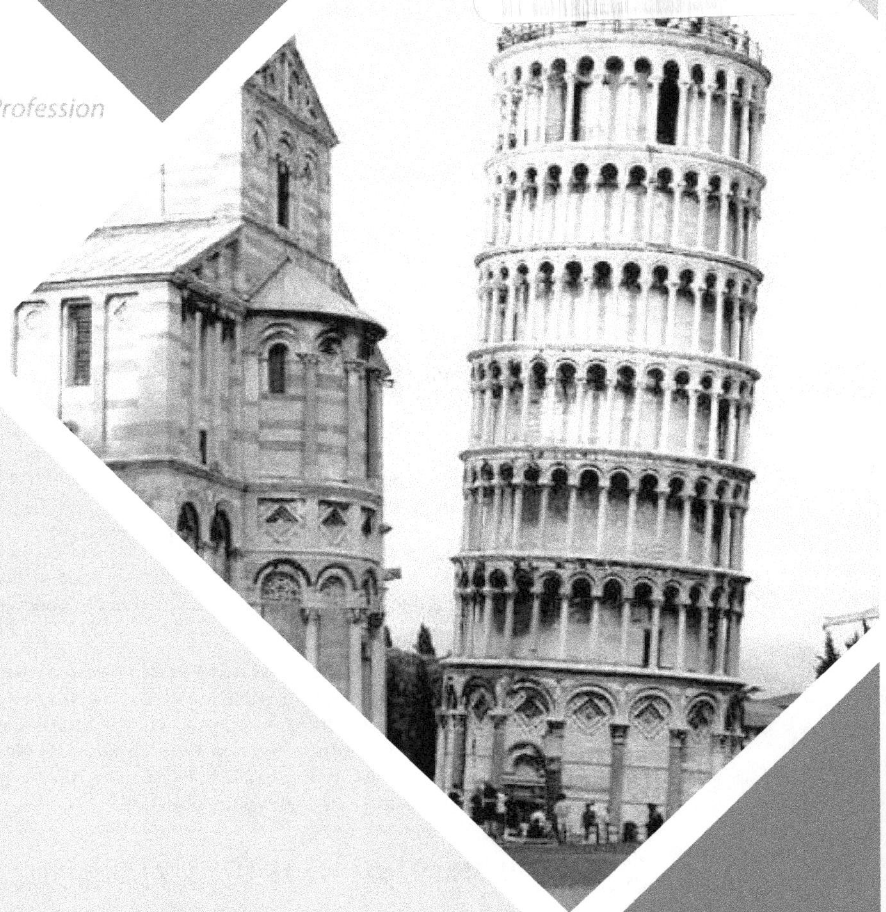

EICS 2011

Proceedings of the 2011 SIGCHI Symposium on

Engineering Interactive Computing Systems

Sponsored by:

ACM SIGCHI

Supported by:

HIIS Laboratory and ifip wg 2.7/13.4 on user interface engineering

Association for
Computing Machinery

Advancing Computing as a Science & Profession

The Association for Computing Machinery
2 Penn Plaza, Suite 701
New York, New York 10121-0701

Notice to Past Authors of ACM-Published Articles
ACM intends to create a complete electronic archive of all articles and/or other material previously published by ACM. If you have written a work that has been previously published by ACM in any journal or conference proceedings prior to 1978, or any SIG Newsletter at any time, and you do NOT want this work to appear in the ACM Digital Library, please inform permissions@acm.org, stating the title of the work, the author(s), and where and when published.

ISBN: 978-1-4503-0778-9 (Digital)

ISBN: 978-1-4503-1386-5 (Print)

Additional copies may be ordered prepaid from:

ACM Order Department
PO Box 30777
New York, NY 10087-0777, USA

Phone: 1-800-342-6626 (USA and Canada)
+1-212-626-0500 (Global)
Fax: +1-212-944-1318
E-mail: acmhelp@acm.org
Hours of Operation: 8:30 am – 4:30 pm ET

Printed in the USA

Foreword

It is our great pleasure to welcome you to the *3rd ACM SIGCHI Symposium on Engineering Interactive Computing Systems – EICS'11* held in Pisa (13-16 June 2011). EICS is an international conference devoted to all aspects of engineering usable and effective interactive computing systems, ranging from graphical interactive systems to those involving new and emerging modalities (e.g. gesture), environments (e.g. ubiquitous ones) and development methods (e.g. model-based design and development).

EICS focuses on tools, techniques and methods for designing and developing interactive systems. EICS brings together people who study or practice the engineering of interactive systems, drawing from Human-Computer Interaction (HCI), Software Engineering, Requirements Engineering, Computer-Supported Collaborative Work (CSCW), Ubiquitous & Pervasive Systems, and Cognitive Engineering fields. EICS encompasses the former conferences and workshops EHCI (Engineering Human Computer Interaction, sponsored by IFIP 2.7/13.4), DSV-IS (International Workshop on the Design, Specification and Verification of Interactive Systems), CADUI (International Conference on Computer-Aided Design of User Interfaces) and TAMODIA (International Workshop on Task Models and Diagrams).

We hope that you will find this year program interesting and thought provoking. The symposium will provide you with a valuable opportunity to share ideas with other researchers and practitioners from institutions around the world. We also wish the best to the next edition, EICS 2012 to be held in Copenhagen, Denmark in June 2012.

We believe that with this third EICS edition, by increasing the diversity of paper presentations, posters, workshops, tutorials, demonstrations and doctoral presentations, we obtained an exciting and interactive program, which stimulates fruitful discussion in the relevant research fields. The distinctive focus of the conference is the engineering of interactive computer systems. Themes include: tools to support the engineering of interactive systems; notations that specify key aspects of interactive behaviour; and models that enable the analysis of interactive systems. There are several papers on context, adaptation, and migration, particularly in relation to engineering ubiquitous systems, as well as papers that discuss engineering issues associated with novel interaction techniques. A further substantial and somewhat novel theme for EICS revolves around interaction with large screens.

Since its beginning EICS has witnessed a growing number of submissions. This year the program contains 14 full papers carefully chosen from a total of 65 submissions (22% acceptance rate). There are also 21 late breaking papers (six of them are presented as posters) as well as a number of doctoral reports, workshop reports, tutorial abstracts and demonstration descriptions. The competition was strong and the selection difficult. The published material originates from 17 countries, including New Zealand, North and South America, China and Europe.

The conference is young and its identity is still evolving. Effie Law and Albrecht Schmidt, our keynote speakers, bring interesting novel perspectives in key topics for the engineering community in next years: user experience and ubiquitous systems. This should provide further useful content for good discussion. Our commitment to industry is underlined by an industrial panel held at the symposium, entitled "Research Agenda for Service Front-Ends", that will provide an interactive discussion forum and a meeting point for industry and academics.

We thank all who contributed to EICS 2011 for their hard work, particularly the Program Committee and the many external reviewers listed in the proceedings, the chairs for doctoral consortium, workshops, demonstrations and tutorials. We also thank Giulio Galesi and the local arrangements team for finding ways of housing the different activities. Lastly, we would like to especially thank our sponsor, ACM SIGCHI, for their continued support of EICS successful symposiums. IFIP WG 2.7/13.4 also accredited this symposium, and we express our gratitude for this.

Fabio Paternò
CNR-ISTI
Conference Chair

Kris Luyten
Hasselt University
Paper Co-Chair

Frank Maurer
Calgary University
Paper Co-Chair

Prasun Dewan
North Carolina University
LBR Co-Chair

Carmen Santoro
CNR-ISTI
LBR Co-Chair

Table of Contents

Session 4: Tools for Graphical User Interfaces

Demo Session

Session 5: Testing

Session 6: Interaction with Large Screens

Session 7: Designing Graphical Interfaces

Tutorial

Workshops

EICS 2011 Symposium Organization

Conference Chair: Fabio Paternò *(CNR-ISTI, Italy)*

Paper Chairs: Kris Luyten *(Hasselt University, Belgium)*
Frank Maurer *(University of Calgary, Canada)*

Late Breaking Results Chairs: Prasun Dewan *(University of North Carolina Chapel Hill, USA)*
Carmen Santoro *(CNR-ISTI, Italy)*

Demonstrations Chairs: Marco Blumendorf *(DAI Labor Technische Universität Berlin, Germany)*
Giuseppe Ghiani *(CNR-ISTI, Italy)*

Doctoral Consortium Chairs: Peter Forbrig *(University of Rostock, Germany)*
Nick Graham *(Queen's University, Kingston, Canada)*

Workshop Chairs: Simone DJ Barbosa *(University PUC-Rio, Brazil)*
Gerrit Meixner *(DFKI, Germany)*

Tutorial Chairs: Greg Philips *(Royal Military College, Kingston, Canada)*
Marco Winckler *(IRIT-ICS, University Paul Sabatier, France)*

Local Organisation Chair: Giulio Galesi *(CNR-ISTI, Italy)*

Program Committee: Simone DJ Barbosa *(University PUC-Rio, Brazil)*
Ann Blandford *(University College London, England)*
Marco Blumendorf *(DAI Labor Technische Universität Berlin, Germany)*
Gaëlle Calvary *(University of Grenoble, France)*
Stéphane Chatty *(ENAC, France)*
Luca Chittaro *(Università di Udine, Italy)*
Karin Coninx *(Hasselt University, Belgium)*
José Creissac Campos *(University of Minho, Portugal)*
Anke Dittmar *(University of Rostock, Germany)*
Gavin Doherty *(Trinity College Dublin, Ireland)*
Peter Forbrig *(University of Rostock, Germany)*
Nicholas Graham *(Queen's University, Kingston, Canada)*
Morten Borup Harning *(Priway, Denmark)*
James Landay *(University of Washington, USA)*
Panos Markopoulos *(Technical University Eindhoven, Netherlands)*
Gerrit Meixner *(DFKI, Germany)*
Jeffrey Nichols *(IBM, USA)*
Philippe Palanque *(University of Toulouse 3, France)*
Fabio Paternò *(CNR-ISTI, Italy)*
Angel Puerta *(RedWhale, USA)*
Carmen Santoro *(CNR-ISTI, Italy)*
Anthony Savidis *(ICS-FORTH, Greece)*
Chris Scaffidi *(Oregon State University, USA)*

Program Committee (continued):

Helen Sharp *(The Open University, UK)*
Noi Sukaviriya *(IBM T.J. Watson Research Center, USA)*
Harold Thimbleby *(University of Swansea, Wales)*
Jan Van den Bergh *(Hasselt University, Belgium)*
Jean Vanderdonckt *(Université catholique de Louvain, Belgium)*
Marco Winckler *(IRIT-ICS, University Paul Sabatier, France)*
Jürgen Ziegler *(Universität Duisburg-Essen, Germany)*

Additional reviewers:

Abdul Rehman Abbasi
Ana Afonso
Dzmitry Aliakseyeu
Margarita Anastassova
Mark Antoniades
Mark Ashdown
Eric Barboni
Thomas Baudel
Gordon Baxter
Karin Bee
Lawrence Bergman
Michael Bernstein
Samit Bhattacharya
Sílvia Amélia Bim
Arnaud Blouin
Christophe Bortolaso
Federico Botella
Matt-Mouley Bouamrane
Judy Bowen
Ruven Brooks
Paolo Buono
Jose Campos
Stefan Carmien
Daniel Cernea
Tsung-Hsiang Chang
Stéphane Chatty
Zebin Chen
Mauro Cherubini
Lydia Chilton
Stéphane Conversy
Enrico Costanza
Nadine Couture
Marco Cristani
Catalina Danis
Laura Dantonio
Alexander De Luca
Asaf Degani
Alexandre Demeure
Epp Carrie Demmans
Prasun Dewan
Alan Dix
Morgan Dixon
Emmanuel Dubois
Mark Dunlop
Sophie Dupuy-Chessa
James Eagan
Florian Echtler
David England
Dominik Ertl
Shamal Faily
David Faure
Jean-Daniel Fekete
Scott Fleming
Federico Fontana
Mathias Funk
Krzysztof Gajos
Yaser Ghanam
Andy Gimblett
Raphael Grasset
Alex Groce
David Gurzick
Mieke Haesen
Michael Haller
Thomas Hansen
Michael Harrison
Björn Hartmann
Benedikt Hauptmann
Tobias Hesselmann
Pazmino Priscilla Jimenez
Alark Joshi
Sasa Junuzovic
Konstantinos Kazakos
Rick Kazman
Kerstin Keil
Sanshzar Kettebekov
Azam Khan
Mary Kiernan
Hyung Nam Kim

Additional reviewers (continued):

David Koop
Volker Kruger
Victor Lòpez-Jaquero
Seth Landsman
Kevin Lano
Grzegorz Lehmann
Catherine Letondal
Sandro Leuchter
James Lin
Steffen Lohmann
Stephan Lukosch
Aran Lunzer
Iglesias José Macìas
Apostolos Malatras
Georgios Marentakis
Nicolai Marquardt
Masood Masoodian
Dimitri Masson
Akhil Mathur
Atif Memon
Jan Meskens
Christian Micheloni
Marino Miculan
Brad Myers
David Navarre
Luciana Nedel
Zeljko Obrenovic
Johanna Octavia
Leif Oppermann
Ipek Ozkaya
Oscar Pastor
Celeste Paul
Heiko Paulheim
Mark Paulk
Eric Paulos
Samuli Pekkola
Robin Penner
Emmanuel Pietriga
Angel Puerta
Wen Qi
Carsten Röcker
Nitendra Rajput
Roberto Ranon
Alberto Raposo
Wolfgang Reitberger
Philippe Renevier-Gonin
Michael Rohs
Licinio Roque
Dirk Roscher
Gustavo Rossi
Daisuke Sakamoto
Luciana Salgado
Ankur Sardana
Chandan Sarkar
Thomas Schlegel
Stacey Scott
Marc Seissler
Bruno Silva
Stéphane Sire
Lucio Davide Spano
Simone Stumpf
Ricardo Tesoriero
Philippe Truillet
den Broek van
Jos Van Leeuwen
Radu-Daniel Vatavu
Maya Venkatraman
Jo Vermeulen
Frederic Vernier
Elena Vildjiounaite
Juergen Vogel
James Wallace
Gerhard Weber
Nadir Weibel
Peter Wild
Wesley Willett
Chancey Wilson
Chadwick Wingrave
Min Wu
Chuang-wen You
Eric Zavesky
Gefei Zhang
Hongbo Zhang

EICS 2011 Sponsor & Supporters

Sponsor:

SIGCHI

Supporters:

ISTI — ISTITUTO DI SCIENZA E TECNOLOGIE DELL'INFORMAZIONE "A. FAEDO"

HIIS Laboratory
The Human-Computer Interaction Group

ifip wg 2.7/13.4 on
user interface engineering

The Measurability and Predictability of User Experience

Effie Lai-Chong Law
Department of Computer Science
University of Leicester
LE1 7RH, Leicester, UK
elaw@mcs.le.ac.uk

ABSTRACT

User experience is an emerging research area with a range of issues to be resolved. Among them, the measurability of UX remains contentious. The key argument hinges on the meaningfulness, validity and usefulness of reducing fuzzy experiential qualities such as fun, challenge and trust to numbers. UX people seem ambivalent towards UX measures. In UX empirical studies, qualitative approaches are predominant, though the popular use of questionnaires in these studies suggests that some form of numeric measures is deemed useful or even necessary. The tension between the two camps (i.e. qualitative design-based and quantitative model-based) stimulates scientific discussions to bring the field forward. As measures may enable us to predict, the concomitant issue of UX predictability is explored. Besides, we look into theoretical frameworks that potentially contribute to a deeper understanding of UX. Of particular interest is theory of memory.

Keywords

User experience, UX Usability, Measurability, Predictability, UX measures, usability measures

General Terms

General.

ACM Classification Keywords

H.5.0 General

INTRODUCTION

User Experience (UX) is a catchy as well as tricky research topic, given its broad applications in a diversity of interactive systems and its deep root in various conceptual frameworks, for instance, psychological theories of emotion. Amongst others, an intriguing controversy about UX is its measurability, which is grounded in the age-old debate of *reductionism versus holism*. Is it theoretically justifiable and empirically practical to operationalise user experience by reducing it to quantifiable constructs? Clearly, different stances on this issue lead to difference choices of approaches to designing for and evaluating user experience. Those in the holistic camp defy the measurability of UX, espousing qualitative approaches such as interaction criticism rooted in literary theory. Their counterparts in the reductionist camp embrace the modeling approaches to understanding the notion of UX, including both *measurement models* and *structural* [33].

We need models, theories and representations to capture and communicate ideas about designing for and evaluating UX, but they are neither the reality nor are they unbiased. Being aware of this is crucial. Irrespective of whether strict formal measurement paradigms are brought to bear on traditional HCI phenomena like usability or emerging ones like user experience, it is the **persuasiveness** of empirical evidence that is ultimately the test of its worth. Furthermore, one may argue that basically everything can be measured, but some things may be more "measurable" than the others; how to estimate the threshold of measurability remains unclear. Above all, measures need to be meaningful, valid and useful.

Research studies on UX have visibly increased during the last two decades, though one may argue that the term user experience being applied in the way it is used today has only commenced since mid-1990s. The change of emphasis from usability to UX in the field of HCI at the turn of millennium has led to a concomitant methodological shift towards *qualitative* approaches from *quantitative* ones, as shown by a recent analysis of UX scientific papers published in the period of 2005-2009 [4]. Nevertheless, mixed-method research designs integrating both approaches are often recommended for triangulating empirical findings.

We posit two theses for the methodological shift instigated by the UX movement: First, the relation between UX and usability remains ambivalent with the UX community striving diligently to claim autonomy and establish a distinct identity from its predecessor – usability - both conceptually and methodologically. Indeed, a common question raised in attempting to demarcate UX is how it can be differentiated from *user satisfaction* – one of the three traditional usability metrics. Being qualitative could arguably be a differentiator. Second, the seemingly unpopularity or distancing from quantitative approaches in the UX research can be attributed to speculations about the measurability of UX qualities (e.g. fun, trust, beauty) and the legitimacy of quantifying them.

In this paper we aim to address this second thesis and its implications. Specifically, we will explore the issue of

EICS'11, June 13–16, 2011, Pisa, Italy.

measurability of UX with reference to the recent research work on definitions, models, evaluation methods, and theoretical frameworks for UX.

WHAT IS UX?

At the outset of this paper we head-plunge into the topic of User Experience without explaining what it is. This way of promoting a notion and retrospectively unpacking it somewhat resembles the uptake of User Experience when it was introduced by Don Norman in the 1990s[1] [39]. It was then followed by rapid adoption of UX in the software industry, thanks to the strong dissemination power of the web and to the deceptive intuitiveness of the concept, as the word 'experience' is casually used in our everyday lives. However, the notion of UX is far more complex than it appears, considering a mesh of psychological, social and physiological concepts it can be associated with. Amongst others, the key concept is *emotion* (or feeling [8]).

Dated back to more than a century ago, the James-Lange Theory of Emotion ([21, 28]) was developed to explicate the intricate relationships between human perception, action and cognition. Accordingly, emotion arises from our conscious cognitive interpretations of perceptual-sensory responses. Put simply, we see and act before we feel. While being aware of volumes of critiques on the James-Lange theory (e.g. [7]) and ongoing debates about the intricate relationships between emotion, cognition and action, we adopt the stance that *UX is a cognitive process that can be modeled and measured* ([14], [33]).

Emotional responses (or experiential qualities) can be instantiated as pleasure, surprise, stimulation, frustration, delightfulness, etc., and their elusiveness renders it especially challenging to quantify them. Nonetheless, attempts have been taken to measure emotion (e.g. [6], [9]) using mixed-method approaches as we will discuss later on.

As mentioned earlier, the question "What is UX?" has been explored in a series of scientific activities (e.g. [32], [42]) resulting in a range of definitions with different foci and underlying assumptions. Consolidating a consensual definition is a daunting and ostensibly impossible mission. The definition proposed by ISO 9241-110: 2010: as "*a person's perceptions and responses that result from the use and/or anticipated use of a product, system or service*" (clause 2.15) is too imprecise or abstract. Note also that in contrast to the ISO definition of usability, identification of UX metrics is yet to be done (or will never be). Nonetheless, a conclusion drawn from the survey attempting to define UX [32] is that user experience in inherently subjective, dynamic and personal.

The recent seminar entitled "Demarcating User Experience" [42] in which thirty UX experienced (NB: another connotation of the word 'experience') researchers and practitioners were involved has resulted in a document named "User Experience White Paper"; its conciseness is a contrast to the extensive discussions from which it has been derived. Accordingly, UX can be viewed as a phenomenon, a field of study or a practice. Whilst in the chapter "UX as a Phenomenon" there is no explicit discussion on the measurability of UX, the chapter on "UX Practice" addresses the issue of UX measures as follows:

> *"No generally accepted overall measure of UX exists, but UX can be made assessable in many different ways... The choice of an evaluation instrument or method depends on the experiential qualities at which the system is targeted, as well as the purpose of the evaluation ... and other (often pragmatic) factors such as time and financial constraints" ([42], p.12)*

The paragraph supports the measurability of UX qualities and highlights the importance of selecting right instruments and methods. Interestingly, the arguments presented therein have primarily been posited by the UX practitioners participating in the seminar. This resonates with Don Norman's claim in a recent interview[2] documented in a blog:

> *"There is a huge need for UX professionals to consider their audience: not the user, but clients and businesses. He [Norman] advocates that we should learn to speak the language of business, including using numbers to sell our ideas."*

Noteworthy is that numbers of some sort are deemed useful (one of the three basic characteristics we uphold for UX measures), primarily because of their brevity and digestibility. A caveat is that such usefulness is contingent on who uses the measures for what purpose. Norman's advocacy is directed at top management executives who need to make (critical) decision on design and development issues within a (very) short period of time. While Norman (see footnote 2) puts emphasis on the **plausibility** of measures to convince the managerial staff, the validity of measures seems not of his major concern.

Usability Measures versus UX Measures

The criterion of plausibility for UX measures seems analogous to the criterion of **persuasiveness** of usability measures [38], though it is addressed in the context of the uptake of usability evaluation feedback by the development team to fix usability problems thus identified. Contrasts and comparisons between usability and UX research and practice have been undertaken; certain concepts, methods, instruments and tools of the former have been "transferred" to the latter[3]. For instance, it is observed that current user experience evaluation methods are largely drawn from usability evaluation methods [43]; some people tend to

---

[1] It is arguable when the term user experience was first used in a way consistent with the meaning currently ascribed to it. According to Peter Merholz, it can be traced back to 1985 in an InfoWorld magazine article authored by Roy Nierenberg (http://www.adaptivepath.com/ideas/the-earliest-use-of-user-experience-as-we-now-think-of-it).

[2] http://www.montparnas.com/articles/don-norman-on-user-experience-design/

[3] However, some of the UX community members resist such a transfer, as mentioned earlier, in order to amputate any connection with usability (whether it is a reasonable attitude is another question).

mistakenly treat the two notions as synonyms. Amongst the set of proposed relationships between usability and UX (e.g. identical, autonomous or exclusive, hierarchical or subsumptive, symbiotic with distinct characteristics), it is increasingly recognized that a threshold level of usability is required for positive user experience, beyond that level a diminishing return may occur [14]. Furthermore, it is intriguing to systematically compare the persuasiveness of usability measures with that of UX measures. For formative (or diagnostic) evaluations, UX measures (e.g. the level of fun derived from playing a game is low with two out of ten) describe the outcome of user interaction without revealing where exactly the problem lies. Qualitative data are required to complement as well as supplement such quantitative results [36]. Conversely, usability measures (e.g. the number of errors occurred when interacting with a game console) may hint the origin of a problem (or sometimes its solution). Hence, generally speaking, UX measures seems less persuasive or even less useful than their usability counterparts, especially from the perspective of the design/development team

Furthermore, some earlier research studies have been undertaken to produce standardized single-score summary usability measures by collapsing a (sub)set of usability metrics ([27], [35]), albeit the validity of the approaches have been challenged. It may be unsurprising if an attempt to produce a single-score user experience measure will be or is already launched. However, it will even be more controversial as the UX qualities are so diverse.

OVERVIEW OF UX MEASUABILITY AND MEASURES

In this section we aim to provide a cursory overview of previous research studies on measuring user experience, arguments for and against the measurability of UX, and UX measures in common use.

Studies on UX Measures

Prior to delving into the historical root of UX and associated arguments for its (non-)measurability, we conduct a somewhat simplified search to illustrate the growth of UX as a research study in general and UX measures as a methodological instrument in particular. Results of searching certain UX-related terms using exact phrases with Google Scholar and ACM Digital Library (DL) (Table 1) provide some rough estimates, though the numbers shown are possibly contaminated by irrelevant noises[4]. However, our concern is the trend rather than the exact figures, and we are also aware that there can be other related search terms and their combinations. Nonetheless, it is intriguing to note that for the terms "user experience measures" and "measure user experience", ACM DL do not return any hit for the 90s and only 4 and 22 hits, respectively, are identified for the last decade (2001-2010). In contrast, for Google Scholar the increases from 0 to 37 and from 3 to 134 hits in response to the two terms are small in absolute number but very high in percentage.

Table 1: Search results about UX terms

	Google Scholar		ACM Digital Library	
	1991-2000	2001-2010	1991-2000	2001-2010
user experience	4950	21900	167	5665
user experience research	18	488	5	115
user experience evaluation	2	294	0	89
user experience measures	0	37	0	4
measure user experience	3	134	0	22

What implication can we draw from these observed patterns? One possible implication is that the notion of user experience needs to be further clarified, scoped and defined, advancing what has enthusiastically been done in the recent years ([32], [42], [44]) to enable UX researchers to operationalise UX qualities. Arguing along this line, a deeper understanding of UX could improve the existing repertoire of UX measures in terms of availability, reliability, validity and sensitivity. However, this view could be rejected by quite a number of UX people.

In fact, the sluggish progress on UX measures suggests that the endeavours of developing UX measures and having them accepted by the HCI community is particularly challenging. A prevailing criticism is that such measures are not sufficiently validated ([4]). Consequently, the research question we aim to explore is:

What are the challenges and obstacles for advancing the research work on measuring UX qualities? Can they be resolved and overcome?

Arguments on Measurability of UX

Before attempting to answer these questions, it is necessary to retrace one step back, asking two basic questions: *Why do we bother to measure at all? What are potential uses of measures?*

A frequently cited quote to argue for the necessity and utility of measurement is from Lord Kelvin (a.k.a. Sir William Thomson, n.d.):

> *"To measure is to know"*
> *"If you cannot measure it, you cannot improve it"*

Lord Kelvin's dictum on measurement has been employed to justify the quantification of theoretical concepts in physical sciences, computer science, engineering and social sciences [3]. Much HCI evaluation aspires to its scientific philosophy. However, while some HCI researchers and practitioners are strongly convinced about the need for measurement, others are highly skeptical about the role of numerical values in providing useful, valid and meaningful assessments and understanding of complex interactions between humans and machines. Some go further and deny the measurability of affective and emotive states such as love, beauty, happiness, and frustration. As a matter of fact, one can measure (almost) anything in some arbitrary way. The compelling concern, however, is whether the measure is *meaningful*, *useful* and *valid* to reflect the state or nature of the object or event in question.

[4] We have no intention to compare the performance of the two search engines.

Concerning their potential uses, UX measures should enable us to know to what extent targeted qualities of a system has been realized and to predict (or project) what values the system can potentially deliver based on its current state. However, whether these assumptions are applicable to UX qualities is a question worthy of further investigation. Current efforts on developing measurement and structural models of UX (e.g., [33]) may allow us to make two kinds of prediction: First, whether assessing an early prototype or even just a design concept provides us sufficient information to predict the UX qualities that the final system/product/service will possibly deliver; Second, whether specific UX qualities will possibly lead to targeted user behaviours (e.g. purchasing or being loyal to a particular system/product/service).

UX Measures

As mentioned earlier, there exists a repertoire of UX measure. Note that in a recent research study of surveying UX evaluation methods [44], UX measures are not explicitly addressed (for instance, it is not included as an attribute in the method description template used in the survey). Strictly speaking, UX qualities[5] (e.g. flow, immersion, challenge, excitement, boredom) to be evaluated should be built upon sound conceptual frameworks, which can inform how such qualities should be defined, scoped and analysed. In essence, theory-informed UX evaluation methods should enable us to collect meaningful data, be their qualitative and quantitative (as it will be argued subsequently, the former can somehow be 'transformed' into the latter). In other words, theories enable us to translate constructs into meaningful measures. Note that emphasis is put on meaningfulness, considering that basically everything can be measured arbitrarily with the numbers so generated being useless and, even worse, misleading and confusing.

In summary, we assert that the measurability is *not* an issue, or making a rather bold claim: There is nothing that cannot be measured. However, it is the design of data collection method (including procedure, technique, tool, and expertise as well as experience of people involved in the process) that is of critical importance to determine the meaningfulness of UX measures.

A query follows naturally from the above discussion is what kinds of UX measures are being in use. In this regard, Bargas-Avila & Hornbaek's [4] study can provide a glimpse, although it is not their aim to meta-analyse the measurability of UX qualities (or UX dimensions, in their words). Specifically, in their systematic reviews of 51 scientific publications of UX, the authors identify how certain UX qualities are measured (Table 2).

[5] UX qualities are also named as experiential constructs, UX constructs, emotional responses, affective responses or some other terms. This is another example of confusion revolving the UX terminologies. Huge effort will be required to clarify them; ontological mapping may help.

Table 2: Measures of UX qualities (adapted from [4])

UX Quality	Type of Instrument	Example
Affect	Scales	SAM
Emotion	Psychophysiology	Heart rate, Eye-tracking,
Fun	Scale, Postgame pictures	Play categories; Coding on 'fun'
Aesthetics	*Scale*	*Appealingness, Attractiveness*
Hedonic	Scale	AttrakDiff
Flow	Scale	Flow State Scale (FSS)

Several remarks need to be made with reference to Table 2: First, the findings presented therein are not fully representative of the ongoing work in UX given the authors' rather strict selection criteria that narrow the scope of papers reviewed (i.e., this limitation is already explicitly acknowledged by the authors). Consequently, some relevant publications are undesirably excluded. For instance, for the UX quality *emotion*, a range of instruments have been developed such as PrEmo [9] and Differential Emotion Scale (DES, [20]) (NB: they are identified in the project ENGAGE[6] and documented in [44] as well). Second, as noted in the column "Type of Instrument", scales are commonly used with most of them, however, being homegrown (cf. standardized ones) and not validated ([4]). The same observation about evaluation of user satisfaction is noted in a meta-analysis of usability studies [18]. Whilst [4] mention that no explanation can be offered, one may argue that UX qualities are highly context-dependent [32], not only *where* but also *when, who* and *how* measures are gauged; the degree of context-dependency of UX measures is likely to be stronger than that of usability ones. Third, the aesthetic quality, irrespective of its inherent fuzziness (cf. "beauty is in the eyes of the beholder"), has attracted visible research efforts aiming to translate it from the related conceptual frameworks ([14], [30]) into measures. In contrast, limited efforts have been invested in translating other ambiguous UX qualities such as challenge (e.g. gaming [34]), trust (e.g. e-commerce [12]) and empathy (e.g. social interaction [46]), though they have been studied qualitatively. In subsequent discussion we will look more closely into the issue of qualitative vs. quantitative.

QUALITATIVE VERSUS QUANTITATIVE

The tension between qualitative and quantitative approaches in HCI is ongoing and may never cease. This issue is inherited from the field of engineering and psychology in which HCI is rooted. UX researchers and practitioners may roughly be divided into two camps, which can be named as "design-based UX research camp" and "model-based UX research camp". The former include Blythe, Cockton, Forlizzi, Gaver, McCarthy, Monk and Wright whereas the latter include Hassenzahl, Mahlke, Sutcliffe, Tractinsky, and van Schaik. Note that the list is not exhaustive, and migration between the two camps, especially from the former to the

[6] http://www.designandemotion.org/society/knowledge_base/tools_methods.html

latter, seems on the rise. Furthermore, proponents of each camp have put forward respective arguments to justify their position.

For instance, Forlizzi and Battarbee [11] – two forerunners of the design-based UX research camp - argue that: "*In interactive systems the challenge is to understand the influence small experiences and emotional responses have on others, as well as the overall view ... emotional responses are hard to understand, let alone quantify.*" [p. 265]. Similarly, Swallow and his colleagues[7] defend qualitative approaches as opposed to the reductionist quantitative ones: "*.... the reduction of experience into a number of factors or processes ... such approaches may be useful for experimental analysis but they can miss some of the insights available in accounts that resist such reduction ... qualitative data provides a richness and detail that may be absent from quantitative measures.*" [pp. 91-92].

In contrast, the model-based UX researchers highlight the use of models: "*First, measurement models of UX are essential: they allow the concept to be measured accurately and, thereby, can aid the evaluation of interactive computer systems. Second, structural models of UX are needed: they establish the structural (antecedent-consequent or cause-and-effect) relations between its components and of these components to characteristics of users and computer systems; consequently, they can inform the design of interactive computer systems.*" ([33], p. 313).

Our stance is that one can and should not claim superiority of one approach to the other, as they have specific strengths, weaknesses and purposes. While arguing for the measurability of UX qualities, we are and should not be dismissive of pure qualitative approaches to understanding such qualities[8]. Indeed, after years of debates, model-based empirical methods embraced in HCI in the 1980s (e.g. GOMS, Fitt's Law) seem losing their ground to analytic methods (e.g. ethnographical methods) emerging in the 1990s. With reference to the recent survey and review work (e.g. [4], [44]), qualitative approaches appear to be a winner in the arena of UX research, as shown by the list of UX data collection methods identified in [4]: *Questionnaires, interviews (semi-structured and open), user observation, video-recordings, focus groups, diaries, probes, collage, photographs, body movements, psycho-physiological, and other methods (e.g. think aloud)*. However, on a closer look, 53% of the studies reviewed [4] have employed questionnaires to yield quantifiable results. This observation suggests the need for some form of numeric values for some sort of reason (e.g., improving the chance of getting a publication accepted; enhancing the receptiveness of evaluation feedback to stakeholders who appreciate or prefer numbers).

For proponents of quantitative approaches, measures provide information about the extent to which the system has (not) met certain UX requirements (e.g. evaluation result should indicate that 75% of gamers rate the degree of fun to be above a threshold value). UX measures also allow us to understand how contextual factors influence the type and extent of UX qualities elicited. However, UX measures do not give us any idea *why* certain emotional responses are elicited. Nonetheless, one may query whether qualitative approaches can provide better insights into a person's cognition and emotion. Psychological research has tackled this challenge for more than a century; today we are still struggling to understand the complex relationship between *what we do* and *what we think or feel*. Are they inseparably coupled, arising in unison, or decoupled, with one triggering the other? Above all, new research methods are required to better articulate the relationship between our action and our feeling. These thoughts lead to our next discussion pertaining to theories on UX.

GLIMPSES OF THEORIES FOR USER EXPERIENCE

While we do not aim to present a thorough literature review of theories that potentially contribute to the deeper understanding of UX as a phenomenon, we highlight several frameworks worthy of further research efforts[9]. Note that theory of judgment, which is relevant and elaborated in the work of Hartmann and his colleagues [14], is not addressed here.

Interestingly, unearthing theoretical roots for UX research is observed to be lagging behind or even remain stagnant [40] as compared to the relatively rich discussions about technological, methodological, and design issues on UX ([42], [44]). Some strong and clear recommendations have been voiced ([26], [31]) that it is necessary to ascribe a high(er) priority to substantiating UX research with sound theoretical frameworks by engaging people of the UX community in scientific discourses. Specifically, Kuutti [26] proposed that more researchers should investigate and experiment with models and theories for user experience. Nonetheless, the criticism that the UX community lacks a thrust for bringing the theoretical front forward may be arguable when looking at the work on experience-centered design (e.g., [1], [15], [47]). For instance, Wright and McCarthy [47] promote a humanistic approach to designing digital technologies that enhance UX. However, there are some confusions and disagreements on the relevance of different theories. Apparently, UX people tend to embrace eclecticism with no single paradigm or set of assumptions being rigidly followed, but drawing upon multiple theoretical approaches to gain complementary insights into UX.

HCI Theories: Activity theory (AT), Distributed Cognition (DC) and Situated Action (SA)

Nardi [37] systematically compares AT with DC and SA. She argues that AT and DC are very close in spirit; the two

[7] Swallow, D., M. Blythe, M., & Wright, P. (2005) Grounding experience: relating theory and method to evaluate the user experience of smartphones. In *Proc. EACE* '05, 91–98.

[8] In contrast, some UX people are strongly dismissive of everything that is quantified and condemn all sorts of statistical analysis on UX qualities.

[9] An upcoming scientific activity in CHI 2011 (a special issue group session [40]) will dedicate to investigating this key issue.

mutually inform and can be merged over time. In contrast, AT, with its rich vocabulary, is considered to be much richer and deeper than SA. The significance of AT in HCI is that it serves as a research time frame long enough to understand users' objects, drawing attention to broad patterns of activity rather than narrow episodic fragments. More important, AT implies a commitment to understanding things from users' points of view, inspiring the inception of the user-centred design approaches [6]. All in all, these theories can be seen as a springboard from which the qualitative approaches in HCI takes off.

Amongst the three traditional HCI theories, we find AT particularly promising to shed light onto the understanding of UX, which is essentially psychological construct determined by actors' motives and needs [16] which are in turn shaped by the socio-cultural context where actors are situated. As an example, in the context of digital educational games, the two seemingly competing motives (i.e. learning and playing) can be seen as inherent inconsistencies within the system and discrepancies between the system and its environment (cf. a traditional formal learning setting of a classroom vs. informal game-based learning). This well exemplifies the notion of contradiction of AT ([24], [25]). On the micro level, contradiction can be seen as *breakdown* [41], which has drawn much research attention in HCI since 1980s [45] and is also broadly used in different disciplines. The breakdown analysis highlights the spontaneous, subjective problems in the use of a technology and connects them to specific aspects of users' action. This notion of breakdown has successfully been applied to analyse UX [34].

Role of Memory

Given the extensive scope of the theoretical work on memory, we will not elaborate models of memory but instead highlight several implications to UX.

According to a medical dictionary[10], memory is defined as: *The mental faculty of retaining and recalling* ***past experience*** *based on the mental processes of learning, retention, recall, and recognition.* By emphasizing the word "past experience", we want to highlight the role of memory in user experience, especially its relevance to understanding the temporal dimension of UX (before: expectation, during: interaction, and after: review) [32]. Hassenzahl and Ullrich's work [17] illustrates the recency effect whereas Karapanos and his colleagues ([22], [23]) in their attempt to develop an instrument for evaluating UX over time argue for the validity of retrospective accounts of experience.

In his recent talk on human happiness[11], Daniel Kahneman posits that happiness is the stream of consciousness resulting from interactions between *experiencing self* and *remembering self.* Particularly intriguing is his interpretation of the notion of *cognitive traps*:

"The first of these traps is a reluctance to admit complexity. It turns out that the word happiness is just not a useful word anymore because we apply it to too many different things. ... The second trap is confusion between experience and memory: basically it's between being happy in your life and being happy about your life or happy with your life. And those are two very different concepts, and they're both lumped in the notion of happiness. And the third is the focusing illusion, and it's the unfortunate fact that we can't think about any circumstance that affects well-being without distorting its importance."

The above description on positive experiential quality – happy- may be applicable to their negative counterparts such as boredom.

Kahneman points out that we have the remembering self and the experiencing self with the major difference being the handling of time. The distinction between the happiness of the experiencing self and the satisfaction of the remembering self has been recognized in recent years, and there have been some efforts to *measure* the two separately. To illustrate this point, Kahneman describes a scenario where somebody is asked how satisfied with her life. The answer so obtained, however, cannot teach one much about how happily she has been living her life, and vice versa. Kahneman further points out that if somebody ranked her life eight on a scale of ten there could still be a lot of uncertainties about how happy she is with her experiencing self. Hence, the correlation is low.

PREDICTABILITY OF USER EXPERIENCE

This brief overview of Kahneman's arguments stimulates us to muse about the predictability of UX. In particular, does the trajectory of UX follow any model, pattern, or rule of 'evolution'? Is user experience predictable? Which *UX factors*[12] should be included and excluded when predicting UX for a specific artifact in a specific context of use? How to address tradeoffs and reciprocal relationships between different UX factors, between different UX qualities and between UX factors and qualities? One can envisage a model of highly complex interdependent, crisscross relationships. Developing and validating such a model is a challenge appreciated by model-based UX researchers. Whether their design-based counterparts want to share their ambition is questionable. Nonetheless, as pointed out earlier on, qualitative data can be coded, counted and, so, quantified, being conducive to computational manipulations. For instance, the number of negative phrases expressed by an expert when evaluating an early design concept with interaction criticism [x] may be useful to predict acceptance or even adoption of a new technology.

To reinstate, there are two levels of prediction. First, we coin it as *UX-factor-quality-loop*: integration as well as

[10] The American Heritage® Medical Dictionary

[11] TED2010 talk (Feb 2010): The riddle of experience vs. memory Retrieved from http://www.ted.com/talks/daniel_kahneman_the_riddle_of_experience_vs_memory.html

[12] UX factor is distinct from UX quality. The former influences how the latter will be instantiated – type, intensity, and extensity. For instance, an organizational culture is a UX factor that may (strongly) influence individual as well as social experiences with a groupware.

interaction of specific UX factors (predictors) allows us to predict which UX qualities (criteria) a user is very likely to experience with an interactive entity of interest. Second, we coin it as *UX-behaviour-loop*: a specific set of user experiences (predictors), be they negative or positive, determines the likelihood a user (or a customer) will likely purchase or adopt a system/product/service (criterion).

In the case of *UX-factor-quality-loop,* the accuracy of prediction hinges crucially on the extent to which an early prototype or a design concept resembles the fully functional and interactive version later on. The issue can then be boiled down to the *fidelity* of design artefacts. It sounds as if we returned back to usability scenario – low vs. high fidelity, discount vs. costly evaluation methods. In the case of *UX-behaviour-loop*, UX accumulated over time may shape cognitive processes and behavioural tendencies.

Above all, as a believer of the eclectic approaches, appreciating the neatness of model-based research and the richness of design-based research, we are convinced that UX can be predicted with an acceptable margin of error. Nevertheless, as it is now we are not able to provide answers to the aforementioned questions concerning predictability of UX. It entails more theoretical and methodological explorations.

CONCLUDING REMARKS

UX as a phenomenon remains quite a mystery to unravel. UX as a study continuously instigates heated debates, stimulating discussions among researchers who espouse different worldviews, which could dichotomously be divided into the qualitative camp (i.e. design-based research) and the quantitative camp (i.e. model-based research). However, quite a number of UX people adopt hybrid or eclectic approaches. UX as a practice is an ongoing negotiation between researchers and practitioners. Practice and research should go hand-in-hand, and the transfer of knowledge between the two should be bidirectional rather than unidirectional. However, their sometimes divergent needs and goals may be difficult to be compromised. For instance, researchers tend to elaborate the process and findings of their work whereas practitioners expect the process to be implemented and findings to be presented in a concise and workable manner. Several studies in usability have been undertaken to investigate the discrepancy between research and practice (e.g. [10], [13]); similar endeavours should also be initiated in UX.

In this paper, we have addressed a number of issues in UX as a study. These issues are not new and remain to be clarified and resolved. All in all, we are convinced about the measurability and predictability of UX. However, the respective issues of meaningfulness and accuracy are something that needs to be worked on. It entails several key requirements: (i) Sound theoretical frameworks for UX to inform the definition and operationalisation of UX qualities and the development of data collection methods; (ii) Effective algorithms to enable the combinatorial integration of a (large) set of UX factors and qualities with reasonable accuracy and efficiency.

Indeed, the key challenge of having accurate prediction is how to represent early design artifacts which are not only *flexible* enough to allow changes in response to evaluation feedback but also '*rigid*' enough with key characteristics being intact in the final prototype. These paradoxical requirements are difficult to address and worthy of further investigations.

REFERENCES

1. Blythe, M., Wright, P., McCarthy, J. & Bertelsen, O.W. (2006). Theory and method for experience centered design. In *Proc. CHI EA '06*. ACM, NY, USA, 1691-1694.
2. Blythe, M., McCarthy, J., Light, A., Bardzell, S., Wright, P., Bardzell, J., & Blackwell, A (2010). Critical dialogue: interaction, experience and cultural theory. In *Proc. CHI EA '10*. ACM, NY, USA, 4521-4524.
3. Bulmer, M. (2001). Social measurement: What stands in its way? *Social Research, 62*(2).
4. Bargas-Avila, J.A., & Hornbæk, K. (2011). Old wine in new bottles or novel challenges? A critical analysis of empirical studies of user experience. In *Proc. CHI'11*. Vancouver, Canada.
5. Boehner, K., DePaula, R., Dourish, P., & Senger, P. (2007). How emotion is made and measured? *Journal International Journal of Human-Computer Studies*, 65(4).
6. Bødker, S. (1990). *Through the interface: a human activity approach to user interface design.* Hillsdale, NJ: Lawrence Erlbaum Associates.
7. Cannon, W.B. (1927). The James-Lange Theory of Emotions: A Critical Examination and an Alternative Theory. *The American Journal of Psychology*. 39 (1/4).
8. Damasio, A. (1999). *The Feeling of What Happens: Body, Emotion and the Making of Consciousness.* Heinemann: London.
9. Desmet, P. (2004). Measuring Emotion. In M.A. Blythe, A.F. Monk, K. Overbeeke, & P.C. Wright (Eds.), *Funology: from usability to enjoyment.* Kluwer.
10. Følstad, A., Law, E. L-C., Hornbæk, K. (2010). Analysis in usability evaluations: an exploratory study. In *Proc. NordiCHI 2010* (pp. 647-650).
11. Forlizzi, J., & Battarbee, K. (2004). Understanding experience in interactive systems. In *Proc. DIS '04*, 261–268. ACM, 2004.
12. French, T., Liu, K., & Springett, M. (2007). A card-sorting probe of e-banking trust perceptions. *BCS HCI (1)*, 45-53
13. Furniss, D., Blandford, A., Curzon, P. (2008). Usability Work in Professional Website Design: Insights from Practitioners' Perspectives. In Law, E., Hvannberg, E., Cockton, G. (Eds.). *Maturing Usability: Quality in*

Software, Interaction and Value (pp. 144-167). London: Springer London.

14. Hartmann, J., De Angeli, A. & Sutcliffe, A. (2008). Framing the user experience: information biases on website quality judgement. In Proc. CHI '08, 855–864. ACM, 2008.
15. Hassenzahl, M. (2010). *Experience Design: Technology for all the right reasons.* Synthesis Lectures in Human-Centered Informatics (no. 8). San Rafael, CA: Morgan & Claypool Publishers.
16. Hassenzahl, M., Diefenbach, S., & Göritz, A. (2010). Needs, affect, and interactive products – facets of user experience. *Interacting with Computers, 22*:353-362.
17. Hassenzahl, M., & Ullrich, D. (2007). To do or not to do: Differences in user experience and retrospective judgments depending on the presence or absence of instrumental goals. *Interacting with Computers 19*(4), 429-437.
18. Hornbæk, K., & Law, E. L-C. (2007). Meta-analysis of correlations among usability measures. In *Proc. CHI 2007*, San Jose, USA.
19. Isomursu, M., Tähti, M., Väinämö, S. & Kuutti, K. (2007). Experimental evaluation of five methods for collecting emotions in field settings with mobile applications. *International Journal of Human-Computer Studies, 65*(4):404–418.
20. Izard, C. E. Libero, D. Z., Putnam, P., Haynes, O. M. (1993). Stability of emotion experiences and their relations to traits of personality. *Journal of Personality and Social Psychology*, 64(5), 847-860.
21. James, W. (1884). What is emotion? *Mind*, ix, 189.
22. Karapanos, E., Zimmerman, J. Forlizzi, J., & Martens, J. (2009). User experience over time: an initial framework. In *Proc. CHI '09,* 729–738. ACM, 2009.
23. Karapanos, E., Zimmerman, J. Forlizzi, J., & Martens, J. (2010). Measuring the Dynamics of Remembered Experience Over Time. *Interacting with Computers*, 22(5):328–335.
24. Kaptelinin, V. (1996). Computer-mediated activity: Functional organs in social and developmental contexts. In B. Nardi (Ed.), *Context and consciousness: Activity theory and human-computer interaction (45-68).* Cambridge, MA: MIT
25. Kaptelinin, V., & Nardi, B.A. (2006). *Acting with technology: Activity theory and interaction design.* Cambridge, MA: MIT press.
26. Kuutti, K. (2010). Where are the Ionians of user experience research?. In *Proc. NordiCHI '10*. ACM, NY, USA, 715-718.
27. Kindlund, E. & Sauro, J. (2005), "A method to standardize usability metrics into a single score", *In Proceedings of CHI 2005 ACM Conference on Human Factors in Computing Systems,* 401-409.
28. Lang, P. J. (1994). The varieties of emotional experience: A meditation on James-Lange theory. *Psychological Review, 101*(2), 211-221.
29. Lange, C. (1887). *Ueber Gemuthsbewgungen*, 3, 8.
30. Lavie, T., & Tractinsky, N. (2004). Assessing dimensions of perceived visual aesthetics of web sites. *International Journal of Human-Computer Studies*, 60(3):269–298.
31. Luojus, S. (2010). *From a momentary experience to a lasting one - The concept of and research on expanded user experience of mobile devices*. Doctoral Dissertation, Acta Universitatis Ouluensis Scientiae Rerum Naturalium A 559, Oulu.
32. Law, E. L-C , Roto, V., Hassenzahl, M., Vermeeren, A., & Kort, J. (2009). Understanding, scoping and defining user experience: a survey approach. In *Proc. CHI '09*, 719–728. ACM, 2009.
33. Law, E. L-C., & van Schaik. P. (2010). Modelling user experience – an agenda for research and practice. *Interacting with Computers, 22*(5):313–322.
34. Law, E. L-C., & Sun, X. (under review). Evaluating User Experience of Adaptive Digital Educational Games with Activity Theory. *International Journal of Human Computer Studies.*
35. McGee, M. (2004), "Master usability scaling: magnitude estimation and master scaling applied to usability measurement", *In Proc. of CHI,* 335-342.
36. Müller, D., Law, E., & Strohmeier, S. (2010). Analysis of the Persuasiveness of User Experience Feedback on a Virtual Learning Environment. In *Proc. of Workshop on Interplay between User Experience Evaluation and System Development* (I-UxSED'10) in conjunction with NordiCHI 2010, Iceland.
37. Nardi, B.A. (1996) 'Activity theory and human omputer interaction', In B.A. Nardi (Ed), *Context and Consciousness: Activity Theory and Human–Computer Interaction* (pp.7–16). Cambridge, MA: MIT Press
38. Nørgaard, M., Høegh, R.T. (2008). Evaluating usability: using models of argumentation to improve persuasiveness of usability feedback. In *Proc. DIS 2008* (pp. 212-221).
39. Norman, D. A. (1990): *The Design of Everyday Things.* New York, Doubleday.
40. Obrist, M., Law, E.L-C., Väänänen-Vainio-Mattila, K., Roto, V., Vermeeren, A., & Kuutti, K. (2011). UX research- which theoretical roots do we build on – if any. In *Extended Abstract CHI'11.*
41. Roussou, M., Oliver, M., and Slater, M.: Exploring activity theory as a tool for evaluating interactivity and learning in virtual environments for children. *Cognition, Technology and Work, 10, (2008*), 141-153
42. Roto, V., Law, E., Vermeeren, A., & Hoonholt, J. (2011). User Experience White Paper. Retrieved from http://www.allaboutux.org/
43. Tullis, T., & Albert, W. (2008). *Measuring the User Experience: Collecting, Analyzing, and Presenting*

Usability Metrics (Interactive Technologies). Morgan Kaufman.
44. Vermeeren, A. P.O.S. Law, E. L-C., Roto, V., Obrist, M., Hoonhout, J., Väänänen-Vainio-Mattila, K. (2010). User experience evaluation methods: current state and development needs. In *Proc NordiCHI 2010* (pp. 521-530).
45. Winograd, T., & Flores, F. (1986). *Understanding computers and cognition: A new foundation for design*. Ablex.
46. Wright, P., & McCarthy, J. (2008). Empathy and experience in HCI. In Proc. CHI'08.
47. Wright, P., & McCarthy J. (2010). *Experience-Centered Design: Designers, Users, and Communities in Dialogue.* Synthesis Lectures in Human-Centered Informatics, ed. John Carroll, no. 8, San Rafael, CA: Morgan & Claypool Publishers.

A Model-Based Approach for Distributed User Interfaces

Jérémie Melchior[1], Jean Vanderdonckt[1], and Peter Van Roy[2]
Université catholique de Louvain
[1]Louvain School of Management, Place des Doyens, 1 – B-1348 Louvain-la-Neuve, Belgium
[2]Computer Science Department, Place Sainte-Barbe, 2 – B-1348 Louvain-la-Neuve, Belgium
+32 10 47 {8379, 8525, 8374} - {jeremie.melchior, jean.vanderdonckt, peter.vanroy}@uclouvain.be

ABSTRACT

This paper describes a model-based approach for designing distributed user interfaces (DUIs), i.e. graphical user interfaces that are distributed along one or many of the following dimensions: end user, display device, computing platform, and physical environment. The three pillars of this model-based approach are: (i) a Concrete User Interface model for DUIs incorporating the distribution dimensions and able to express in a XML-compliant format any DUI element until the granularity of an individual DUI element is reached, (ii) a specification language for DUI distribution primitives that have been defined in a user interface toolkit, and (iii), a step-wise method for modeling a DUI based on the concepts of distribution graph expressing a distribution scenario that can be played namely based on the distribution primitives. A distribution graph consists of a state-transition diagram whose states represent significant distribution states of a DUI and whose transitions are labeled by an even-condition-action representation. The actions involved in this format may call any distribution primitive of the DUI toolkit. In order to exemplify this model-based approach, two simple DUIs are first designed: a DUI for the Pictionary game and a DUI for the Minesweeper game. They are then incorporated into a larger DUI game of the goose where cells may trigger the two other games.

Authors Keywords

Distribution graph, primitives, and scenario, Distributed User Interface, Meta-user interface, Shared displays, Ubiquitous computing, User Interface Toolkit.

General Terms

Design, Experimentation, Human Factors, Verification.

ACM Classification Keywords

C.2.4 [**Computer-Communication Networks**]: Distributed systems – *Distributed applications*. D2.2 [**Software Engineering**]: Design Tools and Techniques – *Modules and interfaces; user interfaces*. D2.m [**Software Engineering**]: Miscellaneous – Rapid Prototyping; reusable software. H5.2 [**Information interfaces and presentation**]: User Interfaces – *graphical user interfaces, user interface management system (UIMS)*.

INTRODUCTION

On the side of the *demand*, end users are more frequently involved in a context of use [21] where domain objects are widespread, where roles and groups are configured in dynamic fashions, thus increasing the need for User Interfaces (UIs) that support them in these multiple configurations. On the side of the *offer*, the market has disseminated a large amount of computing platforms ranging from smartphones to wall screen displays, thus offering a wide spectrum of interaction surfaces to interact with [29]. End users are puzzled by what type of platform they should choose for a particular task, especially when several tasks are distributed in time and space. For instance, when an end user delegates a task to a colleague, parts or whole of this task UI should be transferred as well to the colleague. Even at run-time, an end user may want to ask for advice for a remote colleague, thus requesting to access to the currently running UI.

All these examples strive for a global approach for designing a *Distributed User Interface* (DUI) [5,26,28,35], which is defined as any application UI whose components can be distributed across varying displays of varying platforms that are used by varying users, whether they are working at the same place (co-located) or not (remote collaboration). DUIs have been successfully used in various domains of human activity (e.g., ambient intelligence [22,23], clinical systems [5], economics [14]) and in computer science (e.g., migratory UIs [3,6,25,39], service-oriented architecture [36], ubiquitous computing [7]). DUIs are fundamental because several applications require the integration of distributed interaction devices as functional wholes. There are two main categories in which they can be important. The user needs for DUI and addition to the limited UI development. Many situations need collaboration between users, they share their computing tasks and so they should be able to share their UIs [21]. Current toolkits such as Java Swing or Microsoft Foundation Classes do not support DUIs [34].

The remainder of this paper is structured as follows: the next section reports on some significant DUI related work. Then, a specification language for UI distribution primitives is motivated, defined, and exemplified, based on a model of a Concrete UI [15]. Then, a step-wise method for modeling a DUI based on a distribution scenario represented as a distribution graph involving the abode primitives is presented. A progressive case study will then exemplify how this method can be applied on games that are intrinsically challenging and distributed by nature, first individually, then composed. Finally, a conclusion delivers the main points of this research and presents some future avenues.

RELATED WORK

DUI may be subject to distribution along many dimensions [3,4,11,28] such as user, platform (including various displays/monitors connected to the same computing platform or belonging to the same cluster). Analyzing extensively these distributions is beyond the scope of this paper. Therefore, we only focus on some significant pieces of work to examine some of these dimensions in this state of the art.

User requirements for DUIs

The "display" of the platform dimension is certainly one of the most vivid dimensions of investigation. Beale and Edmondson [4] identified several requirements for distributing or reproducing UI elements from one display to another depending on the task being carried out. They conducted user surveys in order to determine the user behavior induced by using a DUI: they identified the importance of having multiple carets and the complexity of multi-tasking and they suggest design implications for using DUIs in order to support distributed tasks. In particular, they stressed the importance of a multi-tasking model that is partially built at the local level of a single user and at the global level across users when collaboration exists. The global scenario should be also dissolved into local scenario in order to preserve the consistency between common tasks and individual tasks. This observation is fundamental here.

Tan & Czerwinski [33] found out that physical discontinuities had no effect on performance, but found a detrimental effect from separating information within the visual field, when also separated by depth. Grudin [18] highlights usability issues with multi-display such as lack of support and mobile device not used to display. This requirement is acknowledged in Personal Universal Control (PUC) [29], a system that enables controlling a primary platform (such as a desktop or a wall screen) from a secondary platform (such as a PDA or a smartphone). Berglund *et al.* [5] have set user requirements that DUI have to meet: to enable dynamic construction and distribution, to make the best possible use of the available resources, to provide graceful degradation of interaction, to negotiate the interaction resources needs to be handled dynamically and transparent configuration and UI distribution. Distribution also raises concerns for security and privacy [4,20]: when allowing the distribution of a window or application, it allows all users to control or observe all shared windows. But sometimes, users would prefer to avoid users being able to get some windows or applications. Not all users should benefit from sharing the same window, thus requiring control over distribution [12].

Nowadays, more user studies are available on specific DUI setups that provide us with more knowledge on design implications for such DUIs. Yet, in order to allow for the user to get the best potential of interaction capabilities offered by the various devices/displays/platforms for the current task to be carried out, we should enable designers as well as developers to provide users with the best DUI possible for a given set of devices/displays/platforms by described them in a formal way. This is discussed in the next subsection.

System requirements for DUIs

The distribution of UI elements in existing toolkits and frameworks is always at a very high level. Several works [3,6,16] have been done in the domain of migratory applications, where parts or whole of a UI moves from one computing platform to another while preserving the task continuity [3]. WinCuts [34] supports some distribution by clipping areas of interest in windows and arranging them together in order to spare screen space. This distribution is located at the visualization level, not at the UI level. In IMPROMPTU framework [7], only windows can be moved from one wall screen to another through a direct manipulation control. There are however ample possibilities for the granularity of distribution: at the level of applications, windows, widgets, and pixels [11]. Most toolkits supporting distribution support applications [6] and/or windows levels [8,16].

Distributed Programming [37] mainly focuses on the distribution of the functionalities belonging to the functional core of an interactive application [13], leaving the UI distribution aside. DUIs system support remains today only in its infancy. To be able to develop application with fully controllable application, more research has to be done [12]. DUIs could be integrated in domains such as workflows, collaborative tools and for user that would like ubiquitous computing across several devices [3].

Consequently, DUIs allow for the UI to be spread out over a set of displays/devices/platforms taking advantage of their unique properties instead of residing on a single display/device/platform with the interaction capabilities that are constrained on this display/device/platform [3,35]. DUIs have been subject to several studies that investigate further their specific characteristics that may lead to design implications. This includes the use of multiple monitors on the same computing platform by a single user [14,18,38], the use of multiple platforms by a single user with synchronization between [20], exchange of information between platforms belonging to different users [12], moving information between displays on a single platform [28], partition of tasks across displays for a single user [34], sharing common information on a common display while keeping some information private on a own platform [5].

This will allow both designers and developers to enable the underlying system to decide where different DUI portions should be placed in locations that are significant and usable for a distributed task to take place. For instance, the game of Pictionary [27] is a typical example of a distributed task: one player selects a word from a dictionary, a second player draws this word on a surface shared by other players who have to guess what this word is as quick as possible, but below a certain time threshold. The team to which the winning player belongs to receives points. Other tasks are distributed by nature. Sjölund *et al.* implemented a DUI consisting of a remote control GUI on a smartphone that controls Windows Media Player displayed on a TV. Some controls of the Windows Media Player (e.g., play, stop, volume up, volume down) are moved to the smartphone and adapted to this platform at the same time.

Shortcomings of related work

In most of the aforementioned pieces of work, there is almost *no genuine DUI* since UI elements have been developed in such a way that they simply remain in their initial context, while communicating with each other, but without any possibility to be rearranged. Where there is still some distribution of UI elements, it is mainly *predefined* and *opportunistic*: it is impossible to change the distribution of these UI elements because they have been thought in only one particular context of use. For example, the recombinant computing approach induces a small set of DUIs for mobile services such as projecting, printing or storing files [30], but they are predefined. In Sjölund [32], there is no other way to change the repartition of UI elements across the smartphone and the TV. In HyperPalette [2], the distribution of tasks across windows is also predefined, although these windows could be moved. When a distribution is anyway possible at run-time, the UI elements subject to this redistribution are mainly *containers*, such as windows or dialog boxes. For instance, WebSplitter [19] redistributes portions of web pages, WinCuts [34] redistributes window viewports, DistriXML [17] detaches and attaches toolbars depending on the current task. In other words, the *granularity* of UI distributed elements is often *very high*.

In addition, it is not *replicable*. If another user or platform comes in the context of use, it is hard to replicate or migrate on this platform the part that has already been transferred to the first smartphone. In Lightweight services [36], once a service has been selected, it can be distributed to any platform, existing or arriving, but a service can be distributed only once. On the one hand, this does not create any conflict, but on the other hand, it does not support *replication*. For this purpose, there is a need to have an underlying model that captures the various aspects of distribution, which is not the case nowadays. A platform model has been defined in order to accommodate dynamically new platforms or interaction resources coming in play [31], but there is no explicit representation of the distribution logical. Similarly, the Qtk toolkit [27] enables developing DUIs, but there is no underlying model or any representation of replication possible. Models [25] or logical UI descriptions [23] have already been successfully used for partial aspects of DUIs and could expanded with a development method based on primitives for UI distribution explicitly.

To sum up, we are looking for a model-based approach for designing DUIs that support both design-time and run-time distribution of UI with very low granularity and replicability, while being compliant with the DUI goals [35]. In order to address these challenges, we will follow the three pillars of any development method: *models* that capture relevant aspects of the future software (along with a *specification language* that expresses these models), a *step-wise approach* based on the previously defined models, and *software* supporting the step-wise approach. The next section is dedicated to the first pillar (what are the core models required for DUI), the subsequent section is devoted to the second pillar (what is the step-wise method, exemplified on three progressively more complex case studies), and the last section will be about the third pillar (i.e., how the implementation has been achieved).

CORE MODELS FOR DISTRIBUTED USER INTERFACES

The following subsections define respectively the UI model subject to distribution, the models for representing the context of use (i.e., platform, user, and environment), a set of distribution primitives that enable distribution of UI elements specified in the UI model according to the context of use, and a formal language expressing these primitives.

Concrete User Interface (CUI) Model

There has been considerable research and development in defining a *Concrete User Interface* (CUI) model that is independent of any computing platform and implementation language (programming or markup) and their associated User Interface Description Language (UIDL). It is interesting to notice that this is now subject to a common effort under the umbrella of the W3C Incubator Group on Model-Based UIs (). Since the main goal of this paper is to introduce a model-based approach for developing DUIs, we will be using for the purpose of this paper a simple representation of a CUI model. A *CUI model* is hereby defined as recursive hierarchy of containers (e.g., windows, tabbed dialog boxes, group boxes) and individual widgets (e.g., check boxes, push buttons, list boxes, etc.). Widgets are laid out in their containers according to the Box & Glue mechanism [1]: a window is structured into horizontal and vertical boxes, that are in turn, decomposed into boxes, until individual widgets are defined. Each widget is defined as a vector $W=(P_i, V_i)$ where P_i denotes the ith property of the widget and V_i denotes the value of this property (e.g., the widget identifier, the background color of a push button is grey).

An identifier serves as a handle for referring to any particular widget. But it may be convenient to designate a series of widgets that satisfy a certain condition. For this purpose, we introduce the concept of selector. A *selector* consists of a selection of UI element types of a particular CUI model that satisfy a first-order predicate logical formula. In this way, it will be possible to apply a *template* for a selector instead of a (potentially long) sequence of widgets. Four types of selector are defined that will be later on used for addressing UI elements and for specifying source and targets elements of distribution primitives:

- universalSelector: applies the template to all UI elements belonging to a particular CUI, whatever they are.
- elementTypeSelector: applies the template to all UI elements belonging to a particular CUI which correspond to the selector's type (e.g., all containers, all list boxes).
- classSelector: applies the template to all UI elements belonging to a particular CUI which correspond to the selector's type whose definition makes them part of the class (e.g., all containers having an id greater or equal to 10, all list boxes having more than 10 items).
- idSelector: applies the template to only one UI element belonging to a particular CUI: the one whose id property matches the string contained in the parameter.

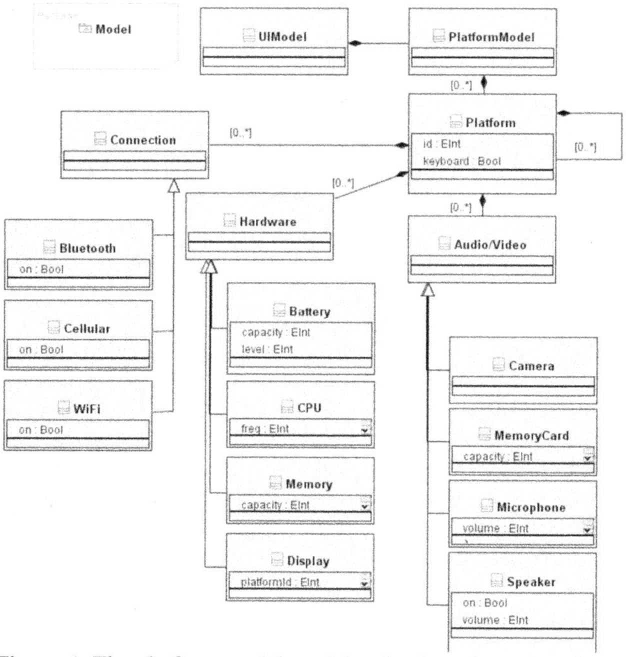

Figure 1. The platform model used for distributed user interfaces.

Platform Model

Again, considerable efforts have been devoted to defining and using models for representing the computing platform operated by the end user. In this work, the user is no longer considered in isolation as a single person carrying out a single task on a single computing platform in a unique environment, which has been the prevalent representation for year. Rather, we consider that a *UI distribution* [5,35] concerns the repartition of one or many UI elements from one or many DUIs in order to support one or many users to carry out one or many tasks on one or many domains in one or many contexts of use, each context of use consisting of users, platforms, and environments. Therefore, the context of use is hereby considered as a cluster of individual components. In order to represent this cluster, we adopted the *Delivery Context Ontology* (DCO) standardized by W3C [10], a subset of which is depicted in Fig. 1. According to DCO, a platform model is divided into one or many platforms. For example, a laptop itself consists of three platforms: the laptop, the display and the keyboard. Each platform has three main categories of components: a *connection* category representing the input and output connections to other devices or to the internet, the *hardware* category that defines the main components such as the CPU, the memory and if the platform has a display or not, and any component linked to the medias (e.g., audio and video).

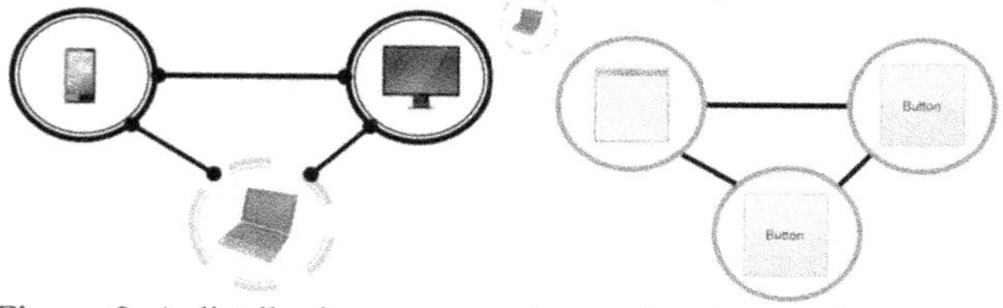

Figure 2. A distribution scene made up of: a cluster of three platforms (a) and an associated graph of CUI models (b).

Devices/ Feature	Mobile Phone	Laptop	Monitor
Battery	YES : 100%	YES : 100%	NO
Bluetooth	YES : OFF	YES : OFF	NO
Camera	YES : 5MP	YES : 1MP	NO
Cellular	YES : HSD-PA	NO	NO
CPU	YES : 1Ghz	YES : 2Ghz	NO
Display	YES : WVGA	YES : SXGA+	YES : HD 1080
Keyboard	YES	YES	NO
Memory Card	YES : 6Go	NO	NO
Microphone	YES	YES	NO
Speaker	YES	YES	NO
WiFi	YES : OFF	YES : ON	NO
Memory	512 MB	2 GB	NO

Table 1. Some properties and their values of the cluster of Fig. 1.

Based on this, a *cluster* is defined by a graph $G=(N_j,R_j)$ which is a set of nodes N_j connected together through R_j relationships. Each *node* consists of a DCO-compliant platform model representing any kind of device or components able to interact with the system (e.g., computers, displays, keyboards and mice are representative examples). Each relationship represents a communication channel (e.g., a Wi-Fi network or a BlueTooth connection) between nodes. Fig. 2a denotes a cluster composed of three platforms: a laptop connected to a flat monitor and a mobile phone, whose descriptions are partially reproduced in Table 1. In order to properly express DUIs, to operate them and to reason about them, it is required to know at time what DUI is residing on which platform of the cluster [21]. For this purpose, we hereby define a *distribution scene* as a cluster in which each node is associated to a CUI model, all CUI models connected to each other by a graph (Fig. 2b). Any cluster node contains a reference to a particular CUI model that could evolve over time. Consequently, a distribution scene holds a two-layer structure: (1) a cluster representing the physical setup of interaction elements and devices and (2) an associated graph of CUI models attached to any element in this cluster that supports some interaction. Not all platforms run a UI at any-time. To depict this, full circles in Fig. 2a represent that no DUI exist for those two platforms at some point (e.g., the starting time). The dashed circle around the laptop means that it holds some DUI.

User and Environment Models

A *User model* is hereby defined as recursive hierarchy of user profiles (e.g., average user, novice, expert) where each user profile is defined as a vector $U=(P_i, V_i)$ where P_i denotes the ith property of the user (e.g., system experience, motivation, task experience, age, background) and V_i denotes the value of this property. An *Environment model* is hereby defined as recursive hierarchy of working places (e.g., ranging from a whole organization to an individual organization cell) where each working place is defined as a vector $U=(P_i, V_i)$ where P_i denotes the ith property of the place (e.g., location, level of stress, light, temperature, organizational responsibilities) and V_i denotes its value.

All models defined so far are defined consistently so as to allow an internal representation for the implementation as a tree of nodes, each node having a vector of properties and values, thus facilitating the handling of models and model elements. This internal representation is not restrictive.

A Catalogue of Distribution Primitives

Definition. As observed in the related work section, the distribution logic of DUIs is often hard-coded and is not represented explicitly, which prevents us from reasoning on how distribution is operated. In order to address this issue, we now provide a catalogue of *distribution primitives* that will operate on CUI models of the cluster. We first define these distribution primitives in natural language, then in an Extended Backus-Naur Form (EBNF) format. In this notation, brackets indicate an optional section, while parentheses denote a simple choice in a set of possible values. In the following definitions, we use only one widget at a time for facilitating understanding. In the EBNF, we will use the four selector mechanism for generalization.

SET <Widget.property> TO {value, percentage} [ON <Platform>]: assigns a value to a CUI widget property or a percentage of the actual value on a platform identified in a cluster. For instance, SET "pushButton_1.height" TO 10 will size the push button to a height of 10 units while SET "pushButton_1.height" TO +10 increases its height by 10%. Note that the platform reference is optional: when it is not provided, we assume that the default platform is used.

DISPLAY <Widget> [AT x,y] [ON <Platform>]: displays a CUI widget at a *x,y* location on a platform identified in a cluster, where *x* and *y* are integer positions (e.g., in characters or pixels). For instance, DISPLAY "pushButton_1" AT 1,1 ON "Laptop" will display an identified push button at coordinates 1,1 on the laptop. UNDISPLAY <Element> [AT x,y] [ON <Platform>] is the inverse operation. DISPLAY <Message> [AT x,y] [ON <Platform>] displays a given message on a designated platform in the cluster (mainly for user feedback in an optional console).

COPY <Widget> [ON <SourcePlatform>] TO [<Widget>] [ON <TargetPlatform>]: copies a CUI widget from a source platform identified in a cluster to a clone on a target platform, thus creating a new identifier. This identifier can be provided as a parameter to the primitive or created automatically by the primitive to handle it.

MOVE <Widget> TO x,y [ON <TargetPlatform>] [IN n steps]: moves a CUI widget to a new location indicated by its coordinates *x* and *y*, possibly in a fixed amount of steps, on a target platform in the cluster.

REPLACE <Widget1> BY <Widget2>: replaces a CUI widget Widget1 by another one Widget2. Sometimes the replacement widget could be determined after a (re-)distribution algorithm, thus giving the following definition: REPLACE <Widget1> BY <Algo:>. This mechanism could be applied to contents and image transformations: images are usually transformed by local or remote algorithms (e.g., for resizing, converting, cropping, clipping, repurposing), thus giving the following definition: TRANSFORM <Image1> BY <ImageAlgo:URL>.

MERGE <Widgets> [ON <SourcePlatforms>] TO [<Widget>] [ON <TargetPlatform>]: merges a collection of CUI widgets from a source platform identified in a cluster into a container widget on a target platform, thus creating a new identifier. Again, when source and target platforms are not provided, we assume that the default platform is used. SEPARATE is the inverse primitive. SEPARATES <Widgets> [ON <SourcePlatforms>] TO [<Widgets>] [ON <TargetPlatforms>]: splits a collection of CUI widgets (typically, a container) from a source platform identified in a cluster into CUI widgets on one or many target platforms.

SWITCH <Widget> [ON <SourcePlatforms>] TO [<Widget>] [ON <TargetPlatform>]: switches two CUI widgets between two platforms. When the source and target platforms are equal, the two widgets are simply substituted.

DISTRIBUTE <Elements> INTO <Containers> [BY <DistribAlgo:URL>: computes a distribution of a series of UI Elments into a series of UI Containers, possibly by calling an external algorithm, local or remote.

EBNF Grammar. In order to formally define the language expressing distribution primitives, an Extended Backus Naur Form (EBNF) grammar has been defined. EBNF only differs from BNF in the usage of the following symbols: "?" means that the symbol (or group of symbols in parenthesis) to the left of the operator is optional, "*" means that something can be repeated any number of times, and "+" means that something can appear one or more times. EBNF has been selected because it is widely used to formally define programming languages and markup languages (e.g., XML and SGML), the syntax of the language is precisely defined, thus leaving no ambiguity on its interpretation, and it is easier to develop a parser for such a language, because the parser can be generated automatically with a compiler (e.g., YACC). Instances of distribution primitives are called by *statements*. The definitions of an operation, a source, a target, a selector and some other ones are defined in Fig. 3 and 4 (excerpt only). The definitions could be extended later to support more operations or features.

```
statement = operation , white_space , source , white_space , "TO" ,
white_space , target ;
operation = "SET" | "DISPLAY" | "UNDISPLAY" | "COPY" |
"MOVE" | "REPLACE" | "TRANSFORM" | "MERGE" | "SWITCH" |
"SEPARATE" | "DISTRIBUTE";
source = selector ;
target = displays | selector , white_space , "ON" , white_space ,
displays ;
displays = display_platform , { "," , display_platform}
display_platform = display , [ white_space , "OF" , white_space ,
platform] ;
selector = identifier , { "," , identifier } | universal ;
display = identifier ;
platform = identifier ;
```

Figure 3. EBNF grammar for distribution primitives (partim).

Examples. In order to illustrate how distribution primitive could behave, we hereby provide a series of progressively more complex examples. In Fig. 4, a display of the platform by default has been modified in the following way: DISPLAY "pushButton_1" AT 5,5 ON "defaultPlatform" followed by SET "pushButton_1.label" TO "B", thus creating a CUI model attached to this platform.

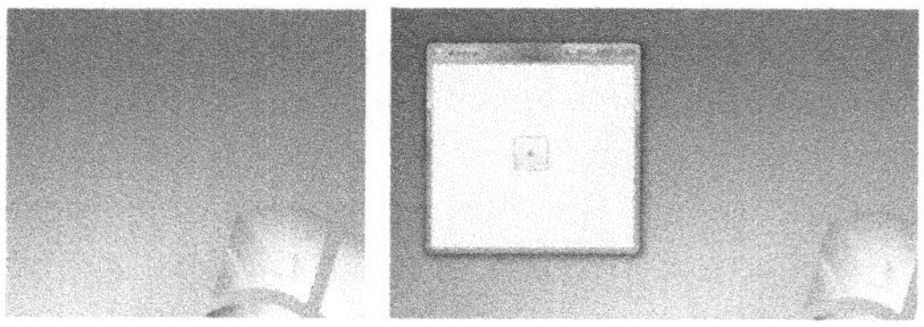

Figure 4. Example of a simple display primitive.

Obviously distribution operations could be more complex than the example provided in Fig. 4. Here is a series of examples for the COPY primitive:

1. COPY button_1 TO shared_display: simple copy of button_1 sent to shared_display without specifying neither an identifier nor a container
2. COPY button_1 TO button_2 ON shared_display: copy button_1 on shared_display and identify it as button_2
3. COPY button_1 TO button_2 ON shared_display of shared_platform: the same but we specify the shared_platform to avoid searching through all the platforms
4. COPY button_1, button_2 TO shared_display: copy button_1 and button_2 to shared_display in a single operation
5. COPY button_1 TO shared_display, my_display: copy button_1 to shared_display and also to my_display
6. COPY button_1 TO shared_display OF shared_platform AND my_display OF my_ipad: copy button_1 to both shared_display and my_display, specifying on which platform is each display
7. COPY * TO shared_display: copy all the graphical components from the current UI to shared_display
8. COPY ALL buttons TO shared_display: copy all buttons to shared_display
9. COPY individuals TO shared_display: copy any individual CUI widgets to shared_display

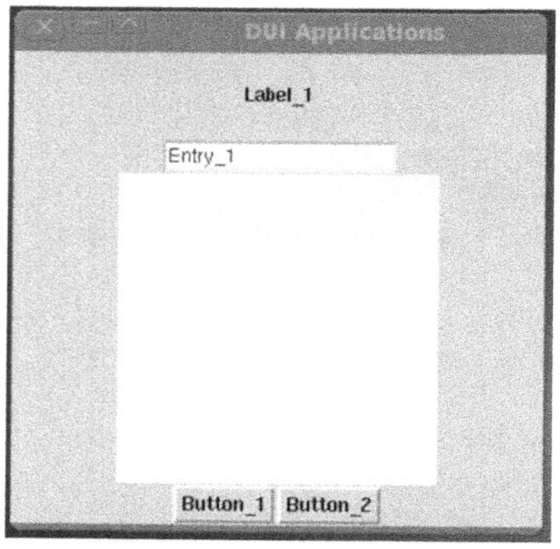

Figure 5. Source CUI for the COPY examples.

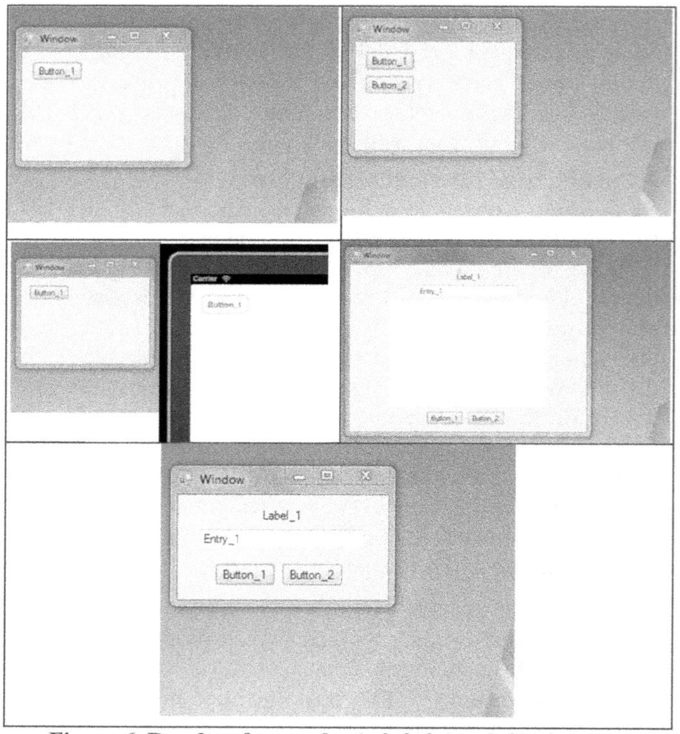

Figure 6. Results of examples 1, 2 & 3 (top left), 4, 8 (top right), 5 & 6 (middle left), 7 (middle right), 9 (bottom).

The source CUI associated to these examples is reproduced in Fig. 5, while the results of the nine above copy operations are reproduced respectively in the different regions of Fig. 6.

Meta-User Interface for Distribution Primitives. The distribution primitives defined in the previous subsection could be called in two ways:

1. *Interactively* through a meta-UI [9] providing a command line equipped with a command language: in this way, one can type any distribution primitive through statements that are immediately interpreted and provide immediate feedback. This meta-UI adheres to usability guidelines for command languages (such as consistency, congruence, and symmetry), but does not provide for the moment any graphical counterpart of each statement or graphical representation of the platforms of the cluster. Actually, each platform is straightforwardly addressed at run-time. It is of course possible to see the results of a distribution primitive immediately by typing it by a "errors and trials" process until the right statement is reached. Fig. 7 reproduces a screen shot of this meta-UI, which also serve as a tutorial to understand how to use the distribution primitives. Indeed, any statement type in the command language can be stored in a list of statements that could be recalled at any time.
2. *Programmatically*: each statement representing an instance of a distribution primitive can be incorporated in an interactive application in the same way since the parser will be called to interpret it. It is therefore no longer needed to program these primitives.

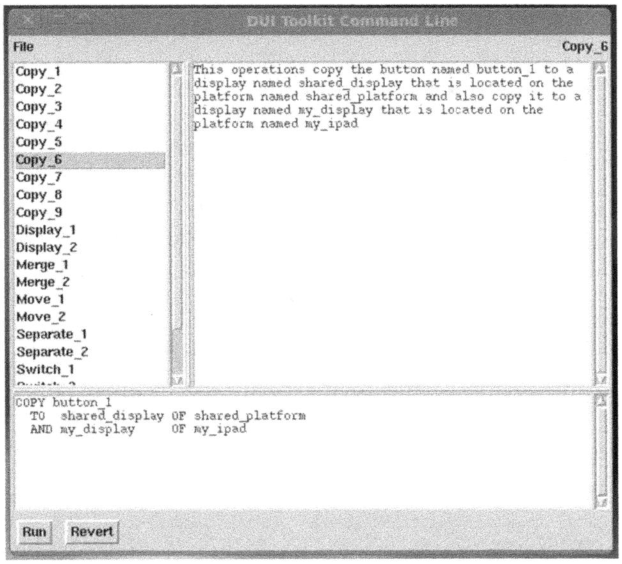

Figure 7. Command Line Interface for primitives.

IMPLEMENTATION

A toolkit has been developed upon the model-based approach. It creates application with UI separated in two-parts: the proxy and the rendering. In Fig. 8, the proxy is represented as a separate part of the application than the rendering. The first keeps the state of the application and ensures the core functionalities, while the second displays the user interface. Application supporting DUI allows the rendering to be distributed on other platforms while the proxy stays where the application has been created. The toolkit works in an environment supported by Microsoft Windows operating systems (XP and newer), Apple Mac OS X, Linux and Android. And we are currently working on the full support for Apple iOS. The applications created with this toolkit are multi-platform. Each graphical component is described as a record containing several keys and values. It ensures compatibility with XML because the keys/values become the name/value pairs of the XML markup. The DUI can be controlled by a command line interface, a meta-UI or even by the applications themselves.

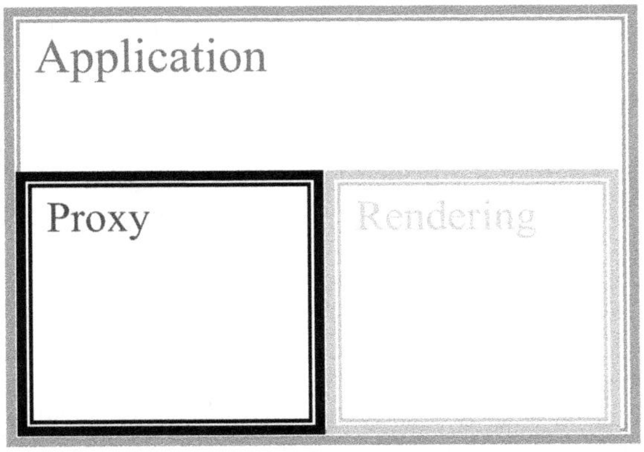

Figure 8. Structure of a DUI application.

A MODEL-BASED APPROACH FOR DUIs

Using the distribution primitives defined and exemplified in the previous section is an appropriate starting point for designing DUIs at a higher level of expression that simple code. After having defined the different models and these primitives, we outline a model-based approach for designing a DUI based on the aforementioned concepts:

1. Build a cluster model of the platforms.
2. Build a CUI model for each platform
3. Assemble models in the distribution scene
4. Write a distribution scenario based on distribution primitives.
5. Develop the distribution scenario

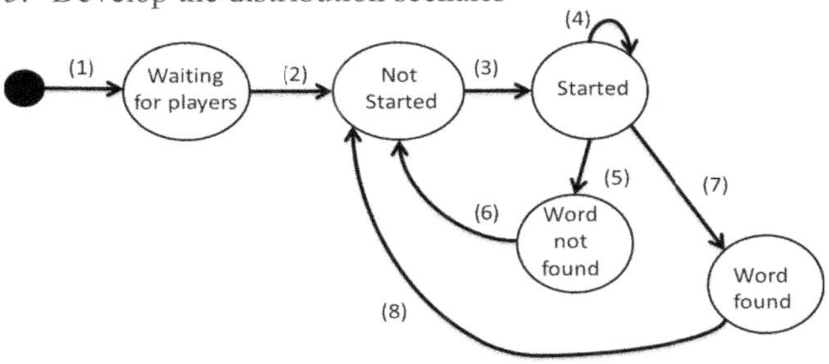

Figure 9. State-machine diagram of the Pictionary.

Pictionary

We now illustrate this method on some examples. A Pictionary game exemplified the mechanisms and evaluates the difference between a local Pictionary and a distributed Pictionary. In Figure 9, the STM shows that to start a game, the Pictionary needs several steps. The players will each have to assign or be assigned to a role. There are three roles: the player, the guessers and the observers. Two players are at least needed because the game needs one drawer and at least one guesser. The distribution does not appear in the states of the Pictionary. The transition can be of two types: with and without distribution. As in any STM, the transitions may have some guarding conditions. For readability issue, we put it apart from the STM. Also, the final state is not display on the diagram. In order to clearly state the transitions, they are all numbered from 1 to 8 and here are the transitions in the form IF condition THEN action:

1. IF new_player_event
   THEN DISPLAY pictionary_UI TO new_player
2. IF nb_player > 1
   THEN DISPLAY assign_UI TO Pictionary_UI OF players
3. IF drawer != null && guesser != null
   THEN UNDISPLAY assign_UI
   DISPLAY draw_UI TO Pictionary_UI OF drawer
   AND guesser_UI TO Pictionary_UI OF guessers
   UPDATE observe_UI TO observers
4. UPDATE draw_UI
5. IF timer <= 0 & !found
   THEN UPDATE draw_UI, guesser_UI
6. UNDISPLAY draw_UI, guesser_UI, observer_UI
   DISPLAY assign_UI TO players

7. IF timer > 0 & found
   THEN UPDATE draw_UI, guesser_UI
8. UNDISPLAY draw_UI, guesser_UI,observer_UI
   DISPLAY assign_UI TO players

The drawer UI (Fig. 10) enables the drawing area. The guessers and observers are able to watch the drawing area but are unable to draw on it. The guessers can try words. A timer runs down until the word is found or until it reaches 00:00. This UI can be translated into a local distribution graph for the device on which the Pictionary is started. For example, a user with a computer and a mobile phone will have the following distribution scene as in Fig. 11 and 12.

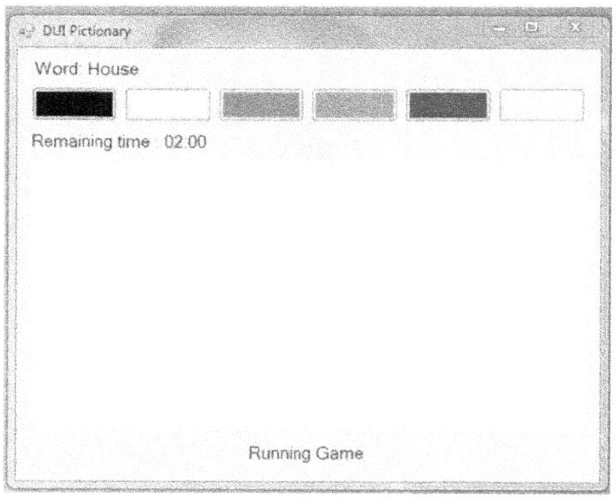

Figure 10. draw_UI enabling drawing area.

Figure 11. The cluster model of the Pictionary.

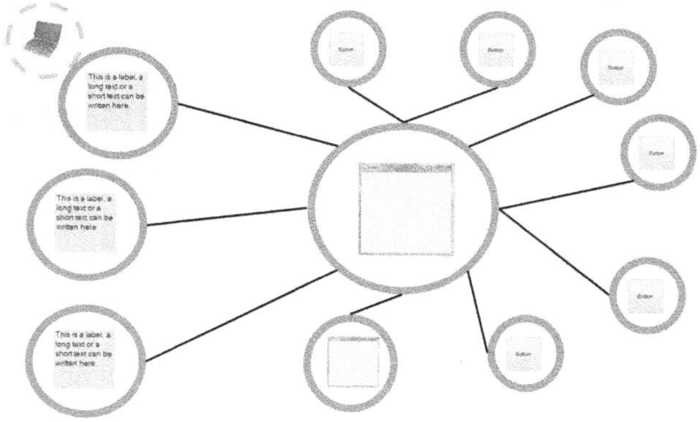

Figure 12. Associated graph of CUI models.

Game of the Goose

We also present an idea of a game that will be a combination of several games as the Game of the Goose. A basic example would be to use the Pictionary, a Minesweeper and a Snake as games to combine. See Figure 13 for the Minesweeper examples of UI. The DUI combination game increases the use of distribution. When a player reaches a case on the board, the game of the case will be loaded and automatically display to its platforms. We may also redistribute the UI through its platforms at his own ease of use.

Figure 13. Example of a Minesweeper game.

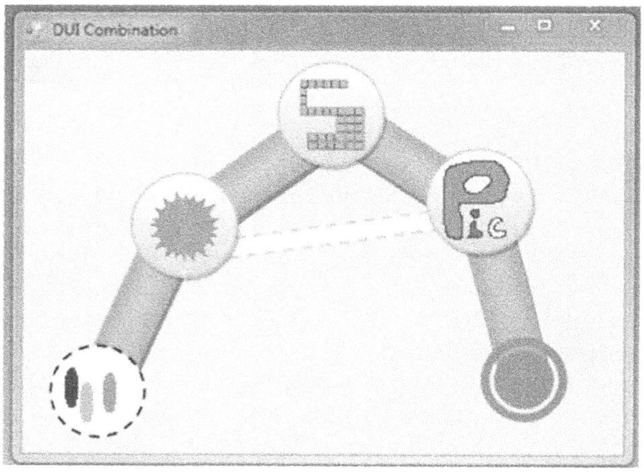

Figure 14. Example of UI for the combination game.

There is a bridge between the Minesweeper and Pictionary games. A win in the Minesweeper game will allow the player to go to the Pictionary while a loss on the Pictionary will send the player back to the Minesweeper. The example shown here is a simple 3-cases game, but the number should be higher for a real game. In the Game of the Goose, there are 63 cases. In order to demonstrate the use of the distribution, we start with a configuration of three devices. The global distribution graph is represented in Figure 15.

Two users, Lucas and Nathan, share Lucas's laptop on which they are currently running the Game of the Goose. This laptop is represented by the dashed circle laptop on the graph. Lucas has connected his mobile phone, while Nathan has connected his own laptop. The Game of the Goose is based on the toolkit and will automatically distribute the UI. Two players have been created in the game and are each linked to a platform. The game starts with the first player, Lucas, and will use Lucas' mobile phone to display the Minesweeper game. The game triggers a scenario of the distribution to distribute the UI allowing Lucas to play and preventing Nathan to access to the game. At this level, the global distribution graph has been changed and is represented in Fig. 16. The scenario used for the distribution is:

DISPLAY minesweeper_UI TO lucas ON mobile_1

Fig. 15. Global distribution graph for the Game of the Goose.

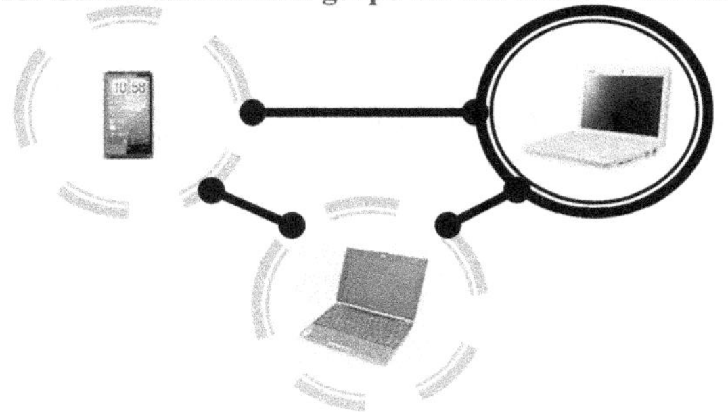

Figure 16. Global distribution graph for the Game of the Goose when Lucas is playing Minesweeper.

When Lucas has finished playing the Minesweeper game, he is now either staying at Minesweeper case if he lost the game or going to the Pictionary if he won. It Is now Nathan's turn, and the UI is now redistribute through the following scenario:

```
UNDISPLAY minesweeper_UI TO lucas ON mobile_1
DISPLAY minesweeper_UI TO nathan ON laptop_2
```

After Nathan's part, it's Lucas turn. They will both play Pictionary. As Lucas is playing, he will be the one that choose the word and that try to make Lucas guess the word. The game is now triggering a new scenario:

```
UNDISPLAY minesweeper_UI TO nathan ON laptop_2
DISPLAY pictionary_UI TO laptop_1
DISPLAY draw_UI TO nathan ON laptop_2
DISPLAY guesser_UI TO lucas ON mobile_1
```

As Nathan wants to choose the word on his laptop, he will manually ask for pictionary_UI to be displayed on his laptop with the following primitive:

```
COPY pictionary_UI TO nathan ON laptop2
```

He is now able to choose the word from pictionary_UI and then draw on the draw_UI. Lucas sees what Nathan is drawing on his mobile phone and has the ability to propose word. If Lucas finds the word, the game stops and Lucas wins. If the time is up and Lucas has not been able to find the word, Nathan wins. The game finishes when one of the player reaches the red dot. Here, Lucas has found the word and has won the Pictionary game. He then won the Game of the Goose as it was the last game before the red dot. Here was an example of a more interesting distribution application.

CONCLUSION AND FUTURE WORK

In this paper we have introduced a model-based approach for designing applications with Distributed User Interfaces. These applications enable the distribution of their UI components in both static and dynamic way. We have first introduced a distribution graph in order to model the distribution space. The distribution graphs help modeling the distribution of the UI and describing the virtual distributed environment of the application. We then introduced a distribution language to describe the distribution statements. These statements can be used in distribution scenarios for automatic and manual distribution. This latter can be through a command line interface or a Meta-UI. No tool has been developed in order to support the distribution graph representation. A toolkit supporting the creation of DUIs and the distribution operations is currently in development and will be introduced in the future. Based on this toolkit, we have exemplified the model-based approach on the example of a Pictionary as basic case-study. Then, we have introduced an example of application that is a composition of games. It exemplifies the use of distribution primitives and scenarios. There is still work to do before releasing the toolkit. We keep working on this model-based approach in order to make it compatible with several approach designing applications. A catalog of the distribution primitives will be released with a complete description of each primitive.

ACKNOWLEDGMENTS

The author would like to acknowledge the support of the ITEA2-Call3-2008026 USIXML (User Interface extensible Markup Language) European project and its support by Région Wallonne

REFERENCES

1. Avrahami, G., Brooks, K.P., and Brown, M.H. A Two-View Approach to Constructing User Interfaces, *ACM Computer Graphics 23*, 3 (July 1989), pp. 137–146.
2. Ayatsuka, Y., Matsushita, N., and Rekimoto, J. HyperPalette: a hybrid computing environment for small computing devices. In: *Proc. of CHI'00* (The Hague, April 1-6, 2000). ACM Press, New York (2000), pp. 133–134.
3. Bandelloni, R. and Paternò, F. Migratory user interfaces able to adapt to various interaction platforms. *Int. Journal of Human-Computer Studies 60*, 5-6 (2004), pp. 621–639.
4. Beale, R. and Edmondson, W. Multiple carets, multiple screens and multi-tasking: new behaviours with multiple computers. In: *Proc. of HCI'07* (Lancaster, September 3-7, 2007). British Computer Society, Swinton (2007), pp. 55–64.
5. Berglund, E. and Bång, M. Requirements for distributed user interface in ubiquitous computing network. In: *Proc. of ACM Conf. on Mobile and Ubiquitous MultiMedia* MUM'02 (Oulu, December 11-13, 2002). ACM Press, New York (2002).
6. Bharat, K. A. and Cardelli, L. Migratory applications. In: *Proc. of UIST'95* (Pittsburgh, November 15-17, 1995). ACM Press, New York, 1995, pp. 132–142.
7. Biehl, J. T., Baker, W. T., Bailey, B. P., Tan, D. S., Inkpen, K. M., and Czerwinski, M. IMPROMPTU: a new interaction framework for supporting collaboration in multiple display environments and its field evaluation for co-located software development. In: *Proc. of CHI'08* (Florence, April 5-10,

2008). ACM Press, New York (2008), pp. 939–948.
8. Chung, G. and Dewan, P. Towards dynamic collaboration architectures. In: *Proc. of CSCW'04* (Chicago, November 6-10, 2004). ACM Press, New York (2004), pp. 1–10.
9. Coutaz, J. Meta-User Interfaces for Ambient Spaces. In: *Proc. of TAMODIA'2006* (Hasselt, October 23-24, 2006). LNCS, Vol. 4385. Springer, Berlin (2006), pp. 1–15.
10. Delivery Context Ontology (DCO), W3C, Geneva, 2010. http://www.w3.org/TR/2009/WD-dcontology-20090616/.
11. Demeure, A., Sottet, J.S., Calvary, G., Coutaz, J., Ganneau, V., and Vanderdonckt, J. The 4C Reference Model for Distributed User Interfaces. In: *Proc. of ICAS'2008* (Gosier, March 16-21, 2008), IEEE Comp. Soc., (2008), pp. 61-69.
12. Dewan, P. and Shen, H. Controlling access in multiuser interfaces. *ACM Trans. Comp.-Hum. Interact. 5, 1* (1998), 34-62.
13. Distributed Programming in Mozart–A Tutorial Introduction, chapter 3: Basic Operations and Examples, accessible at http://www.mozart-oz.org/documentation/dstutorial/node3.html#chapter.examples. Visited on Nov. 21st, 2010.
14. Econometric Modeling & Computing Corporation (EMCC). 2010. Accessible at: http://www.speakeasy.com
15. Eisenstein, J., Vanderdonckt, J., and Puerta, A. Applying model-based techniques to the development of UIs for mobile computers. In: *Proc. of IUI'01* (Santa Fe, January 14-17, 2001). ACM Press, New York (2001), pp. 69–76.
16. Grolaux, D., Van Roy, P., and Vanderdonckt, J. Migratable User Interfaces: Beyond Migratory User Interfaces. In: *Proc. of 1st IEEE-ACM Annual Int. Conf. on Mobile and Ubiquitous Systems: Networking and Services MOBIQUITOUS'04* (Cambridge, August 22-26, 2004). ACM Press (2004), pp. 422–430.
17. Grolaux, D., Vanderdonckt, J., and Van Roy, P. Attach me, Detach me, Assemble me like You Work. In: *Proc. of INTERACT'05* (Rome, September 12-16, 2005). LNCS, Vol. 3585, Springer-Verlag, Berlin (2005), pp. 198–212.
18. Grudin, J. Partitioning digital worlds: focal and peripheral awareness in multiple monitor use. In: *Proc. of the ACM Conf. on Human Factors in Computing Systems CHI'01* (Seattle, 2001). ACM Press, New York (2001), pp. 458–465.
19. Han, R., Perret, V., and Naghshineh, M. WebSplitter: a unified XML framework for multi-device collaborative Web browsing. In: *Proc. of CSCW'00* (Philadelphia, December 2-6, 2000). ACM Press, New York (2000), pp. 221–230.
20. Hutchings, D. R., Smith, G., Meyers, B., Czerwinski, M., and Robertson, G. Display space usage and window management operation comparisons between single monitor and multiple monitor users. In: *Proc. of AVI'04* (Gallipoli, May 25-28, 2004). ACM Press, New York (2004), pp. 32–39.
21. Hutchings, H.M. and Pierce, J. S. Understanding the whethers, hows, and whys of divisible interfaces. In: *Proc. of the Working Conf. on Advanced Visual Interfaces AVI'06* (Venezia, May 23-26, 2006). ACM Press, New Y. (2006), pp. 274–277.
22. Loeser, C., Mueller, W., Berger, F., and Eikerling, H.J. Peer-to-Peer Networks for Virtual Home Environments. In: *Proc. of HICSS'03* (Big Island, January 6-9, 2003). IEEE Computer Society, Los Alamitos (2003), p. 282.
23. Lorenz, A. Research directions for the application of MVC in ambient computing environments. In: *Proc. of the 1st Int. Workshop on Pattern-Driven Engineering of interactive Computing Systems PEICS'10* (Berlin, July 20, 2010). ACM Press, New York (2010), pp. 28–31.
24. Luyten, K. and Coninx, K. Distributed User Interface Elements to support Smart Interaction Spaces. In: *Proc. of the 7th IEEE Int. Symposium on Multimedia ISM'2005* (December 12-14, 2005). IEEE Computer Society (2005), pp. 277–286.
25. Luyten, K., Vandervelpen, C., and Coninx, K. Migratable User Interface Descriptions in Component-Based Development. In: *Proc. of DSV-IS'2002* (Rostock, June 12-14, 2002). Lecture Notes in Computer Science, Vol. 2545. Springer-Verlag, London (2002), pp. 44–58.
26. Luyten, K., Van den Bergh, J., Vandervelpen, Ch., and Coninx, K. Designing distributed user interfaces for ambient intelligent environments using models and simulations. *Computers & Graphics 30*, 5 (2006), pp. 702–713.
27. Melchior, J., Grolaux, D., Vanderdonckt, J., and Van Roy, P. A toolkit for peer-to-peer distributed user interfaces: concepts, implementation, and applications. In: *Proc. of the 1st ACM Symposium on Engineering interactive Computing Systems EICS'09* (Pittsburgh, July 15-17, 2009). ACM, pp. 69–78.
28. Molina, J.P., Vanderdonckt, J., González, P., Fernández-Caballero, A., and Lozano, M.D. Rapid Prototyping of Distributed User Interfaces. In: *Proc. of CADUI'2006* (Bucharest, 6-8 June 2006). Springer-Verlag, Berlin (2006), pp. 151–166.
29. Myers, B. A. 2001. Using handhelds and PCs together. *Commun. ACM 44*, 11 (November 2001), pp. 34–41.
30. Newman, M. W., Izadi, S., Edwards, W. K., Sedivy, J. Z., and Smith, T.F. User interfaces when and where they are needed: an infrastructure for recombinant computing. In: *Proc. of the 15th ACM Symposium on User interface Software and Technology UIST'02* (Paris, October 27-30, 2002). ACM Press, New York (2002), pp. 171–180.
31. Qiu, X. F. and Graham, T.N. Flexible and efficient platform modeling for distributed interactive systems. In: *Proc. of the 1st ACM Symposium on Engineering interactive Computing Systems EICS'09* (Pittsburgh, July 15 - 17, 2009). ACM Press, New York (2009), pp. 29–34.
32. Sjölund, M., Larsson, A., and Berglund, E. Smartphone Views: Building Multi-Device Distributed User Interfaces In: *Proc. of MobileHCI'2004* (Glasgow, 13-16 September 2004). LNCS, Vol. 3160. Springer, Berlin (2004), pp. 507–511.
33. Tan, D.S. and Czerwinski, M. Effects of Visual Separation and Physical Discontinuities when Distributing Information across Multiple Displays. In: *Proc. of INTERACT'03* (Zurich, September 1-5, 2003). IOS Press (2003), pp. 252–260.
34. Tan, D.S., Myers, B. and Czerwinski, M. 2004 WinCuts: Manipulating Arbitrary Window Regions for More Effective User of Screen Space. In: *Proc. of CHI'2004* (Vienna, April 24-29, 2004). ACM Press, New York (2004), pp. 1525–1528.
35. Vanderdonckt, J. Distributed User Interfaces: How to Distribute User Interface Elements across Users, Platforms, and Environments. In: *Proc. of XIth Congreso Internacional de Interacción Persona-Ordenador Interacción'2010* (Valencia, 7-10 September 2010). AIPO, Valencia, 2010, pp. 3-14.
36. Vandervelpen, Ch., Vanderhulst, G., Luyten, K., and Coninx, K. 2005. Light-Weight Distributed Web Interfaces: Preparing the Web for Heterogeneous Environments. In: *Proc. of the 5th Int. Conf. on Web Engineering ICWE'2005* (Sydney, July 27-29, 2005). Springer, Berlin (2005), pp. 197–202.
37. Van Roy, P. and Haridi, S. Concepts, Techniques, and Models of Computer Programming. MIT Press, 2004.
38. Xiaojun, B. and Balakrishnan, R. Comparing usage of a large high-resolution display to single or dual desktop displays for daily work. In: *Proc. of the 27th Int. Conf. on Human factors in Computing Systems CHI'09* (Boston, April 4-9, 2009). ACM Press, New York (2004), pp. 1005–1014.
39. Yanagida, T. and Nonaka, H. 2008. Architecture for Migratory Adaptive User Interfaces. In: *Proc. of the 8th IEEE Int. Conf. on Computer and Information Technology CIT'2008* (Sidney, July 8-11, 2008). IEEE (2008), pp. 450–455.

A Model-based Approach for Supporting Engineering Usability Evaluation of Interaction Techniques

Philippe Palanque, Eric Barboni, Célia Martinie, David Navarre & Marco Winckler
Institute of Research in Informatics of Toulouse
University Paul Sabatier
118 route de Narbonne, 31062 Toulouse CEDEX 9, France
{palanque, barboni, martinie, navarre, winckler}@irit.fr

ABSTRACT
This paper offers a contribution for engineering interaction techniques by proposing a model-based approach for supporting usability evaluation. This approach combines different techniques including *formal analysis* of models, *simulation* and, in particular, *analysis of log* data in a model-based environment. This approach is integrated in a process and is supported by a model-based CASE tool for modeling, simulation and evaluation of interactive systems. A case study illustrates the approach and operation of the tool. The results demonstrate that the log data at model level can be used not only to identify usability problems but also to identify where to operate changes to these models in order to fix usability problems. Finally we show how the analysis of log data allows the designer to easily shape up the interaction technique (as the results of log analysis are presented at the same abstraction level of models). Such as an approach offers an alternative to user testing that are very difficult to configure and to interpret especially when advanced interaction techniques are concerned.

Keywords
Interactive systems modeling, interaction techniques, performance evaluation, model-based usability evaluation.

ACM Classification Keywords
H5.m. Information interfaces and presentation (e.g., HCI).

General Terms
Verification.

INTRODUCTION
The development of interaction techniques to improve users' performance and satisfaction whilst using an interactive system has been a keystone for the research in the Human Computer Interaction field. Since the seminal work of Fitts [14] many refinements of the Fitts' law have been proposed to predict the difficulty for performing interactive tasks on a system, such as McKenzie extending Fitts' law for two-dimensional task [25] or the steering law from Accot & Zhai for constrained movement in trajectory-based tasks [1]. These laws can be applied at design time, indeed, to fine-tune the graphical representation of objects (such as size and shape) or to promote the development of new interaction techniques (e.g. multiple click, Drag and Drop…). In this context, innovation quite often occurs by extending existing interaction techniques. For example, Direct Manipulation enhanced interaction techniques such as Drag and Pop and Drag and Pick from Baudisch et al. [7] extend the Drag and Drop interaction technique by moving closer the possible reactive icons as soon as a drag event is produced. Boomerang of Kobayashi and Igarashi [20] proposes another extension to Drag and Drop interaction by defining mechanisms to suspend and resume a Drag and Drop interaction (after an interruption has occurred for instance). Another extension to standard interaction techniques is the work called "semantic pointing" of Blanch et al. [9] which proposes an adaptation of the control-display ratio based on the interactivity of the object below the mouse cursor. Other extensions have also been proposed taking into account nonstandard input and output devices such MAGIC pointing (which stands for Manual and Gaze Input Cascaded) [36] or Collomb & Hascoët [12] who adapt interaction technique such as Drag and Pop or propose new ones as Drag and Throw and Push and Throw [16] on wall-size display.

When proposing such enhanced interaction techniques, researchers typically build a prototype implementing it and then proceed to comparative assessments of the interaction technique with respect to existing ones. Prototypes are then assessments by the mean of user testing. Any necessary adjustment to improve performance or to fix usability problems are eventually done directly on the prototype. This design process raises the following main issues:

1. **Definition of the precise behavior of the interaction technique**: usually the interaction technique is only described in an informal way using text, screen captures or video (see Drag and Pop page [20]). Such informal descriptions leave a lot of information underspecified such as, for instance in the case of Drag and Pop, the size of the icons, the distance between the reactive icons and the one currently selected, … With more conventional interaction technique (such as Drag and Drop) the same issues remain leaving critical information not precisely defined.

EICS'11, June 13–16, 2011, Pisa, Italy.

2. **Ensuring the correctness of the interaction technique**: interaction technique testing is usually performed in an informal way by means of a sequence of tests. As the behavior of the interaction technique depends on the state of the interactive system and the behavior of the user, tests coverage remains very limited providing no mean to ensure that it will be robust and not fail [35]. Such concerns is well known in the field of interactive systems engineering and one of the only ways to address that problem is by using verification techniques on a formal model.
3. **Tuning the interaction technique to get optimal performance**: one clear example of fine-tuning mean for interaction techniques is the acceleration of the mouse cursor according to the speed movement of the mouse on the table. An efficient acceleration improves significantly selection time but usually remains hidden from the interaction technique description [18]. Each time a new interaction technique is defined, identification of the tunable element and how they have to be tuned are critical. Without an abstract and precise description of the interaction technique, such tuning is made at the code level on objects that are necessarily at a much lower level than the ones describing the interaction technique.
4. **Recording information during the usability tests:** when testing interaction techniques it is very difficult to record pertinent information which is usually at a low level of abstraction i.e. mostly at the level of user interface events [24]. Indeed, most of these events are directly produced by the input devices and thus makes it impossible to understand what happens when several input devices are used in a multimodal way as in a combined click on a bimanual interaction technique.
5. **Interpreting usability tests:** results to improve (both tuning and modification) the interaction technique from usability tests are difficult to interpret as these results usually remain at the event level and thus again are far away from the interaction technique states and behavior. Decisions for improvements are thus hard to make and implementations cumbersome and error prone thus leading to more usability tests than what would have been needed to define and tune the interaction technique.
6. **Reusing and refining interaction techniques**: makes it possible for other researchers and/or companies to reuse what has been proposed and potentially improve it. Building on previous works and knowledge developed in the field is a complex task and requires special means to promote it.
7. **Comparative assessment of interaction techniques**: if only final implementation is available; it is very difficult to determine which usability problems come from the design or from miscoding the interaction technique. Moreover, comparative assessment will require the execution of the same scenarios with all interaction technique being compared. For example, if interruption-tolerant systems are a concern, interruptible scenarios should occur with the same frequency and duration in all user testing sessions.

In order to address these problems, this paper proposes a model-based approach to support parts of the engineering process of interaction techniques. Next section introduces our approach that investigates several techniques including *formal analysis* of models, *simulation* and *analysis of log* data in a model-based environment. In particular we demonstrate how model-based approaches can facilitate the tasks of usability evaluation involving users. The subsequent section illustrates the approach with a case study for the modeling and evaluation a multimodal interaction techniques using two mice in a configuration similar to that embedded into the next generation of aircraft cockpits. Then, we discuss of the advantages and limitations of our approach in particularly with respect to previous works in the field.

APPROACH

The approach proposed in the section is based on models that are used as an input for a series of steps aiming to assess the specification of the interaction technique prior to usability testing with users.

Basic assumptions about the approach

The approach relies on the following assumptions:

- **Use of formal description technique**: the formalism used for describing interaction techniques has a strong impact on the kind of assessments that can be performed [29]. As we shall see, the precise assessment and fine-tuning of interaction techniques requires a complete and unambiguous description of the states of the interaction technique can be in as well as the events triggering state changes and the occurrence of fusion/fission of events.
- **Models must support prototyping:** this means that models run synchronously with user interface prototypes. Model execution is also a main requirement for checking usability properties such as liveness [19]. Moreover, models should be co-executable (i.e. changes in one model trigger changes in all related models in the framework) with any other models or software components use to build the system. Models execution will ensure that system models can be used as a prototype of the expected final application, which means that the prototype behaves exactly as modeled. This requirement implies the prototype is driven by the execution of models and for that there is an appropriate tool support.
- **Evolvability of models:** the approach aims at supporting the fine-tuning of the interaction techniques, which means that models should evolve according to the design of interaction technique until the expected performance fir the system has been reached.

Appropriate models and formalism are essential, but these are just part of the solution. On one hand, we need models to provide developers with a precise description of the system behavior. Based on that, designers can build the system as planned and evaluators can decide which are the most suitable and interesting scenarios to test with users (given that it will be extremely expensive to test all possible scenarios with users only). On the other hand, there must be a bridge between the specifications and the actual application offered to the users. As shown later, the results of *user testing* are directly associated to models instead of the implementation. This is made possible because *models* and *executable prototypes* remain consistent and compatible during the *implementation* phase. For that reason, the approach is heavily dependent of the fact that the formalism is executable and on the tool support which executes them.

So far only ICO [26] and Petshop [4] could support all the aspects described above. The ICO formalism has been demonstrated efficient for describing several techniques including 3D [27] and multimodal [22][30]. ICO models are executable and fully supported by the CASE tool PetShop which has been shown effective for prototyping interactive techniques [28].

Our approach employs methods such as formal analysis to ensure some basic system properties demonstrating the reliability of the interaction technique. It also integrates formal modeling and user testing by exploiting model-based log data. The use of model-based log analysis is very different from "classical" log as in [17] where the information collected is directly related to user's actions on the interface using the input devices (e.g. clicks, move ...) thus far away from higher abstraction elements such as models or code.

The approach in a Nutshell

The general iterative approach for the assessment of interaction techniques is illustrated by Figure 1 (only colored parts are addressed by this paper). It is assumed that early steps such as requirements analysis, design and low-fidelity prototyping have been already carried out previously so that, the process starts by modeling activities.

Different models must be provided including: *task models* (for describing user tasks), *behavioral models* (using the ICO description technique for describing both the general behavior of the interaction technique and the treatment of low level events from input devices). From task models we *extract test scenarios* that are used as input both for the *execution* and the usability evaluation of the prototype (based on the execution of the ICO models). The prototype then follows a usability evaluation plan based on user testing, which produces logs data that can be classical *logs such as video, questionnaires… as well as model-based logs* (that are related to the ICO models).These logs thus support the assessment of the models of the interaction technique, and allow iterating while performance of these techniques does not meet the corresponding requirements. This is represented on Figure 1 by the box decision with its output towards *Interaction Technique OK* or towards *System and Task modeling* if there is still a need for tunings). The main idea is that usability problems discovered with the usability test can now point out these problems on the system models themselves, making it easier for designer both to locate where changes have to be made and additionally how to make them.

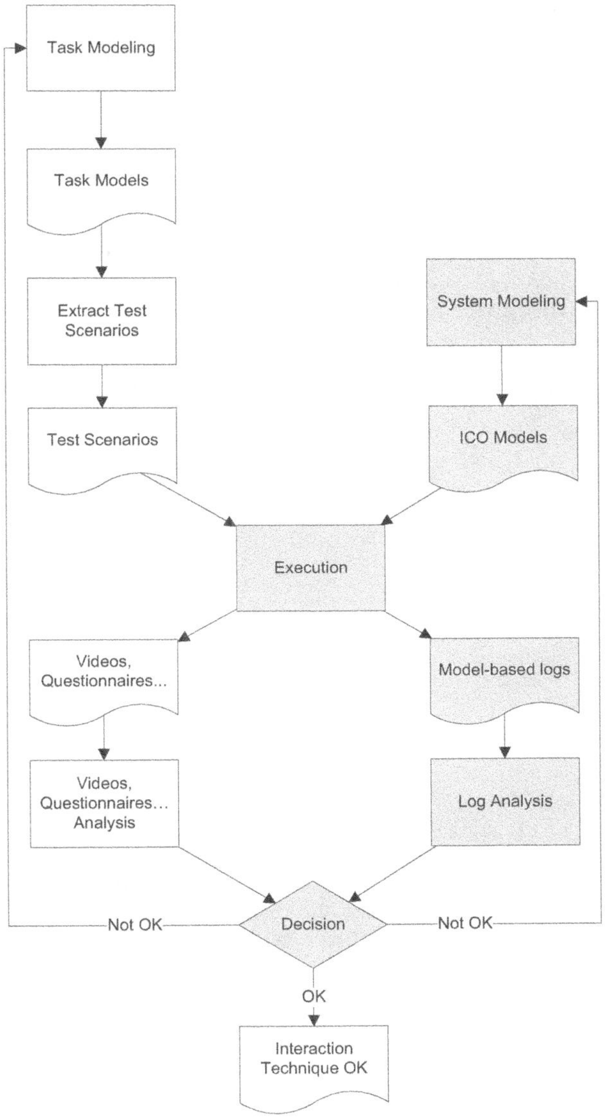

Figure 1. Development process for engineering interaction techniques.

The approach is quite generic but heavily dependent of a tool support and formalism able to support the main assumptions drew about models. In the present case, the approach exploits the ICO notation for describing the entire behavior of the interaction techniques and relies on the tool support Petshop for executing ICO models. Petshop not only support the modeling and execution of ICO models but also ensure the connection of models with the prototype. In previous work we have described how to use the ICO formalism to several techniques including 3D [27] and multimodal [30] interaction techniques. The interested reader can find in [26] a detailed description of the formalism. Iterative prototyping of applications using the ICO formalism have also been fully described in previous work (see [28]) with the help of the tool support PetShop [5]. The rest of the paper details the different steps of the approach. Particular importance is given to model-based evaluation methods which include *formal analysis*, *simulation*, *performance analysis*, and *log data analysis* provided by user testing. These evaluation techniques are better described along the case study which is presented in the next section.

CASE STUDY

The objective of the case study is to present the various phases of the approach on a simple but realistic application which reproduces a classic desktop environment as shown by Figure 2. In this application a set of icons are presented in a window on a grid. The icons can be moved to different locations and deleted once they reach the trash bin icon. The user's goal is to remove all the icons on the user interface.

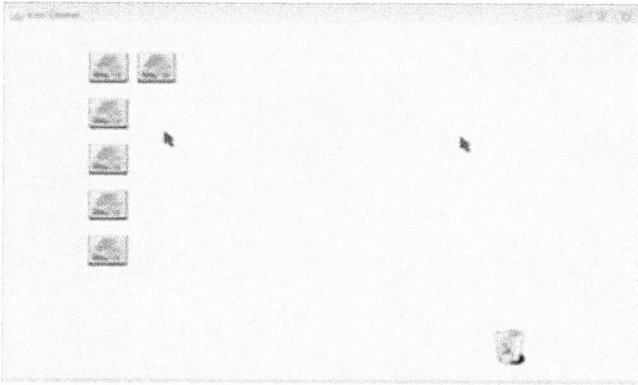

Figure 2. User interface of the case study.

Several interaction techniques could support this goal. However, to illustrate our approach we have investigated an interaction technique based on a *multimodal click* using two mice. To remove an icon from the desktop using the *multimodal click* a user must click on the icon and then on the trash bin. It can also be performed by two users. Indeed, the *multimodal click* is implemented in modern civil aircraft cockpits to allow the interaction of pilot and co-pilot.

Formal specification

Figure 3 and Figure 4 present the ICO models that specify the behavior of the *multimodal click* interaction technique. The Interactive Cooperative Objects (ICO) formalism is a formal description technique designed to the specification, modeling and implementation of interactive systems. It uses concepts borrowed from the object-oriented approach to describe the structural or static aspects of systems, and uses high-level Petri nets to describe their dynamics or behavioral aspects. In addition to these, specific components of the ICO formalism deal with presentation [6] and with command aspects of the interactive systems.

Figure 3 describes the behavior at the dialog level while Figure 4 describes the behavior of the associated mouse transducer. It is interesting to notice that the behavior of the interactive system there is a single model for two mice. In fact, both mice behave exactly the same. At Figure 3 the place *Frame* contains a token that is the reference to the presentation frame which is the user interface of the case study. Place *Trash* contains a token that is the reference to the trash element of the application. Each time a combined click (simultaneous click on both mice) is performed, an event *combinedClick* is received and it fires the *combinedClick* transition: the reference to the icon the target pointer of first mouse is on is stored in *obj1* and the reference to the icon the target pointer of second mouse is on is stored in *obj2*.

Once this transition is fired and consumed, a token is deposited in place *testIcon*. From this place, one transition only can be fired at a time; it will depend on which condition is fulfilled. If the target pointer of the first mouse is on a file icon (*obj1* is an instance of the *Icon* class) and that the target pointer of the second mouse is on the trash icon (*obj2* is equal to *trash*) or conversely, the transition *fileIconAndTrashSelected* will be fired and the file icon will be deleted. In all other cases, the transition *fileIconAndTrashNotSelected* will be fired, but no action will be triggered. In both cases, the token that is present in place *testIcon* will be consumed.

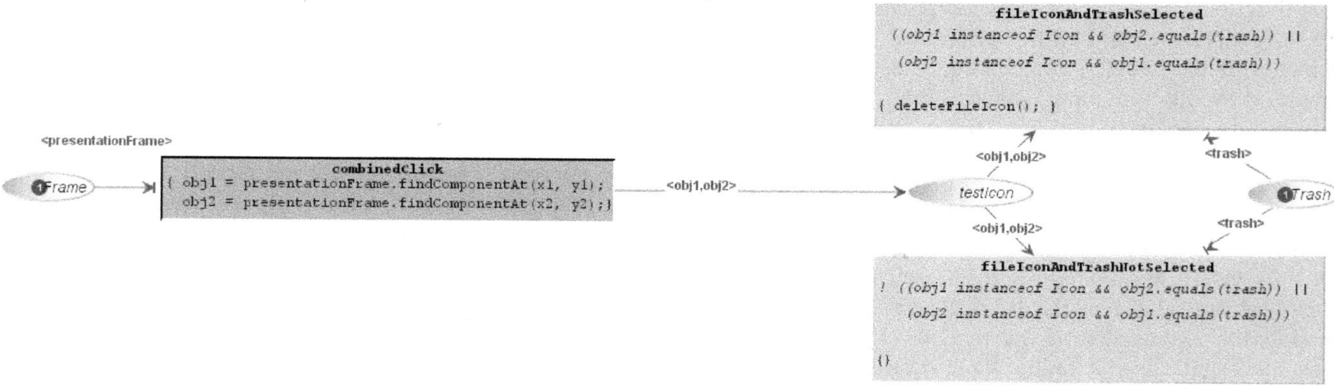

Figure 3. ICO model *combined click* specifying the interaction technique *multimodal click*.

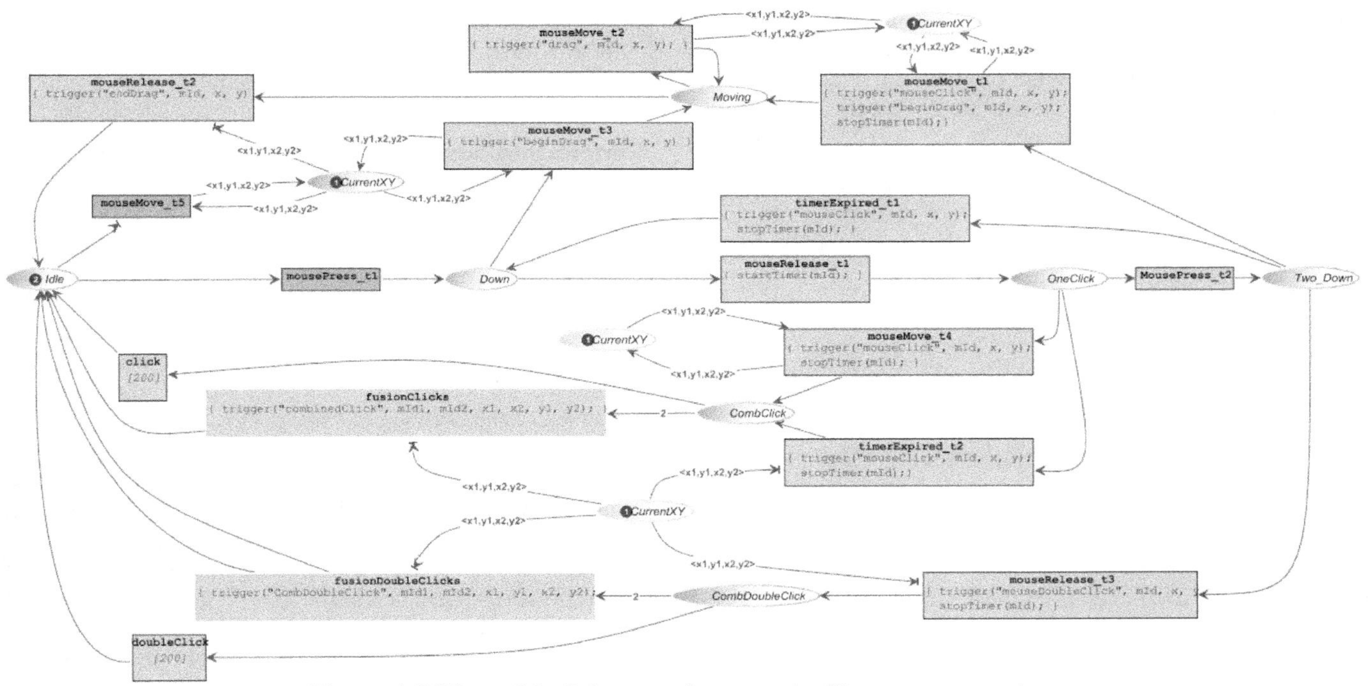

Figure 4. ICO model of the transducer controlling mouse events.

Figure 4 specifies the behavior of the physical interaction between the user and the system. This transducer takes mouse low level events as inputs such as *mouseMove* or *mousePress* and triggers them as higher level events such as *combinedClick* that will be handled by the interaction technique part (Figure 3). Place *currentXY* contains a token that keeps track of the mice target pointers' coordinates. For readability purpose, this place has been demultiplied into virtual places (functionality of the Petshop tool), which are clones of the initial one and are several views of this single place. It avoids overcrowding the figure. Each time a *mouseMove* event is caught (*mouseMove_t1*, *mouseMove_t2*, *mouseMove_t3*, *mouseMove_t4*, *mouseMove_t5*), the current coordinates are updated with the (x, y) deltas that have been done by the target pointers. In the initial state (2 tokens in place *Idle*, one for each mouse), the *mousePress_t1* and *mouseMove_t5* transitions are fireable (users can move or press their mouse). Once a *mousePress* event is caught, the *mousePress_t1* transition is fired and the corresponding mouse token is put into the place *Down.* If a mouseRelease event occurs, the transition mouseRelease_t1 transition will be fired and a timer armed in case of a future double click. The token is put into the *OneClick* place. If a *mouseMove* event occurs, the *mouseMove_t4* transition will be fired. If the timer previously set expires, the transition *timerExpired_t2* will be fired. In both cases, the timer is stopped, a *mouseClick* event is triggered and the token put into the place *CombClick.*

- If all the previously described sequence of events happens for both mice, two tokens are in the *CombClick* place, and the transition *fusionClick* can be fired. It can be fired only in this case because the weight of the corresponding arc is 2. This *fusionClick* transition, when fired, triggers a *combinedClick* event (which will be caught by the interaction technique model, Figure 3) and then deposits the 2 tokens back to the place *Idle*.
- In other cases for the place *CombClick*, if one token arrives in and that no other token arrives in within 200 milliseconds, the *click* transition will be fired and the token will go back to the place *Idle*.

The same principle is applied for the combined double click, which is not detailed here as not used in our case study.

Implementation in the PetShop environment

The described models are then connected to the user interface application software by means of activation functions and rendering functions. The activation function associates each event from the presentation part with the event handler to be triggered and the associated rendering method for representing the activation or the deactivation. For example in Figure 3, when a "combinedClick" event is received, the corresponding event handler which is the transition *combinedClick* is activated and a corresponding service (software in the transition's body) is executed.

The rendering function maintains the consistency between the internal state of the system (place, events) and its external appearance (UI rendering methods) by reflecting system states changes. When a token enters in one place, corresponding rendering events are going to be triggered. In this case study, there is currently no one, but we could for example add a rendering event associated to the place *testIcon* in Figure 3 that would make the mouse pointers blinking before entering into the appropriate transition.

Formal Analysis

Thanks to the CASE tool Petshop, it is possible to verify properties of the ICO model. Figure 5a and Figure 5b represent the invariant analysis of an ICO models presented in Figure 3 and Figure 4, respectively.

a) Analysis ICO model *combinedClick* (see Figure 3).

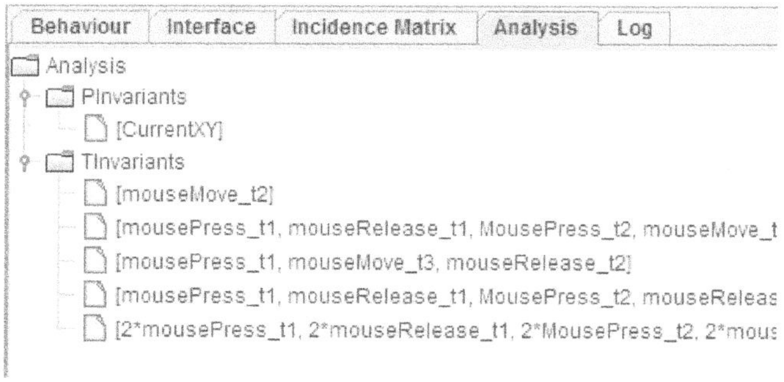

b) Analysis for ICO model *transducer* (see Figure 4)

Figure 5. Invariant Analysis.

The *PInvariants* sub trees in Figure 5a gather place invariants for the models. We can verify that places *Trash*, *Frame* and *CurrentXY* will always contain a token. This means that whatever state the model is in, and whatever events are produced, these places will never lose their resources. The *TInvariants* subtrees gather transition invariants for the models. This set of transition invariants for this interaction technique demonstrates liveness of the transitions handling the mouse events. For example, we can ensure that the user will always be able to move the pointing device from a position to another as the *mouseMove_t2* and *mouseMove_t5* are part of the invariants. According to the result of the analysis process, it can be decided to modify the model. For example, we can decide that the trash bin could not accept more than a certain number of icons. In [29] the interested reader can find a detailed explanation on how to perform such verification in the field of interactive systems.

Models simulation

Thanks to the PetShop environment [4], ICO models can be executed and simulated. This means that events produced by the users while interacting with the input devices will be received by the models that will evolve accordingly. So that the model drives the execution of the interactive systems and that (at the same time) user's actions trigger evolution on the model. Simulation and model-based checking of system specifications have been used to predict usability problems such as unreachable states of the systems or conflicting on events required for fusion. In [8] we provide a more complete account on scenario-based simulations.

Performance analysis

Performance analysis can be done in different ways accordingly to the information provided by models. For example, according to Fitts' law this size of the reactive icon is one of the parameter used for computing the difficulty index of the activity. Variation on this size will thus have an impact on the performance (time to select the Trash) but also the number of errors (an error would consist of moving the icon to be deleted on top of the icon of the Trash and then moving outside). Given that models can provide information such as target screen size, size of icons, etc, predictive information based on Fitt's law can be applied. Interruptions models can also combined with dialog models to assess the system tolerance and performance under different frequencies and duration of interruptions as presented in [31, 33]. If the values provided by the interaction technique are inside the range of values expected for performance, then we can proceed with the step of usability testing with users.

Log analysis of user testing

User testing is a very well-known evaluation technique based on the observation of users performing tasks with a system. It can be used to assess the usability evaluation of interactive systems with respect to its *effectiveness* (i.e. users can perform their tasks), *efficiency* (i.e. tasks can be performed without any unnecessary delay) and *user satisfaction*. Whilst *user satisfaction* is measured with specific questionnaires and interviews, *efficiency* and *effectiveness* are assessed through the execution of controlled tasks. Users can be extremely fast so that it is often difficult to observe all events raised by them. The protocol for conducting user testing is out of the scope of this paper. Our goal is just to demonstrate how user actions during usability testing can be collected and traced back to models. For that purpose, the Petshop tool was enriched with a log tool for assisting evaluators by recording user interactions into a log file. As models are connected to the prototype it is possible to play user interactions directly on models as they were recorded into log files.

In Petshop, each basic Petri net event like transition firing token movements (token added to a place, token removed from a place) is recorded in a single row. Only one log file is generated even if more than one model is involved. Log data are stored in XML files that can be transformed and exported to spreadsheet tools for statistically analysis.

Log files are structured as follows: the first field corresponds to the name of the model concerned by records. The second field represents the type of the Petri net node (i.e. *place* or *transition*). The third field corresponds to the given *node name*. The forth field represents the *action performed* associated to a node; for a transition it can be *fire a transition* whilst for a place the actions are related to the token movement such as *tokenAdded* or *tokenRemoved*. The fifth field represents the *time elapsed* from the start of the application in milliseconds. The last two fields (named *data 1*and *data 2*) represent additional data related to the node type. For a place the field *data1* would represents the number of tokens *added* or *removed* at the same time, the field *data2* would point out to the objects embed by the token. For a transition, the field *data2* is only used to note the substitutions used for firing a transition.

We have asked a user to *delete as fast as possible all icons on our desktop applications using the multimodal click*. The execution of this task generated a huge series of events triggered on the Petshop environment (more than 4000 lines). Due to space reasons, Figure 6 presents a short excerpt of that user testing session. This excerpt will be used hereafter to illustrate different usability problems found with the interaction technique *multimodal click*.

It is noteworthy that the model-based log (presented in Figure 6) records all the change which occurs in the model described by Figure 3 and Figure 4 during the prototype executing; this include firing of each transitions, removal and addition of a token in a place (with the complete print of all the values describing the content of the tokens). It is possible to know which model is in charge of the event by looking at the field *class*.

Two transitions are important to handle the correctness of the interaction technique *multimodal click*. If the transition *fileIconAndTrashSelected* is fired it means that the user complete the deletion of an icon using the interaction technique. If the transition *fileIconAndTrashNotSelected* is fired the user failed to delete the icon but manage to do a proper *multimodal click*. The Figure 6 presents three successful combined clicks (lines 1425-1428, 1435-1438, 2897-2900) and one miss (lines 1699-1702).

In our scenario, the user completes his task after he has removed all icons. We can then calculate the time for completion of the task and the number of missed combined click by hands or with spreadsheet formulas. At this point, log data help to count the number of successful and failed tasks as well as the user performance. However, log data are also useful to understand complex sequences of events that may have led to unexpected user fails whilst trying to delete an icon. For that purpose we should take a look on the events recorded at the transducer level.

	class	type	name	action	time	data1	data2
605	mouse_transducer	transition	mousePress_t1	fire	8000		1*{evt:{mId=>1}}
			...				
609	mouse_transducer	transition	mouseRelease_t1	fire	9900		1*{evt:{mId=>1}}
			...				
613	mouse_transducer	transition	timerExpired	fire	10500		1*{evt:{mId=>1}}
			...				
617	mouse_transducer	transition	click	fire	10700		1*{evt:{mId=>1}}
			...				
650	mouse_transducer	transition	click	fire	10950		1*{evt:{mId=>2}}
			...				
752	mouse_transducer	transition	mousePress_t1	fire	12000		1*{evt:{mId=>1}}
			...				
758	mouse_transducer	transition	mousePress_t1	fire	12010		1*{evt:{mId=>2}}
			...				
761	mouse_transducer	transition	mouseRelease_t1	fire	12020		1*{evt:{mId=>2}}
			...				
774	mouse_transducer	transition	timerExpired	fire	12220		1*{evt:{mId=>2}}
			...				
781	mouse_transducer	transition	click	fire	12420		1*{evt:{mId=>2}}
			...				
794	mouse_transducer	transition	mouseRelease_t1	fire	13010		1*{evt:{mId=>1}}
			...				
1425	CombinedClick_Delete_File	transition	combinedClick	fire	20300		1*{evt:{x1=>40,x2=>400,y1=>40,y2=>400},presentationFrame=>javax....}
1426	CombinedClick_Delete_File	place	testIcon	tokenAdded	20300	1	Icon1,Trash
1427	CombinedClick_Delete_File	place	Frame	tokenRemoved	20300		
1428	CombinedClick_Delete_File	transition	fileIconAndTrashSelected	fire	20300		1*{Icon2,Trash}
			...				
1435	CombinedClick_Delete_File	transition	combinedClick	fire	22100		1*{evt:{x1=>40,x2=>400,y1=>80,y2=>400},presentationFrame=>javax....}
1436	CombinedClick_Delete_File	place	testIcon	tokenAdded	22100	1	Icon2,Trash
1437	CombinedClick_Delete_File	place	Frame	tokenRemoved	22100		
1438	CombinedClick_Delete_File	transition	fileIconAndTrashSelected	fire	22100		1*{Icon1,Trash}
			...				
1699	CombinedClick_Delete_File	transition	combinedClick	fire	23450		1*{evt:{x1=>290,x2=>400,y1=>40,y2=>400},presentationFrame=>javax....}
1700	CombinedClick_Delete_File	place	testIcon	tokenAdded	23450	1	null,Trash
1701	CombinedClick_Delete_File	place	Frame	tokenRemoved	23450		
1702	CombinedClick_Delete_File	transition	fileIconAndTrashNotSelecte	fire	23450		1*{null,Trash}
			...				
2897	CombinedClick_Delete_File	transition	combinedClick	fire	40340		1*{evt:{x1=>120,x2=>400,y1=>120,y2=>400},presentationFrame=>javax....}
2898	CombinedClick_Delete_File	place	testIcon	tokenAdded	40340	1	Icon6,Trash
2899	CombinedClick_Delete_File	place	Frame	tokenRemoved	40340		
2900	CombinedClick_Delete_File	transition	fileIconAndTrashSelected	fire	40340		1*{Icon6,Trash}

Figure 6. Excerpt of a Model-based log provided by PetShop.

In the model *mouse_transducer* (see Figure 4) the transition *click* is fired only when the two clicks are not combined. The substitution contains the ID of a mouse. According to the log the delay between click on mouse 1 (line 617) and click on mouse 2 (line 640) is 250ms. In fact, one of the main assumptions about this interaction technique is that a combined click is counted only if the user clicks on the two mice in an interval of less than 200ms. This makes possible to count number of failed combined click. Based on such as information, the evaluator can decide the means delay of failure for combined click and propose a better value for the trigger.

From the log data produce by our user whilst trying to perform his task, we could extract fine-grained information such as the time between the pressing the first mouse's button with the cursor on an and second mouse click on the trash bin. This time give us the total time for complete a task. The sequence of events described by the lines 752, 758, 761, 774, 781 and 794 are particularly revealing of a usability problem that would be very difficult to found without a model-based log environment. Indeed, it shows that the user failed a combined click when s/he pressed the two mice at the same time but forgot to release the button of first mouse (see *mid at* column *date* 2 in Figure 6) leading to a click after 200ms trigger on the second mouse.

EVOLVABILITY OF MODELS

According to the performance evaluation obtained with the log analysis, some fine tuning can be applied in the model to increase the performance of the interaction technique. This fine tuning can either be done during or before the simulation as in PetShop models can be modified while executed. The data collected during assessment steps, and in particular log data, can then be exploited to assess the performance of the interaction technique. If the performance does not fit the expectations, the log data can be used as input to modify or tune the model that will be simulated again.

As we have seen in our case study, the time of 200ms between two clicks with the two mice was too short in at least one situation. If this scenario is confirmed with more users, it would be reasonable to change the values used in the time interval. Such modification or fine-tuning of the interaction technique is made much easier as the information in the log is already related to the structure of the model.

The parameter used within the case study (time between two clicks) is just an example of what is possible to do, but the approach is generic enough to support the analysis of any parameter while the models explicitly highlight such parameters.

DISCUSSION AND RELATED WORK

Model-based approaches for supporting usability evaluation are not a new idea *per se*. In The HCI community many researchers have described user interface elements by means of models. The interested reader can find a structured state of art of model-based user interface in [26] where the different modeling techniques are categorized by criteria such as: Language (Petri nets-based, state-based, flow-based code-based and constraints-based.), Interaction Coverage (Low Level, Multimodality, Tangible, Fusion, Widget, Rendering and Dialog), Scalability (Toy Example, Case Study or Real Size application), Tool support and Expressiveness (Data Description, State Representation, Event Representation), Time (Quantitative or Qualitative), Concurrent Behavior & Dynamic Instantiation.

Beyond this descriptive aspect, models can also be used to support the evaluation of the user interface for properties (such as liveness and safety) or even for usability. Usability evaluation is a major concern in HCI as it is one of the very few means to assess/ensure matching between a system under design and the users' needs. It is interesting to point, however, previous work combining Model-Based approach and usability evaluation as:

- Paternò et al. [32] which develops MultiDevice RemUsine for remote evaluation of mobile interfaces;
- EvaHelper [3], a framework to help the developer (to perform evaluation on mobile applications) made up of EvaLogger to simplify and EvaWriter to process the log to extract from the log useful data about usability;
- ReModEl [11] (Remote MODel-based Evaluation) composed of a server (containing task structure and task states), a client (for the tester) and another client interface for the usability expert.

In addition, research work following the same philosophy can also be found for the Web domain such as remote automatic evaluation of Web applications based on a combination of web browser monitoring and task models or application, for example AWUSA [34]. Usability evaluation can also be found for more generic (other than mobile and web) purposes as in [13] coupling a workbench for automated usability evaluation called MeMo (Mental Models) and a model based framework for UI generation called MASP (Muli-Access Service Platform). This is similar in [21] with automatic usability evaluation. Lastly, [17] proposes the integration of Analysis of Usability Information from User Interface Events within a compositional model.

However, the scope of these contributions greatly varies accordingly to the formalism used for specifying the application and the tool support available. For example, approaches based on task models cannot capture fine-grained interactions (such as fusion of mouse events in multimodal interaction techniques) that are a basic requirement for evaluation user performance with interaction techniques. Moreover, these previous works propose model-based method to solve a particular problem with the user interface at a time.

Another trick problem is the fact that one should prove that the prototypes behave exactly as specified by models. For example, how to prove that a user will not loose of sight the cursor even if he places the pointer away from screen area? Recently Gimblett and Thimbleby [15] have proposed an approach which consists in the discovery of models able to specify interaction techniques. However, discovery models do not driven the execution of the application. As a consequence, errors related to specific instance of data might occur during the execution of the application and the will never appear in models. Models can be gradually amended but behavior discovery in models is as random as discovery of software flaws with user testing, in the sense that user testing is limited to the scenarios proposed to users; some serious problems can be hidden in rare and difficult to sought possible scenarios.

CONCLUSION AND FUTURE WORK

In this paper we have presented an approach to support testing and evaluation of (multimodal) interaction techniques. The main feature of this approach is that testing and evaluation are based on models. This approach is targeted to novel and complex interaction techniques (including multimodal ones) which are much harder to assess using traditional user testing evaluation methods [23].

More precisely, we have presented ICO and Petshop as a formal approach to support a bi-directional relationship between models and executable prototypes, and to ease user testing by supporting a model-based log analysis. We have demonstrated in the section case study that some problems are very difficult to observe without appropriate tools. Using executable ICO models we were able to discover fine-grained sequences of events that provide evaluators with an accurate description of user actions. These tools not only are useful to observe the events triggered by users but they can also support the activities of identifying the part of the models related to the problem. Additionally, sequences of actions can be then (re)played on the model allowing a multiple inspection of error-prone scenarios.

At first sight, the development process proposed in this work might look familiar to some readers as it combines several existing techniques for supporting the evaluation of interactive systems. The approach is deliberately synergistic as it integrates our previous work on model-based evaluation techniques. It is the combinations of different techniques, rather than a single one that provides a solution for all the claims made in the introduction.

We are currently applying this research to the field of interactive cockpits where standards such as ARINC 661 [2] specification provide recommendations for WIMP interfaces. However, as the captain and first officer are interacting with the KCCU device (Keyboard Cursor Control Unit) the issue of multimodal interaction technique is raised bringing directly to the field of safety critical system problems usually investigated in general public interactive systems.

REFERENCES

1. Accot, J. and Zhai, S. 1997. Beyond Fitts' law: models for trajectory-based HCI tasks. In Proceedings of CHI'97 (Atlanta, USA). ACM, pp. 295-302.
2. ARINC 661 Cockpit Display System Interfaces to User Systems. ARINC Specification 661. Airlines Electronic Engineering Committee 2002
3. Balagtas-Fernandez F., Hußmann H., A Methodology and Framework to Simplify Usability Analysis of Mobile Applications. In Proc. of ASE'2009, p. 520-524.
4. Barboni, E., Ladry, J-F, Navarre, D., Palanque, P., Winckler, M. *Beyond Modelling: An Integrated Environment Supporting Co-Execution of Tasks and Systems Models.* In proceedings of ACM Symposium on Engineering Interactive Systems (EICS'2010), June 19-23, 2010, Berlin, Germany. Pages: 165-174
5. Bastide, R., Navarre, D., and Palanque, P. 2002. A model-based tool for interactive prototyping of highly interactive applications. In Proceedings of CHI '02, pp. 516-517.
6. Bastide R., Palanque P., Le Duc H., and Munoz J. (1998). Integrating Rendering Specifications into a Formalism for the Design of Interactive Systems. Proc. of the 5th Eurographics workshop on Design, Specification and Verification of Interactive systems DSV-IS'98. Springer Verlag.
7. Baudisch, P., Cutrell, E., Robbins, D., Czerwinski, M., Tand-ler, P. Bederson, B., and Zierlinger, A. Drag-and-Pop and Drag-and-Pick: Techniques for Accessing Remote Screen Content on Touch- and Pen-operated Systems. In Proc. of Interact 2003, pp. 57-64.
8. Bernhaupt, R., Navarre, D., Palanque, P., Winckler, M. Model-Based Evaluation: A New Way to Support Usability Evaluation of Multimodal Interactive Applications. In Maturing Usability: Quality in Software, Interaction and Quality (chapter 5). Law E., Thora Hvannberg E., Cockton G. & Vanderdonckt J. (Eds.). Springer Verlag (HCI Series), 2007, p. 96-122.
9. Blanch R., Guiard Y. and Beaudouin-Lafon M. Semantic Pointing: Improving Target Acquisition with Control-Display Ratio Adaptation. In Proceedings of CHI 2004, (Vienna, Austria, April 2004), pp. 519-526.
10. Bowman, Doug A., Hodges, Larry F. Formalizing the Design, Evaluation, and Application of Interaction Techniques for Immersive Virtual Environments. J. Vis. Lang. Comput. 10(1): 37-53 (1999).
11. Buchholz G, Engel J, Märtin C, Propp S. Model-based usability evaluation - evaluation of tool support. HCII 2007, (Beijing, China) pp. 1043-52. Springer-Verlag.
12. Collomb, M. and Hascoët, M. 2008. Extending drag-and-drop to new interactive environments: A multi-display, multi-instrument and multi-user approach. Interact. Comput. 20, 6 (Dec. 2008), pp. 562-573.

13. Feuerstack, S., Blumendorf, M., Kern, M., Kruppa, M., Quade, M., Runge, M., and Albayrak, S. 2008. Automated Usability Evaluation during Model-Based Interactive System Development. In Proceedings of TAMODIA'08 (Pisa, Italy). LNCS, vol. 5247. Springer-Verlag, pp. 134-141.
14. Fitts, P. M. 1954. The information capacity of the human motor system in controlling the amplitude of move-ment. Journal of Experimental Psychology, 47, pp. 381-391.
15. Gimblett, A., Thimbleby, H. User interface model discovery: towards a generic approach. In Proc. of the 2nd ACM SIGCHI symposium on Engineering interactive computing systems (EICS '10). ACM, New York, NY, USA, 145-154.
16. Hascoët, M. 2003. Throwing models for large displays. In: HCI2003, Designing for society, vol. 2. British HCI Group. pp. 73-77.
17. Hilbert, D. M. and Redmiles, D. F. 2000. Extracting usability information from user interface events. ACM Comput. Surv. 32, 4 (Dec. 2000), pp. 384-421.
18. Hinckley, K., Cutrell, E., Bathiche, S., and Muss, T. 2002. Quantitative analysis of scrolling techniques. In Proceedings of CHI'02 (Minneapolis, USA), pp. 65-72.
19. Jiao, L., Cheung, T-Y, Lu, W. Characterizing Liveness of Petri Nets in Terms of Siphon. ICATPN 2002, LNCS 2360, pp. 203-216, Springer-Verlag.
20. Kobayashi, M. and Igarashi, T. 2007. Boomerang: suspendable drag-and-drop interactions based on a throw-and-catch metaphor. In Proc. of the 20th Annual ACM Symposium on User interface Software and Technology (Newport, Rhode Island, USA, October 07 - 10, 2007). UIST '07. ACM, New York, NY, 187-190.
21. Kristoffersen, S. 2009. A Preliminary Experiment of Checking Usability Principles with Formal Methods. In Proc. of ACHI'09. IEEE Computer Society, 261-270.
22. Ladry J-F., Navarre D., Palanque P. Formal Description Techniques to Support the Design, Construction and Evaluation of Fusion Engines for SURE (Safe Usable, Reliable and Evolvable) Multimodal Interfaces. In: ICMI-MLMI 2009, Cambridge, Massachusetts, USA, ACM, p. 135-142, 2009.
23. Lalanne D., Nigay L., Palanque P., Robinson P., Vanderdonckt J., and Ladry J-F. 2009. Fusion engines for multimodal input: a survey. In Proceedings of the 2009 international conference on Multimodal interfaces (ICMI-MLMI '09). ACM, New York, USA, 153-160.
24. Mackay, W.E. Ethics, lies and videotape, in *Proceedings of CHI '95* (Denver CO, May 1995), ACM Press, 138-145.
25. MacKenzie, I. S. and Buxton, W. 1992. Extending Fitts' law to two-dimensional tasks. In Proceedings of CHI'92 (Monterey, United States), ACM, pp. 219-226
26. Navarre, D., Palanque, P., Ladry, J., and Barboni, E. 2009. ICOs: A model-based user interface description technique dedicated to interactive systems addressing usability, reliability and scalability. ACM TOCHI 16,4 (Nov. 2009), pp. 1-56.
27. Navarre, D.; Palanque, P.; Schyn, A.; Winckler, M.; Nedel, L.; Freitas, C. M. D. S. A Formal Description of Multimodal Interaction Techniques for Immersive Virtual Reality Applications. In Proceedings of TC13-IFIP Conference INTERACT 2005, Rome, Italy (12th-16th September 2005). pp. 170-183.
28. Navarre D. Palanque P. Bastide R, and Sy, O. Structuring interactive systems specifications for executability and prototypability. In Proceedings of DSV-IS'2000. LNCS. n° 1946, Springer Verlag, pp. 145-161.
29. Palanque P. & Bastide R. (1995). Verification of an Interactive Software by analysis of its formal specification. Proc. of the IFIP TC 13 Interact'95, pp. 191-197.
30. Palanque, P., Bernhaupt, R., Navarre, D., Ould, M., Winckler, M. Supporting Usability Evaluation of Multimodal Man-Machine Interfaces for Space Ground Segment Applications Using Petri net Based Formal Specification. Ninth International Conference on Space Operations, Rome, Italy, June 18-22, 2006.
31. Palanque, P., Winckler, M., Ladry, J-F., ter Beek, M., Faconti, G., Massink, M. A Formal Approach Supporting the Comparative Predictive Assessment of the Interruption-Tolerance of Interactive Systems In Proceedings of the ACM Symposium on Engineering Interactive Computing Systems (EICS 2009) Pittsburgh, USA. pp. 211-220. ACM Press.
32. Paternò, F., Russino, A., Santoro, C. (2007) Remote evaluation of Mobile Applications. In Proceedings of TAMODIA 2007, Toulouse, France, LNCS Vol. 4849.
33. ter Beek, M., Faconti, G., Massink, M., Palanque, P., Winckler, M. Resilience of Interaction Techniques to Interrupts: A Formal Model-based Approach 12th IFIP TC 13 Conference on Human-Computer Interaction (INTERACT 2009) Uppsala, Sweeden, Springer Verlag, LNCS n° 5727, p. 494-509.
34. Tiedtke, T., Märtin, C., Gerth, N. Awusa, A tool for automated website usability analysis. In: PreProceedings of the 9th Int. Workshop DSV-IS 2002, Rostock, Germany, pp. 251-266 (2002).
35. Yuan X., Cohen M. & Memon A. GUI Interaction Testing: Incorporating Event Context", IEEE Transactions on Software Engineering, 2010, IEEE Computer Society.
36. Zhai, S., Morimoto, C. Ihde, S. (1999) Manual And Gaze Input Cascaded (MAGIC) Pointing. In Proceeding of CHI'99, pp. 246-253.

CAP3: Context-Sensitive Abstract User Interface Specification

Jan Van den Bergh Kris Luyten Karin Coninx
Hasselt University - tUL - IBBT
Expertise Centre for Digital Media
Wetenschapspark 2
3590 Diepenbeek, Belgium
{Jan.VandenBergh,Kris.Luyten,Karin.Coninx}@uhasselt.be

ABSTRACT
Despite the fact many proposals have been made for abstract user interface models it was not given a *detailed* context in which it should or could be used in a user-centered design process. This paper presents a clear role for the abstract user interface model in user-centered and model-based development, provides an overview of the stakeholders that may create and/or use abstract user interface models and presents a modular abstract user interface modeling language, CAP3, that makes relations with other models explicit and builds on the foundation of existing abstract user interface models. The proposed modeling notation is supported by a tool and applied to some case studies from literature and in some projects. It is also validated based on state-of-the-art knowledge on domain-specific modeling languages and visual notations and some case studies.

Author Keywords
User interface design, modeling language, abstract user interface, CAP3, graphical notation.

ACM Classification Keywords
D.2.2 Design Tools and Techniques: User interfaces.

General Terms
Design, Documentation, Human Factors, Languages.

INTRODUCTION
Abstract user interfaces have been discussed in literature for almost 20 years, although the definition of what constitutes an abstract user interface (AUI) has evolved over time together with advances in technology and extension of the scope. This evolution is illustrated by the fact that Limbourg [13, chapter 2] gives two different definitions for abstract user interface model based on the kind of abstraction that is used; abstraction from toolkit or abstraction from interactor type.

In this paper, we will focus on the latter, most recent interpretation of abstract user interface. The former is nowadays usually referenced as concrete user interface.

Despite this long usage of abstract user interface models, there does not seem to be convergence on the language of choice. The reasons for this may be diverse. One reason may be that the needs in different domains may differ significantly. One domain may benefit from a large vocabulary (e.g. interactive web applications), while another domain may prefer a small set of abstractions (e.g. participatory television [25]). Another reason may be that the focus of many research efforts was not the model itself, but the potential benefits for forward or backward engineering (in a specific domain), leading to incomplete descriptions of the modeling language itself in the publicly available literature. Standards such as XForms [5] and ISO 24752:2008 [10] on the other hand are complete but very specific for their domain (websites and universal remote controls).

In this paper we propose the modeling notation (concrete syntax) of CAP3, a new abstract user interface modeling language that builds on previous work. It integrates structural and behavioral specification (similar to what Denim [14] does for low-fidelity user interface sketches). CAP3 includes explicit references to models related to the abstract user interface model, such as domain model, user model or context model. CAP3 refers to the fact that CAP can be interpreted in three different ways that are all appropriate for the modeling language. The first is Canonical Abstract Prototypes; the abstract user interface notation from which most of its concrete syntax is derived. The second is Context-sensitive Abstract Prototypes, which refers to the fact that it can be used to express context-sensitive user interfaces on an abstract level. The third is Configurable Abstract Presentation, highlighting the goal of a configurable notation composed of a core set of symbols and a library of default symbols that can be used when appropriate.

Before introducing the details of CAP3 itself, we present related work and how CAP3 can be used in a user-centered software engineering approach using the MuiCSer process framework [9]. CAP3 is validated using knowledge about domain-specific modeling and visual languages and by discussing how it was applied or could have been applied in some projects.

RELATED WORK

MARIA [23] is an XML-based user interface description language that can be used to describe task models, abstract user interface models and concrete user interface models for service-oriented applications. The description language can be used both at design-time (through a custom editor) and at runtime. The abstract user interface model allows a specification of the dialog (dynamic behavior), the presentation and references to the manipulated data (datatypes are defined ad-hoc through XML Schema [4].) The dynamic behavior is expressed using events, ConcurTaskTrees [18] temporal operators such as concurrency, mutual exclusive choice or sequentiality and event handlers. The presentation of a user interface is described using a composition of interactors. Most of the interactor types are further refined depending on their role or the type of data they are manipulating[1]. The MARIA editor uses an enhanced tree control to modify abstract user interface models and the interactors are abstractions of widgets (as opposed to activities).

UsiXML [13, chapter 3] is also an XML-based user interface description language that can describe user interface models at different levels of abstraction. One of these models is the abstract user interface model. It only discerns two types of abstract interaction objects (*aio*): *abstractContainer* and *abstractIndividualComponent* (aic). Instead of defining different subtypes of aic, it can contain multiple facets but discerns four different types of facets exist (see Table 1). Five different types of relations can exist between the abstract interaction objects: *abstractContainment*, *abstractAdjacency*, *spatioTemporal*, *auiDialogControl* and *mutualEmphasis*. The UsiXML AUI model has a graphical notation [16] that is limited to the structural aspects of the abstract user interface.

Canonical abstract prototypes [6], CAP, is a graphical abstract user interface description language that was created based on practical experience in industry to ease the transition from task models to concrete user interface prototypes. Instead of focusing on making an abstraction of widgets independent from platform and modality, CAP abstracts user activities. Since it is positioned as an alternative to or refinement of paper prototypes during the user interface design process it does not have any formal meta-model, the semantics of each component is defined clearly, but leaves room for some semantic variation. CAP is restricted to the presentation submodel. One can make annotations, to define some behavioral aspects of the user interface.

The MetaSketch editor [20] demonstrated graphical notations for the two major components of the abstract user interface model: the abstract presentation model and the dialog model. A meta-model for these two submodels was realized by extending the UML metamodel [22]. The graphical notation for the presentation model was derived from the Canonical Abstract Prototypes [6] notation, while a custom notation was created for the dialog model. The semantics for the dialog model were derived from the ConcurTaskTrees (CTT) notation [18] while the symbols in the graphical notation were inspired by the UML activity diagram but retained the hierarchical, tree-like structure of CTT.

UMLi [7] specifies an extension of UML (both abstract and concrete syntax) for the specification of user interfaces. It uses a specific new notation for abstract presentations and an extended version of UML 1.x state machines for the specification of the dialog model. UMLi contains six types of abstract interactors, shown in Table 1. It thus supports a set of interactors that is similar to those used in Teallach [1]. The UMLi dialog specification contains specific control flow constructs and explicitly links interactors (and domain objects) to actions and *FreeContainers* to activities. The types of links include presentation (*FreeContainer*), interaction (interactors), confirmation, cancellation and activation (*ActionInvoker*).

CUP 2.0 [26] extends the UML 2 meta-model through a set of stereotypes. It uses similar set of abstractions as UMLi but only contains one type of container and the detailed semantics and syntax are significantly different. It also allows to encode richer relations between interactors, such as *update* and *activate*.

ArtStudio [24] has a limited abstract user interface model that consists of *abstract workspaces* that only defines structural properties.

XForms [5] is an official recommendation of W3C that has a similar level of abstraction as abstract user interface models and was created to embed specification of manipulation and presentation of (complex) system state to XML-documents using the Model-View-Controller architecture. It has a rich feature-set with seven different interactors (see Table 2). These interactors can be logically arranged in *groups*. Specific structures for conditional or repeated display of components are also provided. Fifteen different kinds of actions are provided to handle the effect of specific events on the user interface.

ISO 24752 [10] has a much more limited scope (universal remote controls) and defines a set of interactors that resembles that of XForms. Similar to MARIA, there is also a number of interactors that are aimed to manipulate a certain type of data.

Other approaches, such as PUC [19] or Supple [8], focus more on a description of the state of the application and the commands that can be given to it, complemented with the appropriate labels, to generate appropriate user interfaces and thus differ significantly from the above-mentioned abstract user interface descriptions, although they also describe the user interface on an abstract level.

AUI IN A USER-CENTERED PROCESS

The role of abstract user interfaces in a development process has been discussed in the context of the unifying reference framework by Calvary et al. [3] or as part of usage-centered design [6]. Calvary et al. mention that AUI are an intermediary model to develop multi-device user interfaces. In many

[1] A detailed overview of the interactors can be found in Table 1.

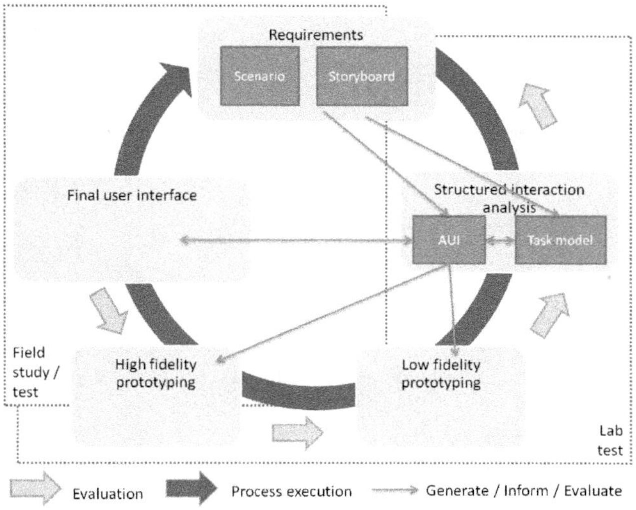

Figure 1. The role of AUI using the MuiCSer process framework.

approaches it is used as a step between the task model (and related models) and the final user interface as discussed by Limbourg [13, chapter2].

In usage-centered design, Canonical Abstract Prototypes (CAP) are used to ease the transition from very abstract specifications to concrete user interface designs. They mention that CAP's graphical notation is useful because it allows to specify the layout as well as the functionality provided by the user interface. This does not mean however that concrete designs must completely follow the layout of the CAP diagrams, but it shows some possibility to use this property to generate pleasing default layouts for the final user interface.

Figure 1 further clarifies the role that an AUI plays in different approaches described in literature by positioning into the MuiCSer process framework [9] for user-centered software engineering. This process framework emphasizes both aspects from user-centered design, such as user evaluations and prototypes at different scales of fidelity, and aspects from (model-based) software engineering, such as structured specifications in e.g. the form of models. An AUI is used as a means to do structured analysis, during the generation, creation or evaluation of prototypes and the final user interface. Some approaches described in literature also generate an AUI directly from an existing final user interface and then use the resulting model to create a user interface for a different platform or interaction paradigm.

Figure 1 also shows that (potential) users of the AUI can have diverse profiles. The professionals involved in *creating* AUI can be interaction designers, information architects, software engineers or developers. Other *users* of the models include designers, who establish concrete designs, and finally also clients and managers, who review the models. This means that the concrete syntax of an AUI should be accessible and readable to people from very diverse backgrounds.

CAP3

Structural Specification

Our CAP3 notation and meta-model builds upon CAP [6] for the specification of the structural aspects. One of the reasons for this decision is motivated that usability of the notation was important from the earliest design of the language, which is important when considering the diverse backgrounds from the potential users of the language as discussed in the previous section.

Another reason to choose for CAP as an AUI is its expressiveness. Table 2 and Table 1 show a comparison of the abstract interactors supported by the different languages. Each row in the Table refers to another type of abstract interactor. For all languages that have a (partial) graphical notation, the symbols for the different kinds of abstract interactors (and facets) are shown in Table 1. The icons for CAP and CUP 2.0 are added in the top-left corner of a rectangle that indicates the actual abstract interactor. The icons for the abstract interactors and facets of UsiXML are shown in the lower-left corner of rounded rectangles. The outline of the rounded rectangle of abstract interactors and facets differs in texture. The symbols for UMLi are the full representation of the abstract interactors; they are not contained in any bounding box.

The columns with vertical text for CAP and MARIA indicate more generic types that are available. In CAP, these more generic types (*tool*, *container*, *active material*) can be used directly in a diagram. It is however unclear whether MARIA allows the more generic types (such as *only_output*) to be used directly in a model. This unclarity and other unclarities in the support for an abstract interactor are indicated by a gray background in the Table. The vertical text *abstractIndividualComponent* in Table 1 is added for UsiXML to indicate that all facets are part of the *abstractIndividualComponent*.

One limitation of CAP is that it has no real knowledge about datatypes, although these can be indicated using appropriate naming. Furthermore, CAP offers no dedicated support for a *secret* interactor (used to model e.g. a password field) nor does it make a distinction between single selection and multiple selection. All these issues can be resolved when transforming CAP from a diagramming notation into a modeling language by adding the necessary attributes to some meta-classes. The latter two issues can be resolved by adding an attribute *isSecret* to the meta-class *Input* and an attribute *maxSelectedElements* to *SelectableCollection*). Knowledge about datatypes is added in a similar fashion. It is also important to note that one cannot choose freely between *submit* and *trigger* for XForms in Table 2, when considering equivalents for a *tool* in CAP.

Although our proposed language, CAP3, follows the conventions of CAP in most cases, there are a couple of deviations:

Repetition Repetition is indicated in CAP by a downwards pointing triple chevron in an *interactor* that contains other

Table 1 — Comparison of abstract interactors among languages.

CAP	MARIA	UsiXML	CUP 2.0	UMLi
tool — (icon)	*control*	*AuiInteractor*		
start/goTo	navigator	Navigator		
stop/end/complete				
perform(&return)				
view			actionComponent	ActionInvoker
select				
create	activator	Command		
delete/erase				
modify				
move				
duplicate				
toggle				
conceptual group	grouping	AuiContainer	groupComponent	Container / FreeContainer
container — element	*only_output* — text / object / description	Output	outputComponent	Displayer
notification	alarm / feedback		outputComponent	
collection	*	*	outputComponent, *	
active material — (icon)	interactive_description	*	*	*
input/accepter				Inputter
editable element	*edit* — position_edit / text_edit / object_edit / numerical_edit / numerical_edit_full / numerical_edit_in_range	Input	inputComponent	Editor
editable collection	*			
selectable collection	*selection* — single_choice / multiple_choice	Selection		
selectable action set	*	Commands or Navigators	*	*
selectable view set	*	Navigators	*	*

Table 1. Comparison of abstract interactors among languages. * denotes that a construct is supported through a combination of abstract interactors. A gray background denotes an unclear support.

	CAP	Standards: Xforms		Standards: ISO/IEC 24752:2008
tool	(tool)	submit or trigger+ Action		TriggerInteractor TimedTriggerInteractor
	start/goTo		send	
	stop/end/complete			
	perform(&return)			
	view			
	select		setindex	
	create		insert setvalue	
	delete/erase		delete	
	modify		setvalue	
	move			
	duplicate		copy	
	toggle		toggle	
	conceptual group	group		Group
container	(container)			Group
	element	output		OutputInteractor
	notification	Action + message		ModalDialogInteractor
	collection	*		
active material	(active material)			
	input/accepter	input secret textarea range		InputInteractor SecretInteractor [type]Interactor RangeInteractor
	editable element			
	editable collection	*		
	selectable collection	select		SelectInteractor
		select1		Select1Interactor
	selectable action set	*		
	selectable view set			

Table 2. Comparison of abstract interactors between CAP and two standardized languages: XForms and ISO 24752-3:2008. * denotes that a construct is supported through a combination of abstract interactors. A gray background denotes an unclear support.

interactors. It is however not clear whether the repetition applies to all contained interactors. In Figure 7(a), for example, it is not clear whether only the information about the film should be repeated or also the *tools* that allow to add or remove film clips. To make it easier to discern that certain elements are repeated they are all contained in a *RepeatedConceptualGroup*, which is depicted by a dashed rectangle (in common with a CAP conceptual group) with a triple downpointing chevron below it. Figure 7 shows this difference between the CAP notation and the CAP3 notation in the interactor *Film Clips*.

Presentation units A presentation unit, which corresponds to a window in a graphical user interface, is depicted in CAP with a rectangle with a flipped corner. In CAP3, every interactor that is not contained in another interactor can indicate a presentation unit. In most cases, this top-level interactor will be a container (as is the *Film Clip Viewer* in Figure 7), but is not necessarily the case. User interfaces on e.g. smart phones may at times only display a single interactor at a time. In CAP3, this single interactor can be a top-level interactor. An example of this is shown in Figure 8.

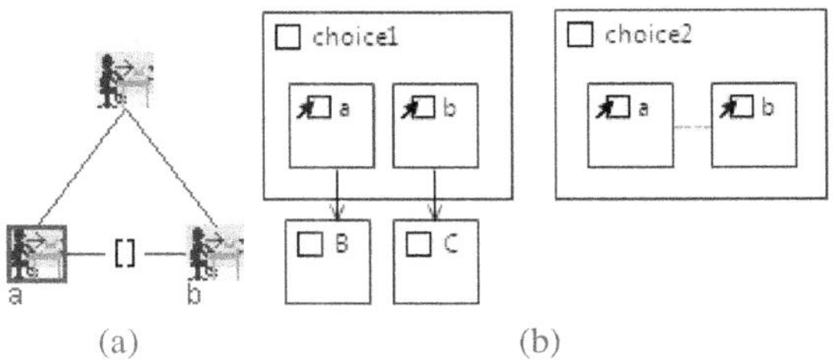

Figure 2. Choice representation using CTT (a) and CAP3 (b).

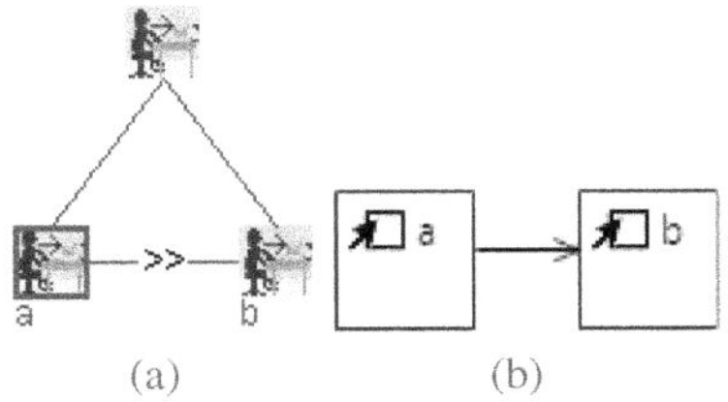

Figure 3. Enabling representation using CTT (a) and CAP3 (b).

In order to keep the language as lean as possible, only the three base interactors (*Tool*, *Container* and *ActiveMaterial*) are considered as required interactors. All other interactors are optional and can be considered part of a standard library rather than part of the language itself. This choice does not conflict with ideas from CAP, which also state that these three interactors can replace all other interactors (see Table 1). Furthermore, Gayos et al. argue that the resulting lack of a selection interactor, which is also the case in their modeling language, can even be beneficial [8].

Similarly additional symbols, such as the *ParticipantElement* and *ActiveParticipantCollection* as used in SPieLan [25] could be placed in a specific library complementing the interactors provided within CAP3 itself. Given appropriate tool support, this enables the creation of reusable modeling language extensions similar to the way reusable extensions are created for programming languages; through the creation of additional libraries.

Behavior Specification

Before adding a dynamic behavior specification to CAP, we considered it good practice to first consider how the dynamic behavior is specified in other abstract user interface languages. UsiXML [13], MARIA [23], and Nobrega et al. [20] all use a similar set of temporal operators. This set is based on, but different from the temporal operators of LOTOS [2]. Differences with LOTOS include, but are not limited to the introduction of new operators such as suspend/resume (|>) and deterministic choice (π). UMLi [7] defines its own set of temporal operators but is explicitly mapped to LOTOS specifications.

In this section we introduce how the behavior of the most commonly used temporal operators can be specified in the proposed notation. Each proposal is compared with a minimal task specification with LOTOS operators. We do not

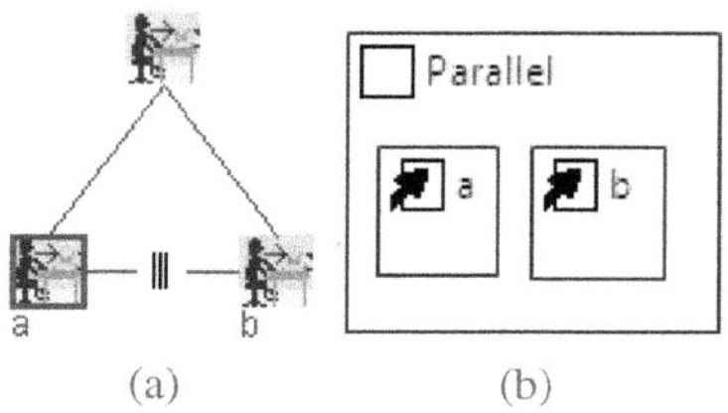

Figure 4. Parallel representation using CTT (a) and CAP3 (b).

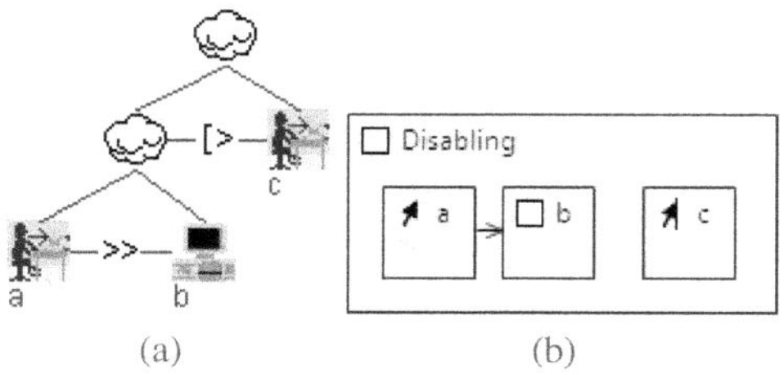

Figure 5. Disabling representation using CTT (a) and CAP3 (b).

discuss the unary optional operator from CTT as an optional interaction task is probably always represented in the user interface, unless a specific constraint is attached. At this moment, we do not consider a specific graphical notation for this operator. The repetition operator is only represented in the graphical notation when it results in a repetition of the interactors, which is not always the case. For example, in the AUI represented in Figure 7, the *Find* interactor may be modeled in a task model as a repeatable task, but it will only be represented using a single interactor.

Figure 2 shows how the choice operator is represented in ConcurTaskTrees notation (CTT) and CAP3. Figure 2(b) shows two options to represent a choice, depending on whether a transition between states is invoked by *a* and *b* or there is no dialog transition as a consequence of an invocation of task *a* or *b* as in Figure 2(a). The former can happen when the parent task of *a* and *b* enables another task or when *a* and *b* are further decomposed into two or more subtasks connected by an enabling operator.

Notice that for both cases we use a notation inspired on UML [22]. The activation of another abstract interactor is based on the UML notation for state transitions, while the notation used in *choice2* is based on the xor-relation, which is used in the UML version of CTT used by Nunes [21]. Instead of relying on a textual notation, we enhance the difference with the other relations through the usage of color (red). We thus increase the number of visual variables we use in the notation, which should make it easier to recognize the relation.

The *Activate* relation (Figure 3(b)) corresponds to the enabling operator in CTT (see Figure 3(a)). Notice that this relation can also be used within a *Container* to denote intra-dialog transitions (see Figure 5(b)) or from a *Tool* or *Active-Material* contained in a *Container* to an abstract interactor outside that *Container* (see Figure 2(b)).

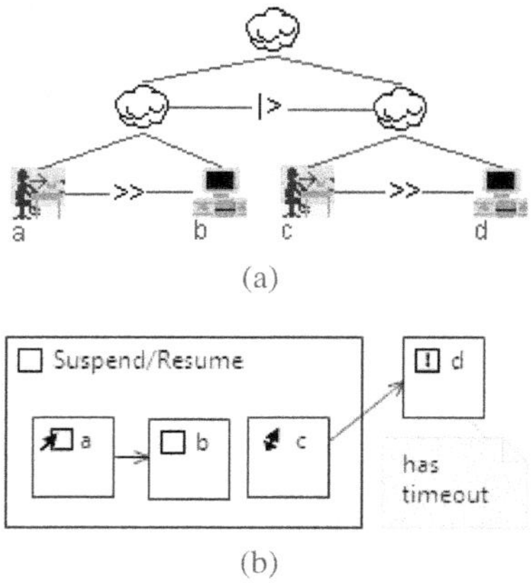

Figure 6. SuspendResume representation using CTT (a) and CAP3 (b).

The parallel temporal operator from CTT (Figure 4(a)), as well as the order independence operator are translated into a single relation CAP3 (Figure 4(b)). As this relation is naturally expressed by containment in the same *Container* in CAP, we keep this notation.

The *End* tool from CAP is especially useful when specifying a disabling relationship as shown in Figure 5(b). This tool disables the complete container in which it is directly contained.

The *PerformReturn* tool is similarly helpful (Figure 6(b)) to specify the suspend/resume temporal operator (Figure 6(a)). Note that reverse direction does not need to be explicitly defined. In Figure 6(b), a notification is shown, which automatically disappears after a certain period. When the notification disappears, the *Suspend/Resume* presentation unit becomes active again.

Inspired by the UML statecharts specification and CAP itself, we decided to use separate notations for information exchange. We still use to convention from CAP to embed a tool in a *Container* to denote that the function in the application core, triggered by the tool *Use* this information. For indicating the other direction, we use an *Update* relation. The notation is inspired on, but different from the UML notation for object flow. We opt for a thicker dotted line and a full arrow head instead of a dashed line and an open arrow head to make the conceptual difference also visually clearer. Figure 7(b) shows several examples of information flow. There is a relationship from the *Find Tool* to the *Film Clips* to indicate the former *update* the latter.

When we compare Figure 7(b) with its original specification in CAP, shown in Figure 7(a)[2], we notice that there is also a difference for the behavior specification: The rather informal notation between parentheses is replaced by an *Update* relationship.

Figure 7(b) also shows another use of a conceptual group; it provides some syntactic sugar to reduce the number of

[2]This diagram is recreated after [6, Figure 2].

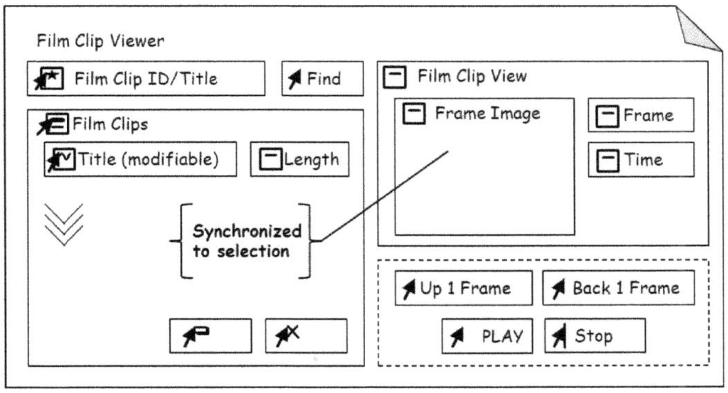

(a) Canonical Abstract Prototypes

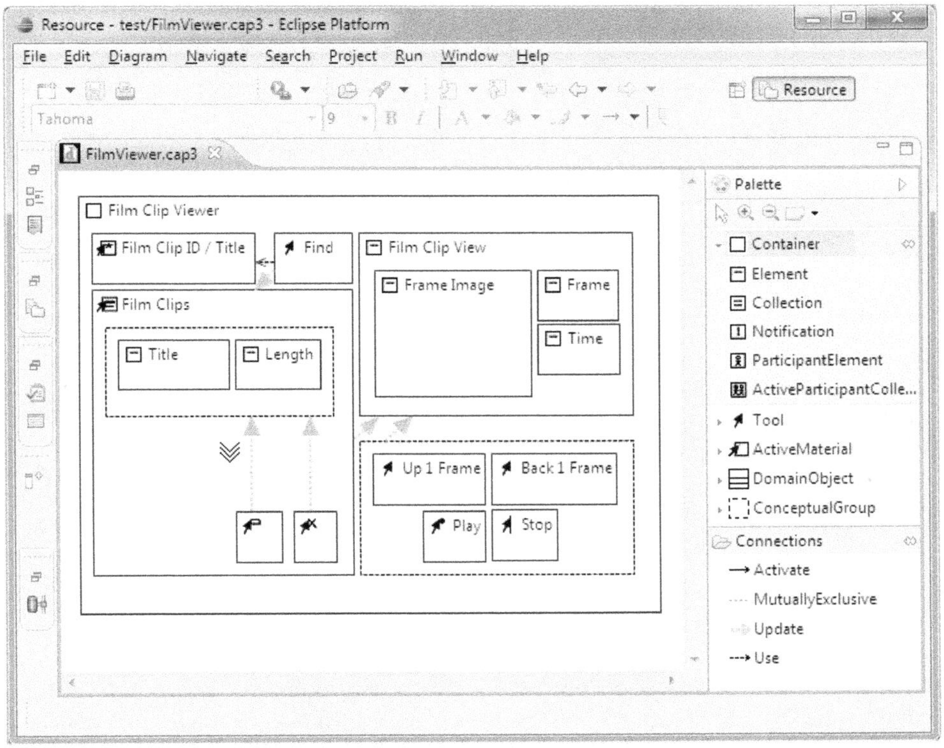

(b) CAP3 specification in Eclipse-based supporting tool

Figure 7. Film viewer example as specified by Constantine (a) and using our tool support (b).

interactor	data display	data modification	navigation
tool		X	X
start/goTo			X
stop/end/complete			X
perform(&return)			X
view			X
select		X	
create		X	
delete/erase		X	
modify		X	
move		X	
duplicate		X	
toggle		X	
container	X		
element	X		
notification			
collection	X		
active material	X	X	
input/accepter	X	X	
editable element	X	X	
editable collection	X	X	
selectable collection	X		
selectable action set			
selectable view set			

Table 3. Capabilities of the CAP3 interactors.

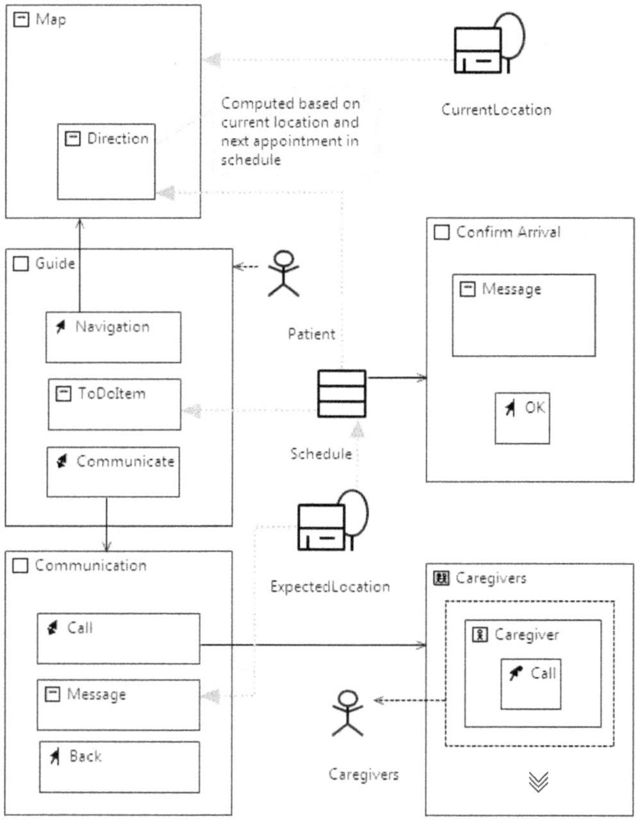

Figure 8. Partial specification of a dementia patient's assistance tool using CAP3.

Update relations. An *Update* relation leaving a conceptual group could be replaced by *Update* relations from each of the tools or active materials it contains to the target of the *Update* relation. This convention is used to avoid that all tools in the lower-right corner would have an *Update* relation with the *Film Clip View*.

Table 4 summarizes the discussion of the relations (except containment) in CAP3. Empty cells in the Table indicate that no constraints are defined. Table 3 lists the CAP3 interactors and their capabilities (data display, data modification and navigation).

These enumerations are the complete subset of elements as defined in CAP. Other interactors that are not part of CAP, can also belong to these groups of interactors. The *ParticipantElement* and *ActiveParticipantCollection* as defined in SPieLan [25], for example, also belong to the interactors that show data; they are specialisations of respectively the *Element* and *Collection* interactors.

Relations to Other Models

With the increasing adoption of context-sensitive user interfaces, multi-user interfaces (such as for social applications) and mixed initiative interfaces, one should take into account that the state of the user interface can not only respond to input by its user, but also by input from sensors. Since this influence is independent of the kind of interactor, it can also be included at the abstract user interface (AUI) level.

In CAP3, we model this influence through the integration of proxies to "domain objects". Each proxy contains a reference to an element of another model. Subtypes of domain objects can include concepts of other models and include the human users of the modeled user interface, things and humans in its environment, the environment itself and the data manipulated through the user interface. These subtypes of domain objects are also considered as library objects.

Figure 8 models the system discussed by Mahmud et al. [15] illustrates how CAP3 can express the influence that domain objects and the environment can have on the user interface. It shows that the user's *current location* is shown on the *map* and that the *message* in the user interface of the *communication* module of the application. It shows that a list of caregivers is shown using the *ActiveParticipantCollection* interactor, introduced in SpIeLan [25]. Figure 8 thus demonstrates how CAP3 supports context-sensitivity on two levels: it can be adapted to the modeling context by adding libraries that contain elements that specialize CAP3 elements, and through the explicit coupling with other models using "domain objects" one can model context-sensitive interactive applications. Figure 8 specifies a mobile application that is not only location-aware but also aware of the reachability of caregivers.

<table>
<tr><th>CTT Operator</th><th>Relation</th><th>Source</th><th>Target</th><th>Parent Interactor</th></tr>
<tr><td>a >> b</td><td>Activate</td><td>interactor (-)
domain object</td><td>interactor</td><td></td></tr>
<tr><td>a ||| b, a |=| b</td><td>no relation</td><td></td><td></td><td>interactor</td></tr>
<tr><td>a |> b</td><td>Activate</td><td>PerformReturn</td><td>interactor</td><td></td></tr>
<tr><td>a [> b</td><td></td><td>End</td><td></td><td></td></tr>
<tr><td>a [] b</td><td>MutuallyExclusive</td><td>interactor</td><td>interactor</td><td></td></tr>
<tr><td>a*</td><td></td><td>interactor</td><td></td><td>RepeatedConceptualGroup (+)</td></tr>
<tr><td>a |[]| b
/</td><td>Update</td><td>interactor (*)
domain object</td><td>interactor (**)
domain object</td><td></td></tr>
<tr><td>/</td><td>Use</td><td>interactor (*)
domain object</td><td>interactor (**)
domain object</td><td></td></tr>
<tr><td colspan="5">(-) only interactors that can trigger navigation</td></tr>
<tr><td colspan="5">(*) only interactors that can modify data</td></tr>
<tr><td colspan="5">(**) only interactors that can show data</td></tr>
<tr><td colspan="5">(+) only applicable when the interactor should be repeated in the user interface</td></tr>
</table>

Table 4. Relations supported by CAP3, the constraints that apply on the source and/or target of these relations, or on the parent interactor.

The authors believe that this very explicit integration of elements of other models should be limited to cases in which these elements actively influence the user interface without interaction from the user, or when the type of user performing the interaction can differ and this distinction is important (such as in the case of collaborative software). In other cases, a more implicit integration through properties that are displayed as part of the labels or not displayed in the diagram at all seems more appropriate. This latter approach is the only mechanism available in modeling languages such as MARIA [23] and UsiXML [13, chapter 3].

DISCUSSION

The abstract user interface modeling language, CAP3, as proposed in this paper demonstrates the possibility to integrate both structural and behavioral aspects of abstract user interfaces into a single consistent language. To assess the language, its expressiveness is compared to that of several other abstract user interface languages (see for example Table 2 and Table 1 for interactors, and Table 4 for the behavior). CAP3 has only been used to describe graphical user interfaces. These comparisons reveal that it has a similar abstraction level as AUI languages that are also used to semi-automatically generate multi-modal and voice user interfaces, such as MARIA [23].

It was applied to some projects in which the authors were involved or that were described in literature (such as the mobile application discussed by Mahmud et al. [15]).

CAP3 (and other AUI modeling languages) were also assessed using state-of-the-art knowledge regarding the construction of domain-specific languages as discussed by Karsai et al. [11] and the perception of visual languages for software engineering[17]. The results of these assessments were overall positive for CAP3. Nonetheless also some points for improvement were identified; namely inclusion of complexity management mechanisms could still improve the language. But this point for improvement is applicable to many software engineering languages.

Some notable positive points regarding the principles discussed by Moody [17] include that all relations differ in one visual dimension and most in two different visual dimensions (Principle of Perceptual Discriminability), an explicit mechanism for including information from other diagrams (Principle of Cognitive Integration) and the symbols suggest their meaning (Principle of Perceptual Immediacy) to at least a significant subset of CAP3's potential users as identified in the discussion on the role of AUI in a user-centered process.

The knowledge about the design of domain-specific languages was applied as demonstrated by the fact that the potential uses and users of the language were identified before the design of the notation, the language is mostly a composition of existing languages (or language elements), it reuses the existing type system provided by EMF ECore, it allows comments (as shown in Figure 8), and syntactic sugar is used appropriately (only in one case, using the *ConceptualGroup*, where it can clearly reduce clutter).

CONCLUSIONS

This paper presents CAP3, a new abstract user interface modeling language to support user-centered development methods. As state-of-art knowledge on domain-specific languages and visual sofware engineering languages propose, it was not created from scratch, but rather builds on existing notations and modeling languages. It integrates the specification of structural and behavioral aspects of user interfaces into a single notation. An approach that was also taken by Denim [14], which was however focused on informal specification using sketches. Denim thus has no model integration, does not allow the integration of contextual information, and uses sketches instead of precise abstractions.

CAP3 has tool support, which is realized on the Eclipse platform using Eugenia [12]. CAP3 is actively used in research projects and validated using state-of-the art knowledge on domain-specific languages and visual software engineering languages.

Future work includes enhancing the tool support for model-transformations, especially to concrete user interfaces.

ACKNOWLEDGMENTS

This work is supported by FWO project Transforming human interface designs via model driven engineering (G. 0296.08).

REFERENCES

1. P. J. Barclay, T. Griffiths, J. McKirdy, J. B. Kennedy, R. Cooper, N. W. Paton, and P. D. Gray. Teallach - a flexible user-interface development environment for object database applications. *J. Vis. Lang. Comput.*, 14(1):47–77, 2003.
2. T. Bolognesi and E. Brinksma. Introduction to the iso specification language lotos. *Computer Networks*, 14:25–59, 1987.
3. G. Calvary, J. Coutaz, D. Thevenin, Q. Limbourg, L. Bouillon, and J. Vanderdonckt. A unifying reference framework for multi-target user interfaces. *Interacting with Computers*, 15(3):289–308, 2003.
4. W. W. W. consortium. *XML Schema*. `http://www.w3.org/XML/Schema`.
5. W. W. W. consortium. *XForms*. `http://www.w3.org/xforms/`.
6. L. L. Constantine. Canonical Abstract Prototypes for abstract visual and interaction. In *Proc. DSV-IS 2003*, Springer (2003), 1–15.
7. P. P. da Silva and N. W. Paton. User interface modeling in UMLi. *IEEE Software*, 20(4):62–69, 2003.
8. K. Z. Gajos, D. S. Weld, and J. O. Wobbrock. Automatically generating personalized user interfaces with Supple. *Artif. Intell.*, 174(12-13):910–950, 2010.
9. M. Haesen, K. Coninx, J. Van den Bergh, and K. Luyten. Muicser: A process framework for multi-disciplinary user-centred software engineering processes. In *Proc. TAMODIA/HCSE 2008*, Springer (2008), 150–165.
10. ISO JTC 1/SC 35. ISO/IEC 24752-3:2008: Information technology – user interfaces – universal remote console – part 3: Presentation template, 2008.
11. G. Karsai, H. Krahn, C. Pinkernell, B. Rumpe, M. Schindler, and S. Völkel. Design guidelines for domain specific languages. In *Proc. DSM 2009*, 2009.
12. D. S. Kolovos, L. M. Rose, S. bin Abid, R. F. Paige, F. A. C. Polack, and G. Botterweck. Taming EMF and GMF using model transformation. In *Proc. MoDELS 2010 (1)*, Springer (2010), 211–225.
13. Q. Limbourg. *Multi-Path Development of User Interfaces*. PhD thesis, Université Catholique de Louvain, 2004.
14. J. Lin, M. W. Newman, J. I. Hong, and J. A. Landay. Denim: finding a tighter fit between tools and practice for web site design. In *Proc. CHI 2000*, ACM Press (2000), 510–517.
15. N. Mahmud, J. Voigt, K. Luyten, K. Slegers, J. Van den Bergh, and K. Coninx. Dazed and confused considered normal: An approach to create interactive systems for people with dementia. In *Proc. HCSE 2010*, Springer (2010), 119–134.
16. F. Montero and V. López-Jaquero. Idealxml: An interaction design tool. In *Proc. CADUI 2006*, Springer (2006), 245–252.
17. D. L. Moody. The "physics" of notations: Toward a scientific basis for constructing visual notations in software engineering. *IEEE Trans. Software Eng.*, 35(6):756–779, 2009.
18. G. Mori, F. Paternò, and C. Santoro. Ctte: Support for developing and analyzing task models for interactive system design. *IEEE Trans. Software Eng.*, 28(8):797–813, 2002.
19. J. Nichols, B. A. Myers, M. Higgins, J. Hughes, T. K. Harris, R. Rosenfeld, and M. Pignol. Generating remote control interfaces for complex appliances. In *Proc. UIST 2002*, ACM Press (2002), 161–170.
20. L. Nóbrega, N. J. Nunes, and H. Coelho. The meta sketch editor. In *Proc. CADUI 2006*, Springer (2006) 201–214.
21. N. J. Nunes and J. F. e Cunha. Wisdom - a UML based architecture for interactive systems. In *Proc. DSV-IS 2000*, Springer (2000), 191–205.
22. Object Management Group. *UML 2.2 Superstructure Specification*, 2009.
23. F. Paternò, C. Santoro, and L. D. Spano. Maria: A universal, declarative, multiple abstraction-level language for service-oriented applications in ubiquitous environments. *ACM Trans. Comput.-Hum. Interact.*, 16(4), 2009.
24. D. Thevenin. *Adaptation en Interaction Homme-Machine : le cas de Plasticité*. PhD thesis, Université Joseph Fourier, 2001.
25. J. Van den Bergh, B. Bruynooghe, J. Moons, S. Huypens, B. Hemmeryckx-Deleersnijder, and K. Coninx. Using high-level models for the creation of staged participatory multimedia events on tv. *Multimedia Syst.*, 14(2):89–103, 2008.
26. J. Van den Bergh and K. Coninx. Cup 2.0: High-level modeling of context-sensitive interactive applications. In *Proc. MoDELS 2006*, Springer (2006), 140–154.

Automated Generation of Device-Specific WIMP UIs: Weaving of Structural and Behavioral Models

David Raneburger, Roman Popp, Hermann Kaindl, Jürgen Falb and Dominik Ertl
Institute of Computer Technology
Vienna University of Technology
Gusshausstrasse 27-29, A-1040 Vienna, Austria
{raneburger, popp, kaindl, falb, ertl}@ict.tuwien.ac.at

ABSTRACT
Any graphical user interface needs to have defined structure and behavior. So, in particular, models of Window / Icon / Menu / Pointing Device (WIMP) UIs need to represent structure and behavior at some level of abstraction, possibly in separate models. High-level conceptual models such as Task or Discourse Models do not model the UI per se. Therefore, in the course of automated generation of (WIMP) UIs from such models, structure and behavior of the UI need to be generated, and they need to fit together. In order to achieve that, we devised a new approach to weaving structural and behavioral models on different levels of abstraction.

Author Keywords
Automated GUI generation, model-based WIMP UI generation, device-specific user interfaces

ACM Classification Keywords
D.2.2 Design Tool and Techniques: User Interfaces

General Terms
Design

INTRODUCTION
Our major rationale for (semi-)automatic GUI generation is to efficiently and quickly provide specific GUIs for multiple devices, generated from a single high-level Communication Model based on discourses [4]. Since any graphical user interface (GUI) needs to have defined structure and behavior, Window / Icon / Menu / Pointer (WIMP) UI generation approaches such as [2, 3, 15], explicitly specify the structure and the behavior of the UI. In the course of our optimized GUI generation for small screens according to a device specification [13], a device-specific model of the structure of the GUI is generated directly from a high-level Communication Model. This approach facilitates the optimization process for the specific device, in contrast to generating an abstract UI model first, and decomposing for small screens later [16].

EICS'11, June 13–16, 2011, Pisa, Italy.

In the course of our automatic generation of the behavior of a WIMP UI from a high-level Communication Model [11], e.g., a UI Behavior Model is generated that is independent of both device and modality. Since this UI Behavior Model and the Structural UI Model are on different levels of abstraction, they do not directly fit together.

In this paper, we show how to *weave* a device-specific Structural UI Model and a device-independent UI Behavior Model to create a consistent and complete screen-based and device-specific UI model. Weaving means here to associate elements of two models that describe the same UI from different points of view to create one model that represents both views. In effect, the resulting *Screen Model* contains both a device-specific Structural Screen Model and a related Behavioral Screen Model. That is, the states of this behavioral model represent the screens of this structural model. Such a Screen Model can be edited interactively by a designer for improving it [12], and from such a screen model the final WIMP UI can be created in a straight-forward manner.

The remainder of this paper is organized in the following manner. First, we provide some background material, in order to make this paper self-contained. Then we explain our new approach to device-specific generation of (optimized) WIMP UIs with a focus on model weaving. Finally, we relate it to other work and provide a conclusion and an outlook.

BACKGROUND
Since our new weaving of structural and behavioral models is embedded in our discourse-based approach to generating WIMP UIs, we provide a brief sketch of this approach as background material. Primarily, the automated generation starts from a *Discourse Model* [4, 11]. Strictly speaking, however, a Discourse Model contains references to objects defined in the *Domain-of-Discourse* and the *Action-Notification Model* [10]. Therefore, the designer has to provide these three models, which are parts of the so-called *Communication Model.*

Our Discourse Model is device- and modality-independent and specifies interaction and communication on a high level, based on discourses in the sense of dialogues. This enables the designer of such models to concentrate on the dialogue structure between the user and the system. The major modeling constructs of a Discourse Model are *Communicative Acts* derived from speech act theory [14]. Communicative

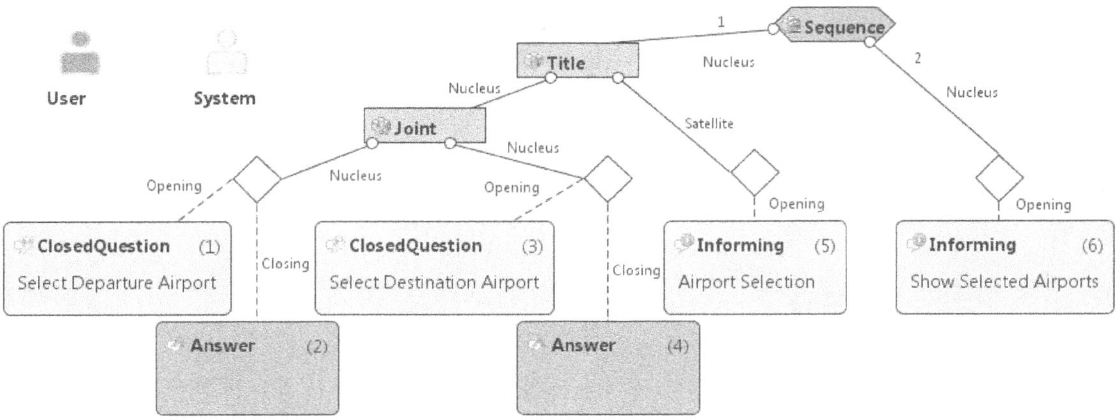

Figure 1. Airport Selection Discourse Model

Acts capture the intention of the communication, like asking a *Question*, *Informing* about new facts, or *Requesting* an action upon receiving the Communicative Act. They are represented by rounded boxes in Discourse Model diagrams like the one shown in Figure 1. Each Communicative Act is assigned to one of the two communication parties defined in the Discourse Model, which is represented by the fill color of the Communicative Acts. Moreover, a Communicative Act specifies the content of the utterance. This content specification refers to objects in the *Domain-of-Discourse Model* and to actions specified in the *Action-Notification Model* (see [10] for more information on these two latter models).

Communicative Acts are normally combined to *Adjacency Pairs* (based on Conversation Analysis [5]), which represent typical turn-takings of communication (e.g., Question–Answer or Offer–Accept). They are represented as diamonds in Discourse Model diagrams. Adjacency Pairs (ADJ) are related with each other via discourse relations, which are partly derived from Rhetorical Structure Theory [6]. They are enriched with procedural relations that allow a precise definition of the interaction flow.

Let us illustrate this modeling approach using a simple excerpt from a flight booking application. In this scenario, the user selects the departure and destination airports. Subsequently, the system informs about the two selected airports. The corresponding Discourse Model is shown in Figure 1.

The airport selection is modeled with two *ClosedQuestion-Answer* Adjacency Pairs, which are related with one another through a *Joint* relation. This defines that both questions can be answered at the same time or in arbitrary order. Additionally, an Adjacency Pair containing only an *Informing* Communicative Act (without any confirmation) is related to the questions via a *Title* relation. This Title relation defines that the Informing Communicative Act conveys information that should be presented either above (e.g., on a GUI) or before (e.g., speech output) the questions. The root relation in this model is a *Sequence*. The Sequence specifies that the airport selection needs to be completed before the informing about the selected airports.

The references from Communicative Acts to their propositional content are given in a shorthand notation (e.g., "Select Departure Airport") in Figure 1. These references link to objects in the Domain-of-Discourse Model and the Action-Notification Model. Figure 2 shows the Domain-of-Discourse Model for our running example. The class *Airport* has the attributes *name* and *airportcode*. The class *Flight* has the attributes *number* and *date*. The relations between these two classes specify that a *Flight* has exactly one departure airport and exactly one destination airport.

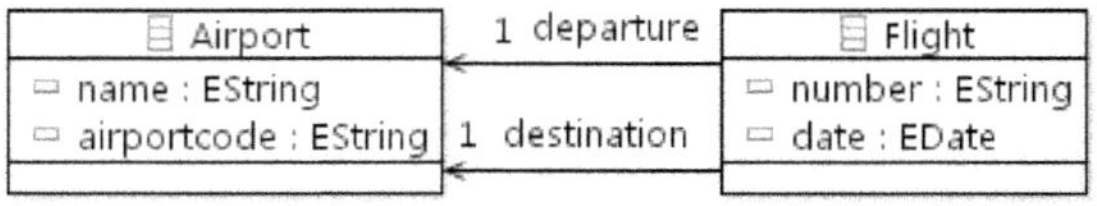

Figure 2. Domain-of-Discourse Model

DEVICE-SPECIFIC WIMP-UI GENERATION

First we sketch how a Communication Model can be transformed both into a device-specific Structural UI Model and in a device-independent UI Behavior Model. Based on that, we describe in detail how these two models are weaved into a consistent, device-specific, screen-based WIMP-UI model — the Screen Model.

The Generation Process

All these model transformations are part of the overall process for automated generation of device-specific WIMP-UIs from a high-level Communication Model, as illustrated in Figure 3. This approach employs model-to-model transformations to derive a Structural UI Model that is already device dependent, and a UI Behavior Model that is independent of device and modality. During these transformations, traces are kept, so that, e.g., the Discourse Model can be accessed in the course of weaving. The separation of structural and behavioral concerns was introduced because the generation approach aims to support different target devices and platforms, as well as modalities.

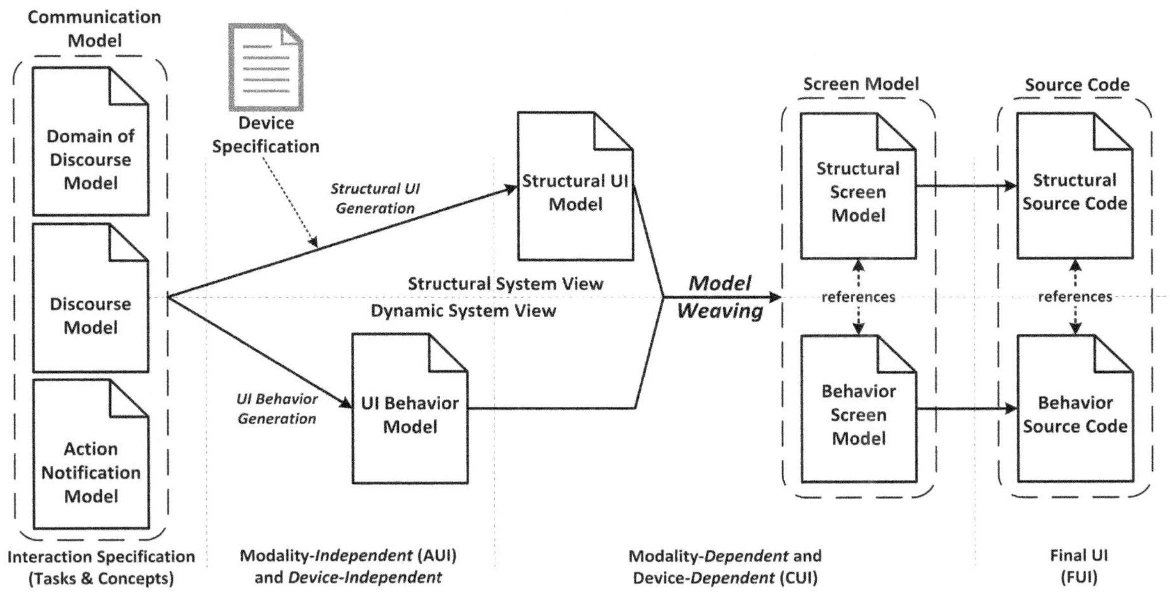

Figure 3. Device-Specific WIMP-UI Generation Process

Figure 3 illustrates the various models in this process according to the Cameleon Reference Framework [1]. It is interesting to see that, in contrast to the behavior models, this process does *not* provide a structural model on the Abstract User Interface (AUI) Level. This intermediate level is not used during the generation process for two reasons. First, in order not to lose information, it would become necessary to replicate the semantic information provided by the Discourse elements, which is used for layout and grouping of the UI widgets. Second, it is not possible to estimate the space-needs of a screen on the AUI level (i.e., not knowing which widgets will be used), hence it would not be possible to apply the optimization described in [13] and sketched below. In contrast to the Structural UI Model, the UI Behavior Model is situated on the AUI level, because it is still independent of device and modality.

Figure 3 also shows that these two models are subsequently weaved to the Screen Model, which is consistent, screen based and device specific. Generation of the final code for structure and behavior from the Screen Model can be done in a straight-forward manner.

Generation of Device-Specific Structural UI Model

The device-specific Structural UI Model is generated out of a Communication Model by a declarative rule-based model transformation process. A GUI designer can specify the required transformation rules in a graphical way by defining a graph pattern on the left-hand side matching parts of the Communication Model, and a GUI structure on the right-hand side that will be inserted into the Structural UI Model, if and when the rule matches and fires. The rules specify traces between Communication Model elements and Structural UI widgets. Such transformation rules can be constrained to specific device properties, like target platform or input modality, and thus can range from device-independent rules to device-specific rules. Rules can also include hints on the space requirements of their results.

The transformation process uses these rules together with a device specification and a conflict resolution strategy to select the matching rule for firing that is most appropriate for the device it is rendering for. Additionally, it calculates the resulting screen size and optimizes the widget selection for the Structural UI Model to fit the device-specific screen size best (for more details see [13]). This transformation process from Task & Concepts Level to Concrete UI Level has the advantage that all semantic information of Discourse Model elements can be directly used to create an optimized device-specific GUI structure. This process exploits the information from the target device specification and encapsulates it in the Structural UI to make it available for further transformations (i.e., Screen Model weaving and code generation).

Figure 4 depicts the Structural UI Model corresponding to our running example. The top *Choice* element contains two *Panels* representing both children of the *Sequence* relation shown in Figure 1. Since we rendered the running example for a very small screen (220×176 pixels), the transformation selects a rule for the *Joint* relation in Figure 1 that splits the information of both branches into two panels that can be displayed alternatively (indicated by the embedded Choice element). Each branch consists of a *List Widget* for selecting an airport that will be rendered as a combo box and a submit button.

Generation of UI Behavior Model

This generation step transforms a Communication Model into a UI Behavior Model. The UI Behavior Model specifies which Communicative Acts are received or can be sent, in principle, at the same time and form a so-called *Presentation Unit*. This transformation step does not consider any

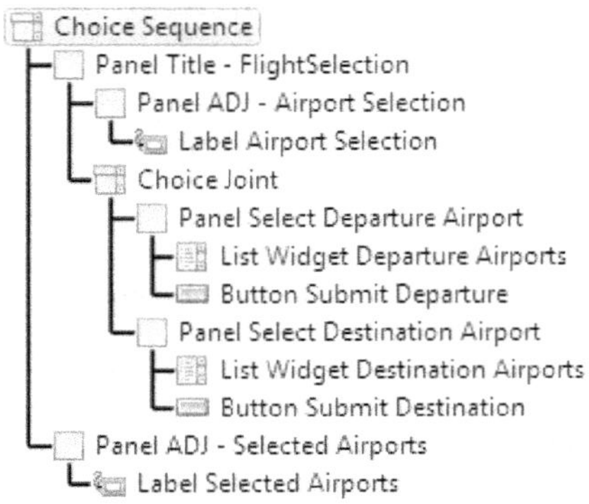

Figure 4. Device Specific Structural UI Model

constraints specific to device or modality. Thus, the UI Behavior Model specifies the flow of interaction (i.e., Communicative Acts) independent of device and modality. The algorithm used to generate the UI Behavior Model is presented in [11]. This model is represented as a state machine with the Presentation Units as its states. The transitions between the Presentation Units are triggered by the Communicative Acts that are sent by the user.

Figure 5 shows the generated UI Behavior Model for our running example. The first Presentation Unit (*PU1 – Airport Selection*) displays the Informing *Airport Selection* and the two ClosedQuestions for the airport selection. It allows the user to send the corresponding answers. The second Presentation Unit (*PU2 – Selected Airports*) presents the selected airports to the user. The Answer Communicative Acts (2 and 4) sent by the user at once trigger the transition between the two Presentation Units.

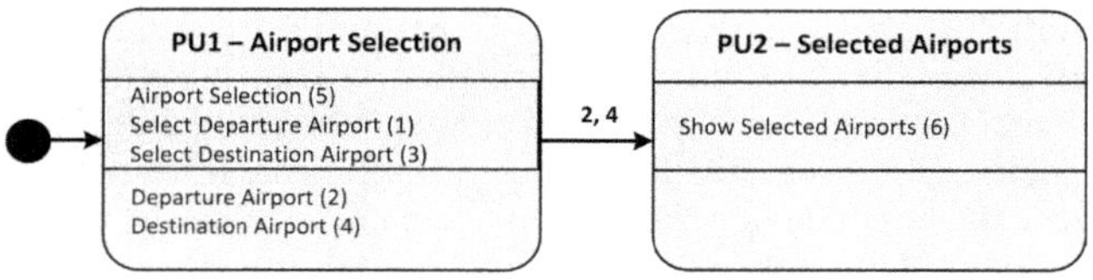

Figure 5. Device Independent UI Behavior Model

Weaving for Generation of Screen Model

The device-dependent Structural UI Model and the device-independent UI Behavior Model are weaved for generating the Screen Model. This resulting model defines both the structure of the WIMP UI and its behavior. It provides the basis for the code generation (see Figure 3).

The Screen Model actually consists of the *Structural Screen Model* and the *Behavior Screen Model*. The Structural Screen Model for our running example is shown in Figure 6 and specifies the concrete screens of the WIMP UI. The corresponding Behavior Screen Model is shown in Figure 7 and specifies the behavior of the WIMP UI, i.e., the possible sequences of screens.

The new weaving process has the following steps. The first step traverses the Structural UI Model top-down and creates

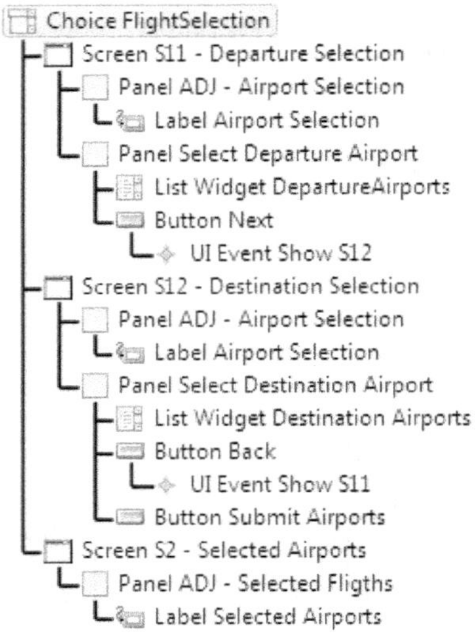

Figure 6. Structural Screen Model

a list of Panels that belong to a screen. The list of Panels is gradually refined according to the containers in the Structural UI Model. A *Panel* means that its Sub-Panels are added to the same screen, whereas a *Choice* element means that the screen is split before the children are added.

The second step uses the traces between the Structural UI widgets and the Discourse elements to create a map that assigns the Communicative Acts that are displayed or can be sent to each screen. Table 1 shows this map for our running example.

Communicative Acts	Panels in Screen
Informing_5, ClosedQuestion_1, Answer_2	Title – FlightSelection, ADJ – Airport Selection, Select Departure Airport
Informing_5, ClosedQuestion_3, Answer_4	Title – FlightSelection, ADJ – Airport Selection, Select Destination Airport
Informing_6	ADJ – Selected Airports

Table 1. Map Communicative Acts from Figure 1 to Screens

Subsequently, this map and the UI Behavior Model are used to create the Structural Screen Model. Each screen consists of the Panels defined in the map. Some Panels, like the *Title – FlightSelection* Panel in our example, may belong to more than one screen. Such Panels are added to the corresponding screens in the Structural Screen Model.

The next step checks whether each Presentation Unit can be mapped directly to a screen, or if a Presentation Unit consists of several sub-screens. No adjustments on the Presentation Units are needed in case of direct mapping, because each Presentation Unit corresponds to a screen. The other case means that screens have been split during the target-device optimization of the Structural UI Model. This implies that *Buttons* need to be added that trigger screen changes between the split screens. We introduce so-called *UIEvents* to model those events that are only specific to the WIMP UI but not defined in the high-level Discourse Model.

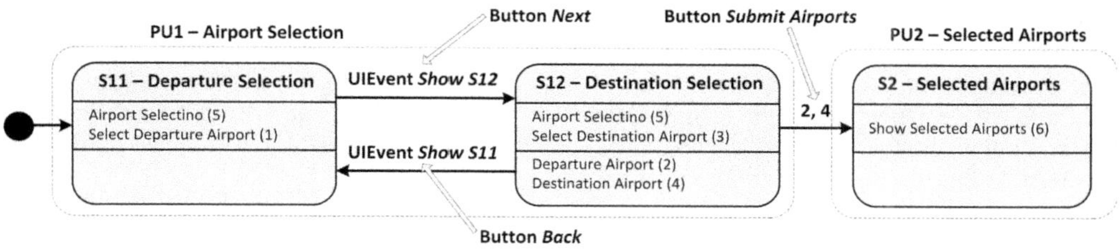

Figure 7. Behavior Screen Model

In the Structural Screen Model of our running example shown in Figure 6, the *Next* Button in Screen *S11 - Departure Selection* and the *Back* Button in Screen *S12 - Destination Selection* trigger the UIEvents for the corresponding screen changes. Additionally, the Buttons that send the Communicative Acts are combined to one Button that sends all Communicative Acts concurrently in the last screen. Which Buttons can be combined is derived from the triggers in the Screen Behavior Model. In our example, this is the *Submit Airports* Button in Screen *S12 - Destination Selection*.

The last step is the adaptation of the Behavior Screen Model. The split screens are added to this model as new states that replace the corresponding original Presentation Unit. Figure 7 shows the resulting model for our running example.

For this example, we chose a target device and a platform that require explicit screen splitting (e.g., a Smartphone with HTML support). Alternatively, if the target platform with the same screen size supported Tabbed Panes (e.g., Java Swing or Java Script for HTML), such a tabbed pane could be used as a container for the two screens in our example. In this case, the screen-splitting would be handled by the Tabbed Pane widget and, therefore, no adaptations in the Behavior Screen Model would be necessary. So, the introduction of UIEvents allows us to support even less powerful target platforms (e.g., Smartphones without Java Script support).

The Screen Model provides a consistent specification of the WIMP UI. The relation between the Structural Screen Model and the Behavior Screen Model is represented by the trigger events. This implies that each state in the Behavior Screen Model corresponds to exactly one screen in the Structural Screen Model and vice versa. Thus, the Screen Model provides a complete and consistent definition of the screens and their possible sequences at compile time. It can be transformed to source code in a straight-forward manner, without any model analysis at runtime. This is especially important for devices with limited capacities (e.g., Smartphones). Moreover, the Screen Model provides a complete WIMP-UI specification at Concrete UI Level and, therefore, a sound basis for manual customization by the designer.

RELATED WORK

The Dygimes Framework [2] combines task specifications with XML-based UI building blocks to generate UIs for mobile computing devices and embedded systems. Such UIs can adapt to the context of use at runtime and thus migrate over devices. Which tasks are enabled in the same presentation is defined by the UI building blocks that need to be provided by the designer.

GrafiXML [7] is an intelligent UI builder that supports the development of UIs for multiple contexts of use (i.e., many users, platforms and environments). The UIs are developed manually in a graphical editor and assigned to a certain context of use. GrafiXML uses UsiXML[1] as its UI specification language. This adds additional power as its UIs can be manipulated or refined in other UsiXML tools as well.

A top-down generation approach that supports the transformation of ConcurTaskTrees (CTT) into UIs for multiple devices is presented in [8]. This approach uses a common task model for all UIs, which is subsequently refined manually by the designer to the System Task model. The System task model is already tailored to the target device and defines which tasks are concurrently enabled and thus belong to the same presentation. System task models are the starting point for the automated UI generation process.

Another CTT-based approach is introduced in [9], which supports the creation of UIs based on pre-existing functionalities in the form of Web services. This approach supports UI refinement in terms of interaction techniques (i.e., modalities or widget selection). Which set of UI elements can be perceived at a given time and thus belong to the same presentation, is still defined by a CTT model.

All these approaches use task models as their highest level of abstraction and provide during the UI generation models on all levels of the Cameleon Reference Framework. The AUI level, however, is independent of modality and platform, but not target-device independent. Therefore, the unique optimization for the target device in the discourse-based approach skips this level for the structural model. This makes the new weaving of structural and behavioral models necessary that we present in this paper.

Our approach is able to fully automatically generate device-specific WIMP UIs out of the same device-independent Communication Model (based on discourses). All the task-based approaches above, in contrast, need one or the other manual intervention by a human designer.

[1] http://www.usixml.org

CONCLUSION & OUTLOOK

When structural and behavioral models are separated in the course of automated generation of WIMP UIs, their consistency is important. Especially when optimizing such UIs for specific (small) target devices, there is an additional difficulty involved through having them on different levels of abstraction. Our new solution involves weaving of structural and behavioral models on different levels of abstraction into a Screen Model, whose structural and behavioral submodels are consistent. They are also complete for straightforward generation of structural and behavioral code of the final WIMP UI.

The implemented generation process is fully automatic so far, but we think it will be important to include a human designer in the future. Especially for larger screens, aesthetic issues (e.g., style or layout) cannot yet be solved satisfactorily through fully-automatic generation of their UIs. To improve the usability of such UIs, we plan to give the designer more control over the UI during the generation process. The Screen Model resulting from our weaving approach will allow the designer to manually customize the UI at an appropriate level of abstraction. Thus, our new Screen Model paves the way for a more powerful semi-automatic WIMP-UI generation as well.

REFERENCES

1. G. Calvary, J. Coutaz, D. Thevenin, Q. Limbourg, L. Bouillon, and J. Vanderdonckt. A unifying reference framework for multi-target user interfaces. *Interacting with Computers*, 15(3):289 – 308, 2003.
2. K. Coninx, K. Luyten, C. Vandervelpen, J. Bergh, and B. Creemers. Dygimes: Dynamically generating interfaces for mobile computing devices and embedded systems. In *Human-Computer Interaction with Mobile Devices and Services*, volume 2795 of *Lecture Notes in Computer Science*, pages 256–270. Springer Berlin / Heidelberg, 2003. 10.1007/978-3-540-45233-1_19.
3. D. Costa, L. Nóbrega, and N. Nunes. An MDA approach for generating web interfaces with UML ConcurTaskTrees and canonical abstract prototypes. In K. Coninx, K. Luyten, and K. Schneider, editors, *Task Models and Diagrams for Users Interface Design*, volume 4385 of *Lecture Notes in Computer Science*, pages 137–152. Springer Berlin / Heidelberg, 2007. 10.1007/978-3-540-70816-2_11.
4. J. Falb, S. Kavaldjian, R. Popp, D. Raneburger, E. Arnautovic, and H. Kaindl. Fully automatic user interface generation from discourse models. In *Proceedings of the 13th International Conference on Intelligent User Interfaces (IUI '09)*, pages 475–476. ACM Press: New York, NY, 2009.
5. P. Luff, D. Frohlich, and N. Gilbert. *Computers and Conversation*. Academic Press, London, UK, January 1990.
6. W. C. Mann and S. Thompson. Rhetorical Structure Theory: Toward a functional theory of text organization. *Text*, 8(3):243–281, 1988.
7. B. Michotte and J. Vanderdonckt. GrafiXML, a multi-target user interface builder based on UsiXML. In *Proceedings of the Fourth International Conference on Autonomic and Autonomous Systems*, pages 15–22, Washington, DC, USA, 2008. IEEE Computer Society.
8. G. Mori, F. Paternò, and C. Santoro. Design and development of multidevice user interfaces through multiple logical descriptions. *IEEE Transactions on Software Engineering*, 30(8):507–520, 8 2004.
9. F. Paternò, C. Santoro, and L. Spano. Model-based design of multi-device interactive applications based on web services. In T. Gross, J. Gulliksen, P. Kotz, L. Oestreicher, P. Palanque, R. Prates, and M. Winckler, editors, *Human-Computer Interaction - INTERACT 2009*, volume 5726 of *Lecture Notes in Computer Science*, pages 892–905. Springer Berlin / Heidelberg, 2009. 10.1007/978-3-642-03655-2_98.
10. R. Popp. Defining communication in SOA based on discourse models. In *Proceeding of the 24th ACM SIGPLAN Conference Companion on Object Oriented Programming Systems Languages and Applications (OOPSLA '09)*, pages 829–830. ACM Press: New York, NY, 2009.
11. R. Popp, J. Falb, E. Arnautovic, H. Kaindl, S. Kavaldjian, D. Ertl, H. Horacek, and C. Bogdan. Automatic generation of the behavior of a user interface from a high-level discourse model. In *Proceedings of the 42nd Annual Hawaii International Conference on System Sciences (HICSS-42)*, Piscataway, NJ, USA, 2009. IEEE Computer Society Press.
12. D. Raneburger. Interactive model driven graphical user interface generation. In *Proceedings of the 2nd ACM SIGCHI Symposium on Engineering Interactive Computing Systems*, EICS '10, pages 321–324, New York, NY, USA, 2010. ACM.
13. D. Raneburger, R. Popp, S. Kavaldjian, H. Kaindl, and J. Falb. Optimized GUI generation for small screens. In H. Hussmann, G. Meixner, and D. Zuehlke, editors, *Model-Driven Development of Advanced User Interfaces*, volume 340 of *Studies in Computational Intelligence*, pages 107–122. Springer Berlin / Heidelberg, 2011. 10.1007/978-3-642-14562-9_6.
14. J. R. Searle. *Speech Acts: An Essay in the Philosophy of Language*. Cambridge University Press, Cambridge, England, 1969.
15. A. Wolff and P. Forbig. Deriving user interfaces from task models. In *Proceedings of the IUI'09 Workshop on Model Driven Development of Advanced User Interfaces*, 2009.
16. X. Xiao, Q. Luo, D. Hong, H. Fu, X. Xie, and W.-Y. Ma. Browsing on small displays by transforming web pages into hierarchically structured subpages. *ACM Transactions on the Web*, 3(1):1–36, 2009.

W^5: A Meta-Model for Pen-and-Paper Interaction

Felix Heinrichs, Daniel Schreiber, Jochen Huber, Max Mühlhäuser
FG Telecooperation, Department of Computer Science
Technische Universität Darmstadt
Hochschulstr. 10, 64289 Darmstadt, Germany
felix_h,schreiber,jhuber,max@tk.informatik.tu-darmstadt.de

ABSTRACT
Pen-and-Paper Interaction (PPI) is used in an increasing number of applications to bridge the digital-physical gap between paper and interactive computer systems. We present W^5, a meta-model for describing PPI, and demonstrate its expressiveness by applying it to several interaction techniques from the literature. In doing so, we derive a set of basic interaction primitives, which can be used to inform the design of development toolkits for PPI and guide interaction designers in a structured exploration of the design space. We present a proof-of-concept implementation for a PPI toolkit based on W^5 in order to demonstrate the practical relevance of our findings.

ACM Classification Keywords
H.5.2 Information Interfaces and Presentation: [Theory and methods]

General Terms
Human Factors, Design, Theory

Author Keywords
Model-based Interactive System Development, Development Tools / Toolkits / Programming Environments, Pen and Tactile Input, Handheld Devices and Mobile Computing, Digital Pen, Anoto

INTRODUCTION
Pen and paper has recently gained some popularity as input modality for digital applications, ranging from note-taking [2] to computer based learning support [9]. These systems use a novel form of human-computer interaction, where the user interacts with a system using a digital pen and normal paper, here referred to as *Pen-and-Paper Interaction* (PPI). To support this form of interaction, applications provide a *Pen-and-Paper User Interface* (PPUI) in addition to, or instead of a graphical user interface (GUI).

As any other interactive application, these applications employ one or more interaction techniques, to trigger application functionality. Thereby, an *interaction technique* consists of *input* combined with appropriate *feedback* [4]. However, interaction techniques in PPUIs differ from those employed in traditional GUIs. For example, unlike a mouse, the pen leaves an ink trail on paper. Using interaction techniques that require the user to mark the same paper area twice will render the content on the paper unreadable. Thus, novel interaction techniques are needed for PPI based applications.

Figure 1. The crop mark selection technique in our prototype

Some examples of interaction techniques for PPUIs have been introduced in the literature. For example, a region on paper can be selected by drawing crop marks [5] (see Fig. 1). Yet, how can PPI interaction techniques be modeled? There is a lack of theoretical models for describing and categorizing such interaction techniques. Such a model should be able to guide researchers in finding new interaction techniques and help interaction designers in selecting appropriate techniques for PPI based applications. Ultimately, an appropriate model could inform the design of development toolkits for PPUIs.

Our contribution to solving this problem is threefold: First, we introduce the W^5 meta-model for modeling PPI. Second, based on this meta-model, we establish a set of primitives that suffice to describe and classify a significant portion of the design space for PPI interaction techniques. Third, we present a proof-of-concept implementation of a PPUI toolkit based on W^5 and the identified primitives to validate our theoretical concepts.

RELATED WORK
The primacy of interaction design in the development of interactive computer systems has been emphasized by Beaudouin-Lafon [1]. Toolkits and models of interaction support the

EICS 2011, June 13-16, 2011, Pisa, Italy.
Copyright 2011 ACM 978-1-4503-0670-6/11/06...$10.00.

designer in the development of appropriate interaction techniques, by providing structuring and reusable components. Basically, PPI is a subset of tangible interaction, for which models exist, e.g. TAC [6]. However, expressing PPI with these models is cumbersome as primitives relevant for PPI, like gesture etc., must be constructed out of generic primitives for tangible interaction. The Resource-Selector-Link (RSL) model proposed by Signer and Norrie [7] has been used to describe PPI, e.g. in the iServer and iPaper framework [8]. Here paper artifacts are modeled as resources, to which links can be established using a certain selector. Although this general link model can be used to describe a broad range of different cross-media links, it does not explicitly model the interaction. To model interaction techniques employed in PPUIs, Steimle proposed a conceptual framework grounded on empirical research [9]. It consists of a syntactic layer of *core interactions* and a semantic layer of *conceptual activities*. Interaction techniques are combinations of core interactions to perform conceptual activities. Described core activities include inking, clicking, moving, altering shape, combining and associating. Conceptual activities are annotating, linking and tagging among others.

W^5 is grounded on this prior work. It forms around the general associative paradigm for PPI modeled in iServer and iPaper [8] to describe its interaction techniques. The semantic and syntactic level described by Steimle [9] are also included. W^5 generalizes the syntactic level, as it uses three dimensions (spatial, temporal, content) which are, in contrast to [9], independent from any application domain. The model of Steimle thus can be derived from our model by picking appropriate representatives from each dimension. However, the two models are not isomorphic: W^5 allows to express interaction techniques that cannot be expressed in the framework introduced by Steimle, e.g. temporal sequences. In contrast to [9], W^5 models PPI, without aspects of tangible interaction. Only input created by touching the paper with a pen is considered, as done naturally while writing or drawing; yet also "clicking" the paper can be described. Input by folding or rearranging paper is not addressed by W^5, although it could be expressed using the external primitive introduced below.

Software support for the interaction designer is also a problem, because in contrast to GUIs, there is no abundance of toolkits for PPUIs. The PaperToolkit [13] aims to provide a generic toolkit, however, it does not explicitly address interaction modeling. As a result, PaperToolkit does not lend itself for combining PPI input primitives into more complex input as it is typical for PPI. Other systems supporting PPI, such as Letras [3] or iServer and iPaper [8] provide the infrastructure needed to support PPI in applications, yet fail to provide the developer and interaction designer appropriate support when it comes to the development of novel interaction techniques.

THE W⁵ META-MODEL

The purpose of W^5 is to describe actions executed by the user with a digital pen in the physical world, that can serve as input to digital applications, i.e. trigger digital functionality. This corresponds to the associative nature of the RSL model [7] introduced by Signer and Norrie, which has been successfully applied to PPI [8]. The application functionality itself and its connection to the input is not described by W^5.

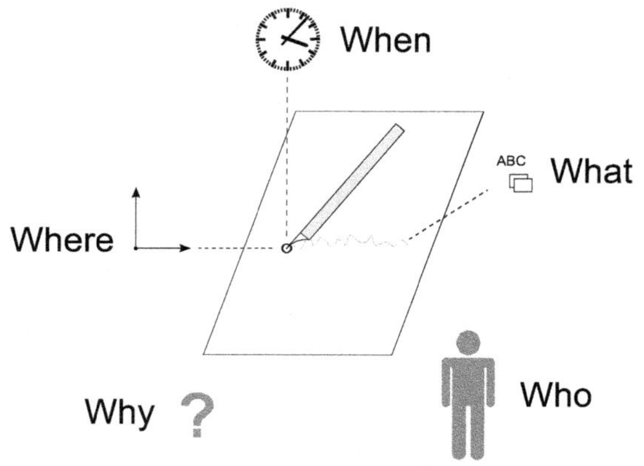

Figure 2. Dimensions of the W⁵ Framework

W⁵ Dimensions

W^5 describes and classifies PPI based on elementary user actions, or *input primitives*, as well as their combinations into more elaborate input expressions. Interaction techniques are combinations of primitives with appropriate feedback. Each action detectable by a PPUI can be classified according to the following five dimensions, as illustrated in Figure 2

- **Where**: Spatial dimension (W_1)
- **When**: Temporal dimension (W_2)
- **What**: Content dimension (W_3)
- **Who**: Originator dimension (W_4)
- **Why**: Contextual task dimension (W_5)

All input primitives fully coincide with one of these dimensions. Spatial primitives (Where) use the location where the user touches the paper with a pen. Temporal primitives (When) use the time when the user touches the paper with a pen. Primitives from the content dimension (What) use the content created by the user with the pen on paper. Gestures or written commands belong to this dimension.

As an example, we consider a spatial input primitive. This input primitive describes touching a certain paper region with the pen. It can be directly used as an interaction technique, e.g. in [8, 2]. In these systems so called paper widgets, or *pidgets*, are used to trigger application functionality. Pidgets are typically marked on the paper with a small iconographic representation of the corresponding application functionality. Another example is a temporal primitive, where the user has to touch the paper with the pen at a certain time. This might be used in a voting system, where the user has to mark a box with an X at the same time the desired choice (out of many) is shown on a screen.

As shown in [9], the perspective on the information ecology cannot be neglected, so the user (Who) and the executed tasks (Why) are also reflected in W^5. These dimensions can also contribute to the interaction techniques supported by a PPUI. Depending on the originator, the system might, e.g., accept or reject a command. The task at hand also can influence available functionality, allowing for example modal interaction in PPUIs. We suggest to use these five dimensions as basis for the design space, i.e., define input primitives for PPI that fully coincide with one of these dimensions.

Composition of Input Primitives

The above input primitives are absolute, i.e., the pen data is compared to an absolute value. Specifying all input by means of absolute input primitives is problematic. To describe more complex input we need means to relate user actions with other user actions. We do so by introducing relative input primitives. Again we consider only input primitives that coincide with one of the five dimensions above.

An example for a relative spatial input primitive is "above" meaning that one input must be performed above another. Another example for a relative input primitive, from the temporal dimension, is "after", meaning that two inputs must be performed in sequence. For example, one can combine two spatial input primitives with the temporal sequence primitive (one shortly after the other) to have something similar to the double-click input known from GUI systems.

W^5 Semantics and Notation

The semantics of W^5 are derived from logic programming. We regard the entire set of pen data PD as facts. Each absolute input primitive is a unary predicate. For example, At_R is *true* whenever PD contains data points that lie inside the rectangle R. *At* is an input primitive from the spatial dimension. The predicate can also be used with a variable, i.e., $At_R(X)$. In this case, all bindings for X that let At_R evaluate to *true* are returned.

Relative input primitives are n-ary predicates. For example, the *Abv* primitive spatially relates two facts. $Abv(X, Y)$ returns all bindings to X and Y so that X is "above" Y.

Example

To illustrate the concept, we apply it to an interaction technique from the literature. In the PapierCraft system, introduced by Liao et al. [5], the user can copy a portion of a document by marking its upper left and lower right corners with a so called crop gesture (see Figure 1 for an example of the crop gesture) followed by a pigtail gesture oriented to the right (east). Using the W^5 framework this is expressed as

$$G_{cs}(X) \wedge G_{ce}(Y) \wedge G_{pgt}(Z) \wedge \curvearrowright (X, Y, Z)$$

Where G_{cs}, G_{ce} and G_{pgt} are input primitives in the content dimension for the two crop marks and the pigtail symbol respectively. $\curvearrowright$ is a temporal relative input primitive indicating a temporal sequence. This can be abbreviated, if we do not reuse any of the variables, emphasizing the hierarchic composition of primitives: $\curvearrowright (G_{cs}, G_{ce}, G_{pgt})$

The EXT Predicate

Because W^5 only describes PPI input, it is impossible to combine non-PPI input with PPI input in W^5 . To remedy this limitation we introduce a special predicate called EXT, that evaluates to true when any relevant non-PPI input happens. This could, e.g., be pressing a button on a keyboard to switch between inking mode and command mode for the UI as in [5].

BASIC INPUT PRIMITIVES

W^5 provides a way to model input in PPUIs. It supports the designer in constructing complex input out of given input primitives. The question arises, which primitives are relevant for implementing PPI? This question has high practical relevance, as such a set could be used to inform the design of PPUI toolkits.

Derivation of Input Primitives

We derive a set of primitives by analysis of interaction techniques described in the literature. In particular we use the interaction techniques described in PapierCraft [5], PaperPoint [8], PaperProof [11] and CoScribe [9].

PapierCraft

Liao et al. describe a set of interaction techniques used in the PapierCraft system [5]. Their interaction techniques use a gesture based command system. Normally, the user uses the digital pen to generate digital ink and annotate a document. In order to invoke some functionality, the user presses a "gesture" button and then specifies a command. A command consists of a sequence of a *command scope* followed by an *intermediate delimiter* and a final *command type*. Commands can be constructed in sequences, e.g., a copy command followed by a paste command. We chose to analyze a copy and paste command using the crop mark selection gesture with an explicit written command, a hyperlink command with a margin bar selection gesture and a stitching gesture to combine two paper artifacts. Other interaction techniques in PapierCraft consist of (sub-)portions of these, or combine them sequentially.

Table 1 presents the employed composition of primitives in formal notation. Copy & paste and hyperlink are split in two lines for the sake of brevity. Formally, the two lines are connected using the temporal sequence primitive described below. Classified in their respective dimensions, used primitives are

- W_1 In the spatial dimension, only the absolute At_X primitive has been used, where X is a region in the absolute paper coordinate system (in the example above $R1$ and $R2$ for two distinct pages)
- W_2 In the temporal dimension, two relative primitives have been used: the simultaneous or parallel primitive $\|$ and the primitive for a temporal sequence $\curvearrowright$. Both have been used in k-ary definitions of sequences or parallelisms of arbitrary length.
- W_3 In the content dimension, two types of primitives have been used: gestures G_X and words W_X, where X cor-

Technique	Formalization
copy & paste	$\| (EXT, \curvearrowright (G_{cs}, G_{ce}, G_{pgt}, G_E, W_{cp}))$
	$\| (EXT, \curvearrowright (G_{cs}, G_{ce}, G_{pgt}, G_W))$
hyperlink	$\| (EXT, \curvearrowright (G_{mb}, G_{pgt}, G_N))$
	$\| (EXT, \curvearrowright (G_{pgt}, G_S))$
stitch	$\| (EXT, \curvearrowright (At_{R1}, At_{R2}, At_{P1}) \wedge \curvearrowright (G_{st}, G_{pgt}, G_S))$

Table 1. Interaction Techniques in PapierCraft

responds to the specific gesture or word respectively. In theory, this is no limitation, as one can define arbitrarily many primitives. However, for practical considerations, the interpretation of X as a parameter for such a primitive might prove useful.

PaperPoint and PaperProof

The PaperPoint [8] and PaperProof [11] system were developed based on the iServer and iPaper infrastructure for PPI. PaperPoint only uses the pidget interaction technique. The input understood by the system can be modeled by using the absolute At_R primitive in the spatial dimension. PaperProof employs gesture based interaction techniques, comparable to PapierCraft. We selected the two interaction techniques for annotation and move described in PaperProof to represent the used interaction techniques. Interestingly enough, the informal notation used in [11] to describe the employed interaction techniques, resembles the structure used in the W^5 meta-model and can be readily transcribed.

As can be seen in Table 2, the description of these interaction technique uses only the DI primitive in addition to the primitives already defined. The DI primitive belongs to the content dimension, and characterizes the need for specifying digital ink, i.e., handwriting or drawing, as part of an interaction technique.

CoScribe

The CoScribe system described by Steimle [9] also introduced a set of PPI techniques. CoScribe differs from the other systems as it incorporates the contextual task domain. Again, we chose a representative subset of the interaction techniques and omitted techniques that either use the same primitives as in PapierCraft, e.g. stitching, or exist as subtechniques or combinations of the chosen techniques. The examined techniques include a technique for creating links between documents and a technique for tagging based on links and an optional written label.

Technique	Formalization
annotation	$\curvearrowright (G_{cs1} \vee G_{cs2} \vee G_{<}, G_{ce1} \vee G_{ce2} \vee G_{>}, DI)$
move	$\curvearrowright (G_{cs1} \vee G_{cs2} \vee G_{<}, G_{ce1} \vee G_{ce2} \vee G_{>}, G_N)$

Table 2. Interaction Techniques in PaperProof

Technique	Formalization
hyperlink	$T_L \wedge \curvearrowright (For_t(At_{R1}), At_{R2})$
tag	$T_T \wedge \curvearrowright (At_{R1}(W_T), For_t(At_{R1}), At_{R2})$

Table 3. Interaction Techniques in CoScribe

The composition of these techniques into input primitives is shown in Table 3. As can be seen, the only primitives used in addition to the primitives defined above are the For_t and the T_X primitives. The former describes an absolute input primitive in the temporal dimension, where t means "executed for a duration of t". The latter describes the contextual task X, which is in this example either "linking" (L) or tagging (T). As can be seen, the only distinction between the two interaction techniques (if we omit the optional label writing action $At_{R1}(W_T)$) here is the contextual task.

Other Systems

Other systems proposed in the literature offer interaction techniques that can be described using the above primitives. Knotty gestures [10] and their associated interaction techniques of tapping, holding, circling and marking are an example for using gestures G_X in combination with absolute spatial At_R and temporal For_T primitives. An interesting observation here is, that the user "creates" the regions for the spatial At_R primitive at run time, i.e. the knot which is used in other techniques, e.g. by tapping. NiceBook [2] presents another recent PPI based note taking application. The used interaction techniques include pidgets, a tagging system comparable to the one described by Steimle [9] and a dog-ear mark. All of these techniques can be described using the previously established primitives. ButterflyNet [12] presents another well-known PPI based note taking application. It supports multi-medial data capture for field biologists and introduces a set of interaction techniques used for associating media. Its interaction techniques are automatic time-based correlation, hotspot association and visual specimen tagging. Of these, only automatic time based correlation requires a primitive not described so far: It associates two actions, i.e. taking a photo and writing something, iff these actions occur within a time interval. This is something less restrictive than the temporal $\|$ primitive defined above, so we denote this as a primitive Int_T, where T marks the interval length.

Overview of Basic Primitives

As we have shown, a relatively small set of *basic primitives*, suffices to model a broad variety of interaction techniques. The overview of basic primitives in the core dimensions is given in Table 4. It must be pointed out, however, that this set of basic primitives does not form a complete basis of the design space. So we conclude, that these primitives are necessary components of a PPUI toolkit – others might however be needed. Regarding the design of PPUI toolkits, we conclude that toolkits need to

(i) support the basic primitives described above

(ii) support be extensibility in terms of new primitives

Primitive		PapierCraft	PaperPoint	PaperProof	CoScribe	Knotty Gest.	NiceBook	ButterflyNet
W_1	At_R	X	X	X	X	X	X	X
W_2	Int_t	-	-	-	-	-	-	X
	$\parallel$	X	-	-	-	-	-	-
	$\curvearrowright$	X	-	X	X	X	X	X
	For_t	-	-	-	X	X	X	-
W_3	G_X	X	-	X	X	X	-	X
	W_X	X	-	X	X	-	-	-
	DI	X	X	X	X	-	X	X
W_4	T_X	-	-	-	X	-	-	-
W_5	-	-	-	-	-	-	-	-

Table 4. Use of primitives in PPI based systems

PROOF-OF-CONCEPT IMPLEMENTATION

To validate our approach and the derived basic primitives, we have implemented a lightweight framework for PPUI development. This framework supports modeling interaction based on the W^5 meta-model and offers system support for basic primitives. Based on it, we have developed three applications employing interaction techniques described in the literature.

The system was implemented based on Letras [3]. Letras provides a generic PPI processing pipeline for Anoto[1] digital pens. Here, we used its pen drivers in combination with a Nokia SU-1B Digital pen. As most parts of Letras itself, our W^5 reference implementation is written in java. We designed it to support rapid development of PPUIs for mobile phones. Therefore, we deployed it on the Android[2] platform for smart phones. It is based on the Android 2.1 API version and has been tested on the Motorola Milestone and the HTC Desire smartphones.

To Letras, we added support for the basic primitives and the W^5 dimensions. Our implementation splits the actual recognition and the structure imposed by the formal description of interaction techniques into separate concerns. First a set of recognizers for the core dimensions allows to detect events along these dimensions. This directly provides support for the absolute primitives, e.g. At_R. All recognizers can be configured to recognize several primitives, e.g. several regions or gestures. When a primitive is recognized, the recognizer issues a corresponding event. Second, relative primitives and complete interaction techniques are modeled as rules. These rules receive the events emitted by the recognizers and fire, iff all required events have been received. This then triggers digital functionality in the application.

Implemented Interaction Techniques

In order to validate the usefulness of our approach, we implemented 3 applications. The first application allows the user take notes using a PPUI and combine these notes with photographs taken with the phone camera. Here, we employed the hotspot association interaction technique described by Yeh [12] as part of ButterflyNet (see Figure 1). The second application allows the user to draw on paper, with a printed palette of various stroke widths and colors. Here we used pidgets to set the drawing mode of the pen, as done e.g. in NiceBook [2]. In the third application, the user can establish cross-media hyperlinks, as described by Steimle [9]. Here we use a similar interaction technique as in CoScribe, where the user draws a vertical line beside the part of the page that should be linked and then associates this page to a web page displayed on the smartphone by a similar gesture, this time using the finger instead of the pen (see Figure 3).

[1]http://www.anoto.com

[2]http://www.android.com

DISCUSSION

A limitation of the W^5 meta-model is that feedback is currently not included. Nevertheless, the input primitives also represent the smallest units capable of providing feedback to the user. Theoretically, the model could be extended here to associate feedback with primitives, however, further research is needed in this direction. Implementations using the W^5 meta-model can assure that it is possible to add hooks in primitives to provide feedback on this level.

An open question is the completeness of the proposed dimensions. The selection has been grounded on study of interaction techniques in the literature, our practical knowledge of PPI design and prior work, as discussed above. However, no final statement on the completeness can be made. Nevertheless, we believe the current selection to represent the lion share of the design space for PPI and to be sufficient for all practical purposes.

The same must be said for the proposed set of primitives. As we have shown, it suffices to model many existing interaction techniques. However, we believe that this set is not complete. Nevertheless, the structuring provided by W^5 may help designers to systematically identify new primitives in the design space. For example, one can clearly see that relative spatial primitives, such as *above*, *below*, *close* etc., have been neglected so far. Additionally, the introduced primitives make only use of four dimensions of W^5. A remain-

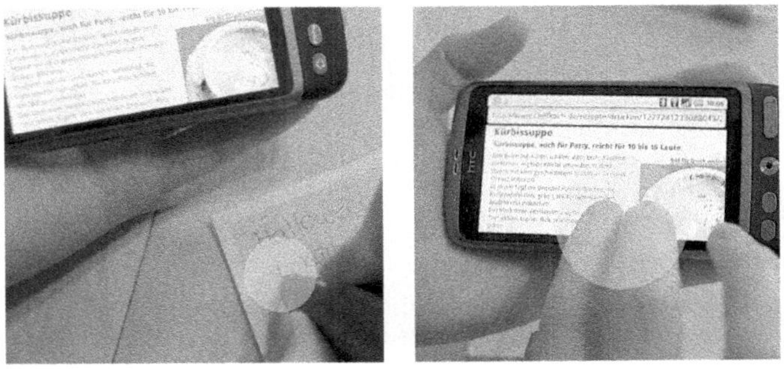

a) b)

Figure 3. A cross-media linking technique of CoScribe in our prototype: a) drawing a marker on paper and b) on the smartphone in sequence to establish a link

ing question is, how these can be extended to systematically incorporate the contextual task (Why) and the originator (Who) dimensions. For example, a PPI based application could develop a user ID primitive in the originator dimension to allow users different actions based on their respective access rights.

Our implementation satisfies the need for supporting the basic primitives, with the exception of the word recognition primitive W_X and the user task primitive T_X. This is because it would require a handwriting recognition sub-system or an explicit task model respectively, which is beyond the scope of a proof-of-concept implementation. The need for extendability in terms of primitives is, however, satisfied: The framework can be extended on the recognizer level, to support additional absolute primitives, and on the rule-level, to support relative primitives.

The implementation using a rule-based system, however, still has drawbacks in terms of developer support: the interaction designer has to maintain active knowledge how the recognizer affects the rules in the system and rules have to be specified programmatically, while having a low re-use factor. This comes from the fact that rules actually serve defining relative predicates along with application logic. A possible solution to this problem would be a domain specific language based on logic programming, that allows to specify interaction techniques more directly and offers a cleaner separation of concerns.

Our proof-of-concept implementation only shows, that the W^5 meta-model and the derived basic primitives can be used to design interaction techniques and explore the design space systematically. What it does not answer, is how huge the benefit in terms of system support for developers actually is. Although the ease of development in our setting proved to be considerable, a comparative study has to be conducted as part of future research.

CONCLUSION

We have presented W^5, a meta-model to describe PPI in interactive computer systems, along with a set of basic primitives. Essentially, W^5 presents a way how the designer can look at and talk about PPI. It can be used to structure the design space and support its exploration, i.e. the systematic discovery and development of new interaction techniques by searching for primitives or combinations thereof that have not been used so far. Additionally, W^5 can be used to inform the design of PPUI toolkits, as we have shown in our proof-of-concept implementation of such a toolkit.

ACKNOWLEDGMENTS

Thanks to Niklas Lochschmidt for his contribution to the implementation of the W^5proof-of-concept. Part of this research was conducted within the ADiWa project funded by the German Federal Ministry of Education and Research (BMBF) under grant number 01IA08006.

REFERENCES

1. M. Beaudouin-Lafon. Designing interaction, not interfaces. In *Proc. AVI '04*, pages 15–22, New York, NY, USA, 2004. ACM.
2. P. Brandl, C. Richter, and M. Haller. Nicebook: supporting natural note taking. In *Proc. CHI '10*, pages 599–608, New York, NY, USA, 2010. ACM.
3. F. Heinrichs, J. Steimle, D. Schreiber, and M. Mühlhäuser. Letras: An architecture and framework for ubiquitous pen-and-paper interaction. In *Proc. EICS '10*, pages 193–198, New York, NY, USA, 2010. ACM.
4. K. Hinckley. *The Human Computer Interaction Handbook*, chapter Input Technologies and Techniques, pages 161 – 176. Lawrence Erlbaum Associates, Mahwah, NJ, USA, 2 edition, 2007.
5. C. Liao, F. Guimbretière, K. Hinckley, and J. Hollan. Papiercraft: A gesture-based command system for interactive paper. *ACM Trans. Comput.-Hum. Interact.*, 14(4):1–27, 2008.
6. O. Shaer, N. Leland, E. H. Calvillo-Gamez, and R. J. K. Jacob. The tac paradigm: specifying tangible user interfaces. *Personal Ubiquitous Comput.*, 8:359–369, September 2004.
7. B. Signer and M. C. Norrie. As we may link: a general metamodel for hypermedia systems. In *Proc. ER'07*, pages 359–374, Berlin, Heidelberg, 2007. Springer-Verlag.
8. B. Signer and M. C. Norrie. Paperpoint: a paper-based presentation and interactive paper prototyping tool. In *Proc. TEI '07*, pages 57–64, New York, NY, USA, 2007. ACM.
9. J. Steimle. Designing pen-and-paper user interfaces for interaction with documents. In *Proc. TEI '09*, pages 197–204, New York, NY, USA, 2009. ACM.
10. T. Tsandilas and W. E. Mackay. Knotty gestures: subtle traces to support interactive use of paper. In *Proc. AVI '10*, pages 147–154, New York, NY, USA, 2010. ACM.
11. N. Weibel, A. Ispas, B. Signer, and M. C. Norrie. Paperproof: a paper-digital proof-editing system. In *Proc. CHI '08*, pages 2349–2354, New York, NY, USA, 2008. ACM.
12. R. Yeh, C. Liao, S. Klemmer, F. Guimbretière, B. Lee, B. Kakaradov, J. Stamberger, and A. Paepcke. Butterflynet: a mobile capture and access system for field biology research. In *Proc. CHI '06*, pages 571–580, New York, NY, USA, 2006. ACM.
13. R. B. Yeh, A. Paepcke, and S. R. Klemmer. Iterative design and evaluation of an event architecture for pen-and-paper interfaces. In *Proc. UIST '08*, pages 111–120, New York, NY, USA, 2008. ACM.

Model-Based Training: An Approach Supporting Operability of Critical Interactive Systems: Application to Satellite Ground Segments

Célia Martinie, Philippe Palanque, David Navarre, Marco Winckler, Erwann Poupart
IRIT - University Paul Sabatier and Centre National d'Etudes Spatiales (CNES)
Campus de Rangueil, Toulouse, France
{martinie, palanque, navarre, winckler}@irit.fr, erwann.poupart@cnes.fr

ABSTRACT
Operation of safety critical systems requires qualified operators with detailed knowledge about the system and how it should be used. Instructional design and technology intends to analyze, design, implement, evaluate, and manage training programs. Among the many methods and processes that are currently in use, the first one to be widely exploited was Instructional Systems Development (ISD) which has been further developed in many ramifications and is part of the Systematic Approach to Training (SAT) instructional design family. One of the key features of these processes is Instructional Task Analysis, particularly the decomposition of a job in its tasks and sub-tasks in order to decide what knowledge and skills must be acquired by the trainee. This paper proposes to leverage this systematic approach using model-based approaches for interactive systems engineering in order to design training programs and thus to improve human reliability. We explain how task and interactive systems modeling can be bound to job analysis to ensure that each trainee meets the performance goals required. Such training ensures proper learning at the three levels of the Rasmussen's Skills Rule Knowledge (SRK). We describe the process for building a training program for operators of satellite ground segments, which is based on and compatible with the Ground Systems and Operations ECSS standard. This process is enhanced with the application of a systematic approach to training, and the use of both a system model and an operator task model.

ACM Classification Keywords
H.5 Information Interfaces and Presentation (I.7). H.5.2 User Interfaces (D.2.2, H.1.2, I.3.6). Theory and methods.

General Terms
Reliability

Author Keywords
Interactive critical systems, formal methods, systematic approach to training.

INTRODUCTION
In the field of HCI, the focus of interest has been for many years biased towards the study of walk-up and use systems. These systems (if "well' designed) are supposed to be called "usable" if the user, after a quick look at the user interface, is able to use it without making mistakes and avoiding a trial-and-error process as the "affordance" of the user interface will drive them through their tasks.

In the action theory [18] users' difficulties are identified along two main lines: the execution gulf and the perception gulf. The corner stone of the design and development processes derived from that theory is that they should be user centered and that such consideration (if "well" mastered) should be sufficient to make hard to use and error prone systems disappear from our environment.

The majority of researchers in the field of HCI took this theory (a quick look at CHI conference proceedings support easily this claim) as a heading for their research program and developed interaction paradigms, interaction techniques user interfaces, input devices … in order to reach the holy grail of easy-to-use walk-up-and use systems. This view has then been extended into emotions and aesthetics considerations [19] where things should not only be usable, but beautiful too.

Other quite different theories have been proposed and one of them is the well-known SRK model described in [23] where a generic model of human behavior is proposed. This model classifies human behavior at three levels: Skill, Rule and Knowledge. These levels define three types of behaviors for a human: skill-based (close to automatic behavior requiring little feedback from the system), rule-based where rules have been built from previous experience and can be used if the situation evolves from standard to unusual and knowledge-based where generic knowledge (or underlying laws of the system) is used to find a solution to new (or never encountered before) situations. An important aspect of that model is that it embeds (in its definition) the fact that human will use different types of knowledge according to their past experience with that situation. One of the key aspects of that model is that human behavior will evolve according to experience and thus provide an explicit manner for coping with impact of operators' training on performance.

As an example, while a bicycle would be perceived (at first glance) with Norman's model as a poorly designed system (as people all fail to use them without a lot of effort and iteration in the execution/perception loop), in Ecological Interface Design (EID) [24] [2] a training program could be identified to allow user to use the bicycle and performance of the couple (user, bicycle) would be evaluated in order to assess the design of the bicycle.

In the field of safety critical systems the approach is much more in line with EID and training program and material is dealt with specific methods and processes as, for instance, in [11], [13], [17] and [26]. However, when it comes to the building of a training program for a graphical interactive system things are getting very difficult especially due to the fact that these systems exhibit a very large number of states (not to say infinite) and that their evolutions is event driven (events being mostly produced by operator's action on input devices). Critical difficulties for defining and building a training program are:

- How to define a training program offering a "reasonable" coverage of the states of the system?
- How to identify among the "infinite" set of states the ones which are very important to be known by the operator?
- How to deal in that program with unlikely events such as failure?
- How to assess the level of training of the operator and especially what is still need to be trained?
- How to assess the evolution of the operator along the 3 SRK levels and how, for instance, retraining is needed?

In this paper we propose a framework for addressing these difficulties. This framework is based on model-based approaches involving both operator tasks and interactive systems models such as the ones described in [1] and integrates systematic approaches to training [28] used in the field of critical systems (namely ADDIE [4]). In order to support training related to operators' activities we use task models and to identify interactive system's states and behavior we use Petri nets-based models of the entire interactive system (including functional core, dialogue and interaction techniques).

The first section of the paper introduces the methods in the fields of systematic approaches to training. This section exhibits some limitations and identifies locations where model-based approaches in the field of interactive systems could provide support to overcome those limitations. Section 3 is devoted to the model-based notations and tools we used that can be found in [16]. We only provide there a quick overview and only recall the main principles. Section 4 is devoted to the presentation of a case study extracted from the ground segment of the satellite PICARD launched in June 2010 and aiming at solar observation. On this case study we will show how integrated tasks and system model-based approaches can support both initial training and on-the-fly training. The example provided describes training aspects of how to switch from a failing Sun Array Driver Assembly (SADA) to the corresponding redundant one in the satellite platform.

TRAINING IN SAFETY CRITICAL CONTEXTS

Computer-Based Training (CBT) and Operational Procedures

Most frequent reason for using CBT rather than human trainers is related to cost-saving and availability of training program for the trainees. In the field of critical systems simulators are usually available (quite often built at the design time of the system prior to the system development) and are reused later on for training purpose. Due to their critical nature, operations of these systems are precisely defined and encompass (beyond the use of the system through its user interface) the definition and training of another artifact called operational procedures. Operational procedures are predefined contexts and sequences of actions that have to be performed by the user in order to operate the system in a given context. These context can be either standard (and thus operations are in a routine mode) or abnormal typically when an alarm occurs (and then the operational procedure describes how to bring the system back to a routine mode).

Related Work on Training Framework for Critical Systems

Systematic Approaches to Training (SAT) type of training development process (detailed in [25] and [28]) are called systematic as they provides a process applicable each time a new training program has to be built.

The most used framework used for training in critical contexts is commonly named Instructional System Development (ISD), which is the name that has been given to it by the U.S. Department of Defense in 1975 [27].

Instructional System Development (ISD)

ISD develops guidelines concerning the design, setup, evaluation and maintenance of an educational or training program. This process is composed of several phases that have to be followed systematically: Analysis, Design, Development, Implementation and Evaluation which forms the acronym ADDIE ([4] and [28]) used to refer to it. It also highlights the importance of:

- Methodology for insuring that a team remains qualified over time,
- Job and tasks analysis of the operators,
- Performance goals and measures expected for the team,
- Training program continual evaluation (external and internal) for each phase.

The first component of ADDIE (the Analysis) is a key aspect of instructional design practices [9] and is a mandatory stage of the training design process. This phase describes in a very simple way how to decompose a job in tasks and sub-tasks. The design and construction of the training program (covered by the Design, Development and Implementation phases of the ISD process), is followed by a performance evaluation that has to be passed by each trainee. The design of these steps is highly based on the type of job and its environment and context is a key aspect in that design process.

Usage in safety critical areas

Safety critical systems can only be operated by qualified operators who know the system, the domain, and which have been trained to apply specific procedures (which might be designed and defined by regulatory independent authorities). In this area, each operator has to be certified before being allowed to operate the critical system.

For this reason, standardization committees have defined training plans development which are usually applicable to specific domains (such as space, air traffic management, nuclear industry …).

We present in this section a set of standards in three domains. It is important to note that these standards typically define some aspect of the process and leave some of it to the companies in charge of the design and constructions of the systems.

Space Domain

The European Cooperation for Space Standardization (ECSS) has defined a set of standards and requirements that are in use in European space activities. Amongst them is the standard for Ground Systems and operations ECSS-E-ST-70C [6], which covers the engineering of the ground segment and mission operations from the end mission analysis to the disposal last phase of the mission. The standard states that the build-up of the operations team training and of the operations team itself starts right after the ground segment system development, verification and release. At the end of this phase, the operators have to be "familiar with the mission" before starting to operate. The standard also indicates a list of steps that have to be performed, such as simulations and rehearsals of operational scenarios. The trained operators then take part in the full ground segment validation. However, this standard does not provide guidelines to ensure that the operators' skills and knowledge has reached a sufficient level to operate ground systems and satellite.

Nuclear Domain

In the nuclear field, IAEA (International Atomic Energy Agency) provides developed guidelines to build a training plan, recruit trainees, evaluate and qualify them as operators. It clearly recommends using one of the Systematic Approaches to Training and describes an ADDIE based process [12].

Air Traffic Management

EUROCONTROL, the European Organization for the Safety of Air Navigation, has put in place a training model for Air Traffic Controllers which is described by several recommendations documents that are referenced by the "EATM Training Progression and Concepts" [8]. As for nuclear domain, it follows a Systematic Approach to Training to "ensure the best use of technology".

The recommendation documents explain in details the various training phases and the importance of objectives and performances together with their description and categorization. The recommendations also contain very precise descriptions of the need to identify Air Traffic Controllers' tasks and what is the core content of several phases of training (objectives of each phase and the related types of training that have to be performed).

INTEGRATING TASKS, SYSTEM, PROCEDURES MODELING AND TRAINING WITHIN SAT

The systematic processes we have discussed above are particularly well adapted to command and control systems and their operations as the list of operators' tasks are typically complex and involve possible catastrophic consequences. Due to that complexity, model-based approaches are particularly well suited as they make it possible to designers to describe in a complete and unambiguous way both behavioral and data aspects. Nowadays, such approaches are prominent in the area of software engineering via the Model Driven Engineering [14] field that emerged from the UML standard [20]. Indeed, as they provide a more abstract description of the system than the implementation code they also provide a unique opportunity for various stakeholders (designers, users, developers …) to comment and propose modifications on the system under design.

Processes and Models

In the Human-Computer Interaction community many researchers have described user interface elements by means of models. The interested reader can find a structured state of art of model-based user interface in [16] where the different modeling techniques are categorized by criteria. However, as pointed out in [3] (where the notion of task-artifact cycle is discussed), dealing only with the system side of socio-technical system is not enough. Indeed, typically; tasks evolve when the system is modified and thus altering one of these two components has an impact on the other one that has to be updated accordingly.

Procedures are a third artifact to be dealt with in this iterative cycle. This artifact is designed by the satellite manufacturer and address very detailed management aspects of the satellite. For instance, a procedure can be a set of activities to be performed by the operator to test the battery level of the satellite. It can be composed of tasks that are executed: by the on-board system, by the operator or by another member of the team. Procedures provide precise guidance to the operators on how to achieve both for routine and failure recovery actions. Thus, as for the task-system cycle, procedures are a different artifact from task model but their design and evaluation heavily depends on both the identified tasks of the operators and the command and control system.

Lastly, training program is also another artifact that has to be designed and assessed according to the identified user tasks the interactive system as well as the defined procedures for operating it. Modifications in any of these artifacts require consistent adjustment in the other three ones. Figure 1 presents this iterative process including the four artifacts and their co-evolution as well as the compatibility assessment activity to be carried out which aims at ensuring conformance and compatibility of the artifacts produced.

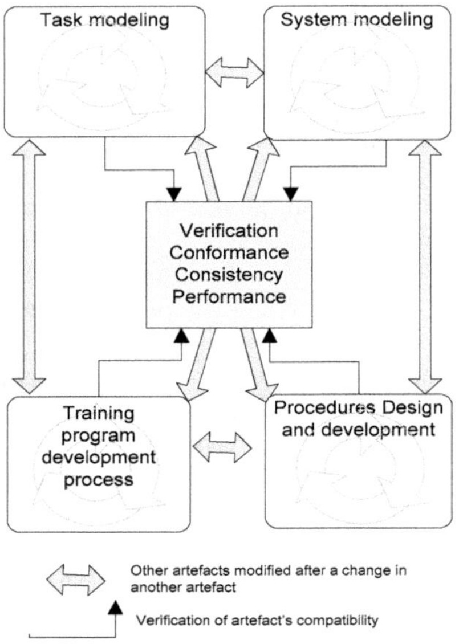

Figure 1. Verification and conformance phase between models

The main contribution of this paper is to propose a similar and more generic perspective on that view by making training a first class citizen. Indeed, we propose to address in a synergistic way tasks-artifact-training cycle.

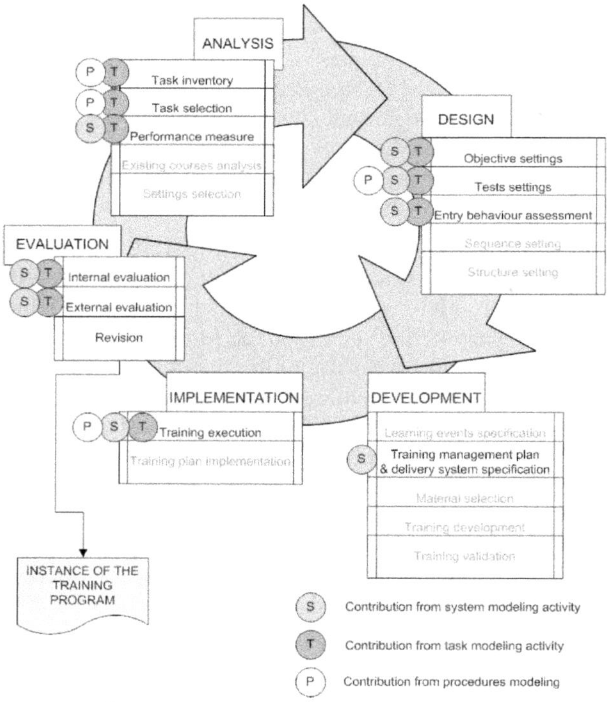

Figure 2. ADDIE ISD model complemented by Task and System modeling activities

Tasks, System, Procedure and Training cycle

Our aim is to exploit modeling techniques and methods (for tasks, procedures and system) within the training development process of command and control systems. As explained before, the design of the training of operations teams follows a generic ISD model included in the entire engineering process and thus benefits from the task and system integrated approach that has been presented before [21] and refined in [15].

Figure 2 presents a detailed view of ADDIE phases and steps of the ISD method. For each phase we have presented in the corresponding box the steps that have to be accomplished. The rounded tokens next to the steps of the boxes represent the fact that a task model, a system model or a procedure model can be useful for performing that step. For instance, in the Analysis phase symbols (S)(T) next to the step "Performance measure" explicit the fact that a model of the command and control system and a model of the tasks can support the definition of performance measures for the training program. As indicated in Figure 2, all the ADDIE phases and steps of the ISD method can be supported by the System, Procedure and Task models:

- Task modeling makes it possible to structure and record the information gathered during the task analysis activities. This activity provides a support to list and select operators' tasks during the Analysis phase of the ADDIE process. It also allows deriving all the possible scenarios for the job and then helps in preparing the training in the Design phase for the objectives and tests definition. A subset of these scenarios can also be used for the Evaluation phase for instance while preparing usability tests.
- System modeling describes the behavior of the system and must include the interactions between the system and the operator in a complete and unambiguous manner. System modeling is done using Interactive Cooperative Objects (ICOs) notation [16], which makes it possible to describe system's behavior in terms of states, state transitions and events and is based on high-level Petri nets. This notation is supported by PetShop (a CASE tool [10] publicly available) making it possible to execute the models and thus directly run the application taking into account user's actions as events triggering models evolution. The modeled interactive systems can then be used to measure operators' performances and to log their actions and behaviors while interacting with the system (thanks to the underlying Petri net notation).
- Together with a critical command and control system usually a set of procedures are defined in order to describe precisely what operators have to do in certain operation context. Such operations might be defined for many different reasons. Structuring collaboration in a shared environment in order to ensure safety is an example of the procedures used in Air Traffic Control. In case of communication system failure in the approach phase of an airport, a standard procedure

(describing in details the entire set of flight levels, speed, beacons …) is available for each airport to the pilot to terminate approach and to land making it possible for ATC to foresee the pilot behavior and to organize the rest of the traffic accordingly. In the case of satellite ground segments, the operators do not have a complete knowledge of the spacecraft and thus some procedures require contacting experts in the failing equipment (engine, solar panels …). Procedure models describe such predefined activities to be carried by the operators and that must be compatible with the operators "standard' task and of course the command and control system they are operating.

Tool-Support for Models Integration

The co-execution environment based on Petshop makes it possible to have an integrated view of all the four types of models. It is important to note that the four models are embedded at runtime and used:

- for driving interaction (system model),
- for providing help to the operators on how to reach their goals (task model),
- for supporting them in the correct and complete use of the procedures and
- for monitoring the progression of the trainees throughout the training program (training program).

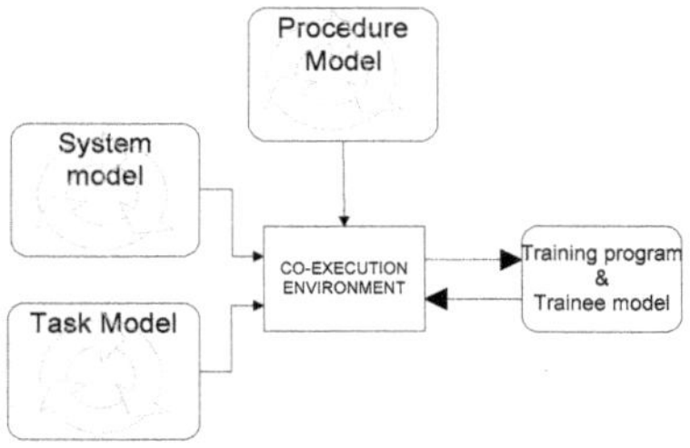

Figure 3. Co-execution environment for enhancing the training development process

Figure 3 shows this integration co-execution approach used at runtime. The dotted line between the environment and the training program box represent the fact that the model of the trainee evolves according to the successes and failures of the operators while performing the training program. It is also important to note that this tool-supported co-execution environment is powerful enough to contribute at various levels of the ADDIE model such as performances measurement (Analysis phase), entry behavior assessment (Design phase), instruction validation (Development phase), training conduction (Implementation phase). This is also described in Figure 2 where training process sub-steps marked by both System and Task modeling activities can also benefit from the co-execution environment.

Impacted training development phases

Similarly, several steps of the ADDIE model are also providing inputs to the Task and System modeling activities (Figure 3 plain arrow) such as task inventory which is an input to the task modeling activity, Tests setting and entry behavior assessment which help to calibrate and adapt the co-execution environment and training specifications which will contain the description of the environment. The modeling and ISD processes can be performed at the same time to enrich themselves and share common practices such as task analysis and procedures identification.

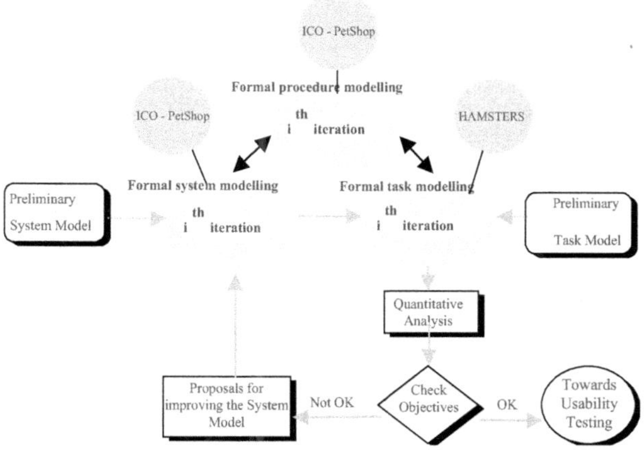

Figure 4. The iterative model-based design life cycle using both tasks and system models

Tool support for model-based training

Interactive systems engineering can involve the production of various models such as task models, user model, domain model, dialog model, training model … that should not be considered independently as they usually co-evolve and represent different views of the same world. When formal description techniques are used, the process of verification and modification of models is iterative and iteration is conditioned by the result of formal verification. This allows proofs to be made on the system model in addition to classical empirical testing once the system has been implemented. Modelling systems in a formal way helps to deal with issues such as complexity, helps to avoid the need for a human observer to check the models and to write code (if executable modelling techniques are considered see [22]). It allows reasoning about the models via verification and validation and also to meet three basic requirements notably: reliability (generic and specific properties), efficiency (performance of the system, the user and the two together) and finally to address usability issues (by means of tasks models for instance to assess effectiveness). Figure 4 presents an example of development process taking into account the integration of system, tasks and procedures models. It also presents (in the grey discs) the notations used for modelling the various elements of the approach.

As stated above, such process in defined in order to be able to engineer the training material and this process will be presented in the case study. We don't present here the expression and verification of properties as this has been previously studied and published and benefits are well known when using formal notations in the field of interactive systems [5].

Making the integration between task and system models possible at tool level requires identifying basic bricks from both notations and supporting tools. As stated in [14] the integration at the tool level is divided into two parts: the first is the editing of the correspondence between the two models while the second consists in a co-simulation of these models.

Correspondence between models

On the task side, the integration relies on the HAMSTERS environment that provides a set of tools for engineering task models (edition and simulation of models). Similarly, on the system side, the integration relies on the ICO environment (Petshop) that provides means for editing and simulating both the system model and the procedure models:

- From the tasks specification we extract the set of interactive tasks (input and output tasks) representing a set of manipulations that can be performed by the user on the system and outputs from the system to the user.
- From the ICO specification we extract the activation and rendering function that may be seen as the set of inputs and outputs of the system model.

The principle of editing the correspondences between the two models is to put together interactive input tasks (from the task model) with system inputs (from the system model) and system outputs (from the system model) with interactive output tasks (from the task model). Setting up this correspondence may show inconsistencies between the task and system model such as interactive tasks not supported by the system or rendering information not useful for the tasks performance. The correspondence edition process is presented on the upper part of Figure 5 where each tool feeds the correspondence editor with information from the API in order to notify it with modifications are done both in the task model and in the system model. The process is exactly the same for establishing the correspondence between task models and procedures models and will be explained in detail in the case study section.

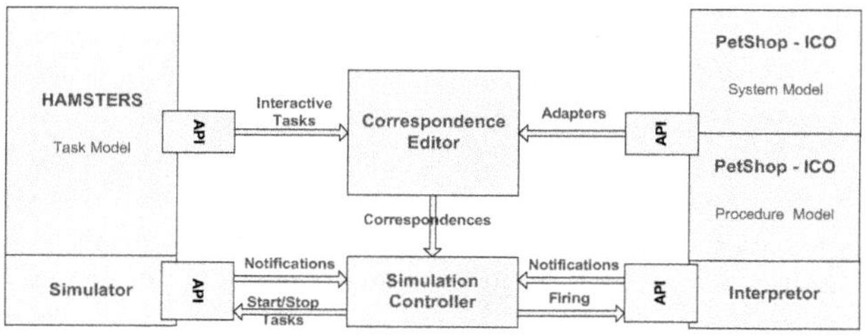

Figure 5. Global architecture of the framework for the co-execution of task, procedures and system model

Co-execution of task and system models

When this correspondence has been set up both HAMSTERS and Petshop tool can run the models simultaneously. We don't present that aspect further more as the interested reader can get a complete description of these concepts in [1].

When the task simulator controls the execution of the system model, the framework behaves as follows: while building a scenario, if the task performed within the scenario is one of the identified interactive input tasks within the correspondence editor, an event is sent to the activation function (simulating the corresponding user event on the user interface), resulting in a user action on the interactive application (from the execution of the model). As a scenario describes a sequence of tasks and as we are able to define a correspondence between an interactive input task and an activation adapter, it is now possible to convert the scenarios into a sequence of firing of event handlers in the ICO specification. In other words, a scenario performed from these tasks can be converted into a sequence of firing of event handlers that directly drive the execution of the ICO specification in exactly the same way as user actions on the user interface would have triggered the same event handlers.

Symmetrically, when the execution is controlled by the execution of the system model, user actions are directly linked to the corresponding tasks from the task model and the user's action on the user interface of the application change the current state of the task model simulation.

Dealing with Training in a Model-Based Manner

Our model-based approach is fully supported by software tools, both at design time (for model editing and models compatibility verification) and at execution time (for co-execution of the various models altogether). This approach to training is fully compliant with Computer Based Training (CBT) approaches, in which we typically find:

- Record session, trainee and trainer information (name, session date …),
- The instructor should provide a list of scenarios used for the entire training as well as a sequence in which they should be trained,
- Log time stamped trainee's action (in order to be able to evaluate the trainee performance and error rate),
- Save scenarios that have been executed by the trainee (check that learning path has been achieved),

Next section is devoted to a case study which will show in detail how these required activities for CBT are fully supported by the approach. This case study focuses on the design of a CBT session, with the articulation between task, system and procedure models. The systematic process to develop a training program is detailed in another case study, available in [13].

CASE STUDY: SATELLITE GROUND SYSTEMS TRAINING

Informal Description of the Domain

The case study presented in the section is an excerpt of the ground segment of the Picard satellite launched by CNES in June 2010 dedicated to solar observation.

We only present the small part making it possible to see in action both the various models and the tools supporting their co-execution and how they can effectively support training activities.

Figure 6 presents a schematic view of a satellite application as defined in the European Standard ECSS-E-70 [10]. The system is split in two parts: the onboard part (the upper one including the spacecraft and called the space segment) and the ground part (made up of antennas for communication and the mission control system) called the ground segment.

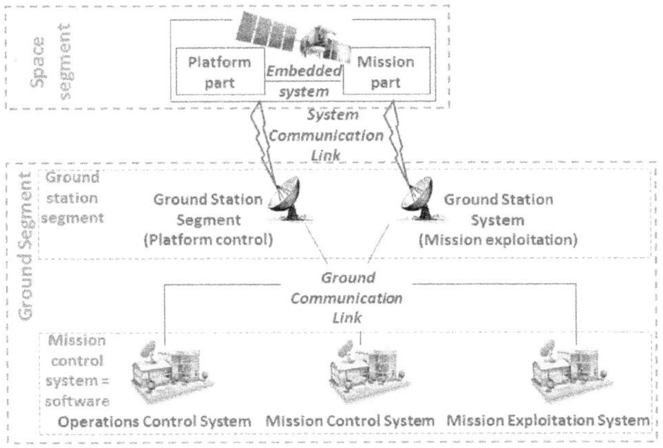

Figure 6. The satellite application domain in a nutshell

The current paper is only concerned about the command and control system in charge of operations (bottom-left icon in the diagram). This control system is in charge of maintaining the spacecraft in operation and is thus heavily dependent of the spacecraft structure and functioning.

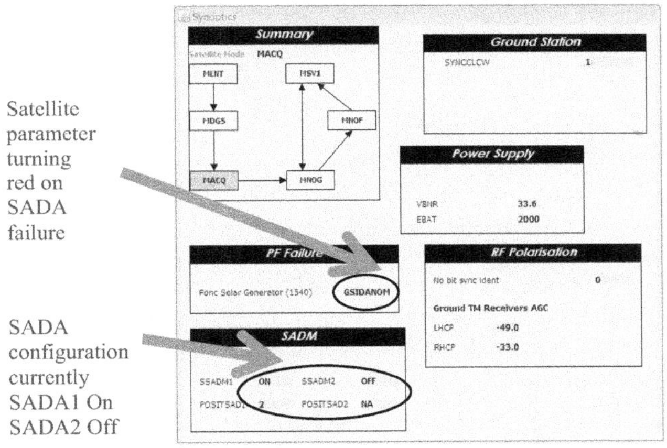

Figure 7. Synoptic for Satellite monitoring

Informal Description of the Case Study

The Operation Ground System we have been studying is the one of the satellites recently launched and called Picard. The Operation Ground Systems is made up of two relatively unconnected components:

- The set of synoptic each of them displaying a number of parameters of the space segment. The number of parameters for a satellite is usually around 10000. Parameters can be battery status, communication link status… For the case study we have rebuilt a subset of Picard synoptic which is presented in Figure 7. The upper oval in that figure highlights the satellite parameter that will change to red color if the SADA (Sun Array Driver Assembly) is faulty. The lower oval represents the current configuration of SADA1 and SADA2.
- The TeleCommand (TC) triggering system allowing the operator to upload commands onto the board system in order to change its current configuration and make the parameters evolve. As for the synoptic we have rebuilt a subset of Picard procedure manager which user interface is presented in Figure **8**. This part of the system has its own user interface allowing the operator to organize, select and trigger procedures (which are made up of a set of TeleCommands).

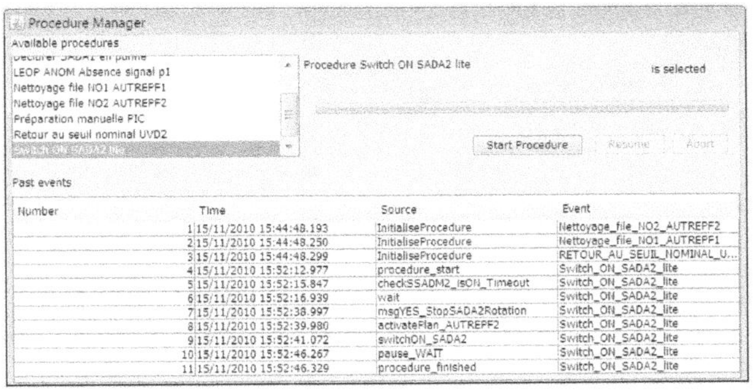

Number	Time	Source	Event
1	15/11/2010 15:44:48.193	InitialiseProcedure	Nettoyage_file_NO2_AUTREPF2
2	15/11/2010 15:44:48.250	InitialiseProcedure	Nettoyage_file_NO1_AUTREPF1
3	15/11/2010 15:44:48.299	InitialiseProcedure	RETOUR_AU_SEUIL_NOMINAL_U...
4	15/11/2010 15:52:12.977	procedure_start	Switch_ON_SADA2_lite
5	15/11/2010 15:52:15.847	checkSSADM2_isON_Timeout	Switch_ON_SADA2_lite
6	15/11/2010 15:52:16.939	wait	Switch_ON_SADA2_lite
7	15/11/2010 15:52:38.997	msgYES_StopSADA2Rotation	Switch_ON_SADA2_lite
8	15/11/2010 15:52:39.980	activatePlan_AUTREPF2	Switch_ON_SADA2_lite
9	15/11/2010 15:52:41.072	switchON_SADA2	Switch_ON_SADA2_lite
10	15/11/2010 15:52:46.267	pause_WAIT	Switch_ON_SADA2_lite
11	15/11/2010 15:52:46.329	procedure_finished	Switch_ON_SADA2_lite

Figure 8. Procedure manager window for the training session**.**

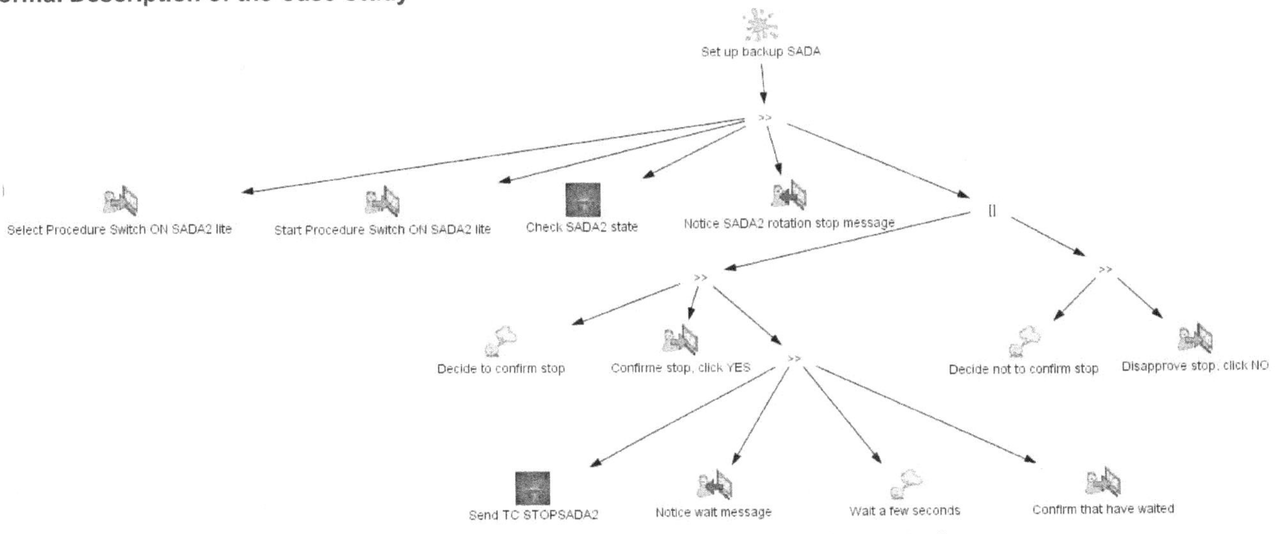

Figure 9. Task model for the procedure “Set up backup SADA”

It is important to note that most satellites are not always in 'visibility' of a ground station. For such satellites (Picard is one of them) the parameters are updated and the TC sent when the satellite is in visibility. Meanwhile it evolves in an autonomous mode (triggering On Board Control Procedure (OBCP) if needed). Indeed, the spacecraft system is a critical system for which fundamental mechanisms (segregation, diversity and redundancy) of dependability are applied at design and runtime.

Case Study Modeling

In this case study, we detail a Computer Based Training session where an operator learns how to switch from a failing Sun Array Driver Assembly (SADA) to the corresponding redundant one. This session is part of the Implementation phase of the ADDIE model (see Figure 2). To make the training appropriate, Analysis, Design and Development phases have been executed prior to the training. On one hand, Tasks, Procedure and System models, as well as the correspondences between them have been set up in the Analysis, Design and Development phases. During the Analysis phase, task inventory and selection have been done by studying operational procedures and sequence plan of events for the mission.

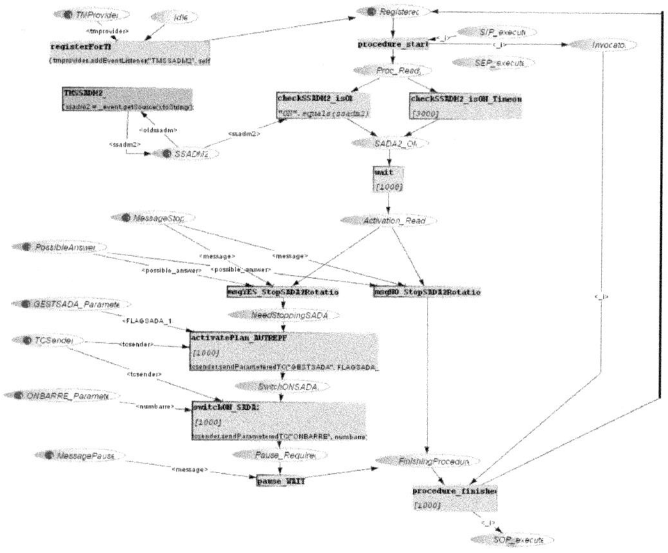

Figure 10. Procedure model "Set up Backup SADA"

Figure 9 shows the resulting task model to switch from a failing SADA to the backup SADA. Concerning the performance measure, an operator is required to ensure the satellite integrity and has then to switch to the redundant SADA as soon as it is detected that the running SADA is failing. This task model makes explicit the relationship between the tasks and the procedure. Indeed, the main goal in that model (top of the hierarchy) is to setup the backup SADA. The first task of the ground operator in order to reach this goal is to select the procedure 'SWITCH ON SADA2 lite' and then to trigger that procedure on the Procedure Manager interface (see Figure 8). The behavior of that procedure is described using the ICO notation and is presented in Figure 10. The task model describes the activity the operator has to perform in interaction with the procedure execution such as deciding to switch of SADA and who is prompted for confirmation by the procedure. That choice is represented by the right-hand side of the task model. Impact of the tasks on the space segment is made by means of the execution of a TeleCommand (TC) represented by the 'system' icon in the task model and in this case is called TC STOPSADA2 (bottom left task of the model). If the failure is not detected rapidly enough by the operator, the satellite will change its mode itself (using an OBCP) to a survival mode and the mission will be delayed and the satellite possibly lost (very seldom case).

In order to follow the ADDIE process, entry behavior assessment, training objectives settings and test settings have been set up in the Design phase. Pre-requisites before entering the training are:

- Trainee is capable of describing the main satellite components and their functionalities (e.g. the fact that SADA is implemented through 2 redundant components,
- Trainee is capable of explaining the main goals of the satellite mission (see ground segment in Figure 6).

Training objective is: validate that, at the end of the session, each trainee is capable of setting up the backup SADA when the running SADA has generated an error.

Test settings describe that the following elements must be available for the session:

- **Prototype of the operation control system.** A part of the ground system application is the Synoptic window (Figure 7) and is used to monitor the state of the satellite. Another part of the application is the procedure manager panel (Figure 8) and is used to select and launch operational procedure and control the satellite.
- **Satellite behavior simulator.** It is used to make interactively evolve the satellite parameters and for example, to trigger various types of satellite failures (such as the SADA failure) (see Figure 11).

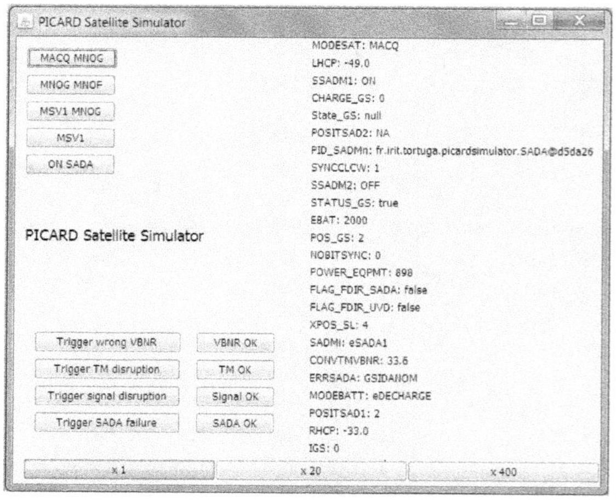

Figure 11. Simulator control window for the training session (lower control button allows trainer to simulate a SADA failure)

In the Implementation phase of the ADDIE process, during the training session, each trainee is provided with a computer that contains the Co-Execution software tool suite. As detailed in the previous paragraph, the tool suite gathers the Task and System models, their correspondences, the satellite ground system applications and a satellite simulator. The trainee then has learnt how to meet the session's goals (Switch to a redundant SADA and potentially avoid the satellite loss) in several ways:

- Understanding the way to switch from a SADA to another while browsing the task model (Figure 9).
- Executing the operational procedure from the task model and visually checking what happens with the Operation Control System. On Figure 12, the model (disc 3) represents the procedure. The progress made on the procedure execution is visible by means of the evolution of distribution of tokens in the places of the model and by the darker transitions highlighting the actions currently available (according to the current state of the procedure),
- Executing the operational procedure from the Operation Control System and visually checking on the task model that she/he is performing accurate actions. This is visible on Figure 12 (disc 2) where the already performed tasks are highlighted in blue color. On that model the procedure has reached its final step made visible as the lower transition in the model is fireable. This is also visible on the user interface of the Operation Control System (Figure 12 disc 4) as the progress bar is full,
- Finding and exploring scenarios to understand the different ways to proceed (not displayed here due to space constraints),
- Recording the scenarios the operator has been through (these scenarios can then be reused by the operation while in operation as a kind of training-based contextual help system). This is represented in Figure 12 where the central window (disc 1) represents the choice left to the operator to carry on with the switching off SADA2 or to abort the current procedure.
- For sake of brevity we have not presented in this paper the system model (corresponding to the behavioral part of the interactive Operation Control System). However, as stated in the section describing the approach, this behavior has a strong impact on operation as, according to the state of that system, some interface elements such as (start procedure button, abort… see Figure 8 and disc 4 on Figure 12) are only available according to the current state of that model.

CONCLUSION AND PERSPECTIVES

In this paper we have proposed a generic approach for designing complex interactive systems in a critical context. These systems require effective training of operators and sometimes training certification prior to allowing them to use the system in real operation.

While training has been extensively studied in psychology and educational science (mostly concerned by the evolution of the mental model of the trainee) this paper is the only research contribution merging contribution in the field of interactive systems engineering with contributions in those field.

We have shown how model-based approaches could provide a unique opportunity for integrating, in a unified iterative process, the four main artifacts i.e. tasks models, operational procedures, training scenarios and interactive system models required to be designed for usable, learnable and dependable command and control systems.

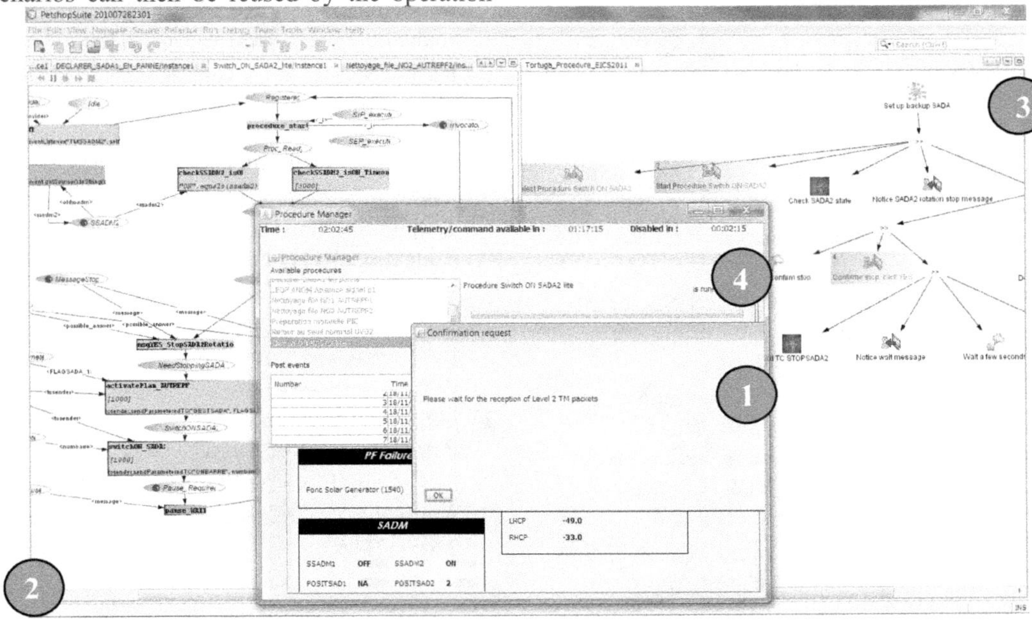

Figure 12. Operation phase: Running (system driven) Procedure (left-hand side) and tasks (right-hand side) models

The case study presented in the paper has been provided by CNES with a long term research project Tortuga. The next step of the project is to address scalability aspects i.e. to apply the approach to a bigger part of the Operation Control Systems, to several larger procedures and to a comprehensive task model of operators of the ground segment.

ACKNOWLEDGMENTS

This work has been partly funded by R&T CNES (National Space Studies Center) Tortuga R-S08/BS-0003-029.

REFERENCES

1. Barboni E., Ladry J-F., Navarre D., Palanque P., Winckler M. Beyond Modelling: An Integrated Environment Supporting Co-Execution of Tasks and Systems Models. In Proc. of EICS '10. ACM, 143-152.
2. Cacciabue. P. C. Human error risk management for engineering systems: a methodology for design, safety assessment, accident investigation and training. Reliability Eng. and System Safety, (2004), 229–240.
3. Carroll, J M., Kellogg, W. and Rosson, M-B.: The Task-Artifact Cycle. In: Carroll, John M. "Designing Interaction: Psychology at the Human-Computer Interface", (1991), Cambridge University Press.
4. Clark, D. R., ISD Concept Map, retrieved January 2010 from http://nwlink.com/~donclark/hrd/ahold/isd.html
5. Dix, A. J., Formal Methods for Interactive Systems, Academic Press, (1991), 0-12-218315-0.
6. European Cooperation for Space Standardization, Space Engineering, Ground Systems and Operations, ECSS-E-70C, 31 July 2008.
7. European Organisation for the Safety of Air Navigation, "ATCO Basic Training – Training Plan", (2003).
8. European Organisation for the Safety of Air Navigation, "EATM Training Progression and Concepts", HRS/TSP-006-GUI-07, 26.03.2004.
9. Gagné, R., The Conditions of Learning and the Theory of Instruction, Holt, Rinehart, and Winston (Eds), (1985).
10. http://ihcs.irit.fr/petshop/, last accessed Nov. 2010.
11. International Atomic Energy Agency, Experience in the use of Systematic Approach to Training (SAT) for Nuclear Power Plant Personnel, Technical Report, IAEA-TECDOC-1057.
12. International Atomic Energy Agency, IAEA Nuclear Energy Series, "Managing Human Resources in the Field of Nuclear Energy", N° NG-G-2.1.
13. Martinie C., Palanque P., Navarre D., Winckler M. A formal approach supporting effective and efficient training program for improving operators' reliability. Safety and Reliability for managing Risk (ESREL 2010), p. 234-243.
14. Navarre, D., Palanque, P., Barboni E. and Mistrzyk, T. On the Benefit of Synergistic Model-Based Approach for Safety Critical Interactive System Testing. Proc. of TAMODIA 2007, (vol. 4849), Springer-pp. 140-154.
15. Navarre, D., Palanque, P., Winckler, M. Task Models and System Models as a Bridge between HCI and Software Engineering. In book "Human-Centered Software Engineering Software Engineering Models, Patterns and Architectures for HCI". Springer (Human-Computer Interaction Series), 2009, pages 357-385.
16. Navarre, D., Palanque, P., Ladry, J., and Barboni, E. ICOs: A model-based user interface description technique dedicated to interactive systems addressing usability, reliability and scalability. ACM Trans. Comput.-Hum. Interact. 16, 4 (Nov. 2009), pp. 1-56.
17. Neitzel, D.K., How to develop an effective training program, IEEE Industry Applications Magazine, May-June 2006.
18. Norman D, The Design of everyday things, Basic Books, 2002.
19. Norman, D. A., Emotion and design: Attractive things work better. Interactions Magazine, ix (4), (2002), 36-42.
20. Object Management Group. Unified Modeling Language (UML) 2.0 Superstructure Specification, August 2003, Ptc/03-08-02, pp. 455-510.
21. Palanque P. & Bastide R, Synergistic modeling of tasks, system and users using formal specification techniques Interacting With Computers, 1997, Academic Press, pp. 129-153.
22. Palanque P., Ladry J., Navarre D. and Barboni E. High-Fidelity Prototyping of Interactive Systems can be Formal too, 13th Int. Conf. on HCI (2009) San Diego CA, USA.
23. Rasmussen, J., Skills, rules, knowledge; signals, signs, and symbols, and other distinctions in human performance models, 1983, IEEE trans. on systems, man and cybernetics, 13, 257-266.
24. Rasmussen, J. & Vicente, K. J., Coping with human errors through system design: Implications for ecological interface design, International Journal of Man-Machine Studies, 1989, 31, 517-534.
25. Reiser R.A., A History of Instructional Design and Technology: Part II: A History of Instructional Design, Educational Technology Research and Development, vol. 49, N. 2, 2001, pp. 57-61.
26. Scott, D.W., Growing a Training System and Culture for the Ares I Upper Stage Project, NASA Technical Report, Number: IEEEAC Paper 1550.
27. U.S. Department of Defense Training Document (1975). Pamphlet 350-30. August, 1975.
28. U.S. Army Field Artillery School (1984). A System Approach To Training (Course Student textbook). ST - 5K061FD9.

MACS: Combination of a Formal Mixed Interaction Model with an Informal Creative Session

Christophe Bortolaso*, Cédric Bach+, Emmanuel Dubois#
University of Toulouse – IRIT-Elipse
118, route de Narbonne 31 062, Toulouse Cedex 9, France
christophe.bortolaso@irit.fr *, cedric.bach@irit.fr +, emmanuel.dubois@irit.fr #

ABSTRACT
In this paper, we propose a collaborative design method combining the informal power of creative session and the formal generative power of a mixed interaction model called MACS (Model Assisted Creativity Session). By using a formal notation during creative sessions, interdisciplinary teams systematically explore combinations between the physical and digital spaces and remain focused on the design problem to address. In this paper, we introduce the MACS method principles and illustrate its application on two case studies.

Author Keywords: Design method, mixed interaction, interaction model, creativity.

ACM Classification Keywords: H5.2. User Interfaces: Theory and Methods.

General Terms: Design, Human Factors, Theory.

INTRODUCTION

Emerging interaction forms, such as Augmented Reality (AR), Tangible User Interfaces (TUI) or pervasive systems aim at combining physical and digital worlds to support the user's interaction with these two worlds. These advanced forms of interaction, hereafter referred to as Mixed Interactive Systems (MIS), are now present in many application domains. However, designing MIS can easily turns out to be a real challenge. Indeed, Shaer and Jacob [19] underline that "*designing and building a TUI requires cross-disciplinary knowledge*" and argue that due to the intrinsically complex nature of these systems, "*designers and developers face too many conceptual, methodological and technical difficulties*". To face those difficulties, a better understanding of the mixed interaction paradigms is required. To do so, a lot of frameworks/models have emerged during the past decade. Some of them support interaction design [6,9], others propose abstract conceptual frameworks [10,11,13,20] which provide a better understanding of the MIS field. Finally others aim at supporting the software design and implementation [19,21]. Although their levels of abstraction vary, they offer a clear definition of the design space and constitute a common terminology supporting interdisciplinary communication. Unfortunately, such design resources are still mainly intended to be used by mixed interaction design experts.

To take advantage of such guiding frameworks and contribute to address some of the MIS design challenges mentioned before, several approaches combining informal sessions and formal models have been recently proposed [5,8,12]. By embedding the use of formal models during creativity sessions, non-practitioners benefit from the structuring power of a guiding framework. However, the existing approaches do not provide a set of guidelines showing how to use such frameworks in creativity sessions. In addition, we state that the atypical nature of mixed interaction for the large audience can easily become a hindrance in a creativity context. Indeed, participants' knowledge is often limited to the few forms of interaction they have ever met. For instance, our daily experience with MSc IT students reveals that their knowledge about this form of interactions is often exclusively limited to the few popular examples (e.g. Nintendo's Wii, tactile devices) while other available technologies offer a large panel of sensors, devices, interaction techniques, etc. As a result, providing an abstract and structured support to the design space exploration appears to be promising for helping design teams in two ways: to envision new and unexpected forms of mixed interactions and, to provide a common terminology between disciplines.

In this paper we present a design method dedicated to MIS, called Model Assisted Creativity Session (MACS). This method is based on the use of a design model to stimulate divergent thinking. In the next sections, we first discuss similar approaches, then detail the core principles of the method and demonstrate how a design model can be seen as a tool to the design space exploration. We finally report the use of the method on two case studies.

RELATED WORK

Although creativity can be regarded as an inexplicable phenomenon, it can also be considered as an everyday activity which is embedded in a social context [7]. Indeed, Amabile [1] defines creativity as the ability to achieve a production that is both *novel* and *adapted* to the context in which it manifests. Moreover, according to the multivariate approach of creativity of Lubart [15], creativity's efficiency relies on many parameters such as individual knowledge, cognitive style, or even personality. For that reason, ensuring the novelty of a creative production turns out to be difficult. However, the adaptation of creative ideas to a defined context can be artificially constrained. For example, Bonnardel showed how creativity benefits from *constrained cognitive environment* [4]. In that way, many creative methods rely on stimulation artifacts, to offer a structured and systematic exploration of the design space.

One of the most famous tools supporting creativity is the Mind Mapping. It allows participants of a creative session to structure their ideas and the relationships between them through hierarchical diagrams. The relationships between suggested ideas may trigger new ideas and new associations. However, because MindMaps are domain independent they do not set any boundaries to the design space. To solve this problem other methods envision the use of specific conceptual notations during creative sessions. For instance, this is the case of Rich Picture [16], in which a facilitator and several participants draw together, at a high conceptual level, a picture depicting stakeholders, relationships and their concerns. The involved graphical notation eases the communication between the participants and provides formalized results that can be used over the design process. Similarly, the Brainstorming Card Game [12] allows participants to explore a TUI design problem by playing with cards representing provocative questions extracted from a framework's concepts. However even if it ensures that all the central issues have been raised at the end of the session, it does not specify how the resulting insights influence the design process.

On the other hand, a corpus of creative methods focuses on a specific part of the design rather than the whole system. For instance, with the Solid Diagrams method [3], designers explore usability properties of tangible manipulation involved in a TUI by creating physical objects with modelling clay. According to the authors, it creates a common ground, crucial for teams who might come from different educational backgrounds. Similarly, Make Tools [22] advocates non-practitioners to build mock-ups depicting the mobile device of their dreams. Authors claim that the unfinished nature of the resulting productions helps people to distinguish them from real objects. As a result they understand them more as design artifacts. For that reason, they emphasize the need of working on abstractions rather than on final products.

Finally, the exploration of the design space by non practitioners has been also recently applied through the whole design process. In [14], formal representations have been used to support communication between museum professionals (i.e. curators and docents) and computer scientists. Through formal representations, combinations of physical and digital media are explored. However, the weakness of their approach lies in the restricted use of a set of predefined technologies (i.e. augmented reality artifacts). As a result, their productions are technologically constrained and their design approach does not allow envisioning innovative forms of interactive systems.

From the methods presented above, we have identified the need to 1) explore combinations between physical and digital spaces, 2) represent ideas through a structure that clearly define the design space of MIS, 3) ease interdisciplinary exchanges and 4) provide a support to produce continuity in the design process through formalized results. We present in the next section the MACS main principles which aim at addressing those needs.

MODEL ASSISTED CREATIVITY SESSION

MACS method aims at adding a support to creativity sessions through the use of an abstract representation. In the following three sections, we present the principles of the method, recommendations for selecting a model and for taking advantage of a model's generativity.

Methods principles

A MACS is built on the basis of a brainstorming session [23]. Usually, five to seven participants produce ideas about a mixed interaction design problem. The session is supervised by a facilitator which has to manage the group dynamics and stimulate the participants with the model dimensions. A session is structured into five steps:

Step 1: Mixed interaction model introduction – The facilitator introduces the key concepts of the model to the participants. This step should not exceed 15 minutes.

Step 2: Case study introduction – The facilitator introduces the case study to the participants. Artifacts related to the case study can be used depending on the granularity of the design problem. As for the step 1, it should not exceed 15 minutes.

Step 3: Ideation and generation of models – This is the central step of the session. The facilitator role is twofold: 1) to help participants in the exploration of the design space by pointing out possible variations on the model dimensions (i.e. based on some basic manipulations detailed in the next section) and 2) to encode the expressed ideas using the model notation. This step should not exceed 90 minutes. At the end of the session, participants review the modeled solutions and select the best ones.

Step 4: Ideas extraction, rearrangement and analysis of the generated models – This step is the first form of post-treatment (i.e. work performed after the session and only by the facilitator). The aim is to select the best modeled solutions through the evaluation of their consistency with the case study requirements. This has to be performed by the facilitator or a group of experts in the model and application domain. Modeled solutions that satisfy all the requirements are first selected. Then rearrangement can be performed: it consists in combining designed solutions that partially cover the requirements, in order to obtain complete solutions. At the end of this step, the extracted modeled solutions are candidates for a second post-treatment which is presented in step 5.

Step 5: Identification of non-discussed issues for further iterations – The aim of this second post-treatment is to identify in the modeled solutions, design dimensions that have not been discussed in step 3 and need further optimization. These issues open the design to further iterations. For example, a generated model can express the need for a communication between a digital concept and the user without describing the representation to adopt (e.g. textual, graphical, 3D, etc.). These problems constitute required optimizations of the system (i.e. future design iterations).

This set of five steps constitutes the basis to conduct a session. Next sections complete the definition of the MACS with details concerning the involved model.

Mixed Interaction model as a generative artifact

We hereafter propose a set of recommendations to select an appropriate model. We believe that the holistic potential of participants' creativity will benefit from the model's generative power [2] by: 1) suggesting dimensions/possibilities which participants were not thinking about and 2) providing a canvas on which ideas can be linked. However model's characteristics may heavily weigh on its ability to support these benefits. On the basis of repeated experiences, we propose the following set of recommendations for selecting an appropriate model.

Provide a graphical notation to be visually perceptible by the participants: The use of a graphical representation will help participants to investigate and better understand their ideas in the conceptual space. Additionally, it helps participants to revisit previously generated ideas by referring to graphical elements and using their spatial cognition to remember the expressed ideas.

Adopt an appropriate level of abstraction: Säde [18] showed that working on too concrete representations narrows the design space, while working on abstractions of a design problem opens it. For that reason, we consider the use of an abstract design model as a good stimulus for a creative context. The model has to be concrete enough to support communication between participants and abstract enough to allow for freedom and creativity. Typically, the concrete side should rely on a concise representation to allow participants linking their ideas with the model's concepts. The abstract side should allow participants to express an idea at a rough grain and to detail it at a finer grain when and if required. To choose the appropriate level of abstraction of a model we propose that: 1) the chosen model has to be explicable in few minutes because in most cases, participants will not be model experts and 2) the number of concepts should be in line with participants' short time memory workload (i.e. 7 ± 2 chunks).

Provide a separate representation of physical and digital spaces: This is specific to MIS and aims to support reasoning about correspondence metaphors and analogies between the two worlds. The model should assist participants in the identification of the involved physical objects, digital concepts and the links between them.

Allow a design point of view to avoid the focus on technological limitations: Dealing with technological problems when exploring the design space of mixed interaction may become an obstacle to the emergence of new ideas. The technical feasibility of an idea should not be evaluated during such a creative session.

Based on this first set of four recommendations, we have identified that high level mixed interaction models such as ASUR [9] or MIM [6] constitutes appropriate candidates to be used in a MACS. In the next section, we further validate the use of ASUR during MACS by illustrating how it constitutes a support to the design space exploration. This validation emerged from observations of the use of ASUR by model experts during design sessions.

Operating the model's generative power

To illustrate how to take advantage from ASUR's generative power, we first provide a brief description and illustration of ASUR. Then, we introduce three generative techniques showing how to explore the design space. This is illustrated with the generation of alternative design solutions of the tangible Google Earth (Figure 1).

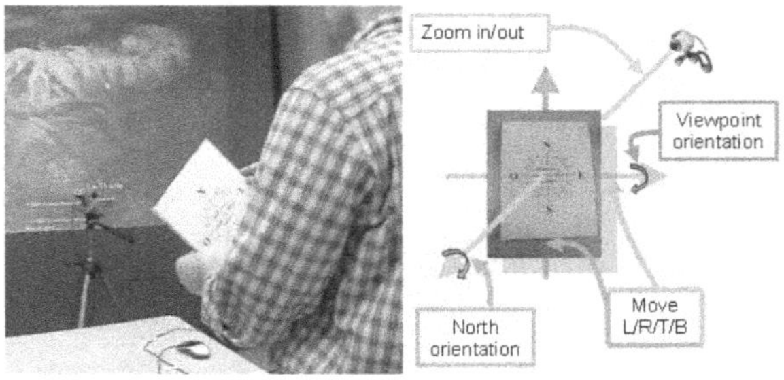

Figure 1: the tangible Google Earth

ASUR description

ASUR [9] originally defines a mixed interactive situation as a set of entities linked by information flows. There are four types of entities: 1) "S" entities (i.e. S_{tool}, S_{object}, S_{info}) depict the computer system, including conceptual computational and storage capabilities, 2) "U" entity refers to the user of the system, 3) "R" entities (i.e. R_{tool}, R_{object}) denote physical entities involved in performing the task and 4) "A" entities (A_{in}, A_{out}) refer to adapters, devices used to bridge the physical and digital worlds. Relationships between entities denote information transfers and are characterized with their representation, language form, medium, dimension, etc. Finally groups precise additional aspects such as the physical proximity of two entities, the representation link between a physical and a digital entity (e.g. particularly relevant in case of tangible user interfaces) and the trigger link which expresses a physical condition that triggers a flow of information between two entities. For example, the model 1 on top left corner of Figure 2 shows an ASUR model of a system in which a user handles steering board (R_{tool}). The position of the steering board is sensed by a camera (A_{in}), which computes and transmit the new coordinates to the Google Earth virtual globe (S_{object}). This one is displayed by a video-projector (A_{out}) in form of satellite images on a three dimensional globe.

Generative techniques

To operate a systematic exploration of the design space with a notation like ASUR, we have identified three elementary manipulations which are detailed in the next paragraphs. Figure 2 illustrates the sequential use of these three techniques. The dotted lines on Figure 2 show the impacted elements after the use of a generative technique.

Split/Group elements. This generative technique consists in splitting an element into several ones or into grouping several elements into one. For example, on the tangible Google Earth (n°1 on Figure 2), the R_{tool} Steering Board allows users to control the four axis of the point of view. When exploring the input possibilities for the user, it is possible to envision splitting the Steering Board into four physical objects, each one controlling one of the four axis (n°2 on Figure 2). The resulting interaction is transformed into a new one in which the mapping between the physical object and the digital map is decoupled. As a result, it opens the solutions to additional questions such as the form of each object and how to interact with it. Concretely this could rely on a multifaceted tactile technology or on the use of four different physical bricks (e.g. translation to the right of one brick might increase the value along one axis)

Materialize/Dematerialize. This generative technique consists in materializing a concept of the digital world to transform it into a physical object or on the other hand dematerializing a physical object into digital information. For example, we have applied this technique on the second model (n°2 on Figure 2) by moving our four physical objects (R_{tool} x 4 in model n°2 on Figure 2) to the digital world. As a result, a new interactive solution appears (n°3 on Figure 2), in which the user interacts directly with four S_{tool} (i.e. digital elements) through the A_{in} Camera. Concretely, this solution could correspond to gesture based interaction, in which the user uses his finger or hand to interact with four displayed widgets; each one respectively moving the point of view to the north, south, east and west. As for the previous example, it opens the design to other considerations such as how the user interacts with these four S_{tool} and what does those widgets looks like.

Add/remove elements. This generative technique consists in adding an element in the diagram. This can be achieved by adding an element and linking it to the other ones, or by breaking a link for inserting a new artifact. We have applied this technique on the third model of Figure 2 in which the

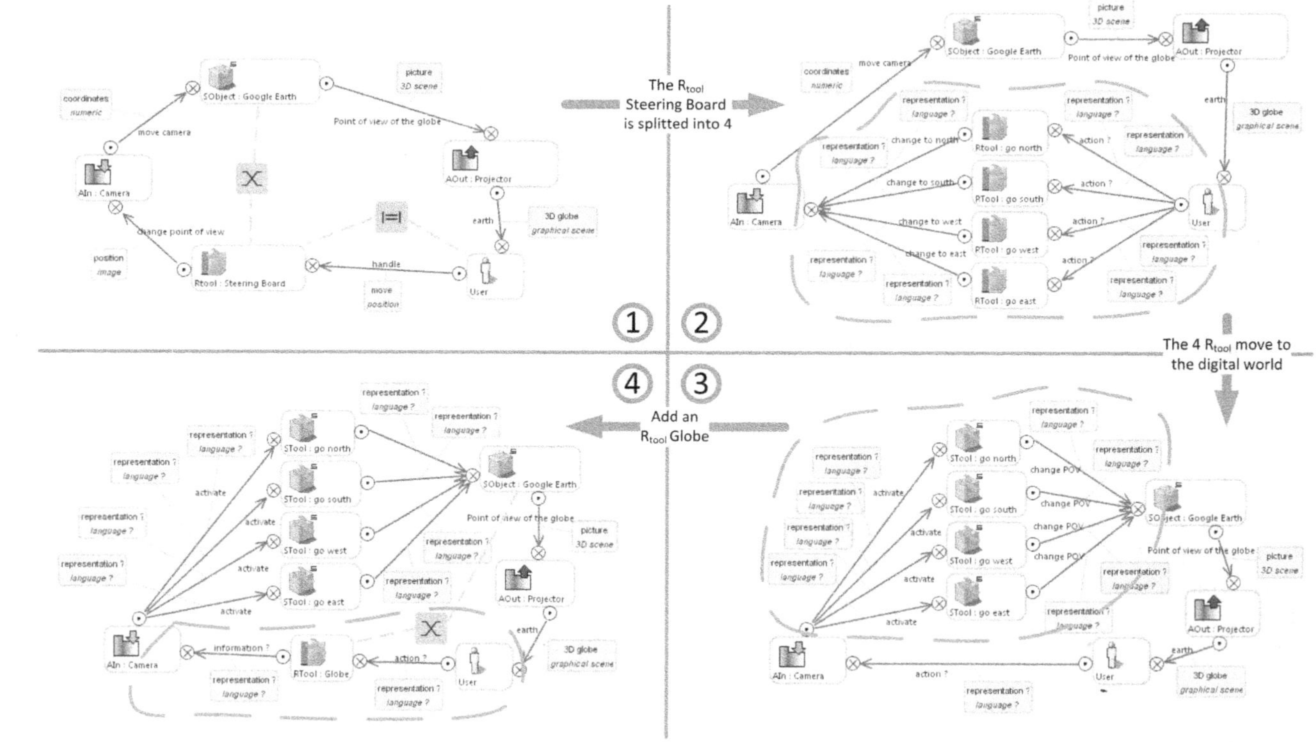

Figure 2: 1) ASUR model of a tangible Google earth; 2) Model 1 after a split action on the steering board (R_{tool} x 4); 3) Model 2 after moving the physical objects (R_{tool} x 4) into digital elements (S_{tool} x 4); 4) Model 3 after adding a physical object (R_{tool})

user directly interacts with four digital elements (S_{tool} x 4 in the model n°3 on Figure 2) through the A_{in} Camera. For example, we have added an element in the user's hands of the third model of Figure 2 to allow him to interact with the four digital tools (n°4 on Figure 2). Concretely, this object can take the form of a globe (R_{tool} in model n°4 on Figure 2) on which the four digital tools and Google Earth pictures would be displayed. The user would have to manipulate (e.g. touch or press for example) the digital widgets to change his point of view on the virtual environment. Of course further considerations have to be considered in this new design setting such as how the user manipulates the globe or how the digital information is displayed on it.

Through successive manipulations of the ASUR model elements, we have shown how to generate new interactive solutions. Based on the Google Earth example, we have generated three different MIS, each involving a different interactive technique. In addition, we have shown that simple modifications can renegotiate the diagram and open the design to additional interrogations. Besides, it is possible to envision applying those manipulations an undefined numbers of times and in any order. However, even if the introduced basic manipulations have an impact on the diagram's syntax, they do not provide any semantic to the elements. For that reason interaction model manipulation has to be considered as a tool for exploring a design space and not as an "idea generator". Providing to the model elements a semantic that links them to a defined application domain undoubtedly requires the contribution of human thinking and a defined methodology.

CASE STUDIES

Over the past years, we have applied MACS several times with different participants and over different scenarios. In this paper, we report the use of MACS on two case studies which aim to: 1) illustrate the use of the method, 2) identify method's strengths and weaknesses and 3) study the influence of the model on the produced ideas.

In the first case-study, two sessions were performed, each one involving a different design team and a different mixed interaction model (ASUR and MIM). The goal was twofold: 1) to identify ways of improving the method by studying the influence of the interaction model on the solutions (i.e. models aggregating the generated ideas) and 2) to test the method's robustness to a model variation.

In the second case study, two sessions were also performed each involving two different design teams but both using the ASUR model. In one session, we used the original version of our method (i.e. as for the 1st case study) and in the second one, we conducted an improved version of the method based on observations made during the first case-study. The goal was to study the influence of these improvements on the resulting solutions.

CASE STUDY 1: TREE OF LIFE INSIDE EXPLORATION

We first applied the method on a case study defined in collaboration with the Museum of Toulouse. This project, called MIME (i.e. Mixed Interaction for Museum Environment) aims at teaching some of the basic notions of cladistics. A low fidelity prototype of this application was previously designed in collaboration with the curators (see Figure 3). It shows a 3D representation of a cladogram in which users can navigate. With this 3D game, visitors are encouraged to explore a 3D cladistic tree and to discover that the complexity of species (tree leaves) depends on the amount of phylogenetic criteria (tree nodes) visited from the root. As a result, the design problem given to the participants was: *"explore and find mixed interactive techniques allowing the visit of the virtual environment representing the tree"*. Consequently, the design space was opened to various input devices, tangible objects, and interactive metaphors. We led two sessions with two different interaction models: ASUR [9] and MIM [6] in order to test the generic aspect of the MACS. The sessions' settings are detailed in the following paragraph.

Implementation of both sessions

The total duration of each session was limited to two hours. Steps 1 and 2 were planned to last 15 minutes and step 3 was limited to a length of 90 minutes and split in two parts: one hour for ideas generation and 30 minutes for debriefing. Steps 4 and 5 were performed after the session only by the facilitator. Participants between the sessions were different in order to avoid the familiarity with the case study. Sessions were recorded with two observers for each one.

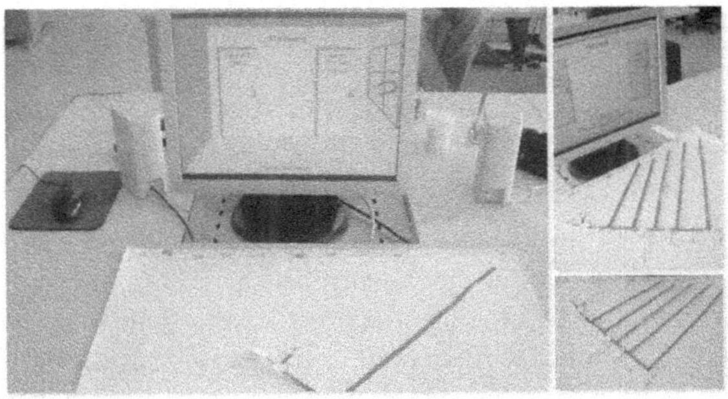

Figure 3: Initial low fidelity prototype of MIME

In order to respect an interdisciplinary context, each design teams was composed of a facilitator, a technical expert, a MIS designer, a usability specialist and a CHI practitioner. One person per profile was selected and with a similar low level of knowledge of the involved model. Despite the museum context of this case study, it was not relevant to involve end-users (i.e. visitors) during this step of the design process. Indeed, the design question is here how to teach cladistic through an interactive experience and not simply how to interact with a 3D cladogram. Therefore, the end-user is rather the curators and docents than the visitors. For that reason, among the participants, most of them had already a long experience in creating museum exhibits.

To better introduce the case study to participants, several artifacts were presented during step 2: 1) a brief scenario showing a nominal use of the application, 2) a task diagram using the KMAD [17] notation pointing out the functionalities, 3) a low-fi prototype (Figure 3) elaborated with the Museum of Toulouse which figures out all of the domain specific data and the navigation in a 3D cladogram and 4) a list of exhibit integration non-functional requirements. As already mentioned, two different models were used by each session: ASUR [9] and MIM [6]. The difference between these two models relies on the aspects of MIS that are represented. MIM describes a MIS as a set of mixed objects and describes the modalities used to link physical and digital properties of these objects. . In contrast, ASUR which has been described in a previous section describes a MIS as a set of entities and communication channels between them.

Session outcomes

Surprisingly, each session produced a set of complete five models. For the ASUR session, each of the five models was related to a different interactive metaphor involving different physical/digital artifacts. For example, one of the models was about using little rocks and a weighing machine to navigate into the tree, each rock representing a node of the tree. Another modeled solution was dealing with a car steering wheel, pedals and gear shift to navigate in total immersion into the virtual environment representing the tree of life. Based on this model, participants have coupled pedals and gear shift (i.e. physical objects) to derive towards a bike handlebar manipulation metaphor. They also envision a direct mapping between the point of view in the tree and the user, by dematerializing the user into a digital avatar. To finish they decide to involve one physical object in the user hands. This one becomes the flashlight of an explorer that allows exploring the tree inside by moving it.

For the MIM session participants mainly focused on the involved modalities and communication languages and on the possible matching between physical and digital worlds. For example, participants envisioned more than seven ways to make the link between an exploration handler (i.e. a physical support with a rabbet in which an object can be displaced to control the motions in the virtual environment.) and the digital world. In another model, they envision to physically represent the tree with animal horns. Finally, another metaphor was related to the use of an object composed of several tabs, each one linked to an exploration action on the virtual environment.

By looking at the produced solutions, sessions have proved to be successful. Indeed, both have produced the kind of results we expected: many modeled solutions addressing the design problem. The introduction of the model has proved to not being a hindrance to participants' creativity because each solution was linked to a different metaphor. However, evaluating the quality of the produced metaphors remains on a subjective expert judgment.

Analysis and feedback

To evaluate the impact of the model on produced ideas, we focused our analysis on a comparison of the produced models of each session based on three metrics: 1) model's concepts exploration, 2) input/output variations in the modeled solutions, and 3) compatibility with the case study in terms of requirements. Those three metrics respectively represent 1) the exploitation degree of model concepts, 2) an indicator of a strong variability source in MIS design, and 3) the modeled solutions' quality regarding to the case study requirements. As a result, those metrics are three leading indicators to study the adequacy of the method within the design process. Our analysis is also completed with qualitative feedbacks extracted from our observations and participants comments. All these analyses have been performed on the basis of an inter-judge agreement involving three researchers and domain experts (museum experts). We discuss these analyses in the next paragraphs.

Model's concepts exploration – To compare the elements constituting the modeled solutions between the two sessions, we defined a common frame of reference between ASUR and MIM. This frame of reference is composed of the main concepts used to represent MIS: physical elements, digital elements, sensing/emitting devices, and communication style. Based on this frame of reference, we characterized the generated modeled solutions of each session. The comparison revealed that the ASUR session triggered the suggestion of many digital and physical entities, whereas the MIM session was more productive in terms of sensors/effectors and communication styles (cf. Table 1). This is in line with the scope of each model involved. Indeed, ASUR is centered on the entities composing the system while MIM is centered on the interaction modalities. This observation confirms that the predominant dimensions expressed in the model influence participants thinking.

Model / Concepts	ASUR Session	MIM Session
Physical elements	12	8
Digital elements	9	1
Sensors/Effectors	7	10
Communication styles	4	12

Table 1: Concepts instantiation of the 1st case study

Input/output variations in the modeled solutions – We also characterized all the elements constituting the modeled solutions in terms of system inputs or outputs. We observed no clear difference between the two sessions (18 inputs for MIM/19 inputs for ASUR, 16 outputs for MIM/15 outputs for ASUR). This tends to show that the model does not influence participants' focus on interaction input/output aspect. Moreover, we observed that some solutions were incomplete: some of them were only composed of system inputs of other ones of system outputs. This result reinforces the need for post-processing in step 4 in which partial solutions are linked.

Compatibility with the functional requirements – We also checked the functional requirements coverage of every modeled solution. We observed only few differences between the two sessions (44% of average compatibility for MIM and 60% for ASUR). However, it reveals for both sessions that most of the generated models did not satisfy all the functional requirements. We believe that participants forgot some requirements during the session. A support should be added in the next sessions to avoid this problem.

Qualitative feedback and suggested improvements – During the debriefings, participants provided many feedbacks about the method. For example, they pointed out that "*the model really helped to come back and remember the produced ideas all along the session*" which is probably due to the graphical notation of the model. We also noticed that all the participants made references to the model, even very early during the sessions. For example, during the MIM session the participants' first reference to the model (i.e. not the facilitator) appeared about 8 minutes after the beginning of step 3; it was about mixed objects, one of the core concepts of MIM: "*Is the visualization of the tree a part of mixed object?*" In case of ASUR participants started to talk about the model about 10 minutes after the beginning of step 3. In addition during the ASUR session debriefing, a participant noticed that "*the model helped me to keep in mind some aspects of the system, such as which physical objects are linked to which functionalities*". This comment was related to the design of the weighing machine solution during ASUR session: on this weighing machine users could put little stones representing the cladogram nodes and leaves. This comment refers to ASUR's mixed proximity concept, meaning that an element in the digital world is represented in the physical world.

Lessons learned and perspectives

The aim of this first analysis is not to measure the performance of our MACS implementations, but 1) to assess the method adequacy within such design situation, 2) to envision new principles and 3) to identify relationships between the session's parameters (case study, model used, etc.) and the generated models. The strengths and weaknesses of the MACS have thus been observed. Indeed, the first case study showed that the method's basic principles were replicable, whatever the team or model. We observed numerous positive influences of the model on the generated ideas and on participants' behavior. For example, participants stayed focused on the design problem and did not switch on irrelevant aspects, such as technological problems. Moreover, the produced solutions have proven to be in adequacy with the design problem and adapted to the application domain (i.e. museum context). Following the use of the post-processing (step 4) on the ASUR session results, an interactive solution has been extracted, prototyped and successfully evaluated in the museum: beyond the replicable nature of the approach this is also a fair indication of its ability to generate context adapted interactive solutions. As a result, we can state at the end of this first use of the MACS that our approach is worthwhile.

However, we also observed during the sessions that multiple references made to the model were not as efficient as we expected. Participants often needed facilitator's interventions to make correct references to the dimensions expressed by the model. It explains why, during the debriefings, several participants suggested the need for a model legend for remembering the concepts' meaning. In addition, we observed that the participants did not remember all of the specificities related to the case study requirements. For those reasons, we developed a stimulation toolbox to help the facilitator during the session. Based on these outcomes, we improved the method and reapplied it on a second case study.

CASE STUDY 2: MANIPULATION OF 3D CLADOGRAMS

With this second case study, called CladiBubble, we have gripped the opportunity to investigate an improved version of MACS. The thematic of this case study also deals with cladistic. Here, the application aims at explaining why some well known groups of species, such as fishes or reptiles, are no longer valid in terms of cladistics. To do so, visitors are invited to manipulate a 3D cladogram in order to bring species spatially close to each other. Then they have to group them with a bubble. Finally the group validity is checked by the application. As a result, the design problem given to the participants was: "*explore and find mixed interactive techniques for manipulating the tree and grouping the species with the bubble*". At this stage of the design, the prototype was in form of a video showing 3D cladogram manipulations and grouping of species with the bubble (Figure 4). As for the first case study, we led two MACS: one, called *improved session*, including some improvements identified through the first case study and another one, called *classic session*, using the same principles than those used in the first case study.

Implementation of both sessions

The conditions were the same as in the first case study. Consequently, the sessions were limited to 120 minutes. Participants between the two sessions were necessarily different to avoid the familiarity with the case study, and participants profiles were also the same (facilitator, technical expert, MIS designer, usability specialist and CHI practitioner) with the same low level of knowledge of the used model. Participants were again different from those involved in case study 1 and across the two sessions. In addition, the ASUR model was the unique model used.

New elements in the improved session

Following the lessons learnt from the firsts MACS, we added a model legend in the improved session. This legend aims to help participants remembering the model elements and their meaning. In addition, we provided a toolbox to the facilitator in form of a set of stimulating sentences (Table

Stimulation goal	N°	Triggering condition	Stimulating sentence example
Adequacy of the generated ideas with the case study	1	Creativity dropping	We have not addressed [untreated feature]? One solution would be [sample solution].
	2	Non completeness of a generated model	This solution allows [feature treated], but does not yet allow [feature untreated], how could [untreated feature] be added?
Optimize the use of the model	3	Global lack of reference to the model	How do your ideas materialize in the model? [explain the construction sequence of the model]
	4	Lack of use for one element of the model	To [feature], are there other potential solutions for these [Element models]?

Table 2: Facilitator's generic sentences

2). These sentences can be used to stimulate participants, in order to help them to make references to the model and to the case study requirements. Each sentence is associated with 1) a goal related to one of the dimension to optimize (i.e. adequacy with the case study and use of the model), 2) a triggering condition revealing to the facilitator when to use the sentence, and 3) the sentence that can be adapted to match the current model and discussion. As a result, during the session, when a triggering condition is activated, the facilitator can use the appropriate generic sentence to stimulate participants. However, to evaluate the impact of this toolbox on the generated ideas, we asked the facilitator to not propose ideas and to be only focused on the triggering of the sentences specified in Table 2.

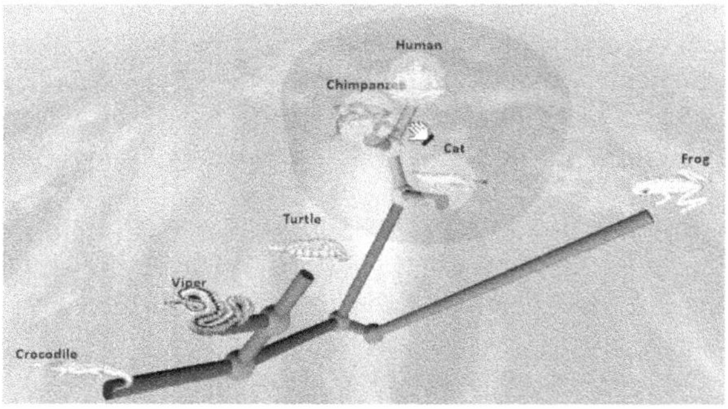

Figure 4: a deformable cladogram and its bubble group

Session outcomes

The two sessions took place in Toulouse with two different design teams. Both sessions were videotaped. The classic session produced 11 ASUR models and the improved session produced 16 ASUR models.

For both sessions (classic and improved), participants have mainly explored the links between the application functionalities (e.g. grabbing a specie, manipulating the tree, grouping species, etc.) and the physical/digital artifacts. Due to the amount of ideas, we do not report here all the modeled solutions, but emphasize the most interesting ones. Surprisingly, some solutions between the two sessions were similar. For example, in both sessions the participants suggested the materialization of each of the digital species into several physical bricks. Another solution proposed in both sessions, was to materialize the bubble's behavior by using a pump to inflate/deflate it. This solution directly refers to the concept of mixed group expressed in ASUR. More specifically in the improved session, participants envisioned the use of a digital shadow to manipulate the tree. It directly relies on a dematerialization of the user into a digital artifact. As for the first case study's sessions, the produced solutions were satisfying: several metaphors and interaction techniques addressing the design problem came out. This is a second empirical proof that the model does not jeopardize participants' creativity. However, in comparison to the first case study, participants have been notably more productive (more than 10 models for each session). This is probably due to the nature of the design problem to address.

Analysis and feedback

We present in the following paragraphs an analysis of the generated solutions which is particularly focused on the influence of the introduced improvements. We reapplied the same metrics than those used in the first case-study, in order to compare the two sessions. Two metrics were relevant in this case: *Model's concepts exploration* and *Compatibility with the required functionalities*. Then, we present qualitative results extracted from participants' feedbacks and video analysis. As for the first case study, the analysis has been performed on the basis of an inter-judge agreement involving three researchers and museum experts. Then we summarize the lessons learnt from these sessions.

Model's concepts exploration – As for the first case study, we characterized and compared the elements from the produced solutions according to the previously introduced frame of reference (cf. Table 3). Through this measure, we noticed an increase in communication styles in the improved session in comparison to the classic session. The participants were notably more productive in terms of diversity of information representation and language. We conclude that participants of the improved session better exploited the exploration potential of the case study. This is a fair indication that the toolbox (n°3 and 4 on Table 2) has a positive influence on the exploration of the design space.

Model / Concepts	Classic Session	Improved Session
Physical elements	17	20
Digital elements	18	15
Sensors/Effectors	30	29
Communication styles	**10**	**32**

Table 3: Concepts instantiation of the 2nd case study

Compatibility with the required functionalities – This second metric aims at studying the influence of the facilitator assistance on the modeled solutions' requirement coverage. For each session, up to three modeled solutions were totally fulfilling the functional requirements, which mean that we noticed no difference between the classic and improved sessions. However we identified in the video that the use by the facilitator of the associated stimulating sentences in the toolbox (n°1 and 2 on Table 2) was very limited. We believe that this is probably due to a difficulty for the facilitator to analyze on-the-fly the requirements compatibility of the current design. Therefore this tends to reveal the need for different tools to help the participants: this is further discussed in the lessons learnt section.

Figure 5: Participants working on a model on the wall

Qualitative feedback – For the improved session, we used a post-session questionnaire, session debriefing and video analysis to collect participants' feedbacks. Regarding the model legend, questionnaires revealed the usefulness of the model legend: to the question, "*Have you used the legend of the model on the table?*" all the participants answered yes, and to the question "*Do you think the legend is useful?*" participants' answers were M=8.5 with an SD=1.2 (on a Likert scale from 1 to 10, 10 being the best). Through the questionnaires' opened questions and during the debriefing, participants stated several times that the legend helped them to express their ideas in the model terms. They also suggested adding a concrete model example in the legend.

With more specific regards to the use of the model, several participants stated that when they had no idea, they randomly used an element/attribute of the model to propose something new. Participants also underlined the helpfulness of the model graphical notation to represent and remember the generated solutions. A participant said: "*the diagram's spatial organization helped me to differentiate a solution from another really quickly*". During the debriefing, participants reported that the model was easy to understand and that the facilitator interventions were helpful to express ideas through the model notation. As a result, we can say that at this stage of the development of the MACS, the use of the ASUR model is no longer a problem, but a useful tool to generate ideas. As an illustration, Figure 5 shows a participant expressing an idea on a displayed model.

Finally, through video analysis, we observed a new and unexpected use of the model: *metaphor derivation*. Indeed, some interactive metaphors have been derived three or four times to produce different interaction techniques, with other physical objects, new types of manipulations and different representations of the digital information. For instance, in the improved session, participants proposed three different uses of the augmented shadow to interact with the cladogram. In those solutions, the metaphor remains the same (i.e. shadow based interaction) but with three different ways of using it to interact with CladiBubble. This way of refining models on a selected metaphor was initially planned to be performed during step 4 of the method, but appears to be done iteratively all along the session.

Lessons learned and perspectives

Testing some improvements through this second case study gives us an opportunity to identify new practices. First, even if the facilitator toolbox enhances the model exploration, this type of real time assistance requires a well-trained facilitator. As a result, it reinforces the need for a dedicated tool that could lighten the facilitator workload. For example, such a tool might allow participants to tick the covered requirements for each modeled solution to get a better idea of which solution addresses which problems. We have also identified a new way of using the model: the iterative metaphor derivation. We envision supporting this practice for the next evolutions of the approach through adapted editing functionalities. For example, advanced copy/paste of elements or the ability of cloning a part of a diagram will notably ease this sort of derivation. Finally, as illustrated on Figure 5, we observed that participants often need to directly point elements on the diagrams. This drives us to envision a direct editing of the model by the participants (and not only by the facilitator). In addition, such a practice may increase the group motivation, which plays a major role in the creativity's efficiency [15]. In that way, design games practices [5] constitutes interesting alternatives. For example, a design game in which the rules are based on model manipulations might motivate participants in a transparent manner. It constitutes a future evolution of the MACS.

CONCLUSIONS AND LIMITATIONS

In this paper, we have stated the importance of providing a method supporting exploration for the complex and variable field of MIS. Based on a literature review of psychology of creativity and design methods in HCI, we have highlighted that the use of a design model during creative sessions may constitute an efficient stimulation to explore the design space of mixed interaction. Such an approach is part of a design stream in which divergent thinking benefits from a structured definition of the design space. The contribution of this paper is thus a design method supporting the articulation of formal and informal design resources.

We have introduced the general principles and development steps of our design method. We have demonstrated how to explore the MIS design space through a basic example. Then, we have illustrated the combination of creative sessions with two different MIS models and on two different case studies. Through these illustrations, we have shown that non practitioners can take advantage of specific mixed interaction models to envision new possibilities. We tried to go beyond the difficulties of evaluating such a method through comparative metrics and qualitative feedback analysis. Obviously a more clinical analysis of the relationships between generated ideas and model influence would be interesting. However, in this paper we focused on analyzing the model influence on the sessions' outputs rather than the way participants play with the model.

Our repeated use of the MACS approach revealed that through the model, the dimensions to explore are clearly defined. As a result, participants stay focused on a mixed interaction problem, and do not switch to irrelevant aspects (e.g. visualization problems, requirements identification, etc.). In addition, our experiences have shown advantages of getting formal models in output of such a method: indeed at the end of the step 4, the extracted models constitute solid materials, appropriate for prototyping or implementing the designed solutions. To conclude, further work on the MACS method will be focused on two aspects: 1) designing tools to support facilitator role and to enable participants to directly manipulate/edit/explore the model by themselves and 2) experience the method on additional case studies and why not, to design UIs other than MIS.

ACKNOWLEDGMENTS

We would like to thank the Museum of Toulouse and more specifically Francis Duranthon. This work is part of ANR-RIAM CARE Project (http://www.careproject.fr)

REFERENCES

1. Amabile, T.M. Social psychology of creativity: A consensual assessment technique. *Journal of Personality and Social Psychology 43, 5* (1982), 997-1013.
2. Beaudouin-Lafon, M. Designing interaction, not interfaces. *Proc. of AVI'04*, ACM (2004), 15-22.
3. Blackwell, A.F., Edge, D., Dubuc, L., Rode, J.A., Stringer, M., and Toye, E.F. Using solid diagrams for tangible interface prototyping. *IEEE Pervasive Computing*, (2005), 18-21.
4. Bonnardel, N. Towards understanding and supporting creativity in design: analogies in a constrained cognitive environment. *Knowledge-Based Systems 13*, 7-8 (2000), 505-513.
5. Brandt, E. et Messeter, J. Facilitating collaboration through design games. *Proc of. PDC'04*, ACM (2004), 121-131.
6. Coutrix, C. and Nigay, L. Balancing physical and digital properties in mixed objects. *Proc. of AVI'08*, ACM (2008), 305-308.
7. Csikszentmihalyi, M. *Creativity: Flow and the Psychology of Discovery and Invention*. Harper Perennial, 1997.
8. Dubois, E., Gauffre, G., Bach, C., and Salembier, P. Participatory Design Meets Mixed Reality Design Models. *Proc. of CADUI'07*, 71-84.
9. Dubois, E. and Gray, P. A Design-Oriented Information-Flow Refinement of the ASUR Interaction Model. *Proc. of EIS'08*, 465-482.
10. Fishkin, K.P. A taxonomy for and analysis of tangible interfaces. *Personal Ubiquitous Comput. 8*, 5 (2004), 347-358.
11. Gaver, B., Boucher, A., Walker, B., and al. Expected, sensed, and desired: A framework for designing sensing-based interaction. *ACM Trans. Comput.-Hum. Interact. 12*, 1 (2005), 3-30.
12. Hornecker, E. Creative idea exploration within the structure of a guiding framework: the card brainstorming game. *Proc. of TEI'10*, ACM (2010), 101-108.
13. Jacob, R.J., Girouard, A., Hirshfield, L.M., and al. Reality-based interaction: a framework for post-WIMP interfaces. *Proc. of CHI'08*, ACM (2008), 201-210.
14. Koleva, B., Rennick-Eggestone, S., Schnädelbach, H., Glover, K., Greenhalgh, C., Rodden, T., Dade-Robertson, M., Supporting the creation of hybrid museum experiences. *Proc. of CHI'09*, ACM (2009), 1973-1982.
15. Lubart, T., Mouchiroud, C., Tordjam, S., and Zenasni, F. *Psychologie de la créativité [Psychology of Creativity]*. Armand Colin, 2003.
16. Monk and S. Howard, "Methods & tools: the rich picture: a tool for reasoning about work context," *interactions, vol. 5*, (1998), 21-30
17. Rodriguez, F.G., Scapin, D.L. Editing MAD* Task Descriptions for Specifying User Interfaces, at Both Semantic and Presentation Levels, *Proc. of DSV-IS'97*, (1997), 215-225.
18. Säde, S. *Cardboard mock-ups and conversations: Studies on user-centered product design*. PhD, University of Art and Design Helsinki, (2001)
19. Shaer, O. and Jacob, R.J. A specification paradigm for the design and implementation of tangible user interfaces. *ACM Trans. Comput.-Hum. Interact. 16*, 4 (2009), 1-39.
20. Shaer, O., Leland, N., Calvillo-Gamez, E.H., and Jacob, R.J.K. The TAC paradigm: specifying tangible user interfaces. *Personal and Ubiquitous Computing 8*, 5 (2004), 359-369.
21. Ullmer, B. and Ishii, H. Emerging frameworks for tangible user interfaces. *IBM Syst. J. 39*, 3-4 (2000), 915-931.
22. Vaajakallio, K. and Mattelmäki, T. Collaborative design exploration: envisioning future practices with make tools. *Proc. of DPPI'07*, ACM (2007), 223-238.
23. Wilson, C.E. Brainstorming pitfalls and best practices. *interactions 13*, 5 (2006), 50-63.

Buffer Automata: A UI Architecture Prioritising HCI Concerns for Interactive Devices

Harold Thimbleby
FIT Lab
Swansea University
h.thimbleby@swansea.ac.uk

Andy Gimblett
FIT Lab
Swansea University
a.m.gimblett@swansea.ac.uk

Abigail Cauchi
FIT Lab
Swansea University
csabi@swansea.ac.uk

ABSTRACT
We introduce an architectural software formalism, *buffer automata*, for the specification, implementation and analysis of a particular class of discrete interactive systems and devices. The approach defines a layer between the physical user interface and the application (if any) and provides a clear framework for highlighting a number of interaction design issues, in particular around modes and undo.

Author Keywords
Buffer automata; modes; undo; interaction programming; structural usability.

ACM Classification Keywords
H.5.2 (D.2.2, H.1.2, I.36) User Interfaces: Theory and methods

General Terms
Design, Theory

1. INTRODUCTION
General purpose programming languages can implement any interactive system, but such systems are not easy to analyse for their interaction properties. Conversely, finite state machines can in principle also describe any interactive system—typically as *enormous* FSMs—but for non-trivial systems they are impractically large and have no clear structure to support insights into human computer interaction issues. In this paper we introduce an extension to FSMs which aims to address this state explosion issue, at least for some systems.

Consider something as simple as a handheld calculator: it has a few basic modes (off, adding, subtracting...) but tracking its states means also tracking (say) 10^8 possible numbers for its display, 10^8 for its memory, 10^8 for the working number, and perhaps 10^8 for any constant (when pressing [=] just adds the current number to the constant). Its full state space thus has at least 10^{32} states; this simple device is at the limits of what can conveniently be handled by current model checking technology (e.g., by exploiting its symmetries), but human users obviously do not conceptualise a state space of this size. Rather (we suggest) users do think about interactive systems a bit like FSMs, but only in terms of their *mode space*, and the exact number values handled by the calculator are abstracted away in the user's mental model—indeed, such abstraction is much of the purpose of the device.

We propose that many simple (but non-trivial) interactive systems can be thought of like this, that is as a manageable space of a few explicit modes combined with a collection of abstracted data values, and that this captures the structure users are aware of and can manage, and abstracts away the structure users ignore details of. There remain many complex interactive systems beyond the reach of such an approach, at least as proposed here (but see section 6); we are particularly concerned at this time with the many devices, from calculators to medical infusion pumps, that we *can* handle clearly and rigorously. Such 'simple' systems still have non-trivial interaction issues, and the approach proposed here exposes and makes explicit some of these issues—and even where it does not resolve them, it provides a framework to support clearer arguments about design choices.

This paper makes the following contributions: we introduce and define *buffer automata*, a new formalism for structuring and thinking about user interfaces; we provide abstract and concrete examples of buffer automata in use; we show that buffer automata provide a new perspective on several issues of interaction design and programming, including modes and undo, and in particular we describe how to automatically compute modes within the formalism. It is our hope that this paper will direct and stimulate further discussion and exploration of some of the issues raised.

We present a review of potentially alternative and contrasting approaches in Section 5; for a short paper, the background literature is perhaps best presented after we first emphasise and examine the focus of our contribution.

2. BUFFER AUTOMATA
As discussed in Section 1, many interactive systems may be thought of as a relatively simple abstract mode space together with various data values which the user may alter. Thinking of the mode space as a 'classic' FSM or automaton, and the data values as being held in buffers where they are manipulated then leads to the idea of a *buffer automaton*.

EICS'11, June 1316, 2011, Pisa, Italy.

Buffers are data values the system keeps track of, such as phone number, radio station, CD track, time now, alarm time, drug infusion rate. *Modes* are significant states of the system, such as on, off, playing, infusing, not infusing, standby. Among other things, modes dictate which buffers are receiving user input, and which are exposed as output. Thus, user actions give rise to input events which are distributed to buffers according to the current mode, modifying buffer values and potentially triggering mode changes. (This mechanism, and the exact relationship between buffers and modes, is explored in Section 2.1.)

In principle a user is generally aware of the current mode(s) of the system and the available actions to change modes; conversely, users do not track exact buffer values, but may know in principle whether they are 'right,' 'wrong,' 'nearly right,' etc. Users rely on systems to keep track of buffer details unless actually interacting with a particular buffer. For example, consider a nurse on a hospital ward with patients connected to drug infusion pumps, asked "is this patient getting an infusion?"; the nurse knows the answer is yes, because earlier they put the device into the infusing mode; when asked "how fast is the patient being infused?" the nurse will probably check the device. Here 'infusing' is a mode, but 'infusion rate' is a buffer.

Another example: a radio can be on or off, and can be tuned in to FM or MW bands; it has 100 possible volume levels and 100 possible tuning frequencies; it responds to events [ON], [OFF], [MW], [FM], [VOLUP], [VOLDN], [TUNUP], [TUNDN]. Modelling this as a 40,000 state FSM ($2 \times 2 \times 100 \times 100$) certainly obscures its structure; modelled as a buffer automaton we have a space of four modes (off/MW, off/FM, on/MW, on/FM) and some independent buffers with simple, well understood behaviour (e.g., for the volume level). Events are cleanly distributed to the various buffers according to mode (when off, everything but [OFF] is ignored, say), and there is no interaction between the buffers in this highly orthogonal device. Variants are possible and explored later in the paper.

Tasks on many systems require a pair of activities: set up one or more buffers (such as the rate of infusion), and make the system do the action with a buffer value (such as perform an infusion). Such systems are well suited to modelling as buffer automata. Of course, any sufficiently complex component could model or even implement an entire system—nothing *needs* to be partitioned into independent modes and buffers. Our proposition is that buffer automata can provide clear descriptions of interactive systems of a particular class, amenable to particular kinds of analysis: the utility of the formalism is its exposure of certain HCI issues such as modes and undo, and as an attempt to model systems closely in terms of how users think of them.

2.1 Buffers and modes

As described above, a buffer automaton is an FSM-like mode space accompanied with a set of buffers (whose structure we define shortly). In fact, while it is possible and may be useful to model the mode space explicitly, we see modes rather as an emergent implicit feature, arising from how inputs are distributed to buffers—thus, the mode space is to be computed, not specified directly. Let us explore this subtlety.

Consider the radio example above. There are on/off and MW/FM 'modes,' combining orthogonally to form a mode space with 4 states; it is precisely the states of *this* space that we refer to when we say *mode*. On/off and MW/FM are not themselves modes: like volume and tuning, they are buffers—data values the user can manipulate—but they are special buffers (only) in that they introduce mode behaviour: they influence how input events are interpreted. This interpretation of the word 'mode' is well-founded: according to [6], a mode is a "*context that changes the interpretation of commands*"; similarly, [11] says "*for any given gesture, the interface is in a particular mode if the interpretation of that gesture is constant*". Our notion of *focus* formally captures this concept—see Section 2.3.

So on/off and MW/FM are just buffers; they happen to have very simple structure, and we can easily model them as 2-state FSMs, but in general this need not be the case: buffers can have rich structure, and even rich buffers may influence mode. Suppose the radio also has a [MUTE] button (another 2-state buffer), which is ignored if the volume is 0—then the volume buffer (modelled as a 100-state FSM, perhaps, corresponding to a physical slider or knob) also contributes to the radio's mode. Every buffer we've seen so far is easy to model as an FSM, but this need not be so (a text entry box is a good counterexample: it *can* be modelled as an FSM, but not naturally), so our definition of buffer, below, is necessarily quite general; 'rich' buffers such as text entry boxes can still influence the system's mode, but perhaps with a greater risk of confusion for the user.

2.2 Definition: Buffers

A buffer is essentially an object for some data along with several functions for manipulating and accessing that object. In order to support undo (see Section 2.5), we structure the object as a *history* rather than a single value, formed from an initial value and a sequence of modifications (perhaps, but not necessarily, corresponding to input events); it is easy to ignore this history if desired, as we shall show by example.

Let $\mathit{FinSeq}(X)$ be the set of finite sequences of elements of X. Given two sets X and Y, the set of *histories* over X and Y, $\mathbb{H}_{X,Y}$ is the set $X \times \mathit{FinSeq}(Y)$. That is, a history has an initial value in X, followed by a sequence of values in Y. Notionally, the Y values modify the initial X value in some sense, although various interpretations are possible (including where $X = Y$ and 'modify' means 'replace').

A buffer is a tuple $(H, \delta, \lambda, \phi)$, with:

- $H\colon \mathbb{H}_{C,I}$ is the buffer's *history*, where C is the buffer's *contents alphabet*, and I is the buffer's *input alphabet*.
- $\delta\colon \mathbb{H}_{C,I} \times I \to \mathbb{H}_{C,I}$ is the buffer's *input function*, which modifies the buffer's history in response to the buffer receiving input events.

  We argue that there are a small number of 'off the shelf' components which can be combined to form all reasonable input functions. For example: *append* to the history; *delete* the history's last element; *reset* by clearing the history; *forget* by replacing the initial value with the result of λ and then performing a *reset*. Additionally, functions like *number, date, name, currencyValue*, etc, provide consistent ways of handling application values.

- $\lambda\colon \mathbb{H}_{C,I} \to C$ is the buffer's *access function*, mapping the buffer's history to some value in C, such as a floating point number. This might perform a fold over the history, or perhaps access its last value, etc; again, a small number of standard functionalities could conceivably cover most real buffers.

- $\phi\colon C \to \mathbb{H}_{C,I}$ is the buffer's *update function*, through which the application in which the buffer is embedded may modify its history and thus its value (see Section 2.6).

FSMs can easily be modelled using this mechanism, but many other structures are possible.

Example: Numerical buffer with direct manipulation. Our radio's volume and tuning buffers might be represented as follows; let $C = \{n \in \mathbb{N} \mid 0 \leq n \leq 99\}$, $I = C$. Then: $\forall x, z \in C \bullet \forall y \in \mathit{FinSeq}(C)$:

$$\delta((x, y), z) = (z, y)$$

That is, the initial value is simply overwritten with new inputs, and the history is never used: whatever number is selected is entered directly, overwriting any previous value.

Example: String buffer with clear and delete. Let $C = \mathit{FinSeq}(\{a, b\})$, the set of finite sequences of a's and b's. $I = \{a, b, \mathit{clear}, \mathit{delete}\}$. Let $\delta\colon \mathbb{H}_{C,I} \times I \to \mathbb{H}_{C,I}$ be:
$\forall x, z \in C \bullet \forall y \in \mathit{FinSeq}(\{a, b\})$

$$\begin{aligned}
\delta((x, y), a) &= (x, y \frown a) \\
\delta((x, y), b) &= (x, y \frown b) \\
\delta((x, y), \mathit{clear}) &= (x, \langle\rangle) \\
\delta((x, \langle\rangle), \mathit{delete}) &= (x, \langle\rangle) \\
\delta((x, y \frown z), \mathit{delete}) &= (x, y)
\end{aligned}$$

(Where $\frown$ is concatenation.) That is, a and b are appended to the history sequence, whereas *clear* and *delete* modify that sequence. Thus, the buffer's history consists of some initial value in C (the empty string, say), followed by a finite sequence of further values in C. Then, let $\lambda\colon C \times I \to C$ be the concatenation of the buffer's history sequence onto its history initial value. This version of the buffer has no maximum length.

2.3 Definitions: Buffer automata, focus and modes

A buffer automaton is a tuple $(\mathcal{S}, L, \mathcal{L}, s_0, \Sigma, \mathcal{F}, \Delta, \mathcal{V})$, with:

- $\mathcal{S}$ is a tuple of buffers. Labels $\in L$ serve as unique names of buffers, and the naming $\mathcal{L}$ is a bijection from labels to buffers. The state of the BA is the state of its buffers; s_0 is the BA's initial state.

- Σ is the BA's input alphabet, the union of each of its buffers input alphabets (which need not be disjoint).

- $\mathcal{F}\colon \mathcal{S} \to \Sigma \to \mathbb{P}(L)$ is the BA's *focus function*, which, given the current state of the BA's buffers, tells us for each input the names of buffers that should receive that input. From $\mathcal{F}$ we derive our formal notion of mode—see below.

- Δ is the BA's derived *input function*, $\Delta\colon \mathcal{S} \to \Sigma \to \mathcal{S}$, which distributes inputs to the BA's various buffers in accordance with $\mathcal{F}$. The definition is omitted here, but is simple: an input is distributed to every buffer which is currently in focus for that input.

- $\mathcal{V}$ is the BA's *visibility function*, $\mathcal{V}\colon \mathcal{S} \to \mathbb{P}(L)$, and determines the names of the visible buffers (and thus what is visible to the user may be computed from their values).

As discussed in Section 2.1, we see mode as a context determining the interpretation of user inputs; assuming (reasonably, for any sane device) that a given buffer's interpretation of its input is always consistent, mode is thus defined solely by the distribution of inputs to buffers—which we can compute trivially given the focus function $\mathcal{F}$. The current mode of a BA is essentially a lookup table telling us, for each buffer (identified by name), which inputs it can receive right now. Thus, we have $\mathit{mode}\colon \mathcal{S} \to \mathcal{L} \to \mathbb{P}(\Sigma)$.

2.3.1 Radio example

Let our radio have the following four buffers:

- *OnOff*, an FSM with states $\{\mathrm{on}, \mathrm{off}\}$, actions $\{\mathit{On}, \mathit{Off}\}$.
- *Band*, an FSM with states $\{\mathrm{mw}, \mathrm{fm}\}$, actions $\{\mathit{MW}, \mathit{FM}\}$.
- *Volume*, with $C = \{0, \ldots, 99\}$, $I = \{v_\uparrow, v_\downarrow\}$, volume values modified with up/down actions, under some sensible interpretation of the buffer's history (e.g. perhaps with wraparound, depending on the physical mechanism used).
- *Tuning*, with $C = \{0, \ldots, 99\}$, $I = \{t_\uparrow, t_\downarrow\}$ (similarly).

Sensible initial BA values might be $(\mathrm{off}, \mathrm{mw}, 0, 50)$, say. Σ is $\{\mathit{On}, \mathit{Off}, \mathit{MW}, \mathit{FM}, v_\uparrow, v_\downarrow, t_\uparrow, t_\downarrow\}$. $\mathcal{F}$ is simple: all events go their respective buffers, unless *OnOff*'s value is off, when *On* goes to *OnOff* and all other events are ignored.

Unlike our earlier conception of the radio, this device actually has only 2 modes: on and off. *Band* has no influence on interpretation of inputs: in effect, we have modelled an old style tuner with a single tuning control for both bands. Instead, let's replace *Tuning* with separate tuning values for MW/FM, better reflecting the operation of a modern radio:

$$\begin{aligned}
\mathit{MWTune} \quad &\text{with} \quad C = \{0, \ldots, 99\}, I = \{t_\uparrow, t_\downarrow\} \\
\mathit{FMTune} \quad &\text{with} \quad C = \{0, \ldots, 99\}, I = \{t_\uparrow, t_\downarrow\}
\end{aligned}$$

Note that *MWTune* and *FMTune* have identical input alphabets; we modify $\mathcal{F}$ so $\{t_\uparrow, t_\downarrow\}$ events are delivered to the appropriate buffer according to the value of *Band*, which is thus now mode-relevant. We still don't have 4 modes however, only 3: off, on/MW, and on/FM. Perhaps that's fine—or perhaps it's possible to turn the volume and tuning knobs while the device is off; a variety of approaches are possible. Even with this simple example we see that thinking concretely about focus and modes brings to light some interesting design questions we might otherwise have ignored.

2.4 Mode space discovery

A buffer automaton's mode space may be discovered using *model discovery* [7] to dynamically explore the state space of all mode-relevant buffers, producing a graph whose nodes are (BA state, focus) pairs; the mode space is then obtained by collapsing together states with identical focus, producing a graph whose nodes are distinct focus values (modes) and whose edges are events which change the mode. Note that the set of mode-relevant buffers must be specified explicitly, otherwise a full exploration of the BA's complete state space would be required just to learn which buffers *are* mode-relevant.

Alternatively, given a suitable representation of $\mathcal{F}$, the mode space can in principle be computed statically. However, as the application may in general modify any buffer freely (see Section 2.6), the statically computed mode space for a given system may be inaccurate, and dynamic discovery is probably safer; at the least, comparing static and dynamic mode spaces tells us something about the BA and application's interaction with each other.

2.5 Undo and history

Common wisdom is that user interfaces should support undo [12]; but, actually, it is more important that they support the user achieving their goals in the face of error. Undo is just one way of recovering from (recognised) error, but often it is not the best strategy. In particular, we argue, undo is often not the right strategy—or not even meaningful—when dealing with mode-changing events. If a nurse accidentally starts an infusion before they intend to, and they notice the error, they wouldn't expect to hit UNDO to fix the problem: they'd hit STOP, triggering another mode change—and that would just be the first step in fixing the error. UNDO probably *couldn't* restore the device to its previous state, due to the physical effect of starting the infusion. Conversely, if the nurse makes a keying error while entering the desired infusion rate, UNDO is a perfectly reasonable approach. This points to another distinction between mode-relevant and non-mode-relevant buffers: the latter can in general use their histories to support undo, whereas the former need not (and often should not); in some cases a mode change represents an action which *can't* easily be undone: that is useful information for designers. This is a rather sweeping generalisation of course, and there will be exceptions; for example, in many simple buffers (such as in our radio), all events have inverses so an explicit UNDO shared between buffers is pointless.

2.6 Buffer automata in context

Conceptually, we see buffer automata as an interpretive and structure-imparting layer between the UI/presentation of an interactive device and its underlying application; after each buffer in focus performs its transition, control is passed to the application to perform access then update operations. The BA is then ready for its next input event. How exactly this is structured is left generic in order to accommodate a wide range of approaches. A typical setting is illustrated in Figure 1. User input is received from the UI and passed to the BA as members of Σ, where it is distributed to various buffers' input functions δ as dictated by $\mathcal{F}$; the application then has the opportunity to read and update buffer values via each buffer's λ and ϕ functions (as well as dealing with other events, such as non-UI I/O, alarms, etc); buffer values are then exposed, subject to $\mathcal{V}$, as views in the UI using some function $V\colon \mathbb{H}_{C,I} \rightarrow \mathbb{V}$ from the buffer's state to the view domain $\mathbb{V}$. How to handle the display of buffer contents, and the role of the function $\mathcal{V}$—the converse of $\mathcal{F}$—and its relationship with modes remains future work to be explored; we note that 'visibility' might in fact involve non-graphical elements such as sound or vibration.

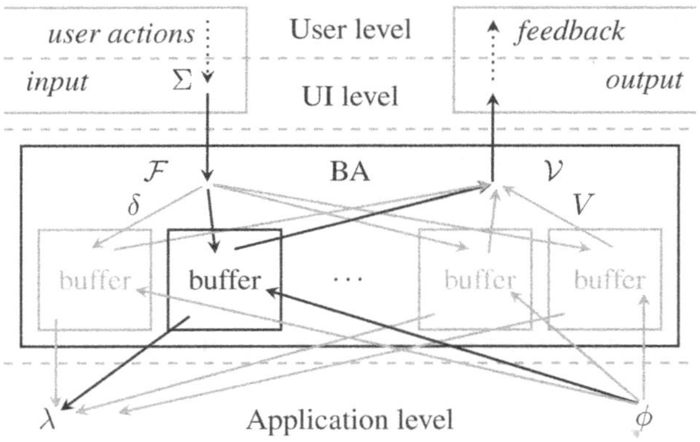

Figure 1. Buffer automata in context. User actions translate to BA inputs in Σ, distributed by $\mathcal{F}$ to each buffer's δ input function; the application reads buffer values via λs and updates via ϕs if necessary; values for feedback are projected by V, filtered according to $\mathcal{V}$.

3. EXAMPLE: PULSE MUSIC SYNTHESIZER

The *Waldorf Pulse* is a 1990s-era electronic musical instrument, controlled remotely for performance via the MIDI protocol, but which may also be programmed via a front-panel interface consisting of 6 knobs, 4 buttons, a 3-character display and 7 LEDs (see Figure 2). There are 69 parameters that control the sound being produced by the instrument (e.g., 'Volume,' 'Arpeggiator Tempo'), where such a collection of parameters is called a *patch*; the Pulse has a memory of 99 patch slots. Patch parameters are edited via the matrix arrangement on the right of the panel: the 69 parameters are arranged in a 6×6 matrix (with some doubling-up—see below), and each of the 6 knobs is dedicated to one column of this matrix. Only one row of the matrix is active at once, as indicated by a red LED to its left and advanced by pressing the large oval Mode button. Finally, the blue Shift button under Mode toggles between parameters where they are doubled up (the red LED flashes when 'shifted'). For example, if the second LED down is flashing, and we rotate the third knob from the left, we modify the 'OSC2 Keytrack' (whatever that means) parameter.

We have simulated the Pulse's patch editing interface using a buffer automaton in Haskell (connected to a web GUI in JavaScript/HTML5 Canvas). Every patch parameter has an associated buffer, and each buffer responds to the events $\uparrow_n$ and $\downarrow_n$ for some column number $1 \leq n \leq 6$. There are also simple buffers for four values associated with modes—see below. We only modelled a single patch, and have not considered the Pulse's memory and related functionality.

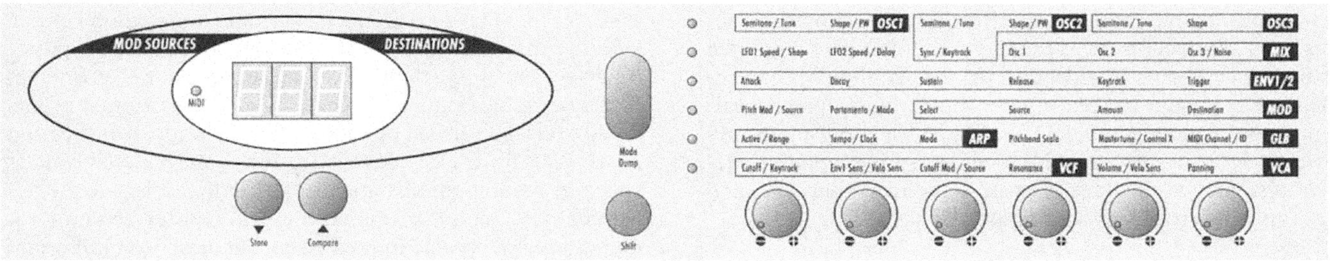

Figure 2. Screenshot from running simulation of Waldorf Pulse control panel. Patch control knobs at bottom right. (Images reproduced from Waldorf Pulse user manual with permission.)

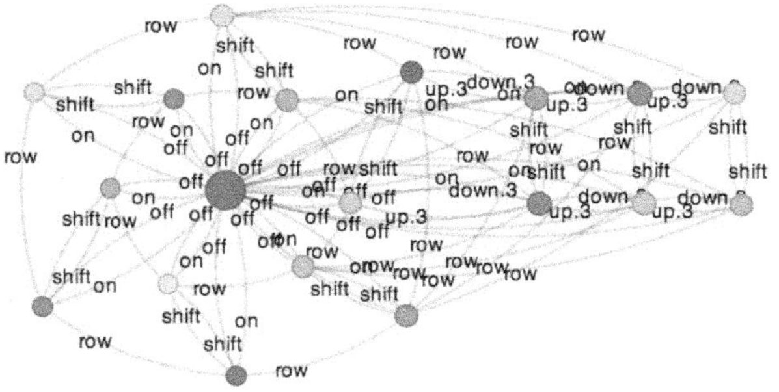

Figure 3. Mode space of Pulse buffer automaton; *row* and *shift* form a regular structure of two concentric hexagons, with off in the centre; *Mod Select* introduces six more modes to the right of the hexagons. Note that this graph is nondeterministic (multiple *row* edges at top-right).

Turning a knob should obviously not modify all 6 (or more) parameters in that knob's column. The Pulse's interface is thus very modeful: how turning a given knob is interpreted depends (at least) on which row of the matrix is active, and (in some cases) whether shift is engaged. The mode-relevant buffers on the Pulse are 'OnOff,' 'Row,' 'Shift' and 'Mod Select' (on row 4, knob 3 controls which 'sub-row' knobs 4, 5, 6 are focussed on)—all of which can be modelled as small FSMs.

We used mode space discovery to compute the Pulse BA's mode space (see Figure 3), which is seen to be quite regular. Our Pulse's focus function is hand-written; we plan to devise a domain specific language (DSL) for describing focus, from which the mode space may be computed directly via abstract interpretation, rather than dynamically by discovery; the dynamic version may however remain useful as a correctness check for comparison against the statically computed version.

4. EXAMPLE: ALARIS INFUSION PUMP

The Cardinal Health Alaris GP volumetric infusion pump [2] is an interactive medical device with 14 buttons, designed to provide patients with controlled delivery of drugs. We modelled the device thoroughly using an interactive *Mathematica* program with a realistic graphical animation that allows user testing to confirm the program is an accurate interaction simulation. The simulation has a transition graph model with 4.8×10^{15} states; such a model is unwieldy and computationally costly to analyse.

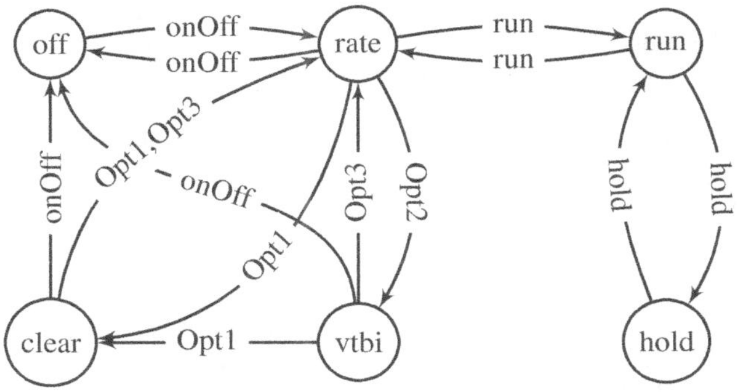

Figure 4. Alaris infusion pump mode space computed from the focus function of our BA model. Mode names are implicit, and have been chosen to reflect each mode's role. Some actions (*Opt1*, etc) correspond to soft buttons; a model using displayed names (e.g., 'VTBI') would have a different, possibly more meaningful, mode structure.

We recently recast this model as a buffer automaton, with 10 buffers: 3 are for numbers in the range 0–999; 6 are interrelated mode-relevant switches: on/off, running/not running, infusing/not infusing, VTBI Mode on/off, clear mode on/off, and alarm silent, beeping or muted. This multiplies up to $2^5 \times 3 = 96$, but (for instance) when the GP is off, it cannot be infusing or alarming, so in fact only 22 combinations are possible, which may be further reduced to just 6 modes with *distinct* input behaviour; mode space discovery finds exactly these modes—see Figure 4.

5. RELATED WORK

A large number of formalisms take an automata-based approach to modelling systems, though most are more general than buffer automata and do not emphasise interaction and HCI concerns as we aim to. A key example is Statecharts [8, 9] (see also the closely-related UML state diagrams), an automata-based visual formalism with a variety of features enabling the representation of many complex systems using structured diagrams with nesting, composition, abstraction, guarded broadcast messaging and history—all of which yield a rich semantics. In contrast, buffer automata try to be a simple formalism that bridges certain user and device perspectives as cleanly as possible, by refusing to represent some controversial features. Very similar comments might be made for very many related formalisms (Petri nets, CSP, ATNs...): each provides a well-defined generalisation that makes the formalism appropriate for some domain (process control, say) but none specifically address human factors or HCI concerns, as is the intention for buffer automata as introduced here. Modechart [10], for example, is a specification language for real-time systems built upon a real-time logic (specifically, RTL). Like BAs, modecharts expose mode explicitly, and aim to aid reasoning about mode-rich systems; Modechart is quite low-level, however, and strongly concerned with timing issues.

Model checking [4] is a well-established technique for automatically verifying a state space model against a logical specification. We have recently seen how this can be applied to interactive systems [1] but this general approach still suffers from the state explosion problem. The BA approach to separating buffers from modes may be compared with the technique of *data abstraction* in model checking. Compositional model checking [3] tries to overcome state explosion by breaking up the model into smaller components; similarly a working theory of hierarchy for buffer automata (see Section 6) would be useful.

6. CONCLUSION

In this paper we have introduced buffer automata, a formalism for describing interactive systems which explicitly separates data entry interactions from mode-changing interactions; we have described how modes emerge from the interaction of buffers via the notion of focus, and thus how to compute a BA's mode space. The formalism introduces a new perspective on the role of undo, and when it is appropriate or not. Imagined and real-world examples demonstrate that BAs are a viable tool for modelling devices of a certain kind in a straightforward and comprehensible manner.

Designers make decisions about UI behaviour, and a BA makes some important decisions explicit. In a conventional program, the UI's structure doesn't relate directly to the user experience; there may be an event loop and UI code sensible to a programmer, but improving the code doesn't necessarily improve the UI or engage with HCI concerns. In contrast, a BA has explicit structures such as the δ function which are *supposed* to be simple. We would argue that a programmer making some δ code simpler improves the user interface design; conversely, programming a Turing Machine inside a δ (which is possible) defeats the object of clarity for the user. By extension, mode-relevant buffers should probably be small and FSM-like to keep the mode space comprehensible.

Future work on buffer automata must explore a number of open issues. The relationship we describe between undo, modes and buffers is convincing but none of the examples in this paper use undo; they are based on real devices, but we should model some other devices which offer undo and check our hypotheses there. Currently, buffer automata have no hierarchical structure; thus, we can't build complex UI elements from simpler ones (as buffer automata), or, realistically, re-use BAs between contexts. One interesting possible line of enquiry here involves positioning BAs as Control components within PAC [5] triads. Similarly, in our current arrangement buffers cannot modify each others' contents or state except via the (analytically opaque) application layer; a working theory of hierarchical buffer automata could possibly overcome this—though we also argue that this is often in fact a desirable feature. Timeouts and other external events could warrant similar treatment. As mentioned in Section 3, we plan for a DSL describing focus and allowing mode space to be computed statically rather than discovered dynamically. Finally, visibility/output of buffer contents remains a relatively unexplored issue, but clearly an important one.

Source code for our BA simulations is available from the authors.

6.1 Acknowledgements

We are grateful to Michael Harrison and our reviewers for many helpful comments; we were funded by EPSRC Grants EP/F020031/1 and EP/G059063/1.

7. REFERENCES

1. J. Campos and M. Harrison. Interaction engineering using the IVY tool. In *Proceedings of the 1st ACM SIGCHI symposium on Engineering interactive computing systems*, 2009.
2. Cardinal Health Inc. Alaris GP volumetric pump: directions for use. Technical report, Cardinal Health, 1180 Rolle, Switzerland, 2006.
3. E. Clarke, D. Long, and K. McMillan. Compositional model checking. In *Proceedings of the 4th Annual Symposium on Logic in computer science*, 1989.
4. E. M. Clarke, O. Grumberg, and D. A. Peled. *Model Checking*. MIT Press, 1999.
5. J. Coutaz. PAC, an object oriented model for dialog design. *INTERACT'87: Proceedings of the 2nd IFIP Conference on Human-Computer Interaction*, 1987.
6. A. Dix, J. Finlay, G. D. Abowd, and R. Beale. *Human-Computer Interaction*. Pearson, 3rd edition, 2004.
7. A. Gimblett and H. Thimbleby. User interface model discovery: towards a generic approach. In *EICS '10: Proceedings of the 2nd ACM SIGCHI symposium on Engineering interactive computing systems*, 2010.
8. D. Harel. Statecharts: a visual formalism for complex systems. *Science of Computer Programming*, 8(3), 1987.
9. D. Harel and A. Naamad. The statemate semantics of statecharts. *ACM Trans. Softw. Eng. Methodol.*, 5, 1996.
10. F. Jahanian and A. Mok. Modechart: A specification language for real-time systems. *IEEE Transactions on Software Engineering*, 20, 1994.
11. J. Raskin. *The Humane Interface*. Addison Wesley, 2000.
12. B. Shneiderman and C. Plaisant. *Designing the User Interface: Strategies for Effective Human-Computer Interaction*. Pearson, 5th edition, 2009.

Formalizing Model Consistency Based on the Abstract Syntax

Frank Trollmann, Marco Blumendorf, Veit Schwartze and Sahin Albayrak
DAI-Labor
Technische Universität Berlin
Ernst-Reuter-Platz 7
10587 Berlin, Germany
{frank.trollmann, marco.blumendorf, veit.schwartze, sahin.albayrak}@dai-labor.de

ABSTRACT
In this paper we define a notion to describe consistency within and between models, which has been identified as important issue when using model-based tools. We introduce the abstract syntax of models as attributed typed graphs and define a formalism of consistency based on this formal description. The application of the formalism is illustrated by an example.

Author Keywords
Model Driven Engineering, Abstract Syntax, Consistency

ACM Classification Keywords
D.2.4 Software/Program Verification: Formal methods

General Terms: Theory

INTRODUCTION
With the increasing utilization of models to address design as well as runtime issues and the quickly growing number of new domain specific modeling languages, model consistency becomes an important issue. Tools and runtime systems read, process, execute and change models and need to take care of consistency issues that can even span multiple related models noted in different languages. This raises an urgent need for a general understanding of model consistency and new ways to ensure this consistency throughout tool chains and within runtime systems.

In this paper, we introduce a formal understanding of consistency. This notion of consistency is based on the abstract syntax of models and the distinction between abstract and concrete syntax as detailed in the next two sections. Afterwards a definition of a way to describe this abstract syntax is presented and it is shown how this description can be used to define internal consistency as well as consistency between models. Thereafter, the formalism is illustrated in an example and the final section concludes the paper and hints to future work.

PROBLEM STATEMENT
With increasing popularity of model based and model driven approaches more and more tools for handling models emerged. In order to be handled correctly by these tools models need to be consistent. We distinguish two kinds of model consistency. Intra-model consistency is the consistency of a model in itself and means that a model is an element of the correct modeling language. Inter-model consistency is the consistency of several models with respect to each other. This kind of consistency requires the information contained in these models to not contradict each other.

One example of an environment that depends on model consistency is a runtime modeling framework. In such a framework a software application results from the interpretation of a set of models. In order to interpret them the framework has to rely on the conformance of each model to its modeling language. If a model is not consistent with respect to its modeling language (intra-model consistency) it cannot be interpreted. An inconsistency between several models (inter-model consistency) can lead to unexpected behavior.

However, due to the variety of models and the heterogeneity of domain-specific modeling languages the definition of consistency is a challenging task. In order to express consistency between models of different modeling languages a common formalism is required. This formalism needs to be able to express intra- and inter-model consistency and has to cope with the heterogeneity of models.

We address these problems by the introduction of the abstract syntax of a modeling language. If the abstract syntax of several models is expressed in the same formalism it can be used to define inter-model consistency between these models. The following section introduces the notion of abstract and concrete syntax of a modeling language and interrelates both. Afterwards a common notion for an abstract syntax and a way of defining model consistency is described.

ABSTRACT AND CONCRETE SYNTAX
In programming languages there is a distinction between abstract and concrete syntax. The concrete syntax of a programming language is the version the programmer works on. The abstract syntax is a representation of the program that can be automatically processed. During the compile process the concrete syntax is parsed into the abstract syntax. Optimization and analysis is done on the abstract syntax.

EICS'11, June 13–16, 2011, Pisa, Italy.

This concept can be borrowed by modeling languages. The concrete syntax of a model is the version that is handled by its designer. In order to be processed by a modeling tool the concrete syntax is parsed into the abstract syntax. The abstract and concrete syntax can be regarded as two models that represent the same aspects of a common system under study.

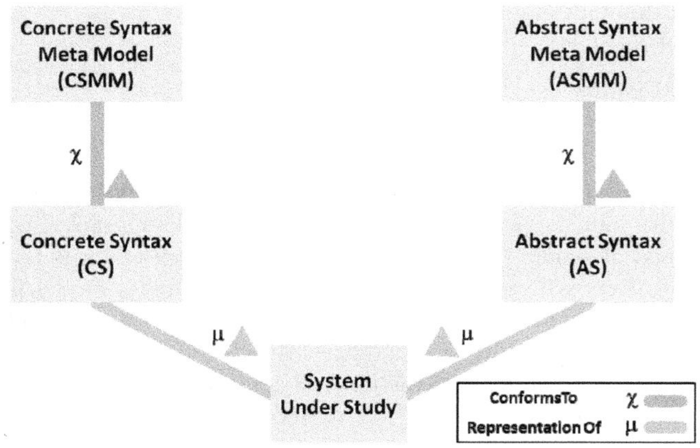

Figure 1. Concrete and abstract syntax and the transformation between them.

This situation is depicted in Figure 1. In this figure we use the terminology introduced by Favre [1]. According to this terminology a metamodel describes a modeling language which consists of a set of models. In Figure 1 both the abstract and concrete syntax are models representing the same system under study but conforming to different metamodels.

If the abstract syntax of two models is expressed in the same formalism it is easier to describe consistency between them. The following section introduces a common basis for the definition of the abstract syntax and a definition of intra- and inter-model consistency on this basis.

DESCRIBING ABSTRACT SYNTAX AS ATTRIBUTED TYPED GRAPHS

In programming languages the abstract syntax of a program is often represented by an abstract syntax tree, containing the functions and expressions of the program.

In fact, most models can be represented by a graph-based structure. For instance many UML tools offer an option to export the models in an XMI format, which can be seen as a tree of XML nodes and thus a graph-like structure. Hermann et. al. use a form of attributed typed graphs to represent the abstract syntax of class and sequence diagrams [2]. Limbourg et. al. use directed attributed typed and labeled graphs as a general representation of models and foundation for their transformational development [3].

A graph consists of nodes and edges between these nodes. In attributed graphs the nodes and edges can be annotated with attributes. An attributed graph can be typed with respect to a type graph. The type graph is an attributed graph that determines possible node and edge types. Typing is represented by a mapping between the typed graph and its type graph. An attributed graph with a morphism to a type graph is called an attributed typed graph (AT-Graph). A formal definition of AT-Graphs is given in [4].

We choose AT-Graphs as the formal basis of the abstract syntax. The language of this abstract syntax consists of a set of AT-Graphs. Its metamodel, the abstract syntax metamodel (ASMM), describes this set. We define that for a given modeling language all models are typed over the same type graph. This means the abstract syntaxes of models for one modeling language use the same set of node and edge types.

Accordingly, the ASMM of a modeling language contains the common type graph. In some cases not all graphs typed over this type graph are considered valid models. Most modeling languages have additional structural requirements. For instance a Finite State Machine needs an initial state to be valid. In order to express these requirements the ASMM contains an additional set of graph constraints as defined by Ehrig et. al. [5]. An atomic graph constraint consists of a graph morphism $a : P \rightarrow C$. A graph G fulfills this constraint if every occurrence of P inside of this graph also contains the structures defined in C. A graph constraint is a boolean formula over atomic constraints. A formal version of the ASMM is given in Definition 1.

Definition 1. An abstract syntax metamodel $asmm = (TG, cons)$ consists of an attributed type graph TG and a set of attributed typed graph constraints $cons$ that are typed over TG.

The ASMM describes the abstract syntax modeling language as the set of all attributed typed graphs that are typed over the type graph TG and fulfill the graph constraints $cons$.

Intra-model consistency is defined as the conformance of a model to this metamodel. If the model is correctly typed and fulfills the constraints it is conform to the metamodel and is called intra-model consistent. This is formally defined in Definition 2.

Definition 2. A model m in abstract syntax is intra-model consistent with respect to its metamodel $asmm = (TG, cons)$ if m is typed over TG and fulfills all constraints in $cons$.

Using this definition and the abstract syntax metamodel a modeling framework or tool is able to judge whether a model is consistent by checking whether the abstract syntax of the model is correctly typed and fulfills all constraints. Both can be checked automatically.

In order to define inter-model consistency we need a way to interrelate the abstract syntaxes of two or more models. For this purpose we define a composite model as a model that is composed of a set of other models. This is illustrated in Figure 2.

This figure shows a composite model in abstract syntax for two models A and B. The composite model contains both models. In compliance with our definition the abstract syntax of a composite model consists of an attributed typed graph. The containment relationship on the level of the abstract syntax denotes that the composite model contains the abstract syntaxes of the contained models as subgraphs. A formal definition of this relation can be found in Definition 3.

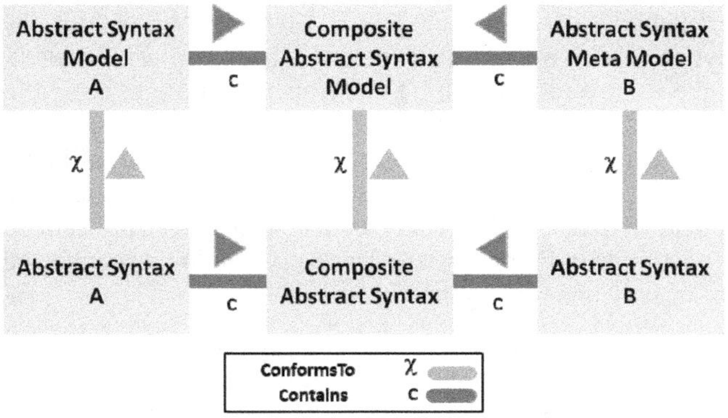

Figure 2. A composite model of two models A and B.

Definition 3. A model m in abstract syntax is a composite abstract syntax of $n \in \mathbb{N}$ models in abstract syntax $m_i, i \in \{1, \dots, n\}$ if $\bigcup_{i=1,\dots,n} m_i \subseteq m$

The composite abstract syntax can also contain additional nodes and edges. These elements can be used to interrelate elements in the contained models and describe their relation.

Since the composite abstract syntax contains the union of the contained abstract syntaxes its type graph also has to contain a union of their type graphs. The relation between the composite ASMM and the ASMMs of the contained models is a containment relationship. Since the ASMM of the composite model is defined in compliance with Definition 1 this relation is defined as a component-wise containment of the type graphs and constraints. A formal definition of the composite abstract syntax metamodel is given in Definition 4.

Definition 4. An abstract syntax metamodel $asmm = (TG, cons)$ is a composite abstract syntax metamodel of $n \in \mathbb{N}$ abstract syntax metamodels $asmm_i = (TG_i, cons_i), i \in \{1, \dots, n\}$ if $\bigcup_{i=1,\dots,n} TG_i \subseteq TG$ and $\bigcup_{i=1,\dots,n} cons_i \subseteq cons$.

The type graph and constraints in the composite ASMM can contain additional elements. The type graph can contain additional node and edge types. They can be used to interrelate elements in the contained type graphs. The set of constraints can contain additional constraints. These constraints can be used to specify consistency requirements between the contained models that cannot be expressed on the layer of the individual models.

Since the composite abstract syntax metamodel still conforms to Definition 1 it is possible to define inter-model consistency of a set of models as intra-model consistency in their composite model. The definition can be found in Definition 5.

Definition 5. A set of n models $m_i, i \in \{1, \dots, n\}$ in abstract syntax that are contained in a composite abstract syntax m are inter-model consistent if m is intra-model consistent.

Since inter-model consistency is a special case of intra-model consistency it can be validated with the same mechanisms.

The next section shows how the abstract syntax of two models can be described as AT-Graphs and how intra- and inter-model consistency can be expressed.

EXAMPLE

This section introduces an example for the described formalisms. For this example we assume a simplified runtime interpreter which interprets two models. The interpretation results in a software application.

The two interpreted models are a user interface model (UI model) and a state model. The UI-Model describes all windows that belong to this application as well as their layout and user interface elements. The state model is described as a finite state machine (FSM) and defines the states the application can be in. Each window in the user interface model is associated to one state. Whenever the state becomes active this window is shown. The transitions between states are associated to user interface elements. The transition fires whenever the user performs a certain action on the corresponding user interface element.

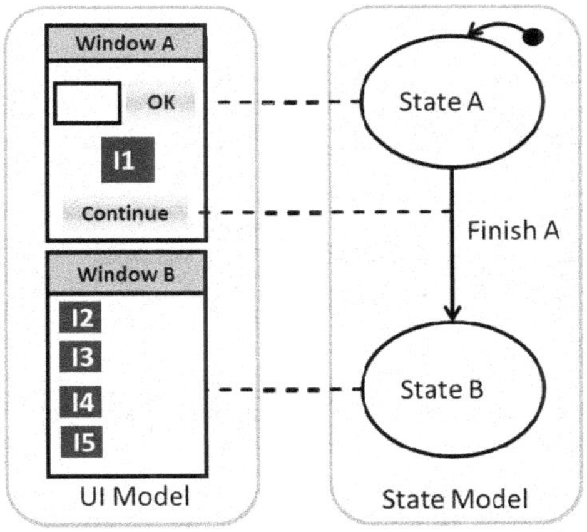

Figure 3. Both models and their connection in concrete syntax.

Figure 3 shows an example of both models in concrete syntax. The application in this example contains two states A and B. Accordingly the state model contains two states and a transition between them and the UI model contains two windows, one for each state.

The interrelations between both models are indicated by dashed lines. Each window is related to its respective state. The button labeled "continue" is connected to the transition from *State A* to *State B*. Whenever this button is clicked the transition is fired. Accordingly *Window A* is closed and *Window B* is opened when *State B* is reached.

In order for the framework to work correctly several consistency requirements have to be fulfilled. On one hand the used UI model and state model have to conform to the correct metamodel. For instance an unknown user interface element in the UI model cannot be interpreted by the framework. According to this, both models have to be intra-model consistent.

In addition, the following inter-model consistency requirements have to be fulfilled:

1. Each state has to be associated to a window. A state without a window can cause problems. If such a state is reached the interpreter cannot show any user interface to the user and consequently there are no user interface elements that could trigger a state change. Thus the application is in a dead-lock.
2. The user interface element associated to a transition has to be contained in the window that is associated to the origin state of this transition. If this is not the case the UI element is not shown when the transition is enabled. This means the transition can never fire.

The remainder of this chapter introduces the abstract syntax of both models and their composite model and shows how these consistency requirements are modeled.

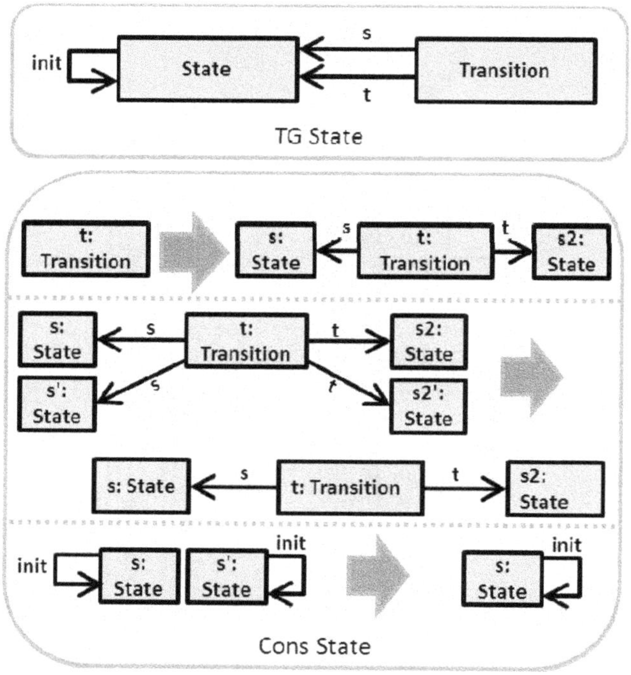

Figure 4. The abstract syntax metamodel of the state model.

Figure 4 shows the abstract syntax metamodel of the state model. It consists of the type graph *TG State* and a set of constraints *Cons State*. For the purpose of this paper we focus on a limited version of the type graph of a FSM. This type graph contains the node types: *State* and *Transition* and edges denoting which states are the source (*s*) and target (*t*) of a transition. In addition an edge *init* marks the initial state. Figure 4 also shows three of the constraints of this model. These first two constraints specify a transition to contain exactly one source and target. The first constraint can be read as: "if a transition exists it is always connected to at least one source and one target state". The second constraint specifies that a transition cannot have more than one source and target state. The third constraint specifies that only one initial state can exist.

Figure 5 shows an excerpt from the abstract syntax metamodel of the UI model. The type graph contains the types *Window* and *UI Element*. The type *UI Element* inherits several specific UI elements which are indicated in this figure. Amongst others, there are layout containers, labels and buttons. The window is connected to all of its UI elements via the edge type *ui elem*. The edge type *root* identifies the root layout of the window. The sample constraints in Figure 5 state that every window is connected to exactly one root element.

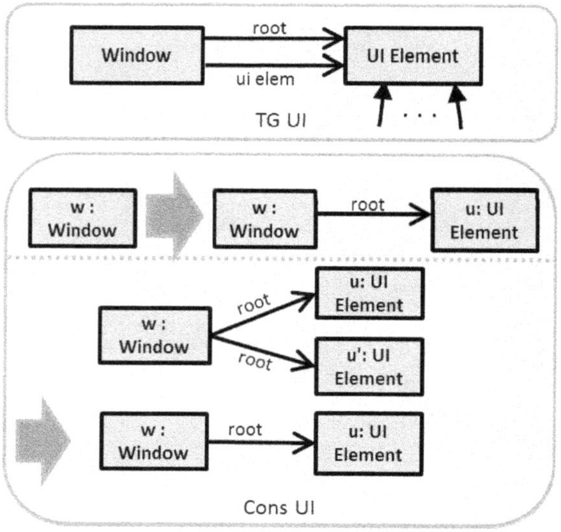

Figure 5. The abstract syntax metamodel of the UI model.

The inter-model consistency requirements are reflected in the composite model. Figure 6 shows the abstract syntax metamodel of the composite model. The type graph of this metamodel contains the type graph of the state model (upper part) and the type graph of the UI model (lower part). In addition it contains the type *State 2 Window* which establishes the relation between the state and its window and the type *Transition 2 UI* which denotes which UI element causes the transition to fire.

The constraints in the composite ASMM are responsible for ensuring that inter-model consistency requirements 1 and 2 hold. The first constraint can be read as "if there is a *State*, it has to be connected to a *Window* via a *State 2 Window* element". This ensures requirement 1. The second constraint can be read as "if a *UI Element* is a trigger for a transition, this *UI Element* has to be contained in the *Window* that is associated to the source of this *Transition*". This ensures requirement 2.

The abstract syntax of our example in Figure 3 is an attributed typed graph over the type graph in Figure 6 that has to fulfill all constraints. This graph is depicted in Figure 7. It contains the abstract syntax of the state and UI model. The abstract syntax of the state model is depicted in the upper part of the composite abstract syntax. It consists of nodes for both states and the transition between them. The abstract syntax of the window model is depicted on the lower part of this figure. It contains two windows. The content of both windows is indicated by three dots. The composite abstract syntax also contains the additional elements that establish the relation between both models. Each state is connected to a window by a *State 2 Window* node. The transition is connected to the commit button in *Window* A by a *Transition 2 UI* node.

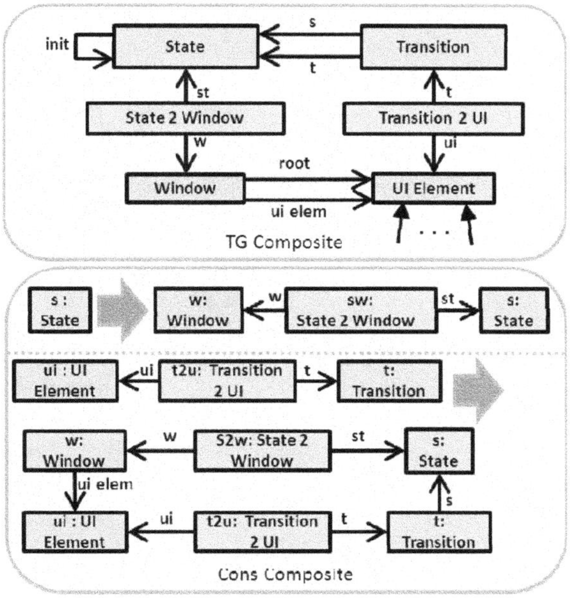

Figure 6. The abstract syntax metamodel of the composite model.

The model also fulfills the constraints, introduced in this section. The FSM contains one initial state and a transition that is connected to exactly one source and target state. Thus it fulfills the constraints from the ASMM of the state model. The abstract syntax of the state model is thus intra-model consistent with respect to its metamodel. Each window is also connected to exactly one root element (even if this is only indicated in the figure). Thus the UI model is intra-model consistent with respect to its ASMM

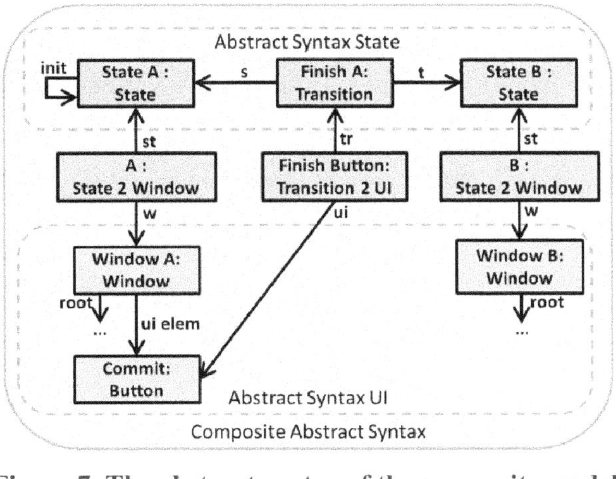

Figure 7. The abstract syntax of the composite model.

Both inter-model consistency requirements are also fulfilled. Each state is connected to a window and the commit button that triggers the transition *Finish A* is contained in *Window A* which is connected to the source state of this transition. Thus the model in Figure 7 is intra-model consistent with respect to the ASMM in Figure 6. Thus the contained state and UI model are inter-model consistent.

RELATED WORK

With the wide utilization of UML with its different models and the advent of domain specific languages for model engineering, intra- and inter-model consistency have been widely discussed.

Triple Graph Grammars, as introduced by Schürr [6], are a widely researched formal way for model to model transformation. For instance, Brandt et al. describe the abstract syntax of models as AT-Graphs [7]. In this approach the abstract syntaxes are interrelated by using a Triple Graph Grammar that describes how they can be constructed jointly. This approach is appealing for the joint construction of models and enables to generate one interrelated model from the other. In order to check for consistency both models have to be parsed with the grammar. The theory of Triple Graph Grammars still has to be extended to interrelate more than two graphs.

Usman et al. conveyed a Survey regarding different techniques for consistency checking between UML models [8]. The approaches are classified regarding the intermediate representation the consistency is checked on. The presented approaches are only able to interrelate special kinds of UML models and have not yet been applied as a general way to represent model consistency. The survey paper also introduces several consistency types and analysis parameters which can be a good starting point for future work.

A classification of the types of relationships between models participating in a software development process and possible inconsistencies is presented in [9]. Based on this classification, a set of requirements for generic inconsistency detection and a reconciliation mechanism is derived, which is suitable to serve as basis for future work on our formalism.

The idea of consistency checking via merges was first explored by Easterbrook and Chechik and applied in the framework for merging and reasoning about multiple, inconsistent state machine models [10]. Based on this approach, [11] aims at checking system consistency with respect to defined requirements. As requirements are addressed by different models, inconsistencies might be missed and it is difficult to take the heterogeneous (i.e. expressed in different languages) specifications into account. Thus it is proposed to translate heterogeneous requirements into model fragments which are instances of a common metamodel and to use model composition to merge these fragments into one unique model. Recent work of Sabetzadeh et al. [12] discusses model consistency checking through model merging. They present a technique for global consistency checking, supported by the TReMer+ tool [13] and identify patterns for consistency rules in conceptual modeling. Similar to our approach models are introduced as graphs and inter-model consistency is ensured through model merging. Lacking an abstract or, as they call it, logical model the approach cannot handle heterogeneous models yet. Additionally, it also focuses on conceptual and not so much formal models.

Finally, [14] proposes an alternative approach to model consistency by representing models by sequences of elementary construction operations. This allows the expression of structural and methodological consistency rules as logical constraints on these sequences. While aiming at being meta-model independent, the approach requires the definition of the constructional operations for each language.

CONCLUSION

This paper introduces a formalism for describing the abstract syntax of models as attributed typed graphs. Based on this formalism it is possible to describe consistency within models and between models in a homogenous way. This enables automatic validation of both types of consistency. Based on the introduced formalisms modeling tools and frameworks are able to check the contained models for consistency in order to spot possible problems early.

This paper also indicates the application of this notion of consistency in a small example. In the future, we plan to practically apply the approach to ensure consistency for adaptive user interfaces, generated at runtime on basis of a set of models.

Furthermore, we intend to work on extensions of this theory. There are additional formalisms like inheritance edges in type graphs and nested graph constraints that can considerably add to the expression power of the introduced formalism. Triple Graphs are also an appealing starting point for an alternative to our theory that will be explored in the near future. Using this technique it is possible to interrelate models without having to merge them. In this area we plan to explore the use of the Triple Graph formalism but slightly defer from the traditional theory of Triple Graph Grammars.

REFERENCES

1. Favre, J. M., Towards a basic theory to model model driven engineering, in *In Workshop on Software Model Engineering, WISME 2004, joint event with UML2004*(2004)
2. Hermann, F., Ehrig, H. and Taentzer, G. A typed attributed graph grammar with inheritance for the abstract syntax of uml class and sequence diagrams, in *Electron. Notes Theor. Comput. Sci. 211* (Amsterdam, April 2008), Elsevier Science Publishers B. V., 261-269.
3. Limbourg, Q., Vanderdonckt, J, Transformational Development of User Interfaces with Graph Transformations, in *CADUI* (2005), Kluwer, 104-118
4. Ehrig, H, Prange, U, Taentzer, G., Fundamental Theory for Typed Attributed Graph Transformation, in *ICGT* (Berlin, 2004), Springer berlin / Heidelberg, 161-177
5. Ehrig, H., Ehrig, K., Habel, A., Pennemann, K., Theory of Constraints and Application Conditions: From Graphs to High-Level Structures, in *Fundam. Inf. 74* (Amsterdam, 2006), IOS Press 135-166
6. Schürr, A., Specification of Graph Translators with Triple Graph Grammars, in *Proceedings of the 20th International Workshop on Graph-Theoretic Concepts in Computer Science* (London, 1995), Springer-Verlag, 151-163
7. Brandt, C., Hermann, F., How Far Can Enterprise Modeling for Banking Be Supported by Graph Transformation?, in *Graph Transformations* (Berlin, 2010), Springer Berlin / Heidelberg, 3-26
8. Usman, M., Nadeem, A., Kim, T., Cho, E., A Survey of Consistency Checking Techniques for UML Models, *in Advanced Software Engineering and Its Applications* (Los Alamitos, 2008), IEEE Computer Society, 57-62
9. Easterbrook, S., Chechik, M., A Framework for Multi-Valued Reasoning over Inconsistent Viewpoints, in *In Proceedings of International Conference on Software Engineering* (2001), IEEE Computer Society Press, 411-420
10. Perrouin, G., Brottler, E., Baudry, B., Le Traon, Y., Composing Models for Detecting Inconsistencies: A Requirements Engineering Perspective, in *Proceedings of the International Working Conference on Requirements Engineering: Foundation for Software Quality (REFSQ2009)* (Amsterdam, 2009), Springer Lecture Notes in Computer Science (LNCS)
11. Sabetzadeh, M., Nejati, S., Liaskos, S., Easterbrook, S., Chechik, M., Consistency Checking of Conceptual Models via Model Merging, in *15th IEEE International Requirements Engineering Conference (RE 2007)* (2007), IEEE, 221-230
12. Sabetzadeh, M., Nejati, S., Easterbrook, S., Chechik, M., Global Consistency Checking of Distributed Models with TReMer, in *In 30th International Conference on Software Engineering (ICSE'08)* (2008)
13. Mao, X., Shan, L., Zhu, H., Wang, J., An adaptive casteship mechanism for developing multi-agent systems, in *Int. J. Comput. Appl. Technol.*(Geneva, 2008), Inderscience Publishers, 17-34
14. Blanc, X., Mounier, I. Mougenot, A., Mens, T., Detecting model inconsistency through operation-based model construction, in *Proceedings of the 30th international conference on Software engineering* (Leipzig, 2008), ACM, 511-520

Combining Aspect-Oriented Modeling with Property-Based Reasoning to Improve User Interface Adaptation

Arnaud Blouin
IRISA, Triskell, Rennes
arnaud.blouin@inria.fr

Brice Morin
SINTEF ICT, Oslo
brice.morin@sintef.no

Olivier Beaudoux
ESEO-GRI, Angers
olivier.beaudoux@eseo.fr

Grégory Nain
INRIA, Triskell, Rennes
gregory.nain@inria.fr

Patrick Albers
ESEO-GRI, Angers
patrick.albers@eseo.fr

Jean-Marc Jézéquel
IRISA, Triskell, Rennes
jezequel@irisa.fr

ABSTRACT
User interface adaptations can be performed at runtime to dynamically reflect any change of context. Complex user interfaces and contexts can lead to the combinatorial explosion of the number of possible adaptations. Thus, dynamic adaptations come across the issue of adapting user interfaces in a reasonable time-slot with limited resources. In this paper, we propose to combine aspect-oriented modeling with property-based reasoning to tame complex and dynamic user interfaces. At runtime and in a limited time-slot, this combination enables efficient reasoning on the current context and on the available user interface components to provide a well suited adaptation. The proposed approach has been evaluated through EnTiMid, a middleware for home automation.

Author Keywords
MDE, user interface, context, adaptation, aspect, runtime, malai

ACM Classification Keywords
H.5.2 Information Interfaces and Presentation: User Interfaces—*Theory and methods, User Interface Management Systems (UIMS)*; D.2.1 Software Engineering: Requirements/ Specifications—*Methodologies*; H.1.0 Information Systems: Models and Principles—*General*

General Terms
Design

INTRODUCTION
The number of platforms having various interaction modalities (*e.g.*, netbook and smart phone) unceasingly increases over the last decade. Besides, user's preferences, characteristics and environment have to be considered by user interfaces (UI). This triplet <platform, user, environment>, called context[1] [8], leads user interfaces to be dynamically (*i.e.* at runtime) adaptable to reflect any change of context.

UI components such as tasks and interactions, enabled for a given context but disabled for another one, cause a wide number of possible adaptations. For example, [14] describes an airport crisis management system that leads to 1,474,560 possible adaptations. Thus, an important challenge is to support UI adaptation of complex systems. This implies that dynamic adaptations must be performed in a minimal time, and respecting usability.

The contribution of this paper is to propose an approach that combines aspect-oriented modeling (AOM) with property-based reasoning to tackle the combinatorial explosion of UI adaptations. AOM approaches provide advanced mechanisms for encapsulating cross-cutting features and for composing them to form models [1]. AOM has been successfully applied for the dynamic adaptation of systems [20]. Property-based reasoning consists in tagging objects that compose the system with characterizing properties [14]. At runtime, these properties are used by a reasoner to perform the adaptation the best suited to the current context. Reasoning on a limited number of aspects combined with the use of properties avoids the combinatorial explosion issue. Although these works tackle system adaptation at runtime, they do not focus on the dynamic adaptation of UIs. Thus, we mixed these works with Malai, a modular architecture for interactive systems [4], to bring complex and dynamic user interface adaptations under control. We have applied our approach to EnTiMid, a middleware for home automation.

The paper is organized as follows. The next section introduces background research works used by our ap-

[1] In this paper, the term "context" is used instead of "context of use" for conciseness.

proach. Then, the process to create an adaptive UI using our approach is explained. Next, the adaptation process that is automatically executed at runtime is detailed. Following, our approach is evaluated through EnTiMiD, a middleware for house automation. The paper ends with the related work and the conclusion.

BACKGROUND

The work presented in this paper brings an interactive system architecture and a software engineering approach together. Thus, this section starts with the presentation of the Malai architecture. The software engineering approach applied to Malai to allow complex UI adaptations at runtime is then introduced.

The Malai Architecture

The work presented in this paper is based on Malai, an architectural model for interactive systems [4]. In Malai a UI is composed of presentations and instruments (see Figure 1). A presentation is composed of an abstract presentation and a concrete presentation. An abstract presentation is a representation of source data created by a Malan mapping (link ①). A concrete presentation is the graphical representation of the abstract presentation. It is created and updated by another Malan mapping (link ②) [5]. An interaction consumes events produced by input devices (link ③). Instruments transform input interactions into output actions (link ④). An action is executed on the abstract presentation (link ⑤); source data and the concrete presentation are then updated throughout a Malan mapping (link ⑥).

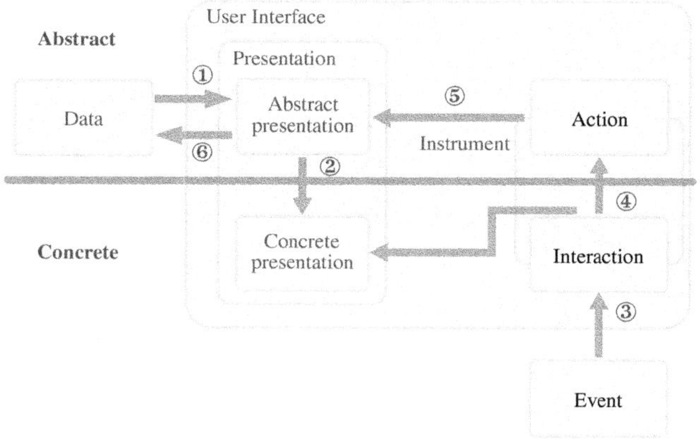

Figure 1. Organization of the architectural model Malai

Malai aims at improving: 1) the modularity by considering presentations, instruments, interactions, and actions, as reusable first-class objects; 2) the usability by being able to specify feedback provided to users within instruments, to abort interactions, and to undo/redo actions. Malai is well-suited for UI adaptation because of its modularity: depending on the context, interactions, instruments, and presentations, can be easily composed to form an adapted UI. However, Malai does not provide any runtime adaptation process. The next section introduces the research work on dynamic adaptive system that has been applied to Malai for this purpose.

Dynamically Adaptive Systems

The DiVA consortium proposes an adaptation metamodel to describe and drive the adaptation logic of Dynamically Adaptive Systems (DAS) [14]. The core idea is to design DAS by focusing on the commonalities and variabilities of the system instead of analyzing on all the possible configurations of the system. The features of the system are refined into independent fragments called *aspect models*. On each context change, the aspect models well adapted to the new context are selected and woven together to form a new model of the system. This model is finally compared to the current model of the system and a safe migration is computed to adapt the running system [20].

The selection of the features adapted to the current context is performed by a reasoning mechanism based on multi-objective optimization using *QoS Properties*. QoS properties correspond to objectives that the reasoner must optimize. For example, the properties of the system described in [14] are security, CPU consumption, cost, performances, and disturbance. The importance of each property is balanced depending on the context. For instance, if the system is running on battery, minimizing CPU consumption will be more important than maximizing performances. The developer can specify the impact of the system's features on each property. For example, the video surveillance feature highly maximizes security but does not minimize CPU consuming. The reasoner analyzes these impacts to select features the best suited to the current context.

If DiVA proposes an approach that tames dynamic adaptations of complex systems, it lacks at considering UI adaptations. The following sections describe the combined use of Malai and DiVA to bring adaptations of complex interactive systems under control.

CONCEPTION PROCESS

This section describes the different steps that developers have to perform during the conception of adaptable UIs. The first step consists in defining the *context* and the *action* models. Then a *mapping* between these two models can be defined to specify which context elements disable actions. The last step consists in defining the *presentations* and the *instruments* that can be selected at runtime to compose the UI.

All these models are defined using Kermeta. Kermeta is a model-oriented language that allows developers to define both the structure and the behavior of models [21]. Kermeta is thus dedicated to the definition of executable models.

Context Definition

A context model is composed of the three class models *User*, *Platform*, and *Environment* that describe each context component. Developers can thus define their own context triples without being limited to a specific context metamodel.

Each class of a class model can be tagged with QoS properties. These properties bring information about objectives that demand top, medium, or low priority during UIs adaptation. For instance, Listing 1 defines an excerpt of the user class model for a home automation system. Properties are defined as annotations on the targeted class. This class model specifies that a user can be an elderly person (line 3) or a nurse (line 6). Class *ElderlyPerson* is tagged with two properties. Property *readability* (line 1) concerns the simplicity of reading of UIs. Its value *high* states that the readability of UIs must be strongly considered during adaptations to elderly people. For instance, large buttons would be more convenient for elderly people than small ones. Property *simplicity* (line 2) specifies the simplicity of the UI. Since elderly people usually prefer simple interaction, this property is set to *high* on class *ElderlyPerson*.

```
1 @readability "high"
2 @simplicity "high"
3 class ElderlyPerson inherits User {
4 }
5
6 class Nurse inherits User {
7 }
```

Listing 1. Context excerpt tagged with QoS properties

By default properties are set to "low". For example with Listing 1, property *readability* is defined on class *ElderlyPerson* but not on class *Nurse*. It means that by default *Nurse* has property *readability* set to "low".

All the properties of the current context should be maximized. But adapting UIs is a multiobjective problem where all objectives (*i.e.* QoS properties) cannot be maximized together; a compromise must be found. For example, a developer may prefer productivity to the aesthetic quality of UIs even if maximizing both would be better. Values associated with properties aim at balancing these objectives.

Our approach does not provide predefined properties. Developers add their own properties on the UI components and the context. The unique constraint for the developers is to reuse in the context model properties defined in UI components and *vice versa*. Indeed, properties of the current context are gathered at runtime to then select the most respectfully UI components towards these properties. The efficiency of the reasoner thus depends on the appropriate definition of properties by the developers.

Actions Definition

Actions are objects created by instruments. Actions modify the source data or parameters of instruments. The main difference between actions and tasks, such as CTT tasks [22], is that the Malai's action metamodel defines a life cycle composed of methods *do*, *canDo*, *undo*, and *redo*. These methods, that an action model must implement, bring executability to actions. Method *canDo* checks if the action can be executed. Methods *do*, *undo*, and *redo* respectively executes, cancels, and re-executes the action. An action is also associated to a class which defines the attributes of the action and relations with other actions.

```
1  abstract class NurseAction inherits Action { }
2
3  class AddNurseVisit inherits NurseAction,Undoable{
4   reference calendar : Calendar
5   attribute date     : Date
6   attribute title    : String
7   attribute event    : Event
8
9   method canDo() : Boolean is do
10   result := calendar.canAddEvent(date)
11  end
12  method do() : Void is do
13   event := calendar.addEvent(title, date)
14  end
15  method undo() : Void is do
16   calendar.removeEvent(title, date)
17  end
18  method redo() : Void is do
19   calendar.addEvent(event)
20  end
21 }
22
23 class CallEmergencyService inherits NurseAction{
24   // ...
25 }
```

Listing 2. Excerpt of nurse actions

Listings 2 defines an excerpt of the home automation action model in Kermeta. Abstract action *NurseAction* (line 1) defines the common part of actions that nurses can perform. Action *AddNurseVisit* (line 3) is a nurse action that adds an event into the nurse calendar (see method *do* line 12). Method *canDo* checks if the event can be added to the calendar (line 9). Methods *undo* and *redo* respectively remove and re-add the event to the calendar (lines 15 and 18). Action *CallEmergencyService* in another nurse action that calls the emergency service (line 23).

Mapping Context Model to Action Model

Actions can be disabled in certain contexts. For instance elderly people cannot perform actions specific to the nurse. Thus, action models must be constrained by context models. To do so we use Malan, a declarative mapping language [5]. Because it is used within the Malai archetecture, the Malan language has been selected. Context-to-action models consists of a set of Malan expressions. For instance, one of the constraints of the home automation system states that elderly people cannot perform nurse actions. The Malan expression for this constraint is:

```
ElderlyPerson -> !NurseAction
```

where *NurseAction* means that all actions that inherit from action *NurseAction* are concerned by the mapping.

Another constraint states that nurses can call ambulances only if the house has a phone line. The corresponding Malan expression is:

```
House[!phoneLine] -> !CallEmergencyService
```

where the expression between brackets (*i.e.*, *!phoneLine*) is a predicate that uses attributes and relations of the corresponding class of the context (*i.e. House* in the example) to refine the constraint.

By default all the actions are enabled. Only actions targeted by context-to-action mappings can be disabled: on each context change, mappings are re-evaluated to enable or disable their target action.

Presentation Definition

Developers can define several presentations for the same UI: several presentations can compose at runtime the same UI to provide users with different viewpoints on the manipulated data; defining several presentations allows to select at runtime the presentations the best suited to the current context. For instance, the calendar that the nurse uses to add visits can be presented through two presentations: 1) a 2D-based presentation that displays the events of the selected month or week; 2) a list-based presentation that shows the events into a list widget.

```
class Agenda {
  attribute name   : String
  attribute events : Event[0..*]
  attribute dates  : Date[0..*]
}
class Event {
  attribute name        : String
  attribute description : String
  attribute place       : String
  reference date        : Date
  attribute start       : TimeSlot
  attribute end         : TimeSlot
}
//...
```

Listing 3. Excerpt of the 2D-based abstract presentation

```
@aestheticQuality "high"
@space "low"
class AgendaUI {
  attribute title        : String
  attribute linesUI      : LineHourUI[0..*]
  attribute handlerStart : Handler
  attribute handlerEnd   : Handler
  attribute eventsUI     : EventUI[0..*]
  attribute datesUI      : DateUI[0..*]
}
class EventUI {
  attribute x      : Real
  attribute y      : Real
  attribute width  : Real
  attribute height : Real
}
//...
```

Listing 4. Excerpt of the 2D-based concrete presentation and its QoS properties

Listings 3 and 4 describe parts of the 2D-based presentation of the nurse agenda. Its abstract presentation defines the agenda model (see Listing 3). An *Agenda* has a name, contains *Event* and *Date* instances. An event has a name, a place, a description, a starting and an ending *Timeslot* instances. A time-slot specifies the hour and the minute. A date defines its day, month and year.

The concrete presentation defines the graphical representation of the nurse agenda (see Listing 4). The graphical representation of agendas (class *AgendaUI*) contains representations of days, events, and time-slot lines (respectively classes *DayUI*, *EventUI* and *LineHourUI*). These representations have coordinates x and y. Classes *DayUI* and *EventUI* also specify their width and height. An agenda has two handlers associated to the selected event. These handlers are used to change the time-slot of the selected event.

Similarly to context models, presentations can be tagged with QoS properties. These properties provide context reasoner with information about, for example, the easiness of use or the size of the presentation. For instance, the 2D-based and list-based presentations have characteristics well-suited for some platforms and users. Listing 4 shows the QoS properties of the 2D-based presentation defined as annotations: the 2D-based presentation optimizes the aesthetic quality (property *aestheticQuality "high"*) but not space (property *space "low"*). By contrast, the list-based presentation optimizes space to the detriment of the aesthetic quality.
While properties specified on contexts define objectives to optimize at runtime, properties on presentations declare characteristics used to select appropriated presentations depending on the current context and its objectives. For instance, if the current context states that the the aesthetic quality must be highly considered, the 2D-based presentation will be selected.

Instrument Definition

Instruments transform input interactions into output actions. Instruments are composed of links and of a class model. Each link maps an interaction to a resulting action. Instrument's class model defines attributes and relations the instrument needs. Widgets handled by instruments and that compose the UI are notably defined into the class model of instruments.

VisitTypeSelector is an instrument operating on the nurse agenda. This instrument defines the type of visit to add to the agenda. The selection of the type of visit can be performed using different widgets: several toggle buttons (one of each visit type) or a list can be used. While toggle buttons are simpler to use than a list (a single click to select a button against two clicks to select an item of a list), lists are usually smaller than a set of toggle buttons. The choice of using such or such widgets thus depends on the current context: if space is a prior objective, list should be privileged; otherwise, toggle buttons should be selected.

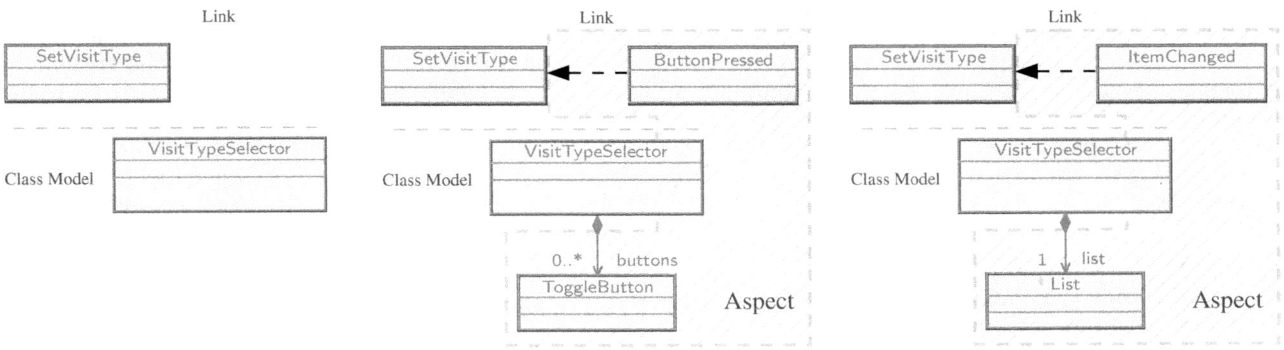

(a) Incomplete instrument (b) Completed using toggle buttons (c) Completed using a list

Figure 2. Instrument *VisitTypeSelector*

One of the contributions of our work consists of being able to choose the best suited interaction for a link at runtime: while defining instruments, developers can let interactions undefined. Interactions and widgets are automatically chosen and associated to instruments at runtime depending on the current context. For instance, Figure 2(a) describes the model of instrument *VisitTypeSelector* as defined by developers. This model is composed of an incomplete link that only specifies the produced action *SetVisitType*; the way this action is performed is let undefined. The class model of this instrument only defines a class corresponding to the instrument (class *VisitTypeSelector*). This class model will also be completed at runtime.
Figure 2(b) corresponds to the model of Figure 2(a) completed at runtime. Toggle buttons have been chosen to perform action *SetVisitType*. The interaction corresponding to the click on buttons (interaction *ButtonPressed*) is added to complete the link. A set of toggle buttons (class *ToggleButton*) is also added to the class model. This interaction and these widgets come from a predefined aspect encapsulating them. We defined a set of aspects for WIMP[2] interactions (*i.e.* based on widgets) that can automatically be used at runtime to complete instrument models.
Figure 2(c) corresponds to another completed model. This time, a list has been chosen. Interaction *ItemChanged*, dedicated to the handle of lists, completes the link. A list widget (class *List*) has been also added to the class model. This widget and its interaction also come from a predefined aspect.

Figure 3 presents an example of the instrument *TimeslotSetter* completed with interactions. This instrument changes the time-slot of events of the nurse agenda (action *SetTimeslotEvent*). Figure 3(a) shows this instrument completed with a drag-and-drop interaction (*DnD*) and handlers. Handlers surround the selected event. When users drag-and-drop one of these handlers the time-slot of the event is modified. This interaction and these handlers were encapsulated into an aspect defined by the developer.

Figure 3(b) shows another aspect defined by the developer for instrument *TimeslotSetter*: when the current platform supports bi-manual interactions, such as smartphones or tabletops, time-slot setting can be performed using such interactions instead of using a DnD and handlers.

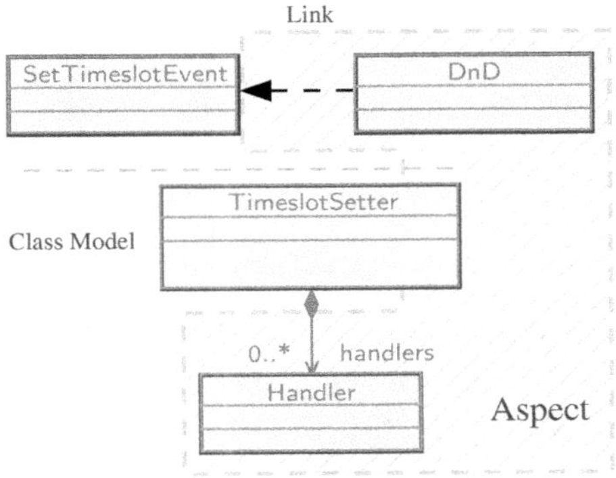

(a) Completed using a drag-and-drop interaction

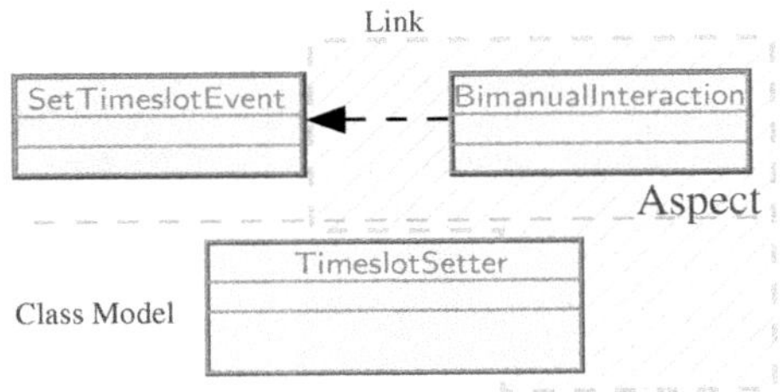

(b) Completed using a bimanual interaction

Figure 3. Instrument *TimeslotSetter*

Such flexibility on interactions and widgets is performed using QoS properties. Widgets and interactions are tagged with properties they maximize or minimize. Widgets are also tagged with properties corresponding to simple data type they are able to handle. For in-

[2]" *Windows, Icons, Menus and Pointing device*"

stance, the toggle button widget is tagged with four properties: property *simplicity high* means that toggle buttons are simple to use; property *space low* means that toggle buttons do not optimize space; properties *enum* and *boolean* mean that toggle buttons can be used to manipulate enumerations and booleans. At runtime, these properties are used to find widgets appropriate to the current context.

ADAPTATION PROCESS AT RUNTIME

This section details the adaptation process at runtime. This process begins when the current context is modified. The *context reasoner* analyzes the new context to determine actions, presentations, interactions, and widgets that will compose the adapted UI. The *weaver* associates WIMP interactions and widgets to instruments. The *UI composer* adapts the UI to reflect the modifications.

Reasoning on Context

The context reasoner is dynamically notified about modifications of the context. On each change, the reasoner follows these different steps to adapt actions, presentations, instruments, interactions, and widgets, to the new context:

```
1 foreach Context change do
2   Re-evaluate mappings to enable/disable
    actions
3   Disable instrument's links that use disabled
    actions
4   Enable instruments's links that use enabled
    actions
5   Disable instrument's links which interaction
    cannot be performed anymore
6   Disable instruments with no more link enabled
7   Select presentations by reasoning on
    properties
8   Select interactions/widgets for instruments by
    reasoning on properties
9 end
```

Algorithm 1. Context reasoner process

The process of enabling and disabling actions (line 2 of Algorithm 1) is performed thanks to the context-to-action mapping: if the change of context concerns a mapping, this last is re-evaluated. For instance with the home automation example, when the user switches from the nurse to the elderly person, mappings described in the previous section are re-evaluated. Actions that inherit from `NurseAction` are then disabled.

Once actions are updated, instruments are checked: instrument's links that use the disabled, respectively enabled, actions are also disabled, respectively enabled (lines 3 and 4). Links using interactions that cannot be performed anymore are also disabled (line 5). For example, vocal-based interactions can only work on platforms providing a microphone. Instruments with no more link enabled are disabled (line 6).

Presentations that will compose the UI can now be selected (line 7). This process selects presentations by aligning their properties with those of the current context. In the same way, WIMP interactions and widgets are selected for instruments (line 8) using properties. These selections can be performed by different kind of optimization algorithms such as genetic algorithms or Tabu search. These algorithms are themselves components of the system. That allows to change the algorithm at runtime when needed.

We perform this reasoning on properties using the *genetic algorithm* NSGA-II [12]. Genetic algorithms are heuristics that simulate the process of evolution. They are used to find solutions to optimization problems. Genetic algorithms represent a solution of a problem as a chromosome composed of a set of genes. Each gene corresponds to an object of the problem. A gene is a boolean that states if its corresponding object is selected. For example with our UI adaptation problem, each gene corresponds to a variable part of the UI (the nurse actions, the toggle button aspect, the list aspect, the different presentations, *etc.*). The principle of genetic algorithms is to randomly apply genetic operations (*e.g.* mutations) on a set of chromosomes. The best chromosomes are then selected to perform another genetic operations, and so on. The selection of chromosomes is performed using fitness functions that maximize or minimize objectives. In our case, objectives are properties defined by the developer. For instance readability is an objective to maximize. For each chromosome its readability is computed using the readability value of its selected gene:

$$f_{readability}(c) = \sum_{i=1}^{n} prop_{readability}(c_i)x_i$$

Where $f_{readability}(c)$ is the fitness function computing the readability of the chromosome c, c_i is the gene at the position i in the chromosome c, $prop_{readability}(c_i)$ the value of the property *readability* of the gene c_i, and x_i the boolean value that defines if the gene c_i is selected. For example :

$$f_{readability}(001100111001011) = 23$$

The fitness functions are automatically defined at design time from the properties used by the interactive system.

Chromosomes that optimize the result of fitness functions are selected. Constraints can be added to genetic algorithm problems. In our case a constraint can state that the gene corresponding to the calling emergency service action can be selected only if there is a line phone in the house.

When genetic algorithms are stopped, they provide a set of solutions that tend to be the best ones.

Weaving Aspects to Complete Models

Once interactions and widgets are selected, they must be associated with their instruments. To do so, we reuse the process proposed in the DiVA project to weave aspects with models. An aspect must specify where its content (in our case the interaction and possible widgets and components) must be inserted: this is the role of the *pointcut*. In our case pointcuts target instruments and more precisely an action and the main class of the instrument. An aspect must also define its *composition protocol* that describes how to integrate the content of the aspect into the pointcut.

Composing and Updating the User Interface

The goal of the UI composer is two-fold: 1) It composes the selected presentations and widgets at startup. 2) Once composed, the UI composer updates the UI on context changes if necessary. Because modifications of the UI must be smooth enough not to confuse the users, the UI must not be recomposed from scratch using 1). The existing UI must be updated to minimize graphical changes and to keep usability.

EVALUATION

Our proposal is based on two hypotheses: 1) it tames the combinatorial explosion of complex interactive systems adaptations; 2) adaptations performed using our proposal are well adapted to the current context. We evaluated these two hypotheses by applying our proposal to EnTiMid, a middleware for home automation. Each component of the UI of EnTiMid is developed with the Kermeta implementation of Malai. At the end of the conception time, executable models are compiled as OSGi components [25] to run on the top of DiVA. The use of OSGi permits instruments, actions, and presentations to be easily enabled and disabled at runtime.

The experiments described in this section have been performed on Linux using a laptop with a Core2Duo at 3.06GHz and 4Gb of RAM. Each result presented below is the average result of 1000 executions.

EnTiMid: a Middleware for Home Automation

EnTiMid is a middleware for home automation. It notably addresses two issues of the home automation domain, by providing a sufficient level of abstraction.
The first issue is about interoperability of devices. Built by many manufacturers, devices are often not compatible with one another because of their communication protocol. EnTiMid offers a mean to abstract from these technical problems and consider only the product's functionalities.
The second issue is about adaptation. Changes in the deployed peripherals or in the user's habits imply changes in the interactive system dealing with the home. Moreover, many people with different skills will have to interact with the interactive system, and the UI must adapt to the user. Considering models at runtime, EnTiMid permits such dynamic adaptation.

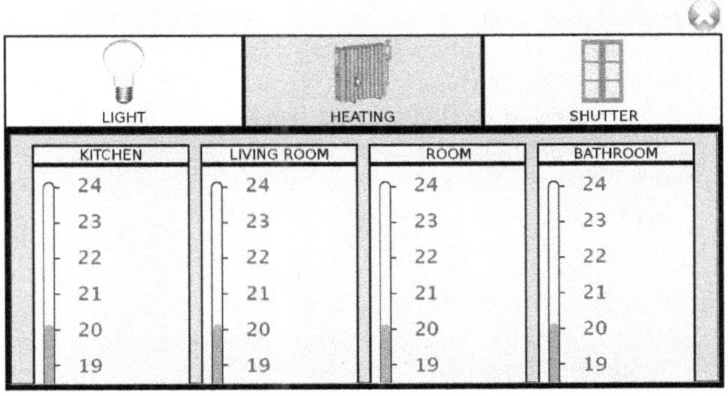

Figure 4. Part of the EnTiMid UI that controls the lights, the heaters, and the shutters of the home

Figure 4 shows a part of the EnTiMid's UI that manages home devices such as heaters, shutters, and lights. A possible adaptation is if the home does not have any shutter, related actions will be disabled and the UI adapted to not provide the shutter tab.

Hypothesis 1: Combinatorial explosion taming

We evaluate this hypothesis by measuring the adaptation time of five versions of EnTiMid, called v_1 to v_5. These versions have an increasingly level of complexity, respectively around 0.262, 0.786, 4.7, 42.4, and 3822 millions of configurations. These different levels of complexity have been obtained by removing features from version v_5. A configuration defines which components of the interactive system are enabled or disabled.

The adaptation time starts after a change of context and ends when the UI is adapted accordingly. The adaptation time is composed of: the time elapsed to select the optimal possible configuration in a limited time; the time elapsed to reconfigure the interactive system and its UI.

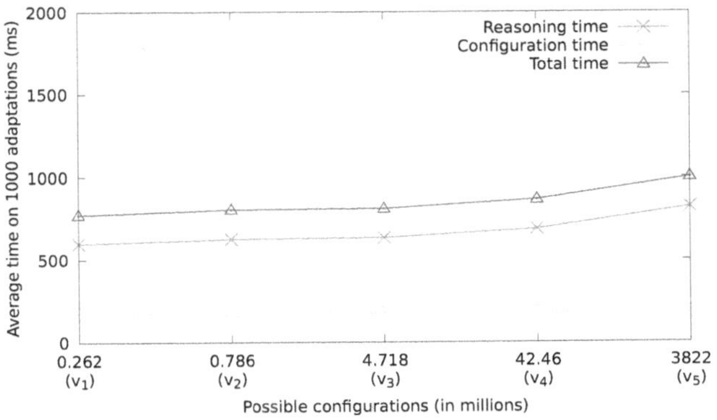

Figure 5. Average adaptation time of EnTiMid using an increasingly number of possible configurations

Figure 5 presents our results using the reasoner based on the NSGA-II genetic algorithm. It shows that the reasoning time remains linear between 600 and 800ms. That because the parameters of the reasoner (*e.g.* the number of generations, the size of the population) are automatically modified in function of the complexity of the system to run between 500 and 1000ms. Figure 5 also shows that the configuration time (*i.e.* when the system and its UI are modified) remains constant around 200ms. That brings the full adaptation time to around 1 second for the most complex version of EnTiMid.

Hypothesis 2: Adaptations quality

Finding a configuration in a limited time makes sense only if the configuration found is of good quality. Thus, we now evaluate the quality of the configurations found by the genetic reasoner in the limited time-slots described above. We compared these configurations with the optimal configurations. Optimal configurations are configurations giving the best results using the fitness functions. These optimal configurations have been computed by an algorithm exploring all the solutions. Such computations took 4.5s, 10s, 480s, and 7200s for respectively v_1, v_2, v_3, and v_4. We were not able to compute the optimal solutions of v_5 due to time and resource constraints.

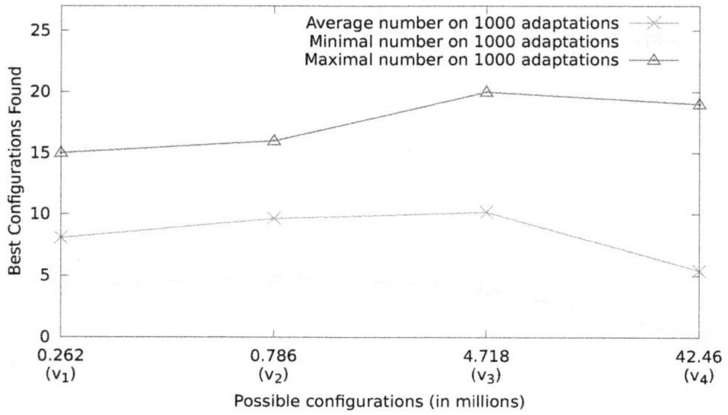

Figure 6. Comparison between the optimal solutions and solutions found by the genetic reasoner

Figure 6 presents the number of optimal configurations found by the genetic reasoner with v_1, v_2, v_3, and v_4. In average the reasoner always found optimal configurations for every version of EnTiMid tested. However, the performance slightly decreases while the complexity increases. For example with v_4, several adaptations among the 1000 performed did not find some of the optimal configurations. This result is normal since we cannot obtain same quality results in the same limited time for problems whose complexity differ.

We can state that the genetic reasoner gives good results for EnTiMid. But it may not be the case for less complex or different interactive systems. One of the advantages of our proposal is that the reasoner is also a component that can be selected in function of the context. For instance with a simple interactive system (*e.g.* 10000 configurations), the selected reasoner should be a reasoner that explores all the configuration since it will not take more than 0.5s.

Threats to validity

An important remark on this evaluation is that in our current implementation the configuration quality does not include the evaluation of the usability of adaptations, nor the user's satisfaction. For example our process may perform two following adaptations provoking big changes in the UI, that may disturb the user. Such evaluations can be performed by:

- The reasoner while selecting a configuration. In this case, the previous UI will be integrated into the genetic algorithm under the form of fitness functions maximizing the consistency of the adapted UI.
- A configuration checker that would evaluate the best configuration among the best ones found by the reasoner.

The configurations found by the genetic reasoner mainly depend on the properties defined on the components of the interactive systems. The developers have to balance them through simulations to obtain good results [14].

This paper does not focus on the UI composition. The UI composer used in this evaluation is basic and takes a negligible amount of time during the reconfiguration. The use of a more complex composer will slow down the configuration process.

RELATED WORK

The conception of dynamic adaptable systems has been widely tackled in the software engineering domain [20]. Software engineering approaches use model-driven engineering (MDE) to describe the system as a set of models. These models are sustained at runtime to reflect the underlying system and to perform adaptations. This process thus bridges the gap between design time and runtime. Yet these approaches do not focus on the adaptation of UIs. For example in [9], Cetina *et al.* propose an approach to autonomic computing, and thus to dynamic adaptation, applied on home automation. This approach lacks at considering the system as an interactive system whose UI needs adaptations.

Based on MDE, UI adaptation has been firstly tackled during design time to face the increasing number of platforms (*e.g.*, Dygmes [11], TERESA [19] and Florins *et al.*. [15]). These adaptation approaches mainly follow the CAMELEON top-down process composed of 1) the task model 2) the abstract UI 3) the concrete UI 4) the final UI [8]. Using the CAMELEON process, developers define several concrete UIs using one abstract UI to support different platforms. Users and the environment have been also considered as adaptation parameters, such as in UsiXML [18] and Contextual ConcurTaskTrees [3]. A need to adapt at runtime UIs thus appear to face to any change of user, environment and platform.

Approaches have been proposed to consider models of UIs at runtime [2, 24, 6]. In [7, 6], Blumendorf *et al.*

propose a framework for the development and execution of UIs for smart environments. Their proposal shares several points with ours: the use of a mapping metamodel to map models; they consider that bridging design time and runtime implies that models are executable. However, they focus on the link between the models and the underlying system while we focus on the adaptation of complex interactive systems.

In [24], Sottet *et al.* propose an approach to dynamically adapt plastic UI. To do so, a graph of models that describe the UI is sustained and updated at runtime. The adaptation is based on model transformations: in function of the context change, the appropriate transformation is identified and then applied to adapt the UI. This process follows the event-condition-action paradigm where the event is the context change and the action the corresponding transformation. The main drawbacks of this approach are that: transformations must be maintained when the interactive system evolves; the development of complex interactive systems will lead to the combinatorial explosion of the number of needed transformations.

CAMELEON-RT is a conceptual architecture reference model [2]. It allows the distribution, migration, and dynamic adaptation of interactive systems. Adaptations are performed using rules predefined by developers and users, or learned by the evolution engine at runtime. A graph of situations is used to perform adaptations: when the context changes, the corresponding situation is searched into the graph. The found situation is then provided to the evolution engine that performs the adaptation. This approach focuses on the usability of adaptations. However, it can hardly deal with complex systems because of the need to define a graph of situations.

ReWiRe is a framework dedicated to the dynamic adaptation of interactive systems [26]. As in our approach, ReWiRe's architecture uses a component-based system that facilitates the (de-)activation of the system's components. But ReWiRe suffers from the same main limitation than CAMELEON-RT: it can hardly deal with complex systems because of the increasing complexity of the ontology describing the whole runtime environment.

In [13], Demeure *et al.* propose a software architecture called COMETs. A COMET is a task-based interactor that encapsulates different presentations. It also embeds a reasoner engine that selects the presentation the more adapted to the current context. While we define a unique reasoner for the entire interactive system, COMETs defines one reasoner for each widget. We think that tagging widgets with properties that a global reasoner analyzes is a process that requires less effort than defining several reasoners.
The approach presented in [17] is close to COMETs where UI components can embed several presentations and an inference engine deducing from the context the presentation to use.

In [23], Schwartze *et al.* propose an approach to adapt the layout of UIs at runtime. They show that the UI composer *must* also be context-aware to layout UIs in function of the current user and its environment. For example, our reasoner decides the components that will compose the UI, but not their disposition in the adapted UI. It is the job of the UI composer that analyzes the context to adapt the layout of the UI accordingly.

DYNAMO-AID is a framework dedicated to the development of context-aware UIs adaptable at runtime [10]. In this framework, a forest of tasks is generated from the main task model and its attached abstract description. Each task tree of this forest corresponds to the tasks possible for each possible context. Because of the combinatorial explosion, such process can be hardly scalable to complex interactive systems.

In [16], Gajos and Weld propose an approach, called Supple, that treat the generation of UIs as an optimization problem. Given a specific user and device, Supple computes the best UI to generate by minimizing the user effort and respecting constraints. This approach is close to our reasoning step. However, Supple is not MDE-driven and only consider user effort as objective while our approach allows developers to define their own objectives.

CONCLUSION
Adapting complex interactive systems at runtime is a key issue. The software engineering community has proposed approaches to dynamically adapt complex systems. However, they lack at considering the adaptation of the interactive part of systems. In this paper, we have described an approach based on the Malai architectural model and that combines aspect-oriented modeling with property-based reasoning. The encapsulation of variable parts of interactive systems into aspects permits the dynamic adaption of user interfaces. Tagging UI components and context models with QoS properties allows the reasoner to select the aspects the best suited to the current context. We applied the approach to a complex interactive system to evaluate: the time spent adapting UIs on context changes; the quality of the resulting adapted UIs.

Future work will focus on the consideration of adaptations quality during the reasoning process. It will assure consistency between two adapted UIs. Work on context-aware composition of UIs will be carried out as well.

ACKNOWLEDGMENTS
The research leading to these results has received funding from the European Communitys Seventh Framework Program FP7 under grant agreements 215412

(http://www.ict-diva.eu/) and 215483 (http://www.s-cube-network.eu/).

REFERENCES

1. International Workshop on Aspect-Oriented Modeling. http://www.aspect-modeling.org.
2. L. Balme, A. Demeure, N. Barralon, J. Coutaz, and G. Calvary. CAMELEON-RT: A software architecture reference model for distributed, migratable, and plastic user interfaces. In *EUSAI*, pages 291–302, 2004.
3. J. V. d. Bergh and K. Coninx. Contextual concurtasktrees: Integrating dynamic contexts in task based design. In *Proc. of PERCOMW '04*, page 13, 2004.
4. A. Blouin and O. Beaudoux. Improving modularity and usability of interactive systems with Malai. In *Proc. of EICS'10*, 2010.
5. A. Blouin, O. Beaudoux, and S. Loiseau. Malan: A mapping language for the data manipulation. In *Proc. of DocEng '08*, pages 66–75, 2008.
6. M. Blumendorf, G. Lehmann, and S. Albayrak. Bridging models and systems at runtime to build adaptive user interfaces. In *Proc. of EICS'10*, 2010.
7. M. Blumendorf, G. Lehmann, S. Feuerstack, and S. Albayrak. Executable models for human-computer interaction. In *Proc. of DSV-IS'08*, 2008.
8. G. Calvary, J. Coutaz, D. Thevenin, Q. Limbourg, L. Bouillon, and J. Vanderdonckt. A unifying reference framework for multi-target user interfaces. *Interacting With Computers*, 15(3):289–308, 2003.
9. C. Cetina, P. Giner, J. Fons, and V. Pelechano. Autonomic computing through reuse of variability models at runtime: The case of smart homes. *Computer*, 42:37–43, 2009.
10. T. Clerckx, K. Luyten, and K. Coninx. DynaMo-AID: A design process and a runtime architecture for dynamic model-based user interface development. In *Proc. of EIS'04*, 2004.
11. K. Coninx, K. Luyten, C. Vandervelpen, J. V. den Bergh, and B. Creemers. Dygimes: Dynamically generating interfaces for mobile computing devices and embedded systems. In *Proc. of MobileHCI'03*, pages 256–270, 2003.
12. K. Deb, A. Pratap, S. Agarwal, and T. Meyarivan. A fast and elitist multiobjective genetic algorithm: Nsga-ii. *IEEE Transactions on Evolutionary Computation*, 6:182–197, 2002.
13. A. Demeure, G. Calvary, and K. Coninx. COMET(s), a software architecture style and an interactors toolkit for plastic user interfaces. In *Proc. of DSV-IS'08*, pages 225–237, 2008.
14. F. Fleurey and A. Solberg. A domain specific modeling language supporting specification, simulation and execution of dynamic adaptive systems. In *Proc. of MODELS'09*, 2009.
15. M. Florins and J. Vanderdonckt. Graceful degradation of user interfaces as a design method for multiplatform systems. In *Proc. of IUI '04*, pages 140–147, 2004.
16. K. Gajos and D. S. Weld. Supple: automatically generating user interfaces. In *Proc. of IUI '04*, pages 93–100, 2004.
17. A. Hariri, D. Tabary, S. Lepreux, and C. Kolski. Context aware business adaptation toward user interface adaptation. *Communications of SIWN*, 3:46–52, 2008.
18. Q. Limbourg, J. Vanderdonckt, B. Michotte, L. Bouillon, M. Florins, and D. Trevisan. UsiXML: a user interface description language for specifying multimodal user interfaces. In *Proc of WMI'2004*, 2004.
19. G. Mori, F. Paternó, and C. Santoro. Design and development of multidevice user interfaces through multiple logical descriptions. *IEEE Transactions on Software Engineering*, 30:507–520, 2004.
20. B. Morin, O. Barais, G. Nain, and J.-M. Jézéquel. Taming Dynamically Adaptive Systems with Models and Aspects. In *Proc. of ICSE'09*, 2009.
21. P.-A. Muller, F. Fleurey, and J.-M. Jézéquel. Weaving executability into object-oriented meta-languages. In *Proceedings of MODELS/UML'2005*, pages 264–278, 2005.
22. F. Paternò, C. Mancini, and S. Meniconi. ConcurTaskTrees: A diagrammatic notation for specifying task models. In *Proc. of INTERACT '97*, pages 362–369, 1997.
23. V. Schwartze, S. Feuerstack, and S. Albayrak. Behavior-sensitive user interfaces for smart environments. In *Proc of ICDHM '09*, pages 305–314, 2009.
24. J.-S. Sottet, V. Ganneau, G. Calvary, J. Coutaz, J.-M. Favre, and R. Demumieux. Model-driven adaptation for plastic user interfaces. In *Proc. Of INTERACT 2007*, pages 397–410, 2007.
25. The OSGi Alliance. OSGi service platform core specification, 2007. http://www.osgi.org/Specifications/.
26. G. Vanderhulst, K. Luyten, and K. Coninx. ReWiRe: Creating interactive pervasive systems that cope with changing environments by rewiring. In *Proc. of the 4th International Conference on Intelligent Environments*, pages 1–8, 2008.

Showing User Interface Adaptivity by Animated Transitions

Charles-Eric Dessart, Vivian Genaro Motti, and Jean Vanderdonckt
Université catholique de Louvain, Louvain School of Management
Louvain Interaction Laboratory, Place des Doyens, 1 – B-1348 Louvain-la-Neuve (Belgium)
{vivian.genaromotti, jean.vanderdonckt}@uclouvain.be – Phone: +32 10 478525

ABSTRACT
In order to reduce the inevitable end user disruption and cognitive perturbation induced by adapting a graphical user interface, the results of the adaptation could be conveyed to the end user by animating a transition scenario showing the evolution from the user interface before adaptation to the user interface after adaptation. A transition scenario consists of a sequence of adaptation operations (e.g., set/change a property of a widget, replace a widget by another, resize a widget) belonging to a catalogue of operations defined as an Extended Backus-Naur Form grammar. Each transition operation has a range from a single widget (e.g., this "Ok" button) to a selection of widgets based on a selector mechanism (e.g., all validation widgets of this family of interfaces). A transition scenario is built either automatically by any adaptation algorithm or interactively by a specific editor for designers. An animator then executes the animation scenario by parsing each adaptation operation one by one or in a grouped mode and by rendering them by an animated transition on a user interface model. The type (e.g., wipe, box in, box out) and parameters (e.g., animation speed, pace, direction) of each animated transition have been selected based on usability guidelines for animation. A user study suggests that a transition scenario reinforces understandability and trust, while still suffering from lag.

Author Keywords
Adaptation, adaptivity, animation, transition operation, selection mechanism, transition operation, visual transition.

General Terms
Design, Experimentation, Human Factors, Verification.

ACM Classification Keywords
D2.2 [**Software Engineering**]: Design Tools and Techniques – *Modules and interfaces; user interfaces.* D2.m [**Software Engineering**]: Miscellaneous – Rapid Prototyping; reusable software. H.5.1 [**Information interfaces and presentation**]: Multimedia Information Systems – *Animations.* H5.2 [**Information interfaces and presentation**]: User Interfaces – *User-centered design.*

INTRODUCTION
User Interface (UI) adaptation typically consists in modifying parts or whole of a particular interface in order to address specific needs required by an end user or a category of end users. Adaptation falls into two categories depending on who is in control of the adaptation process [7,11,24]: *adaptability* refers to as the ability of the end user to adapt the UI, *adaptivity* refers to as the ability of the system to adapt the UI. Mixed-initiative adaptation exists when both the end user and the system cooperate towards the UI adaptation goal. Adaptivity, although expensive to develop, has demonstrated several benefits [27] and is largely used in a wide range of domains of human activity, such as ambient intelligence [13], automotive [30], electronic commerce [33], algorithmic [26], and information systems [11].

Some of the main shortcomings of adaptivity are [8,27]: *end user disruption* caused by a behavior that is unexpected by the end user and *cognitive perturbation* when the end user, confronted to a new UI, must reconcile with this UI by imagining the correspondence between the UI before and after adaptation. Between the UI before adaptation and the UI after adaptation, there is nothing than a big whole, thus reinforcing the cognitive perturbation. Cognitive psychology [19] refers to this phenomenon as "cognitive destabilization", meaning that any user is mentally destabilized when confronted with anything unexpected, unprecedented, or unpredicted contents. The end user remains in this stage of cognitive destabilization until a "re-stabilization" restores a relation between the past and the newly presented contents. The end user does not suffer from these shortcomings in adaptability since the end user remains in control (therefore knowing what she is doing), as opposed to the system is in control in adaptivity (therefore the end user does not know what the system is doing). In order to address this challenge, animated transitions are applied to showing how the adaptivity process has been conducted in order to explain to the end user what has been adapted, and perhaps why.

The remainder of this paper is structured as follows: the next section reports on some related work. Then, the full process of adaptation by animated transitions is introduced, motivated, and defined. The software architecture supporting the implementation of animating transition is explained, and exemplified. A user study is then conducted in order to determine what the impact of animated transition over the end user is. Finally, a conclusion delivers the main points of this research and presents some future avenues.

RELATED WORK
Animated transitions and support for adaptivity are two main fields of research that are related to this work since its originality lies in considering the former for the latter.

EICS'11, June 13–16, 2011, Pisa, Italy.

Animated transitions

Animation [1, 35] has been widely used as a general technique for supporting end users in understanding different types of contents: evolution of a dynamic process (e.g., a mechanical process) [34, rule 2.4*18], a chronological sequence of events over time (e.g. a country demography) [12] or complex graphics (e.g., earth rotation) [39] and statistics [20]. It has also been used to represent various types of relations between elements [34, rule 2.4*19], such as sequences, important [35] or spatial connections [3], causal relations [41], for organizing diagrams [5], and for searching in 3D tree-maps where task times and user performance were improved [4]. Small animated icons could convey functionality better than static icons of the same size [1].

Animated transitions [2,4,20] in interactive systems are aimed at conveying to the end user a transition between states, views or scenes, e.g., to foster a smooth transition between two scenes, menus [22] or images [23]. Animated transitions improve feedback on users' actions [31], to notify display changes [29], and to improve situation awareness in a distributed environment. Sliding and blinking animated transitions were used to convey a context change on a menu [22] or images [23] on a mobile device with a positive impact on perception and conception of change.

Cartoons-inspired visual effects [10,28,38] have also been added to achieve a more realistic, if not lifelike, visual effect in the transition. Animated help better explains a GUI usage to the end user [36].

In order to be effective and usable, animated transitions need to be carefully designed as they are subject to a series of intrinsic shortcomings: they may require more cognitive workload than static images [41], animation is always the first display element attracting the end user's attention [21] whatever the animation goal is, they may cause user distraction [41], their duration always induce some lag [35], the animated objects should not exceed a certain threshold [9]. To minimize lag, an animated transition should be fast, but not too fast, otherwise the end user may completely overlook the animated transition. Typical duration may range from 300 msecs to several secs, depending on the complexity of the transition and other user- and situation-specific factors such as familiarity, expectation, attentiveness, and perceptual abilities that are difficult to predict [2].

Animated transitions may induce a significantly positive impact on understanding display changes, whether it is for notifying value changes in controls of a GUI [2], for updated contents in a web page [37], such as web navigation [14] or for evolving data in a dynamic display [12]. Different techniques support end users in perceiving and understanding screen changes, mainly based on animation between states [22,23], perhaps supplemented by sound [32].

Mnemonic rendering [6] consists of an image-based technique that buffers all changes of a fast-changing dynamic display and restitutes these changes under the end user's control via a memory jog. *DiffIE* consists of highlighting web page contents that have been updated since last visit [37]. A positive value has been demonstrated on how people interact with the web page and understand their contents. For instance, some users confessed they initially perceived some contents as static although they were dynamic. *Phosphor widgets* rely on afterglow effect in order to leave some visual reminiscence of changes of values of widgets (e.g., the value change of a slider, the check/uncheck of a check box, a new selection in a radio box). Rhetorical Structure Theory (RST) is exploited to apply Flash multimedia animated transitions on web pages to explain how web navigation has been transformed [14]. *Differentiated transitions* [31,32] are animated transitions that support explaining a process over time in a way that is reflected in the visual effect. For instance, the transfer time, the network bandwidth, and the file size are explicitly represented in an animated transition depicting a file transfer. RST, respectively Mnemonic rendering, force end users to wait for, respectively to replay, the display changes, thus inducing some lag [35]. DiffIE does not induce such a drawback (since the highlighting is almost instantaneous), nor Phosphor widgets (since the afterglow effect does not stop user in their tasks). Differentiated transitions actually animate the task while being executed [31], thus not representing any hindrance for achieving the end user's task. The aforementioned techniques certainly contribute to improving the perception of display changes over time, but they do not address the perception of UI adaptation over time, even if UI adaptation could be considered as a certain type of screen change. More importantly, they are not capable of recording the adaptation process to replay or explain it afterwards. RST [14] is the only one applying animated transitions on an abstract UI description of a web page. In our work, the animated transitions are applied on a general-purpose GUI model, but could be equally interpreted with any similar User Interface Description Language (UIDL).

Support for adaptivity of user interfaces

Adaptivity has been subject to many pieces of work that lead to a recognition of a series of benefits vs. costs [7,11,17]. In particular, adaptive UIs are able to optimize task completion time and rate [27], to induce a positive impact on accuracy [18], human performance [15,25], predictability [18], situation awareness [15,25] and workload [25]. Adaptivity has also been revealed effective when the UI should be adapted to the constraints imposed by any loss of screen resolution [15], like on mobile devices [16].

In this work, animated transitions show to the end user how an adaptivity process has led to an adapted GUI. It is expected that all benefits of animated transitions will establish a feeling of continuity between the UI before and after adaptation, thus impacting the end user's disruption and the cognitive perturbation discussed in the introduction. To our knowledge, this combination remains unexplored.

WHICH TRANSITION FOR WHICH ADAPTATION?

In order to address the problem of determining which animated transitions are considered adequate to mimic an adaptation operation, this section first provides a catalogue of such adaptation operations to be supported by the animator. It then reviews usability guidelines and cognitive psychology principles for animation for establishing a mapping between adaptation operations and animated transitions.

A Catalogue of Adaptation Operations

Adaptation operation is hereby defined as any transformation performed on any UI element in order to adapt the UI for the ultimate benefit of an end user interacting in a certain context of use. Such adaptation operations may involve a series of actions that are intended to obtain a certain global effect on the initial UI before adaptation until the final UI after adaptation is obtained (Fig. 1). Each adaptation operation produces a *transient UI being adapted* (Fig. 1), which consists in an intermediary UI stage during adaptation. Usually, the end user does not perceive any of these transient UIs, being presented only with the initial and the final UIs, which cause the end user disruption and the cognitive perturbation. The whole sequence of adaptation operations conducted for the UI adaptation is called the *adaptation scenario*, that could involve a wide spectrum of adaptation operations which fall into five categories [15,16,17]:

1. *Resizing operations*: are aimed at changing a widget size in order to optimize screen real estate, aesthetics, and visual design [40]. For instance, an edit field could be enlarged/shortened in height and/or length to take less space and to be subject to various alignments.
2. *Relocating operations*: are aimed at changing a widget location in order to reduce the screen space consumption. For instance, "Ok", "Cancel", and "Help" push buttons could be relocated to the bottom of a dialog box.
3. *Widget transformations*: are aimed at replacing one or a group of widgets by another widget or another group of widgets ensuring the same task, perhaps with some degradation [16]. For instance, an accumulator that consists of list boxes with possible values and chosen values could be replaced by a multi-selection list, which could be in turn replaced by a multi-selection drop-down list.
4. *Image transformations*: are aimed at changing the size, surface, and quality of an image in order to accommodate the constraints imposed by the new context of use, namely the display/platforms constraints.
5. *Splitting rules*: are aimed at dividing one or a group of widgets into one or several other groups of widgets that will be displayed separately. For instance, a dialog box is split into two tabs in a tabbed dialog box.

A single adaptation operation could be performed on a single UI element in isolation (e.g., resizing an individual or a compound widget) or several related UI elements concurrently (e.g., resizing a group of aligned edit fields). Therefore, we will define an *Adaptation Operation Language* (AOL) for expressing one adaptation operation on one element at a time first and then, this will be generalized to several UI elements together.

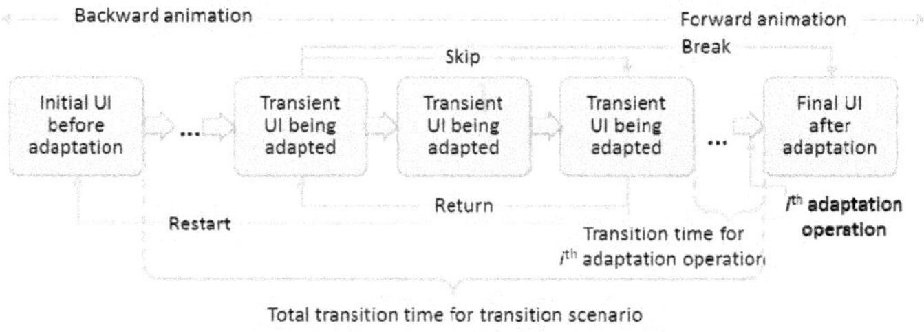

Figure 1. Timeline of the animation process.

Adaptation Operation Language. We now provide a catalogue of adaptation operations belonging addresses the five aforementioned categories. For this purpose, each adaptation operation is defined in an Extended Backus-Naur Form (EBNF) format to form a grammar. In this notation, brackets indicate an optional section, while parentheses denote a simple choice in a set of possible values.

SET <Element.property> TO {value, percentage}: assigns a value to a widget property or a percentage of the actual value. For instance, SET "pushButton_1.height" TO 10 will resize the push button to a height of 10 units while SET "pushButton_1.height" TO +10 increases its height by 10%.

DISPLAY <Element> [AT x,y]: displays a UI element whose identifier is provided at a *x,y* location where *x* and and *y* are integer positions (e.g., in characters or pixels). For instance, DISPLAY "pushButton_1" AT 1,1 will display an identified push button at coordinates 1,1 on a designated display. UNDISPLAY <Element> [AT x,y] is the inverse operation. DISPLAY <Message> [AT x,y] displays a provided message.

MOVE <Element> TO x,y [IN n steps]: moves a UI element to a new location indicated by its coordinates *x* and *y*, possibly in a fixed amount of steps.

REPLACE <Element1> BY <Element2>: replaces a widget Element1 by another one Element2. Sometimes the replacement widget could be determined after an adaptation algorithm, thus giving the following definition: REPLACE <Element1> BY <AdaptationAlgo:>. This mechanism is similar for image transformations: images are usually transformed by local or remote algorithms (e.g., for resizing, converting, cropping, clipping, repurposing), thus giving the following definition: TRANSFORM <Image1> BY <ImageAlgo:URL>.

DISTRIBUTE <Elements> INTO <Containers> [BY <DistribAlgo:URL>: computes a distribution of a series of UI Elments into a series of UI Containers, possibly by calling an external algorithm, local or remote.

Selection mechanism. In the above definitions of adaptation operations, only one UI element is provided as parameter at a time. Obviously, an adaptation operation could have a scope of several UI elements together. For this purpose, a selection mechanism is introduced that defines a scope of UI Elements that could serve as a parameter. A *Selector* consists of a definition of the UI Element types to which the adaptation operation applies, and a series of property declarations that define the operations. Four major types of selector scope are considered that replace <Element> or <Elements> fields in the previous definitions:

1. universalSelector: applies the adaptation operation to all UI elements belonging to the current GUI of concern. For instance, SET "universalSelector.backgroundColor" TO "Ivory" will change the background color of the entire GUI into ivory.
2. elementTypeSelector: applies the adaptation operation to all elements belonging to the selector's type (e.g., all containers, all list boxes). For instance, SET "elementTypeSelection.foregroundColor=pushButton" TO "lightGrey" will set the foreground color of all push buttons of the current UI to light grey.
3. classSelector: applies the adaptation operation to all elements belonging to the selector's type whose definition makes them part of the class (e.g., all containers having an ID greater or equal to "CC2", all list boxes having more than 10 items).
4. idSelector: applies the template to only one element belonging to the GUI of concern: the one whose id attribute matches the string contained in the parameter. The idSelector is used by default and should not be necessarily specified.

Animated transitions for an adaptation operation

On the one hand, usability guidelines [1,9,10,15,21,28,35, 40,41] exist that recommend an animated transition for a particular usage that has been proved effective and/or efficient to some extent. On the other hand, cognitive psychology provided a series of high-level principles that could be converted into design guidelines. For instance, the visual animation dynamicity should be appropriate to the animated transition: "wipe from left" is considered less disruptive when explaining a process that is demonstrated from left to write, other animations like "appear", "fall from top" are considered too disruptive and/or too visually impactful. "Venetian blinds" should be used when the process evolves to a significantly different stage, which is not appropriate for a local change. In order to decide which animated transition is appropriate for which adaptation operation, some major animated transitions are defined in Table 1 and classified into five families in Table 2 that will then be used in establishing mappings summarized in Table 3. Presentation software [20,26] and animation [1,10,21, 35] have introduce a large amount of varied animated transitions. Therefore, animations selected in Table 1 have been chosen according to the following criteria: they are the most frequently used techniques that are described in a consistent way throughout the literature, they are easy to implement, they convey a message that is simple enough to be understood while being flexible enough to allow some variation. In order to group these selected animated transitions, we clustered them into five families based on visual properties [41] (e.g., visual differentiation, clarity, density) based on the literature [28,35,40] (Table 2):

Icon	*Name*: **definition**
	*Horizontal scroll from right*: to display the next element from a sequence of UI elements
	*Horizontal scroll from left*: to display the previous element from a sequence of UI elements
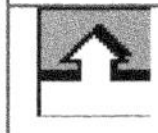	*Vertical scroll from bottom*: to proceed with a step-by-step reasoning, a continuous subject or a long passing over, or a movement
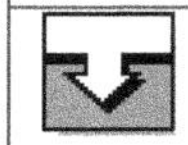	*Vertical scroll from top*: to move back in a step-by-step reasoning, a continuous subject or a long passing over, or a movement
	*Diagonal replacement from top/bottom left corner*: to go back to the previous page or Screen or UI element
	*Diagonal replacement from top/bottom right corner*: to move to next page or screen or UI element
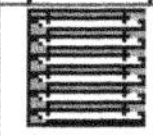	*Venetian blinds*: to present a completely different topic, to provide a feeling of coordinated time, to convey a significant transition
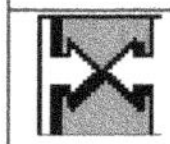	*Barn door close*: to close a transient screen (e.g., an information screen, the About... splash screen), to close a current scene, to signify game over
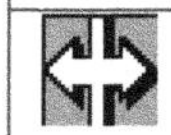	*Barn door open*: to open a transient screen, to initiate a new step, to open a new window or UI element, to launch a game, a simulation
	*Iris open*: to show more detailed information about a particular topic
	*Iris close*: to show more general information about a particular topic

Table 1. Definitions of some major animated transitions.

F1	Scroll, Diagonal replacement, Wipe
F2	Checkers, lines, columns, blinds, barn door open/close
F3	Cover, uncover
F4	Open, close, Box in, Box out, Iris open/close
F5	Cutting, Black transition

Table 2. Five families of animated transitions.

1. *F1 family* gathers animated transitions that simply recover the old element by a new element (i.e, in our context any UI element, but in general, it could be any graphical object of a display or an entire display such as a graphic, a presentation slide, or an overhead). The main variation lies in the way the new element is presented with respect to the old one, which is usually the direction or the shape of the animated transition.
2. *F2 family* gathers animated transitions that divide the old element into regions that are further subject to partial overlapping when transitioning to the new element.
3. *F3 family* gathers animated transitions that present the new element on top of the old element by moving it in some way. The new element is therefore perceived as it "flies" over the old element.

4. *F4 family* gathers animated transitions of type double "blinds" or "windows". The new element is divided into two regions and progressively appears on top of the old element because the blinds have been opened or closed.
5. *F5 family* gathers specific animated transitions that do not induce any movement or overlapping of the new element, but that simply makes the old element disappearing for the new element by a sharp visual effect.

Table 3 motivates the selection of animated transition for each adaptation operation that was previously defined. Animated transitions from F5 should be reserved for highly-changing regions of the display. Per se, there is no direct adaptation operation that is directly appropriate to this kind of transition, except the complete display/replacement of a significant region. For the moment, this animated transition was not incorporated in the Animator for this reason, but this may change depending on users' feedback. We hereby define a *transition scenario* as a sequence of adaptation operations rendered by animated transitions based on Table 3.

USER CONTROL ACTIONS

The critical success factor for an animation beyond its appropriateness (as discussed in the previous section) resides in the user's capability to govern the pace and duration of the animation. This is also applicable to our animated transitions in the transition scenario. In order to provide some user control over the whole animation process, thus keeping control over the total transition time of the animation scenario (Fig. 1), the user may want to operate some actions either in the *forward animation* (e.g., to understand the evolution of the adaptation process) or in the *backward animation* (e.g., to come back to a previously applied animated transition). These actions are made available in the Animator through keyboard shortcuts as follows:

- *Skip* (Pg Dn): terminates the current animated transition and skips to the next one in the transition scenario. This user action is motivated by the end user need to stop an animated transition as soon as it is understood by users.
- *Break* (End): terminates the current transition scenario. This is probably the most important user action since the end user should be able to terminate the animation at any time, as recommended by Smith & Mosier [34].
- *Return* (Pg Up): escapes from the current animated transition and returns to the previous one in the transition scenario. This user action is motivated by the end user need to come back to a previously animated stage when there is a disruption in the understanding.
- *Restart* (Home): starts again the current transition scenario from the first animated transition. This user action is motivated by the end user need to replay entirely the transition scenario in case of misunderstanding.

Adaptation operation	Animation family, animated transition with justification
SET that modifies the length of a UI element into a larger value (absolute or relative)	Horizontal scroll/wipe from left (F1): this operation minimizes the visual change since only the right part resulting from the enlarging is changing. For edit fields, for instance, this is particularly appropriate because it gives the feeling that the field is really expanding
SET that modifies the height of a UI element into a larger value (absolute or relative)	Vertical scroll/wipe from bottom (F1): this operation minimizes the visual change since only the right part resulting from the enlarging is changing
DISPLAY that displays a new UI element at a certain position	Uncover (F3), Box out (F4), or Iris open (F4): these operations all induce a progressive display of a new UI element at once, thus creating the illusion that it is coming from the empty.
UNDISPLAY that undisplays a new UI element at a certain position	Cover (F3), Box in (F4), or Iris close (F4): these operations all induce a progressive disappearing of a existing UI element at once, thus creating the illusion that it is shrunk to an empty/white region.
REPLACE that substitutes a UI element by another one	Bam door open (F2): this operation affects the entire visual aspect of the previous one and the new one.
DISTRIBUTE that computes a distribution of a series of UI Elments into a series of UI Containers	Bam door open (F2) or Iris open (F4): these operations enable the visualization of an entire group at once, instead of showing every little display change individually
MOVE that moves a UI element to a new location indicated by its coordinates x and y, possibly in a fixed amount of steps	Ideally, the UI movement could be represented by an animation depicting the movement itself. But practically, this would induce a very long animation, thus increasing again the lag. Therefore, we preferred to adopt a disappearing of the UI element from its original location and an appearing to its target location. Depending on these locations, vertical, horizontal or diagonal replacements (F1) are selected. For instance, when a UI element disappears from a top left location to a bottom right location, a diagonal replacement from top/bottom left corner is selected, thus creating the illusion that the element moves from one location to another. Consistently with this direction, when a UI should only move linearly (either vertically or horizontally), a vertical/horizontal scroll is selected instead.

Table 3. Mapping table between adaptation operation and animated transition.

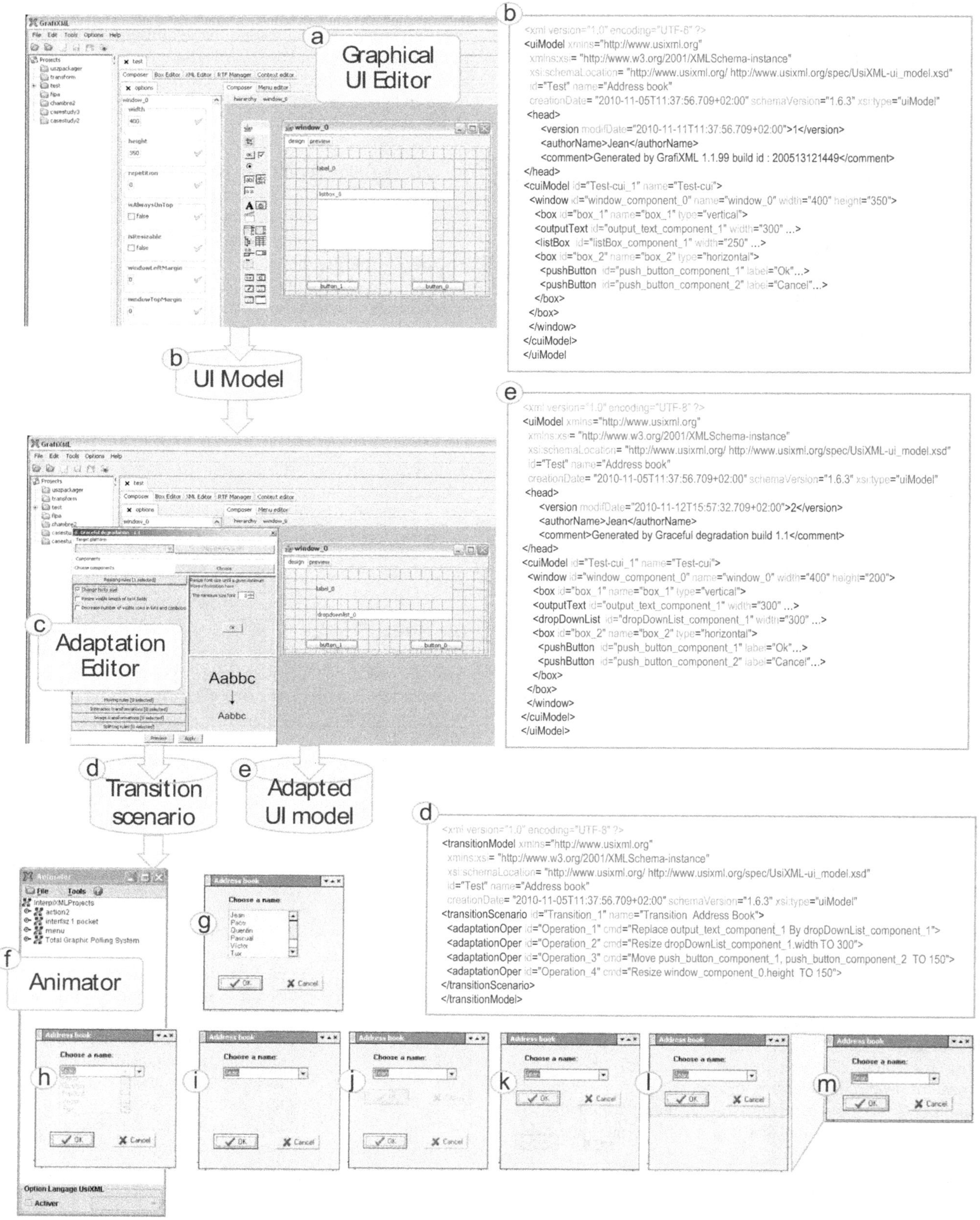

Figure 2. Process of adaptation rendered by a transition scenario.

- *User-Break* during *n* msecs or *n* secs, until *m* next transition/end (Space with repetition): stops momentarily the animated transition. This user action is motivated by the end user need to pause or stop as long as the space bar is pressed, depressed so as to allow time enough to understand the adaptation operation being animated.
- *Acceleration* (CTRL+A): increases the speed of the animation scenario. This user action is motivated by the end user need to speed up the animation pace when there is no problem of understanding when the understanding of the animated transitions is fine-grained or obvious.
- *Deceleration* (CTRL+D): decreases the speed of the animation scenario. This user action is motivated by the end user need to slow down the animation pace when there is a need to allow more time for understanding of the animated transition.

PRODUCING A TRANSITION SCENARIO

After having defined adaptation operations and animated transitions that are adequate for conveying the message of a particular adaptation operation, the process of adaptation rendered by a transition scenario (Fig. 2) is now explained, along with the implementation of software that supports it.

Step1: Producing a User Interface Model.

Fig. 2a reproduces a screen shot of a *Graphical UI Editor* with which the designer can edit the initial UI before adaptation. As in any UI builder, the designer drags widgets from a palette and drops them onto a working surface area where they can be assembled, grouped, and aligned. The GrafiXML was developed that exports the results of the design phase into a Concrete User Interface (CUI) model (Fig. 2b) that is stored in UsiXML, a XML-compliant UIDL that is partially reproduced in Fig. 2b. A CUI model basically consists here of a recursive hierarchy of containers and widgets that are expressed independently of any programming or makup language. The editor today consists of about 20,000 LOC implemented in Java 1.5 with various libraries (e.g., Castor, Jakarta, Jdom, LiquidINF, Looks, Xalan, and Xerces) and stores models in a MySQL V5.0 database. This editor today supports two UIDLs: UsiXML (http://www. usixml.org) and XAML (http://archive.msdn.microsoft. com/XAML/), and could be extended to other UIDLs through a set of XSLT transformations provided that equivalent concepts exist.

Step 2: Producing an Adapted User Interface Model.

Fig. 2c reproduces a screen shot of an *Adaptation Editor* with which the designer can apply any adaptation operation defined in the aforementioned catalogue on the initial UI in order to obtain the final UI after adaptation. For this purpose, control panels are provided to let the designer applying any adaptation operation desired on the UI being designed in the Graphical UI Editor. Any such operation, once executed, is stored in a log file. Each line of the log file is an instruction compatible with the EBNF format for adaptation operations. All lines of adaptation then form a transition scenario stored in an independent XML file for a transition model (Fig. 2d). "Undo", respectively "Redo" operations cancels, respectively duplicates, the last operation in the file. Fig. 3 reproduces another panel of this Adaptation Editor in which the designer is applying a selection of UI elements based on the selection mechanisms introduced in order to apply widget substitution. The *Adaptation Editor* consists of 2,600 LOC implemented in Java 1.5 with some libraries (Jdom, JSearch, Xalan, and Xerces). The adapted UI is maintained in an adapted UI model (Fig. 2e).

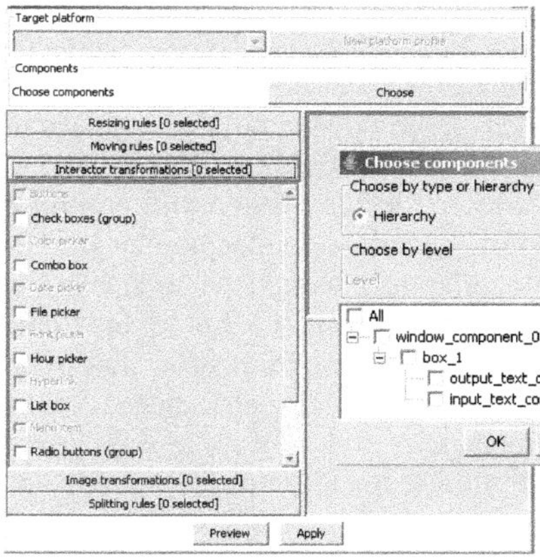

Figure 3. Some control panels of the adaptation editor.

Step 3: Rendering a Transition Scenario.

Fig. 2f reproduces a screen shot of an *Adaptation Editor* that opens a transition scenario to be applied to a UI model. For this purpose, the transition scenario file (Fig. 2d) is parsed and animated transitions corresponding to each line of the scenario (according to Table 3) is produced, equipped with the user actions described in the previous section. An animation is then produced that shows the transition from the UI before adaptation until the UI after adaptation is reached (Fig. 2g to m). The *Animator* consists of 1,100 LOC implemented in Microsoft Expression Studio. This environment has been selected for the following reasons: it is already compliant with XAML, a XML-compliant UIDL for CUI; all UI elements of a GUI expressed in XAML are vector-based and logical operations could be performed on them; animated transitions of Tables 1 and 3 are already built-in with some options (like speed, duration); MS Expression Studio comprises five products: Expression Blend (for building GUIs for Silverlight, Windows, and Surface), Expression Blend SketchFlow (for prototyping these GUIs), Expression Web (for building Web GUIs), Expression Design (for creating graphic assets for the Web or Silverlight, Windows, and Surface), and Expression Encoder (for preparing video assets for the Web or Silverlight, Windows, and Surface). In our case, we used Expression design to develop the animated transitions based on the AOL defined previously and Expression Blend for the Animator itself.

In the next subsections, we examine when adaptation operations could be grouped together in order to reduce the animation duration while not decreasing its main quality. Animations could then be executed in series or in parallel.

Grouping similar adaptation operations

On the one hand, grouping similar adaptation operations into one single animated transition instead of playing the same animated transition several times for several similar adaptation operations makes sense. This would decrease animation duration (thus reducing animation lag [35]) and produce a global animation at once (thus improving the understandability of the whole adaptation process executed through the transition scenario). For instance, instead of moving up two horizontally aligned push buttons one after another (as in Fig. 2j, k), they could be moved all at once. Similarly, a same adaptation operation performed on a series of physically adjacent widgets could lead to a grouped animated transition: right resizing a column of edit fields could be done at once in one single animated transition. *On the other hand*, grouping similar adaptation operations should consider human limitations: no occlusion, no overlapping should be induced; the cognitive load of the animated transition should be minimized; the amount of widgets subject to animation should be reduced. Psychophysics research has revealed that average end users cannot track more than five objects in movement [9]. Therefore, the EBNF allows specifying grouped adaptation operations, but it does not check whether any such limitation occurs.

Grouping dissimilar adaptation operations

It is also possible to consider grouping dissimilar adaptation operations under certain conditions. Typically, such a grouping could be made possible when several different animated transitions affect the same widget but in different ways. For instance, replacing a list box by a drop down list while enlarging the resulting widget is acceptable as long as the associated animated transitions affect different portions of the same widget or non-overlapping regions in the same container. In contrast to similar operations where all operations could be performed at once, in this case the transitions cannot be executed all at once, but in a way that could be perceived together, e.g. by fading in/out. This situation is acceptable provided that the amount of transitions per widget does not exceed a certain threshold.

USER STUDY ON SUBJECTIVE PERCEPTION

After describing how a transition scenario could be dynamically produced at run-time, we report on a user study on the subjective perception of end users when confronted to a transition scenario of animated transitions showing UI adaptivity. The purpose of the study was to examine whether the transition scenario helps users to understanding it.

Participants

We conducted a user trial of 20 users (6 female, 14 male) who were recruited from a database of volunteers coming from different disciplines (e.g., marketing, finance, pharmacy, medicine) and having different ages and background.

Method

The participant's task was to watch 3 transition scenarios: a *personal information form* as a simple scenario to foster initial understanding of the whole process; an *address book* adapted for a PDA (Fig. 2g to m) as a moderately-complex scenario to illustrate other adaptation operations, and the *connexion* between the two previous ones as a more complex example in order to illustration dialogue and navigation. Then participants had to demonstrate their appreciation of the animation process by answering a questionnaire made up of a section of 12 closed questions and 3 open questions (i.e., what are the aspects that you liked the most, what are the aspects that you disliked the most, what do you suggest in order to improve the quality of the animation). In the closed part of the questionnaire, we asked the participants to respond to a series of positive statements on a scale of one to five (1 = strongly disagree, five = strongly agree). The first two statements on the questionnaire tested user satisfaction with the two interfaces. The statements were:

1. I liked the animation process
2. I liked the animation interface
3. I preferred the animation over no animation at all
4. The animation is easy to use
5. The animation is easy to control
6. The animation is easy to understand
7. The animation is easy to follow
8. The animation is easy to progress (forward an.)
9. The animation is easy to revert (backward an.)
10. The animation represents the adaptation
11. The animation is fast
12. I would recommend using the animation

Results and Discussion

The cumulated histogram in Figure 4 summarizes the responses to the statements included in the questionnaire. The distribution for statement #1 revealed that nobody had a negative feeling about having an animation of the transition scenario (neither orange nor red areas). But some participants were concerned about the Animator UI: the distribution of responses for statement #2 shows this, while the preference (statement #3) follows a similar trend. Participants appear, however, to show a preference for the animation over no animation at all ($p = 0.031$ for a one-tail t-test with 19 degrees of freedom). But this does not mean that the animation should always come automatically, as suggested in statement #4: participants seemed to appreciate the animation effects, but do not appreciate the time consumed by the animation, especially when the total animation time is long. Rather, they prefer to keep control over the transition scenario with user actions, but it turns out that they do not know exactly what user action to undertake since they do not know what the next adaptation operations are.

Forward animation (statement #8) is perceived in a better way that the backward animation (statement #9). The last statement (#12) on the questionnaire verifies the results of the global perception responses by asking the participants to respond to a recommendation statement: three quarters of the participants were confident in recommending the animation transition as a mechanism for showing the adaptation. These results are more moderate than the initial statements.

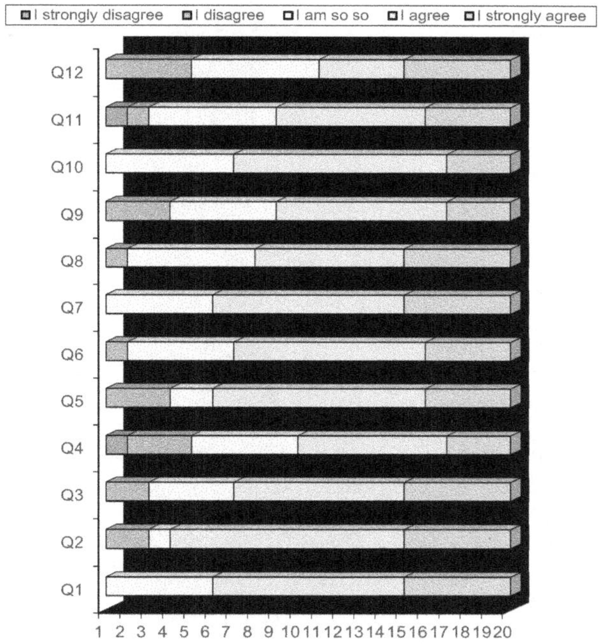

Figure 4. Distribution of participants's responses.

When asked to freely comment on potential improvements to the transition scenario, users had several suggestions. Six of the twenty participants suggested some mechanisms for grouping more animated transitions together while animating the scenario. Several participants recommended finding out such mechanisms in order to reduce the total time. Therefore, the lag problem [35] is still important. Participants however recognized that the animation is adequately shown by the animation (statement #10), which is confirmed by several informal comments. Participants perceive less disruption since there is a transition between the UIs before and after adaptation and felt less perturbation. In addition, some participants confessed that they felt more trust in the system when an animation shows the adaptation, but that this could be reinforced by on-demand explanation. They also said that, if they see some transition like that for one or two UIs subject to adaptation, they would trust more the system and ask less the animation in the future.

CONCLUSION

This paper presented a method for showing the adaptation process to the end user by animating its transition scenario from the UI before adaptation until the UI after adaptation is reached. A user study was conducted to determine what the subjective perception of the transition scenario on end users was. This study revealed some advantages (e.g., global appreciating, a perception that the end user disruption and the cognitive perturbation were reduced, increase of trust), but also some shortcomings to be addressed in the future (e.g., enabling faster animation, including on-demand explanation of why this or that adaptation operation has been executed), better capabilities to bypass, group or compact some adaptation operations. In the near future, conducting an experimental study to determine the exact cognitive load of each animated transition and their adequacy with respect to the adaptation operation would be welcome. In this work, we only established such an adequacy based on cognitive psychology and usability guidelines for animation, which is a qualitative approach. A quantitative approach is a desirable for the next step, although different factors may influence these results that are hard to quantify.

ACKNOWLEDGMENTS

The authors would like to acknowledge the support of the ITEA2-Call3-2008026 UsiXML (User Interface extensible Markup Language) European project and its support by Région Wallonne DGO6 as well as the FP7-ICT5-258030 Serenoa (Multidimensional context-aware adaptation of Service Front-ends) project supported by the European Commission. The authors would like also to thank the anonymous reviewers, particularly the one who has been the most criticizing, thus triggering new directions to explore and to generalize the work already done.

REFERENCES

1. Baecker, R. and Small, I. Animation at the interface. In: B. Laurel (Ed.), *The Art of Human-Computer Interface Design*. Addison-Wesley, New York (1990).
2. Baudisch, P., Tan, D., Collomb, M., Robbins, D., Hinckley, K., Agrawala, M., Zhao, S., and Ramos, G. Phosphor: Explaining Transitions in the User Interface Using Afterglow Effects. In *Proc. of ACM Symposium on User Interface Software Technology UIST'2006* (Montreux, October 15-18, 2006). ACM Press, New York (2006), pp. 169-178.
3. Bederson, B.B. and Boltman, A. Does Animation Help Users Build Mental Maps of Spatial Information? In *Proc. of IEEE Symposium on Information Visualization InfoVis'99*. IEEE Computer Society Press, Los Alamitos (1999), pp. 28–35.
4. Bladh, T., Carr, D.A., and Kljun, M. The Effect of Animated Transitions on User Navigation in 3D Tree-Maps. In *Proc. of the 9th Int. Conf. on Information Visualization InfoVis'2005*. IEEE Computer Society, Los Alamitos (2005), pp. 297–305.
5. Bétrancourt, M. and Tversky, B. Animation, can it facilitate? *Int. J. of Human Computer Studies 57*, 4 (2002), pp. 247–262.
6. Bezerianos, A., Dragicevic, P., Balakrishnan, R. Mnemonic Rendering: An Image-Based Approach for Exposing Hidden Changes in Dynamic Displays. In *Proc. of ACM Symposium on User Interface Software Technology UIST'2006* (Montreux, Oct. 15-18, 2006). ACM Press (2006), pp. 159-168.
7. Browne, D., Totterdell, P., and Norman, M. (Eds.). *Adaptive User Interfaces*. Computers and People Series. Academic Press, Harcourt Brace Jovanovich Publishers, London (1990).
8. Bunt, A., Conati, C., and McGrenere, J. What role can adaptive support play in an adaptable system? In *Proc.of the 9th Int. Conf. on Intelligent User Interfaces IUI'2004* (Funchal, Jan. 13-16, 2004). ACM Press, NY (2004), pp. 117-124.
9. Cavanagh, P. and Alvarez, G. Tracking multiple targets with multifocal attention. *Trends in Cognitive Science, 9*, 7 (July 2005), pp. 249–354.
10. Chang, B.-W. and Ungar, D. Animation: From Cartoon to User Interface. In *Proc. of ACM Symposium on User Interface Software Technology UIST'93* (Atlanta, November 3-5, 1993). ACM Press, New York (1993) pp. 45–55.
11. Dieterich, H., Malinowski, U., Kuhme, T., and Schneider-Hufschmidt, M. State of the art in adaptive user interfaces. In: Schneider-Hufschmidt, M., Kuhme, T., Malinowski, U. (Eds.),

Adaptive User Interfaces Principles and Practice. Elsevier Science Publishers B.V., Amsterdam (1993), pp. 13–48.
12. Dunn, C. The Use of Real-Time Simulation by Means of Animation Film as an Analytical Design Tool in Certain Spatio-Temporal Situations. *Ergonomics, 16* (1973), pp. 515–519.
13. Escribano, J.G., Manrique, G.M., Haya Coll, P.A. iFaces: Adaptive User Interfaces for Ambient Intelligence. In *Proc. of IADIS Int. Conf. on Interfaces and Human Computer Interaction IHCI'2008* (Amsterdam, July 25-28, 2008). InderScience.
14. Fialho, A.T.S. and Schwabe, D. Enriching Hypermedia Application Interfaces. In *Proc. of 7th Int. Conf. on Web Engineering ICWE'2007* (Como, July 16-20, 2007). LNCS, Vol. 4607. Springer-Verlag, Berlin (2007), pp. 188-193.
15. Findlater, L. and McGrenere, J. Impact of screen size on performance, awareness, and user satisfaction with adaptive graphical user interfaces. In *Proc. of the 26th ACM Conf. on Human Factors in Computing Systems CHI'2008* (Florence, April 2008). ACM Press, New York (2008), pp. 1247–1256.
16. Florins, M., Montero, F., Vanderdonckt, J., and Michotte, B. Splitting Rules for Graceful Degradation of User Interfaces. In *Proc. of 8th Int. Working Conference on Advanced Visual Interfaces AVI'2006* (Venezia, 23-26 May 2006). ACM Press, New York (2006), pp. 59–66.
17. Gajos, K.Z., Czerwinski, M., Tan, D.S., and Weld, D.S.. Exploring the design space for adaptive graphical user interfaces. In *Proc. of 8th Int. Working Conference on Advanced Visual Interfaces AVI'2006* (Venezia, 23-26 May 2006). ACM Press, New York (2006), pp. 201–208.
18. Gajos, K.Z., Everitt, K., Tan, D.S., Czerwinski, M., and Weld, D.S. Predictability and accuracy in adaptive user interfaces. In *Proc. of the ACM Conf. on Human Factors in Computing Systems CHI'2008* (Florence, April 5-10, 2008). ACM Press, New York (2008), pp. 1271–1274.
19. Gardiner, M. and Christie, B. *Applying Cognitive Psychology to User Interface Design*. John Wiley, New York (1987).
20. Heer, J. and Robertson, G. Animated Transitions in Statistical Data Graphics. *IEEE Transactions on Visualization and Computer Graphics 13*, 6 (Nov. 2007), pp.1240-1247.
21. Hong, W., Thong, J.Y.L., and Tam, K.-Y. Does Animation Attract Online Users' Attention? The Effects of Flash on Information Search Performance and Perceptions. *Information Systems Research 15*, 1 (2004), pp. 60–86.
22. Huhtala, J., Mäntyjärvi, J., Ahtinen, A., Ventä, L., and Isomursu, M. Animated Transitions for Adaptive Small Size Mobile Menus. In *Proc. of the 12th IFIP TC 13 Int. Conf. on Human-Computer Interaction Interact'2009* (Uppsala, August 24-28, 2009). Lecture Notes in Computer Science, Vol. 5726, Springer-Verlag, Berlin (2009), pp. 772-781.
23. Huhtala, J., Sarjanoja, A.-H., Mäntyjärvi, J., Isomursu, M. and Häkkilä, J. Animated UI transitions and perception of time: a user study on animated effects on a mobile screen. In *Proc. of ACM Conf. on Human Aspects in Computing Systems CHI'2010*. ACM Press, New York (2010), pp. 1339–1342.
24. Jameson, A. Adaptive Interfaces and Agents. In: Jacko, J.A., Sears, A. (Eds.), *Human–Computer Interface Handbook*. Lawrence Erlbaum, Mahwah (2003), pp. 305–330.
25. Kaber, D.B. and Endsley, M.R. The effects of level of automation and adaptive automation on human performance, situation awareness and workload in a dynamic control task. *Theoretical Issues in Ergonomics Science 5*, 2 (2004), pp. 113–153.
26. Kerren, A, Stasko, J., Algorithm Animation, Introduction of Software Visualization, State of the Art Survey. LNCS, Vol. 2269. Springer-Verlag, Berlin (2002), pp. 1-15.
27. Lavie, T. and Meyer, J. Benefits and costs of adaptive user interfaces. *Int. J. of Hum.-Comp. Stud., 68* (2010), pp. 508–524.
28. May, J., Dean, M.P., and Barnard, P.J. Using Film Cutting Techniques in Interface Design. In *Human-Computer Interaction*, Vol. 18, Lawrence Erlbaum Ass. (2003), pp. 325–372.
29. Rensink, R.A., O'Regan, J.K., and Clark, J.J. To see or not to see: the need for attention to perceive changes in scenes. *Psychological Science 8*, 8 (1997), pp. 368–373.
30. Rogers, S., Fiechter, C.N., and Thompson, C. Adaptive user interfaces for automotive environments. In *Proc. of the IEEE Symposium on Intelligent Vehicles Dearborn*. IEEE Computer Society Press, Los Alamitos (2000), pp. 662–667.
31. Schlienger, C., Dragicevic, P., Ollagnon, C., and Chatty, S. Les transitions visuelles différenciées : principes et applications. In *Proc. of IHM'2006* (Montréal, 18-21 April 2006). ACM Int. Series, Vol. 133 (2006), pp. 59–66.
32. Schlienger, C., Conversy, S., Chatty, S., Anquetil, M., and Mertz, Ch. Improving Users' Comprehension of Changes with Animation and Sound: An Empirical Assessment. In *Proc. of Interact'2007* (Rio de Janeiro, 2007). LNCS, Vol. 4662, Springer-Verlag, Berlin (2007), pp. 207–220.
33. Sherman, R., Alpert, J.K., Karat, C., Carolyn, B., and Vergo, J. User attitudes regarding a user-adaptive e-commerce web site. *User Modeling and User-adaptive Interaction 13*, 4 (2003), pp. 373–396.
34. Smith, S.L. and Mosier, J.N. Design guidelines for the user interface software. Technical Report ESD-TR-86-278 (NTIS No. AD A177198), U.S. Air Force Electronic Systems Division, Hanscom Air Force Base, Massachusetts (1986).
35. Stasko, J. Animation in User Interfaces: Principles and Techniques. In *Proc. of User Interface Software '93*, pp. 81–101.
36. Sukaviriya, P. and Foley, J. Coupling a User Interface Framework with Automatic Generation of Context Sensitive Animated Help. In *Proc. of ACM Symposium on User Interface Software Technology UIST'90* (Snowbird, Oct. 1990). ACM Press, New York (1990), pp. 152–166.
37. Teevan, J., Dumais, S.T., Liebling, D.J., and Hughes, R. A Longitudinal Study of How Highlighting Web Content Change Affects People's Web Interactions. In *Proc. of ACM Conf. on Human Aspects in Computing Systems CHI'2010*. ACM Press, New York (2010), pp. 1353-1356.
38. Thomas, B.H. and Calder, P. Applying Cartoon Animation Techniques to Graphical User Interfaces. *ACM Trans. on Computer-Human Interaction 8*, 3 (Sept. 2001), pp. 198–222.
39. Tucker, J.B. Computer Graphics Achieves New Realism. *High Technology* (June 1984), pp. 40–53.
40. Vanderdonckt, J. and Gillo, X. Visual Techniques for Traditional and Multimedia Layouts. In *Proc. of 2nd ACM Workshop on Advanced Visual Interfaces AVI'94* (Bari, 1-4 June 1994), ACM Press, New York (1994), pp. 95–104.
41. Ware, C., Neufeld, E. and Bartram, L. Visualizing Causal Relations. In: *Proc. of IEEE Symposium on Information Visualization InfoVis'99*. IEEE Computer Society Press, Los Alamitos (1999), pp. 39–42.

Engineering JavaScript State Persistence of Web Applications Migrating across Multiple Devices

Federico Bellucci, Giuseppe Ghiani, Fabio Paternò, Carmen Santoro
CNR-ISTI, HIIS Laboratory
Via Moruzzi 1, 56124 Pisa, Italy
{federico.bellucci, giuseppe.ghiani, fabio.paterno, carmen.santoro}@isti.cnr.it

ABSTRACT

Ubiquitous environments call for user interfaces able to migrate across various types of devices while preserving task continuity. One fundamental issue in migratory user interfaces is how to preserve the state while moving from one device to another. In this paper we present a solution for the interactive part of Web applications. In particular, we focus on the most problematic part, which is maintaining the JavaScript state. We also describe an example application to illustrate the support provided by our migration platform.

ACM Classification: H5.2 [Information interfaces and presentation]: User Interfaces. - Graphical user interfaces.

Keywords: Migratory User Interfaces, Multi-device Environments, User Interface Adaptation, Continuity.

General Terms: Design, Experimentation, Human Factors.

INTRODUCTION

Recent advances in the capability of digital devices together with their progressive mass market penetration has led users to expect to be able to carry out their tasks in any context and in a seamless way regardless of the possibly changing settings.

In order to address this kind of challenging scenario, we propose our approach for migratory interactive applications, which are applications that are able to preserve the state reached after some user interactions using a specific device, and then resume such state within a new version of the application that has been migrated to the new device. The proposed architecture for migratory user interfaces is composed of a number of software modules, which support the dynamic generation of user interfaces adapted to various types of target devices and implementation languages, with the state updated to the one that was created through the source device.

The range of opportunities that migratory applications open up can be beneficial in radically different application domains: for instance, applications whose tasks require time to be carried out (such as games, business applications) or applications that have some rigid deadline and thus need to be completed wherever the user is (e.g.: online auctions). We focus on Web applications, which have limited support for state persistence and continuity across various types of devices. Thus, if for some reason users have to change device, the information entered can be lost and then they have to start over their interactive session on the new device from scratch.

Previous solutions for supporting migration [1] proposed techniques for the migration of entire applications, but this does not usually work because of the different interaction resources of the various devices. Kozuch and Satyanarayanan [5] proposed a migration solution based on the encapsulation of the volatile execution state of a virtual machine, but only limited to migration of applications among desktop or laptop systems. Chung and Dewan [2] proposed that, when migration is triggered, the environment starts a fresh copy of the application process in the target system, and replays the saved sequence of input events to the copy. However, this solution can have performance issues if such a sequence is long. Quan et al. [7] proposed to collect user parameters into an object called user interface *continuation*. Programs can create UI continuations by specifying what information has to be collected from the user and supplying a callback (i.e., a continuation) to be notified with the collected information. However, differently from them, we support the possibility of pausing the performance of a task, and then afterwards being able to resume the performance on a new device from the point the user left off. A toolkit for Distributed User Interfaces was proposed in [6], though our solution differs in that Web applications can be migrated without posing any constraint on the authoring technique to use for developing the applications. Other solutions for migratory interfaces [4] were able to manage only the state of forms and their adaptation process was not able to manage the

EICS'11, June 13–16, 2011, Pisa, Italy.

associated scripts. In this work, we present a solution able to preserve the state during a Web migration, including not only the input entered by the users through the various interaction techniques available in the Web page, but also the state referred by JavaScript code (including Ajax scripts). In particular, the latter point represents the main contribution of this paper, since it has not been addressed in previous work on migratory user interfaces.

MIGRATION SOFTWARE ARCHITECTURE

Our solution is mainly a server-based approach. We did not implement our solution as a browser extension because our idea was to be as general as possible thus allowing users to freely choose whatever browser they like. In our solution we just suppose the existence of the desktop version of the page to be migrated. Also, we do not consider a migration occurring between two existing different versions of the application (e.g. migration from an existing desktop version to an existing mobile version of the same application). Rather, we judged more challenging and interesting to migrate such desktop version by means of dynamically building a new version suitable for the target device.

The proposed software architecture is illustrated in Figure 1. First, there is a device discovery phase (1), which allows the various devices available in the environment to discover each other. This is done through a communication between the Migration Server and the so-called "Migration Control Panel", a Web application (implemented in HTML and JavaScript) running on each migration device and allowing the user to manage the various migration features. In order to support the device discovery phase, the Migration Control Panel periodically announces itself (via Ajax requests) to the Migration Server, and then gets the list of available target devices. After this discovery step, and supposing a desktop-to-mobile migration, every time the browser currently running on the desktop requests a page via the Migration Control Panel (2), this request is captured by the Migration Proxy of the Migration Platform (3), which calls up the page concerned from the application server (4). Before sending the page back to the client device, the Migration Proxy annotates the page.

Annotations consist in modifying the accessed page in order to enable its migration. In particular, it includes i) adapting the links included in the page (to route any following connection through the Migration Proxy so as to support migration of pages that are accessible from the currently visited page), ii) adding IDs to the page components which can potentially be subject to migration (e.g. "DIV", "TABLE", "FORM"); iii) including appropriate JavaScript code in the original Web page so as to support the various migration features (e.g. capture and transmission of the current state of the page).

The Migration Control Panel also enables the user to trigger the page migration (5). When a migration trigger occurs, such a trigger has the effect of "waking up" a script method previously included in the original Web page in the annotation phase. Such a script method sends the DOM of the source page together with the current application state to the Migration Server (6). The communication between Migration Control Panel and the Web page is possible because the Migration Control Panel window keeps a reference to the Web page window, and thus can access data and structures of the Web application, which arrive via the Migration Proxy.

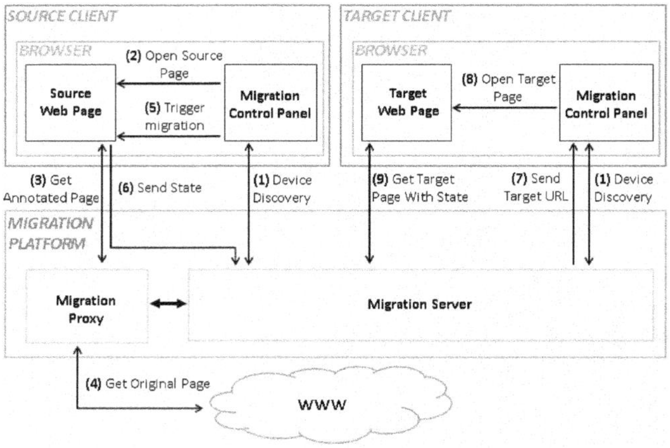

Figure 1. An overview of the migration architecture.

Once the Migration server has obtained the information about the current context in which the interaction is taking place (document, application state, focus), it generates the page for the new device with a state consistent with that of the original page, and sends its URL to the Migration Control Panel of the target device (7), which opens it in a new window (8). The new window shows the target page with state persistence obtained from the Migration Server (9).

The process which supports the generation of the page for the target device starting from the source device page is actually divided into a number of steps carried out by the Migration Server. First, by getting the DOM of the current page (which provides a description of the Web page considered) and the state of the page (namely: values contained within forms, currently selected options, etc.), the Migration Server returns as output a new page which is the original one enriched with the state information received in input (therefore, in the new page the form fields contain the updated values, etc.). Then, such resulting page undergoes a phase of reverse engineering, which builds the corresponding logical description from (X)HTML, CSS and JavaScript implementations. It is worth mentioning that when the Web application contains Flash or Java applets, then they are either replaced with alternative content provided by the application developers or they are passed "as is" to the target device, if it is able to execute them. The output of this reverse engineering phase (which is a concrete UI description for the desktop platform) is then transformed to a corresponding concrete UI description for the target platform, by mapping concrete interface elements on the source device into ones that are more suitable for the interaction resources available in the target device. Afterwards, the Migration Server analyses such a target logical description containing all the various presentations and identifies the currently focused presentation. Finally, the identified logical presentation is then transformed in order to build the corresponding implementation for the target device, which is sent to the target client so that the user can load the adapted page with the state resulting from the interactions occurred on the source device and then continue the interaction with the new version of the page.

The state that we preserve is composed of the values associated with all the forms elements, the current focus, the cookies, and the state of the JavaScript code. The last one has shown to be the most problematic aspect, which was not supported by previous solutions for migratory user interfaces and, thus, in this paper we discuss extensively its solution, whose importance also derives from the increasing use of JavaScript code.

MANAGING JAVASCRIPT STATE WITHIN MIGRATION

The problem of correctly managing the JavaScript state in migratory Web applications is a critical point, and since Web applications are becoming more and more interactive, it is likely to play an even more important role in the future. Indeed, if the state associated with JavaScript variables is not properly saved and restored, inconsistencies can be experienced when the user migrates to the target device. This means that exceptions could be raised due to the fact that some variables no longer exist in the new version uploaded on the target device, or even worse, no exception is raised, but some variables might hold incorrect values (namely, ones that are different from those held when the migration was triggered).

To capture and restore the JavaScript state of a Web application we basically use JavaScript code (automatically included in the concerned Web page by the Migration platform). Regarding the format for saving the state, we use the JavaScript Object Notation (JSON), since it is a lightweight format and in addition the JSON serialisation/parsing support is natively integrated within most currently available browsers.

The data types that are supported by the standard JSON format are: i) primitive types (Number, String, Boolean, null); ii) arrays (like [value1, value2, ...]); iii) associative arrays (also known as "Maps"), like {key1: value1, key2: value2, ...}. However, just using a standard JSON serialiser is not sufficient, since – as we will see – some problems are not appropriately handled by using it alone (object references, non-numeric properties of arrays, timers, …). In the following sections we describe the main issues we have addressed regarding the capture and restoration of migration JavaScript state, and the associated solutions we adopted. As we will see, such solutions include using a JavaScript library (*dojox.json.ref* [3]), which we have customized in order to properly handle specific issues. More specifically, we made a number of modifications to this library in order to serialise the objects that are not handled by standard JSON (Dates, array properties, DOM elements) and we manage the serialisation of objects that do not appear in global variables (e.g. timers), by using a library-independent mechanism explained in the following section.

Global and BOM variables

In JavaScript code, every object/variable defined in the global environment is simply a property of the global Window object (which in turn represents the browser window). In order to programmatically capture the values of the user-defined *global* variables, we use the JavaScript *for..in* statement, which enumerates the properties of objects (without knowing their names in advance). However, there are some window properties that, though enumerated, should not finally be included in the migration state. These are the properties belonging to the so-called Browser Object Model (BOM), an interface provided by the browser, which makes available a number of "utility" properties (e.g. the address of the page currently loaded in the browser, the reference to the DOM root, the history produced by using "Back" and "Forward" browser buttons). Such properties should be excluded from the migration state since on the one hand some of them are *browser-dependent*, while, on the other, some properties (like the reference to the DOM root) are already handled by the migration platform, thus they are useless for migration purposes. The mechanism we use to exclude the BOM-related variables is to create a "filter" list for each browser considered (Internet Explorer, Safari, Opera, Firefox, Chrome). This support works with any web application.

Object References

This case refers to when the migration platform has to serialise two variables or properties that refer to the same value and the value type is non-primitive (then, it is a type different from Number, Boolean, etc.). For instance:

```
var x= <anObject> ;
var y = x ;
```

In this situation, standard JSON would i) serialise twice <anObject> and ii) serialise it into two separate objects (one for the x variable and the other one for y). Instead, in our solution the result of the serialiser is that the y variable is associated with a unique *reference* to the x variable. With this mechanism (called *object referencing*) we avoid duplication of value serialisation and preserve, after migration, the fact that the *y* variable will continue to refer to the *x* variable.

Circular References

A special case of object references is represented by *circular references*. We have circular references when there is a variable, which is defined through another variable, which in turn is defined through the first one. Let us consider the following JavaScript excerpt:

```
var johnJohnson = {
      name : "John" ,
```

```
        father : {
          name : "Paul" ,
          son : johnJohnson
        }
};
```

By using standard JSON, the variable *johnJohnson* could not be correctly serialised, since standard JSON serialises every object through its value and therefore an endless recursion will result, eventually raising an exception. In our case, in order to correctly preserve the object state, we serialise the *reference* to the object (not the value). This has been done by exploiting the *dojox.json.ref* library, which in correspondence of the value of the "son" property puts *a reference* by using a *path-based referencing* mechanism. The latter technique supports the identification of an object property by specifying its location within the object's structure. Thus, in this case, in order to identify the "son" property of the object we provide the *path* that goes from the root of the tree (where the tree represents the object), to the leaf (representing the property involved).

Timers

Timers are generally used when the developer wants to include some time dependency within the code (e.g. indicating that a certain portion of the code should be executed after a specific number of seconds). They are handled through the methods *setTimeout* and *setInterval* (resp.: to activate a single timer which triggers a handler at its end; to repeat a portion of code after a specific time interval); and through the *clearTimeout* and *clearInterval* methods (resp.: to stop a currently active timer, which is identified by an ID; and to clear a timer set with the *setInterval* method). In the following example *handler* is the code excerpt to run after *ms* milliseconds have elapsed; *timerId* is the identifier associated with the timer:

```
var timerId = setTimeout (handler , ms);
clearTimeout (timerId);
```

Timers can affect the state in two possible manners: first, we can have timers that are currently active/pending at the time when the migration occurs; secondly, in the code we might have variables containing references to timers. Unfortunately, the ECMAScript APIs neither offer methods enabling to access the state of an active JavaScript Timer, nor do they allow enumerating the list of active Timers.

In order to cope with this issue and allow the correct restoring of timers after migration, in our solution we override the standard behaviour of *setTimeout* by adding additional code able to appropriately handle the state of timers. More specifically, the solution we adopted creates a global/public list of Timers, by adding a Timer object to such a list every time the *setTimeout* (or *setInterval*) is invoked. Since such a list is global, it will be easily accessed in the global state. The timers of such a list will be updated by a single "central" timer which will invoke at regular intervals the update function of each active timer. In order to correctly restore timers after migration, in the target device we build a list of timers starting from the global/public list of timers saved in the state and then, by re-starting the central timer, all the connected timers will also be re-started. In this way, the active timers will be consequently restored in the target device.

Dates

The Date object is used to work with dates and times. Standard JSON does not support the serialisation of a Date object since it serialises it as a *void* object. The *dojox.json.ref* library provides only a partial solution for this problem. Indeed, it correctly serialises the Date object into an ISO-UTC –formatted string, but it is not able to re-convert it again into a Date object without explicitly instructing the deserialiser with a list of Date property names. However, even doing this, the solution was not able to cover some situations, for instance when an object has multiple properties of Date type at different nesting levels and the same name. In this case only the first occurrence was correctly preserved with that technique. Our solution is simpler and more general: we encapsulate the ISO-formatted date in an object holding a property that marks the object in such a way that the deserialiser can quickly identify and correctly restore the object as a Date Object.

Properties dynamically assigned to objects

In JavaScript all the non-primitive data types (like associative arrays, arrays, strings, functions...) are objects and, as such, can have *dynamically assigned* properties. Such properties are saved in the state by standard JSON only if the object containing them is an *associative array* (or *Map*), otherwise (namely, if they are included by other types of objects) they are ignored. An example of this problem can occur while serialising the following excerpt:

```
var array = [value1 , value2];
array.dynProp = someValue;
```

In order to manage this issue, we have identified a solution that successfully manages saving such dynamic properties also for other types of objects apart from associative arrays. So far we have implemented this solution for managing arrays, though our solution is easily extendible to other cases. In our solution we appropriately modified the *dojox.json.ref* serialiser in such a way that it encapsulates each array in an object holding a property that contains all the array's dynamic properties.

References to DOM nodes

The JavaScript of a web page can access the DOM tree nodes by reference (e.g. to read or modify them). Thus, the persistence of such references is needed in order to preserve the state.

Indeed, one of the most common operations carried out on the DOM tree is to find a node by providing its identifier (by using the *getElementById* method, which provides a reference to a DOM node that has a unique ID). Unfortunately, standard JSON is not able to correctly serialise JavaScript variables containing references to DOM nodes. The following cases can happen: either the concerned element has an ID, or it does not have an ID, or it does not belong to the DOM.

Consider the following excerpt:

```
var element = getElementById("myHtmlElement");
var image = new Image("imageSource");
```

In our solution, when an object of type HtmlElement is actually a reference to a DOM node, we verify whether it has an ID. In this case, such an ID is saved within the state, otherwise our solution assigns an ID to it. In the remaining case (when the object does not belong to the DOM, like the *image* variable included in the above code excerpt), the value of the object is saved by storing the values of all of its public properties using the JavaScript library JsonML (http://jsonml.org/).

SAVING, TRANSMITTING AND RESTORING THE STATE WITHIN THE MIGRATION PLATFORM

In this section we focus on how the migration platform supports the saving, transmission and restoring of the JavaScript state of Web pages. The core of our solution is represented by the JavaScript *JSStateMigrator* library we have developed for this goal. Such a library has two main methods:

- *saveState():* saves the current JavaScript state into a JSON message represented by a Map object, and includes all the global variables of the application and their properties;
- *loadState()*, takes as input parameter the JSON message representing the state of the migrated application and restores it within the target device.

In the following sections we describe them further.

Saving the State

The *saveState()* method works in the following way. As previously mentioned, we use the *for...in* statement as the main mechanism for saving the value of all the JavaScript global variables (which are properties of the window object). As also noted before, we added to the *for...in* cycle a condition to check whether a certain property has to be excluded since it belongs to the BOM variables. After having done this, we create a JSON message containing a couple (key, value) for each property of the concerned global object. It is worth noting that the serialised JavaScript state is no longer in standard JSON, because the serialised properties are enriched with additional information that will enable the custom deserialiser to correctly handle special objects that cannot be [de]serialised by using standard JSON (e.g. Date objects, array properties with non-numerical keys, DOM elements, or even HTML elements which are not in the DOM). However, the entire JavaScript state is now included in such a JSON message.

Transmitting and restoring the state

Regarding the transmission of such a JSON message, this is carried out by an AJAX request directed to the Migration Server. Through such a request, the client passes both the DOM of the page and the JavaScript state to a servlet (which is on the Migration Server). According to such information, the servlet creates the corresponding page. This means that first the servlet identifies the <body> element of the page derived from the received DOM. Then, it appends a JavaScript function, whose goal is to update the JavaScript variables contained in the page, to the current content (if any) of the *onload* attribute of the <body> element. After having done such modifications to the page, the servlet stores the updated page (containing the up-to-date state) in a specific location of the server, and also stores the JSON message received from the AJAX script in a file. According to such information, the server then builds the URL from which the target device browser will load the page with the updated state. So, by analysing the received JSON message the target device browser will be able to restore the state in the target device (*loadState()* method). This is done by deserialising all the properties of the abovementioned JSON object and restoring them onto the corresponding global variables. Then, the pending timers are also created and the central timer is started again (as explained above). So, the actual restoring of the JavaScript state of the Web application is carried out within the client, after the Web page has been loaded.

AN APPLICATION EXAMPLE: JS-TETRIS

To show an example application, we consider a Web (XHTML+JavaScript) implementation of Tetris (http://www.gosu.pl/tetris/), a widely known arcade game. The considered game (see Figure 2) is composed of a 12x22 grid, in which objects with different geometrical shapes fall to the bottom of the game board. The player controls the pieces by moving/rotating them, trying to make them fit each other so as to compose a horizontal line through them. When this occurs, the line(s) of pieces disappear and the score increases. As the horizontal lines are completed, the game becomes more difficult (e.g. the pieces fall progressively faster). Alternatively, if the player leaves holes within the horizontal piece rows, they do not disappear but start to pile up, until the player is no longer able to play, and the game will end. The UI of the game is composed of a number of nested DIV elements. First, there is the top level DIV (representing the whole game), which in turn is vertically decomposed into a DIV element (for the menu) and another DIV element (with the game board).

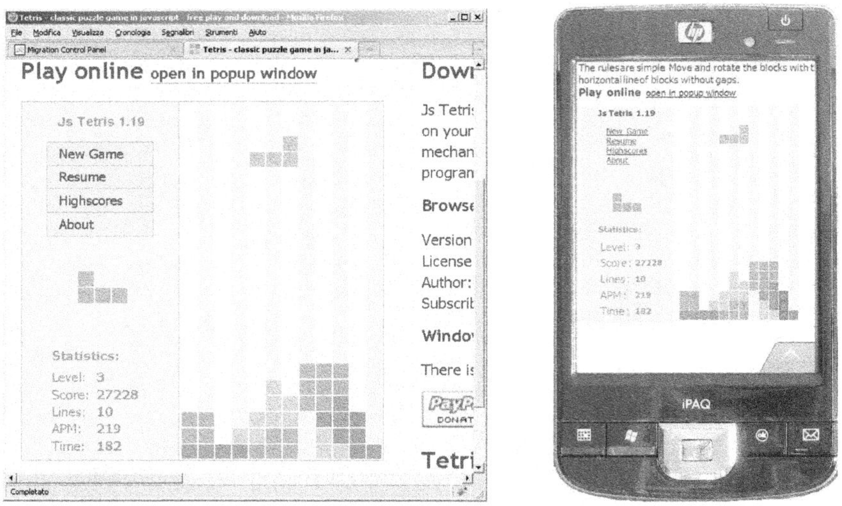

Figure 2: Desktop-to-mobile Migration of the Example

The menu is in turn composed of a number of DIV elements, each of them including a menu item (the control buttons, the next piece, the score data, ...). The board area is a DIV element which initially contains only the twelve vertical columns, which act as guides for the pieces. However, as soon as the game progresses, such elements will contain the various small, elementary squares (each of them represented by a DIV element) composing each game piece. The game layout and the initial positioning of its elements are handled by an associated CSS stylesheet.

All the JavaScript code is included within the constructor function *Tetris*, instantiated after the Web page is loaded, and then saved in a global variable. Within this function, various nested functions are defined: *start*, *reset*, *pause*, *gameOver*, *random*, as well as *up, down, left, right, space* in order to control the pieces. In addition, other constructor functions are defined such as *Window*, *Keyboard*, *Area*, *Puzzle*, *Stats*, *HighScores*, which define corresponding properties of the game. In addition, in the Tetris code there is also the definition of some anonymous functions, which are assigned to properties of DOM nodes, for instance ($("tetris-menu-start").onclick is for starting a new game). Finally, there are also additional properties defining the board area (*unit*, *areaX*, *areaY*). In the desktop-to-mobile migration of the Tetris game (see Figure 2) our migration platform exploits some of the features for managing the JavaScript state we described before. Indeed, this game has object references such as references to HTML elements, and timers.

CONCLUSIONS AND FUTURE WORK

In this paper we have presented our approach for supporting JavaScript state persistence and, consequently, task continuity in interactive Web migratory applications, and describe its application to a case study in the game domain. Future work will be dedicated to carrying out a number of user tests to assess the usability of the presented solution on various case studies.

ACKNOWLEDGMENTS

We gratefully acknowledge support from the Artemis EU SMARCOS and the ICT EU SERENOA projects.

REFERENCES

1. Bharat, K. A. and Cardelli L. Migratory Applications. In proceedings of User Interface Software and Technology (UIST '95), 1995, pp. 133-142.
2. Chung, G., Dewan P. A mechanism for Supporting Client Migration in a Shared Window System, Proceedings UIST'96, pp.11-20, ACM Press.
3. Dojox.json.ref library, available at http://docs.dojocampus.org/dojox/json/ref
4. Ghiani, G., Paternò F., Santoro C. On-demand Cross-Device Interface Components Migration, Proceedings Mobile HCI 2010, pp. 299 – 308, 2010, ACM Press.
5. Kozuch, M., Satyanarayanan, M. Internet Suspend/Resume, Proceedings of the Fourth IEEE Workshop on Mobile Computing Systems and Applications (WMCSA'02) IEEE Press, 2002.
6. Melchior, J., Grolaux, D., Vanderdonckt, J., Van Roy, P. A toolkit for peer-to-peer distributed user interfaces: concepts, implementation, and applications. Proceedings ACM EICS 2009: 69-78.
7. Quan, D., Huynh, D., Karger, D. R., and Miller, R. User interface Continuations. Proceedings 16th ACM UIST Symposium. 2003. ACM Press, pp. 145-148.

If Their Car Talks to Them, Shall a Kitchen Talk Too? Cross- Context Mediation of Interaction Preferences

Elena Vildjiounaite, Vesa Kyllönen, Jani Mäntyjärvi
VTT Technical Research Center of Finland
Kaitoväylä 1, 90571 Oulu, Finland
Elena.Vildjiounaite@vtt.fi, Vesa.Kyllonen@vtt.fi, Jani.Mantyjarvi@vtt.fi

ABSTRACT
So called "smart products" try to recognise user context and to deliver relevant information upon own initiative, e.g., to advise to buy a windscreen washing liquid or to stir an overheated meal. As variety of usage situations grow, it may become difficult for the users to configure interaction manually in every new case, e.g., to specify via which modalities to deliver different message types. This work proposes several strategies to predict interaction preferences of individual users and user groups for a new context, based on preferences of these and other users in other contexts and preferences of other users in the target context. In the experiments with the smart products' configurations, set by 21 test subjects for different contexts (new and known tasks in cooking and car servicing domains, performed alone and in a group), the best of the proposed preferences mediation strategies allowed to predict on average 75% of settings, chosen by individuals and groups.

Author Keywords
Interaction adaptation, multi-user adaptation, context

ACM Classification Keywords
H5.m: Miscellaneous; H.5.2: User Interfaces

General Terms
Design, Human Factors

INTRODUCTION
Smart products are emerging applications, aiming at helping humans in performing different kinds of their everyday tasks. They may recognise speech commands and user context via various sensors, deliver information and just-in-time reminders on different topics and via various output modalities. Although generally useful, proactivity of smart products may be also annoying if they push information too frequently or via wrong modalities. In this paper we attempt to predict for different contexts, which aspects of input/ output functionality are more likely to annoy the users than to please. We call these aspects of functionality "interaction features": for example, sensor-based activity recognition is one feature; capability to deliver reminders is another feature and so on. Interaction features may be configured differently (take different states), for example, activity recognition can be enabled or disabled; for reminders one of the following states can be chosen: disabled; GUI-only reminders delivered just once; GUI-only repeated reminders, intensifying until the user reacts; audio + GUI reminders delivered just once; audio + GUI repeated reminders, intensifying until the user reacts.

Although it is possible to always enable all available input functionality and to adapt only output, our first user study with the cooking assistant prototype [1] has shown that it is infeasible to assume that users would not care whether activity recognition is enabled or disabled if recognition results are not used in any way. Many test subjects said that tracking is annoying independently on how the data is used, because tracking "does not allow to feel like left alone". Additionally, disabling unnecessary functionality in sensor nodes and mobile applications helps to prolong battery life.

The contribution of this paper is the following: first, using interaction preferences of 21 test subjects, we study how individual preferences for one application domain (car servicing or cooking) can help in predicting his/ her preferences for another application domain. This type of reasoning can be called cross-domain mediation of user preferences [2], but we consider application domain as context type. Second, we study how interaction preferences of individuals for a new task (cooking a new recipe or handling a new car servicing problem) can help to predict their preferences for dealing with a known task in the same application domain (thus we consider task type as context). Third, we study how interaction can be adapted to social context (to multiple users, involved in a same task), either by combining individual preferences for the same domain, or by using joint group preferences for another domain. To the best of our knowledge, we are the first who studied how interaction preferences for one context can help in predicting preferences for another context.

MEDIATION SCENARIO
As number of usage contexts for smart products may be fairly large, it would be useful if the products could predict interaction preferences for each user for a new context immediately when this context emerges, using interaction histories of this user and some other users. Thus when a target user (or a target user group) enters new context, for

EICS'11, June 13–16, 2011, Pisa, Italy.

example, launches the cooking assistant for the first time, interaction preferences of this user (or this group) for the target context (e.g., whether to enable audio output or not) should be predicted based on the following data:

- Interaction history of the target user/ group in some other context(s) (e.g., the target user used the car assistant alone, or the target group used the car assistant);
- Interaction histories of other users (or other groups) in the same context(s) as that of the target user/ group and in the target context (e.g., other users used both assistants alone, or other users used both assistants in groups).

This scenario assumes limited amount of available data, but does not require fine-grain ranking of interaction features – it is only needed to select for each feature a state from a finite number of possible states.

MEDIATION OF INTERACTION PREFERENCES

The main research questions regarding cross-context mediation of interaction preferences are the following:

- What affects interaction preferences stronger: differences between persons or contexts (or both)?
- If interaction preferences of some users are similar to each other in one context, will they remain similar to each other in another context?

In order to get first insight into these research problems, we tested the following mediation strategies:

- *Straight*: straightforward use of preferences, acquired in some other context, in the target context (assuming that preferences depend on users rather than contexts).
- *Unified*: take preferences, acquired in another context, and add to each preference value positive or negative feature-dependent and context transition-dependent "shifting cost" (assuming that desired trade-offs between usefulness and annoyance depend rather on contexts than on persons, and "shifting cost" reflects these trade-offs).
- *kNN*: find in other contexts users/ groups, similar to the target user/ group, and apply collaborative filtering method to their preferences in the target context (assuming that users, similar to each other in one context, would remain similar in other contexts too).
- *kNN-E*: same as *kNN* strategy, but user similarity measure is context transition-dependent (assuming that users, similar to each other in one context, would remain similar in other contexts too, but similarities in users' attitudes towards some features may be more important for this context transition than similarities in their attitudes towards other features).

The two former simple strategies were chosen because they do not require sharing of individual preferences and complex computation (and thus suit well to resource-constrained inexpensive products). We assume that "shifting cost" for *Unified* strategy should be determined by domain experts, but in this study we found it with differential evolution algorithm [3]: for each target user a vector of feature-dependent "shifting costs" was optimised to minimise prediction error for all non-target users.

The two latter strategies employ the idea of collaborative filtering, proved to work well in many areas (although in most cases tested in one context only). As selected feature states served as preference values and thus rating scales of users did not differ, we found "like-minded" users with cosine similarity measure. In *kNN* strategy equal weights of all features were used. In *kNN-E* strategy we used feature-dependent weights, optimised via differential evolution [3]: for each non-target "test user" we found users, expressed similar (according to current distance measure) preferences in non-target context(s), and used their preferences in the target context for predicting preferences of the "test user" in the target context. The overall prediction error for all non-target "test users" served as penalty function in differential evolution algorithm, and it produced new vector of feature weights. After certain number of iterations evolutions stopped, and the found weights were used for predicting preferences of the target user.

STRATEGIES TO BUILD GROUP PROFILES FROM INDIVIDUAL PREFERENCES

One approach to decide on joint preferences of a group of persons, involved in a same task, is to mediate group preferences from another context by the same strategies as proposed above. This is impossible, however, if the group members did not collaborate together earlier. Thus it makes sense to build group profiles also by combining individual preferences for the same context. After a preliminary user study with the cooking assistant [1] we concluded that the following combination strategies may be feasible to use:

- *Democratic*: use average of individual preferences in choosing feature states. For example, "audio output" can be in "on" or "off" states; "on" state will be selected if the majority of group members would select it alone
- *Aggressive*: choose the most visible state if anybody in a group would have chosen it for individual use. E.g., audio + GUI repeated reminders would be selected if anybody in a group would select them alone, even if all other group members would use softer reminders alone
- *Shy*: choose the least visible state if anybody in a group would have chosen it alone. E.g., reminders would be disabled if anybody in a group would disable them alone, despite individual preferences of all other group members
- *No sensors*: if anybody in a group does not rely on sensor-based tracking alone, probably he/ she is expert in this task and thus may want to take responsibility for it. Thus use his/ her individual preferences and ignore preferences of others. If there are more than one expert in a group, apply *Democratic* strategy to their preferences; if there are no experts in a group, use *Default* strategy

- *Default*: ignore individual preferences of all group members and use default settings (all features in most visible states, but explanations delivered only via GUI). Strictly speaking, it is not a combination strategy, but it preserves privacy of group members and is easy to use.

COOKING AND CAR ASSISTANTS PROTOTYPES

The prototypes are mobile applications, running on Nokia N900 phone. They have similar interfaces (shown in Figure 1) and functionality: they perform step-by-step guiding through cooking and car servicing tasks respectively. The prototypes aim at helping users in the following ways:

- Deliver primary task-related information: instructions how to perform each recipe or car servicing task step;
- Deliver product-initiated reminders, e.g., to add water or to stir a meal; to check that two car parts are correctly fixed to each other before starting to attach a third part;
- Deliver complimentary information: health and tool tips, e.g., suggestions to replace certain recipe ingredients by healthier food products or suggestions to buy most appropriate lubricant for car servicing;
- Deliver explanations, e.g., that interface change was caused by a message from a sensor-augmented object.

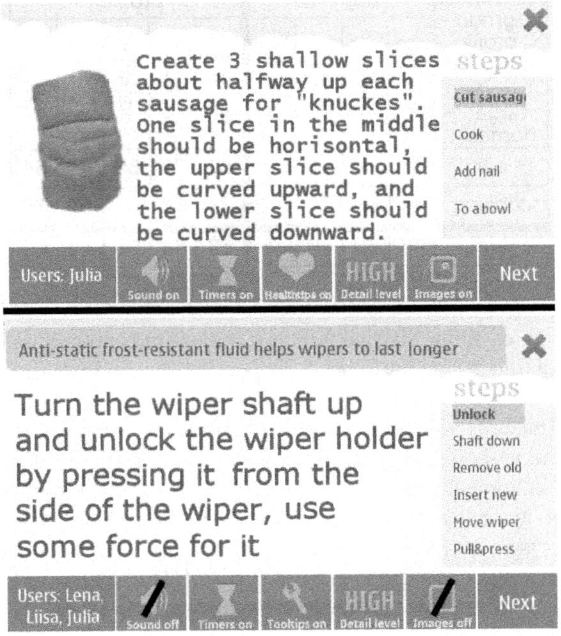

Figure 1. Top: instructions in the default cooking assistant interface; bottom: instructions and a tool tip in a customised car assistant interface.

The prototypes can deliver information via GUI (text and images) and/ or audio messages. Information delivery is supposed to be triggered by both explicit user input (GUI controls and speech commands) and implicit input (recognition of users' actions). During this study audio and sensor data processing was performed by the laptop instead of the phone, but the test subjects believed that the phone is capable of doing it. Recognition of users' actions is achieved by analysis of motion data from sensor-augmented objects, sent via Bluetooth. For example, a significant tilt of a cutting board indicates that sausages were cut and thrown to boiling water and thus the first cooking step is finished. This event detection triggers displaying of next step instructions. On the other hand, a failure to detect certain event within a step-dependent timeout may trigger a reminder regarding the required action.

In Figure 1 the cooking assistant guides through "Hallowing sausages" recipe steps, and the car assistant – through wiper changing task steps. Controls in the bottom of the GUI allow to quickly disable/ enable most potentially annoying features (audio output, reminders and tips), to select level of instructions' details and to hide/ show images, so that text can be displayed in a larger font. Controls for disabling/ enabling inputs (sensor-based activity recognition and speech processing), as well as for finer output customisation (e.g., for enabling audio output for instructions and reminders, but disabling it for health or tool tips) do not fit to the main screen. Thus capability to predict interaction preferences for new contexts is important for saving users from menu navigation efforts.

PREFERENCES ACQUISITION

The user group consisted of 21 subjects (11 females, 10 males) aged from 17 to 75 years old. They were biologists, accountants, businessmen, physicists etc, and none of them ever heard about smart products prior to our first user study [1]. All subjects reported that they cook well-known meals at least once per month, cook new recipes at least several times per year and cook together with friends (usually known recipes) at least several times per year. The subjects had less experience in car servicing: four males reported that they sometimes repaired their cars themselves, while others performed only minor car servicing tasks.

During the study the prototypes instructed how to cook "Hallowing sausages" and how to replace windscreen wipers (see Figure 1); they delivered step-by-step instructions, explanations, a health or a tool tip and a reminder. The cooking assistant reminded not to overcook sausages as they may deform, and the car assistant suggested to test whether a wiper was properly attached to a shaft (we used real wipers and a shaft, but disconnected them from a car for user convenience). Reminders were first delivered via a text box. If the users did not react, audio message was spoken: "Sorry, may I interrupt? Have you done …". At another step the cooking assistant delivered a health tip: an advice to dilute ketchup (used for painting sausages) to make it less salty was given to hypertonic users, and an advice to add garlic (as it helps against viruses) – to others. As Figure 1 shows, the car assistant delivered a tip regarding the type of windscreen washing liquid, allowing wipers to last longer in our climate. Audio presentation of tips (if enabled) took place shortly after audio presentation of instructions. We also demonstrated how sensor-based recognition of user actions may facilitate hands-free operation: cutting board tilt indicated that sausages were put to boiling water, and triggered transition to the "cook [sausages]" step, where cooking timer was activated. Acceleration of a wiper indicated that "remove old [wiper]" step was complete, and next step instructions were shown.

All subjects first interacted with the cooking assistant and then with the car assistant. First the subjects had to fulfil the tasks alone and to configure the prototypes for individual use. In order to reduce affect of navigation cost on preferences acquisition, we asked to mark on a paper preferred states of those buttons which were not available in the main screen, and added them to the profiles manually. Individual settings were stored for each subject for two task types: known recipe/ car servicing procedure vs. a new one. After collecting individual profiles we created ten groups of three persons, well acquainted with each other, and asked each group to configure the prototypes for joint use. As our subjects cooked together only well-known recipes, group preferences can only be compared for "dealing with a known task together" context.

EXPERIMENTAL RESULTS

In our study all subjects, who enabled reminders, preferred to use them in full (audio + GUI repeated reminders). All subjects preferred default settings for explanations: enabled, but delivered via GUI only. Thus in the tests we used the following feature states: audio output of instructions on/off; images on/off; instructions presentation in detail vs. concisely; health/ tool tips on/off; audio output of health/ tool tips on/off; speech recognition on/off; sensor-based activity recognition on/off, repeated GUI + audio reminders on/off. The two latter features in this study do not fully correlate as reminders can be based on timing or step importance, while sensor-based activity recognition can be used for facilitating hands-free operation.

available context	cook new	cook known	cook new & known	car new	car new	car known	car new & known	cook new	AVERAGE
target context / strategy	car new	car known			cook new	cook known			
Straight	75	58	-	87	75	58	-	67	70
Unified	83	62	-	85	76	65	-	76	74
kNN	88	71	88	79	71	61	82	74	77
kNN-E	88	71	86	79	76	68	82	71	78
default	87	74			71	40			68

Table 1. Percent of correct predictions for mediating individual preferences

Table 1 presents, which percent of feature states was correctly predicted by different strategies for individual use. Expression "car known" in Table 1 denotes "known car servicing task" context, expression "cook new & known" denotes the case when preferences for both new and known cooking tasks were assumed to be available. In cases when data of two contexts was used in predictions, similarity calculation was based on concatenated vectors of preference values for these contexts. Applying *Straight* and *Unified* strategies to concatenated vectors does not make sense, so results for these strategies are not shown. The last column presents average preferences of the tested strategies over all context transitions. Neighbourhood size for *kNN* and *kNN-E* strategies was five. The accuracy of the *kNN-E* is an average value, obtained by repeating for each target user the procedure of optimising similarity measure on data of all other subjects and then using this measure in predictions for the target user. The result of *Unified* strategy was obtained in the same way.

Table 2 presents, which percent of feature states was correctly predicted by different mediation and profile combination strategies for group use; the last row presents an average over two domains. Mediation strategies were applied to group profiles in the same was as they were applied to individual profiles.

Confidence intervals (at 95% level) for the accuracies, presented in Tables 1 and 2, ranged from 0.5% to 1.2%.

strategy to predict group profile / target domain	from other domain				from individual profiles				
	Straight	Unified	kNN	kNN-E	Default	Democratic	Aggressive	No sensors	Shy
car	42	70	76	71	80	78	83	84	64
cooking	44	68	76	79	26	51	50	52	75
average	43	69	76	75	53	64	66	68	69

Table 2. Percent of correct predictions for group preferences

The tables show, that on average in our study individual and especially group preferences depended on context stronger, than on persons (as *Unified* strategy, which takes into account only differences between contexts, achieved higher accuracy than *Straight* strategy, which takes into account only differences between persons). This is due to significant difference between application domains in our study: the test subjects perceived cooking largely as leisure activity (especially cooking a known recipe), while car servicing as a risky activity. Consequently, the car assistant was usually configured to ensure correctness and efficiency of procedures: for example, many subjects enabled tool tips also for known tasks and said that "you never know which mistakes can cost you a lot". The cooking assistant was often configured to ensure least annoyance, especially for cooking known recipes: for example, many of those subjects, who were interested in health tips, disabled audio output of health tips, while many others disabled health tips completely and explained that "when I need this information, I'll search the web myself" (none of our subjects had a strict diet due to health problems).

On the other hand, certain individual preferences appeared to be valid across contexts: for example, some subjects always disabled sensors, explaining that "sensors are too much because computers do not have rights to check me"; others disabled audio output because they "always prefer to read then to listen". Many busiest middle age subjects disabled audio output because they "wanted some piece", while eldest subjects liked audio output due to vision problems. Young subjects were more inclined to enable images for known tasks than others and explained that they "generally like icons". These stable characteristics did not allow *Straight* strategy to fail completely.

Group decisions were also significantly affected by domain differences: in car domain often full responsibility for the task was delegated to male group member(s) (even if they had little experience in car servicing), and they accepted it and configured the car assistant according to own preferences, or default settings were used because the group was afraid to make mistakes even in a known task. On the contrary, in cooking domain group members did not try to delegate responsibility to more experienced persons, and generally the groups cared less about efficiency than about social aspects. For example, one group decided that "it is impolite to talk to computers in presence of other humans" and disabled speech recognition; another group decided that "it is impolite to allow anything else [the cooking assistant] to talk here" and disabled all interaction features except for instructions' presentation via GUI upon user request.

The tables also show, that on average collaborative filtering – based strategies *kNN* and *kNN-E* succeeded better than other strategies. This result suggests that both individuals and groups, similar to each other in one context, to some extent remain similar in other contexts too.

RELATED WORK

Mediation of user preferences across contexts is a new topic, emerged in the domain of collaborative filtering – based movie recommender systems, where number of available user ratings is significantly greater than number of interaction data in our study. The work [2] proposed several mediation approaches: to use ratings from different domains as if they belong to the same domain; to compute user similarity in a way reflecting correlations between domains; to generate recommendations in all domains independently, and then to combine their ranks in a domain-dependent way. Our *Straight* strategy reflects the former approach, while our *kNN* strategy corresponds to the latter approaches due to the limited amount of available data.

The work [4], also in the domain of movie recommender systems, proposed to learn user similarity measures for each dataset of movie ratings with genetic algorithm. Such datasets differ in rating scales, but users' attitudes towards movies do not differ (e.g., if a user likes comedies, he/she will rate them positively in all datasets), while in our study a person could like e.g. sensor-based activity recognition in car domain and dislike it in cooking domain. Consequently, the work [4] uses genetic algorithm for transformation of ratings across datasets, while we use differential evolution method for discovering, towards which interaction features the subjects express similar attitudes in different contexts.

Use of individual preferences in multi-user adaptation was studied also in recommender systems for movies, tourist attractions and TV programmes, e.g., in the works [5 - 7], where three ways to create group profiles were proposed: 1) to learn a joint group profile; 2) to merge individual preferences into a joint profile and then to use this profile in ranking; 3) to calculate individual ranks for each group member and to use them in decision making. We did not test the first approach because it requires fairly long interaction histories. We did not test the second approach because the work [6] has shown that it does not succeed very well in cases when individual preferences differ from each other significantly. For the third approach several ways to combine individual preferences were proposed, e.g., to average individual ranks or to use preferences of one group member while ignoring others ("dictator" strategy) [7]. We adopted this approach and selected strategies, suitable for our scenario (e.g., our *Democratic* strategy corresponds to strategies, called in other works "average" and "utilitarian". We were not able to test "dictator" strategy because we did not have enough data to detect dictators. Our *No sensors* strategy is based on the assumption that most experienced person in a group would dictate, and this strategy worked well in car domain, but in cooking domain preferences of inexperienced and young group members were not ignored. Our *Aggressive* strategy is essentially a union of positive preferences regarding proactive behaviour of smart products, while our *Shy* strategy can be viewed as interaction-specific "least misery" strategy – if users feel more miserable when a smart product becomes more difficult to ignore.

Works outside of recommender systems domain are not very relevant to this study: works on interaction adaptation are mainly concerned with adapting interface layout. The majority of works on cooking assistants aim at helping individuals in a certain context (e.g., to cope with distractions from cooking [8] or to eat healthier [9]) and do not consider context-dependency of users' preferences. Applications for cars mainly aim at driver support.

CONCLUSIONS

This work presented the results of studying, how knowledge regarding interaction preferences of individuals and groups in one context can help in predicting their preferences in another context. Several strategies for mediating individual preferences were proposed and tested in four contexts: new/ known car servicing task and new/ known cooking task. Several strategies for mediating group profiles from another context, as well as for building group profiles from individual profiles, acquired in a similar context, were tested for the cases when a group is involved in cooking of a known recipe and in performing a known car servicing task. Due to users' perception of cooking as a creative leisure activity and of car servicing as a task to be performed accurately, individual and group preferences for cooking guidance differed significantly from each other and from that for car servicing guidance, while preferences of individuals and groups for car servicing tasks differed from each other less significantly. Consequently, *Straight* strategy, which adapts only to users, but not to context transitions, slightly outperformed other strategies only in predicting individual preferences for a known car servicing task, based on preferences for a new car servicing task, because only in these contexts the test subjects had same goals – to avoid mistakes.

Despite significant difference between the tested contexts, on average collaborative filtering-based mediation strategies *kNN* and *kNN-E* achieved fairly high prediction accuracies, and both benefited from availability of longer interaction histories. This result suggests that although users' choices strongly depend on context, in some aspects like-minded users remain similar to each other in many contexts. *kNN-E* strategy is both context transition-adaptive and user-adaptive, and it succeeded best of all in predicting group choices in cooking domain (79.1±1.2% accuracy at 95% confidence level), while straightforward use of car servicing preferences in cooking resulted in 44.2±1.2% accuracy, and attempt to launch the cooking assistant with default settings – in 26% accuracy. *kNN-E* strategy also succeeded best of all in predicting individual preferences for cooking a known recipe, based on individual preferences for a known car servicing task (with 68.4±0.9% accuracy). This context transition was very difficult for predictions because preferences of many subjects coincided in car domain but differed in cooking domain (that's why *kNN* strategy, which adapts only to users, but not to context transitions, achieved significantly lower accuracy of 61.0±1.0% - it failed to find the right neighbours).

Among all tested strategies for cross-context mediation of preferences, *kNN-E* strategy requires more computational power, but no domain-specific knowledge and thus can probably succeed in many contexts both for individuals and groups, except that it can not deal well with users who are very different from others. *kNN* strategy requires less computational power and suits for cases when differences between users matter, but the target context does not differ dramatically from contexts where like-minded users/ groups are found (as for example transition between "cooking a new recipe" and "cooking a known recipe" contexts in this study). *Unified* strategy, which adapts to context transitions, but not to users, requires very little computational power if "shifting costs" are set by domain experts. This strategy can be used in cases when the target context differs dramatically from other contexts (for example, in this study *Unified* strategy predicted individual preferences for cooking a known recipe, based on individual preferences for a known car servicing task, with 65.1±1.2% accuracy, because it simply disabled most of annoying features). *Default* strategy appeared to be the worst, except that it can be used in domains where user mistakes are known to be costly (but this will not work for domain experts).

Among tested strategies for building group profiles by combining individual preferences, *Shy* strategy succeeded best of all in cooking domain because of the subjects' desire to be polite, while *No sensors* strategy (use preferences of the most confident group member) – in car domain.

In future we would like to acquire interaction data in longer term use of smart products. We would be also interested to compare two ways to select controls in the main screen: according to feature annoyance, as it is done now, or according to prediction accuracy for feature states (as interface adaptation approaches usually consider navigation costs). First experiments on predicting interaction preferences, presented in this paper, seem encouraging for further work on this problem.

ACKNOWLEDGMENTS

This research was conducted within the SmartProducts EU project, grant number 231204. We thank all participants of the user study for their goodwill and open discussions.

REFERENCES

1. Vildjiounaite E. et al., Designing Socially Acceptable Multimodal Interaction in Cooking Assistants, in *Proceedings of IUI* (2011)
2. Berkovsky, Sh., Kuflik, T., Ricci, F., Mediation of User Models for Enhanced Personalisation in Recommender Systems, *UMUAI* (2008) 18: 245-286
3. Storn, R., Price, K., Differential Evolution – A Simple and Efficient Heuristic for Global Optimization over Continuous Spaces, *Journal of Global Optimization*, 11 (1997), 4: 341 – 359
4. Anand D., Bharadwaj, K., Adaptive User Similarity Measures for Recommender Systems: A Genetic Programming Approach, in *Proceedings of ICCSIT* (2010), 121-125
5. Jameson, A., Smyth, B.: Recommendation to Groups, In: Brusilovsky, P., Kobsa, A., Nejdl, W., (eds.): *The Adaptive Web* (2007), 596-627
6. Yu, Z., Zhou, X., Hao, Y., Gu, J.: TV program recommendation for multiple viewers based on user profile merging, *UMUAI* (2006) 16: 63--82
7. Senot, Ch., Kostadinov, D., Bouzid, M., Picault, J., Aghasaryan, A., Bernier, C., Analysis of Strategies for Building Group Profiles, *Proceedings of UMAP* (2010)
8. Tran, Q. T., et al. Cook's Collage: Déjà vu Display for a Home Kitchen, in *Proceedings of HOIT* (2005)
9. Chi, P., Chen, J., Chu, H., Lo, J., Enabling Calorie-Aware Cooking in a Smart Kitchen, in *Proceedings of Persuasive Technology conf.* (2008), 116-127

Hayaku: Designing and Optimizing Finely Tuned and Portable Interactive Graphics with a Graphical Compiler

Benjamin Tissoires [1,2]
[1] DSNA DTI R&D
7, avenue Edouard Belin
31055, Toulouse,
France
tissoire@cena.fr

Stéphane Conversy [2]
[2] Université de Toulouse, ENAC, IRIT
7, avenue Edouard Belin
31055, Toulouse,
France
stephane.conversy@enac.fr

ABSTRACT
Although reactive and graphically rich interfaces are now mainstream, their development is still a notoriously difficult task. This paper presents Hayaku, a toolset that supports designing finely tuned interactive graphics. With Hayaku, a designer can abstract graphics in a class, describe the connections between input and graphics through this class, and compile it into runnable code with a graphical compile chain. The benefits of this approach are multiple. First, the front-end of the compiler is a rich standard graphical language that designers can use with existing drawing tools. Second, manipulating a data flow and abstracting the low-level run-time through a front-end language makes the transformation from data to graphics easier for designers. Third, the graphical interaction code can be ported to other platforms with minimal changes, while benefiting from optimizations provided by the graphical compiler.

Author Keywords
Human-Computer interfaces, User Interface Design, Methods and Applications, Optimization

ACM Classification Keywords
H.5.2 User Interfaces: GUI.

General Terms
Design, Languages

INTRODUCTION
Interactive graphics development is a notoriously difficult task [18, 19]. In particular, rich interactive systems design requires finely-tuned interactive graphics [13], which consists of a mix of graphical design, animation design and interaction design. Subtle graphics, animations and feedback enhance both user performance and pleasure when interacting [16]. The success of the iPhone demonstrates it: finely tuned widgets, reactive behavior, and rich graphics together make the iPhone interface superior to other products. Designing such systems is a recent activity that has rarely been supported explicitly in the past. Yet, their quality is essential for usability. Unfortunately, developing such software is not reachable by all stakeholders of interactive system design. This requires highly trained specialists, especially when it comes to using very specific graphic concepts *and* optimize the rendering and interactive code. Hence, there is a clear need for making interactive graphical programming more usable.

Moreover, even within a given style of computing (either web or mobile), new means of thinking, designing and developing interfaces arise every couple of years. For example, we successively saw the rise of Java2D, Adobe Flash, Adobe Flex, Microsoft dot net, XAML, SVG, WMF, Web 2.0 interfaces programmed in javascript in the browser (with the Canvas and HTML5), OpenGL etc.[1]. In order to design and develop interactive systems on those platforms, interface designers have access to a plethora of toolkits, usually incompatible with one another. This results in the failure of *reusability*, one of the most praised property in computing: designers have to redevelop existing software in order to port it to another platform, with the associated drawback of not reusing well crafted and tested software. For example, the menu subsystems that have reached a good level of usability in traditional desktop platforms (i.e. Windows or MacOSX) are poorly imitated in Web 2.0 interfaces, where the user is for instance required to follow a tunnel strictly when navigating in a hierarchical menu. Hence, there is a need for the ability to reuse existing software, especially if we assume that new platforms will keep appearing in the future (see WebGL for example).

This paper addresses the two requirements presented above: design usability and reusability of finely-tuned interactive gra-phics. In particular, we introduce Hayaku, a toolset that targets interactive graphics that Brad Myers refers to as the "insides" of the application [21], and that no widget toolkit can support. After a review of related works, we present the exact audience that we target, and the requirements of such an audience. We then present the toolset using three use cases, and some of the internal mechanisms that implement

[1] ..., Cairo, Qt, Prefuse, Protovis, iPhone SDK, Open Handset Alliance's Android, Palm WebOS to name a few more

EICS'11, June 13–16, 2011, Pisa, Italy.

its features. We finally provide a number of elements to evaluate the toolset according to our claims. Related Work This work is related to two topics in the user interaction software and technology community: methods to design interactive systems, and graphical toolkits.

Interactive System Design Methods

Chatty et al. [6] present a method and associated tools to involve graphic designers in interactive system design and development. Programmers and graphic designers first agree on a conceptual and simple SVG skeleton of the scene. While programmers code the interaction with a low quality representation, graphic designers can work on their design in parallel. Since programmers and designers respect a contract, the production of the final system consists in the replacement of the low quality representation by the designer's one. However, the tools oblige the graphic designer to use a library to transform the high-level language (SVG) to a lower-level one (a Tk-like canvas) with a lesser expressive power. This hinders exploration of alternative design since changing gra-phics implies many manipulations to reflect the change in the final application. Furthermore, when optimizing code, the approach falls back to a sequential process: programmers have to wait for designers' solutions before optimizing by hand the rendering code, and designers have to wait for optimizations to assess if their design is usable.

Microsoft Expression Blend makes heavy use of XAML to describe the graphical parts of the application. Like Intuikit, the aim is to separate the graphical description from the functional core of the application. The designer can produce one design per C# class that has to be drawn, but he still needs to manipulate the low level code in order to implement interactions and animations. The concept of "binding" allows programmers to link the graphical shapes and the source objects. The Adobe Flex and Flash suite also provides a means to separate the graphical description from the functional core. However, even if the designer can rely on Flash to build her graphical components, she has to develop the rest of the application using the ActionScript language. Furthermore, there is no abstraction of the graphics, nor a way to express properties with a data-flow. Finally, even if Flex runs on a variety of platforms in its own window, it is not possible to embed the graphics among the graphical scene of another application.

Toolkits

Many toolkits address the problem of performance: Prefuse [14], Jazz [4], Piccolo [3], and Infoviz Toolkit (IVTK) [9] for instance. Performance is maximized by using specialized data structures explicitly (tables for Prefuse and IVTK), or hidden data structures (spatial tree for Piccolo). The first limitation of this approach is that the language used to describe graphics is both inappropriate and not rich enough: describing graphics in Java code with SwingStates [1] is verbose, Java concepts do not match graphics exactly, and rich graphics created with tools for graphic design cannot be directly used in the toolkit. Rich graphics toolkits exist, such as Batik[2], but they are not efficient performance-wise. Furthermore, the problem with these toolkits is that even if they are efficient, they force the toolkit user to work with a specific language and a specific run-time. For instance, users of toolkits can not use Prefuse to write a C or C++ application.

Other works use compiler-like optimizations to produce efficient graphical code (Java3D, LLVM [15] with Gallium3D[3] in Mesa). However these tools are only accessible to low level graphical programmers that manage to write code for the graphic card directly. They are not supposed to be used by the average interactive application developer, with basic understanding of the factors that accelerate rendering.

The solution we propose here consists in helping the production of efficient code for heavy graphics handling. In order to compile the graphical part, we rely on a dataflow, and a mechanism that is able to track the dependencies between input data and graphical elements. Dataflow has been used in graphical interactive toolkits (Icon [8] for the input, and Garnet [25] for the constraints), and have been showed to help building interactive systems efficiently. However, the main difficulty with such a system is to make it fast for both graphical rendering *and* the dependency updating mechanism.

This point is addressed in [24], which introduces a compile chain for interactive graphical software. This work shows that using a graphical compiler (GrC) together with a dataflow leads to good performance. However, the tools were more a proof of concept than a real toolset: the authors present a way to implement optimizations, but do not detail how programmers of the graphical interface can connect all parts together. Another problem of the GrC is that it generates a program that is linked to the runtime of the GrC. This forces the designer to describe all graphical parts of the application with the GrC. However, when dealing with high performance applications, there are parts of the code that the programmer still wants to write manually, in order to maximize the performances. Meanwhile, this programmer may not want to write every piece of the software, if only because they already exist.

The work we present in this paper improves on the concepts described in [24]. In particular, we show how our new tool can help the programmer and the graphic designer to use graphical compiling in a simpler manner, and what benefits can be gained from the new functionalities. We also improve it by allowing it to be modular and thus producing embeddable components. Finally this modularity allows us to turn this proof of concept into a real compiler that can handle multiple graphics back ends and run-time modules.

TARGET AUDIENCE AND REQUIREMENTS

The work presented here targets members of interactive system design teams. A large body of work aims at supporting interactive system design. For example, Participatory Design (PD) partly aims at facilitating production and communication between all designers, be they user-experience specialists, graphic designers, users, programmers [17]. PD employs multiple means to elicit design and communicate it

[2] http://xmlgraphics.apache.org/batik/

[3] http://wiki.freedesktop.org/wiki/Software/gallium

efficiently in groups where people do not share the same culture. Use cases in the form of stories, drawings and mock-up [5], paper prototypes [23]: all tools aim at maximizing expression, exploration by iteration and understanding by culturally different designers.

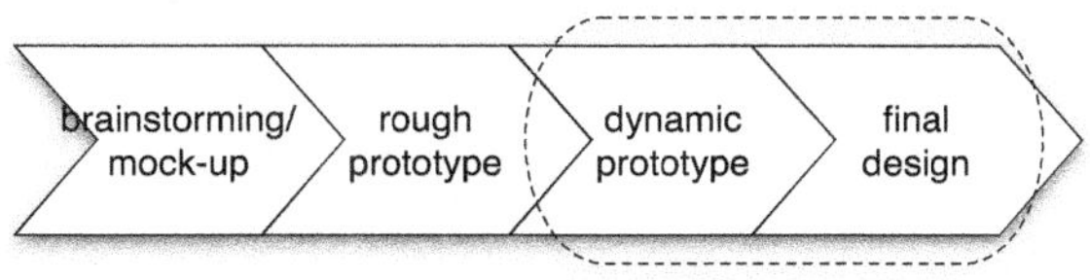

Figure 1. Targeted activity

After these tools have led to initial static prototypes, the designers have to work on dynamic, graphical interactive prototypes [2] [6] (figure 1). As said in the introduction, part of the work is the design of finely-tuned interactive graphics, which consists in a mix of graphical design, animation design and interaction design. The quality of the artifacts designed during this stage in the process is essential for usability. The overall user experience of interacting depends on how well all features (be they graphical, animation, behavior) mix together: the designer must address all concerns at the same time, and dispatching the task between a graphical designer and a programmer does not work anymore. Hence, this activity requires designers with skills in graphic design, animation, interaction design and programming. Our work especially targets this kind of designers.

As demonstrated by Artistic Resizing [7], we think that technical support has a great influence on the experience of designers engaged in the activity. A recent survey analyzes how designers design and program interactive behaviors with current tools [19]. Among the findings, the designers expresses that "the behavior they wanted were quite complex and diverse [...] and therefore requires full programming capabilities"; that "the design of interactive behaviors emerge through the process of exploration [...] and that today's tool make it difficult to iterate on behavior or revert to old versions"; "Details are important, and you never have them all until full implementation"; "I can represent very exactly the desired appearance. However, I can only approximate the backend behaviors"; and they want to do "Complex transitions / animations."

Based on these concerns, we propose a set of requirements for our tools. Similarly to paper prototypes in PD, tools should *maximize expression, exploration, and communication* between designers. Maximizing expression requires rich graphics, hence a toolset should be able to handle *heavy graphical* scenes, with lots of *subtle* graphical properties. Designing such scenes requires efficient design tools, such as vector graphics editors. However, in order to be usable in interactive system, the toolset should *deliver enough performance*. Maximizing exploration implies a system in which changing things (e.g. a graphical property) should be as inexpensive as possible, i.e. with as *little manipulation as possible* required to reflect the change in the subsystems.

TOOLKIT DESIGN AND CONCEPTUAL MODEL

Designing a system that addresses all the requirements above is beyond the scope of this paper. In this work, we describe Hayaku, a tool set that partly addresses these requirements. In particular, we address *richness of expression, exploration, performances*, and *reusability*. Hayaku mainly focuses on the rendering part of the application. It also provides hooks to implement interaction with the user and communication with the rest of the application. The functional part of the application (what happens in the system when the button is pressed for instance) is out of the scope of the paper.

General Idea: the Interaction Designer is in Charge

As said before, this activity requires designers with skills in graphic design, animation, interaction design and programming. Omniscient individuals that possess all skills are rare, if existing. In order to tackle this problem, teams include specialists in each domain, and design is distributed among the members of the team. In particular, graphical designers and computer scientists (or more precisely interaction programmer) are among the kind of specialists involved in the design of interactive software.

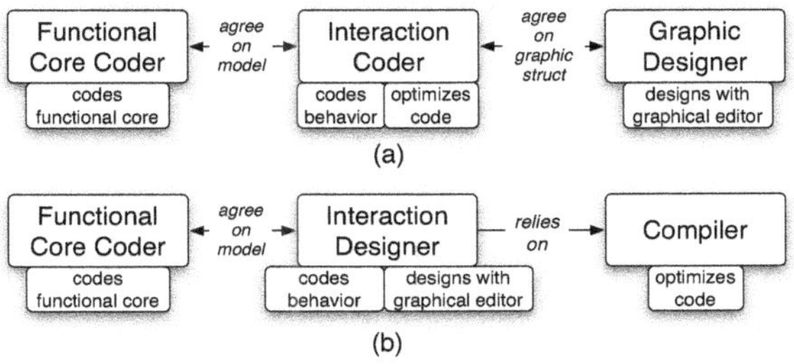

Figure 2. Role repartition with Intuikit and XAML (a) and role repartition with Hayaku (b).

The general idea of our approach is wider than the Intuikit approach [6]: instead of acknowledging the irreconcilability between graphical designers and interaction programmer, and maximizing communication between two different specialists, we tried to make the programmer's concerns accessible to the graphical designer. More precisely, what we target is a graphic designer that has basic programming skills, and that the tool empowers. As depicted in Figure 2, Hayaku provides the required graphical expressive power, while offloading optimizations to the graphical compiler. This turns the *interaction coder* and the *graphic designer* into an *interaction designer*. Again, we assume that the artefacts produced at this stage in the design should be done with all concerns (graphics and code) in mind, and thus by a unique person, or a very close team that share tools and artefacts. The approach is similar to Artistic Resizing: instead of describing with code the behavior of graphical elements under size change, Artistic Resizing enables graphic designers to express the behavior with means closer to their knowledge.

We provide the interaction designer with a tool chain that uses a standard vector graphics editor (Inkscape or Adobe Illustrator) as its first link. This has two advantages: the designer leverages on her experience with such tools, and she can express graphics using the full expressive power of the tools. The other links of the toolchain consist in a compile chain that takes two inputs: graphics elements edited with the graphical editor, and abstractions of graphical element to control them. The remaining of this section enumerates the main features of Hayaku. One of the contributions of this work is the identification of those features. The goal of the paper is to present the concepts used by the tool, and show why they are adapted to the activity we target. Though there is not enough information to fully describe the system because of limited space, the concepts presented here can be used by readers if they want to design a similar system.

Abstract and Control Graphical Elements The graphic editor stores the drawings in an SVG description. SVG drawings are like "classes" of graphical objects. In order to use SVG drawings in a real application, the designer has to provide three descriptions, all written in JSON[4]. The first one is the "conceptual language" shared with the functional core coders, and serves as a bridge between the functional core and interactive graphics. As in [6], the designer and the rest of the team must agree on a common data structure, or "models" which also acts as classes of concepts. This language is illustrated by the right part of Figure 3. The second one describes how the models defined in the first description is related to SVG graphics, by connecting fields of the models to nodes and attributes in SVG drawings with a mini, data-flow-like functional language. It is similar to a stylesheet. In Figure 3, the connections are represented by the lines between the SVG part and the abstract model part. Finally, the last description is the "scene", i.e. a list of instances of the classes (not represented on Figure 3).

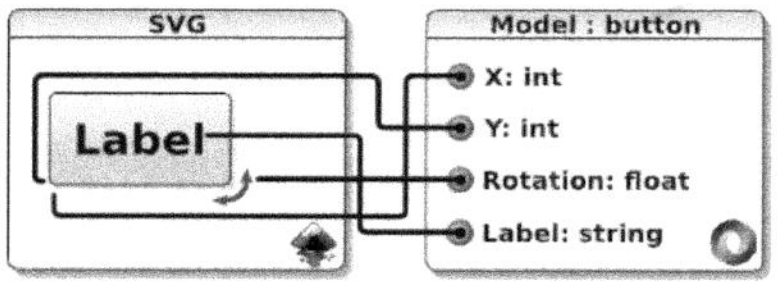

Figure 3. Representation of the connections (the black lines) between the graphical classes (the SVG) and the model.

Though this conceptual model of application design seems complex, it is no more than existing ways of writing code: the first JSON description can be considered as a class definition, the second one as a stylesheet, while the last one corresponds to the instantiation phase of classes at the launch of a program. The only addition is the SVG description, which corresponds to "graphical classes" definitions.

Fast Application Generation

Hayaku includes a compiler that takes the SVG description and the three JSON files as input, and generates an application. The compiler uses various strategies to maximize compile speed and launch speed of the generated application. This allow for rapid fixes and tests, and thus efficient exploration of design.

[4]Javascript Object Notation

Fast and Portable Code Generation

As many compilers, the graphical compiler is able to optimize the generated code. Thanks to a data-flow analysis, and user-provided hooks, the code allows the use of complex graphics (expressive power) with a rendering speed compatible with interaction. Furthermore, the compiler is able to target different graphical back-ends, such as OpenGL or Cairo. This guarantees that the design is portable.

Generate Whole Application or Embeddable Code The compiler can generate either a stand-alone application, or embeddable code. With traditional toolkits, embedding is often limited to a window that the host application displays next to its own windows. The kind of embedding that we target is more useful: graphics should appear inside an existing scene of the host application. Such embeddable code allows for creation of dynamic applications, in which the number of graphical elements is not known at compile-time. This also allows designers to use the compiler as a translation tool between SVG and a run-time environment. More generally, this transforms our toolset in a toolkit for graphical toolkit design (a toolkit of toolkits).

USE CASES

In order to illustrate our approach, we describe how to use Hayaku to implement three different kinds of applications. Though the descriptions look like a tutorial, they enable to understand and assess how a designer is supposed to use the features provided by the tool, and help evaluate how efficient the features are at supporting the designer's activity. The first one is a basic multi-touch application that enables multiple users to move and resize simple graphical objects. It is not very rich in terms of graphics, but since it is simple, it allows for a gentle introduction and short code examples. The second one is a more graphically complex application: a resizeable keyboard with a fish-eye effect that is activated only if the size of the keyboard is too small. The last example is a generic pie-menu that can be reused in an existing application.

Figure 4. A simple multi-touch application.

Writing a Simple Application

This test-case consists in writing a simple multi-touch application (Figure 4). The interaction consists in controlling in a simple and natural way each of the "heads" that appears on Figure 4. The properties that users of the application can control are the position, size and rotation of each shape.

For the designer, the first phase consists in defining four *graphical "classes"* (here the "head"-shapes) with Inkscape, and save them in a SVG file.

```
{  "model": "SMILEYS",
   "classes": [  {
       "name":"Object",
       "extends":null,
       "attributes": {
           "ID":"key",
           "X0":"vint", "Y0":"vint",
           "SCALE":"vfloat",
           "ROTATION":"vfloat",
           "PRIORITY":"vfloat",
           "Picked_Key":"vint" }},
     { "name":"Object_0",
       "extends":"Object",
       "attributes": {}}]}
```

Figure 5. Model of the multi-touch widget.

```
{"model":"SMILEYS",
  "objects": [
  {"className":"Object_0",
   "file":"demo.svg",
   "graphicalItems": [
   {"name":"smiley_svg",
     "connections":
     {"X0":"smiley_svg.transform.tx",
       "Y0":"smiley_svg.transform.ty",
       "SCALE":"smiley_svg.transform.scale",
       "ROTATION":"smiley_svg.transform.rotation",
       "PRIORITY":"smiley_svg.transform.priority"},
     "picking":
     {"Picked_Key":"smiley_svg"}}]}]}
```

Figure 6. Connection between the model of the multi-touch widget and the graphic parts (smiley_svg).

```
{  "name":"Smileys",
   "model":"SMILEYS",
   "content": [
   {  "type":"Object_0",
      "attributes": {
          "ID":0,
          "ParentID":0,
          "X0":100, "Y0":100,
          "SCALE":0.5,
          "ROTATION":0.0,
          "Picked_Key":-1 }}] }
```

Figure 7. Instantiation of the multi-touch widget.

```
def translate(self,dx,dy):
    self.x0.set(self.x0.eval() + dx)
    self.y0.set(self.y0.eval() + dy)
def rotate(self, dr):
    self.rotation.set(self.rotation.eval() + dr)
def zoom(self, z):
    if self.scale.eval() + z >= 0.1:
        self.scale.set(self.scale.eval() + z)
```

Figure 8. The Python code of the three commands to control the graphical objects.

The third phase consists in defining the *connections* between the model and the graphical part (Figure 6), again in a JSON file. Connections are straightforward and need no explanation. The fourth description pertains to the *scene*, in another JSON file. This file consists in instantiating the different elements of the graphical scene (Figure 7).

The designer has to provide the reactive part of the application, i.e. the connection between input events and reaction of the graphical objects. Since Hayaku focuses on the rendering part only, it does not provide any multi-touch capabilities. Rather, it is up to the designer to describe with the run-time language and input toolkit how events act on the conceptual model, by updating the corresponding fields of the instances. However, when generating the code corresponding to the conceptual model, the toolset offers the possibility to concatenate user-defined code. This enables the designer to abstract behavior (see Figure 8). Furthemore, Hayaku provides a picking mechanism that can be called from user-defined code.

In order to test and launch the application, the interaction designer edits a Python script that contains a call to the function *load* with the three JSON files as arguments (the model, the model-to-svg connection, and the scene). She then launches the command *hayaku* with the script as a parameter. If the compile phase succeeds, Hayaku launches the generated application.

The compilation time for this example is 2.2 seconds the first time. Further recompilations requires 1.9 secs only. The first time of compilation is longer due to some tools that need to be embedded in the final application and that does not need to be recompiled each time a change occurs (OpenGL shaders and utility functions). The application takes less than one second to launch, and runs at 515 frames per second (see Table 2). Again, this application is simple and not demanding in terms of computation power. Still, it shows that the toolkit is reactive enough to deal with high-rate incoming data.

A Fish-eye Keyboard

The second application is a 40 auto-expanding keys keyboard, designed for motor-disabled users (Figure 9) [22]. The keyboard consists in two parts: the keyboard itself, and a one line screen to display the result. The caps-lock key is fully functional: the key mapping changes accordingly. The key *"123"* toggles the numeric mode. Finally, the keyboard can be resized, and at low sizes the keys close to the cursor expand thanks to a fish-eye effect [10].

Figure 9. The test application in action.

This example demonstrates the ability of the toolkit to handle rich graphics with high rendering performance. The design of the keyboard uses a full vectorial description for its components. This leads to high quality graphics even when the keyboard is resized. The design also uses rich graphic properties: gradients, transparency, shadows...

Realisation

The graphical part of the application has been realised with Inkscape (Figure 10). In a first SVG file, the designer creates a key by using eight separate graphical layers. The layers are grouped and named in a unique SVG component. In order to build the global composition, the keys are then cloned, organized and modified to generate an artwork of the final keyboard. The creation of the upper area, including the text display, the backspace key and a background with a gradient completes this artwork. The whole keyboard contains 400 graphical elements.

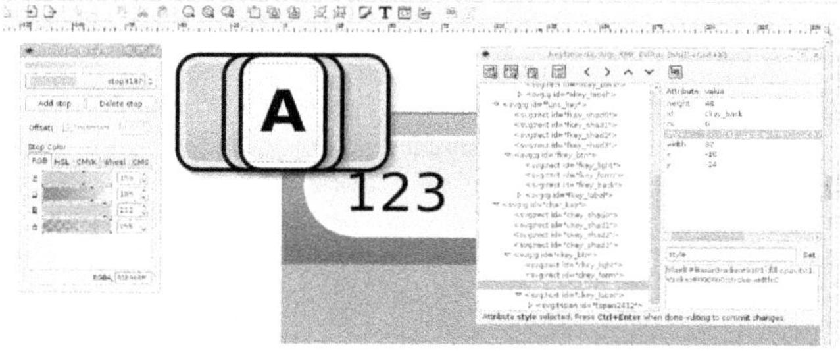

Figure 10. The SVG description of the different components of the keyboard, realized with Inkscape.

Once the global composition is satisfactory, three examples of the different type of keys are put in a separate SVG file, to serve as “graphical classes” : *char_key*, *func_key* and *enter_key*. The graphical components correspond to the component described in the model, and are named accordingly. The blocks that describe the background and the display of the result are also added to this file. A parent class *Key* has been defined to handle the common properties of the different keys. The class is inherited by the different types of key (*char*, *func* and *enter*).

The layout of the keyboard is given in the JSON *scene* file. However, Hayaku does not provide a visual editor for the scene. Thus, the designer has to provide it. Since the production of this file can be laborious, a script has been written to produce it. This script allows the interaction designer to rapidly change the layout of the keyboard by changing some variables in the script, instead of a bunch of values and parenthesis into the JSON file.

The fish-eye effect is implemented by computing the distance between the cursor and each key, and by using this distance to set the scaling property of the key accordingly. Each time the cursor moves, a redraw is triggered, and the key is scaled with is current scale before being drawn.

A Generic Pie-menu

To assess that Hayaku can be considered as a toolkit of toolkits[5], we implemented a generic pie-menu (Figure 11). The objective was to provide an implementation-independent description in order to use it inside an actual, existing application (Figure 12). The pie-menu we designed includes a feedback when flying over a slice: the underlying slice is enlarged. Thus we can not use a mere circle, but several distinct slices. We also need to be able to control the number of elements inside the menu.

[5]here, Hayaku can be considered as a toolkit for building a widget

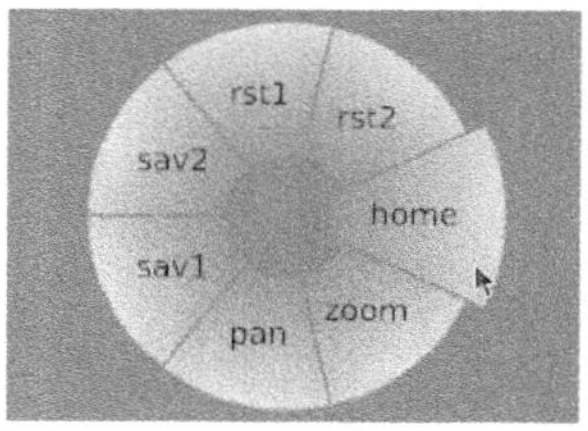

Figure 11. The pie-menu in action.

Realisation

The design in itself resembles the design of the keyboard: we designed the pie-menu to be a set of slices. Each slice has 7 main graphical parameters: a *position*, a *label*, an *angle*, an *internal radius*, an *external radius*, a *rotation*, and a *color* parameter. To describe the scene, we wrote a script similar to the one that generated the keys in the keyboard. The script generates the slices and their parameters according to the number of slices.

The behaviour part maps the picking value of each slice with a callback that changes the internal radius, the external radius and the color as needed. High-level events, such as “*menu 7 has been selected*”, have to be generated by the behaviour part, since Hayaku only provides the graphical part of the application.

Embedding in an Existing Application

We have embedded the pie-menu into an existing radar-like application for Air Traffic Control (see Figure 12). This application is written in C++ and makes extensive use of OpenGL. The application is extensible, and provides a mechanism for loading dynamic external libraries. We used this mechanism to plug our pie-menu into this system.

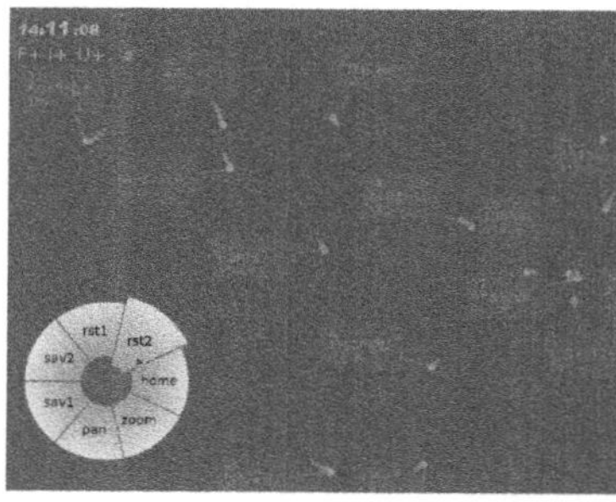

Figure 12. The pie-menu inside a real application.

The steps involved were the following. First, we had to write a C++ class that interacts with the dynamically loaded objects generated by Hayaku. This class is the glue that links the host application and the generated interactive graphics, and factorizes the setup code for all embedded Hayaku code. Then we wrote a subclass specific to the pie-menu, to handle the pie-menu behaviour with respect to user interaction. This subclass represents 112 lines of code. It is a transcription in C++ of previously written Python code, developed during the prototyping phase of the pie-menu widget. As

Figure 12 shows, the pie-menu smoothly integrates into the host application, and does not reduce the frame rate.

This use case shows that it was possible to externalize the creation of widgets and reuse them in other applications. However, in general, existing systems do not support extensions with external dynamic plug-in: in this case, the code generated by Hayaku must be embedded at source-level. The glue between the original code and the graphical part is simpler (just a "#include" at the beginning). Drawing is initiated by calling the exported *draw* function.

TOOLKIT IMPLEMENTATION

How the Toolset Works

The command *hayaku* automatically calls the GrC. The GrC then creates a directory named *BUILD* in which it places all its productions. The JSON files are transformed into Python ones, and a set of C files and their headers are written. Then, the GrC calls *gcc* to compile those C files and produce the object files that can be embedded into C applications. It generates a dynamic library that can be either linked to the runtime of the GrC, or embedded into an existing application.

To reduce compile time, the compiler is able to detect parts that have been modified between two successive compilations, and compiles those parts only. In addition, we designed a monitoring system on the files, and the recompilation occurs automatically whenever a file is modified and saved. The change is automatically reflected in the generated application while it is still running. For example, changing the color of one of the shapes in the example above with Inkscape, and saving the SVG file automatically updates all shapes of this class in the running application. This illustrates the advantage of separating graphics from behavior and using data-flow mechanisms: since the graphical pipeline is clearly delimited, the toolset is able to trigger it at any time, without affecting the behavior of the whole application. Such tools reduce the time needed between envisioning an idea and testing it.

Generation of Portable Code

As we already said in the previous sections, the designer produces the graphical shapes thanks to SVG files. The abstractions and connections between those graphical shapes and the models are given through JSON files. Then, Hayaku loads them into the GrC.

The GrC in itself is written in Python. The GrC is able to produce different types of outputs, in terms of target language and run-time (currently C and Java), and in term of graphical backend (currently OpenGL, and partly Cairo). To be able to reuse the code of the transformations, we implemented our own partial class mechanism. We separate the description of the intermediate languages and the transformation between them. At the beginning of the compile chain, the GrC chooses which languages and transformations it needs to produce the final code by attaching the transformation functions to the descriptions nodes. The trees that are generated can then be transformed just by visiting each node. This mechanism allows us to modularize the graphical compiler and thus to plug different behaviour at different stages as needed.

Generation of Static and Semi-static Code

Most examples are instances of application in which the number of objects is not variable (sliders, pie-menus, keyboard). For other types of applications, such as radar image where the number of flights is in theory not bounded, the data-flow architecture does not allow for simple description and handling of dynamic creation of objects. In this case, Hayaku provides two strategies.

The first one is to consider the number of elements to be displayed bound by an upper limit [24]. This requires to start the application with a pool of available invisible graphical objects, which are allocated to any new data that appear during run-time. In practice, this strategy works well: for example, the number of flights in a sector is bounded by regulation agencies in order to enable a limited numbers of controllers to handle the traffic. It comes at the expense of internal handling of invisible objects (which may hinder performance uselessly) and longer compile time. But the benefits outweigh the drawbacks, since it helps keeping the application simple to write and understand.

The second strategy consists in generating pieces of specific interactive graphical code that can be reused in a larger program. In the radar image, this would consist in designing the graphics for a single flight, and generating the corresponding display code. The main program would then manage creation of new flights and deletion of disappearing ones, and use the display code whenever necessary. With this solution, the compile time is reduced, since the graphical code is not unrolled as in loop unrolling for instance, and the constraint of the upper limit of objects is removed.

Generated code must follow a number of requirements to make it embeddable. First, the generated code has to keep the state of the application. For instance, when working with OpenGL applications, the drawing code has to keep the pipeline in the same state it was before its use. A second requirement is to produce "human readable" code. Since most of the time a designer will connect the generated code to the other application, the names of the functions that are exported have to be understandable by the programmer. For instance, *set0_25_2_1* is less readable than *set_component0_key25_backgroundColor_red*.

Picking Support

The generated code must provide a way to send back information. For instance, when the end-user moves the mouse, the code has to inform the caller that the picking state changed. Hayaku provides a picking mechanism, together with a callback system. The host application has to register callbacks if it wants to be notified by the graphics code, or by the underlying dataflow. Care must be taken when handling picking. For example, a usual picking algorithm consists in rendering the scene in a tiny rectangle around the cursor, and storing each graphical object that owns pixels actually rendered in the rectangle. Applying the same algorithm in a multitouch application requires as many passes as the number of touches, which is costly. Instead, we used a one-pass color-keying algorithm [12]. Each graphical shape is assigned a unique color in an associative array, and rendered with their unique solid color in an off-screen buffer. Picking shapes consists in reading back the color of the pixel under each touch, and retrieving the corresponding shape from the color with the associative array.

PRELIMINARY EVALUATION

As with any method that aims at supporting design, evaluating a toolset requires controlled experiments, with multiple design teams under different conditions (with or without the tested toolset for example). Such an experimentation is a heavy task, and is beyond the scope of this paper. However, we provide in this section a preliminary evaluation in terms of descriptive power, performance, and usability.

Descriptive Power

We provide two dimensions of analysis to evaluate the descriptive power of the toolkit: the size of the class of visualizations that can be described by the toolkit in a reasonable amount of work, and the simplicity of the description of typical applications. A toolset must target the right balance between the class size and simplicity. A thin class may indicate that the toolset is so specialized that the benefits provided are not very significant. On the other hand, expanding the class usually comes at the expense of simplicity.

Class of Application: previous work showed that the GrC is able to handle basic WIMP interaction (sliders) and graphical scene with a large number of objects, such as a radar image. We showed with the use-cases of this paper that Hayaku can implement multiple types of interactive graphical software: interactors (pie-menus), graphically rich interactive software (fish-eye keyboard), and multitouch applications.

As said before, most examples are instances of application in which the number of objects is not variable (sliders, pie-menus, keyboard). For other types of applications, such as radar image where the number of flights is in practice bounded, a strategy consists in picking objects in a pool of available invisble objects. Hayaku enables to use a second strategy that relies on embeddable, generated code, thus expanding the class of applications.

Using a graphical editor also enables the designer to expand the class of representation he can employ. However, we did not try to design very dynamic applications such as graphical editors with Hayaku because we think that Hayaku is not made for that kind of applications. We suspect that writing such systems would require to twist the conceptual model of application design so much, that it would be too cumbersome to do.

Simplicity: Despite our research in the literature, we could not find a clear definition for simplicity. Thus, we measured it in terms of compactness of the code required to describe interactive graphics, by providing the number of lines of code (LOC) of previously described examples. (Table 1). As said before, the JSON description of the scene (the graphical components of the interface) has been judged as "laborious", and a Python script to produce it has been required. It corresponds to the "generator" column. For example, the 890 LOC for the keyboard have actually been generated by the 210 lines of code generator. As we can see, the amount of code is in the hundreds, which is low considering the richness and variability of the three examples.

use case	conceptual model	model to SVG	scene	generator of the scene
multi-touch	43 LOC	90 LOC	54 LOC	∅
keyboard	129 LOC	199 LOC	890 LOC	210 LOC
pie-menu	40 LOC	42 LOC	102 LOC	46 LOC

Table 1. The number of lines of code (LOC) of the different examples.

Performance

In Table 2, we show the performances of the three use-cases, compiled with Hayaku, and rendered through OpenGL. For each example, we show the frame rate of the produced code (C+OpenGL), and the time needed to compile it. We differentiate "first compile-time" from "re-compile time", because Hayaku caches some computation between two consecutive compile phases (text fonts for example). The most significant time is the re-compile time, since a designer using Hayaku will spend most of her time doing small increments to her description, and will launch recompilation from time to time.

use case	frames per second	first compile time	re-compile time
multi-touch	~515 f.p.s.	2.2 sec	1.9 sec
keyboard	~136 f.p.s.	29.1 sec	8.6 sec
pie-menu	~400 f.p.s.	10.2 sec	2.9 sec

Table 2. The performances of the different examples.

If performances may not be as good as expected, they could be much higher (8.6 sec re-compile time for the keyboard). The implementation of the toolkit we show here is a prototype (written in the Python language), and could be improved in many ways. For instance, the produced OpenGL code does not use Vertex Buffer Objects, which could significantly improve the run-time performances. In addition, the internal data structures of Hayaku and the GrC (graphs of tiny Python objects) should be changed to decrease compile time.

Usability

Evaluating the usability of a toolkit is an open research problem [20]. For this purpose, we discuss how Hayaku ranks against Cognitive Dimensions of Notation [11], which help make explicit what a notation (i.e a language) is supposed to improve, or fails to support. Cognitive dimensions are based on activities typical of the use of interactive systems. We chose to evaluate the following activities: *incrementation, transcription, modification*, and *exploratory design*; along the following dimensions: *closeness of mapping, hidden dependencies, premature commitment, progressive evaluation, abstraction, viscosity*, and *visibility*.

Closeness of Mapping: the designer creates (*incrementation*) drawings directly into a graphical editor: it is very *close* to the final product, at least closer than textual graphical language. This allows the use of existing *exploratory design* tools (inkscape), and thus maximizes this property. *Modification* of the graphics is eased since it modifies in turn an SVG file that keeps the same properties (e.g. naming), which in turn is compiled i.e. transformed computationally. Porting can be considered as a *transcription*, and is efficient thanks to the use of a compiler with multiple front-ends and back-ends. The front end of the compiler is the conceptual model JSON file. Since the interaction designer designs the conceptual model, she can make it as close as possible to the domain she models. Hence, closeness of mapping is maximized. However, setting the link between the graphics, the conceptual models, and the data-flow language requires a switch of notation (a graphical editor vs a textual notation).

Hidden Dependencies: the dataflow we provide is not entirely visible. It is difficult for the designer to know exactly what happens once the models and transformations are given. However, the designer is mostly interested in the part of the data-flow he wrote. The part of the data-flow generated by the compiler is less susceptible to be read and understood, except for debugging purpose. *Premature Commitment*: using a graphical compiler inherently prevents premature commitment. For example, changing the run-time environment can occur at any time during the design process. Furthermore, changing a property of the graphics may require a simple recompile to be reflected in the application. Moreover, as Hayaku relies on style-sheets to link the graphical model to the graphical shapes, the design can be rewritten several times without having to rewrite the behaviour part. However, the structure of the graphics must not change too often, since other descriptions rely on it (see viscosity). *Progressive Evaluation:* evaluating a recently modified graphics is immediate. However, evaluating the behavior with respect to the interaction requires to launch the software. Clearly, a tool such as artistic resizing is needed for this kind of activity and concerns.

Abstraction: Hayaku relies on JSON files to *abstract* the graphical model, the connections and the graphical scene. However, if this language is well adapted to represent abstract data, and forces the user to keep it abstract, it is not very well adapted to the human that needs to write it into his/her text editor. In particular, the connection between the models and the graphics would be better defined directly in a graphical editor.

Viscosity: the conceptual model requires all graphical elements to be declared in the JSON file. Hence, if a graphical element is used multiple times (such as the key element in the keyboard example), a change in the "prototype" requires propagating the change in all instances of that element. A solution to this *viscosity* problem is to design a small program that generates all instances from a prototype in a JSON file. This program can be considered as another link in the compile chain, and helps abstract concepts from the conceptual model of the application to be designed.

A change in the conceptual model itself must be reflected into the connection description, and the scene description. This is the problem that the programmer of a C++ class encounters when he adds a field for example: he has to update all calls of the class constructor if a parameter to set up the field is required. Various mechanisms exist to cope with this problem (e.g. a default value), but none is implemented in Hayaku. Similarly, a change in the graphical structure (i.e. the hierarchy of SVG elements) can have a large impact on the model-graphics connection description.

Visibility: currently, the *visibility* of the toolkit is limited. For example, JSON files tend to be verbose and long, which hinders searching or exploratory understanding.

EARLY FEEDBACK FROM DESIGNERS

We provided Hayaku to the graphical designer of the original Fish-Eye Keyboard, and we asked him to recreate it. This designer is used to both design graphics and write interaction code. The designer praised the reliability of the rendered scene. Since Hayaku relies on a graphical compiler, the final generated code does not suffer from a trade-off between speed and power of expression. The final rendered scene is then very close to a static one, produced by Inkscape for instance. Thanks to the expression power of SVG, the graphic designer is not limited when dealing with graphics.

The designer found that one of the most interesting thing was to design the graphical objects by keeping in mind their graphical behaviour during the interaction. This behaviour has been defined by targeting the graphical properties that need to be *connected* to the models in the graphical scene. The evolution of the parameters are then described, either "relatively" with a mathematical expression (similar to the one-way constraints in Garnet [25]), or with a value computed by the behaviour part. For example, the anchor of the shape of a key depends on its width ("FORM_X0": "(self. WIDTH - 100) / -2"): since the width depends on the distance with the cursor, the anchor is updated automatically. Considering all the inputs and outputs of the generated application as a data flow simplified the work of the designer. For instance, implementing the global resize of the keyboard took around 10 minutes, the time needed to understand and implement the solution to connect the two variables screen_width and screen_height to the application. The "connections" allow the graphic designer to quickly build complex behaviour, such as the "fish-eye" function of the keys.

However, there still are some pitfalls. The main problem was the hand writing of the different JSON files. This has been judged as laborious, since the coherence between those files had to be maintained manually. Furthermore, writing a JSON file for the scene is also annoying, since a scene can contain many similar elements. As explained, a solution to this problem is to write a script that generates the scene, which makes it more controllable.

CONCLUSION

In this paper, we have identified that there is a lack of tools to support designers in producing graphically rich, finely tuned and highly reactive graphical applications. We have presented Hayaku, a toolset that aims at supporting this activity, by turning the interaction coder and graphical designer into an interaction designer. The interaction designer writes the program in a high-level, known language (SVG) and through JSON files that abstract the graphical elements. He then compiles it into an runnable application or embeddable code.

Like the keyboard example shows, the compile time hinders design exploration, and must be improved. We have developed Hayaku in Python in order to prototype it rapidly, and we are aware that parts of the code are sub-optimal (notably trees traversal). Many optimizations can be done to improve that part of the toolset. Future works also include expanding the sets of back ends, both for graphics platform and languages. Finally, using multiple JSON files as a description language is cumbersome, especially when describing the connection between models and graphic models. Specialized tools must be designed, such as a graphical editor.

REFERENCES

1. Appert, C., and Beaudouin-Lafon, M. SwingStates: adding state machines to Java and the Swing toolkit. *Software: Practice & Exp. 38*, 11 (2008), 1149–1182.
2. Beaudouin-Lafon, M., and Mackay, W. Prototyping tools and techniques. In *The Hum. Comp. Inter. Handbook*, A. Sears and J. A. Jacko, Eds. CRC Press, 2007.
3. Bederson, B., Grosjean, J., and Meyer, J. Toolkit design for interactive structured graphics. *IEEE Transactions on Software Engineering 30*, 8 (aug. 2004), 535 – 546.
4. Bederson, B. B., Meyer, J., and Good, L. Jazz: an extensible zoomable user interface graphics toolkit in Java. In *Proc. of UIST '00* (2000), ACM, 171–180.
5. Buxton, B. *Sketching User Experiences: Getting the Design Right and the Right Design*. Morgan Kaufman, 2007.
6. Chatty, S., Sire, S., Vinot, J.-L., Lecoanet, P., Lemort, A., and Mertz, C. Revisiting visual interface programming: creating GUI tools for designers and programmers. In *Proc. of UIST '04* (2004), ACM, 267–276.
7. Dragicevic, P., Chatty, S., Thevenin, D., and Vinot, J.-L. Artistic resizing: a technique for rich scale-sensitive vector graphics. In *Proc. of UIST '05* (2005), ACM, 201–210.
8. Dragicevic, P., and Fekete, J.-D. Support for input adaptability in the ICON toolkit. In *Proc. of ICMI '04* (2004), ACM, 212–219.
9. Fekete, J.-D. The InfoVis Toolkit. In *Proc. of InfoVis'04* (October 2004), IEEE Press, 167–174.
10. Furnas, G. W. Generalized fisheye views. *SIGCHI Bull. 17*, 4 (1986), 16–23.
11. Green, T. R. G. Cognitive dimensions of notations. In *Proc. of HCI'89* (1989), Cambridge University Press, 443–460.
12. Hanrahan, P., and Haeberli, P. Direct WYSIWYG painting and texturing on 3D shapes. In *Proc. of SIGGRAPH'90* (1990), ACM, 215–223.
13. Hartmann, B., Yu, L., Allison, A., Yang, Y., and Klemmer, S. R. Design as exploration: creating interface alternatives through parallel authoring and runtime tuning. In *Proc. of UIST '08* (2008), ACM, 91–100.
14. Heer, J., Card, S. K., and Landay, J. A. Prefuse: a toolkit for interactive information visualization. In *Proc. of CHI '05* (2005), ACM, 421–430.
15. Lattner, C., and Adve, V. LLVM: A Compilation Framework for Lifelong Program Analysis & Transformation. In *Proc. of CGO'04* (Mar 2004).
16. Mertz, C., Chatty, S., and Vinot, J.-L. The influence of design techniques on user interfaces: the DigiStrips experiment for air traffic control. In *Proc. of HCI Aero IFIP 13.5* (2000).
17. Muller, M. Participatory design: The third space in HCI. In *The Hum. Comp. Inter. Handbook*, A. Sears and J. A. Jacko, Eds. CRC Press, 2007, 1061–1081.
18. Myers, B. Challenges of HCI design and implementation. *Interactions 1*, 1 (1994), 73–83.
19. Myers, B., Park, S. Y., Nakano, Y., Mueller, G., and Ko, A. How designers design and program interactive behaviors. In *Proc. of IEEE VL/HCC '08* (2008).
20. Myers, B. A. Usability issues in programming languages. Tech. rep., School of Computer Science, Carnegie Mellon University, 2000.
21. Myers, B. A., and Rosson, M. B. Survey on user interface programming. In *Proc. of CHI* (New York, 1992), CHI '92, ACM, 195–202.
22. Raynal, M., Vinot, J.-L., and Truillet, P. Fisheye keyboard: Whole keyboard displayed on small device. In *Proc. of UIST '07: poster session* (Oct 2007).
23. Snyder, C. *Paper Prototyping: The Fast and Easy Way to Design and Refine User Interfaces (The Morgan Kaufmann Series in Interactive Technologies)*. Morgan Kaufmann, April 2003.
24. Tissoires, B., and Conversy, S. Graphic Rendering Considered as a Compilation Chain. In *DSV-IS'08* (2008), no. 5136 in LNCS, Springer, 267–280.
25. Vander Zanden, B. T., Halterman, R., Myers, B. A., McDaniel, R., Miller, R., Szekely, P., Giuse, D. A., and Kosbie, D. Lessons learned about one-way, dataflow constraints in the Garnet and Amulet graphical toolkits. *ACM Trans. Prog. Lang. Syst. 23*, 6 (2001), 776–796.

Specifying and Implementing UI Data Bindings with Active Operations

Olivier Beaudoux
ESEO Group, GRI Team
Angers, France
olivier.beaudoux@eseo.fr

Arnaud Blouin
INRIA, Triskell Team
Rennes, France
arnaud.blouin@inria.fr

Olivier Barais, Jean-Marc Jezequel
Univ. of Rennes 1, Triskell
(barais, jezequel)@irisa.fr

ABSTRACT

Modern GUI toolkits propose the use of declarative data bindings to link the domain data to their presentations. These approaches work fine for defining simple bindings, but require an increasing programming effort as soon as the bindings become more complex. In this paper, we propose the use of active operations for specifying and implementing UI data bindings to tackle this issue. We demonstrate that the proposed approach goes beyond the usual declarative data bindings by combining the simplicity of the declarative approaches with the expressiveness of active operations.

ACM Classification Keywords

D.2.2 Software Engineering: Design Tools and Techniques—*Computer-aided software engineering (CASE), User interfaces*

General Terms

Algorithms, Design, Languages

Author Keywords

Data binding, active operation, GUI

INTRODUCTION

The problem of linking domain data to their presentations has appeared very early in computer science. The Model-View-Controller (MVC) design pattern has been introduced with the SmallTalk-80 language to formalize and implement such a linking [13]. The main drawback of this pattern is that the view is bound to a specific model: the view has to observe the model and refresh its state on model changes. Consequently, applications must adapt their domain data to the specific models bound to their possible views. The Java *Swing* API applies such a schema; for example, displaying a collection of elements within a *JTable* requires adapting the collection by implementing interface *TableModel*[8].

EICS'11, June 13–16, 2011, Pisa, Italy.

The concept of data binding can be seen as an evolution of MVC that avoids such a drawback. A data binding is a "controller" that binds the model and the view: it observes the model and updates the view whenever the model changes; conversely, it observes the view and updates the model whenever the view changes. The concept of data binding is very close to the controller of the PAC model where the Controller binds the Abstraction and the Presentation [6]. Recent GUI toolkits propose the data binding as the first-class object for linking models and views. However, as this paper will illustrate, they all suffer from two main limitations: 1) they offer a limited expressiveness so that hand-programming is often required when the complexity of the bindings grows; 2) they are platform-dependent implying that a data binding written within a given GUI toolkit must be entirely rewritten to be used within another one.

In this paper, we propose the use of active operations for specifying and implementing UI data bindings. The concept of active operation extends the usual concept of operation by allowing the result of an operation to be re-evaluated afterward. For example, usual operation $b := a.select(f)$ constructs collection b containing each element of collection a that satisfies predicate f [18]; the active version of this operation does more: it adds into b (respectively removes from b) any element newly added into a (respectively removed from a) that satisfies f. Active operations formalize and generalize our initial work on active transformations in the context of GUI [3, 2]; the mathematical definition of action operations is provided in [4].

Our proposal aims at combining the simplicity of the declarative approaches with the expressiveness of active operations, which is achieved through: a *unified* and *platform-independent* language for specifying data bindings; the use of simplified *class diagrams* (Ecore documents) for representing both the models and the views; a formalism for *implementing* the specification of bindings independently from the final implementation language; a *compatibility* schema with GUI toolkits.

The remainder of this paper is split into five sections. The first section presents, through three examples, our language used to specify data bindings with active operations. The second section explains why and how the specification of active operations must be translated before being implemented. The third section focuses on the implementation of active operations on GUI platforms. The fourth section introduces works related to data binding. The fifth section complements the previous section by comparing our proposal with the declarative data bindings of three representative Rich Internet Application (RIA) toolkits. The paper ends with a conclusion on our work and its perspective.

SPECIFYING ACTIVE OPERATIONS

This section introduces active operations through three complementary examples. These examples have been carefully designed to illustrate the expressiveness of active operations for specifying various UI data bindings. They have also been motivated to illustrate the limitation of usual binding mechanisms.

The following specifications of active operations are expressed using our own domain specific language (DSL) that is close to the OCL language [18].

Example 1 - A Simple XML Editor

Figure 1 gives the model of a simple XML editor. The left part represents a simplified XML document model; the right part represents the model of a tree widget; the middle part represents bindings between these two models.

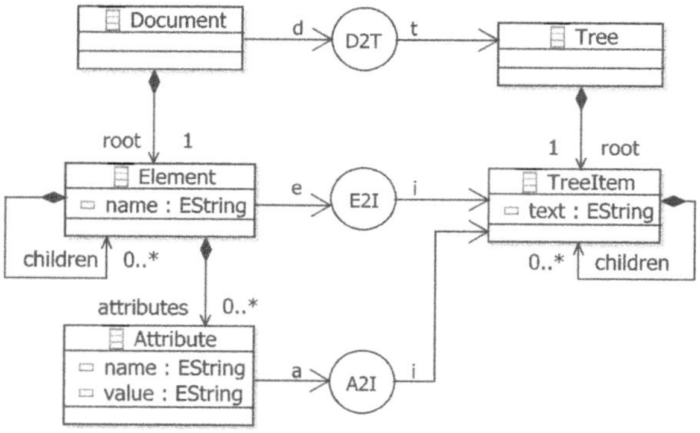

Figure 1. A Simple XML Editor

Binding *D2T* binds XML document *d*, instance of class *Document*, to tree widget *t*, instance of class *Tree*, as follows:

```
t.root := d.root.map(E2I)
```

Expression *c.map(f)* applies function f to each element e of collection c, and maintains a link (called a *trace*) between e and the element returned by *f(e)*. In the example, the root element of document d is bound to the root item of tree t through binding *E2I* defined as follows:

```
1 i.text := "<" + e.name + ">"
2 i.children :=
3     e.attributes.sortedBy(a | a.name).map(A2I) +
4     e.children.map(E2I)
```

The *text* of tree item i displays the *name* of element e surrounded by angle brackets. *Children* of item i result from concatenating *attributes* of element e sorted by their *name* and mapped to tree items (line 3), with *children* of element e recursively mapped to tree items (line 4). Finally, binding *A2I* displays the *name* and *value* of attribute a into tree item i:

```
i.text := "@" + a.name + "=" + a.value
```

All the previous bindings are *unidirectional*. The next example illustrates how active operations can be used to define *bidirectional* bindings.

Example 2 - A Directory Editor

Figure 2 gives the model of a directory editor. The left part represents a directory d of contacts; the right part represents the model of a list widget l; three text-fields *ff*, *lf*, and *pf*, are used to respectively edit the first-name, last-name and phone number of the contact selected from the list widget l; finally, a fourth text-field *tf* is used to filter the content of the list so that a user can quickly find a contact within a large directory.

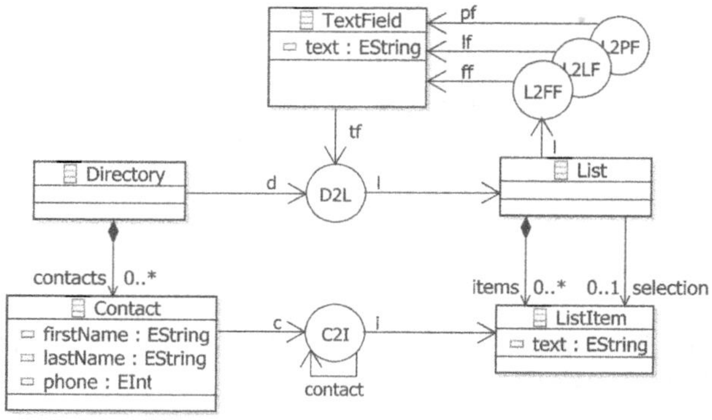

Figure 2. A Directory Editor

Binding *D2L* binds list of contacts *d*, instance of class *Directory*, to list widget *l*, instance of class *List*. The binding has a second argument *tf*, instance of class *TextField*, used to filter the list:

```
1 l.items := d.contacts
2     .sortedBy(c | c.lastName + c.firstName)
3     .select(c | tf.text.isEmpty() or
4                 c.lastName.startsWith(tf.text))
5     .map(C2I)
```

The list of contacts is first sorted (line 2); a simple string concatenation is here used to specify a sort on the *lastName* and then on the *firstName* of the contacts. The resulting list is then filtered through the *select* operation (lines 3-4): if text-field *tf* is empty, all the contacts are selected; otherwise, only contacts whose last-name starts with the text-field content are selected. Each resulting contact c is then mapped to a list item i by calling binding *C2I* (line 5), which is defined as follows:

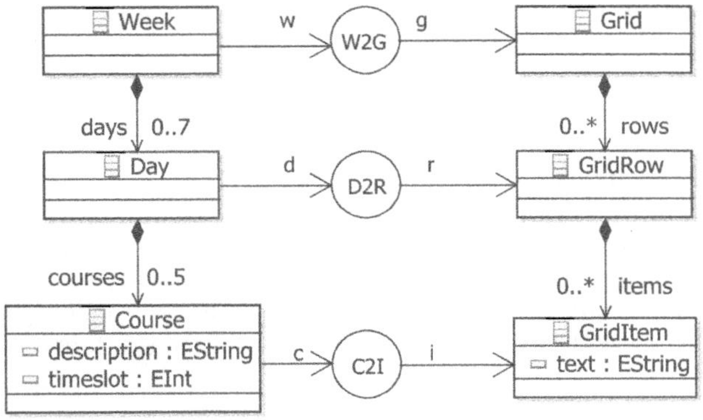

Figure 3. An academic calendar

```
1  i.text := c.firstName + " " + c.lastName
2  i.contact := c
```

This binding displays each contact in the list widget with their first and last names (line 1). A *trace* of binding *C2I*, represented by reverse arrow *contact* in figure 2, is then set (line 2).

Binding *L2PF* binds text-field *pf* used to edit the *phone* number to the selected item of the list *l*, as follows:

```
1  pf.text := l.selection.contact.phone.toString()
2  l.selection.contact.phone := pf.text.toInteger()
```

The *phone* number of the selected contact is converted into a string displayed into text-field *pf* (line 1); conversely, the *text* of text-field *pf* is converted into an integer that represents the phone number of the selected contact (line 2). Text-field *pf* must be designed to restrict the editing to integers; this must be achieved at the GUI platform level, but *not* by the binding itself. Binding *L2PF* is *bidirectional*: if the user changes the selection, the text-field is automatically updated; conversely, if the user changes the text-field content, the phone number of the selected contact is automatically updated. Infinite loop on such a bidirectional binding is avoided by only notifying changes on *new* values: if the new value does not differ from the previous one, no notification is performed by the property setter method.

Only path assignments, along with an optional conversion, can be used in a bidirectional way [4]. If no conversion is required between two properties, the double use of operator := defines a *bidirectional assignment* that can be shortened with the operator =, such as binding *L2FF* illustrates:

```
ff.text = l.selection.contact.firstName
```

Contrary to the previous binding, no conversion is required here. Binding *L2LF* is similar to *L2FF* for property *lastName*.

These bindings illustrate the bidirectionality feature of active operations; however, as within example 1, these bindings remain quite simple. The next example uses intensively active operations to achieve a complex binding.

Example 3 - An Academic Calendar

Figure 3 gives the model of an academic calendar. The left part represents a simplified model of a weekly academic calendar; the right part represents the model of an HTML-like table widget; the middle part represents bindings between these two models.

Binding *W2G* binds week *w*, instance of class *Week*, to grid widget *g*, instance of class *Grid*. It maps *days* of week *w* to *rows* of grid *g* by calling binding *D2R*:

```
g.rows := w.days.map(D2R)
```

Binding *D2R* binds day *d* to a grid row *r*, which consists of populating relation *r.items* from relation *d.courses*. Figure 4 synthesizes the principle of binding *D2R* through a simple example: collection *ts* contains all the predefined time-slots of the calendar (for example, time-slot 0 corresponds to slot 9:05-9:55am); day *d* contains two courses *a* and *b* respectively located on time-slots 1 and 4. The resulting grid-items *r.items* of grid-row *r* must contain empty grid-items (noted $i_\varnothing$) that represent the free time-slots, and non-empty grid-items (noted i_a and i_b) that represents courses *a* and *b*.

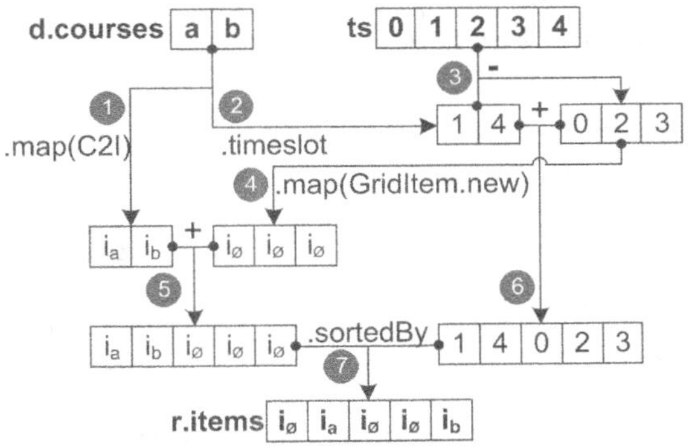

Figure 4. Principle of binding *D2R*

The collection (i_a, i_b) is computed by mapping courses *d.courses* through binding *C2I* ①. The collection of free time-slots $(0, 2, 3)$ is computed by subtracting *d.courses.timeslot*[1] equals to $(1, 4)$ ②, from collection *ts* representing all defined time-slots (0..4) ③. The collection of empty grid-items $(i_\varnothing, i_\varnothing, i_\varnothing)$ is computed by mapping collection of free time-slots with function *GridItem.new* ④. The two collections of grid-items are

[1]Expression *d.courses.timeslot* is a path, which is a specific operation detailed in the next section.

then concatenated to form the collection of all grid-items $(i_a, i_b, i_\emptyset, i_\emptyset, i_\emptyset)$ ⑤. Such a collection is however not ordered accordingly to time-slots. Since time-slot numbers represent positions, the "order collection" $(1, 4, 0, 2, 3)$, resulting from the concatenation of a and b time-slots and the free time-slots ⑥, is used to sort the grid-items ⑦: operation *sortedBy* sorts collection $(i_a, i_b, i_\emptyset, i_\emptyset, i_\emptyset)$ with order $(1, 4, 0, 2, 3)$ that gives the position of each item after sorting.

The previous principle is quite complex due to the calendar model that does not divide a day into time-slots. However, this proposed model is a simplification of a calendar model that allows a time-slot to contain multiple courses and a course to span multiple time-slots. This simplified model has been designed to illustrate that active operations allow the definition of bindings between "something missing" (a time-slot without any course) to a UI object (an empty grid-item).

Binding *D2R* is specified with our DSL as follows, and illustrates the expressiveness of our DSL:

```
ts := seq(0 to 4)
courseTS := d.courses.timeslot
freeTS := ts − courseTS
items := d.courses.map(C2I) +
        freeTS.map(n | GridItem.new)
r.items := items.sortedBy(courseTS + freeTS)
```

Binding *C2I* finally binds the text of the not-empty grid-item i to the description of its corresponding course c, as follows:

```
i.text := c.description
```

TRANSLATING ACTIVE OPERATIONS

The previous section focuses on the specifications of bindings. However, as this section will illustrate, these specifications cannot be executed on a target platform as is: they must be *translated* into an active implementation. Such a translation uses again our own DSL by introducing new specific operations, thus making the translation process independent from the final implementation language and platform. Moreover, some of the new operations motivated by the translation might be useful at the specification level, such as example 3 illustrates through its use of operation *sortedBy*.

Paths

Paths extend the dotted notation of OOP so that the dot symbol can be applied more than once on collections [18]. For example, expression *d.contacts.firstName* represents a path that returns a *flattened* collection, as the OCL operation *collect* does [18], containing the first-name of all contacts of directory *d*. The dedicated operation *path* must be used for implementing path on collections on top of an OOP language; in binding *L2FF* of example 2, expression:

```
ff.text = l.selection.contact.firstName
```

must be *translated* into:

```
ff.text = l.selection
    .path(s | s.contact).path(c | c.firstName)
```

Observability

Usual loops can be used to implement usual operations on collections. For example, expression *b := a.collect(f)* computes collection b by converting each element e of collection a into element *f(e)* within collection b; operation *collect* is easy to implement using a loop, as follows:

```
a.each(e, i | b.add(f(e), i) )
```

The previous code states that each element e at position i within collection a must be converted to the corresponding element *f(e)* at the same position i within b.

Making an operation active, such as operation *collect*, requires the *observability* of collections: an observable collection is a collection from which additions and removals can be observed [1, 9]. We have proposed in [4] to extend usual loops with *active loops* that manage collection observability and allow implementing active operations as usual loops do for implementing the usual operations. For example, the previous usual loop that implements operation *collect* can be easily translated to the following active loop:

```
1 a.eachAdded(e, i | b.add(f(e), i) )
2 a.eachRemoved(e, i | b.remove(i) )
```

This code states that: each element e *newly* added into a results in adding the converted element *f(e)* into b (line 1); each element e *newly* removed from position i within collection a results in removing the corresponding element from b (line 2).

Such a translation process from usual loops to active loops works fine for operations *collect*, *map* and *path*. However, it must be augmented for operations *select* and *sortedBy*, as explained in the next section.

Selection and sort

The following expression:

```
minors := persons.select(p | p.age < 18)
```

computes collection *minors* that contains persons p under 18. The active loop of such a *select* operation can be easily translated from a usual loop. This loop works fine whenever a person is added or removed from collection *persons*; however, it fails whenever the age of a person goes above 18: this last change is not captured by the active loop. We thus propose to *reify* predicate function f involved in expression *c.select(f)* into a *predicate collection* represented as a sequence of booleans. The predicate collection related to the previous example is defined by the following expression:

```
persons.path(a | a.age).predicate(a | a < 18)
```

If *persons* contains three people with ages 16, 42 and 12, this expression returns predicate collection $true, false, true$. By *overriding* operation *select*, the previous example should be translated into:

```
minors := persons.select(
    persons.path(a | a.age).predicate(a | a < 18)
)
```

The same problem arises with operation *sortedBy*. For example, binding *E2I* of example 1 sorts attributes of element *e* by their name:

```
e.attributes.sortedBy(a | a.name)
```

If an attribute *a* is added or removed from *e.attributes*, the active loop updates correctly the resulting collection. However, any change to *a.name* is not captured by the active loop. We thus propose to *reify* the order function *f* involved in expression *c.sortedBy(f)* into an *order collection* represented as a sequence of integers. In the previous example, the order collection is defined by the following expression:

```
e.attributes.path(a | a.name).ascendingOrder()
```

If element *e* defines three attributes named "first", "second" and "last", the previous expression returns order collection $\{0, 2, 1\}$ that gives the position of names after the sort. By *overriding* operation *sortedBy*, the previous example should be translated into:

```
e.attributes.sortedBy(
    e.attributes.path(a | a.name).ascendingOrder()
)
```

Order collections are also useful for solving various ordering problems, independently from the translation phase. For example, they have been used in the specification of binding *D2R* to bind courses and free time-slots with grid-items.

Tuples

Anonymous functions *f* involved in active operations, such as *b := a.select(f)*, may require more than one argument. For example, binding *D2L* includes a selection based on two arguments *tf* and *c*:

```
d.contacts.select(c |
    tf.text.isEmpty() or
     c.lastName.startsWith(tf.text)
)
```

The reified version of this *select* operation uses a *tuple* from which a *predicate* operation is performed, as follows:

```
d.contacts.select(
    (d.contacts.lastName, tf.text).predicate(n,t |
        t.isEmpty() or n.startsWith(t)
    )
)
```

By doing so, the predicate collection is updated whenever *d.contacts.lastName* or *tf.text* changes. Tuples can thus be used for extending the initial scope of operation select to multiple arguments; a similar extension can be applied to other active operations, such as operation *collect*[2].

IMPLEMENTING ACTIVE OPERATIONS

The previous section explains the translation of binding specifications to their active implementation, independently from the target GUI platform. This section explains how to make the final implementation *compatible* with a given GUI platform so that its widgets can be reused. It gives theoretical and experimental results regarding performances of the final implementation.

Implementing Active Operations on a GUI Toolkit

In order to evaluate the use of active operations for UI data binding, we have implemented active operations on top of the Flex GUI platform [12]. Flex has been chosen for its own internal binding mechanism, its rich set of widgets, and its ability to pass anonymous functions as function arguments. All the three examples presented in this paper have been implemented with the resulting *ActiveFlex* project; more details about the Flex implementation can be found within the project.[3].

Figure 5 gives an overview of our *ActiveFlex* model that extends Flex classes with active operation capabilities.

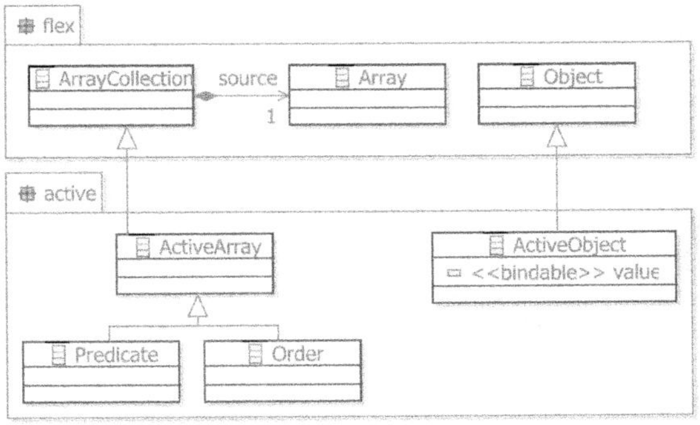

Figure 5. ActiveFlex model

The Flex API defines a built-in data binding mechanism accessible through classes *ArrayCollection* and *Object*. An *ArrayCollection* represents an observable and ordered collection of elements; it is bound to a source *Array* that holds the elements. Array collections can be bound to Flex widgets displaying collections to users, such as widget *List*. Consequently, our class *ActiveArray* inherits from this Flex *ArrayCollection* class so that instances of *ActiveArray* returned by active operations can be bound to such Flex widgets. Class *Predicate* defines predicate collections and adds usual boolean operations to class *ArrayCollection*; class *Order* defines or-

[2] Such an extension is however out of the scope of this paper.
[3] *ActiveFlex* is available under GPL license at `http://gri.eseo.fr/software/activeflex.html` .

der collections by providing operation *and* that allows sorting on multiple criteria.

Any class derived from the Flex class *Object* can mark any of its attribute as *bindable*: by doing so, the bindable attribute can be bound to Flex widgets displaying simple values, such as a text-field or a check-box. Our class *ActiveObject* thus defines its content through attribute *value* that is marked as bindable so that any active object can be bound to such Flex widgets.

The following MXML code[4] illustrates how simple the binding of the *TreeItem* of example 1 to a Flex *mx:Tree* widget is:

```
<mx:Tree dataProvider="{tree.root}" ... />
```

Object *tree* is an instance of our class *Tree*. The *mx:Tree* is bound to the *tree.root*, which is an instance of our *TreeItem* class; the *mx:Tree* then uses internally: the *children* property to recursively construct the tree content, and the bindable property *label* to display the content of each tree item. Any Flex widget can be bound to an instance of our classes *ActiveArray* or *ActiveObject* similarly.

Such a scheme can be applied to any RIA toolkit that proposes a declarative data binding mechanism, such as with WPF/Silverlight [16] or JavaFX [10]. Toolkits without data binding capabilities require more coding effort. For example, the use of active operations on top of the Swing toolkit requires implementing Java interfaces such as *TableModel*, *TreeModel* or *Document* within active collection and/or object classes.

Theoretical Complexities

Table 1 summarizes the best-case (C_{min}), average-case (C_{av}) and worst-case (C_{max}) complexities of active operations (see [4] for more details on computation of these complexities).

	C_{min}			C_{av}			C_{max}		
Operation	I	+	-	I	+	-	I	+	-
collect	n	1		n					
path	n	1		n					
select	n	1		n					
predicate	n	1		n					
not, and, or	n	1		n					
sortedBy	n	1		n					
asc.Order	n	1		$n.log_2\, n$	n		n^2	n	
and	n	1		n					
union	n	1		n					
difference	n	1		n^2	n		n^2	n	
intersection	n	1		n^2	n		n^2	n	

Table 1. Complexities of active operations

Columns labeled "I" give complexities for the initial construction of the operation result; columns labeled "+" (respectively "-") give complexities for updating the result when an addition (respectively a removal) occurs on the source collection. Initial constructions mainly cost a linear time since they globally use elementary operation *add* in the best-case (*i.e.* append); subsequent mutations also cost a linear time due the required shifting. These results only vary for sorting that requires two loops, and for difference/intersection that must check the presence with operation *contains* which costs a linear time.

The previous complexities are asymptotic. However, the *translation cost* representing the amount of time and memory used by the intermediate operations that appear during the translation should be also taken into account. For example, expression:

```
c.select(e | f1(e.p1) and f2(e.p2))
```

must be translated into expression:

```
c.select(c.path(e|e.p1).predicate(f1) and
         c.path(e|e.p2).predicate(f2))
```

This last expression includes 2 paths ($n_{pa} = 2$), 2 predicates ($n_{pr} = 2$), plus 1 boolean expression ($n_{pr} - 1$), and thus costs 5 intermediate active collections and operations. A similar principle can be applied to operation *sortedBy* that can be based on multiple criteria (n_{cr}). Table 2 synthesizes such a cost.

Operation	Translation cost
union, diff., inter.	0
collect	0
path	1
select	$n_{pa} + 2 \times n_{pr} - 1$
sortedBy	$n_{pa} + 2 \times n_{cr} - 1$

Table 2. Translation cost

The previous complexities of *individual* operations can be used to compute complexities of an *overall* binding. Let us consider the binding defined by example 1 (the XML editor) for a source XML document with a depth d, a number of child elements per element n_e, and a number of attributes per element n_a, both common to all elements. For simplification purpose, we consider that $n_e = n_a = n$. Document thus counts $N_e = \frac{n^d-1}{n-1}$ elements, and $N_a = n \times N_e$ attributes; the tree widgets counts $N_i = N_a + N_e$ items. By considering that $N = n^d \gg 1$, we have: $N_e \simeq n^{d-1} = N/n$ and $N_a \simeq N_i \simeq n^d = N$. Number $N = n^d$ thus represents the overall and approximate number of both document nodes and tree items, while n represents the cardinality of each relation. The worst-case complexity of the associated binding is given by the complexity of the sort that binding *D2R* performs, and thus costs $\mathcal{O}(n^2)$. The initial construction of the tree widget requires N_e sort operations, and thus costs $C_{init} = N_e \times \mathcal{O}(n^2)$, *i.e.* $C_{init} = \mathcal{O}(N \times n)$. Mutations cost a linear time for all operations within the binding, *i.e.* $C_{update} = \mathcal{O}(n)$.

[4]MXML is the Flex XML dialect used to specify user interfaces.

The ratio N between these two complexities well illustrates the interest in making active binding operations, rather than recomputing all the resulting tree widget content. The next section illustrates that our experimental results match these theoretical ones.

Experimental results

Our experimental measurements focus on two objectives: verifying that our theoretical complexities match the measured performance; comparing the cost of active operations with the cost of widget rendering. They have been performed on a PC running Windows XP on top of an Intel Pentium 1.8 GHz + 1 GB RAM and an ATI FireGL 128 MB. Figure 6 gives the performance of initial construction of the tree widget for the XML document defined in the previous section with depth 3 ($N = n^3$). Axis x represents number n, and axis y gives time performance in ms.

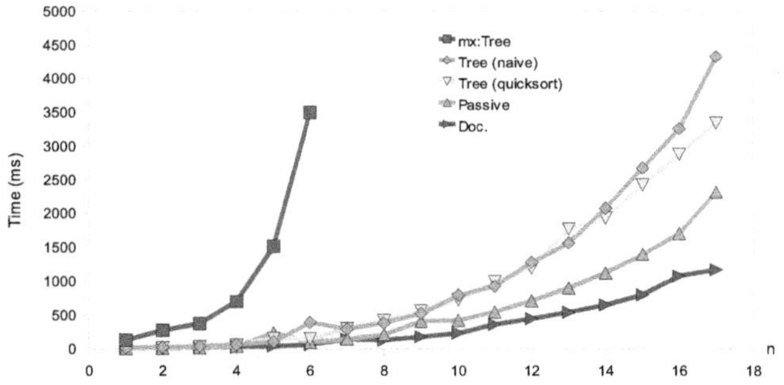

Figure 6. Construction performance

The five curves represent respectively: the XML document construction (curve "Doc.") that includes the creation of instances of classes *Document*, *Element* and *Attribute*, and the establishment of their relation; the "passive" data binding (curve "Passive") that represents the usual operations that can be used (only) for the initial construction; the tree construction (curve "Tree (naive)") that represents the binding uses to build the target instances of class *Tree* and *TreeItem* with active operations; the tree construction that uses a quicksort-based algorithm (curve "Tree (quicksort)") instead of a naive one (previous curve); finally, the tree widget rendering (curve "mx:Tree") performed by the Flex engine to display the graphical content of the widget. Curve "Doc" tends to $0,25 \times N$, thus illustrating that the document construction is linear. Curve "Tree (naive)" gives the performance of the bindings in the worst-case since it uses a naive implementation of the sort that costs $\mathcal{O}(n^2)$; it tends to $0,052 \times N \times n$, thus matching the expected theoretical result. Curve "Tree (quicksort)" tends to $0,18 \times N \times log_2 n$; the expected logarithmic dimming effect appears for a significant value of n (here around 14). Curve "Passive" tends to $0,028 \times N \times n$, which is around half the curve "Tree (naive)": this illustrates that the translation cost is around 1, as expected (one intermediate order collection is here required). Finally, curve "mx:Tree" tends to $0,6 \times N \times n^2$, which probably results from the traversing required for computing location y of each tree-item i. This location may be recursively computed by summing heights h of the previous-sibling items of i: $y(i) = \sum_j h(i.sibling[j])$; in turn, computing the height of a node consists of summing the height of its children: $h(i) = \sum_j h(i.children[j])$. The overall layout includes N computation of y, so that the complexity tends to $N \times n^2$.

This experimentation illustrates that complexity of data bindings can often be neglected regarding the complexity of rendering complex graphics, such as a tree. Simpler widgets, such as a list widget, can however require complexity comparable to the one of the associated binding. Experiments performed on example 2 with a large list of contacts confirms this point: because the binding performs a sort, displaying the list can become faster than performing the binding, but for a large number of list items (around 10.000 in our experimentation).

Figure 7 gives the performance of the addition of an attribute; performance of its removal is very close to this curve, and is thus not shown in the figure. In both cases, updating the document (curve "Doc.") takes a constant and negligible time; data binding takes a linear time $t(ms) = 0,015 \times n$, as expected (curve "Tree"); the Flex tree widget does not have to compute new y locations: this rather consists of applying a vertical offset in the display buffer, which requires a constant time around 150 ms (curve "mx:Tree").

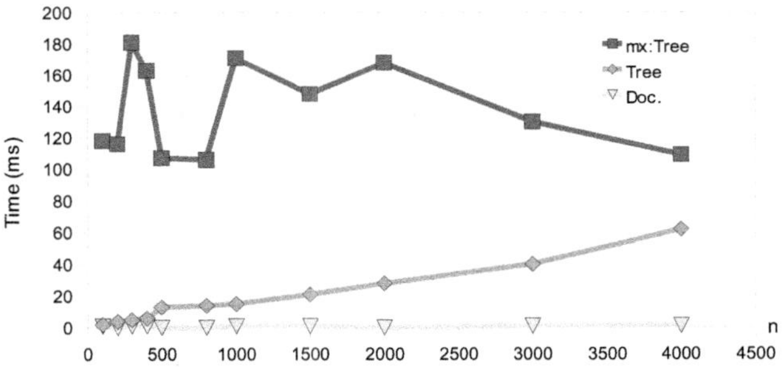

Figure 7. Addition performance

These performances illustrate that the time required to refresh a drawing is often bigger than the time for computing a binding. In the previous example, the update time for the Flex tree and the active operations become equal when n reaches $150/0,015 = 10.000$, which represents a really huge XML document (10^{12}nodes for a depth of 3).

RELATED WORKS

Constraint systems have been widely used for defining data bindings in the context of GUI. The Garnet toolbox proposes the use of "formula", expressed in Lisp, to bind an object value to other object values: the formula is reevaluated whenever the values within the formula change, like in spreadsheets [14]. The Rendezvous architecture defines the concept of "active value": an active value is a variable used as en entry point to constraint definitions (also expressed in Lisp); when the value changes, the constraint is reevaluated to reflect the change [11]. Similarly, but within a C++ infrastructure, the Amulet environment allows the definition of constraint through "formula" that bind object values [15]. However, all these constraint-based systems are limited to the binding of object values: they do not address the binding of collections, and are thus limited to simple widgets such as text-field or combo-box.

The *JFace* toolkit defines interfaces *IObservableValue* and *IObservableCollection* that respectively allow the observation of values and collections [9]. These interfaces are implemented in classes that can be used for representing "bindable" data in both the model and the view. This approach defines the required foundation classes for data binding; however, it is a pure *programmatic* approach where bindings must be implemented rather than being declared. The *ObjectEditor* toolkit uses a more subtle approach that consists of extending the JavaBean syntax so that data bindings appear in a more declarative way [7]. Moreover, this toolkit extends the scope of data binding to action binding that allows user actions to be bound to "do", "undo" and "redo" methods. However, *ObjectEditor* offers a low expressiveness regarding data binding capabilities.

RIA toolkits, such as WPF [16], Flex [12], and JavaFX [10], have adopted a *declarative* approach to data binding. The aim of these approaches is to simplify the process of writing bindings: rather than being implemented, bindings are declared. These approaches work fine for simple bindings where the view does not differ much from the model; they however lose their simplicity as soon as the complexity of the model is increased, which often results in requiring some low level programming that contradicts the initial aim of the declarative approach. The next section focuses on proving these limitations.

Using rule-based incremental transformation languages solves the previous limitations of declarative data bindings. The incremental XSLT processor *incXSLT* allows the incremental execution of XSLT transformations [17]. However, XSLT concerns source XML documents and target text documents, which makes it difficult to use on various GUI platforms. Moreover, XSLT is a complex language that does not match well the required simplicity of data binding. Using a *mapping* language, such as Malan [5], combines the benefits of the simplicity of data bindings and the expressiveness of transformation languages. However, this higher level approach postpones the problem of executing the mappings: for example, active operations can be generated from a mapping so that the mapping can be executed on a target platform.

COMPARISON WITH BINDINGS OF RIA TOOLKITS

From our knowledge, recent RIA toolkits offer the best data binding mechanisms. This section compares our approach with three representative RIA toolkits: Flex [12], WPF[16], and JavaFX [10]. It illustrates why the three examples presented in this paper cannot be fully implemented by using their data binding capabilities.

Active Operation Capabilities

Table 3 summarizes the capabilities of active operations presented throughout this paper. The capabilities belong either to active collections, active objects, or both.

Category	Capability	Collection	Object
Math.	*union*	√	√
	intersection	√	√
	difference	√	√
	tuple	√	√
View	*select*	√	√
	sort	√	n/a
	multiple views	√	√
Transf.	*collect*	√	√
	path	√	√
	map	√	√
Bidir.	bidir. assignment	n/a	√
	+ conversion	n/a	√

Table 3. Active operation capabilities

Category "Math" includes the usual mathematical set operations, and the definition of tuples; tuples are useful in operations such as *select(f)* and *collect(f)* with more than one parameter in *f*. Category "View" (in the database sense) includes operations *select* and *sort*; it also defines the ability for an active collection or object to be treated more than once by an active operation (such as *select* and *sort*), thus allowing *multiple views* on a common model. Category "Transformation" concerns operations *collect*, *path* and *map*, that allow a progressive transformation from the source to the target. Finally, category "Bidir." defines the bidirectional assignment used to perform two-way bindings on active objects; this functionality is supplemented by a reversible conversion.

All these capabilities have been illustrated in the 3 examples presented at the beginning of this papers. The next section discusses if and how these capabilities are present within the data binding mechanisms of the three RIA toolkits Flex, WPF and JavaFX.

Comparison with RIA Toolkits

Table 4 summarizes the data binding capabilities of the three RIA toolkits Flex, WPF and JavaFX.

As mentioned earlier, instances of the Flex class *ArrayCollection* can be bound to collection widgets, and bindable properties defined within instances of class *Object* can be bound to simple widgets [12]. These two capabilities are equivalent to operation *map* on collections

	Flex		WPF		JavaFX	
	Coll.	Obj.	Coll.	Obj.	Coll.	Obj.
Math op.						
select	(√)		√			
sort	(√)	n/a	√	n/a		n/a
m. views			√	√	√	√
collect		√		√	√	√
path		√		√		√
map	√	√	√	√	√	√
assign.	n/a	√	n/a	√	n/a	√
+ conv.	n/a		n/a	√	n/a	

Table 4. binding capabilities of RIA toolkits

and on objects. Bidirectional assignment is possible through property binding, but without conversion. A path can be specified when binding two properties; however, paths cannot be defined on collections. It is also possible to define a "transformation function" within a property binding, which is analogous to operation *collect* for a single object. All the other capabilities are not available with Flex. Operations *select* and *sort* exist on class *ArrayCollection*, but they do not return new collections: they rather modify the source model directly; this does not separate well the model from the GUI. Moreover, these operations cannot use "active" parameters (for example, through tuples).

WPF offers richer binding capabilities than Flex [16]. Operations *select* and *sort* return new bindable collections, and thus allow the definition of multiple views; bidirectional conversion is also possible. However, math operations and transform operations *collect* and *path* remain undefined for collections.

JavaFX has adopted a radically different strategy for defining bindings: rather that proposing a bunch of binding artifacts, such as with Flex or WPF, JavaFX introduces new language *keywords* dedicated to the definition of bindings [10]. Consequently, JavaFX bindings are clearer than that of Flex or WPF since they are based on very few constructs, while Flex and WPF bindings use many different artifacts that often require low level *ad hoc* programming. However, as table 4 illustrates, important features are unavailable in JavaFX thus making it not as expressive as expected.

Implementing the Examples using RIA Toolkits

Regarding example 1, Flex data binding cannot be used to bind XML documents to the tree widget since this requires *union* operations. The example could be built by coding a specific data provider that implements Flex interface *ITreeDataDescriptor*. This practice is similar to the implementation of Swing models, and thus does not respect the initial philosophy of binding. Filtering contacts in example 2 is impossible with Flex binding: this requires the programming of an *ad hoc* code that recomputes the filtering whenever the user changes the filtering text. Moreover, sorting and filtering the contacts must be specified by altering the code of the model: the design of the GUI thus impacts the source model, which contradicts the fact that binding clearly separates the model and its GUIs. Finally, example 3 cannot be implemented by using Flex binding. This is due to the free-time slots objects that are not present in the source model, and thus cannot be bound to grid-items.

As with Flex, example 1 cannot be implemented using WPF binding due to the lack of operation *union*. Example 2 is easier to implement than with Flex due to WPF view capabilities; however, the active filtering of contacts again requires the development of *ad hoc* code. But most of all, implementing example 2 with WPF requires a bunch of data binding artifacts: "bidirectional converters" must be programmed by implementing interface *IValueConverter*; "data templates" must be defined with the XAML document[5] for implementing functions that define the text of the tree items; and "observable collection" must specify the filtering and sorting of contacts in a programmatic way. The developer thus needs to juggle with multiple artifacts, and with both programmatic and declarative paradigms. Example 3 cannot reap benefit from WPF binding and must be implemented from scratch.

Due to the lack of view capabilities, examples 1 and 2 cannot be implemented using JavaFX binding. As with Flex and WPF binding, example 3 is not feasible with JavaFX.

Discussion

Data binding of RIA toolkits are simple to use for simple bindings. Their binding mechanisms remain sufficient as long as the source models do not differ much from the target models. Moreover, these mechanisms allow binding to existing relational databases and/or XML documents directly, thus making them attractive in an enterprise context. In counter part, the offered binding capabilities become insufficient to address various and/or complex problems. These toolkits often require multiple artifact juggling that alter the initial simplicity of the declarative approach. Moreover, each RIA toolkit proposes its own data binding mechanism. Consequently, a binding written in WPF cannot always be translated to a Flex or JavaFX binding: they are all platform dependent and do not share a common model.

The use of active operations for specifying and implementing data binding removes such limitations. A single DSL is used for specifying the bindings, and translating them before being implemented; it is thus platform-independent. The resulting implementation performances are good for the initial construction of operation results, and very good for updating these results. In counter part, active operations have to be implemented through a dedicated compiler; however, RIA toolkits also require some hidden code generation

[5]XAML is the XML dialect used by WPF to specified user interfaces.

(for example, to implement paths between two bound properties). Active operations currently do not provide mechanisms for binding UI directly with databases or XML documents. However, such an issue is not specific to the domain of active operations: it concerns the serialization and deserialization of models on different data platforms.

CONCLUSION

This paper presents how to reap benefits from active operation expressiveness and easiness for specifying and implementing UI data bindings. Active operations offer the ability to reevaluate the result of the operations in real-time while the user interacts with the system. The proposed approach overcomes the limitations of data binding mechanisms provided by modern UI toolkits. These limitations are: GUI bindings are platform-dependent and lack at defining complex bindings. It is based on a single DSL, mainly inspired by OCL, that allows both the specification and the platform-independent implementation of data bindings. Active operations have been implemented on top of the Flex RIA toolkit; the resulting ActiveFlex API offers good performance for the initial construction of active operation results, and very good ones regarding their updates.

The next step of our work is to implement a compiler that will generate active implementations from any active operation specification. Such a compiler would generate the implementations on various GUI platforms. Since our approach offers a great expressiveness, we will use and evaluate it in the context of "Information Visualization" in order to confront its performance to large models.

REFERENCES

1. D. H. Akehurst. *Model Translation: A UML-based specification technique and active implementation approach.* PhD thesis, University of Kent, 2000.
2. O. Beaudoux. XML active transformation (eXAcT): Transforming documents within interactive systems. In *DocEng '05: Proceedings of the 2005 ACM symposium on Document engineering*, pages 146–148. ACM, 2005.
3. O. Beaudoux and A. Blouin. Linking data and presentations: from mapping to active transformations. In *DocEng '10: Proceedings of the 2010 ACM symposium on Document engineering*, pages 107–110. ACM, 2010.
4. O. Beaudoux, A. Blouin, O. Barais, and J. M. Jezequel. Active operations on collections. In *MoDELS '10: Proceedings of the 13th ACM/IEEE International Conference on on Model Driven Engineering Languages and Systems (LNCS 6394)*, pages 91–105. Springer, 2010.
5. A. Blouin, O. Beaudoux, and S. Loiseau. Malan: A mapping language for the data manipulation. In *DocEng '08: Proceedings of the 2008 ACM symposium on Document engineering*, pages 66–75. ACM, 2008.
6. J. Coutaz. PAC, on object oriented model for dialog design. In *Interact'87*, 1987.
7. P. Dewan. Increasing the automation of a toolkit without reducing its abstraction and user-interface flexibility. In *EICS '10: Proceedings of the 2nd ACM SIGCHI symposium on Engineering interactive computing systems*, pages 47–56. ACM, 2010.
8. R. Eckstein, M. Loy, and D. Wood. *Java Swing.* O'Reilly, 2002.
9. Eclipse Foundation. JFace data binding. `http://wiki.eclipse.org/index.php/JFace_Data_Binding`.
10. R. Field. JavaFX language reference (chapter 7 - Data binding). `http://openjfx.java.sun.com/current-build/doc/reference/ch07s01.html`.
11. R. D. Hill. The Rendezvous constraint maintenance system. In *UIST'93: Proceedings of the 6th annual ACM symposium on User interface software and technology*, pages 225–234. ACM, 1993.
12. C. Kazoun and J. Lott. *Programming Flex 2.* O'Reilly, 2007.
13. G. E. Krasner and S. T. Pope. A description of the model-view-controller user interface paradigm in smalltalk80 system. *Journal of Object Oriented Programming*, 1:26–49, 1988.
14. B. Myers, D. Giuse, R. Dannenberg, B. Zanden, D. Kosbie, E. Pervin, A. Mickish, and P. Marchal. Garnet: comprehensive support for graphical, highly interactive user interfaces. *Computer*, 23(11):71–85, 1990.
15. B. Myers, R. McDaniel, R. Miller, A. Ferrency, A. Faulring, B. Kyle, A. Mickish, A. Klimovitski, and P. Doane. The Amulet environment: new models for effective user interface software development. *IEEE Transactions on Software Engineering*, 23(6):347–365, 1997.
16. C. Sells and I. Griffiths. *Programming Windows Presentation Foundation.* O'Reilly, 2005.
17. L. Villard and N. Layaida. An incremental XSLT transformation processor for XML document manipulation. In *WWW '02: Proceedings of the 11th international conference on World Wide Web*, pages 474–485. ACM, 2002.
18. J. B. Warmer and A. G. Kleppe. *The object constraint language: getting your models ready for MDA.* Addison-Wesley.

GUIDE2ux: a GUI Design Environment for Enhancing the User eXperience

Jan Meskens[1] **Matthias Loskyll**[2] **Marc Seißler**[3] **Kris Luyten**[1] **Karin Coninx**[1] **Gerrit Meixner**[2]

[1]Hasselt University – EDM – IBBT
Wetenschapspark 2, 3590 Diepenbeek, Belgium
{firstname.lastname}@uhasselt.be

[2]German Research Center for Artificial Intelligence (DFKI)
67663 Kaiserlautern, Germany
{firstname.lastname}@dfki.de

[3]University of Kaiserlautern
67663 Kaiserlautern, Germany
{marc.seissler}@mv.uni-kl.de

ABSTRACT

For the design and development of graphical user interfaces, designers have to take various guidelines, standards and target platform characteristics into account. This is often a hard and time consuming activity because guidelines are spread over multiple documents using different styles, and furthermore it requires considerable effort to verify whether a design will work well on the targeted device. We propose GUIDE2ux, a design environment that (1) identifies and shows usability problems automatically and (2) facilitates designers to verify their designs on the target device easily. With GUIDE2ux, we make design standards more accessible for designers and help them to improve and test the user experience of their designs.

ACM Classification Keywords

H.5.2 Information interfaces and presentation: User Interfaces – Graphical user interfaces, Prototyping

General Terms

Design

Author Keywords

Design tools, Guidelines, User Experience, Jelly

INTRODUCTION

Today, many types of computing devices such as smart phones, tablet PCs, interactive TVs and notebooks exist. In order to create usable User Interfaces (UIs) for these different devices, designers commonly create a series of prototypes. The realization of concrete prototypes allows designers to try out their design ideas on the actual target device. Those prototypes will help to uncover design problems and to generate suggestions for new designs.

User interface prototypes are mostly constructed by means of design tools such as Adobe Flash or Microsoft Expression Blend. Typically, those tools allow designers to design the visual layout of a UI using direct manipulation. With the advent of those tools, designers are acquiring increased control in creating interactive prototypes. Nevertheless, a recent large scale survey revealed several issues with current design tools [7]. Two issues are particularly interesting in the field of interactive prototyping:

1. the difficulty to check whether a design follows standardized design rules or usability standards. Doing these checks manually is difficult because these rules and standards are often described using broad principles and contain a lot of ambiguities;
2. the difficulty to verify whether a design will be compatible with the target device (e.g. suited for the screen resolution, processing power, interaction capability, etc.).

A lot of work has been done concerning the first issue, mainly in the area of automatically checking web-based user interfaces. MAGENTA checks web sites according to usability and accessibility criteria in order to improve web interac-

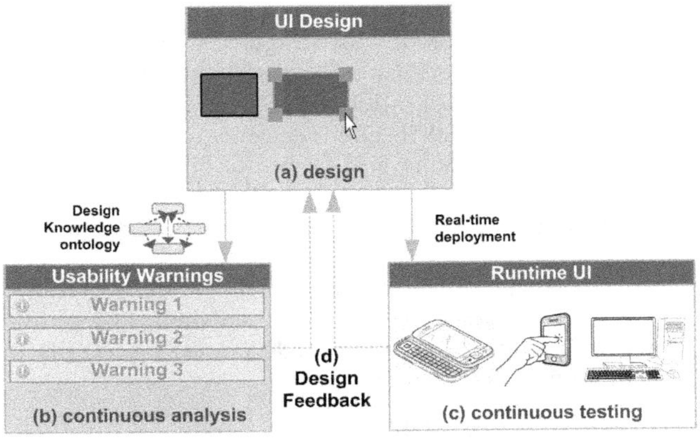

Figure 1. While designing a GUI in GUIDE2ux (a), the tool provides feedback (d) about the design by showing whether predefined design rules are violated (b) and by allowing designers to inspect a design immediately on the target device (c).

tion for different typologies of users [11]. NAUTICUS has been developed with the intent of automatically checking whether a Web site is usable for users interacting through screen readers [6]. The work of Vigo et al. [21] considers device-specific features (e.g., screen size or support for particular picture formats) for the evaluation of mobile web guidelines to produce device-tailored reports. Most of these approaches can only target web-based user interfaces, while we want to target graphical user interfaces for more than one platform. These approaches also provide no means to verify whether a design is compatible with the target device constraints.

The second issue, checking the compatibility of a design with the target device, has been addressed by *"live UI design"* systems such as Page Tailor [4], Morphic [13] and User Interface Facades [19]. Those approaches allow designers to edit a Graphical User Interface (GUI) directly on the target device while the GUI is running. This way, designers can always test their prototypes while designing the UI. However, most live editing systems are difficult to employ on mobile devices with constraints such as limited input (e.g. only a soft input panel) or low screen resolutions.

In this paper, we explore how we can extend GUI design tools (1) to visualize how well a design fits usability standards and style guidelines, and (2) to reveal the run-time characteristic of a design to verify its compatibility with the target device. Such tool support would allow designers to adjust UI designs, even before the UI has been completed [9]. These changes are less expensive compared to changes that are made as a result of a traditional evaluation, which usually takes place after the interface or prototype has been built [15].

This paper proposes GUIDE2ux, a **GUI** **D**esign **E**nvironment for **E**nhancing the **U**ser e**X**perience. It allows designers to gradually verify and improve their designs. Using GUIDE2ux, designers create UI prototypes using a design environment which is similar to traditional GUI builders (Figure 1-a). This design environment is implemented using Jelly [14], an open source multi-device graphical design environment. While designing a GUI, GUIDE2ux shows whether a design violates predefined usability rules (Figure 1-b) and it deploys all design changes immediately to the target device, allowing designers to test their designs (Figure 1-c). This way, GUIDE2ux provides feedback for designers to improve their designs iteratively (Figure 1-d).

In summary, the main contribution in this paper are:

- GUIDE2ux, a multi-device design environment that improves the accessibility of usability standards and guidelines, and reduces the effort needed to test and verify a GUI design on the target device;
- an evaluation of GUIDE2ux against proposed heuristics for UI design tools.

GUIDE2UX

This section discusses the most important interaction techniques and UI elements that GUIDE2ux offers to provide instant feedback about a GUI design. To illustrate these features, we show how GUIDE2ux can be used to construct a touch-screen *food menu application*, which allows customers to browse through restaurant menus.

The Design Workspace

GUIDE2ux' design workspace is structured similar to existing GUI builders: it contains a *toolbox* (Figure 2-a) showing the available widgets for the target platform; a *canvas* (Figure 2-b) supporting direct manipulation to build a UI; and a *properties panel* (Figure 2-c) to change the style properties of the user interface elements on the canvas. Currently, GUIDE2ux supports three computing platforms: mobile (Android and Windows Mobile), desktop (.NET and Java Swing) and web-based (using Adobe Flex).

In general, designers create a GUI in GUIDE2ux by placing widgets from the toolbox on the canvas and dragging them around until the resulting layout is visually appealing. This similarity with existing GUI builders allows designers to reuse their knowledge of existing tools in the GUIDE2ux design environment. Figure 2 shows the GUIDE2ux design environment while designing the GUI design for the food menu application.

Usability Warnings

While designing a user interface, GUIDE2ux continuously verifies if the design is structured conform a predefined set of usability rules. If the design does not follow these rules, usability warnings are shown in a separate tabbed panel (see Figure 2-d, first tab page). For example, the label "pasta" of the selected radio button in Figure 2 does not start with an upper-case letter. As shown in the warnings panel, this does not correspond to a predefined rule, stating that every label should start with an upper-case letter except for specific cases. This warning will disappear when the designer makes the first letter of this radio button upper case.

Each warning can be further explored by the designer (Figure 2-e) by simply right-clicking the warning. In cases when the warning is not relevant, the designer can also choose to hide the warning and avoid cluttering with irrelevant data. When further exploring a warning, this warning is displayed in a separate window together with a clear example showing when this warning occurs and how it can be resolved (see Figure 2-f). If the designer decides to remove the warning, the system will neglect the rule causing this warning in the future.

Design Tips

Besides usability warnings, GUIDE2ux provides tips about the widgets that are used in the design. Tips are no strict usability rules, they provide advise on how the usage of certain widgets could be improved. For example, in our food menu application, GUIDE2ux advised to place the title ("Select food type") of the radio button list on the left or on top of this list.

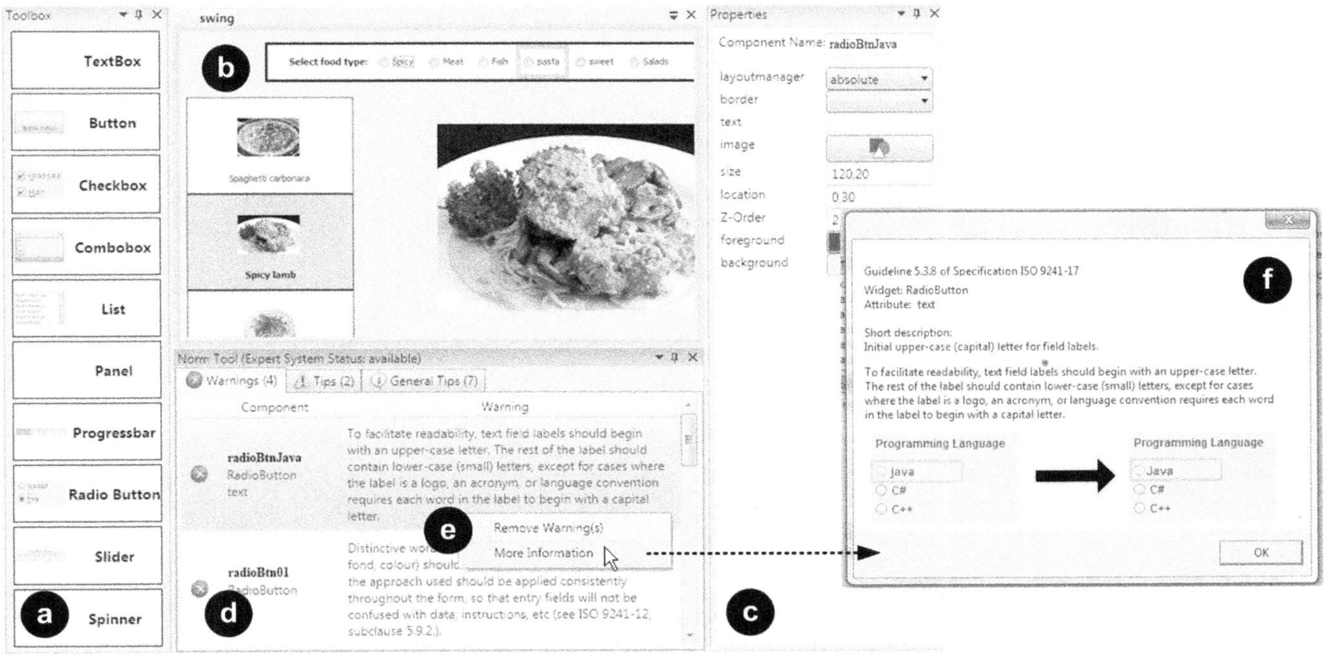

Figure 2. The GUIDE2ux design environment provides usability warnings about the designed GUI. Every usability warning can be inspected in detail.

GUIDE2ux also gives general tips about the designed interface. For example, while designing the food-menu touch screen application, general tips about touch screen design will be shown. In this example, the system provides general tips about e.g. the fat finger problem: "a finger is larger than a mouse pointer: buttons should be large enough for a finger to touch easily".

Real Time Deployment

While designing a user interface, GUIDE2ux deploys every design change in real time to a running version of the user interface on the target device. This allows designers to test the UI immediately on the target device and to verify whether the design takes the constraints of this device into account. Such test-driven GUI design approach helps to uncover wrong design decisions early in the design process and to generate ideas for new -better- designs [10].

To benefit maximally from GUIDE2ux' real-time deployment, the target device and the PC running the GUIDE2ux environment have to be located close to each other. During the construction of the food-menu UI, real-time deployment can help to detect some usability problems with the top-bar for selecting the desired food type. In the design shown in Figure 2, radio buttons are used for this purpose. However, while testing these radio buttons, it will be clear that those are difficult to use on a touch screen. Due to the fat finger problem, the feedback of a radio button (checked or unchecked) remains invisible underneath the finger. This can inspire to replace the radio buttons by other widgets such as large toggle buttons, where it is immediately visible whether they are checked or not.

REPRESENTATION OF DESIGNER KNOWLEDGE

After describing the most important fundamentals of knowledge representation using ontologies, this section discusses the details of our designer knowledge ontology.

Fundamentals of Knowledge Representation

Knowledge-based systems model knowledge, commonly human expert knowledge, of a certain problem domain. The knowledge base depicts a key component of such a system. Methods of explicit knowledge representation such as ontologies support the semantic processing of data by machines, i.e. the interpretation of electronically stored pieces of information with regard to their content and meaning. Ontologies consist of three basic structures, namely classes (or concepts), relations and instances. In addition, restrictions, rules and axioms can be defined in order to model complex coherences. Another great advantage of ontologies is the possibility to draw inferences over the explicitly modeled knowledge, thereby deriving new knowledge that is contained implicitly in the knowledge base. To this end, a reasoner system is needed, which depicts a piece of software that is able to interpret logically defined facts and axioms and to infer logical consequences.

Ontology-based Implementation of the Knowledge Base

GUIDE2ux uses usability rules as *"designer knowledge"* to verify GUI designs automatically. Therefore, it is important to select the rules and recommendations that we can extract from existing standards and to find an appropriate representation for these rules. To experiment with our automatic design evaluation approach, we decided to use the standards series ISO 9241 "Ergonomics of Human System Interaction"

[1] and the guideline VDI/VDE 3850 "User-friendly Design of Useware for Machines" [2] as knowledge sources.

Currently we follow an informed manual approach to extract rules from text because we did not wanted to be constrained by a specific guideline markup to automate this step. Eventually, we envision that rules related to a guideline can be provided and shared within the design community. Based on the textual description of the usability knowledge, the premise, the conclusion and logical conjunctions of each rule as well as the concerned widgets and attributes of a user interface need to be identified in a first step. Figure 3 shows an example of the transformation from the textual description to a semi-formal representation of the rule. Concerning the extraction of design rules, attention must be paid to the fact that some of the rules contained in the norms and guidelines cannot be represented formally because they are too vague. Therefore, we make a distinction between two kinds of rule knowledge: warnings and tips. If it is possible to check whether a widget, its attributes and its relationship to other widgets comply with the defined usability rules, a corresponding violation of the rules can be displayed as a warning. If an automatic validation is not possible - take for example a rule that refers to the subjective perception of the user - the matching rule is shown as a tip only.

After having transformed the textual description to the semi-formal representation, we describe the design rules contained in the different standards in a formal manner using an extensible ontology, which is modeled in the Web Ontology Language (OWL) and with the help of the ontology editor Protégé. OWL gives enough expressive power to represent simple rules including logical expressions. It is also possible to integrate more sophisticated rules using SWRL (Semantic Web Rule Language), which easily integrates with OWL. Figure 4 shows a high-level overview of the ontology. As the basic structure of this ontology, the different interaction objects of a user interface and their attributes have been modeled on the basis of the UIML (User Interface Markup Language) specification. The rules contained in the different standards are translated into logical expressions in a second step. Then, they are connected with the corresponding widgets and their attributes with the help of ontological relations. Rules are assigned either to individual widgets or to widget-attribute-pairs. Depending on the interaction of the developer with the design tool, a semantic query can be performed, which retrieves the matching rules from the ontology, resulting in a list of warnings and tips.

ARCHITECTURE AND IMPLEMENTATION

This section describes GUIDE2ux' underlying architecture and discusses how we integrated the designer knowledge ontology as part of our design environment. The flow and different components of the architecture are outlined in Figure 5, and will be clarified step-by-step throughout this section.

Design Environment

The GUIDE2ux design environment is implemented using the open source Jelly multi-device design framework that is written in .NET [14]. This framework provides a graphical design environment that can target various platforms such as Windows Mobile, Adobe Flex, Java Swing and Android.

Command Object Architecture

Our architecture supports automatic UI evaluation and real-time deployment using the "Command Object Model" [3]. Every action supported by our GUI builder is implemented as a command object. Each time a designer interacts with the design environment to perform a design action, a command object will be executed (Figure 5-1). When the execution of a command object is finished, it notifies the design evaluation module (Figure 5-2) and the real-time deployment module (Figure 5-5).

The current version of the GUIDE2ux design environment supports a wide variety of design actions that can trigger automatic design evaluation and real-time deployment. Example operations include *direct manipulation* actions for resizing, moving or rotating widgets on the design tool's canvas, actions for *adding* or *removing* widgets and *property update* actions for changing the property values in the properties panel.

Design Evaluation Module

When a command object has been executed, the design evaluation module analyses the corresponding design update. To

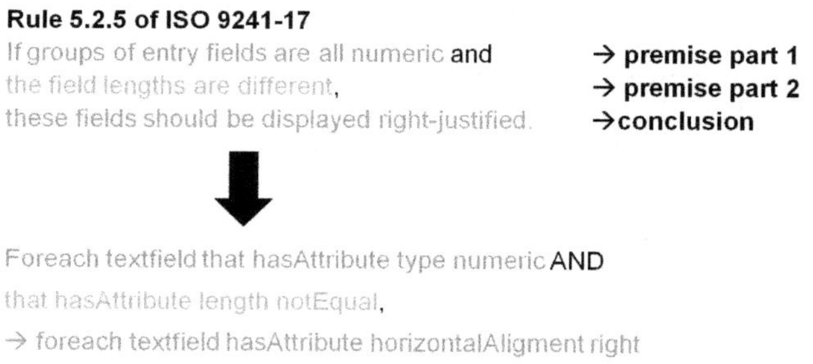

Rule 5.2.5 of ISO 9241-17
If groups of entry fields are all numeric and
the field lengths are different,
these fields should be displayed right-justified.
→ premise part 1
→ premise part 2
→conclusion
Foreach textfield that hasAttribute type numeric AND
that hasAttribute length notEqual,
→ foreach textfield hasAttribute horizontalAligment right

Figure 3. Example of the manual transformation of design rules

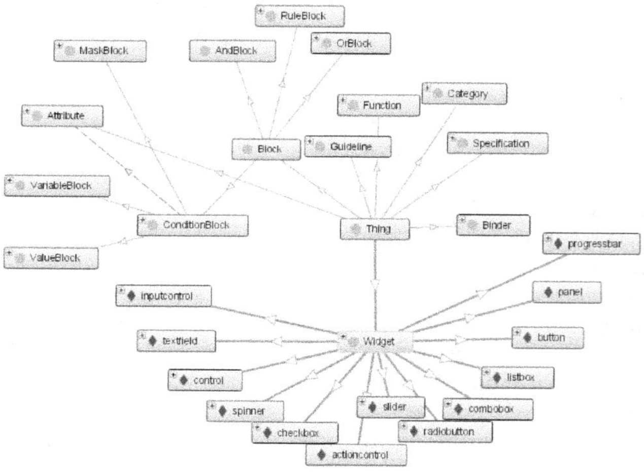

Figure 4. High-Level overview of the ontology

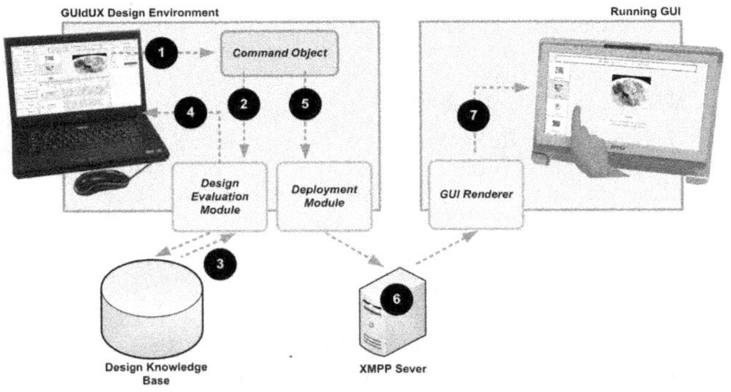

Figure 5. The architecture of GUIDE2ux. Every design action is executed using a command object (1), which evaluates the design (2) using a design knowledge base (3) and updates the displayed usability warnings (4). At the same time, this command object deploys (5) the design change to a GUI renderer (6) on the target device, which updates the running GUI (7).

this end, it deploys our ontology, which contains knowledge about usability rules and the concerned widgets and attributes. With the help of the OWL API 3.0 [8] and the Reasoner FaCT++ [20] we developed methods to perform queries against the ontology. The widgets and attributes that are updated in the design are compiled into semantic queries, which retrieve the matching tips and warnings from the ontology (Figure 5-3). When receiving the tips and warnings from the ontology, the design evaluation module will update GUIDE2ux' usability warnings panel accordingly (Figure 5-4).

It is important to note that the design evaluation module is implemented as a separate service that is loosely coupled with the design environment. Such a service oriented architecture makes it possible to implement custom evaluation modules in different programming languages or using custom types of usability rule representations. For example, the current evaluation module perfectly interfaces with Jelly (written in .NET) although it is implemented in Java.

Real-Time Deployment Module

The real-time deployment module is responsible for updating the running GUI on the target device. It serializes every design action received from the command object (Figure 5-5) into an XML description. This description is sent to the target device using the Extensible Messaging and Presence Protocol (XMPP) protocol (Figure 5-6). On the target computing device, a GUI renderer receives these design updates and updates the running version of the GUI accordingly (Figure 5-7).

We implemented the communication between the design environment and target device using XMPP, which provides the required functionalities to build cross-platform distributed applications [17]. Several open-source XMPP libraries exist in different programming languages, which makes it possible to implement live running GUI renderers for several types of computing devices.

QUALITATIVE EVALUATION

In this section, a qualitative evaluation of GUIDE2ux is summarized based on the evaluation framework of Olsen [16] to assess user interface system research. We discuss two important attributes that help to evaluate the effectiveness of a user interface system: reducing solution viscosity and power in combination.

Reducing solution viscosity

According to Olsen [16], good UI design tools reduce solution viscosity, which means that they minimize the effort required to iterate on many possible design solutions. Three ways in which a tool can reduce solution viscosity are flexibility, expressive leverage and expressive match.

Flexibility

A UI design tool is flexible if it is possible to make rapid design changes that can then be evaluated by the users. GUIDE2ux clearly supports the flexibility claim, since it deploys every design change in real time to the target device where it can be evaluated by the designers.

Expressive leverage

Expressive leverage [16] is where designers can accomplish more by expressing less. GUIDE2ux achieves leverage by automatically visualizing usability warnings. Using our tool, designers can take standards and usability warnings into account without having to explore these guidelines and usability standards manually. This is an important achievement because designers have historically experienced difficulties following design guidelines (e.g. [9, 5, 18, 12]).

Expressive match

Olsen [16] defines expressive match as an estimate of how close the means for expressing design choices are to the problem being solved. GUIDE2ux adheres to this principle by showing an interactive version of the design directly on its target device. This is a very close expressive match because we want to facilitate designers to experience themselves whether parts of a GUI are well suited for the target device or not.

Power in combination

Power in combination refers to the way UI tools can support new components to create new solutions. This can be supported by minimizing the cost of adding new components and by making these components easy to use and to combine.

GUIDE2ux represents design rules using an ontology. Because of the clear structure of the modeled knowledge base and its separation from the implementation of the design environment, new usability standards can be included in an efficient manner. Our ontology supports the integration of multiple usability standards, which allows designers to take usability warnings from all of these standards into account.

DISCUSSION AND FUTURE WORK

In this paper, we presented GUIDE2ux, a GUI design environment, which supports designers to build high-quality user interfaces in two ways: (1) by incorporating design rules to automatically verify whether the designed GUI complies with usability standards, and (2) by employing design changes immediately to the target device itself. We believe that our approach improves the accessibility of usability standards and guidelines by formalizing the design knowledge with the help of ontologies, which can be easily extended by additional usability standards. Furthermore, the real-time deployment capability of GUIDE2ux can help to reduce the effort needed to test GUIs on the target device.

We assessed the value of GUID2ux's contribution through a qualitative evaluation. Based on these findings, we will continue the development of GUIDE2ux. As part of future research, additional and thorough validations will be done in order to estimate the value of GUIDE2ux for UI designers and developers.

GUIDE2ux currently uses standards for analysing GUI designs. Although standards are suitable to extract basic principles for designing user interfaces - e.g. the orientation of interface elements - they lack a detailed description of design aspects. While this is due to the nature of standards - they usually don't limit their application to certain domains - it limits the feedback developers can get from our design tool. To cope with this problem, additional standards, guidelines and style guides will be evaluated with respect to their suitability to be formalized and integrated in our approach.

Acknowledgments

Part of the research at EDM is funded by ERDF (European Regional Development Fund) and the Flemish Government. The AMASS++ (Advanced Multimedia Alignment and Structured Summarization) project IWT 060051 is directly funded by the IWT (Flemish subsidy organization).

REFERENCES

1. ISO 9241: Ergonomics of Human System Interaction, 1996.
2. VDI/VDE 3850: User-friendly Design of Useware for Machines, 2000.
3. T. Berlage. A selective undo mechanism for graphical user interfaces based on command objects. *ACM Trans. Comput.-Hum. Interact.*, 1(3):269–294, 1994.
4. N. Bila, T. Ronda, I. Mohomed, K. N. Truong, and E. de Lara. Pagetailor: reusable end-user customization for the mobile web. In *Proc. MobiSys '07*, pages 16–29. ACM, 2007.
5. J. A. Borges, I. Morales, and N. J. Rodríguez. Guidelines for designing usable world wide web pages. In *Proc. of CHI '96*, pages 277–278. ACM, 1996.
6. F. Correani, B. Leporini, and F. Patern. Automatic inspection-based support for obtaining usable web sites for vision-impaired users. *Universal Access in the Information Society*, 5(1):82–95, 2006.
7. V. Grigoreanu, R. Fernandez, K. Inkpen, and G. Robertson. What designers want: Needs of interactive application designers. In *Proc. VL/HCC'09*, pages 139–146. IEEE Computer Society, 2009.
8. M. Horridge and S. Bechhofer. The owl api: A java api for working with owl 2 ontologies. In *OWLED*, volume 529 of *CEUR Workshop Proceedings*. CEUR-WS.org, 2008.
9. M. Y. Ivory and M. A. Hearst. The state of the art in automating usability evaluation of user interfaces. *ACM Comput. Surv.*, 33(4):470–516, 2001.
10. S. R. Klemmer, B. Hartmann, and L. Takayama. How bodies matter: five themes for interaction design. In *In Proc. DIS '06*, pages 140–149, 2006.
11. B. Leporini, F. Patern, and A. Scorcia. Flexible tool support for accessibility evaluation. *Interacting with Computers*, 18(5):689–890, 2006.
12. J. Löwgren and T. Nordqvist. Knowledge-based evaluation as design support for graphical user interfaces. In *CHI '92: Proceedings of the SIGCHI conference on Human factors in computing systems*, pages 181–188, 1992.
13. J. H. Maloney and R. B. Smith. Directness and liveness in the morphic user interface construction environment. In *Proc. UIST '95*, pages 21–28. ACM, 1995.
14. J. Meskens, K. Luyten, and K. Coninx. Jelly: A multi-device design environment for managing consistency across devices. In *Proc. AVI'10*, pages 289–298. ACM, 2010.
15. J. Nielsen. *Usability Engineering*. Morgan Kaufmann Publishers Inc., San Francisco, CA, USA, 1993.
16. D. R. Olsen, Jr. Evaluating user interface systems research. In *UIST '07: Proceedings of the 20th annual ACM symposium on User interface software and technology*, pages 251–258. ACM, 2007.
17. J. S. Pierce and J. Nichols. An infrastructure for extending applications' user experiences across multiple personal devices. In *Proc. UIST '08*, pages 101–110. ACM, 2008.
18. F. d. Souza and N. Bevan. The use of guidelines in menu interface design: Evaluation of a draft standard. In *Proc. of INTERACT '90*, pages 435–440. North-Holland Publishing Co., 1990.
19. W. Stuerzlinger, O. Chapuis, D. Phillips, and N. Roussel. User interface façades: towards fully adaptable user interfaces. In *Proc. UIST '06*, pages 309–318. ACM, 2006.
20. D. Tsarkov and I. Horrocks. Fact++ description logic reasoner: System description. In *In Proc. of the Int. Joint Conf. on Automated Reasoning (IJCAR 2006*, pages 292–297. Springer, 2006.
21. M. Vigo, A. Aizpurua, M. Arrue, and J. Abascal. Automatic device-tailored evaluation of mobile web guidelines. *The New Review of Hypermedia and Multimedia*, 15(3):223–244, 2009.

GRIP: Get better Results from Interactive Prototypes

Jan Van den Bergh, Deepak Sahni, Mieke Haesen, Kris Luyten, Karin Coninx
Hasselt University - tUL - IBBT
Expertise Centre for Digital Media
Wetenschapspark 2
3590 Diepenbeek, Belgium
author@uhasselt.be

ABSTRACT

Prototypes are often used to clarify and evaluate design alternatives for a graphical user interface. They help stakeholders to decide on different aspects by making them visible and concrete. This is a highly iterative process in which the prototypes evolve into a design artifact that is close enough to the envisioned result to be implemented. People with different roles are involved in prototyping. Our claim is that integrated or inter-operable tools help design information propagate among people while prototyping and making the transition more accurately into the software development phase.

We make a first step towards such a solution by offering a framework, GRIP, in which such a tool should fit. We conducted a preliminary evaluation of the framework by using it to classify existing tools for prototyping and implementing a limited prototyping tool, GRIP-it, which can be integrated into the overall process.

Author Keywords

Prototype, Tool support, Interaction Design, Classification

ACM Classification Keywords

H.5.2 [Information interfaces and presentation]: User Interfaces-*Prototyping, User-centered Design.*

General Terms

Design, Documentation

INTRODUCTION

Prototyping is an integral part of development and testing of design ideas in user-centered design methods. It helps interaction designers to define user interfaces, and evaluate usability issues in early stages of design. Many current tools, however, do not support the complete set of tasks of an interaction designer and other team members very well. They may be excellent at one, or even several points, but do not support the transition between different stages in the user-centered design process, and especially to implementation and more generally software engineering very well.

EICS'11, June 13–16, 2011, Pisa, Italy.

We are not the first to notice problems with the tool support for both user-centered design and software engineering. Seffah et al [17] also noticed the problem and stressed both the need for "computer-assisted usability engineering" tools as well as a framework to share best practices between software engineering and user-centered design. Grigoreanu et al [8] focused on tool support for designers and noticed similar issues: tools should better support the "flow" of the design process and support the evaluation and communication about the look-and-feel of an application. Campos et al [4] also noticed the problem with the flow. They have a more software engineering focus, and noticed that in early user interface design stages there was a frequent change in workstyle. They thus proposed a tool, CanonSketch, that supports different workstyles and a framework that allows to evaluate tools on their support for different workstyles.

We propose a framework, GRIP, that complements the workstyle framework by Campos et al [4] and focuses on the flow of information between different roles involved in the creation, evaluation and implementation of *digital interactive prototypes*. The framework is based on a literature study and our own experience and validated through its application to existing research and commercial tools used for prototyping. GRIP focuses on the relations between artifacts involved in the prototyping process.

To illustrate the use of the GRIP framework, we developed tool, GRIP-it. The tool is based on the functionalities provided by framework. It addresses the specific problems that occurs in the early design of prototypes (for example integration of design artifacts).

PROTOTYPING

User-Centered Design (UCD) processes typically include several iterations of prototyping. Because of the multidisciplinary approach in UCD projects, team members with different backgrounds are involved, and design artifacts are transferred between these people frequently.

Team members that are involved in prototyping usually have one of the following roles: interaction designer, human-factors and ergonomics expert and software developer and end user [9]. In the remainder of this paper, we will make the distinction between the aforementioned roles to provide a clear under-

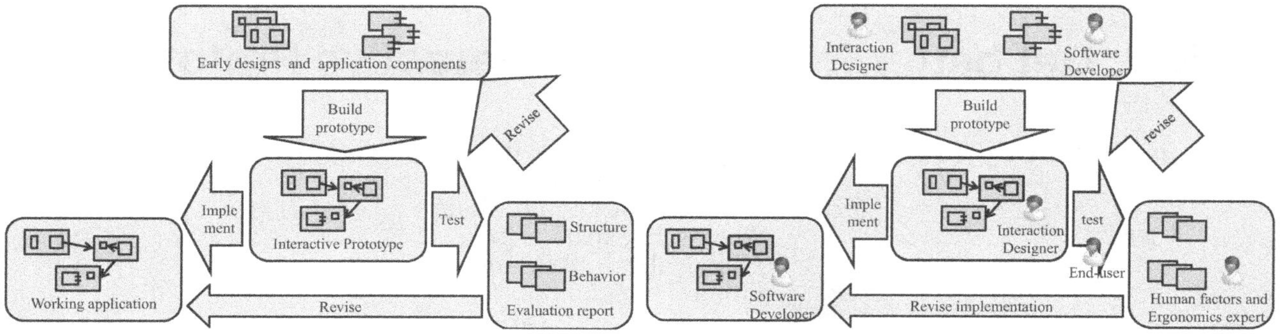

(a) Artifact view (b) People view

Figure 1. GRIP Framework

standing of what type of practitioner is involved for a particular prototyping activity. Nevertheless, we are aware that team members can combine several roles in a UCD project.

Besides the involvement of a multidisciplinary team in prototyping, the cooperation with end-users is inevitable. The level of involvement of end-users in UCD can vary according to the type of project and prototype that will be designed and developed. In general, end users will be involved during a user needs analysis before any prototyping takes place, and in the evaluation of several prototypes [9, 16]. In some projects, participatory design allows end-users to be involved in prototyping activities as well [14]. In this paper we mainly consider end-user involvement before prototyping activities and during design evaluations, but participatory design activities are not excluded.

The most accessible and ubiquitous tool to translate design ideas into visible User Interface (UI) designs is pencil and paper [3, 19]. Sketches can be easily understood by all team members, including end-users. Usually, an interaction designer is in charge of creating these designs, but all team members can be involved in brainstorm sessions. End-users can be involved in early evaluations of these sketches, which is the cheapest and quickest way to collect feedback.

Despite the reduced cost and time investments to create and evaluate sketches, these paper prototypes cannot contain all interactions exemplifying content and other application components [19]. Therefore, in the prototyping process sketches may very soon evolve into digitally created interactive prototypes using prototyping software or UI toolkits, which often have a longer lifespan [1]. This level of prototyping involves interaction designers. Once interactive behavior needs to be included in the prototypes, software developers contribute by developing a working application. Usability evaluations are conducted by human-factors and ergonomics experts or interaction designers and result into evaluation reports.

The involvement of team members with diverse backgrounds demands extra efforts to transfer designs and accompanying information (such as design decisions and evaluation reports). Each team member may prefer another prototyping tool to contribute to the prototyping process [1]. Furthermore, it is likely that some information gets lost during these transfers. Some prototyping tools support the creation and transfer of UI designs. However, a general tool for interaction design that supports the entire prototyping process, described above, is lacking.

GRIP FRAMEWORK

The GRIP framework defines the required artifacts and stakeholders that participate in the prototype development process. We discern four groups of artifacts: Early designs and application components, Evaluation reports and a Working application (Figure 1(a)). We classify the different roles involved in the creation, evaluation and further usage of prototypes as follows: *Interaction designer*, *Human factors and Ergonomics expert*, *Software developer* and *End user*. The involvement of each role is explained in more detail below and is illustrated in Figure 1(b).

The Interaction designer plays a crucial role in the creation of prototypes as he is responsible for the creation of *(early) designs* (depicted by wireframes) and the creation of the combined prototype. Note that in subsequent iterations, he may be assisted by a visual designer to create more detailed designs. UI designs (or even sketches) can be combined with *software components* (depicted by the UML symbol for software components) to create *interactive prototypes* (depicted by interconnected wireframes).

These interactive prototypes should be tested by experts and at least some of the time involve end-users of the application. The results of these tests are documented by the human factors and ergonomics expert in an *evaluation report.* Notice that this evaluation report contains an evaluation of the look and feel (*structure* and *behavior*). We make no assumptions about the form of this report, but it preferably presents the interpretation of the results, as well as the supporting data in a format this is understandable by all stakeholders. Understanding the evaluation results and the implications this has for the implementation may be beneficial to convince software developers to *revise* the software components used or the actual *working application.* Similarly visual and interac-

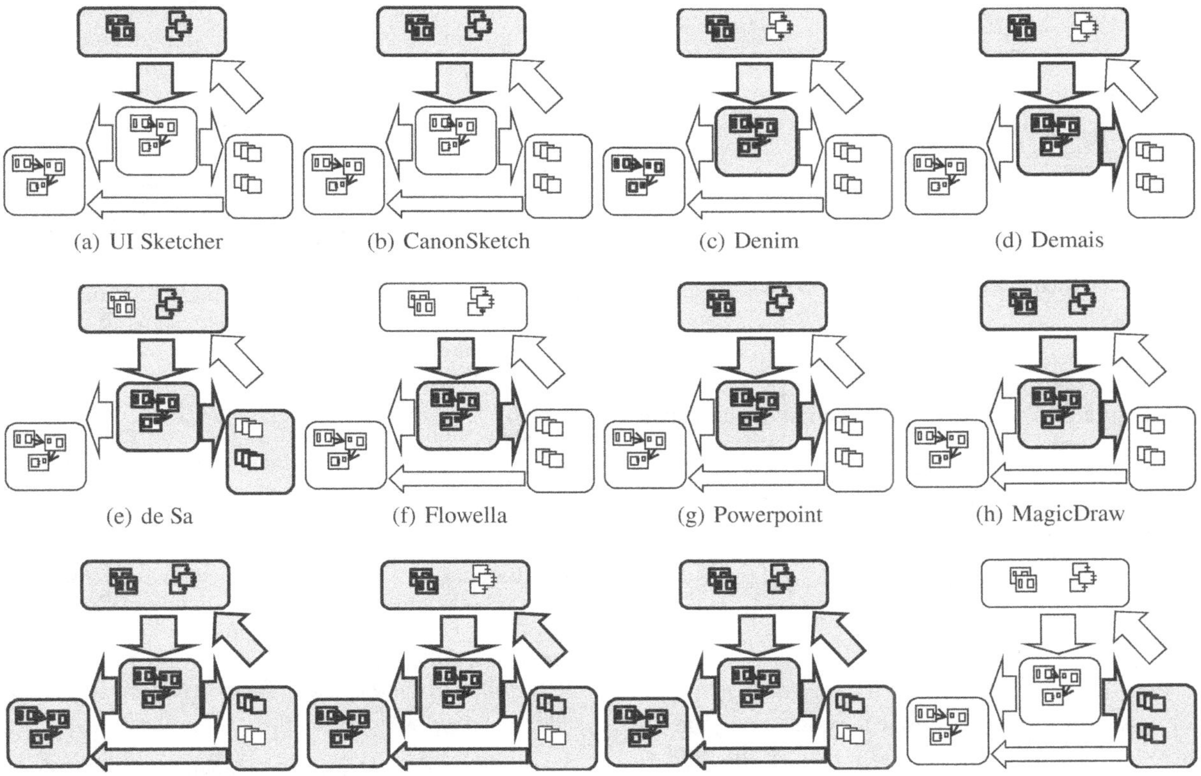

(a) UI Sketcher (b) CanonSketch (c) Denim (d) Demais

(e) de Sa (f) Flowella (g) Powerpoint (h) MagicDraw

(i) SketchFlow (j) ProtoShare (k) JustInMind (l) ClickTale

Figure 2. GRIP Framework applied for commercial and research prototyping tools

tion designers need this information to revise their designs or the integration thereof in the interactive prototype.

To optimize the flow of information it is useful in some situations that the interactive prototype can (at least partly) be exported to a format that allows the software developer to access the prototype from within his programming environment. This to ensure an optimal flow of information and a minimal duplication of efforts.

To illustrate the coverage of the ideal tool set, we use the line weight and the background color of the different parts of the diagram. In this way, one can instantly grasp the features. As the ideal tool set covers all activities and artifacts, all activities (arrows) and artifacts have the same line weight and background color in Figure 1. Support for an activity can be accomplished in a variety of ways. The fact that an interactive prototype can be exported as a website supports the testing of a prototype, and the ability to export a design as a picture, may enable the creation of an interactive prototype.

CLASSIFYING PROTOTYPING TOOLS

This section and Figure 2 illustrate how GRIP can be applied to classify and/or compare a diverse set of existing tools for the support they can provide for prototype development and evaluation. The tools are both research and commercial, selected to differ in scope and target users. To visualize the capabilities of the tools, we adapt the line weight and the background color of the activities (arrows) and artifacts (rounded rectangles and specific illustrations). The line weight of activities and artifacts that are not supported is reduced and their background color is removed. For example, UI Sketcher [18] (Figure 2(a)) and CanonSketch [4] (Figure 2(b)) support the creation of (early) designs, but not the creation of application components. The illustration of application components thus gets a white background and has a reduced line weight. Since (early) designs are supported, the rounded rectangle and the early designs illustration retain the original line weight and background color. Both tools are focused on creating designs, but not on the creation of interactive prototypes.

Figure 2(d) illustrates that Demais [2] enables the creation of interactive prototypes (using a diversity of media formats and sketches). Denim [11] supports sketch-based prototyping of both navigation and web page structure (Figure 2(c)). Denim has a feature that exports the design into html for testing, but not with the aim of further development. MS PowerPoint (Figure 2(g)) allows the creation of interactive presentations that can be used for testing but does not facilitate the export of design evaluation data. MS PowerPoint can be imported in MS Expression Blend to a SketchFlow [12] (Figure 2(i)) specification. This SketchFlow specification can be executed in a web-based runtime that supports annotations on the user interface structure. Furthermore, the SketchFlow specifications can include custom components

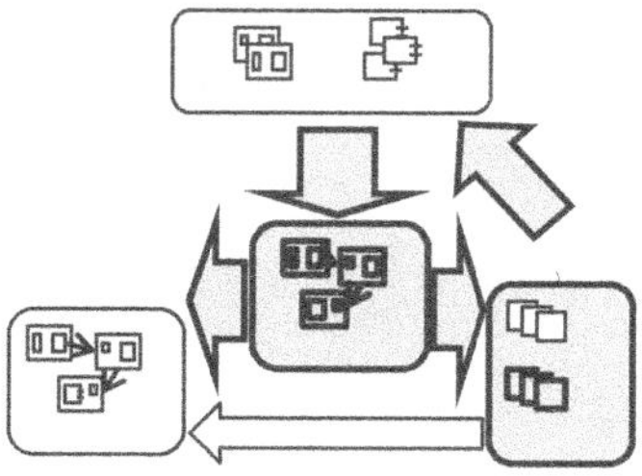

Figure 3. GRIP framework to identify new tool

and are saved in XAML [13], which can be the basis for further development. ProtoShare [15] (Figure 2(j)) and JustinMind [10] (Figure 2(k)) also allow the creation of interactive prototypes, but export the prototypes to regular webpages, which can be annotated using their hosted services. Web-based prototypes can also offer insights on user behavior using services such as ClickTale [5] (Figure 2(l)). Flowella [7] (Figure 2(f)) is a prototyping tool, developed by Nokia, focusing on building of interactive prototypes for mobile devices from designs (exported as images). The exported prototypes can be executed both on desktops and on the targeted mobile devices.

A special case of a prototyping tool is proposed by de Sà et al [6], as shown in Figure 2(e). The goal of this tool is to allow end-users to create complete interactive prototypes within specific domains. To enable this, a specific set of software components and media can be combined to create complete interactive prototypes that can be executed on mobile devices on a specific runtime that logs all actions, enabling replay.

MagicDraw (Figure 2(h)), a modeling tool, allows the creation of interactive prototypes, realized as models, but with a concrete Windows look-and-feel.

GRIP FOR EXPLORING NOVEL TOOLS

Based on our experience and an analysis of the state of the art using the GRIP framework, we identified a combination of features that was not present in literature and seemed to be promising. The requirements for this tool, GRIP-it, are shown using the GRIP framework in Figure 3. The tool should be able to use early designs, but also software components, to create an interactive prototype (especially for tablet or other touch-based devices). One should be able to use the prototype as a starting point for implementation and be able to analyse interaction logs of user tests.

It complements existing tools such as SketchFlow (Figure 2(i)), ProtoShare (Figure 2(j)) and JustInMind (Figure 2(k)) since the evaluation support is concentrated on the behavior rather than the structure of the interface. It also uses both (early) designs and components as input rather than mainly components as documented in Figure 2(e).

GRIP-it Tool

Our tool support for the GRIP framework facilitates the connection between the creation and evaluation of prototypes at early stages of interaction design. This section discusses the most important artifacts that were implemented in the tool. A screenshot of our tool is shown in Figure 4. An *interaction designer* uses pre-defined prototypes, which can be scanned sketches on paper, digitized sketches or images to create the user interface design (Figure 4, A-1). Besides creating and editing the designs, the *interaction designer* can add interactive components to the early designs (Figure 4, A-2). The clickable areas of the user interface can be defined by adding resizable interactive regions to the digitized sketches (Figure 4, B). Similarly, multimedia (including image and video components) can be added to the designs to provide a first impression of possible content in the user interface. Once this prototype is finished, *interaction designers* can save the prototype (Figure 4, A-3) in XAML [13] and revise it based on suggestions of a *human factors and ergonomics expert* without having to create a new prototype. Software developers could use this format to start programming a working application.

This tool has the advantage that as soon as an interactive prototype is available, one can immediately explore or evaluate it (Figure 4, C). There is an option to give visual feedback for successfully registered taps. This is especially useful on some tablet devices as some force is required to successfully register a tap.

After the prototypes are being evaluated, a *human factors and ergonomics expert* can analyze how *end users* performed the task. A visual log of the interaction or an export in CSV format can be used for the analysis. The log shows every tap (or click on a desktop system) during an evaluation session using color-coded dots(Figure 4, D). Since these dots focus on direct interaction with the prototype, they provide enough details to compare design decisions such as different navigation options, interaction aspects (such as size of interactive region), and placement of controls. All screens that the user interacted with, are available in a corresponding order (Figure 4, D-1) and team members can opt to show only a subset of the chronologically ordered taps (Figure 4, D-2).

Expert Review

An expert review of the preliminary GRIP-it tool was conducted to evaluate the ideas of the GRIP framework. In contrast to interviewing or surveying practitioners about their opinion of the GRIP framework, presenting a concrete instance of the framework stimulated the experts involved to think about practices in which this type of tool can be used, and possible features that can be supported by the GRIP framework and instances of it, such as our tool.

Three HCI researchers, having 4 to 7 years of experience in prototyping, participated in the expert review. Each of them has a different background: computer science, cognitive psychology and cognitive ergonomics, and sociology. Besides doing research of prototyping and user-centered design within their respective domains, they all participated in various prototyping processes. They received no specific rewards for their participation except for a promise to be kept informed about eventual future versions of the tool.

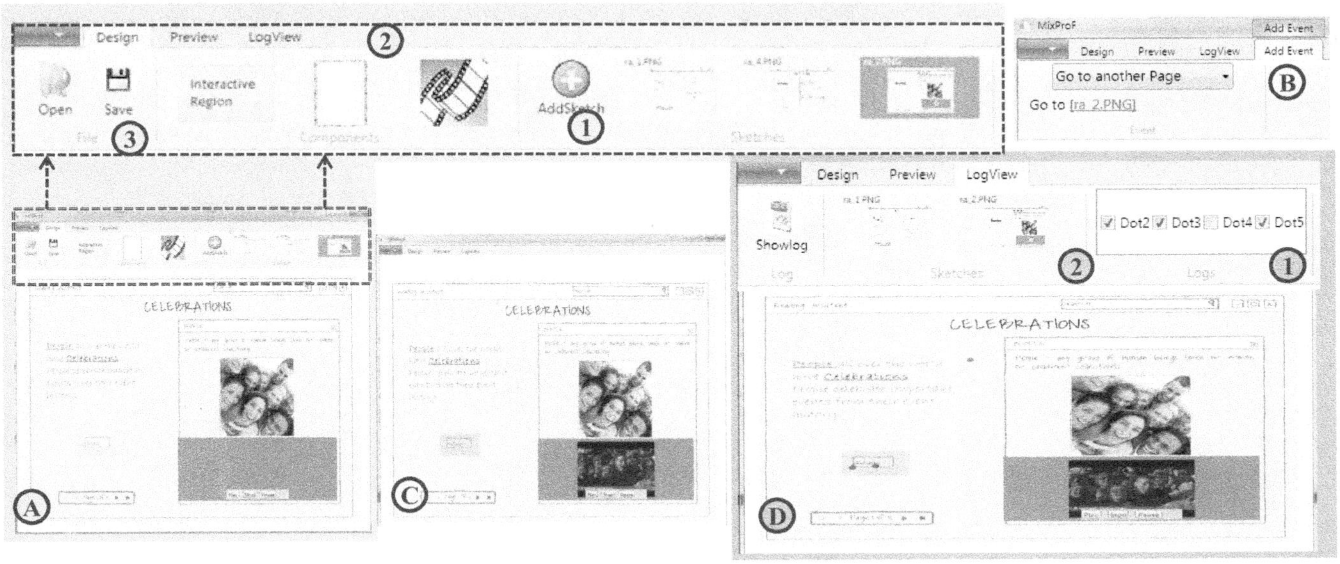

Figure 4. Screenshot of our (revised) tool prototype. Designers create interactive prototypes (A, B), one can explore the prototypes (C), visual logs of prototype explorations are provided (D).

Before the review, there was a briefing session to present the tool, its goals and some examples of UI designs created by the tool. Analogous to cognitive walkthroughs [20], the experts received written instructions, including a list of tasks, and were asked to write a short report regarding their feedback and findings. Furthermore, the tool and some examples of interactive prototypes created using the tool were provided to the experts. Afterwards, the experts presented their findings in a report and provided reasons behind the problems, and possible suggestions. This expert review differs from a typical cognitive walkthrough because we did not ask the experts to focus on ease of learning. We were interested in feedback concerning GRIP-it.

According to the feedback, the general idea of a tool that combines prototyping and the evaluation of UI designs before any working prototype is available, is appreciated by all the experts. One of the experts mentioned: *"The application could be useful for designers when creating UIs to illustrate the interactivity of their design drafts"*. Another expert reports: *"Evaluating these sketched prototypes including interactive features of a prototype is interesting for evaluating a first prototype of an application"*. Furthermore, one of the experts remarks: *"The application could replace paper prototypes and Wizard of Oz experiments. It allows an easy trial of a good way to test alternative interfaces"*. Consequently, this type of tools is suitable to support both the creation and the early evaluation of interactive UI designs.

During the evaluation of the interactive behavior of UI designs, our tool logs actions of participants on the screen. One of the experts assessed this feature as follows: *"The fact that the system logs where the test participant has clicked in the prototype can be very useful"*. Furthermore, this expert recommends to add various visualizations of the logs and to relate more information to the existing dots, such as time information and a path that shows the navigation actions of a test participant.

One of the experts favors the support for iterative design in the GRIP-it tool. Since only the evaluation of UI designs was considered in this expert review, this expert reports: *"I am very curious about the design feature in this tool, and the interplay between designing and evaluating. A good balance between these two tasks, and features that enhance iterative design, according to the logs, would be very interesting."*. Another expert mentions that a more advanced version of the tool could be used in co-design sessions, which includes participatory design into the scope of GRIP. Further remarks of the experts concern detailed feedback on the UI of the tool, including comments regarding the size and placement of UI widgets. Most of these detailed comments are already taken into account in GRIP-it as shown in Figure 4.

More general comments suggested to provide an export feature, specifically to better support testing with a larger number of people over the Internet with support for logging and the possibility to also include a questionnaire. Inclusion of a wizard-like interface was another suggestion. These suggestions of the experts on the UI design of the tool will be considered for future iterations.

Although this expert review is a preliminary evaluation of the tool, the feedback of the experts acknowledges the ideas supported by the GRIP framework and encourages us to continue the development of the tool. In this review, the experts, all having relevant experience in several prototyping projects, appreciate this prototyping tool that provides features to easily and quickly add interactive behavior to sketched prototypes. By supporting the creation as well as the evaluation of prototypes, the iterative approach and cooperation within multidisciplinary teams can be benefited.

CONCLUSION AND FUTURE WORK

This paper reports on GRIP, a framework to address tool support for interaction design in (early) design prototyping. We believe GRIP complements earlier work in identifying areas where tool support is needed to improve integration design practices in prototyping. We showed how the framework can be used to compare existing tools for (early) prototype development as well as to identify opportunities for identifying potentially interesting tool support. The latter was illustrated using our GRIP-it tool.

The findings described in this paper have potential to stimulate insightful discussion among researchers. This has been demonstrated through the expert review carried out with researchers from different disciplines with experience in creating interactive prototypes. Our work has not only generated interest among researchers from technical but also among researchers from social science background. Some insightful feedback that the paper already generated includes its contribution in integration towards needs of designers.

The GRIP framework allows to identify areas of attention for prototyping tools that could be beneficial for their adoption. More refinement and analysis on how GRIP fits together with other frameworks is needed to enable more detailed analysis and more focused discussion of tool support for interactive prototyping. One sign of this is that vastly different tools such as Denim (Figure 2(c)), Demais (Figure 2(d)) and MagicDraw (Figure 2(h)) are almost identical. It is however a good thing that commonalities between these tools can be easily identified.

The results of the expert review learned us that there is a desire to have a more advanced version of a tool along the lines of the GRIP-it tool. Future work for GRIP-it includes addressing these more advanced requests, such adding the capability to create questionnaires, and richer visualization options to better understand the results across different evaluation sessions.

ACKNOWLEDGMENTS

This work is partially supported by the IBBT Gr@sp project and the AMASS++ IWT SBO project, IWT 060051. We thank the expert reviewers and anonymous reviewers for their suggestions to improve the presentation of the paper.

REFERENCES

1. Arnowitz, J., Arent, M., and Berger, N. *Effective Prototyping for Software Makers (The Morgan Kaufmann Series in Interactive Technologies)*. Morgan Kaufmann Publishers Inc., San Francisco, CA, USA, 2006.

2. Bailey, B. P., Konstan, J. A., and Carlis, J. V. Demais: designing multimedia applications with interactive storyboards. In *MULTIMEDIA '01*, ACM (New York, NY, USA, 2001), 241–250.

3. Buxton, B. *Sketching User Experiences getting the design right and the right design*. Morgan Kaufmann, 2007.

4. Campos, P. F., and Nunes, N. J. Towards useful and usable interaction design tools: Canonsketch. *Interacting with Computers 19*, 5-6 (2007), 597–613.

5. ClickTale. Customer experience analytics by clicktale. `http://clicktale.com/`.

6. de Sá, M., Carrio, L., Duarte, L., and Reis, T. Supporting the design of mobile interactive artefacts. *Advances in Engineering Software 40*, 12 (2009), 1279 – 1286. Designing, modelling and implementing interactive systems.

7. Flowella. Create prototypes before writing a line of code - forum.nokia. `http://www.forum.nokia.com/Library/Tools_and_downloads/Other/Flowella`.

8. Grigoreanu, V., Fernandez, R., Inkpen, K., and Robertson, G. G. What designers want: Needs of interactive application designers. In *VL/HCC* (2009), 139–146.

9. International Standards Organization. *ISO 13407. Human Centred Design Process for Interactive Systems*. Geneva, Swiss, 1999.

10. Justinmind. `http://www.justinmind.com`.

11. Lin, J., Newman, M. W., Hong, J. I., and Landay, J. A. Denim: finding a tighter fit between tools and practice for web site design. In *CHI '00*, ACM (New York, NY, USA, 2000), 510–517.

12. Microsoft. Sketchflow - UI Prototyping Tool. `http://www.microsoft.com/expression/products/Sketchflow_Overview.aspx`.

13. Microsoft. Xaml overview (wpf). `http://msdn.microsoft.com/en-us/library/ms752059.aspx`.

14. Muller, M. J., and Kuhn, S. Participatory design. *Commun. ACM 36* (June 1993), 24–28.

15. ProtoShare. Wireframing and prototyping tool. `http://www.protoshare.com/`.

16. Redmond-Pyle, D., and Moore, A. *Graphical User Interface Design and Evaluation*. Prentice Hall, London, 1995.

17. Seffah, A., and Metzker, E. The obstacles and myths of usability and software engineering. *Commun. ACM 47* (December 2004), 71–76.

18. UI-Sketcher. The User Interface Sketching Tool - iPad app. `http://uisketcher.com/`.

19. Warfel, T. Z. *Protoyping: A Practitioner's Guide*. Rosenfeld Media, 2009.

20. Wharton, C., Rieman, J., Lewis, C., and Polson, P. The Cognitive Walkthrough Method: A Practitioner's Guide. Tech. rep., Institute of Cognitive Science, University of Colorado, 1993.

PageSpark: An E-Magazine Reader with Enhanced Reading Experiences on Handheld Devices

Jiajian Chen
Georgia Institute of Technology
Atlanta, GA 30318 USA
jchen30@mail.gatech.edu

Jun Xiao
HP Labs
Palo Alto,
CA 94304 USA
jun.xiao2@hp.com

Jian Fan
HP Labs
Palo Alto,
CA 94304 USA
jian.fan@hp.com

Eamonn O'Brien-Strain
HP Labs
Palo Alto, CA 94304 USA
eamonn.obrien-strain@hp.com

ABSTRACT

In this paper we present PageSpark, a system that automatically converts static magazine content to interactive and engaging reading apps on handheld reading devices. PageSpark enhances the reading experience in three general aspects: page layout reorganization, page element interactions and page transitions. We explored and implemented several design variations in each aspect with the prototype running on the iPad. Participants from our initial user study showed strong interest of using PageSpark over existing magazine reading apps.

Author Keywords

PageSpark, document analysis, page segmentation, page transition, page layout.,

ACM Classification Keywords

H.5.1. Information interfaces and presentation (e.g., HCI): Multimedia Information Systems.

General Terms

Algorithms, Design, Human Factors.

INTRODUCTION AND RELATED WORK

The fast development in both mobile services and digital publishing is transforming people's way of consuming media content. A growing range of e-readers and tablets, such as the iPad and Kindle, are available for people to read digital magazines, newspaper and books. These reading appliances are handheld, lightweight, and have superior displays compared to traditional PC monitors. However, interaction design for such reading devices is still an active research area in need of attention to make the reading experience as relaxing and engaging as reading prints.

Various researches have been conducted to develop better user interaction mechanisms for common tasks such as emailing and web-browsing on mobile devices with small displays. For example, Wobbrock et al. presented WebThumb and discussed interaction techniques for a small screen browser [6]. Lank and Phan described a *focus+context* sketching on Pocket PC devices [4]. The main focus of our research, however, is on e-reader devices that are close in size and resolution to traditional books, and on improving reading experience for e-magazines.

Figure 1. PageSpark UI snapshots for PC World Magazine.

Not surprisingly, the prevailing interaction metaphor for e-readers models after paper and their appearance and affordance. Seminal studies, such as the one published by Adler et al. looked at how people use paper documents in their everyday life and discussed design implication for digital reading devices [1]. However, such studies often centered on professional and work related scenario and the comparison between reading on paper and reading on screen often dwelled on reading speed and comprehension.

Reading magazines, we argue, is often more for recreational purpose than for information gathering. The readers' task goal, if there is any, is not to study or learn the content but to follow and enjoy the storyline. Digital publishing brought a range of features to books that would not be possible in print, such as built-in dictionary and search. However, because of the linear, narrative nature of the magazine content, we believe presentation and appearance play crucial roles rather than hyper-textual navigation structures. Wilson et al. suggested that visual cues should be adapted to exploit the potential of the medium [5].

PageSpark offers an attempt to achieve that. It automatically converts static PDF magazines to interactive multimedia apps running on the iPad. The iPad is our platform of choice because of its form factor and display, and iOS programming interface, but our design concepts and developed technologies may well be extended to other tablets and e-reader platforms. Similarly, our analysis engine only works on PDF files now because the PDF format is prevalent in digital distribution of magazine content, but other document analysis technologies that work on web content or scanned document images may well be incorporated into the PageSpark system.

SYSTEM ARCHITECTURE

There are three main components in PageSpark. Given input of a PDF magazine (e.g., National Geographic), first we use our PDF segmentation algorithms to analyze the content of each page to extract its text and image. Each text and image ("information block") is labeled for its semantics, such as an article title and author name, and stored separately. Second we compute the reading order of the text content of the articles, link multi-page images and articles and generate an XML description file for this magazine. After these two offline steps, PageSpark parses the XML and maps the semantics of the mark up in runtime into interactive behaviors in the app that runs on the iPad. The system architecture of PageSpark is shown below.

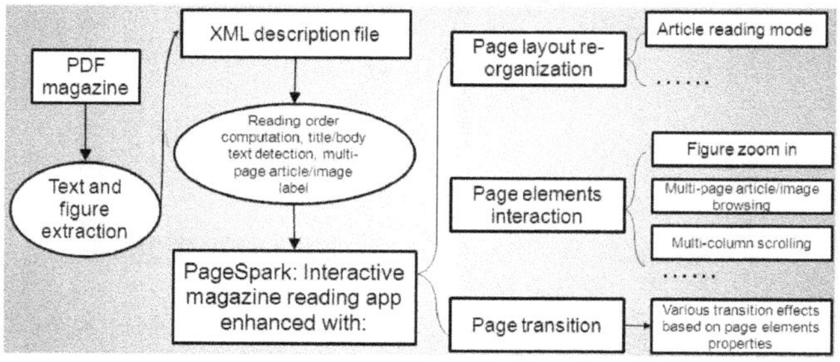

Figure 2. System architecture.

PDF SEGMENTATION ALGORITHM

Even though PDF (portable document format) files truthfully preserve the intended visual appearance of electronic documents, they do not maintain logical and semantic structures such as paragraphs, titles and captions that are more meaningful for readers to interact with. The goal of our PDF segmentation is thus to identify these semantic structures from unstructured internal PDF data utilizing some visual properties.

Text Grouping

In PDF files, the text is represented as words with attributes of font name, font size, color and orientation [3]. The task of text grouping is to group words into text lines, and group text lines to text segments/paragraphs. Currently we only deal with text of horizontal and vertical orientations.

To group words into lines, we start a new line and add an available word to the line. We then look for available words to add to the line on both the left and the right ends. The conditions for a word to be added to the line are: 1) the difference between the font size of the words and the font size of the line must not exceed one point, 2) the horizontal distance between the word's bounding box and the line bounding box must be less than the nominal character space for the font and it is the smallest among all available words, 3) the vertical overlap between the word bounding box and the line's must be more than 40%. When no word can be added to the current line, we start a new line. It should be pointed out that we do not require words in a line to have the same font style. This is based on our observation that many documents include URL links and names that have different font styles. For each text line, we compute and maintain two key metrics of font size and central location weighted by lengths of words. To group text lines into segments, we sort the text lines in top-down fashion. We start with a new segment and add an available line to it. We grow the segment by adding lines to it (see Figure 3 (a)).

Image Object Segmentation

The need for image segmentation arises due to two reasons: 1) A PDF image object may contain multiple semantic image objects,2) the bounding box of an image object may overlap with other image objects or text regions and thus limits the display and interaction options. We classify foreground/background pixels by computing color distance. The connected component analysis is followed to identify image objects from foreground pixels (see Figure 3(b)).

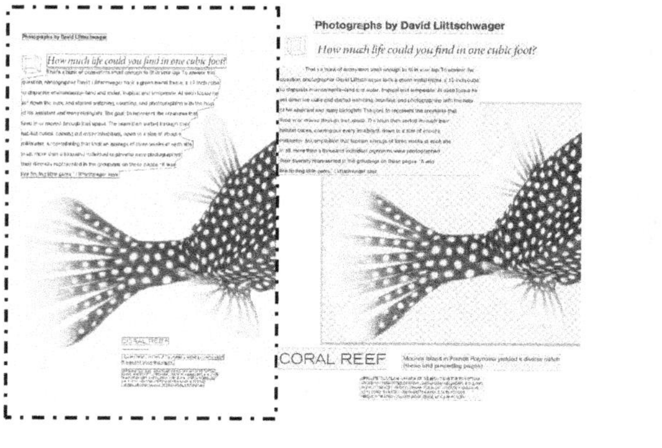

(a) (b)

Figure 3. An example of the PDF segmentation.

XML DESCRIPTION

We proposed an XML based description format to organize the results of PDF segmentation. In this format every information block in each page is stored as a node in a hierarchical tree structure in an XML file. An example of a node is shown in Figure 4.

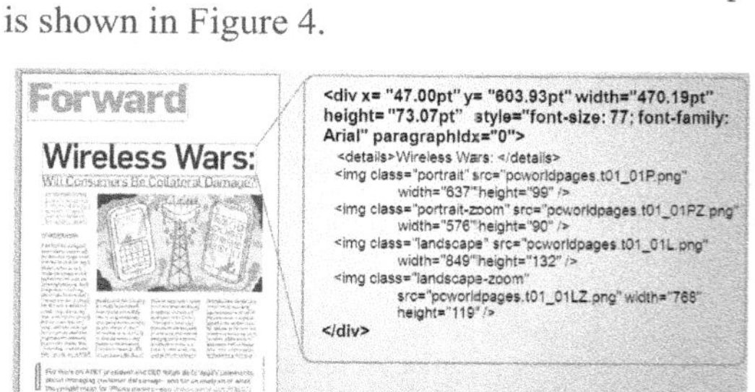

Figure 4. Segmentation result of an magazine page and its XML description of the 'wireless war' information block.

INTERACTION DESIGN

PageSpark enhances user's reading experiences beyond simple zooming and paging in three general aspects based on page segmentation analysis: page layout reorganization, page elements interaction and page transition. Page layout reorganization intelligently computes and reorganizes article content for better reading. Page elements interaction allows users to interact with every piece of text and image content of the article. Page transitions add visually appealing effects to increase reader engagement.

Page layout reorganization

The first enhancement we designed is page layout reorganization. Our goal is increasing readability by reorganizing the layout of page contents. Magazine articles usually have a multi-column style. We found that the font size in the columns is usually too small to read easily even on handheld devices with middle-size displays in portrait view. Traditional PDF readers allows user to zoom in to look, but it is not a good solution from readers' perspective. Modern e-readers such as Kindle or Sony Reader provide specially designed format with proper font size for e-pubs suitable for reading on these devices, but it requires a format redesign of the content. We designed an 'Article Reading Mode' to cope with this problem. In this mode, PageSpark leverages the result of PDF segmentation and automatically puts all text content of an article together to form a clear single reading scroll, as shown in Figure 5.

To form a single reading column in the correct order we use the following rule-table based heuristic algorithm to compute the reading order for each text block in the article.

Rule Set	Rank
Font size and style	1
TextBlock.origin.x	2
TextBlock.origin.y	3
TexBlock Column Width	4

Table 1. Rule table for computing reading order.

Given a set of text blocks of an article, we run a two pass algorithm to compute the reading order for each block. In the first pass, based on the rule table we distinguish titles, footnotes with the main body text. We also create several buckets based on the width of information block to find a group of blocks that has smallest variation in width. Combining these two steps we can distinguish main body text from other types of information blocks. In the second pass, we compute the reading index of each main body text block based on its position in the original page layout.

We animate the transition between the original page layout and the article reading mode. When use taps inside the content of an article on the original PDF page, text blocks of this article pop up and fly to form the long article reading scroll. It also zooms in and scrolls to the exact location in the article where user's finger touches.

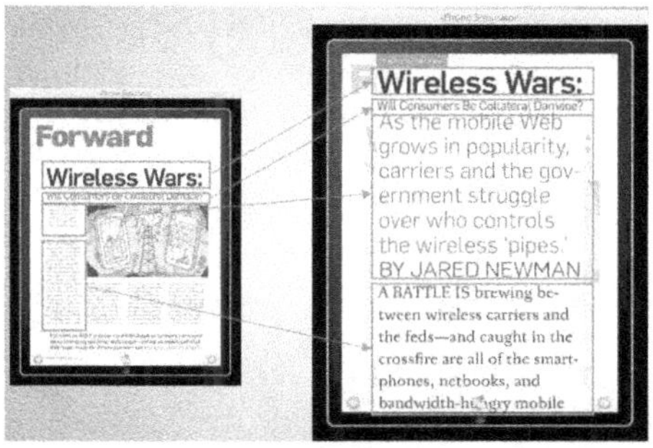

Figure 5. Article reading mode of a page in portrait view.

The article reading scroll takes 75% of width of the screen (576 pixels) in the portrait mode on the iPad. In the meantime the original page is rendered semi-transparently as the background. User can tap the background to switch back to the ordinary page view. We choose these parameters because we find that these settings make reading multi-column articles much easier not only on the iPad, but also on other devices with middle-size displays.

Page elements interaction

In general the goal of page elements interaction is make every piece of the magazine page interactive. There are many possible design variations for page elements interactions. We implement three enhancements to demonstrate the possibilities: multi-column scrolling, multi-page article/image browsing, and single figure zooming in.

In the previous section we presented the article reading mode. We found this mode is very useful for reading article in portrait. However, we found in general a multi-column article is readable on the iPad in landscape mode. In this case, we designed and implemented a multi-column scrolling mechanism to enhance reading experiences. Braganza et al. concluded from their studies that horizontal paging with multi-column layout is superior to scrolling in terms of performance and user preference [2]. But we found that the main problem is that by the time the user finishes reading the last line of the previous column, s/he has to scroll the whole page all the way back to the top to read to the next column. The continuity of reading, as a result, is lost. In PageSpark we render each column of the article independently in landscape mode. Therefore, each column of the article is independently scrollable to provide continuous reading experiences for the users.

Figure 6. User can scroll each single column of the article.

The second feature, multi-page article/image browsing allows user to get a quick overview of an article or image than spans multiple pages. When the user taps the margin area of a page that belongs to a multi-page article or image spread, the current page zooms out and its adjacent article/image pages slide in to form an overview of the whole article or image. User can quickly jump to any page of the article by tapping a thumbnail in this mode, as shown in Figure 7.

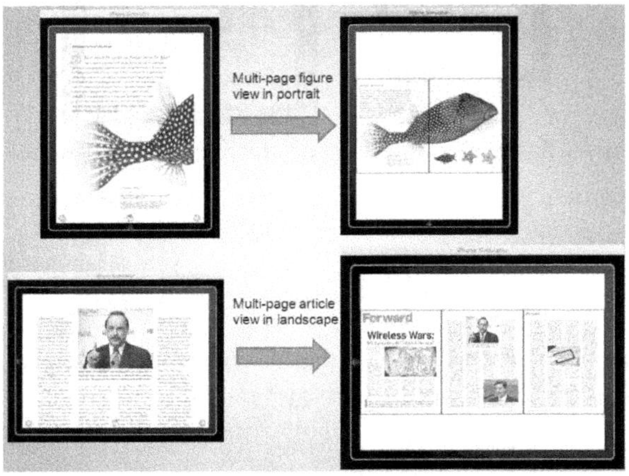

Figure 7. Multi-page article/image browsing mode.

Lastly, single figure zooming, is a feature that zooms in a figure when user touches it, fits the figure to the screen size and fades out the background page.

Page transition

Another key enhancement of PageSpark compared with existing PDF magazine readers is that we apply various visually-appealing transition effects intelligently to different document elements. The purpose of applying these transitions is to better convey the content structure to the readers by distinguishing text from images, and headings and titles from body text and callouts in animations and transitions. We pre-defined many types of transition effects. When user switches between article pages each information block (e.g., text, figure, title) has its corresponding transition effect (e.g., fade in/out, slide in/out, and cross-dissolve). Besides the article page transition, we also designed and implemented several special transitions for ads pages, such as highlighting.

USER STUDIES

In a preliminary user study we interviewed and observed 10 people to gather information of their reading behaviors on handheld devices. We discussed with them about extra value for digital magazines as well as any discomfort of reading them on screen vs. on paper. This preliminary study provided us many insights to build PageSpark prototype.

In a post user study, we tested our system with a full 155 page national geographic magazine. We asked 10 participants to freely interact with the magazine in PageSpark, and in a traditional PDF reader on the iPad. We interviewed them after this session and asked open ended questions. People expressed a strong preference of using PageSpark over the PDF reader to view the magazine. Using PageSpark, participants showed a greater level of engagement. One explanation is simply the fun of seeing how the system reacts and the novelty of the system. But tangibility and responsiveness are often mentioned by the users as the main reason they like the system. They commented that PageSpark made the magazine "live".

DISCUSSIONS AND FUTURE WORK

PageSpark enhances reading experiences in three general aspects. We have implemented one instance for each aspect, but we just touched the tip of an iceberg. There are many design variations that can be explored under the PageSpark's general framework for different types of digital content.

For example, besides the article reading mode, we can apply other types of page layout reorganization, such as removing unrelated content or adding additional content. This may not be suitable for professionally designed magazines, but it may be useful for web articles since web pages often contain a large number and area of unrelated content, such as ads.

For the page elements interaction, we can break the linear structure of the magazine and provide a more natural non-linear navigational help for the readers. For example, since we can extract the semantic meaning of any page entities, names and keywords found on the pages can be indexed for search. User can then simply tap a photographer's name to retrieve all the photos taken by this photographer across the entire magazine collection.

Finally, for the page transition, we may apply different transition templates or styles for different types of content. For example, static print advertisement can be automatically converted into animated display ads using the PageSpark system. The key, however, is to find the right balance between attention grabbing and being annoying.

REFERENCES

1. Adler, A., Gujar, A., Harrison, B. L., O'Hara, K., and Sellen, A. A diary study of work-related reading: Design implications for digital reading devices. *CHI' 98*, pp. 241-248. New York, NY.
2. Braganza, C., Marriott K., Moulder P., Wybrow, M. and Dwyer T. Scrolling behavior with single- and multi-column layout, Proceedings of *WWW'09*.
3. Chao H. and Fan J. Layout and Content Extraction for PDF Documents, *DAS*'04, *LNCS* 3163, pp. 213–224.
4. Lank, E. and Phans, S. Focus+context sketching on pocket PC. *CHI '04*. pp.1275-1278.
5. Wilson, R., Landoni, M. and Gibb, F. (2002) A user-centred approach to e-book design. The Electronic Library, 20 (4).
6. Wobbrock, J., Forlizzi, J., Hudson, S. and Myers, B. WebThumb: interaction techniques for small-screen browsers. *UIST'02*. pp.205-208.

A Research Framework for Performing User Studies and Rapid Prototyping of Intelligent User Interfaces Under the OpenOffice.org Suite

Martin Dostál and Zdenek Eichler
Dept. Computer Science
Palacký University Olomouc, CZ
{dostal, eichlerz}@inf.upol.cz

ABSTRACT
We introduce a research framework which enables to use the OpenOffice.org as a platform for HCI research, particularly for performing user studies or prototyping and evaluating intelligent user interfaces. We make two contributions: (1) we introduce an innovative hybrid logging technique which provides high-level, rich and accurate information about issued user commands, command parameters and used interaction styles. Our logging technique also avoids an unwanted requirement for further complex processing of logged user interface events to infer user commands, which must be performed on most loggers these days. (2) Our logging tool acts as a component object in OpenOffice.org with an easy-to-use Application Program Interface (API) which enables, along with deep OpenOffice.org programmability, to use OpenOffice.org as a research framework for developing and evaluating intelligent user interfaces.

Author Keywords
user studies, logging, intelligent user interfaces, prototyping

ACM Classification Keywords
D.2.2 Design Tools and Techniques: User Interfaces

General Terms
Human Factors, Design development.

INTRODUCTION
HCI (Human-Computer Interaction) researchers and practitioners often perform user studies to evaluate user interfaces. The methods used are either qualitative or quantitative. Quantitative parameters are observed by measuring the user's interaction with the studied interface. It is usually done by human observation, recordings of the screen contents or using specialized software that automatically collects measured data about user interaction. User studies may either be performed on research prototype software or real software applications. The advantage of software prototypes is that they are usually developed in a short time and also that the implementation of logging facilities is not difficult. However, the limitation is that prototypes do not represent real applications known by users and usually offer only limited functionality. That is why prototypes may be limited in terms of ecological validity. Unfortunately, an additional implementation of logging facilities into a third-party-developed software is usually either not feasible or technically demanding and difficult since it requires deep integration with the internal structure of the application.

EICS'11, June 13–16, 2011, Pisa, Italy.

RELATED WORK TO LOGGING USER ACTIVITY
Loggers automatically capture user interface events or other types of appropriate events triggered by an application. The captured data is stored in a file called a *log*. This approach overcomes some disadvantages of human observation and screen-recording systems; logging is usually light on system resources, the data can be further analyzed by corresponding software and logging can be used for short- as well as long-term analysis on a virtually arbitrary number of users.

User Interface Event-Based Logging
User interface event loggers are based on recording low-level (e.g., keyboard input, cursor movement or window resizing) and high-level (e.g., menu or toolbar selection) user interface events generated by running applications [4]. Such loggers are called *user interface event-based loggers* and represent the most widely-used approach today, e.g., MSTracker [7], AppMonitor [1] or RUI [5]. User interface event-based logging provides very detailed, fine-grained, low-level, user interface event-centered data which is useful for a certain kind of user studies such as determining the optimal size and layout of user controls. The logged data must be further extensively processed in order to infer user commands from user interface events. Unfortunately, this is not a simple task. In fact, the researcher must write an interpreter of logged events, which could be a laboured task, since common software applications usually contain hundreds of user commands. For instance, a font selection in standard font dialog would typically result in 10–150 logged user interface events.

User Command-Based Logging
In User Command-Based logging, a logger directly captures issued user commands at the level of the underlying func-

tion call, not at the level of user interface events. The logging mechanism is thus entirely separated from the user interface elements and, consequently, the corresponding user interface events. Unfortunately, it has one serious disadvantage: since it is essentially independent of the user interface representation and user interface events, it is not possible to retrieve information about the interaction style used to invoke a user command. User Command-Based logging has been used scarcely until today because there is no standard way to capture such information at the level of APIs provided by the operating system. Linton used this approach in the OWL [6] system to log user activity in Microsoft Word for Macintosh. However, OWL has two strong limitations. First, OWL is not able to capture the used interaction style, as we explained above. Second, OWL cannot record the parameters of invoked user commands (we can get information about font change but not about what font or size was selected) due to technical limitations.

A Hybrid Approach

We propose a hybrid approach to logging that combines both the mentioned methods. Basically, our logging technique is based on the User Command-Based logging using a modified macrorecorder framework in OpenOffice.org which provides information about the issued commands and their parameters. User Command-Based logging is surrounded by recording certain user interface events such as opening a menu or opening a window in order to capture information about the interaction style used. Combination of both the logging techniques provide high-level, semantically rich and accurate information about user activity including the interaction style used. Although it may not be obvious, the implementation and internal architecture of such a kind of logger is quite complex and requires considerably deep integration with the internal architecture of the application.

OPENOFFICE.ORG INTERCEPTOR

Our tool is called "OpenOffice.org Interceptor" (OOI). It is based on the above-mentioned hybrid logging approach. OpenOffice.org Interceptor emerged as a by-product of our research focused on novel adaptive interfaces (adaptive interfaces dynamically adjust the user interface in order to satisfy the user's requirements observed from application usage) [7]. We focused on a real software suite instead of developing prototypes or mock-ups, in order to evaluate the developed system with appropriate ecological validity. Furthermore, office suites are one of the most widely used kinds of software. In particular, the strengths of OpenOffice.org relevance to HCI research lie in the following facts: (1) it provides widely-known and widely-used office applications, (2) it is widely programmable and can be used to develop custom applications under the OpenOffice.org suite. It uses internally a component object model called UNO (Universal Network Objects) that provides an extensive API for programming using various programming languages, including OpenOffice.org BASIC which is easy to learn and use even for a non-experienced programmer. In particular, the programmability is useful for the preparation of study tasks or prototyping user interfaces. (3) OpenOffice.org functionality can be extended using components called *extensions*. The

Action	Initiated	Executed
`Bold`	`toolbar`	`toolbar`
`FontColor`	`toolbar`	`toolbar`
`InsertTable`	`menu`	`dialog`
`Zoom`	`toolbar`	`dialog`

Time	User	Application
`2009-04-20 18:12:55:165`	`Dostal`	`Writer`
`2009-04-20 18:13:02:400`	`Dostal`	`Writer`
`2009-04-20 18:13:29:022`	`Dostal`	`Writer`
`2009-04-20 18:12:41:889`	`Dostal`	`Writer`

Parameters
`Bold: true;`
`FontColor: 65535;`
`TableName: Sallary;Columns: 2;Rows: 4;Flags: 9;`
`Zoom.Value: 110;Zoom.ValueSet: 28703;Zoom.Type: 0;`

Table 1. Log Sample

logging process is able to differentiate between the interaction style used to *initiate* a particular user command and to *execute* such a user command. In most cases, the initiation and execution style used to invoke a user command would be identical, except for user commands that are executed using a dialog. For instance, saving a file can be initiated and executed using a menu, a toolbar or a keystroke whereas the "Save As" (save file under a different file name) user command is always executed from the "Save As" dialog. Logged data can be exported to a CSV (Comma Separated Values) file. We present a log sample of four records in Table 1. Note that key press events (except keystrokes) are not logged due to preserving privacy. Interceptor logs the following information:

- User command name – a string identifying the name of performed user command, e.g., "Bold" or "InsertTable".
- Names and values of the commands parameters – a string of parameters that have been applied to the user command, e.g., "TableName: Sallary;Columns: 2;Rows: 4;Flags: 9;".
- Interaction style used to initiate the user command – may be either one of "menu", "pop-up menu", "toolbar" or "keystroke".
- Interaction style used to execute the user command – may be either one of "menu", "pop-up menu", "toolbar", "keystroke" or "dialog".
- Username – a string identifying the user. This parameter may be set in the OOI settings.
- Time and date – time and date of a user command completion in `YYYY-MM-DD hh:mm:ss:msc` format.

Internal Architecture

The internal architecture is quite complex and extensive to describe. Basically, the logger is composed of three parts: (1) the user-command-logging framework, (2) the interaction-style-detection framework and (3) the API implementation. The user-command-logging framework is built upon the OpenOffice.org macrorecording framework which receives most user commands issued in an OpenOffice.org application. About ten percent of user commands can not be captured by the macrorecorder and thus must be handled using other techniques. The interaction style detection is implemented using similar techniques as user interface event-based loggers use. The logger hooks some user interface events, e.g., window events or keypress events using the so-called *listener* objects provided by the UNO API. The implementation of the interaction style detection is quite complex due to the internal architecture of the OpenOffice.org suite, which completely separates user commands from user interface representation. For any reader interested in the implementation issues we published a technical report [2] which provides a detailed description of the OOI architecture and implementation.

RAPID PROTOTYPING OF INTELLIGENT USER INTERFACES

HCI researchers interested in studying or prototyping new user interfaces usually develop prototype or mock-up applications which are used to perform further user studies in order to investigate interfaces on users. Prototypes are sometimes quite difficult to develop particularly for a non-experienced programmer. Such prototype applications usually contain a logging mechanism to provide further treatable data for a user study. For some studies, the downside of prototypes or mock-up applications is that such applications provide limited functionality and also its ecological validity may be limited.

OpenOffice.org suite uses internally a component object model called UNO (Universal Network Objects), that also provides an extensive API for OpenOffice.org programming using various programming languages. In fact, UNO is a component model that manages OpenOffice.org internal objects. UNO provides a runtime environment that can be accessed from several programming languages using the so-called language bindings acting as an interface between UNO and programming languages. An UNO component is specified using a meta-language called UNOIDL that describes the program interface of a component. UNO components can be developed in JAVA, C++ or Python. In addition, UNO components can be used (although not developed) in OpenOffice.org BASIC, OLE automation or .NET CLI. OOI is implemented as such an UNO component, so that it can be used in any programming language with a UNO binding. The program interface is extremely easy to use, only two steps should be done in order to use our logging API:

1. Create a UNO service (initiate the OOI) and create a listener object.

2. Provide an implementation of the `ooi_listen` subroutine which acts as a callback. This subroutine is issued by OOI when a user command is performed with parameters as described above.

Figure 1 depicts an implementation of a simple adaptive menu for OpenOffice.org Writer written in OpenOffice.org

```
Global PopupMenuContainer As Object
Global MenuBar As String
Global MenuBarSettings As Object
Global ModuleCfgMgr As Object
Global ooi As Object
Global ooi_listener As Object

Sub RegisterLogHandler
InsertMenu("Favorites")
ooi = createUnoService(_
 "org.openoffice.oointerceptor.XOOInterceptor")
ooi_listener = createUnoListener("ooi_", _
 "org.openoffice.oointerceptor.XOOInterceptorListener")
ooi.addOOInterceptorListener(ooi_listener)
End Sub

Sub ooi_listen(action, initiated, executed, time,_
               user, application, parameters)
 For i = 0 to PopupMenuContainer.getCount() - 1
  item = PopupMenuContainer.getByIndex(i)
  If item(0).Value = ".uno:" + action Then
   PopupMenuContainer.removeByIndex(i)
   Exit For
  End If
 Next i
 MenuItem = CreateMenuItem(".uno:" + action, action)
 PopupMenuContainer.insertByIndex(0, MenuItem)
 ModuleCfgMgr.replaceSettings(MenuBar, MenuBarSettings)
 DisplayTextStatusBar("Action: " & action & _
 ", initiated: " & initiated & ", executed: " & _
 executed & ", time: " & time & ", user: " & _
 user & ", application:" & application & _
  ", parameters: " & parameters)
End Sub
```

Figure 1. Adaptive menu source code

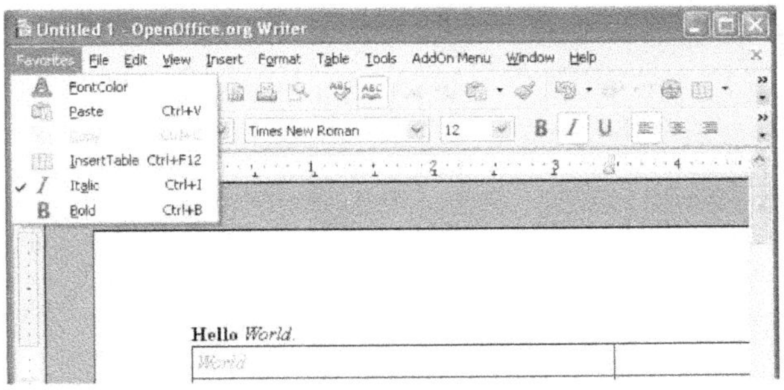

Figure 2. OpenOffice.org Writer with adaptive menu

BASIC. The program displays the information about a recently performed user command in the status bar of the primary window and creates a new menu category called "Favorites" which contains recently issued user commands as depicted in Figure 2. The code structure includes the following tasks: the `RegisterLogHandler` subroutine creates OOI objects for accessing the logging API. The `ooi_listen` subroutine removes the user command from the menu (if it already exists) and then adds the user command at the top of the "Favorites" menu. After that, information about the user command is displayed in the status bar. Other used subroutines are auxiliary, see the complete source code at `http://dostal.inf.upol.cz/oo-interceptor.html`. Note that the complete program contains no more than 78 lines of code. The page contains also a demonstration video with the above-described example.

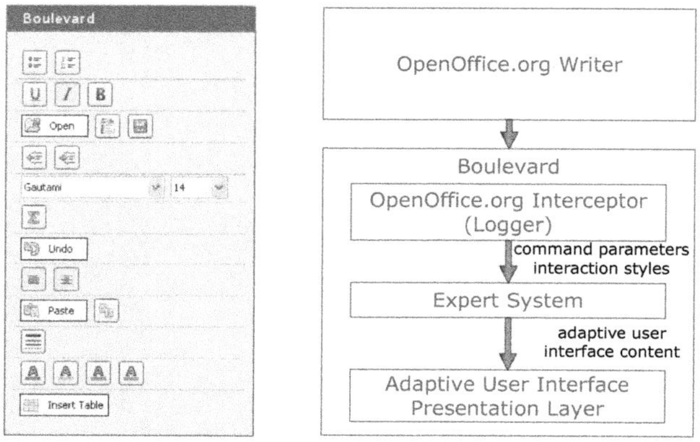

Figure 3. Boulevard: screenshot (left), system architecture (right)

A Real Application of the Interceptor

OpenOffice.org Interceptor is used as a component responsible for logging user activity in the adaptive user interface called "Boulevard". Basically, it is an expert system-based software tool for automatic personalization of the OpenOffice.org Writer user interface. It provides a panel container (see Figure 3) with the user interface adjusted to user's preferred commands, parameters and interaction styles. The expert system performs an intelligent organization of user commands in the panel container, which is based on continuous evaluation of user activity in the word processor. The user activity is captured by OOI.

PERFORMING USER STUDIES

We performed a comparative study on invoking commands using menu, toolbar and the aforementioned Boulevard. The measurement was performed using the OOI. The study analyzed task times and error rates on selecting user commands. The study was participated by 12 users (9 males and 3 females) aged 21 to 53 (M=28.75 years). Users had to select a particular user command in OpenOffice.org Writer according to instructions on the computer screen which depicted which command should be selected and which interaction style should be used. The task was composed of three parts. In the first part, the user selected a sequence of 60 commands using a toolbar; in the second part the user selected a sequence of 60 commands using a menu and finally, the third part was devoted to selecting a sequence of 75 user commands using the Boulevard. The logged data had been analyzed statistically. Overall, the users were able to select the desired user command at the first attempt in 62.7 % of cases for toolbar, 53.3 % of cases for menu and 66.4 % of cases for Boulevard. On the other hand, users failed (i.e., were not able to select the demanded command during 30-seconds long period) in 8 % of cases for the menu part, 2.4 % of cases for the toolbar part and 1.3 % of cases for the boulevard part of the experiment. Average task completion times were 5.29 secs for toolbar (Mdn=4.29, Sd=3.93), 8.94 secs for menu (Mdn=7.50, Sd=5.00) and 5.43 secs for Boulevard (Mdn=4.17, Sd=4.27). Repeated measures ANOVA showed a significant effect of interaction style on task completion time ($F(2, 22) = 63.76, p < .001$, partial $\eta^2 = 0.85$). Pairwise comparisons using t-test with a Bonferroni adjustment showed significant differences in the task completion time between menu and toolbar $p < .001$ and between menu and Boulevard $p < .001$. A significant effect of interaction style on average error rate has been found using repeated measures ANOVA ($F(2, 22) = 12.9, p < .001$, partial $\eta^2 = 0.54$). Pairwise comparisons using t-test with a Bonferroni adjustment showed significant differences in average error rate between menu and toolbar $p = .012$. The results described here are sketchy, appropriate details and discussion on this matter can be found in [3].

CONCLUSION

This paper has introduced a research framework for the OpenOffice.org software suite based on the proposed hybrid logging approach. It enables logging of high-level and semantically rich user activity information with several features not covered by the current loggers, such as accurate logging of user command parameters, avoiding further log processing requirements. The provided program interface enables prototyping and evaluation of intelligent user interfaces under the OpenOffice.org suite. Our tool is easy to use and requires almost no user involvement. We use OOI for our HCI research and believe that our logger could be useful for other HCI researchers and practitioners. That is why we have decided to offer OOI free for public use. The authors will provide OOI upon e-mail request. Additionally, please see the demonstration videos at `http://dostal.inf.upol.cz/ooi.html` where OOI features are presented.

REFERENCES

1. J. Alexander and A. Cockburn. Appmonitor: a tool for recording user actions in unmodified windows applications. *Behavior Research Methods*, 40(2):413–421, May 2008.
2. M. Dostál and Z. Eichler. The implementation of logging user activity in the openoffice.org interceptor. Technical report, Palacký University of Olomouc, Olomouc, Czech Republic, March 2010. http://dostal.inf.upol.cz/data/hci/ooi-techreport.pdf.
3. M. Dostál and Z. Eichler. Fine-grained adaptive user interface for personalization of user interface of a word processor. In *Proceedings of the HCI International 2011*, 2011.
4. D. M. Hilbert and D. F. Redmiles. Extracting usability information from user interface events. *ACM Comput. Surv.*, 32(4):384–421, December 2000.
5. Kukreja, Urmila, Stevenson, E. William, Ritter, and E. Frank. Rui: Recording user input from interfaces under windows and mac os x. *Behavior Research Methods*, 38(4):656–659, November 2006.
6. F. Linton, D. Joy, H.-P. Schaefer, and A. Charron. Owl: A recommender system for organization-wide learning. *Educational Technology & Society*, 3(1), 2000.
7. J. Mcgrenere. *The Design and Evaluation of Multiple Interfaces: A Solution for Complex Software*. PhD thesis, University of Toronto, 2002.

Tell Me Your Needs: Assistance for Public Transport Users

Bernd Ludwig (*), Martin Hacker (+), Richard Schaller (+), Bjoern Zenker (*)
*Chair for AI +Embedded Systems Institute
University of Erlangen-Nuremberg
Haberstr. 2, D-91058 Erlangen
ludwig,martin.hacker,richard.schaller, bjoern.zenker@cs.fau.de

Alexei V. Ivanov, Giuseppe Riccardi
Department of Information Engineering and Computer Science
University of Trento
I-38050 Povo di Trento
riccardi,ivanov@disi.unitn.it

ABSTRACT
Providing navigation assistance to users is a complex task generally consisting of two phases: planning a tour (phase one) and supporting the user during the tour (phase two). In the first phase, users interface to databases via constrained or natural language interaction to acquire prior knowledge such as bus schedules etc. In the second phase, often unexpected external events, such as delays or accidents, happen, user preferences change, or new needs arise. This requires machine intelligence to support users in the navigation real-time task, update information and trip replanning. To provide assistance in phase two, a navigation system must monitor external events, detect anomalies of the current situation compared to the plan built in the first phase, and provide assistance when the plan has become unfeasible. In this paper we present a prototypical mobile speech-controlled navigation system that provides assistance in both phases. The system was designed based on implications from an analysis of real user assistance needs investigated in a diary study that underlines the vital importance of assistance in phase two.

Author Keywords
mobile navigation, replanning, plan execution monitoring

ACM Classification Keywords
H.5.1 Information Interfaces and Presentation: Multimedia Information Systems; H.5.2 Information Interfaces and Presentation: User Interfaces

General Terms
Algorithms, Experimentation, Human Factors, Languages

INTRODUCTION
With the availability of GPS enabled smart phones and mobile devices constantly growing, more and more applications provide location based services to their users. Many of them compute suggestions for points of interest (POI) and therefore fall in the class of recommender systems ([2, 4]).

EICS'11, June 13–16, 2011, Pisa, Italy.

However, people, tourists and residents (with a bunch of every day affairs) often need further assistance: they have to complete a task involving of a series of POI. In order to implement this requirement in an application, we need to consider some implications for the recommendation algorithm: Firstly, as it has to provide a solution for the user's task, it should not recommend just individual POIs, but a set of them: *the computation of recommendations needs to be not only context-aware, but task-aware*. Secondly, assistance aims at providing support to users in executing the task (phase two). At any time, users may wish to start interacting with the system and modifying the tasks according to needs which came up while completing the task: *the computation of recommendations needs to be interactive* as well. When user communicate new needs, the system must adapt its solution (replanning). It is this kind of assistance that distinguishes systems that support the user in both phases from such that provide only recommendations in phase one.

In this paper we present our design methodology how we have developed systematically a navigation system of the type discussed above. As a first step we conducted a diary study to assess assistance needs of pedestrians and public transport (PT) users. The results of the survey were formalized using Concurrent Task Trees (CTT) in order to identify and understand which kinds of problems have to be solved for providing assistance. Building upon this analysis we could specify the necessary components of the hybrid system architecture and the requirements for the user interface.

ASSISTANCE NEEDS ON PUBLIC TRANSPORT USAGE
In order to better understand the assistance and information needs of PT users, we conducted a pilot user study. For this step of requirements engineering, nine participants who use PT regularly for private and business purposes kept a diary about their trips within a period of two weeks. The diary contained a questionnaire for each one-way trip, collecting some general information about the trip and contextual factors. Furthermore, the subjects could record their assistance needs emerging on the trip (see Figure 1(a)). In order to capture as many requirements as possible, we asked the participants to record "any question or problem" they were concerned with on the trip. To allow for objective interpretations, we also collected as much background information as possible in the questionnaire. For a quantitative analysis of the user responses, we classified all recorded needs (i.e. the

Q1 Explain information or assistance need
Q2 Indicate reasons why you had this need
Q3 Where and when did it come up during the trip?
Q4 Indicate the relevance of a solution for this need: (very relevant – not relevant)
Q5 Does this need come up often? (just today – sometimes – often)
Q6 Could you find a solution? If not, please indicate why.
Q7 If you found a solution was it hard to find (hard – easy) and satisfactory (satisfactory – not satisfactory)? Why?

(a) Questionnaire used in the user survey

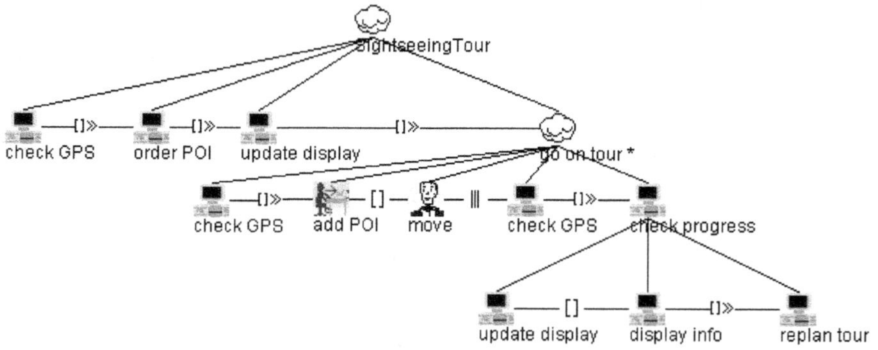

(b) Concurrent task tree for the task of organizing and executing a tour consisting of a set of POI. The task is hierarchically decomposed in phase one (`check GPS` ⟩⟩ `order POI` ⟩⟩ `update display`) and phase two `go on tour` (see the text for more details).

Figure 1. Requirements engineering based on a diary study and the resulting task analysis

Pa	arrival time of a certain means of public transport
Pc	live information about public transport connection or line
Pd	departure time of a certain means of public transport
Pd+	departure time under additional external constraints
Pg	geographic information about PT facilities, e.g. bus stop
Pl	duration of a trip
F	solution how to organize a foot walk without using PT
F+	as above under additional constraints mentioned explicitly
T	solution how to organize a trip using public transport
T+	as above under additional constraints mentioned explicitly
fee	information about the price of a trip or how to acquire a ticket
n.a.	other type of information or no information need involved
?	requested information out of the public transport domain

Table 1. The tags used to label the collected data.

information retrieval need	**type**	?	Pa	Pc	Pd	Pd+	Pg	Pl	fee	n.a.
	abs.	11	4	16	9	2	3	1	4	32
	rel. (%)	13	5	19	11	2	5	1	5	39
find solution for a task	**type**	?	F	F+	T	T+	n.a.			
	abs.	1	2	5	6	17	51			
	rel. (%)	1	2.7	6	7.3	21	62			
verify own proposal for a solution	**type**	Pc	T	T+	n.a.					
	abs.	4	1	3	74					
	rel. (%)	5	1	4	90					
verify information from external sources	**type**	Pc	n.a.							
	abs.	2	80							
	rel. (%)	2	98							
describe external circumstances	**type**	Pc	n.a.							
	abs.	1	81							
	rel. (%)	1	99							

Table 2. Information needs registered by users in the diary study

answers to the questions in Fig. 1(a)) according to the type of missing information that underlies the assistance need using the schema in Table 1.

From the collected data we observe that people need support in *deciding* about a sequence of actions to complete complex tasks: Table 2 indicates that a large portion of requests concerns usual information retrieval tasks with a given set of search parameters – most of them concerned with departure and arrival times of trains, busses, trams, and subways: 35 out of 82 diary entries involved an information retrieval assistance need resulting from a lack of such information (see the information types Pa, Pc, Pd, Pd+, Pg, Pl). 19% addressed information about live data on PT, such as *current delays* or *extraordinary changes of stops*. Obviously, people are unsure about the information necessary to decide how to complete a task. Even more interesting is that the need to *find solution for a task* is involved in 38% of all diary entries. In these cases, users did not know how to solve a PT task or – even more complicated – how to integrate a PT trip into a more complex task as one step of a solution. Examples of such problems are: *The recommended bus is late. Should I wait for the next one or should I start walking towards the train station? Whatever, I still have to find a cash machine as I need some money urgently.* In this example, assistance requires problem solving: a solution starting in the current situation consists of multiple steps to be executed in a certain order. Moreover, often from the diary entries it can be concluded that assistance to the user requires updating the recommendation to new needs or changes in the current situation: While executing a part of the solution for a complex task, this process is often interrupted by tasks resulting from new information needs. An example for this is the following problem recorded in the diaries: *Is it possible to buy something in the shop over there quickly without missing my bus?* In this example, the new need *to buy something in the shop over there* is communicated. In order to provide assistance in such a case, an assistance system must be capable to *replan* a solution for a complex task comprising both the interrupted (*take a bus*) and the interrupting task (*buy something*).

Two major conclusions can be drawn from these results: Firstly, at any point of time, the interface must allow the user to express new needs and to require assistance in solving tasks related to these needs. The task trees for an application contain all activities and sequences of these activities. A flexible user interface allows users to refer to any activity

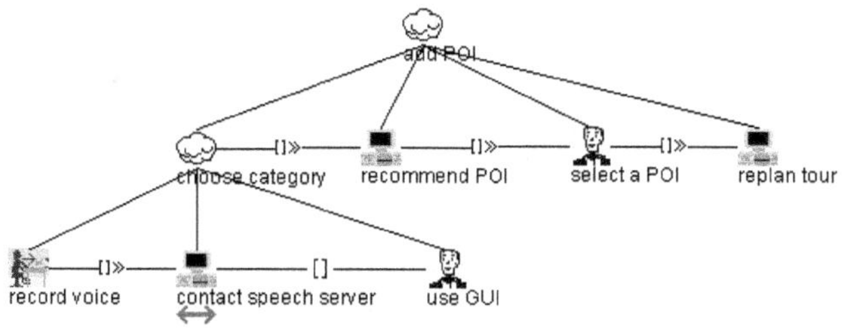

Figure 2. CTT for the task to communicate a new assistance need

at any time in order to express a need. The system must find the activities necessary to satisfy the identified need (planning a solution). Secondly, modifications of a solution are required when external events not foreseen in phase one prevent parts of the solution from being executed (replanning).

TASK ANALYSES TO MODEL ASSISTANCE

As the second step of our design methodology we performed a task analysis by constructing Concurrent Task Trees (CTT, see [5]). Due to space constraints, we just discuss the CTT for `SightseeingTour` in Figure 1(b): For executing this task, it is preassumed that the user has already selected a set of POI in phase one (see Figure 3(a) and (b)). The task is solved by recommending an order in which all POI can be visited with minimal effort to get from one to the next. This order depends on the current position of the user (see tasks `check GPS` and `order POI`). Finally, the route is displayed (`update display`) on the mobile device (see Figure 3(c)). This concludes phase one. In phase two, the task progress depends on live information gathered while the user is on tour: The phase two task `go on tour` iterates until all POI have been visited or the user explicitly abandons sight seeing. Users may visit the POI in the recommended order, but they can also deviate arbitrarily from it: in this case, the tour will be replanned by computing an optimal order for the remaining POI.

As far as the interaction between user and system is concerned, at any point of time during a tour users can activate the context menu of the application in order to communicate a change of their intentions: According to the Concurrent Task Tree in Figure 2, they can ask for a recommendation of nearby POI either by speech input (`record voice`) or by using the GUI (`use GUI`). The fact that there are always two modalities for input at the user's disposal, is important for the reliability of the user interface. Whenever it is too difficult to pronounce e.g. the name of a POI, the user can select it from a list on the screen. Anyway, in order to successfully complete the task, it is necessary to replan the tour: the selected POI is added to the list of POI in the tour as the next POI to visit. This strategy of replanning is based on the simplifying assumption that a communicated change of the user's intentions must have an immediate impact as the user communicates an urgent assistance need.

IMPLEMENTATION

As the third step of our design methodology, on the basis of the CTT discussed above, we implemented the interface that allows users to express their information needs in spoken language as well as using the GUI. The system is implemented as an Android application following the client-server paradigm: while the time-critical replanning for small, local problems is done on the mobile phone, the generation of complete tours and speech recognition run on the server. In order to transmit speech data from the phone to the server the application executes a phone call to a SIP phone number. The server propagates the signal to speech recognizers for English, German or Italian. The result is returned to the mobile application for further processing. Solutions for tasks are computed on the phone. The system continuously monitors the state of execution for the current solution and initiates replanning as to be discussed below.

Replanning As discussed in the previous section, in many cases when users require assistance they need support for solving a complex task in which a set of POI is involved: in particular, to solve the task it is necessary to visit each POI in the set once (Travelling Salesman Problem). An exact solution for this problem is computationally expensive. The problem becomes even harder if task constraints such as time tables, opening hours or limitations for the time available to complete the task have to be taken into account. In this case, it is necessary to drop some POI. This problem belongs to the class of Orienteering Problems [9], for which we implemented an approximative solution using a genetic algorithm and a constraint solver. Optimization is based on the minimization of the overall travel time, the most important criterion inferred from the user survey presented in [7]. To evaluate this algorithm, we implemented a prototypical assistance system for tourists in Trento[1]. It computes sightseeing tours across the Trento city center.

User Interface At any point of time, users can tell the system about changes in their preferences (see Fig. 3(a)). For the natural language understanding component we use the system described in [3]. After shaking their mobile phone, users can start speaking (e.g. "I would like to eat something in a restaurant.") or push a button. A list of possible locations is presented. Next, users can choose a destination that matches the query. Now, the route is replanned with the chosen location being the next sub-goal[2] (Figure 3(c)). Note that as a consequence the ordering of POI may be rearranged as the system always tries to minimize the overall trip length.

Evaluation Although the system has been successfully tested by staff members[3], the evaluation of the usability is still an ongoing work. In the next evaluation step the system will be used as a tool for collecting more data about the users' assistance needs. Test persons will be able to record their needs using the application instead of the paper questionnaire from the pilot study. In this way, we expect to gain additional data about the users' needs and feedback about the application which we can exploit for evaluation purposes.

[1]This work was partly funded by the LIVEMEMORIES project funded by the Autonomous Province of Trento (Italy).

[2]Our next version allows to place the new goal anywhere in the list.

[3]for a demo video see `http://www.rose-mobil.de/aktuelles.php`.

a) b) c)

Figure 3. Screenshots illustrating the task of adding a POI to the tour.

RELATED WORK

The work on Cyberguide [1] started the research on mobile tourist guides and gave initial contributions to the design of these systems. The proposed model implements spatial awareness of the mobile device and history tracking, but it lacks the recommendation function. A more sophisticated mobile context-aware city guide is COMPASS [8]. The authors use context both as a soft and hard criterion for recommendations. This work focusses on the system architecture and the user study, evaluating the usefulness of a context-aware guide, whereas the recommendation step is described briefly. City Guide [6] is a mobile information system that has been evaluated extensively in a user survey. The system features a planner for a tour comprising a set of user-selected POI. The field study in which the system has been tested demonstrates the high acceptance of such information systems. In contrast to our system, City Guide does not support assistance for PT and the recommendation of POI. The systems presented so far lack the capability to provide assistance with PT connections. In this field numerous applications are available, e.g. a German web portal[4] lists more than 40 applications for Germany. However, almost all applications are proprietary developments of local PT providers. Most of them offer the same information also available from a PC at home and only a few of them take the current position into account. Moreover, the applications are not compatible. Therefore, a user needs at least one application for each city. Finally, the applications neither support phase two nor do they recommend solutions for complex tasks. As a consequence, they cannot replan a solution for a task in order to react on information obtained during the trip.

CONCLUSIONS AND FUTURE WORK

From our analysis of the state of the art we conclude that research about methodologies and system architecture for assistance in phase two is still at the beginning. Our system indicates that it is feasible to build assistance systems supporting complex tasks from the perspective of the user. This can be achieved by integrating different problem solving algorithms in a hybrid system architecture. This approach from the system designer perspective needs to be complemented by a user centered approach: using e.g. CTT one can specify how all the components work together towards a solution of a task that can satisfy the assistance needs of the user. We are aware of the fact that the system for Trento does not completely cover all the assistance needs entailed in our diary study. Therefore, we do not consider the system as sufficient proof of concept for assistance in phase two. Its benefit, however, is that we are now able to conduct user studies in which test persons will use the phone to report their needs. To analyze the performance of the genetic algorithm on the mobile, we are working on a system that computes tours on the phone. Our focus for future work lies in the conditional dependencies between recommending POI at a certain step of a solution for a task and planning the steps of the solution. This amounts to modelling explicitly the effects not just of actions as steps of the solution, but also of decisions on the planning process. For this purpose, the genetic algorithm will be combined with planning techniques.

[4] `http://www.fahrplanauskunftssysteme.de`

ACKNOWLEDGEMENT

This work was supported by the Embedded Systems Initiative (`http://www.esi-anwendungszentrum.de`).

REFERENCES

1. Abowd, G., Atkeson, C., Hong, J., Long, S., Kooper, R., and Pinkerton, M. Cyberguide: A mobile context-aware tour guide, 1997.
2. Baltrunas, L., Ricci, F., and Ludwig, B. Context relevance assessment for recommender systems. In *Proceedings of the 2011 International Conference on Intelligent User Interfaces*, ACM Press (2011).
3. Dinarelli, M., Stepanov, E., Varges, S., and Riccardi, G. The luna spoken dialogue system: Beyond utterance classification. In *Proceedings of the 35th International Conference on Acoustics, Speech, and Signal Processing (ICASSP)* (Dallas (USA), March 2010).
4. Hinze, A., and Buchanan, G. Context-awareness in mobile tourist information systems: Challenges for user interaction. In *Proceedings of the International Workshop on Context in Mobile HCI*, University of Salzburg (Salzburg, Austria, September 2005).
5. Paternó, F. *Model-Based Design and Evaluation of Interative Applications*. Springer, 2000.
6. Riebeck, M., Stark, A., Modsching, M., and Kamalek, J. Studying the user acceptance of a mobile information system for tourists in the field. *Information Technology and Tourism 10* (2008), 189–199.
7. Schrader, J., Zenker, B., and Schaller, R. Rose – Auf dem Weg zur mobilen Assistenz. *KI – Kuenstliche Intelligenz 24* (2010), 153–157.
8. van Setten, M., Pokraev, S., and Koolwaaij, J. Context-aware recommendations in the mobile tourist application compass. In *AH*, P. D. Bra and W. Nejdl, Eds., vol. 3137 of *Lecture Notes in Computer Science*, Springer (2004), 235–244.
9. Vansteenwegen, P., Souffriau, W., and Oudheusden, D. V. The orienteering problem: A survey. *European Journal of Operational Research 209*, 1 (2011), 1 – 10.

Multi-user Chorded Toolkit for Multi-touch Screens

Ioannis Leftheriotis
Ionian University
Tsirigoti sq. 7, Corfu, Greece
midmandy@gmail.com

Konstantinos Chorianopoulos
Ionian University
Tsirigoti sq. 7, Corfu, Greece
choko@ionio.gr

ABSTRACT

In this work, we present the design and implementation of a chorded menu for multiple users on a large multi-touch vertical display. Instead of selecting an item in a fixed menu by reaching for it, users make a selection by touching multiple fingers simultaneously on any place of the display. Previous research on multi-touch toolkits has provided basic access to touch events, but there is no support for advanced user interface widgets, such as chords. For this purpose, we extended the open-source PyMT toolkit with an architecture that supports alternative user interaction strategies with chorded menus. In addition, we built a multi-user extension that supports chords for two or more users. Chords could be used for having user-aware MT applications. Our toolkit is open source and has been designed as a widget that could be integrated into broader interaction frameworks for multi-touch screens.

Author Keywords: Multi-touch, toolkit, chord, large display, PyMT, multi-user, architecture.

ACM Classification Keywords: H5.m. Information interfaces and presentation: Miscellaneous.

General Terms: Design.

INTRODUCTION

In this work, we designed and implemented a chord selection technique, which is suitable for large multi-touch (MT) displays. The system was implemented with the PyMT programming framework [4]. In accordance to researchers who have highlighted the need for novel set of MT programming toolkits [9] being reusable [7], we found that the available MT programming toolkits support neither chorded interaction, nor multiple users. Thus, we developed a novel chorded selection interaction technique that leverages the unique characteristics of MT interaction. We have also found that most of the MT toolkits do not have support for multiple users. Although there have been some multi-user MT systems, some of them require the users to wear special receivers, which is not convenient.

The design and implementation process has been guided by a case study of a simple drawing application. The application provides a menu of four different shapes: an empty circle, a line, a rectangle and a full/painted circle as depicted in Figure 1. Every shape can be drawn with just two fingers, using only one hand or both of them. For example, when user wants to draw a circle he/she firstly selects the circle item from the menu. Then, he/she touches the MT display with the first finger and then with the second one. The center of the circle would be the middle point between the two fingers and the diameter of the circle would be equal to their distance. Lines are drawn with two fingers too. A line is drawn between each two touches when the line item is selected. Finally, defining two opposite corners draws the rectangle. In the next section, we describe the design process for replacing the fixed menu with a chorded one for the case of the above drawing application.

INTERACTION DESIGN

During the process of designing a multiple-touch chorded menu for our drawing application, a number of different menus were designed and evaluated. (see Table 1)

Fixed selection
- needs more time than other methods
- move to menu constantly
+ traditional menu, known to most users
+ novice users feel comfortable
Fixed area chorded selection
- using only one hand - restricted area - for menu selection
+ faster menu selections than traditional menu
Free chorded selection
- supports only one user
- select menu items from all over the multi-touch screen
+ fastest menu selection
Multi-user Chorded selection
- restricted interaction area
- window manipulation policy is needed
+ supports multiple users

Table 1: Different types of selection techniques

Fixed selection

In almost every desktop computer, a mouse is an essential input device. Therefore, we considered a transition from the mouse click to the single-finger touch. The first implementation of a MT menu is the traditional menu with the four shapes (Figure 1). Users have to choose the shape they want to draw and just touch the appropriate button in the upper side of the screen. The system indicates their selection and they are able to draw by touching their two fingers. In Figure 1.a the user has selected the line button and draws a single line. The drawing application shows two small circles for every touch as a feedback. Whenever the user lifts one finger the line is painted on the virtual canvas. Although the above scenario of menu selection is familiar, it does not leverage the benefits of multiple touches in the menu selection process. The next step was to create a menu that allows multi-finger selection.

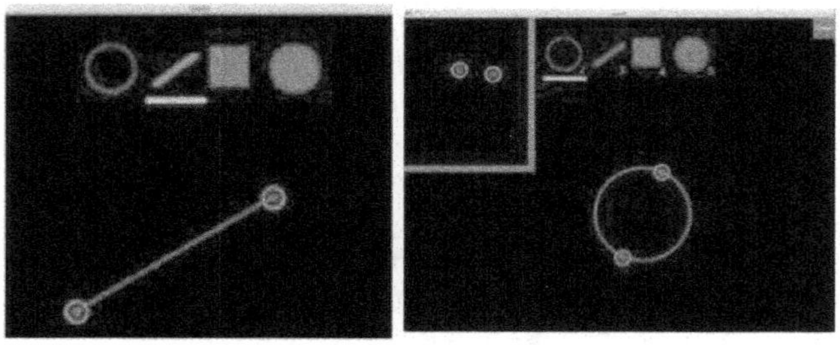

Figure 1: a) Traditional menu embedded in a MT environment. b) fixed are chords. In both cases, users draw a shape with two fingers.

Fixed area chorded selection

Although the above scenario of menu selection is familiar to desktop users, it does not leverage the benefit of multiple touches. In previous work, there have been chord keyboards that allow switching between modes (pressing the shift button by touching down a number of fingers in a MT display in order to write in capitals) [8] but these methods are used basically for improving user performance and they are not the main way of making ambiguous selections. The main objective is to empower the user to choose an item from the menu without touching the menu itself. For this purpose, a small portion of the MT display next to the menu was reserved. There, a user can touch the display with as many fingers as indicated in the status bar (Figure 1.b).

We placed the fixed chord area next to the status bar on the upper left part of the screen, in order to be accessible by the non-dominant hand of a right handed user (Figure 1.b). The design of this multi-finger menu was based on Guiard's Kinematic Chain (KC) model[2]. According to this model, the non-dominant hand sets the frame of reference in which the dominant hand works. In our drawing application, the non-dominant hand selects items from the menu and the dominant hand draws the relative shape. Such asymmetric movements are very common in our everyday life and that is because the non-dominant hand is considered to be coarser than the dominant hand. [5]

Even though the fixed area multi-finger menu selection technique keeps busy both hands and thus improves selection times, it has some limitations. First of all, the user has again to move his left hand to a specific area in the MT display. If he/she holds his hand above that area constantly in order to change his/her selections rapidly, he/she is obliged to draw with only one hand (his right one), which could be really difficult for larger shapes or for larger MT screens. For those reasons, another more flexible multi-finger menu selection technique emerged.

Free chorded selection

In large-scale vertical MT displays, the selection of items (e.g., on a fixed menu) requires excessive physical movement of hands, or even the body of the user, Instead of having a constantly reserved part of the screen as a MT selection area, users should be able to make direct contextual selections. In our new design, users can select the shape they want by just touching down the appropriate number of fingers wherever they want to draw on the screen (see Figure 2.a). Then, they are able to draw the shape with two fingers, as before. We also provided a status indicator, which allows the user to understand which shape has been chosen and how many fingers he/she has to touch on the display to change to another shape. In contrast to the traditional contextual menu, this technique is a one-step action and it has the affordances to support modes. Moreover, this technique affords a two-handed inter-changeable interaction [6], where user can interchange or use in parallel two hands to perform selections

For example, in the drawing application (Figure 2.b), the first two fingers are reserved for drawing the shapes. In order to draw a painted circle, the user has to touch six fingers somewhere in the screen firstly, (that is using his both hands), and then draw it with his two fingers.

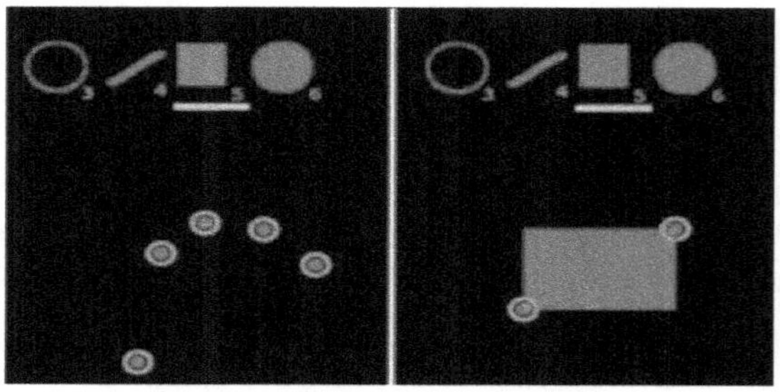

Figure 2: a) In this example, user chooses the rectangular by touching five fingers on the screen, b) rectangular is drawn

One other important aspect apart from the use of multiple fingers on a MT display is the simultaneous use of more than one user. In this condition, the menu techniques presented here do not work. Thus, the next step was to augment the multiple finger menu selection techniques to allow more than one user interactions.

Multi-user Chorded selection

On a collaborative framework for a large display, users should interact simultaneously with the MT screen. While a user is drawing in a window that popped-up another user could have touched the MT screen with his fingers to generate another pop-up window for another shape.

We realized that the free chord technique would not allow chorded modifiers for more than one user, because it regarded every finger to be part of the same chord. In order to deal with this issue, we decided to go a backward step in the chorded modifiers design process. A modified version of fixed area multi-finger selection found to be the solution.

We have developed a multi-user MT component that allows users to touch multiple fingers on any place of the display just as before. Each time a user makes a selection of a shape a new pop-up window indicates the selected shape. In Figure 3 the interaction design of the system is presented.

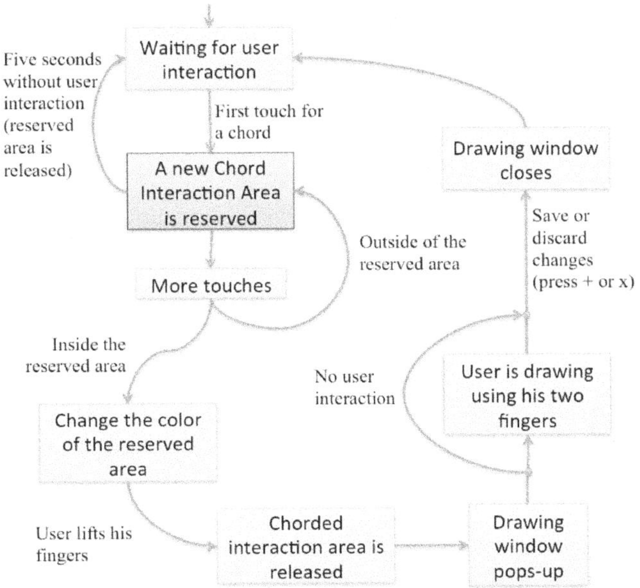

Figure 3: The interaction design of the system

The user, then, is able to draw that specific shape in that window only. The window has a close button (x button), an add button (+ button) and an undo button (Figure 4). The pop-up windows are dynamic: 1) they can be moved anywhere, and 2) users can change their sizes. For instance, if the user wants to draw a line, which is beyond the limits of the window, he/she must use the reversed pinch gesture to enlarge it and therefore becoming able to draw the line in it. In the same way, the chords are performed in a circular area around the first touch of the user, which is about the user's hand size. Chorded areas remain active for a specific period of time (e.g. 5 seconds)

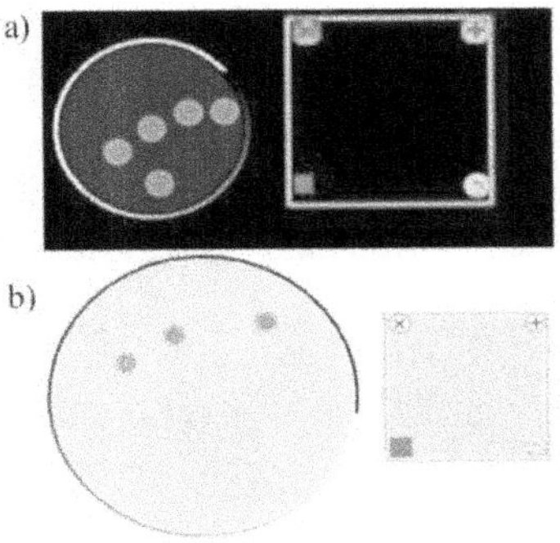

Figure 4: Chorded circular area and the respective drawing window. a) prototype, b) final version

In addition, a number of restrictions on the relationships between the pop-up windows should be applied. For example, the pop-up windows should not overlap or at least when this happens strict rules should apply, such as allowing drawing only in the front window. Moreover, those windows should be almost invisible in order to allow user to see the image of the background. If we would like to make them more MT oriented we could permit window moving among users or scaling.

SYSTEM DESIGN AND IMPLEMENTATION

The multi-user chorded selection technique has been built on top of the fixed chorded selection functions. In a multi-user environment, users dynamically reserve a small circular area, which is as large as ones palm (diameter is 15 cm). In the following subsections the architecture and the implementation of the system are described.

Architecture

The main architecture of the Toolkit presents three different levels (Figure 5). The system is based on the PyMT event engine. When the appropriate event is called a chorded event layer is created. Multiple chorded event layers are allowed since it's a multi-user Toolkit. If the chord is recognized then the respective Window event layer is created. Drawing, text, and images go up one level on the appropriate visualization layer.

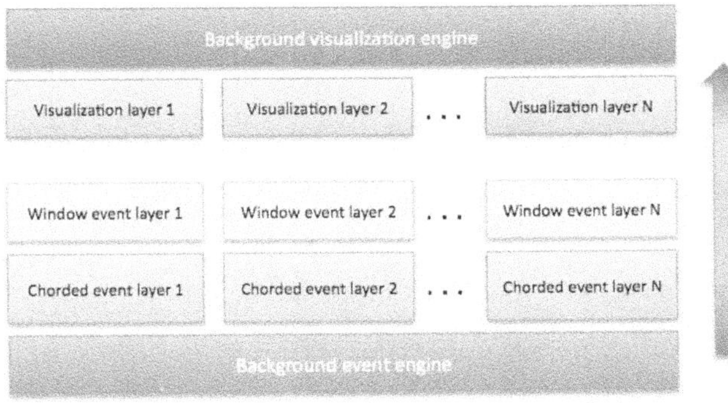

Figure 5: The architecture of the MT Toolkit for Multi-user interaction.

The different layers are represented with different classes. Each class takes parameters from the previous level. For instance a chorded event layer updates the window event layer with the event that three fingers touched the surface. Thus the window created will be accordingly chosen.

Implementation

In an effort to build upon other MT toolkits we implemented a system that is based on the architecture described in the previous subsection. A simple MT drawing application with the PyMT framework[4] was developed. We found that the PyMT framework is very suitable for quick prototyping, as well as for simulating MT with a variety of input devices, such as the track pad of Apple notebooks. In this way, our system is easy to demonstrate without the use of a full MT set-up. Nevertheless, an MT installation and field testing is required in order to adapt the parameters of the system to the scale of users and their environment. For instance, in Figure 6 the system is being tested with two users in a vertical MT screen.

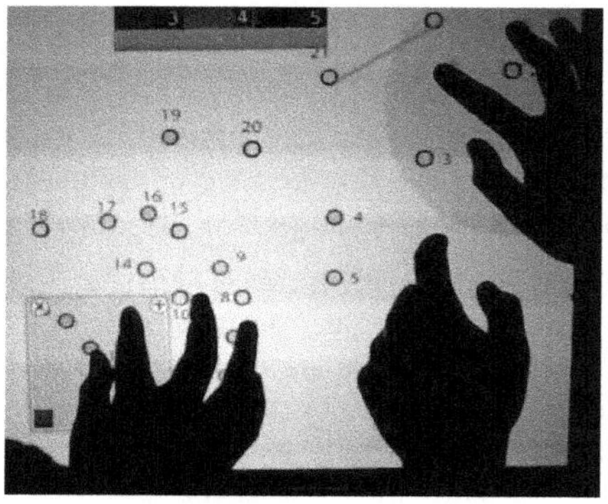

Figure 6: Two users working with the chorded Toolkit on a drawing task

Although PyMT has great support for basic touch, images, and windows, it lacks a set of window manipulation policies, which are necessary for multiple users interaction. For example, it is difficult to understand which window is on top or how many windows are occluded. In our implementation, both chorded interaction areas and drawing windows were MT widgets and thus we were able to count the number of touches, an important element of chorded interaction technique. Furthermore, we suggest that the buttons (exit, add, undo) used are an essential part of a multi-user collaborative application. In the current implementation, when the user has finished working, the changes are integrated in the Background visualization engine of PyMT. Thus, when the users finish their drawing and close the pop-up windows the shapes that they drew integrate in the same MT display. The next version will provide support for a screen object buffer.

DISCUSSION

Although the chorded menu is considered to be a "mouse impossible" application, an alternative design could be used for selection with a mouse. Menu items could be added in a right-click contextual menu that would pop-up at the point of interaction. Then, user would be able to select an item with his left-click. Nevertheless, the contextual menu is a two-step interaction, while the chord is an atomic action. One more limitation of our menu selection techniques is that they allow up to eight different menu items as long as we have ten fingers and we have to use our two fingers for drawing. But, as it is shown in [6] eight different items in a menu is an effective number of menu elements and as far as the depth of the menu is concerned, a MT application could reserve a suitable chord of fingers which could permit it.

CONCLUSION

In this research, we presented a toolkit for multi-user chorded selections on MT screens. The main contribution is the idea of using chords in a MT collaborative environment for menu selections, as well as a working toolkit and a set of example applications. Although a chording system was absent from MT Toolkits we believe that it would be integrated in future MT Toolkit updates for being simple, fast, atomic and essential for selection without the traditional buttons that overflow desktop applications (especially in larger MT installations). Finally, we suggest that MT screens demand fluid interaction techniques such as chording.

ACKNOWLEDGMENTS

We would like to thank our pilot users for their patience during the experiments. Moreover, we thank the NUI community and particularly the PyMT project team. The work reported in this paper has been partly supported by project CULT (http://cult.di.ionio.gr). CULT (MC-ERG-2008-2308940 is a Marie Curie project of the European Commission (EC) under the 7th Framework Program (FP7).

REFERENCES

1. Fitzmaurice G., Khan A., Pieké R., Buxton B., Gordon K., Tracking menus, In *Proc. UIST '03*. 5:2, 71-79.
2. Guiard, Y.,Asymmetric Division of Labor in Human Skilled Bimanual Action: The Kinematic Chain as a Model,*Journal of Motor Behavior 19*, 4 (1987), 486-517.
3. Han, J. Y., Low-cost multi-touch sensing through frustrated total internal reflection. In *Proc. UIST 2005*, ACM Press (2005), 115–118.
4. Hansen T., Denter C., Virbel M., Using the PyMT toolkit for HCI Research, Forum on Tactile and Gestural interaction, Lille(France), (2010).
5. Jiao, X., Deng, H., and Wang, F. An Investigation of Two-Handed Manipulation and Related Techniques in Multi-touch Interaction. *Conference on Machine Vision and Human*, (2010).
6. Kiger, J., The depth/breadth trade-off in the design of menu-driven user interfaces, *International Journal of Man-Machine Studies 20*, 2 (1984), 201-213.
7. Kris Luyten, Davy Vanacken, Malte Weiss, Jan Borchers, Shahram Izadi, and Daniel Wigdor. Engineering patterns for multi-touch interfaces. In Proc. EICS '10, ACM Press (2010), 365-366.
8. Westerman, W., Elias, J., Multi-touch system and method for emulating modifier keys via fingertip chords, United States Patent RE40153, (1998).
9. Wigdor, D., Fletcher, J., and Morrison, G. (2009). Designing user interfaces for multi-touch and gesture devices. *Ext. Abstracts CHI 2009*, ACM Press (2009), 2755-2758.

UI-Driven Test-First Development of Interactive Systems

Judy Bowen
Department of Computer Science
The University of Waikato
Hamilton
New Zealand
jbowen@cs.waikato.ac.nz

Steve Reeves
Department of Computer Science
The University of Waikato
Hamilton
New Zealand
stever@cs.waikato.ac.nz

ABSTRACT

Test-driven development (TDD) is a software development approach, which has grown out of the Extreme Programming and Agile movements, whereby tests are written prior to the implementation code which is then developed and refactored so that it passes the tests. Test-first development (TFD) takes a similar approach, but rather than relying on the testers to infer the correct tests from the requirements (often expressed via use cases) they use models of the requirements as the basis for the tests (and as such have a more formal approach). One of the problems with both TDD and TFD is that is has proven hard to adapt it for interactive systems as it is not always clear how to develop tests to also support user interfaces (UIs). In this paper we propose a method which uses both formal models of informal UI design artefacts and formal specifications to derive abstract tests which then form the basis of a test-first development process.

Author Keywords

Interactive system design, test-first development, formal specification.

ACM Classification Keywords D.2. Software Engineering: D.2.2. Design Tools and Techniques: User Interfaces

General Terms

Design, Reliability

INTRODUCTION

The test-driven development cycle follows a pattern of short iterations: write a test which is failed; write just enough code to pass the test; refactor the code. This is repeated until the implementation is complete [2]. Once the code is finished the tests then act as a regression test suite and if there are new requirements for subsequent versions tests can be added to the test suite which drive the new code in the same way. Tests are developed from the requirements of the code which may be expressed as use cases or scenarios, and as such rely on the skill of the developer to translate these into comprehensive tests.

EICS'11, June 13-16, 2011, Pisa, Italy.

TDD assumes no pre-defined plan for constructing the code beyond the requirements (which drive the tests). Test-first development takes a similar approach but instead of assuming that the tests can be directly inferred from the requirements with no other development steps, it instead uses models developed from requirements as the basis for the tests.

Test-driven development can be problematic for interactive systems as the development of the UI is more usefully built in conjunction with users and with a full understanding of their needs beyond the functional requirements. Kent Beck (often credited with the re-invention and popularization of TDD) says of TDD:

"*I'm not submitting this as something everyone should do all the time. I have trouble writing GUIs test-first, for example*" [3].

Because TFD allows for pre-development modelling and uses these models as the basis for the tests, it appears that this might be more suitable for interactive system development. For example, it might enable user-centred design (UCD) artefacts, such as prototypes (which as an abstraction of the intended design are themselves a type of model) to be used to help drive test creation. However, there is still no immediately obvious way to use these artefacts in this way.

In previous work we have shown how abstract tests can be derived from formal models of user interfaces and system specifications. Our work is based on the premise that a UCD approach has been used in conjunction with formal system development (by way of specification and/or refinement) [4]. We have subsequently described how such tests can be instantiated for post-implementation model-based testing as well as used as the basis for user evaluations of the UI [5].

In this paper we discuss how the same automatically generated abstract tests can be used as the basis for a TFD approach for interactive software. We again place this work in the context of a formal development process incorporating UCD techniques for the UI, and show how TFD can ensure consistency throughout the development process as well as ensuring that subsequent refactoring (due perhaps to changes in requirements or feedback from users) maintains the consistency between UI and functional core.

We present a methodology of our approach and details enabling others to replicate our work, but do not attempt to present an evaluation in this paper, rather we leave that for future work.

The contributions this paper proposes are a method for combining the benefits of TFD and functional TDD for interactive systems. This method is based upon existing sound principles of user-centred design and functional specification. These support the development of robust, usable systems and incorporate models of design artefacts, which are easy to produce and maintain, which provides both a formal and user-centred description of interactive systems.

BACKGROUND AND RELATED WORK

UI testing is an essential, yet complex, requirement of software development. Not only must we ensure that the interface is usable and understandable by the target group of users, but also that it provides all of the necessary required functionality to the user by interacting correctly with the functional core of the system. As such it can be a time-consuming and expensive process involving both human-based testing (by way of user evaluations and usability testing) as well as extensions to traditional functional testing which often do not include (or which use methods which are not appropriate for) UI testing. One of the challenges is dealing with the complexity of the UI, which may present the user with a large number of possible interactions at any given time, so the state space of possible interaction paths is often unmanageable in terms of both modelling and testing.

One of the first issues we face when testing UIs is finding the right tool. UIs are designed for human interaction and as such do not lend themselves naturally to automated testing. Record and playback testing is a technique often used to test UIs. A user (usually one of the developers or testers) interacts with the software to exploit particular functionality and the sequence of interactions is recorded and can subsequently be played back automatically to repeat the test. This approach can, however, be time-consuming and prone to needing constant revision, in that as soon as a change is made to production code the test needs to be re-recorded and then re-run. These tools also require most, if not all, of the UI to be complete, and so are most useful in post-implementation testing. Another problem is that the tests are generated in a runtime environment and then stored as scripts which are not easy to read or interpret.

Abbott [6], a JUnit extension for Java Swing applications, partially solves some of these problems by recording the tests and defining them at a more abstract level (so they are not coupled to co-ordinates of widgets as is common in record and playback tools) making the mechanism more robust to changes. It also allows tests to be defined using an XML script editor so that they can be used for TDD. An extension to such tools are the simulated interaction testing tools which interact with UIs of a system in the manner of a user (*i.e.* by way of mouse clicks and widget activation) based on scripted or coded commands. For example, the FEST tool, which we have previously used for model-based testing [4], is an extension to Abbott which allows developers to write unit tests for UIs written in Java based on simulated interaction. Similar tools, such as Ranorex [14], exist for the Microsoft .NET platform. The simulation tools can have similar problems to the record and playback methods, as the tests are often tightly coupled to the code, and both methods still rely heavily on expertise to create the correct tests to ensure full coverage.

These problems of UI testing are equally true in a TFD process, with the added difficulty that there is a requirement to consider not only *how* to test the interactive parts of the system (what sort of method and tools to choose) but also what sort of tests should be included. While the functional specification may lend itself well to the derivation of tests, the UI design artefacts do not.

TFD has been adopted by the Agile community, along with many other practices such as prototyping from the UCD community. In [8] Hellmann *et. al.* take a similar approach to ours to trying to solve the difficulties encountered using TFD for interactive systems. Their work uses prototypes – or rather scenarios of interaction sequences derived from prototypes – as the basis for tests for simple systems with UIs consisting of limited widgets. As such they have moved the burden of the work of creating the tests into that of creating the scenarios of interaction sequences, but with no consideration of correctness or coverage, which is not a focus of their work in the same way that it is in ours.

In order to consider what sort of tests we might use, and how these can be derived, we can look at model-based approaches to post-implementation testing. Memon et al. [11][12] use reverse-engineering techniques to create models of interactive systems and from these automatically generate tests which (try to) exercise all paths throughout the UI and can be used for regression testing. Similarly, Gimblett and Thimbleby [7] have developed an algorithm for discovering models of UIs, producing a finite directed graph which can be analysed to discover design defects or structural usability concerns. While both of these approaches are post-implementation, the methods for using models derived by UI inspection to develop tests may suggest useful ways forward for TFD. In particular, Gimblett and Thimbleby's method of using the model discovery and analysis as a lightweight approach, which is part of a collection of methods to try and increase formality and correctness, sits well with our own approach to lightweight modelling.

We have shown in previous works how simple abstract models of a user interface (which may be based on a design such as a prototype or an actual implementation) can capture required information about UI designs and behaviours while avoiding state explosion via abstraction. We have also shown how we can use these models to derive abstract tests which can then be used as the basis for model-based testing. By automatically generating tests from models we can ensure the coverage of the UI functionality, the consistency of the testing process and reduce the burden of test derivation.

Functional test driven development (FTDD) [1] tries to improve UI code and its inclusion within the testing process by delaying the UI development until later (after much of the functional core has been developed using standard unit tests) and then exercising UI tests. In addition, the tests are used both for development and to act as a requirement specification. There is an additional requirement that the tests be specified in such a way that they are unambiguous (and compatible with the chosen testing framework) but at the same time can be understood by non-technical subject matter experts as well as by multiple development teams who inherit both the code and test-defined specification as the project moves through development phases. These are challenging aims, and this area of research currently suffers from lack of tool support.

Our intention is that by keeping the tests tied to the UCD artefacts, we achieve simplicity and unambiguity by already having a specification which can be understood by users and developers alike. Our UI models are lightweight and easily updated as new requirements are added, and there is an automated process for producing abstract tests ensuring consistency. In addition, the UI models are linked to the existing formal system specification which forms part of the basis for the instantiated tests, and so we do not rely solely on the tests themselves to provide such a specification.

THE TEST-FIRST PROCESS – OUR APPROACH

In this paper we use the UISpec4J testing framework [15] which is a simulated interaction testing tool for Java Swing applications which works alongside JUnit [10]. While this has the usual disadvantage of simulated interaction tools of requiring tests which are tightly coupled to application code (in order to simulate interaction on a widget the test must refer to the type and one of the properties of the widget) this is less of a problem with TFD as we already have models which give us information about the type of the widgets. Also, the UISpec4J framework supports tests that are easy to write (often considered an important goal of TFD) by providing wrapper classes with interaction methods (such as click and double click for Buttons) for Swing component classes, enabling a higher level of abstraction than is possible when directly interacting with the Java Robot class. Another advantage of UISpec4J (and similar tools) is that we can use it within standard IDEs, such as Eclipse, which then provides all of the usual support for the test code that we expect from such tools.

As the tests are written first we can use the naming conventions from the model also and continue this in the implementation. As in any testing process having the correct tests (in terms of both coverage and behaviour) is essential to ensure a correct end result. It is not enough to develop a system which satisfies a set of tests if the tests are missing crucial parts of the functionality or UI, or are incorrectly defined.

Starting with the requirements (both user and functional) we develop a set of models which consist of a functional specification and UI models derived from the UCD process (including user requirements, task analysis, prototyping *etc.*) The models are created when we are happy we have satisfied all of the requirements within our functional and user requirement descriptions. From the UI models we then automatically derive a set of abstract tests using the PIMed tool [13]. We use these tests in conjunction with the specification and the prototypes as the basis for the test-first process. Figure 1 illustrates the process.

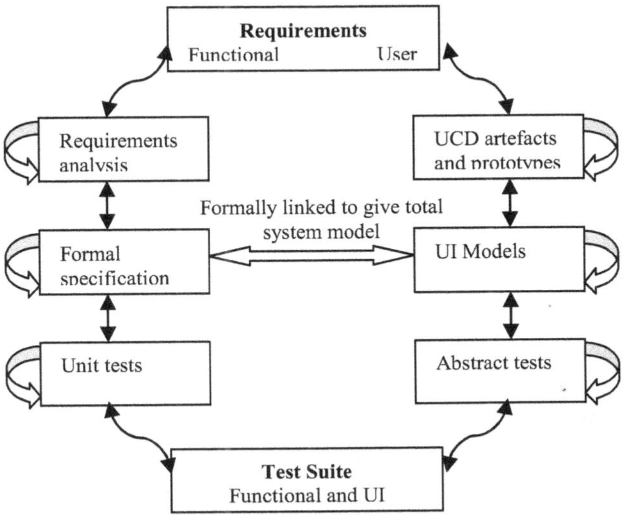

1: Process Flow

Unlike a test-driven approach where we define the tests as we go along and can satisfy them in any way that is appropriate, we have additional constraints given by the prototypes and UI models which act as a guide. It is not enough to test that a particular function is accessible from the UI, it must also meet the design given in the prototype by providing a correctly typed widget, and when we come to the layout of the UI (during the code refactoring stage) we use the prototype to inform how this should be done. The actual development steps are then the same as in a test-driven process:

- Write a test
- Check that the test is failed
- Write enough code to pass the test
- Refactor

The abstract tests derived from our models determine what the next test is (we describe this process later) and as part of the refactoring we must also ensure that we continue to satisfy the layout and designs created as part of the UCD process. Once we have reached a certain point in the development (which might be defined to when a specific set of states of the model have been implemented or a given amount of the development finished, whichever is most appropriate) we can extend the testing process to include users, who can begin to interact with the software to ensure that usability is also being satisfied, and if necessary refactor designs to maintain this. The automated tests show that we are following the agreed designs and specification but by adding humans into the equation of testing we may find additional issues that were not obvious from the paper prototypes.

While the UISpec4J tests can still be difficult to read and understand for those unfamiliar with the framework, we include the abstract test within the comments and documentation for each concrete test, making it easier to relate the test code to the model-generated abstract tests and thereby easier to understand the test suite.

The tests we derive allow us to examine the expected behaviours of the UI in terms of the resulting functionality. We are not interested in making sure that default component behaviour works, such as does a button click occur when the cursor is positioned over it and the mouse button clicked (we assume the programming language will take care of this), but rather what happens to both the UI and system state when such an action occurs.

In the next section we describe the Simple Calendar application which is used as an example throughout the rest of this paper.

SIMPLE CALENDAR EXAMPLE

The example application we use in this paper is that of a simple calendar which can be used to record events associated with particular dates. This example is based on a real-world system, but has been simplified to make the modelling and explanations required suitable for description in this research publication.

Requirements and Specification

The functional requirements for SimpleCalendar are as follows:

The application is a calendar which incorporates a diary allowing events to be assigned to days, which can then be viewed in the calendar overview. As well as a month-by-month view, the application provides the ability to view the events of a single day and to add, edit and remove events for any visible day. The calendar view can be changed to move forward and backward between months.

The application should provide the following functionality to users:

- A visual display of a single month where any events assigned to days in that month are visible
- The ability to view the previous month
- The ability to view the next month
- The ability to view the events of a single day
- The ability to add new events to any day
- The ability to edit any existing events in the calendar
- The ability to remove any existing events in the calendar

Based upon these requirements a functional specification was created using Z [9]. In fact any formal specification language can be used, we use Z for convenience. The user requirements were broken down into tasks and subtasks, and prototypes were developed of the possible UI. The specification and prototypes were validated and refined until we were satisfied we had correctly described all of the requirements and that the UI was satisfactory for the intended users of the system. Standard UCD processes were followed whereby the users validated the prototypes (we did not, of course, expect them to understand or comment on the formal specification) and the formal experts validated the specification.

UI Design Prototypes and Models

UI prototypes for each of the states of the UI had been developed and these were then modelled as presentation models and presentation interaction models (PIMs). Presentation models describe the narrative of a prototype by describing each state of the UI in terms of its component widgets, their type, and their associated behaviour. The prototype for the main opening UI for simple calendar is shown in figure 2. The presentation model for this part of the UI is:

MainView is

(QuitButton, ActionControl, (Quit)),

(PrevArrow, ActionControl, (S_PrevMonth)),

(NextArrow, ActionControl, (S_NextMonth)),

(DayDisplay, ActionControl, (I_DayView)),

(DayDisplay, Responder, (S_PrevMonth, S_NextMonth, S_AddEvent, S_RemoveEvent, S_EditEvent)),

(ShowMonth,SValResponder (S_PrevMonth, S_NextMonth)),

(ShowYear, SValResponder, (S_PrevMonth, S_NextMonth))

The behaviours associated with widgets are defined either as S-Behaviours (denoted by prefixing the name with S_) which are behaviours which relate to underlying functionality of the system, or I-Behaviours (denoted by prefixing the name with I_) which relate to interactive behaviours which change the state of the UI. Widgets may have more than one behaviour associated with them and either generate these behaviours (and as such are categorised as an Action Control or a sub-type of Action Control) or they respond to behaviours (and are categorised

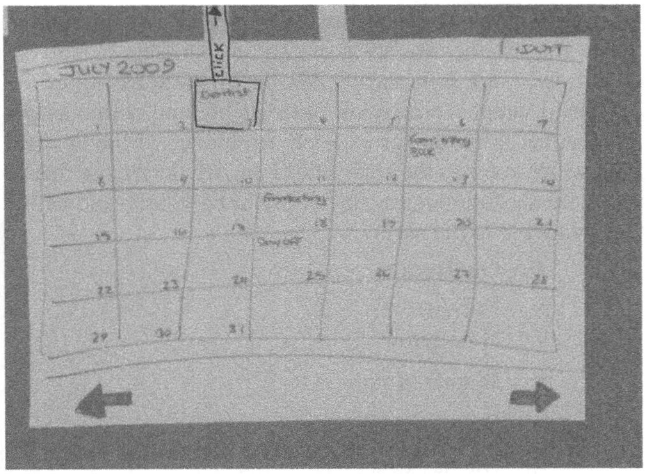

2: Prototype for opening screen of simple calendar

as a Responder or a sub-type of Responder). Widgets which both generate and respond to behaviours are described twice within the model.

The second part of the model is the PIM which is a state transition diagram showing how the UI moves between states as a result of the I-Behaviours. The PIM for Simple Calendar is given in figure 3.

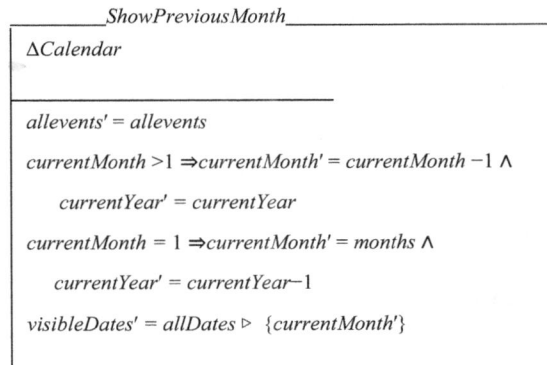

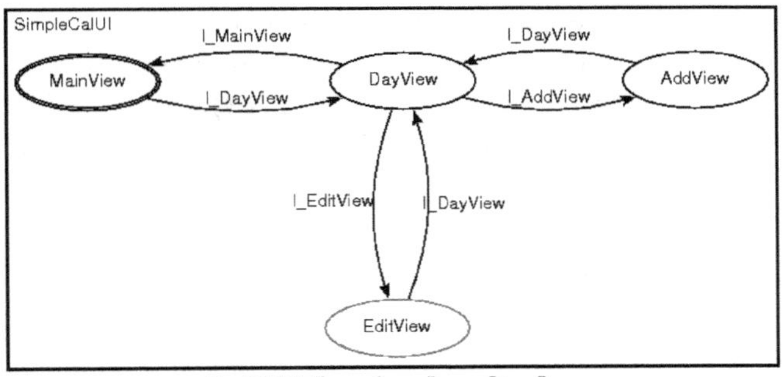

3: PIM for simple calendar

The final part of the model is the PMR which shows how the S-Behaviours defined in the presentation model relate to operations in the functional specification (and corresponds to the horizontal double arrow in figure 1). The PMR for Simple Calendar is:

{ S_PrevMonth ↦ ShowPreviousMonth,

S_NextMonth ↦ ShowNextMonth,

S_RemoveEvent ↦ DeleteEvent,

S_UpdateEvent ↦ EditEvent,

S_AddEvent ↦ AddEvent,

S_ShowEvent ↦ SelectSingleEvent ,

S_ShowSingleDay ↦ SelectSingleDay }

Each of the operations listed on the right of the relation are defined within the Z specification, for example the ShowPreviousMonth operation is:

ShowPreviousMonth

$\Delta Calendar$

$allevents' = allevents$

$currentMonth > 1 \Rightarrow currentMonth' = currentMonth - 1 \wedge$

$\quad currentYear' = currentYear$

$currentMonth = 1 \Rightarrow currentMonth' = months \wedge$

$\quad currentYear' = currentYear - 1$

$visibleDates' = allDates \rhd \{currentMonth'\}$

Abstract Tests

Once the models were complete we used the PIMed tool to generate the abstract tests. These tests describe the conditions of the presentation model in first order logic where all of the conditions on each of the UI states are defined. That is, each state is described by a series of predicates which give the requirements for the widgets of that state. The *MainView* state, for example, contains (among others) the following tests.

$State(MainView) \Rightarrow Visible(DayDisplay) \wedge Active(DayDisplay) \wedge$
$\quad hasBehaviour(DayDisplay, I\_DayView)$

$State(MainView) \Rightarrow Visible(PrevArrow) \wedge Active(PrevArrow) \wedge$
$\quad hasBehaviour(PrevArrow, S\_PrevMonth)$

Each test describes the conditions on one of the widgets of one of the states of the UI. The *Visible* and *Active* predicates have the (expected) meaning that in this state of the UI the named widget must be both visible and available for interaction (which is not always the case, sometimes particular widgets might not be enabled in particular states) and the *hasBehaviour* predicate gives the designated behaviours for the widget. Widgets which respond to behaviours rather then generate them result in a test predicate called *resBehaviour*.

Using the Tests in a TFD Process

With the complete set of abstract tests derived from the models we now move on to development. The abstract tests must be instantiated into concrete tests in a way which supports the TFD process. The tests can be divided into categories as follows:

- Test of state
- Test of widget instantiations
- Test of I-Behaviours

- Test of S-Behaviours

The first category defines what it means to be in a particular state of the UI. Each of the abstract tests relates to a particular state, so for example the test:

State(MainView) ⇒ *Visible(DayDisplay)* ∧ *Active(DayDisplay)* ∧ *hasBehaviour(DayDisplay, I_DayView)*

is only of interest when we are in the *MainView* state. Our first set of concrete tests defines each of the states so we can determine which we are in. From the PIM we also determine the start state of the system. The states of Simple Calendar are:

- MainView
- DayView
- AddView
- EditView

and the start state is *MainView*. We can now write our first test which is to ensure that when Simple Calendar is started a window which can be identified as *MainView* is visible.

Within our test class we create a reference to an instance of the SimpleCalendar class (although this does not exist of course as the test is the first thing written) which we call *sysEx* and which will be used as the basis for all of the tests (UI and functional). We also create a reference to the UISpec4J class Window which handles all of the UI testing for an identified window and which we call *calExUI.*

UISpec4J follows the JUnit convention of providing setup and teardown methods, so we instantiate the references we have declared within the setup method which ensures we use the same instances throughout the testing process. The first test we write looks for an active window once the application is started (we will subsequently test that this window matches the start state, once we have defined the state tests).

In order to run the test we must start writing the application code, and in keeping with the TFD process aim to write the smallest amount required to satisfy the test. In order to make the test compile and run we need to satisfy the variable declarations by creating a class template for both *SimpleCalendar* and *MainView.* This gives us a failing test, and we then pass it by extending the description of *MainView* so that it creates a visible window which is instantiated when *SimpleCalendar* starts up. Of course if we strictly follow the mantra of "write the smallest amount of code possible to pass the test" we could just define the *SimpleCalendar* class and have it contain a reference to a Java Window and then subsequently refactor this into two separate classes, but as is usual in TFD (and TDD) we balance the process with some informed design knowledge which enables us to make steps that are larger than the bare minimum and give a more realistic development process (while remaining mindful of not over-constraining ourselves by making big decisions too early).

Now for each of the states of the PIM we develop a test to determine whether we are correctly in that state or not. To be correctly in a state means that the UI state has all of the described widgets which are both visible and active as per the abstract tests. So for example from each of the abstract tests which refer to the state *MainView* we determine that in this state the following widgets should be visible and active (*i.e.* available to the user):

- QuitButton
- PrevArrow
- NextArrow
- DisplayMonth
- DisplayMonth
- DisplayYear
- DayDisplay

which we capture with the following test:

```
public void testMainViewState(){
 calExUI.getButton("Quit").isEnabled();
 calExUI.getButton("Quit").isVisible();
 calExUI.getButton("Prev").isEnabled();
 calExUI.getButton("Prev").isVisible();
 calExUI.getButton("Next").isEnabled();
 calExUI.getButton("Next").isVisible();
 calExUI.getSwingComponents(cont.getClass(),
    "DisplayMonth")[0].isVisible();
 calExUI.getSwingComponents(cont.getClass(),
    "DisplayYear")[0].isVisible();
 calExUI.getSwingComponents(cont.getClass(),
    "DayDisplay")[0].isVisible();
 calExUI.getSwingComponents(cont.getClass(),
    "DayDisplay")[0].isEnabled();
 }
```

When this test is passed we are certain that we have a correctly defined state, in terms of the component widgets (we consider the behaviour of these widgets later). The state tests also have the effect of ensuring all non-behavioural widgets (such as text entry fields) are correctly defined and available for use. As we will also want to reuse this test (and the other state tests) later when we write the tests to ensure correctness of behaviours, we generalise the state tests so that each of them receives a UISpec4J Window as a parameter and then checks the given window for the relevant widgets. We can then write a single test called "TestUIStates" which calls all of the state tests, and then we can subsequently call any of the state tests individually as required within other tests. We are not concerned at this stage as to the *type* of the widgets (in order to pass the test we can define each of them as a JButton, or any other type of Java Swing widget) but as part of the refactoring we refer to the models to ensure that we make a correct choice. This is what we mean by using the models to support the tests within the development process.

For some of the widgets we may not yet have considered their concrete type. For example, while many widgets described as *ActionControls* in the presentation model may be instantiated as JButtons, this is not necessarily the case. In the example above for `testMainViewState` we have written a test which expects some of the widgets to be JButtons, whereas others we just abstractly describe as SwingComponents. However, this has implications as testing progresses as it affects the methods we can invoke on them within the test. The UISpec4J Button class, for example, has a click() method allowing us to simulate user interaction, whereas the SwingComponent class does not have such a method.

Those widgets we have defined as Buttons pass the test because this is how we have instantiated them in the first version of the code. However, if we subsequently refine them to a different type of widget we would then get a failing test, not because of problems with the code, but due to the way we have defined the test. There is, therefore, a trade-off between being specific enough early on to make interaction simulation easy or being more general and having to write more detailed test code to interact with the widgets.

We can, of course, refactor the tests to match more specific widgets once the code has been refactored. This may not seem like an ideal solution as changing the tests to match the code seems to go against the principles of TFD. However, as we will show later, the tight coupling of the UI code with the tests means that sometimes this is a necessity.

There is one other element of state that needs to be tested and that is modality. The presentation model and PIM inform us which of the windows and dialogues in the UI are modal (by showing the availability, or not, of their behaviours in conjunction with other states). From the Simple Calendar models we know that *DayView*, *AddView* and *EditView* are all modal and so we add this condition to each of the relevant state tests and update our code in order to pass the tests.

Once we have created tests for each of the states, and then the necessary classes and code to ensure that the tests are passed, we begin refactoring to tidy up the code, remove duplication and set the UI layout in accordance with the design prototypes. As such, defining the UI layout becomes part of the refactoring process and is informed by the design models.

After the state tests have all been passed and the first stage of refactoring has taken place, we have UIs for each state of the system. Some examples of these are shown in figures 4 and 5.

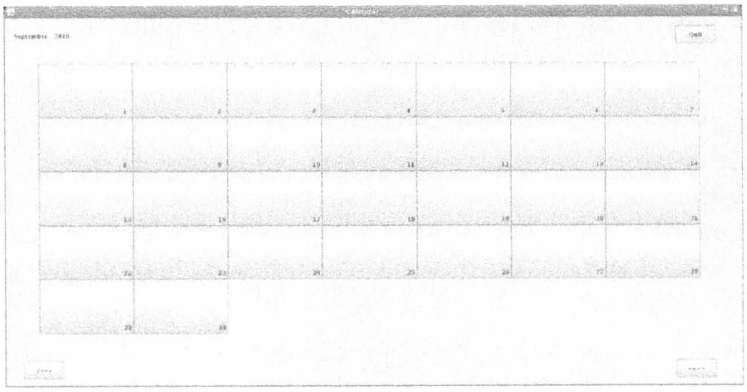

4: Main View

One of the things that has happened during refactoring is that a new class has been created which combines the code for *AddView* and *EditView*. In the first version of the code each was defined in its own class, but as the code for these two classes was almost identical refactoring led to them being combined. We have added a Boolean value which sets the state of the UI to either add or edit and which will be used to control the elements which are different. The next step is to write the tests for the I-Behaviours. From the set of abstract tests we identify those relating to I-Behaviours and for those tests where widgets have multiple behaviours we split them into smaller tests with single behaviours.

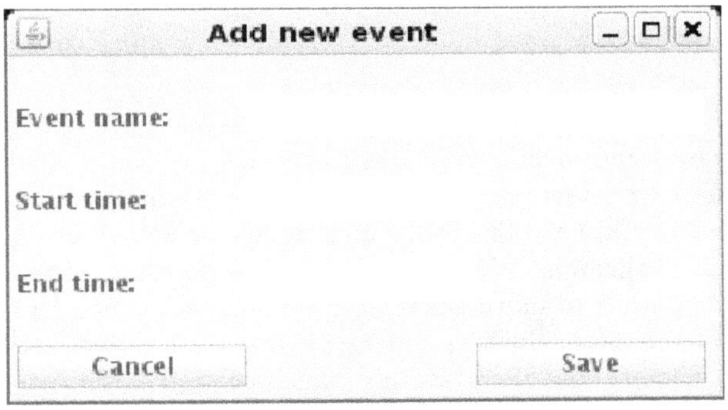

5: Add View

For example, the test:

$$State(AddView) \Rightarrow Visible(SaveButton) \wedge Active(SaveButton) \wedge hasBehaviour(saveButton, I\_DayView, S\_AddEvent)$$

is split into two new tests:

$$State(AddView) \Rightarrow Visible(SaveButton) \wedge Active(SaveButton) \wedge hasBehaviour(SaveButton, I\_DayView)$$

and

$$State(AddView) \Rightarrow Visible(SaveButton) \wedge Active(SaveButton) \wedge hasBehaviour(SaveButton, S\_AddEvent)$$

For each state we identify the required widgets and test that activating the widget changes the state as defined by the I-Behaviour. For example, in *MainView* we test that a widget called *dayDisplay* changes the UI state from *MainView* to *DayView*. We already know that the widget exists from the earlier state test and to ensure we have reached the correct state we capture the window after the behaviour has occurred and call the relevant state test with this window as the parameter.

When we test the *I_DayView* behaviour from the UI we are initially interested in only one instance of the *DayDisplay* widget and so just arbitrarily use the first available instance which performs the required command and ensures that the user can get from here to the *DayView* state. When we add the functional tests we will need to extend this to ensure that each visible day of the month has the correct behaviour *i.e.* goes to the correct day view.

As there is a requirement for windows to be modal we use a specific window interceptor in UISpec4J which handles modal windows. A consequence of this is that you must specify within the test the widget which closes the modal window (to return control to the test suite) which means each test of a state change to a modal window ends up testing two I-Behaviours: the behaviour which moves to the modal state as well as the behaviour which takes the user out of that state. Where there is more than one way to exit a modal window (as in the case of *AddView* where we could use either the *Save* button or the *Cancel* button) then we must, of course, ensure both are tested.

After we complete each I-Behaviour test and implement the code to ensure they are passed, we again refactor. At this stage we now have a working UI (albeit with no functionality) and this is a good time to extend the testing to user evaluation. We can repeat the automated tests by asking users to move between different states of the UI (or to just explore the UI) and check that their experience is satisfactory and there are no human-centred errors which could not be captured by the automated testing. In our example there were no changes to be made, but if there are then we must amend the models as necessary, reproduce the abstract tests and extend the test suite as required.

Next we move on to test the non-behavioural widgets. Having already ensured that they exist in the correct states, and are visible, we must rely on the widget type information given in the presentation model to understand what other properties we must test. In Simple Calendar all of the non-behavioural widgets have the type 'Entry', *i.e.* they are used to provide a way for users to enter information. Our tests then are to ensure that it is possible to enter information into each of the entry widgets. We do this by using UISpec4J windows and identifying the relevant widgets within those windows and using the `setText()` method to enter pre-defined strings. Note that the UISpec4J `setText()` method attempts to put text into the field using simulated keystrokes and does not use the underlying Java Swing `setText()` method of the widget. We then use assertions to ensure that the contents of the entry widgets match the pre-defined strings. Extending the code to pass these tests and subsequent refactoring did not lead to any changes in the appearance of the UI, but just added functionality.

The final sets of tests relate to the S-Behaviours. These are the behaviours linked to underlying system functionality. As such the meanings of these behaviours are given by the functional specification. The tests we write for these behaviours relate both to the underlying system state and the UI. S-Behaviour tests fall into two categories. There are widgets which generate S-Behaviours (typically defined as *ActionControls* like JButtons) where a user interaction causes a function to be activated, and those which respond to S-Behaviours (typically widgets which display dynamic data) where system functionality (which may or may not be user initiated) causes a widget to change its state. Just as we did with the I-Behaviour tests we first simplify the abstract tests by splitting them into single behaviour tests. We write the tests for S-Behaviour generating widgets first, and will complete the process with the S-Behaviour responding widgets. We do this for convenience, as generally the responding widgets rely on some of the code which we will write to satisfy the generating tests.

For each S-Behaviour we write a test that both invokes the widget which has the behaviour we are testing and performs the functionality testing based on the defined operation in the specification. As an example, consider the following abstract test:

$$State(AddView) \Rightarrow Visible(SaveButton) \land Active(SaveButton) \land hasBehaviour(SaveButton, S\_AddEvent)$$

Our test consists of the UISpec4J code to interact with the *SaveButton* widget in *AddView* and a unit test to ensure the correct functional behaviour occurs following the interaction. We find the definition of *S_AddEvent* by its related operation in the Z specification, which is *AddEvent*, and which is defined as follows:

AddEvent

$\Delta\ Calendar$

$i?: EVENT$

$selectedDay?: Day$

$(i?, currentMonth \mapsto selectedDay?) \notin allevents$

$allevents' = allevents \cup \{(i?, currentMonth \mapsto selectedDay?)\}$

$currentMonth' = currentMonth$

$currentYear' = currentYear$

$visibleDates' = visibleDates$

This gives us the requirements for the test. We are interested in the observation of the system called *allevents* and input values called *i?* of type *EVENT* and *selectedDay?* of type *DAY*. If the *i? selectedDay* pair does not exist in the set *allevents*, then after the operation it will have been added (denoted in the Z schema by the primed observation *allevents'*). The *currentMonth*, *currentYear* and *visibleDates* observations remain unchanged by the operation.

For this test we are only interested in the behaviour of the system state and not in any UI displays which may related to the display of events – these are considered later when we write the S-Behaviour responder tests. We start with a test that checks the number of events that currently exist in the system state, interacts with the UI to add an event and then uses an assertion to check that the number of events has increased by one. We then extend the test to ensure that the event which has been added is the correct one (*i.e.* that it matches the entered information), and finally we try and add the same event to the set and check that the size of the event set does not change.

When we write the S-Behaviour tests, we order them for convenience. That is, we write the test for *S_AddEvent* before the test for *S_DeleteEvent* as in order to test delete we first need to be able to add an event.

The final set of tests for the UI functionality are the S-Behaviour responder tests. We leave these until last as they rely on S-Behaviours which will have been (mostly) coded as part of the previous set of tests. For some of these tests we are only interested in part of the related operation. For example, when we test the responders for *S_ShowSingleDay* (which are the displayDate and displayMonth widgets) we are only interested in the parts of the operation relating to the date. The rest of the operation has already been tested as part of the S-Behaviour generating widget tests (*e.g.* the dayButton widget in *MainView*). We could, of course, take the approach of always testing complete operations and combining generating and responding widget tests as necessary to accommodate this. However, the approach we have taken enables us to make the tests smaller (and therefore easier to develop from) and allows us to rely on the structure of the abstract tests rather than grouping things together based on the functional specification.

Once the abstract tests have all been concretised the final step is to ensure that there are no parts of the formal specification which are not related to the UI functionality which still need to be implemented. For example, system functionality which is not available to users (perhaps interacting with operating system calls or network capabilities) will not be included in the abstract tests which have been generated from the UI models. We identify these as any operations in the specification not related to S-Behaviours in the PMR. In the Simple Calendar example there is an operation called *Init* which meets this criterion. *Init* is described as follows:

Init

$Calendar$

$actualMonth? : MONTH$

$actualYear? : \mathbb{N}$

$allevents = \emptyset$

$visibleDates = allDates \rhd \{currentMonth\}$

$currentMonth = actualMonth?$

$currentYear = actualYear?$

This leads to a test that ensures that on start up the set of events is empty and the *currentMonth* and *currentYear* observations are set to the input values *actualMonth?* And *actualYear?*. For Simple Calendar these inputs are obtained from the operating system. The *visibleDates* observation is the set of all dates constrained by the *currentMonth*. Once the code has been written to ensure these tests are passed the implementation is complete.

Conclusions

We set out to find a suitable approach for supporting TFD for interactive systems by using abstract tests which can be automatically generated from UI models as the basis for the test development. Our intention was to find a suitable tool for running the tests (which could integrate both system and UI functionality) as well as providing a re-usable method for determining what tests should be written, with the aim of ensuring full coverage of all parts of the system to be implemented.

The work we have presented here provides a repeatable process which can be used for any interactive system and consists of the following steps:

- Designing the UI following a UCD process
- Formally modelling the system specification
- Developing models of the UI designs
- Automatically generating abstract tests
- Concretising the abstract tests
- Creating any required additional functional tests

This method enables TFD to be used for interactive systems in an integrated manner, *i.e.* both system and UI can be developed using the TFD approach with tests for all parts of the system being created, and run, using the same tool within a standard IDE.

We chose to start development from the UI behaviour tests and UI state tests, which meant we constructed the UI first and added system functionality last. However, we could just as easily have taken the reverse approach with very little difference, although the advantage of the first approach is that we quickly have a semi-functioning user interface which means we can begin user testing earlier on in the development.

What we have presented in this paper is the detail of *how* we propose TFD for interactive systems may be achieved.

Evaluating this to determine its ease of use, success, scalability *etc.* is part of ongoing work.

The method we have described here could be used with any simulated interaction testing tool and is not tied to the UISpec4J framework. However, while UISpec4J is not without its limitations, we did find that in most cases it was suitable for our requirements. In the cases where its inbuilt classes could not handle behaviours we wanted to assign to widgets (such as double clicking on a listbox item) it was fairly straightforward to extend its functionality to handle this (using the Mouse class for example). This did mean that there were times when we had to write tests in a more long-winded way to compensate for this, but we were able to replicate all of the interaction we needed.

By taking a TFD approach rather than TDD, we have been able to incorporate UI models developed as part of a UCD process and use these as the foundation for tests and development. This assists with supporting interactive systems with well-designed UIs; it is a recognised problem that this is often not the case in TFD and TDD. We have shown in this paper that TFD can be successfully applied to interactive systems and that by using formal models as the basis for the tests we can automatically generate abstract tests. This provides a structured and easy to use framework, which does not require input from a test expert, which can be used by anyone wishing to develop interactive systems in this way.

For the small example application used in this paper we have assumed we require 100% test coverage, and the size of the system means that this was not overly onerous in terms of test generation. However, it still remains to be seen how this will scale to larger systems as well as defining how decisions should be made regarding levels of test coverage with respect to which areas should be considered critical and which optional.

In summary, we have investigated the lack of support for (integrated) TFD for interactive systems and propose a solution based on developing abstract tests from UI models and using these as the basis for the test development. The benefits of this approach are: the ability to automatically generate the abstract tests, ensuring that coverage remains consistent without the need to rely on experienced test writers; tests which are easy to understand and relate back to initial specifications and models; a set of integrated tests which can subsequently be used for regression testing for all parts of the system; a lightweight approach with an underlying sound theory based on the specification and models.

REFERENCES

1. Andrea, J. Envisioning the Next Generation of Functional Testing Tools. *IEEE Software 24*, 3, 58-66, May/June 2007.
2. Beck, K. *Test-Driven Development by Example*. The Addison-Wesley Signature Series, 2003.
3. Beck, K. Aim, Fire. *IEEE Software 18*, 5, 87-89, September 2001.
4. Bowen, J. and Reeves, S. UI-Design Driven Model-Based Testing, in *Electronic Communications of the EASST 22 : Formal Methods for Interactive Systems*, 2009.
5. Bowen, J. and Reeves, S. Developing usability studies via formal models of UIs, in *Proceedings of the 2nd ACM SIGCHI Symposium on Engineering interactive Computing Systems* (Berlin, Germany, June 19 - 23, 2010). EICS '10. ACM, New York, NY, 175-180.
6. Dutta, S. Abbot - A Friendly JUnit Extension for GUI Testing, *Java Developer Journal*, pp 8-12, April 2003. (http://abbot.sourceforge.net)
7. Gimblett, A. and Thimbleby, H. User interface model discovery: towards a generic approach, in *Proceedings of the 2nd ACM SIGCHI Symposium on Engineering interactive Computing Systems* (Berlin, Germany, June 19 - 23, 2010). EICS '10. ACM, New York, NY, 145-154.
8. Hellman, T., Hosseini-Khayat, A. and Maurer, F. Supporting Test-Driven Development of Graphical User Interfaces Using Agile Interaction Design, in , *Proceedings of the 2010 Third International Conference on Software Testing, Verification and Validation Workshops*. IEEE 2010.
9. ISO/IEC 13568. *Information Technology - Z Formal Specification Notation - Syntax, Type System and Semantics*. First edition. Prentice-Hall International series in computer science. ISO/IEC 2002.
10. JUnit. http://junit.sourceforge.net.
11. Memon, A., Banerjee, I. and Nagarajan, A. GUI Ripping: Reverse engineering of graphical user interfaces for testing, in, *Working Conference on Reverse Engineering*, 260, 10th Working Conference on Reverse Engineering (WCRE 2003), 2003.
12. Memon, A, Nagarajan, A. and Xie, Q. Automating regression testing for evolving GUI software. *Journal of Software Maintenance and Evolution: Research and Practice 17*, 1, 27-64, Jan/Feb 2005.
13. PIMed. An editor for presentation models and presentation interaction models. Available from: http://www.cs.waikato.ac.nz/Research/fm/PIMed.html
14. Ranorex. http://www.ranorex.com
15. UISpec4J. http://www.uispec4j.org

Test Case Generation from Mutated Task Models

Ana Barbosa
Universidade do Porto
Faculdade de Engenharia
Departamento de Engenharia Informática
Rua Dr. Roberto Frias, s/n
4200-465 Porto
PORTUGAL
ei05089@fe.up.pt

Ana C. R. Paiva
Universidade do Porto
Faculdade de Engenharia
Departamento de Engenharia Informática
Rua Dr. Roberto Frias, s/n
4200-465 Porto
PORTUGAL
apaiva@fe.up.pt

José Creissac Campos
Departamento de Informática/CCTC
Universidade do Minho
Campus de Gualtar
4710-057 Braga
PORTUGAL
jose.campos@di.uminho.pt

ABSTRACT
This paper describes an approach to the model-based testing of graphical user interfaces from task models. Starting from a task model of the system under test, oracles are generated whose behaviour is compared with the execution of the running system. The use of task models means that the effort of producing the test oracles is reduced. It does also mean, however, that the oracles are confined to the set of expected user behaviours for the system. The paper focuses on solving this problem. It shows how task mutations can be generated automatically, enabling a broader range of user behaviours to be considered. A tool, based on a classification of user errors, generates these mutations. A number of examples illustrate the approach.

Author Keywords
Task models, model based GUI testing

ACM Classification Keywords
H.5.2. Information interfaces and presentation: User Interfaces. D.2.5. Software Engineering: Testing and Debugging.

General Terms
Human Factors, Reliability

INTRODUCTION
Graphical User Interfaces (GUIs) are nowadays the pervasive means of interaction between users and computer systems. Clearly, the quality of the GUI is a determining factor in the decision to use a system or not. At the very least, it will have an impact in the effectiveness, efficiency and satisfaction with which the system is used [1].

GUI quality is a multifaceted problem. Two main aspects can be identified. For the Human-Computer Interaction (HCI) practitioner the focus of analysis is on *Usability*, how the system supports users in achieving their goals (which can range from being productive to having fun, depending on the specific system being considered). For the Software Engineer, the focus of analysis is on the quality of the implementation (from the degree of coverage of requirements, to the maintainability of the code). Clearly there is interplay between these two dimensions. Usability will be a (non-functional) requirement to take into consideration during development, and problems with the implementation (e.g., *bugs* in the code) will create problems to the user, hindering usability.

In a survey of usability evaluation methods, Ivory and Hearst [2] identified 132 methods for usability evaluation, classifying them into five different classes: (User) Testing; Inspection; Inquiry; Analytical Modelling; and Simulation. They concluded that automation of the testing process is greatly unexplored. Automating the testing process is a relevant issue since it will help reduce analysis costs by enabling a more systematic approach to testing.

Another possible division of evaluation methods is between those that require users to use the system, and those that rely on models or simulations of the system for the analysis. In the first case, the costs remain high due to the need for testing sessions with real users of the system to be carried out. Moreover, and given the high costs of user testing, the analysis will not be exhaustive in terms of all the possible interactions between the users and the system. This means that problems with the implementation might remain unnoticed during the analysis. In the second case, an assumption is being made that the implementation will be faithful to the model. This begs the question of how to test the implementation (ideally, without resorting to human users).

The ability to automatically generate, and run, relevant test cases on a target GUI would support the analysis of the implementation while reducing costs. The problem, then, is that while there are several tools for GUI testing, many such tools do not automate the generation of test cases and/or the testing process.

EICS'11, June 13-16, 2011, Pisa, Italy.

Model-based testing methods automate the generation of test cases from a model of the system under test. However, these methods present several difficulties. In the particular case of interactive systems, one such problem is the need to build detailed models of the GUIs [3]. One way to overcome these difficulties is to increase the level of abstraction of the models. In [4], it is shown how task models can be used to achieve this goal of using more abstract models in the model based testing of GUIs. Task models, however, describe the normative operation of a system only. They do not capture the common mistakes that users might make, or alternatives to the expected normative usage.

This paper focuses on user errors, and examines the feasibility of using task models to test GUIs against erroneous user behaviour in a model-based testing setting. It achieves this by building on the existing approach described in [4]. The approach uses ConcurTaskTrees (CTT) [5] as the task modelling notation. This paper proposes an algorithm to carry out changes to the original models (mutants) by introducing typical user errors. For a definition of this algorithm Reason's user errors classification [6] was used. Then several existing applications were analyzed in order to detect patterns in the construction of their task models. The proposed algorithm detects those patterns in the task model and provides a strategy for generating mutants capturing the effect of the different types of errors on them.

To validate the approach, the CMTTool (CTT Model Transformation Tool) was developed. This tool takes a task model and applies the algorithm defined in the approach, thus generating several mutants of the task model for testing purposes. To assess the quality of the generated models, the approach was applied in the model-based testing of a number of GUI applications. The results obtained by analyzing these case studies showed that the approach allowed the detection of faults arising from unexpected behaviours of the users. This shows evidence that the approach supports the inclusion of typical erroneous user behaviour in the automated task models based testing of user interfaces.

In the next four sections, the paper discusses task models and model-based GUI testing (State of the Art); presents the proposed approach and associated tool support (The Approach and the Tool); presents a number of examples of application of the tool to real GUIs (Case Studies); and ends with a discussion of the results and pointers for future and ongoing work (Conclusions and Future Work).

STATE OF THE ART

Task Models

In the context of interactive systems development, a task is an activity that should be performed in order to reach a particular goal. Used as a requirements analysis artefact, task models capture knowledge about the work the system to be developed will be supporting. Used as a design artefact, task models are a representation of the system's interactive layer logic, and describe assumptions about how the user will interact with the device. In any case, task models are usually normative. They describe the *correct* procedures users (should) follow to achieve defined goals in the system.

Several task-modelling languages have been proposed over the years. Some relevant examples include GOMS (Goals, Operators, Methods, Selection Rules) [7], UAN (User Action Notation) [8], TKS (Task Knowledge Structures) [8], or CTT (ConcurTaskTrees) [9]. These are all examples of the family of hierarchical task analysis notations, the most common approach to task analysis. In this style of approach, the task model is a hierarchical decomposition of tasks into sub-tasks that must be carried out to achieve a given goal. For a discussion of alternative approaches see, for example, [7].

GOMS focus is on user behaviour. The actions users perform on the interface, and how they select which actions to use. TKS focus on the knowledge needed to use the system. UAN and CTT describe both user and system actions. UAN defines a language to describe user actions at the level of mouse and keyboard events. Tasks are described in a tabular notation relating user actions to system responses and user interface states. CTT defines a language to describe the temporal relationships between tasks (based on the LOTOS specification language [10]). The notation does not fix the level of abstraction used to model atomic tasks.

CTT has become a popular language for task modelling and analysis, due to its graphical notation, formal semantics and tool support. The TERESA tool [9] supports editing and analysis of CTT models, and a number of features relating to the animation of task models that have proven useful in our work.

Model Based GUI Testing Tools

Model Based Testing (MBT) has been widely investigated for API testing (e.g., [11-12]), and therefore MBT based approaches are more common for API than for GUI testing. However, approaches applying MBT for GUI testing do exist, e.g., Memon's work [13-14], and Paiva's work [15]. They differ in the kind of model they use and in the coverage of the test criteria used to guide the test case generation process. However, both authors have concerns with the effort required to construct the models.

The tool developed by Memon (GUITAR) generates test cases from an Event Flow Graph (EFG) model. In the EFG, a directed edge from one node to another represents an event-flow relationship between two events. Memon tried to diminish the effort in constructing the model by developing a GUI ripping tool to extract EFG from an existing GUI [14].

In his following work [13], Memon generates a sub-graph of the EFG by removing nodes and edges that are not observed in the usage information obtained from the application's real users, and augments it with probabilistic information in each node (event) that describes the occurrence probability of the event. Test cases are then generated taking into account the probability of the events occurring.

Another problem faced when considering model-based GUI testing related to the mapping between events in the model, and physical actions in the GUI. The GUI Mapping tool developed by Paiva [15] is an extension of the model-based testing tool Spec Explorer, developed by Microsoft Research. The GUI model is written in Spec# with state variables to model the state of the GUI and methods to model the user actions on the GUI. Spec Explorer generates a finite-state machine (FSM) by exploration of the Spec# model and then test cases are generated from the FSM according to coverage criteria like full transition coverage.

To run tests automatically over a GUI some additional (intermediate) code is needed to simulate the user actions on interactive GUI controls. The GUI Mapping Tool generates such code automatically, based on the mapping between model actions and GUI controls where corresponding real actions occur. Although the intermediate code is generated automatically, Paiva agrees that the effort needed for the construction of Spec# GUI models is too high. Similarly to Memon, she also tried to diminish the effort in constructing a model by using a reverse engineering process to extract a preliminary model from an executable GUI. This model is completed afterwards and validated in order to generate test cases. Another attempt to reduce the time spent with GUI model construction was described in [16] where a visual notation (VAN4GUIM) is designed and translated to Spec# automatically. The aim was to have a visual front-end that could hide formalism details from testers. However, a VAN4GUIM model is in an abstract level lower than task models. Another attempt to reduce the effort in constructing GUI models is to increase the level of reuse. In [17], Cunha tried to increase reuse by identifying recurrent GUI behaviour (UI patterns) and defining test strategies for each of those patterns.

Following on from [4], the approach described in this paper addresses the issue of diminishing the effort in the construction of GUI models by increasing the level of abstraction of those models to task models.

THE APPROACH AND THE TOOL

CTT Task Models

A task model in CTT is a tree of nodes, where the goal is at the root of the tree and leaves are atomic tasks. Temporal operators relate adjacent pairs of nodes at the same level in the tree.

The Case Studies section presents several examples of CTT task models. Four different types of tasks can be identified in those examples: interaction tasks ( ) are atomic tasks representing user input to the application; application tasks ( ) are atomic tasks representing application output to the user; user tasks ( ) are atomic tasks representing decision points on the user's part; abstract tasks ( ) are used to structure the model and appear as internal nodes in the tree.

The semantics of the model is defined by the possible traversals of the tree. Tree traversal is done left to right in a depth first fashion, and is governed by the temporal operators relating pairs of nodes (plus two additional operators that are applied to single nodes – see below). A total of eight operators can be used [5]:

- choice operator ([]): T1 [] T2 means that one of T1 and T2 will happen;
- order independency operator (|=|): T1 |=| T2 means that T1 and T2 will happen in any order;
- concurrent operator (|||): T1 ||| T2 means that T1 and T2 will happen concurrently (the operator |[]| is used to express information exchange between the tasks)
- disabling operator ([>): T1 [> T2 means that T2 interrupts T1 (which will not be resumed);
- suspend/resume operator (|>): T1 |> T2 means that T2 suspends T1, but T1 resumes once T2 has finished;
- enabling operator (>>): T1 >> T2 means that T2 happens after T1 is finished ([]>> is used to express information exchange between the tasks);
- iterative operator (*): T1* means task T1 happens repeatedly;
- optional operator ([ ]): [T1] means task T1 might happen or not.

Consider the task model in Figure 15 (the last in the paper). The goal of the task (the root of the tree) is to start the Unit Converter ("Start UnitConverter"). To achieve the goal the user starts by opening the unit converter ("Press OpenUnitConverter"), after which (enabling operator) the system responds by showing it ("Show UnitConverter"). After the unit converter is displayed, repeatedly (iterative operator applied to "AreaConvert") the user enters digits ("Enter Digit") and the system responds with displaying results ("Display Results"). Information about the digits entered in "Enter Digit" is passed to "Display results" (enabling operator with information exchange).

As mentioned above, CTT does not define the level of abstraction for writing the atomic tasks in the models. Neither does it constrain how tasks are to be named. In order to automatically generate oracles from the task models, some conventions about how CTT atomic tasks should be named were defined in [4]. More specifically, a set of valid keywords to be used when writing atomic task names was defined. These keywords are also used here and are:

- Start <*task*> — defines the start of a new task (and creates a new namespace);
- Enter <*field*> <*value*> [<*type*>] — the user enters *value* of type *type* in *field* (String is the default type and can be omitted);
- Press <*button*> [<*window*>] — the user presses *button* in *window*, if the window is not specified the current window is assumed;
- Show <*window*> — the application opens *window* as a non-modal window;
- ShowM <*window*> — the application opens *window* as a modal window (i.e., it must be closed before the user can interact again with the parent window);
- Display <*value*> <*window*> — the application displays *value* in *window*;
- Close [<*window*>] — the application closes *window*, if the window is not specified then the current window is assumed.

These keywords were inspired by the Framework for Integrated Tests (FIT) [6]. Describing the process that lead to this specific set of keywords is outside the scope of this paper. The process is described in [4].

Typical mistakes of the user

According to Reason, in [18], the cognitive process of performing tasks is divided into three stages. The first stage consists in planning. During this stage the objective of the task, and the sequence of actions to achieve that objective, the plan, are identified. The second stage consists in storing the plan in memory until it is executed. The third stage involves implementing the plan (implementation of agreed actions).

During this cognitive process errors may arise, associated with each stage. In [18], three types of user errors are identified: slips, lapses and mistakes. The errors of type slips correspond to the implementation stage of the cognitive process, and consist in the wrong execution of an action, e.g., the user performs the sequence of actions in the wrong order. Lapses are errors that occur during storage and consist of the incorrect omission of an action, e.g., the user forgets to perform one action. Mistakes are a type of errors occurring in the planning phase and are the establishment of a wrong plan to achieve the objective, i.e., the plan chosen for achieving the objective is not adequate.

The first two types of errors (slips and lapses) can be represented in the task model by the omission of tasks, changes in the operators, changes in the order of the tasks or combinations of these approaches. The third type of errors (mistakes) can be represented, using the elaboration of different strategies to achieve the objective. Each strategy corresponds to a different task model, thereby checking which is the strategy followed by the application under test.

Methodology

The task-based MBT methodology proposed in this paper takes the above types of errors into consideration and comprises five main steps (Figure 1).

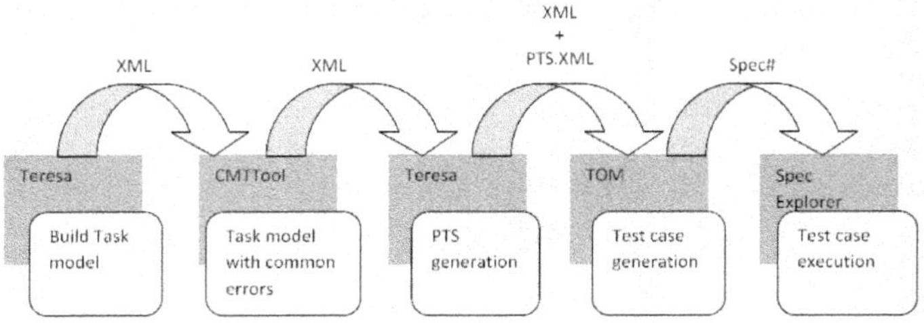

Figure 1: Methodology

The first step corresponds to the design of the task model using the CTT notation. This model is exported to XML file, by using the Teresa tool [19]. The second step is the introduction of typical user errors in the original model producing model mutants. This step is carried out by the CMTTool developed in this work. CMTTool will take the original task model and perform various transformations, constructing new XML files. The mutated models allow testing the GUI against errors, such as slips and lapses. For each mutant, the corresponding finite state machine (PTS – Presentation Task Set) will be generated and exported to XML, using the Teresa tool [19]. In the case of errors of type mistake, several task models will be developed, each corresponding to a different strategy to achieve the goal. In this case, it is not necessary to construct mutants with the CMTTool, jumping directly to the PTS generation step for each of those models. The fourth step generates a Spec# test oracle from the models, mutants, and their PTSs. This generation is automated, using the TOM tool [4, 20]. Finally, Spec Explorer [21] will generate test cases (according to coverage criteria) from the test oracles constructed previously and will execute them.

Transformation algorithm

An algorithm was designed to introduce user errors, such as slips and lapses, in the original task model, i.e., to construct model mutants. This algorithm was designed so that it could work for any task model without depending on the specific GUI that was being modelled.

The first step was to study task models and the CTT operators described above, and define strategies to introduce typical user errors in such models. The goal is not to cover all possible mutations but only those that reflect typical user errors. This has the advantages of focusing the testing activity, helping control scalability problems. Currently, the approach considers leaf tasks only, but it can be extended to consider tasks at other levels in the task tree. The strategies are described in the sequel.

Sequence of tasks

Two interaction tasks, T1 and T2, defined in sequence related by CTT operators such as >> or []>>, have to be executed in the order they are defined. In these situations, it is interesting to test if the execution order is indeed relevant because, if the GUI allows it, the user may interact with it performing those tasks in the wrong sequence. So, the algorithm generates a mutant with those tasks in an opposite order.

In the case of two tasks related by the operator []>>, e.g., T1[]>>T2, where there is passage of information from T1 to T2, the algorithm changes the order of the tasks and deletes the pre-condition of T2 if it depends on the information passed between them. Otherwise, it would be impossible to generate afterwards test cases with the execution of T2 before executing T1.

When the last task of a sequence of tasks is an application task, the algorithm does not change its order because it will be a task performed by the application as a result of executing the task sequence and will be used to check if the result obtained by executing the tasks is the one expected.

Non-mandatory order
A sequence of tasks with no mandatory order is a set of tasks separated by operator |=|. In this case, what matters is to test whether, in fact, tasks can be performed in any order. So, it would be necessary to test if the result obtained by executing T1>>T2 is the equal to the one obtained by executing T2>>T1. Excluding application tasks, the algorithm generates several mutants with all possible combinations of task orders and replaces the operator |=| by the sequence operator >>.

Optional/mandatory task
Sometimes, the users forget to execute one of the tasks needed to achieve a goal. In a CTT model it is possible to distinguish between optional tasks (within brackets) and mandatory tasks (without brackets). It may be useful to test if optional tasks are effectively optional and if the mandatory tasks are effectively mandatory.

For a sequence of tasks T1>>[T2]>>T3 in which T2 is optional, the algorithm generates four mutants with the following sequence of tasks:

1. T1>>T2>>T3,
2. T1>>T3 to check if the T2 is really optional,
3. T1>>T2 to check if T3 is really mandatory,
4. T2>>T3 to check if T1 is really mandatory.

In the case of a mandatory task, mutants are generated with the task removed. In the case of a sequence of tasks T1>>T2[>T3 where T2 executes until T3 starts, the mutant omitting T2 will be T1>>T3.

If the operator []>> is used between two tasks, e.g., T1>>T2[]>>T3, when the tool generates the mutant T1>>T3 it deletes the pre-condition of T3 if it depends on the information passed by T2 to T3.

Task choice
When a sequence of tasks is separated by the choice operator [], e.g., T1[]T2[]T3, it means that the user can choose to perform one of those tasks. For each set of tasks separated by [] operator, the algorithm generates mutants, keeping one of those tasks and omitting the other ones. The result of executing the test cases generated will say if the set of tasks are really a choice. For the sequence T1[]T2[]T3, the algorithm generates 3 mutants: one with task T1, one with task T2 and another with task T3.

Disabling
T1[>T2 means that task T1 is active until T2 is performed, and that at any time during the execution of T1, T2 can be performed. This can also lead to errors when the user attempts to perform T1 after performing T2. Thus it becomes necessary to test if T1 is really disabled after performing T2. The tool generates a mutant with the following sequence of tasks T1>>T2>>T1', where T1' is a copy of the task T1 to check if the execution of T2 disables T1.

Iterative task
A task followed by *, e.g., T*, means that T can be executed iteratively. When an iterative task has a sequence of subtasks ending with a task of type "Press" and all the other tasks are interaction tasks of the type "Enter", the model may describe a form filling interface. A behaviour that may be useful to test may be to check if between following iterations, the previous inserted information is kept or is throw way. A typical user error is to forget to fill out a required field and fill only that field in the second iteration assuming the all the other information is kept filled. However, not all interfaces record information from one to the following iteration, so, most of the times, the user has to re-fill all fields. One way to simulate these errors is to omit a mandatory task in the first iteration, and perform only that task in the next iteration, thus checking if the information was recorded between iterations.

Test case generation and execution
The tool TOM [4, 20], generates test oracles in Spec# [22] transforming the atomic tasks of the task model in model actions. Afterwards, these oracles are used by the Spec Explorer tool [21] for the generation and execution of tests.

In Spec#, actions can be of several types: controllable, probe, observable and scenario. CTT interaction tasks correspond to controllable actions in Spec#, because they describe user actions. CTT application tasks correspond to probe actions in Spec# because they represent actions that only read the system state without updating it. These tasks allow checking if the application is in the desirable state at a certain time.

For test case generation, the Spec Explorer tool [21] allows the definition of the domain values for the actions' parameters. With this information, Spec Explorer generates a finite state machine (FSM) by exploring the Spec# model and afterwards generates test cases according to a coverage criterion. To execute the test cases, a mapping is needed between actions of the model and methods of an adapter code that will simulate those actions on the GUI under test. After establishing this map, the tests can be executed automatically by Spec Explorer and the GUI Mapping Tool [15] after which a test report is generated.

CASE STUDIES

Several case studies were conducted over some existing web applications in order to evaluate the approach. Each case study was used to test some of the typical errors of the user, based on the test strategies proposed. The selected applications were:

- an online hotel reservation system (*Online Vip Hotels reservation*);
- the houses' search menu of a real estate agent (*Search houses*);
- the login page of a wiki system (*DokuWiki*);
- a currency converter (*Currency convertor*); and
- unit converter (*online converter*).

Online Vip Hotels reservation

VIP Hotels Group owns a chain of hotels in various regions. Through his address, www.viphotels.com, you can access various features. The online booking functionality allows searching available rooms in hotels of the group for the selected dates and afterwards the booking may be performed. Only the search functionality was tested in this case study. Figure 2 shows the menu of online reservations.

Figure 2: Vip Hotels online reservation.

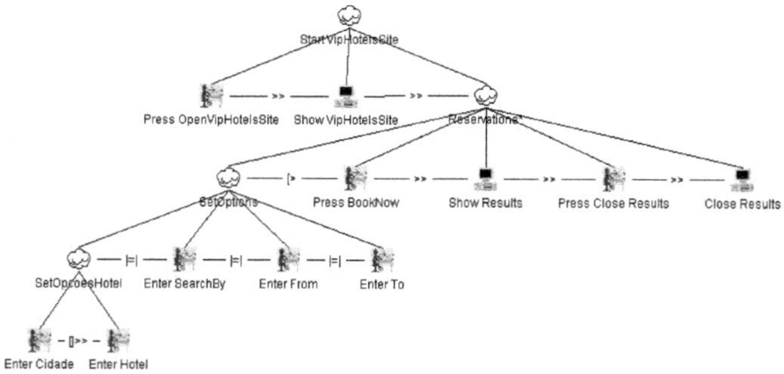

Figure 3: Task model of the Vip Hotels online reservation menu

As can be seen by examining the model in Figure 3, after opening the Vip Hotels group page, the Hotel Reservations menu is immediately available. The menu options can be chosen in any order. However, the city (*Cidade*) must be selected before the hotel. This happens because the list of hotels to choose depends on the chosen city (there is a dependency between those tasks because the first one passes information to the second). After filling in the requested information, it is possible to see, in a new window, the search results (rooms available) by performing the task "Press BookNow". The CMTTool is used to generate mutants according to the predefined algorithm. One of the mutants generated for this case study will be analyzed in the sequel.

A typical user error is to exchange the order of a sequence of tasks. One of the mutants generated exchanged the order of "Enter Cidade" and "Enter Hotel" tasks (Figure 4).

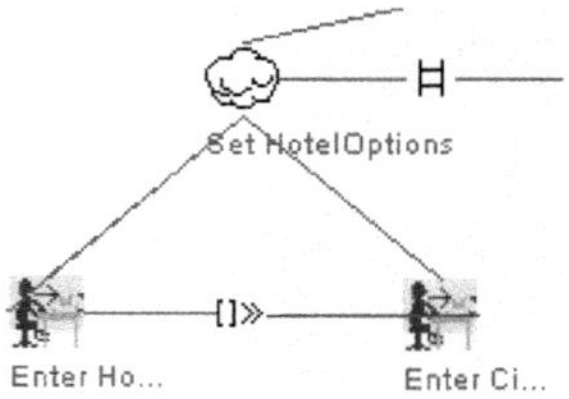

Figure 4: Detail of the mutated model

The TERESA tool generated the PTS and afterwards, the TOM tool generated the Spec# model. Test cases were generated and executed with Spec Explorer. The input values used were:

- City (*Cidade*) = Lisboa;
- Hotel = Vip Inn Berna;
- Search by = Rooms;
- From = 2/09/2010;
- To = 30/09/2010.

The Vip Hotels online reservation allows choosing the hotel first and then the city however, after selecting the hotel and afterwards the city, the value of the hotel changes to its default value which is "All". Then, when performing "Press BookNow" the results obtained are different from the ones obtained by executing the tasks in their original order. To avoid this kind of user error, the interface should be made less flexible, allowing setting the value of the Hotel only after setting the city (*Cidade*) value.

Search houses

The website of Agimoura (www.agimoura.com) has a set of features to buy, sell, search houses, among others. In this case study, only the quick search feature properties were analyzed in greater detail. It is a simple search for which information must be provided, such as: the type of housing, the type of information to configure the search (e.g., County, Place, Price, Reference, Type, etc.) and details about the information selected to configure the search (Figure 5).

Figure 5: Search houses menu.

One typical error that may occur is the case where the user forgets to perform one of the mandatory tasks, e.g., filling in one of the search options ("SetOpcoes") (Figure 6). To describe this situation, the algorithm generates a mutant with the task "Enter Info" omitted.

When executing the test cases generated by spec Explorer, for the above mutation, it was not possible to press the search button at the end because this button was disabled. So, it is possible to conclude that it is really mandatory to fill in the "Enter Info" field.

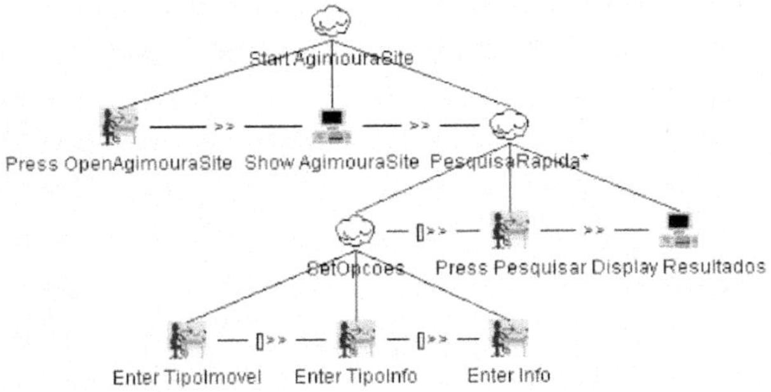

Figure 6: Task model of the Agimoura website

One interesting point to notice here is that, when testing GUIs with mutated models, such as this one, a failing test does not necessarily indicates a problem. It might instead be showing that the user interface prevents erroneous user actions from occurring.

DukuWiki

This case study aimed to test the Login/Password dialog (Figure 7) of the wiki-type DokuWiki.

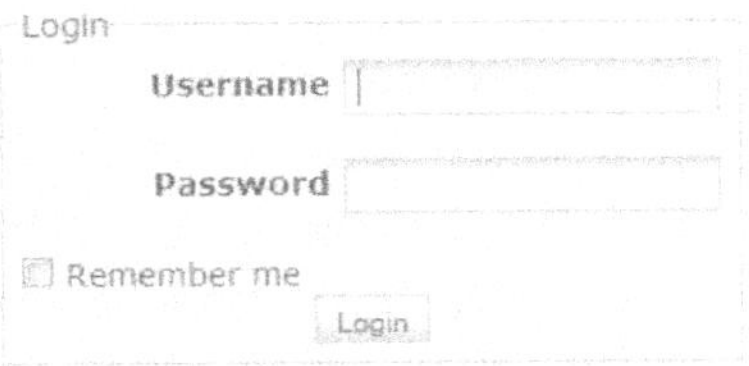

Figure 7: Login of the DokuWiki

As can be seen in the task model of Figure 8, there is an iterative task in the model: "Login". The goal was to test if, in following iterations, the inserted information is saved. To test this situation, the algorithm generates several mutated models, e.g., Figure 9.

As can be seen in the model of Figure 9, the task "Enter Password" was omitted from the first iteration of the cycle and executed in the second iteration, in order to check if the login information is kept between successive iterations.

To perform this check it was necessary to create two types of probe actions. The first one ("Display LoginResults") checks the failure of the sign-in process after the first iteration. This should happen because the password field is not filled. The second one ("Display LoginResults_Copy") verifies the success of the sign-in process at the end of the second iteration, indicating whether or not there was recording of information. After executing the generated test cases, it was possible to conclude that the login information is recorded between successive iterations.

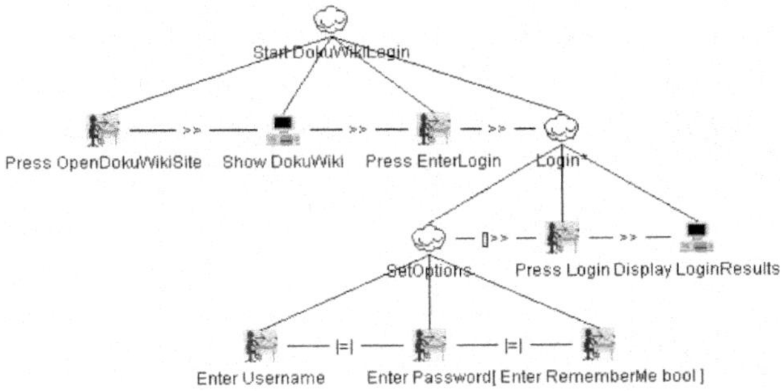

Figure 8: Task model of the login

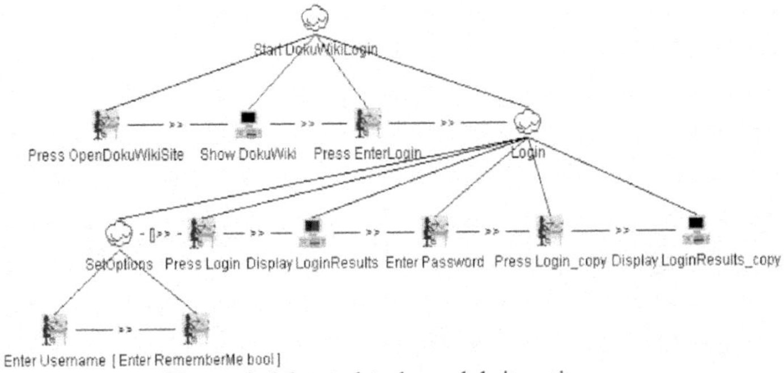

Figure 9: Mutated task model: iterations

Currency converter

The XE Converter is a universal currency converter to convert an amount from one currency to another. This application can be accessed at the following URL: www.xe.com/ucc/. Figure 10 shows the menu of this application.

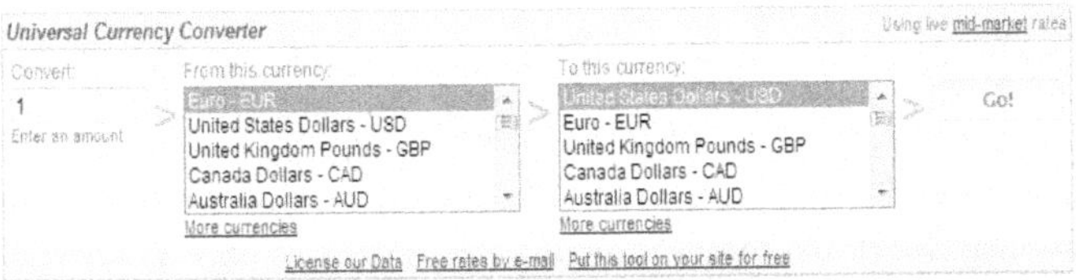

Figure 10: XE converter

As can be seen in the model in Figure 11, after accessing the converter, it is possible to select the conversion options you want (task "SetOptions"). The sub-tasks within "SetOptions" can be performed in any order until "Press Go!" is performed. Thereafter, the previous tasks are no longer active, they are disabled ([> operator), and the result of the conversion is displayed. The algorithm generates several mutants of the model.

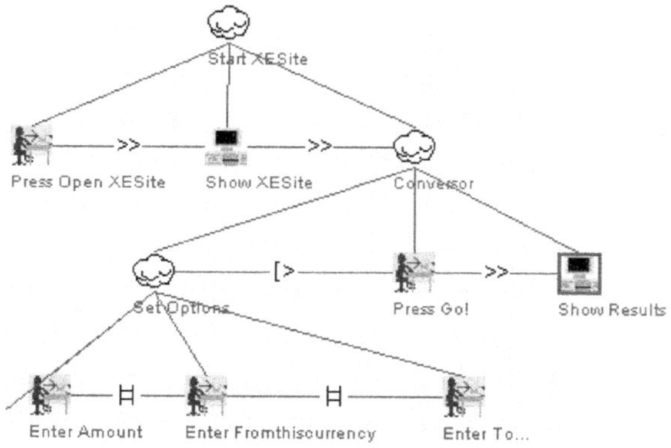

Figure 11: Task model of the XE converter

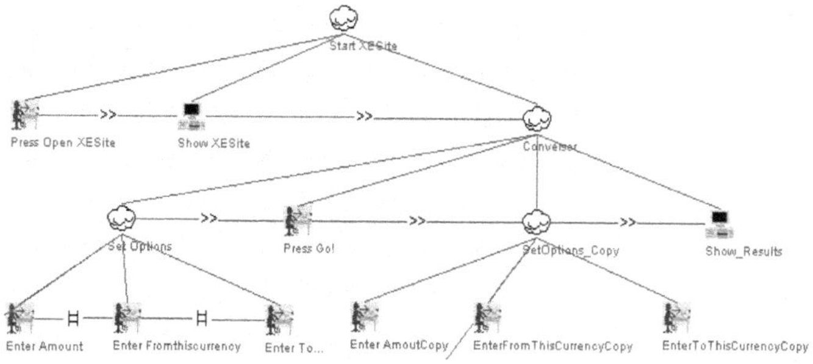

Figure 12: Mutated task model: disabling tasks

The one that checks if the tasks are really disabled is shown in Figure 12. As can be seen in the Figure 12, the task "SetOptions" is repeated (with the name "SetOptions_Copy") after the "Press Go!" task. The input values used to execute the test cases were:

- amount: 1;
- from this currency: Euro - EUR;
- to this currency: United States Dollars - USD.

During the execution of the test cases, it was possible to verify that the tasks within "SetOptions_Copy" were not available.

Online converter

The online converter (see the form depicted in Figure 13) (www.peters1.dk/webtools/conversion.php?sprog=en) was used to test the approach regarding mistakes, i.e., the use of wrong plans to achieve a goal. Two different plans were built: Figure 14 and Figure 15.

The plan described by Figure 14 models entering several digits at the input value field ("Enter Digit"), and at the end "Press Submit" to see the conversion result.

The plan described in Figure 15 models entering one digit at a time, and seeing the result after each input digit without the need to perform a specific action for that. That is, it models a user that is assuming the system will react to each digit press by updating the result values.

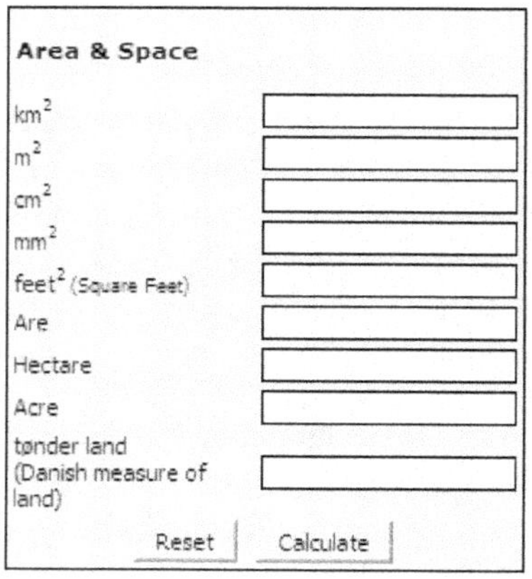

Figure 13: Online converter

Both plans were tested against the online converter application. Results showed that Plan B is not supported by the software application. This happens because the result values are updated only after the Calculate button is pressed, and not after entering each input digit as was expected.

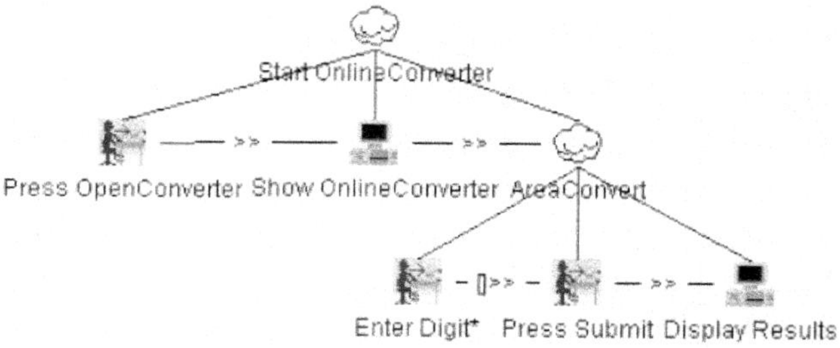

Figure 14: Plan A to convert units

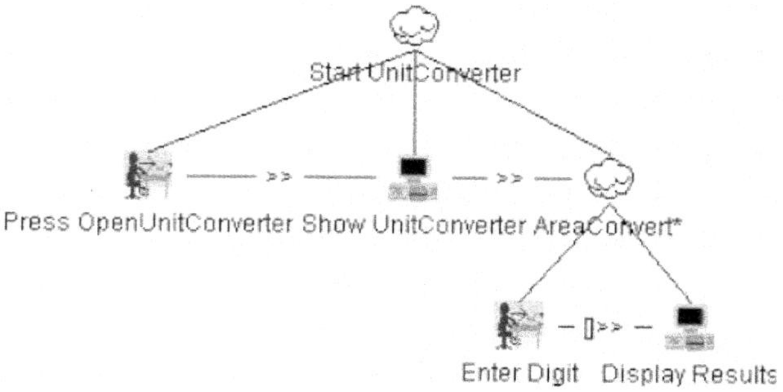

Figure 15: Plan B to convert units

CONCLUSIONS AND FUTURE WORK

Model-based testing automates the generation and execution of test cases from a model of the system under test. However, the need to build detailed models of the systems under test creates a barrier for the adoption of this testing approach. Previous work has looked at the possibility of using task models in the model based testing of GUIs [4]. Task models, however, describe the normative operation of a system only. They do not capture the common errors that users might make, or alternatives to the expected normative usage they might consider. This was initially addressed by manually introducing changes in the task models (i.e., creating mutations of the task models). This paper builds on this previous work by developing an automated approach to the generation of these mutations.

Using a number of cases studies, the paper shows how it is possible to systematically introduce changes in a task model in order to generate behaviours corresponding to errors users typically make. This mutation process is supported by the CMTTool, which was built specifically to the effect. Together with the TOM tool, it supports a process of model-based testing of GUIs from task models, where the test oracles focus on expected user behaviour, both correct (via the original task model), and erroneous (via the task's mutations). Hence, together the two tools increase the degree of coverage of the more likely user behaviours of the model based testing approach.

The user interfaces used in the case studies were small and targeted at experimenting with different types of tasks. As such, they did not bring into light scalability problems. Investigating scalability is an area for future work. Nevertheless, for large models where this problem may be visible, the approach can always be applied to sub-models of the original one.

The CTT language is currently a popular task modelling language due to its tool support and precise semantics. As such, it should present a low barrier for the use of the approach. One drawback of the current status of the approach however, is the number of different tools that must be brought together for its application. To solve this, we will have to bring all the tools together in a single deliverable. Now that all the pieces are in place, the process should be made easier.

The GUI Mapping tool, in particular, uses proprietary software libraries and cannot be made available. We are working on an alternative tool based on an open library.

While we believe that the mutations being used enable us to capture relevant user interface problems, we do not yet have the data to back this claim. To this end, we plan to carry out a study comparing the results of applying the approach against problems actually felt by users. This will enable us to assess the quality of the mutations by determining the degree of coverage achieved. Once user data is available, the fact that the testing approach is automated means we will be able to experiment with different mutations to determine the best set of mutations, and further explore scalability issues.

At a more technical level, an area where work is being carried out is in automating the generation of the input values to be used during the testing process. To that end, we are studying the possibility of integrating formal models of the application into the task model, in order to be able to rigorously analyse the input data types, partitioning them into equivalence classes.

ACKNOWLEDGMENTS

The authors wish to thank José Luís Silva, the author of the TOM tool, for making the tool available, and for his support with using it.

José Campos acknowledges support from the CROSS project (An Infrastructure for Certification and Re-engineering of Open Source Software), funded by *Fundação para a Ciência e Tecnologia* (Portugal) through grant PTDC/EIA-CCO/108995/2008.

REFERENCES

1. ISO 9241-11. Ergonomic requirements for office work with visual display terminals (VDTs) -- Part 11: Guidance on usability. First Edition ed. 1998: International Organization for Standardization.
2. Ivory, M.Y. and M.A. Hearst, The State of the Art in Automating Usability Evaluation of User Interfaces. ACM Computing Surveys, 2001. 33(4): p. 470-516.
3. Paiva, A.C.R., Automated Specification-Based Testing of Graphical User Interfaces, in Department of Electrical and Computer Engineering. 2007, Engineering Faculty of Porto University (Ph.D thesis): Porto. p. 228.
4. Silva, J.L., J.C. Campos, and A.C.R. Paiva. Model-based user interface testing with Spec Explorer and ConcurTaskTrees. in 2nd International Workshop on Formal Methods for Interactive Systems. 2007. Lancaster, UK.
5. Paternò, F., Model-Based Design and Evaluation of Interactive Applications. 1999, London, UK: Springer-Verlag.
6. Mugridge, R. and W. Cunningham, Fit for Developing Software: Framework for Integrated Tests. 1st Edition ed. 2005: Prentice Hall. 384.
7. Card, S.K., T.P. Moran, and A. Newell, The Psychology of Human-Computer Interaction 1986: Lawrence Erlbaum Associates. 469.
8. Hamilton, F., Predictive evaluation using task knowledge structures, in Conference companion on Human factors in computing systems: common ground. 1996, ACM: Vancouver, British Columbia, Canada. p. 261-262.
9. Mori, G., F. Paternò, and C. Santoro, CTTE: Support for Developing and Analyzing Task Models for Interactive System Design. IEEE Transactions on Software Engineering, 2002. 28(9).
10. Bolognesi, T. and E. Brinksma, Introduction to the ISO specification language LOTOS. Computer Networks

and ISDN Systems - Special Issue: Protocol Specification and Testing, 1987. 14(1).

11. Hartman, A. and K. Nagin. The AGEDIS Tools for Model Based Testing. in ISSTA'04. 2004. Boston, Massachusetts, USA: Springer.

12. Jacky, J., et al., Model-Based Software Testing and Analysis with C#. 2007: Cambridge University Press. 366.

13. Brooks, P.A. and A.M. Memon, Automated GUI testing guided by usage profiles, in Proceedings of the 22nd IEEE international conference on Automated software engineering (ASE'07). 2007, IEEE CS: Washington, DC, USA. p. 333-342.

14. Memon, A., I. Banerjee, and A. Nagarajan. GUI Ripping: Reverse Engineering of Graphical User Interfaces for Testing. in Proceedings of the 10th Working Conference on Reverse Engineering (WCRE'03). 2003. Washington, DC, USA: IEEE CS.

15. Paiva, A.C.R., et al. A Model-to-implementation Mapping Tool for Automated Model-based GUI Testing. in Proceedings of the 7th International Conferece on Formal Engineering Methods (ICFEM'05). 2005.

16. Moreira, R.M.L.M. and A.C.R. Paiva, Visual Abstract Notation for GUI Modelling and Testing: VAN4GUIM, in Proceedings of the 3rd International Conference on Software and Data Technologies (ICSOFT'08), J. Cordeiro, et al., Editors. 2008, INSTICC Press: Gaia, Portugal.

17. Cunha, M., et al., PETTool: A Pattern-Based GUI Testing Tool, in 2nd International Conference on Software Technology and Engineering (ICSTE'10). 2010. p. 202-206.

18. Reason, J., Human Error. 1990: Cambridge University Press.

19. Paternò F. Santoro C. Mäntyjärvi J., Mori G., Sansone S., Authoring pervasive multimodal user interfaces, International Journal of Web Engineering and Technology, vol. 4 pp. 235 - 261. Inderscience Enterprises Ltd, 2008.

20. Campos, J.C., J.L. Silva, and A.C.R. Paiva, Task models in the model-based testing of user interfaces. Technical Report, 2009, Universidade do Minho.

21. Veans, M., et al., Model-based testing of object-oriented reactive systems with Spec Explorer, in Formal Methods and testing: an outcome of the FORTEST network. 2008, Springer-Verlag. p. 39-76.

22. Barnett, M., K.R.M. Leino, and W. Schulte. The Spec# Programming System: An Overview. in CASSIS'04 - International workshop on Construction and Analysis of Safe, Secure and Interoperable Smart devices. 2004. Marseille.

Rapid Development of User Interfaces on Cluster-Driven Wall Displays with jBricks

Emmanuel Pietriga[1,2] **Stéphane Huot**[2,1] **Mathieu Nancel**[2,1] **Romain Primet**[1]

[1]INRIA
F-91405 Orsay, France

[2]LRI - Univ Paris-Sud & CNRS
F-91405 Orsay, France

ABSTRACT

Research on cluster-driven wall displays has mostly focused on techniques for parallel rendering of complex 3D models. There has been comparatively little research effort dedicated to other types of graphics and to the software engineering issues that arise when prototyping novel interaction techniques or developing full-featured applications for such displays. We present jBricks, a Java toolkit that integrates a high-quality 2D graphics rendering engine and a versatile input configuration module into a coherent framework, enabling the exploratory prototyping of interaction techniques and rapid development of post-WIMP applications running on cluster-driven interactive visualization platforms.

General Terms

Design, Human Factors, Performance

Keywords

Wall Displays, Clusters, Interaction, Toolkit, Prototyping

ACM Classification Keywords

H.5.2 Information Interfaces and Presentation: User Interfaces. - Graphical user interfaces.

INTRODUCTION

Over the last decade, wall-sized displays have evolved from experimental, CRT monitor-based setups to sophisticated arrays of tiled projectors or LCD panels. The latter are often called *ultra-high-resolution* displays to emphasize their significantly higher display capacity compared to projector-based *very-high-resolution* displays. They typically accommodate several hundred megapixels, and are driven by clusters of computers. As an example, the setup depicted in Figure 1 uses 32+1 graphic processing units in 16+1 computers to display $20480 \times 6400 \simeq 131$ megapixels on a $5.5m \times 1.8m$ surface ($\simeq 100dpi$). These displays enable the visualization of truly massive datasets. They can represent the data with a high level of detail while retaining context [14], and enable the juxtaposition of data in various forms. To make them interactive, wall-sized displays are increasingly coupled with advanced input devices, e.g., motion-tracking systems, wireless multitouch devices, in order to enable multi-device and/or multi-user interaction with the displayed data [14, 15]. These interactive ultra-high-resolution displays can be used in many application domains, including command and control centers, geospatial imagery, scientific visualization, collaborative design and public information displays.

These new environments pose new research challenges. From a *computer graphics perspective*: how to render complex graphics at high frame rates, taking advantage of the cluster's computing and rendering power. From a *human-computer interaction perspective*: how to design effective visualizations that take advantage of the specific characteristics of large, ultra-high-resolution surfaces; how to design interaction techniques that are well-adapted to this particular context of use, and how to handle the multiple and heterogeneous input devices and modalities typically used in this context. Finally, from a *software engineering perspective*: how to enable the rapid prototyping, development, testing and debugging of interactive applications running on clusters of computers, providing the right abstractions.

In this paper, we focus on the latter research question, that we consider essential to foster more research and development from the HCI perspective. We present jBricks, a Java toolkit for the development of post-WIMP applications executed on cluster-driven wall displays, that extends and integrates a high-quality 2D graphics rendering engine and a versatile input management module into a coherent framework hiding low-level details from the develeoper. The goal of this framework is to ease the development, testing and debugging of interactive visualization applications. It also offers an environment for the rapid prototyping of novel interaction techniques and their evaluation through controlled experiments, such as the one we recently conducted about mid-air pan-and-zoom techniques for wall-sized displays [14].

Background and Motivation

The parallel-rendering techniques developed over the last ten years enable the efficient display of 3D graphics on tiled displays driven by clusters of computers. This is usually done by sending already rendered images to the cluster nodes, or by sending geometry and performing compositing operations to produce the final wall-sized image. Different techniques exist, including *sort-first* and *sort-last* pipelines as well as various hybrid solutions. Well-known frameworks include Chromium [9], Equalizer [8] and SAGE [11]. See Ni *et al.* [15] for a comprehensive survey.

EICS'11, June 13–16, 2011, Pisa, Italy.

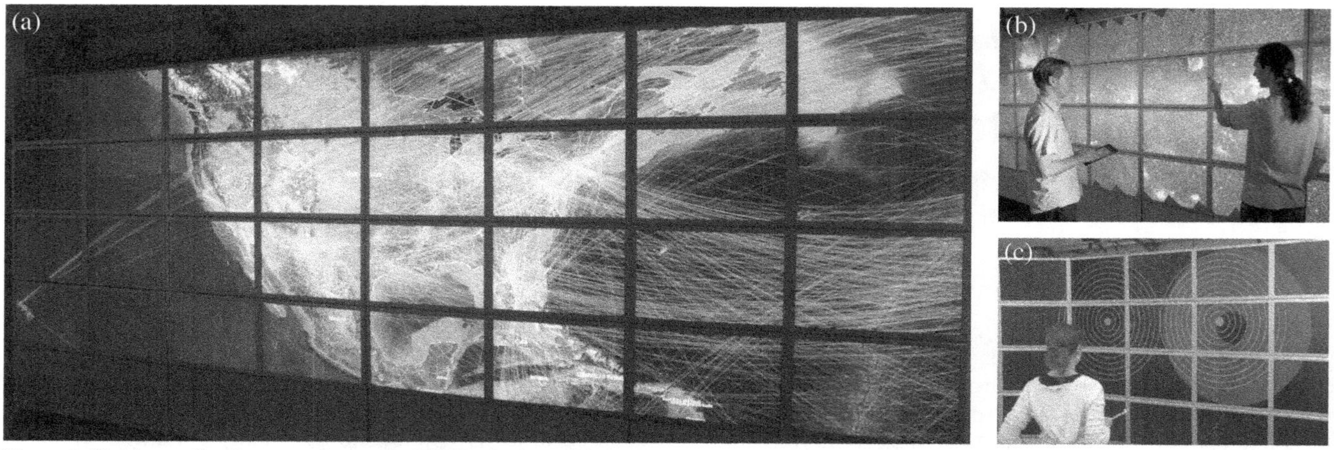

Figure 1. jBricks applications running on the WILD platform (32 tiles for a total resolution of 20 480 × 6 400 pixels). (a) Zoomed-in visualization of the North-American part of the world-wide air traffic network (1 200 airports, 5 700 connections) overlaid on NASA's Blue Marble Next Generation images (86 400 × 43 200 pixels) augmented with country borders ESRI shapefiles. (b) Panning and zooming in Spitzer's Infrared Milky Way (396 032 × 12 000 pixels). (c) Controlled laboratory experiment for the evaluation of mid-air multi-scale navigation techniques [17].

However, not all wall display applications use 3D graphics. With the introduction of ultra-high resolution, high-quality 2D graphics open wall-sized displays to new applications, e.g., in astronomy, geospatial intelligence and visual analytics at large, to give a few examples. These applications essentially combine very large bitmap images, high-quality text and 2D vector graphics, e.g., satellite imagery augmented with data layers, or information visualization techniques for the display of large datasets, e.g., for the visual exploration of large networks (Figure 1-a). However, there is currently no good solution for the distributed rendering of high-quality 2D graphics on cluster-driven wall displays.

Low-level 3D graphics APIs such as OpenGL are currently the main solution for developing cluster-driven visualizations. They work well for the high-performance visualization of textured 3D scenes, but are ill-suited to programming high-quality 2D graphics interfaces, lacking appropriate support for the management and efficient rendering of text, line styles, arbitrary 2D shapes and WIMP widgets. This was already observed for desktop application programming [4], and remains true for cluster-driven wall-displays. Pixel streaming approaches à la SAGE work well when combining different windows of relatively limited size from different applications, potentially running on different machines. They would however not work for full-screen, highly-dynamic visualizations on ultra-high-resolution displays: updating hundreds of megapixels forming a single coherent image at an interactive refresh rate would require significantly more network bandwidth than is commonly available and would put an extremely heavy load on the node in charge of rendering the image to be streamed.

Rich interactive 2D desktop applications, usually termed post-WIMP applications, are typically developed with structured graphics toolkits [1, 5, 10, 16] that provide useful abstractions on top of low-level APIs. They enable rapid prototyping and development of advanced interactive visualizations. Our goal is to offer a structured graphics toolkit capable of running transparently on cluster-driven wall displays and capable of handling a wide range of input devices and modalities. From a graphics perspective, this requires hiding the complexity entailed by having to distribute rendering on multiple computers. While our focus is on expressiveness and ease-of-use, we also pay attention to scalability issues, adapting ideas originally developed for efficient distributed 3D rendering to our context, such as the use of a multicast protocol to transmit updates to cluster nodes, and a culling algorithm adapted to zoomable user interfaces. From an input management perspective, this requires going beyond the basic redirection mechanisms found in existing distributed rendering frameworks that only support conventional input devices, i.e., mouse and keyboard operated from the master computer. For now, support for other devices is mostly achieved *via* ad hoc solutions (drivers or libraries) that are strongly integrated and statically linked within applications. This approach is not generic and flexible enough when exploring and prototyping novel interaction techniques [7]. An alternative approach consists in providing high-level abstractions of input modalities that enable association and runtime substitution of devices. It has proven successful in other domains, including physical ubiquitous computing [3], virtual reality (Gadgeteer for VR Juggler [6]) and in the more general context of post-WIMP applications (ICon [7], Squidy [12]), and we adapt it to interactive wall displays.

jBricks FRAMEWORK ARCHITECTURE

The framework is essentially composed of two independent modules: one for managing all graphical operations, and one for handling input. The two modules are loosely coupled. They communicate via a dynamic plugin architecture and network sockets using high-level protocols such as OSC. This makes the framework highly flexible: modules can be instantiated multiple times and can run on different nodes.

Structured Graphics

Our goal is to provide an API and feature-set similar to those of desktop structured graphics toolkits [1, 5, 10, 16] while i) hiding the complexity entailed by distributed rendering, ii) promoting ease of learning and ease of use, and iii) enabling code reuse: visualization components initially developed for desktop computers should run on cluster-driven wall displays with minimal changes to the original application code. With these high-level objectives in mind, we chose to extend an existing structured graphics toolkit rather than start developing a new one from scratch.

We used the open-source ZVTM toolkit [16], that supports most Java2D drawing primitives but offers higher-level abstractions that ease the management and manipulation of graphical objects: rendering is handled in retained mode, meaning that the toolkit retains a complete model of the objects to be rendered. ZVTM follows a monolithic approach, as opposed to a polylithic one[1]. Experience has shown that monolithic approaches are conceptually easier to handle by developers, generate less lines of code and require managing a smaller number of objects [5]; properties that we consider of high importance for rapid UI development.

Featured types of graphical objects include polygons of arbitrary shape, splines, Swing widgets, bitmap images and high-quality text, with support for advanced stroke and fill patterns. Those objects (*Glyphs*) are placed on infinite drawing surfaces (*Virtual Spaces*) that are observed through one or more *Cameras*. A camera renders the objects that lie in its viewing frustum in a *View*, that corresponds to a window on the screen. The toolkit makes it easy to create zoomable user interfaces (cameras can be smoothly panned and zoomed). It supports multiple independent views, as well as *Portals* (views within views) [4], multiple layers within a view (each corresponding to a different camera), as well as a variety of built-in focus+context visualization techniques. Cameras and glyphs can be animated using various pacing functions.

Cluster-based Structured Graphics Rendering

jBricks' extension of ZVTM to render graphics on cluster-driven tiled displays is conceptually straightforward. It takes an approach similar to what *sort-first* algorithms do for parallel rendering of 3D graphics in retained mode: as ZVTM already enables multiple cameras to observe a given virtual space, implementing tiled rendering basically consists in sharing that virtual space between all cluster nodes and setting one camera per display tile. Each camera's viewing frustum is configured so that their juxtaposition forms an overall coherent image from the user's perspective, according to the physical layout of display tiles.

Distributed Virtual Spaces. jBricks adopts a client-server model [15]: as shown in Figure 2, a single instance of the application runs on a *client node*, generating the geometry (populating virtual spaces with glyphs) and distributing it to *render servers* running on *cluster nodes*. Virtual spaces and glyphs contained therein are broadcast to all cluster nodes. They are replicated and kept synchronized as glyphs are added, removed, or have their properties changed. Parallel rendering frameworks for 3D graphics have mainly focused on the visualization of static-geometry models where only the camera(s) are manipulated interactively. The applications that jBricks aims to support typically manage much more dynamic objects, both in terms of geometry and visual

[1] *Monolithic* toolkits primarily use compile time inheritance to extend functionality, while *polylithic* toolkits primarily use run-time composition to do so, typically using a scene graph [5].

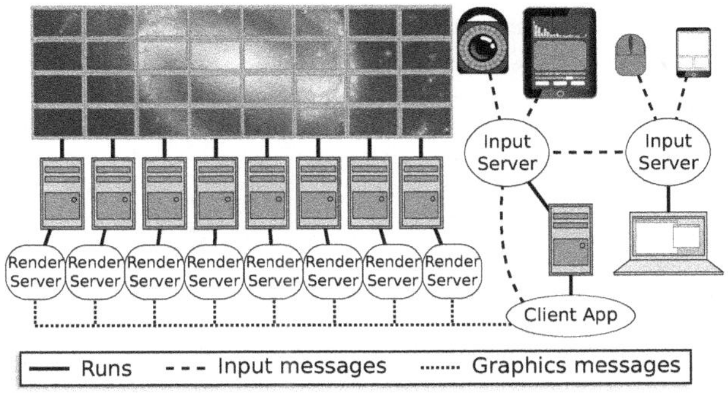

Figure 2. Example jBricks configuration: wall's graphics client and input server for motion tracker and tablet run on client node; input server for mouse, keyboard and smartphone run on user's laptop.

appearance (color, stroke, font, etc.), potentially requiring a lot of network bandwidth. Multicast communication can greatly decrease bandwidth requirements for those updates [13]. We use JGroups (`http://www.jgroups.org`) as our group communication layer, that provides reliable messaging over IP multicast. Over this layer, we exchange atomic changes called `Delta`, which are serialized Java objects representing a new value for a given glyph attribute, propagated to the corresponding glyphs on render servers.

Performance. As noted by Bederson and Meyer [4] about zoomable user interfaces: *"Smooth real-time interaction is crucial. If the system becomes slow and jerky, the metaphor dies"*. The use of a multicast protocol for updating glyphs enables us to smoothly animate several hundred property changes simultaneously and independently of the number of render servers. Camera animations do not require significant bandwidth, as moving a camera only requires updating a maximum of three double-precision floating point values per frame. A more serious bottleneck when panning and zooming is the frame rate achieved by render servers. ZVTM already implements efficient culling algorithms for zoomable user interfaces. Glyphs get projected and rendered for a given camera only if they lie in that camera's viewing frustum. jBricks benefits from this directly: each server renders only the glyphs that will eventually be visible in the associated tile, which significantly decreases the computational and rendering load for scenes with high object counts.

Preliminary tests have shown that visualizations containing up to 200,000 objects could be rendered at interactive frame rates on the platform depicted in Figure 1. jBricks also benefits from Java2D's OpenGL pipeline, and from ZVTM's spatial indexing and dynamic external resource (un-)loading mechanisms. These were developed to support multi-scale navigation in very large datasets, such as gigapixel bitmap images decomposed recursively as a region quadtree. We adapted these mechanisms in jBricks to work in a distributed context, enabling the interactive visualization of very large images. Example images that have been visualized include the 26 gigapixel panorama of Paris (354 048 $\times$ 75 520 pixels) and Spitzer's Infrared Milky Way (Figure 1-b), that can be freely panned and zoomed on a wall display.

Programming. jBricks adds cluster support to ZVTM by monkey-patching the original toolkit using AspectJ, without altering its source code. This makes the cluster extension module small ($\simeq$ 3 000 lines of code vs. $\simeq$ 39 000 for ZVTM) and facilitates forward compatibility. This also keeps API changes to a minimum: virtual spaces, glyphs, animations and most other constructs are managed through the original ZVTM API; low-level mechanisms for distribution to render servers are hidden from the developer. Only cameras and views get created and managed in a slightly different manner. The tiled display's geometry has to be declared: number of rows and columns, size of each screen (pixels), options such as whether to paint pixels behind the bezels separating the tiles (overlay approach) or ignore them (offset approach). *Clustered Views* replace regular ZVTM views: a clustered view is divided into blocks, each block corresponding to a tile and render server. Render servers can be instantiated multiple times on a single node if that node drives multiple tiles. ZVTM-based desktop applications, originally written to run on single hosts, can be adapted to run on a cluster-driven large displays by changing as little as four lines of code. Render servers are instances of a generic display program that is part of jBricks, meaning that developers only have to modify the client application and do not have to run application-specific code on cluster nodes. This enables a quick development and deployment lifecycle. It is also interesting to note that the client application and render servers can run anywhere, including on the same computer, which facilitates development outside the cluster platform.

Advanced Input & Interaction

Wall-sized displays are often augmented with a complex interactive environment, made of heterogeneous input modalities ranging from actual input devices (e.g., mouse, 6-DOF devices, tablets), to the output of interactive systems used for input (e.g., motion-tracking system software, multi-touch table tracker, mobile device sensors interpreter). jBricks's cluster extension to ZVTM handles all aspects related to graphics distribution and rendering, but supports little beyond basic input redirection for conventional devices. An input management system is required to handle the multiple input channels and to ease their fusion so as to eventually deliver high-level input events to applications, that make the description of complex interaction techniques easier [10].

We identified three main requirements for such an input management system. The system should be able to handle various kinds of distributed input in a *generic* way to allow easy substitution of input modalities, and should provide generic output to several distributed applications, no matter whether they were specifically developed for this platform or not. The system should be *extensible*, making it easy to support new devices and functionalities with re-usable processing functions or interaction techniques. Finally, the system should be *adaptable*, enabling runtime addition of new devices and changes to the input configuration.

With these objectives in mind, we developed the jBricks Input Server (jBIS), the distributed input and interaction management system of jBricks. jBIS is built on top of the FlowStates toolkit [2], that combines the ICon [7] and SwingStates [1] libraries. ICon's dataflow model can handle multiple devices and describe advanced interactions efficiently [10]. Its visual editor makes it simple to connect them to application input endpoints (Figure 3). SwingStates extends the Java language with state machines and provides a simple yet powerful programming language that simplifies the description of interaction logics on the application side. FlowStates integrates these two models seamlessly: state machines are instantiated as dataflow processing devices that can be graphically connected to input devices or to other state machines in the dataflow configuration.

Input handling. Thanks to the ICon library, the jBricks Input Server has built-in support for various regular and advanced input devices: mouse, keyboard, various tablets, Nintendo Wii remotes, VICON motion-trackers, interactive pens, etc. These input devices are instantiated as dataflow processing devices that can be connected to adapters or application devices through the dataflow editor (see the mouse device in Figure 3). These dataflow components are high-level structured representations of input devices (or classes of input devices) with typed output slots mapped to the various channels of the input device they handle.

We extended ICon to support generic devices through various protocols with specific dataflow devices that can receive and send OSC, Ivy or TUIO messages. This approach provides an implicit way of performing automatic device registration thanks to the addressing mechanism of these protocols: each input source that sends a message addressed to a specific receiving device in a running configuration is implicitly considered. For instance, a jBIS' OSC receiver device can listen to messages addressed to `/jBIS/position` with two arguments, x and y. This device will then externalize the corresponding output slots. These will be updated each time that a new `/jBIS/position` message is received, wherever it comes from: a smartphone running an application that sends OSC messages from touchscreen events, the tracking software of an interactive table, mouse movements from a laptop running another instance of the jBIS, etc.

Interaction configuration. Input configuration and the lower-level description of interaction techniques (typically the connection to inputs) get specified in jBIS with an ICon dataflow configuration. ICon provides an extensive library of adapter devices, e.g., math or logic operators, control structures, flow control. These can be used to manipulate and transform the raw values of input channels into higher-level data structures (e.g., the mult device in Figure 3). The jBIS built-in library also extends the basic processing devices of ICon with platform-specific ones, adapted to interactive wall-sized displays: for instance, the *pointed tile* dataflow component returns the display tile that is intersected by a 3D vector received as input (typically modeling the user's arm). More than simple low-level processing components, these higher-level devices are close to the re-usable interaction techniques of [10], offering several levels of granularity to the user when building an input configuration.

The jBricks Input Server also includes a plug-in mechanism for the creation of custom dataflow devices with FlowStates [2]: state machines are instantiated as dataflow components, and their transitions are triggered by the connected inputs (pointing and pan-zoom in Figure 3). Programmers can use this descriptive and straightforward approach to extend the jBIS library and to describe some parts of the interaction logic of an application, or even more generic libraries that can be used with multiple applications running on the platform.

Link with application/visualization software. In jBricks, the higher-level interaction logic (manipulation of objects, graphical feedback) is encoded in the client application (Figure 2) developed with ZVTM. The link between the jBIS and this application can be established in two ways. The first solution consists in using specific dataflow devices in the input configuration to deliver high-level interaction events to the application through a networking protocol such as OSC; the client application interprets these messages and reacts accordingly. The other solution consists in using the plug-in mechanism of jBIS to implement application-specific devices that will be instantiated as endpoints of the dataflow. These plugins can define their own protocol to communicate with the client application, or even encapsulate it, enabling direct communication as the client node is running in the same process (same Java Virtual Machine) than jBIS.

Finally, jBIS can be controlled remotely, so that applications can trigger commands (start/stop/change the input configuration) or dynamically install a plugin. Several jBIS instances can run simultaneously, communicating through networking dataflow devices (Figure 2). This modularization, based on the description of partial input configurations, reinforces the flexibility and adaptability of the platform as partial configurations can easily be substituted.

The architecture of jBricks and the resulting development and configuration tools make it possible to develop applications outside the platform, i.e., on a simple laptop, and then deploy and run them on an actual cluster-driven wall display. On the graphics side, changes to the client application are minimal (four lines of code) and can easily be managed using, e.g., command line options or Maven profiles. On the interaction side, the jBricks Input Server makes it easy to dynamically reconfigure and adjust inputs according to available devices and modalities. In the following section, we illustrate these principles with a short scenario showing how jBricks can be used for the prototyping and implementation of interaction techniques for a controlled experiment on a wall-sized display.

jBricks IN ACTION

Abelard and Eloïse need to prepare an experiment to compare one-handed mid-air interaction techniques for selection of very small targets on wall-sized displays. They consider two techniques: a very precise bi-modal pointing technique, and a cursor-centered pan & zoom technique.

They first describe the two techniques with state machines (Figure 3) and plan to implement and configure them as follows. The pointing technique will be operated with a gyroscopic mouse and will feature a coarse mode – i.e., ray-casting – and a precise mode – i.e., relative pointing with a low CD gain. Precise mode will be triggered using the right

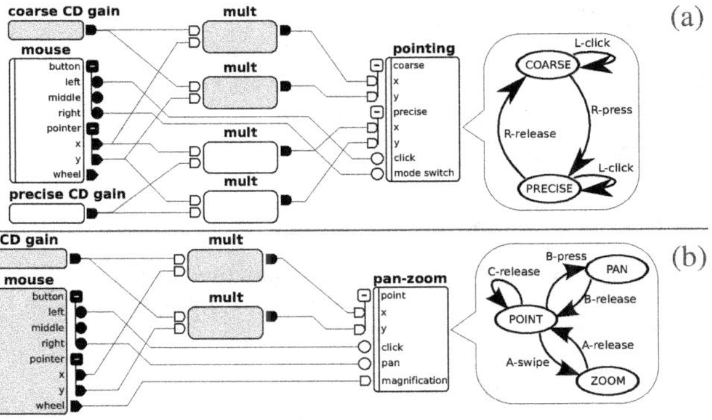

Figure 3. jBIS configurations of the pointing (a) and pan & zoom (b) techniques and their corresponding state machines. A mouse is used to control the techniques and simulate unavailable devices.

mouse button; target selection using the left button (Figure 3-a). The pan & zoom technique is operated with an iPod Touch. Vertical thumb movements control the zoom factor, ray-casting of the user's arm controls the cursor's position. Two small areas at the bottom of the iPod's screen trigger panning and target selection, respectively (Figure 3-b).

Prototyping

As jBricks' graphics and input modules are loosely-coupled, Abelard can work on the experiment's graphics while Eloïse implements and configures the two interaction techniques.

Abelard is working on the graphics part of the experiment. Using ZVTM, he creates an application that displays the targets, cursor appearance and textual instructions on his personal computer without having to worry about the specifics of the cluster-based wall display environment. He just needs to consider the actual dimensions of his graphical scene (in this case, a 20000×7000 pixel area). To make the entire scene visible on his screen, he sets the zoom factor higher than it will eventually be in the real experiment (a straightforward operation in a zoomable user interface).

Meanwhile, Eloïse implements each technique as a FlowStates state machine and encapsulates them in a jBricks Input Server plugin, making them available as dataflow processing devices. During this early prototyping stage, Eloïse focuses on developing the interaction logic, using a basic version of the graphics interface provided by Abelard. She does not need to work on the actual hardware platform either. She runs jBIS on her laptop and uses a regular mouse to simulate the actual input devices that will be used eventually (motion-capture system, gyroscopic mouse, iPod Touch). In this testing configuration, ray-casting with the motion-capture system and gyroscopic mouse are replaced by mouse coordinates; the mouse wheel and buttons are used in lieu of touch events. The output ports of the mouse device are connected to the technique devices, pan-zoom and pointing (Figure 3), the two modes of the pointing technique being simulated by applying constant multipliers to the mouse coordinates (the mul and CD gain processing devices). Later, these configurations will be slightly modified to handle the actual input devices to be used in the experiment.

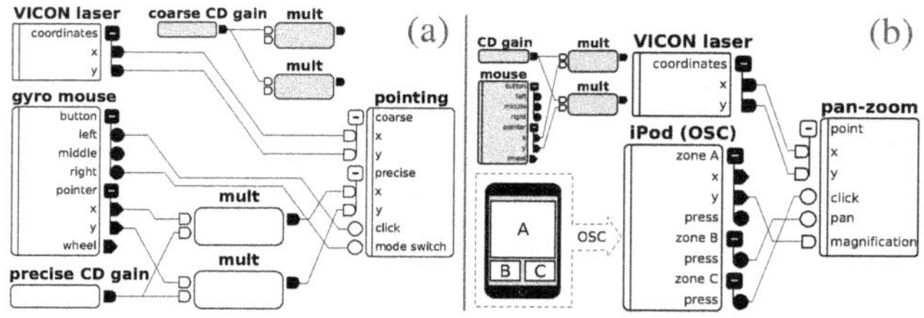

Figure 4. jBIS configurations of the final pointing (a) and pan & zoom (b) techniques. The simulation inputs (in grey) can be reused at any time simply by changing the connections.

Porting to the Wall Display Hardware Platform

On the input side, Eloïse substitutes the devices used for prototyping on her laptop with the platform's actual devices, as shown in Figure 4. The regular mouse can be directly substituted with the gyroscopic mouse, with only a CD gain adjustment (changing the value of precise CD gain, Figure 4-a). jBIS has built-in support for the 10-camera motion tracking system in the room (the VICON laser device). For the iPod Touch, Eloïse uses a built-in OSC receiver device in her input configuration to receive touch events from a freely-available application running on the handheld (Figure 4-b). To deploy the client application on the actual hardware, Abelard only needs to add a few jBricks instructions describing the *Clustered View*. He then embeds the application into the jBIS plugin made by Eloïse. The client application is launched by jBIS; it has access to the state machines' output and will react according to the chosen interaction technique.

Further iterations, switching back and forth between the simplified configuration running on personal computers and the one for the actual wall display hardware is straightforward. Abelard and Eloïse can also easily add new techniques by implementing new state machines and test several input configurations for each of them.

CONCLUSION

The jBricks framework extends and integrates state-of-the-art structured graphics and input management toolkits to enable the rapid development of post-WIMP applications for cluster-based wall displays equipped with advanced input devices and modalities. Its architecture and features enable easy deployment and reconfiguration, allowing developers to partially implement and debug their applications on conventional hardware such as a single laptop or workstation.

We have successfully used jBricks for the rapid prototyping of novel interaction and visualization techniques, and to run controlled experiments for their evaluation [14]. It is also used for the development of various applications for the visualization of large datasets in other disciplines: astrophysics, social network analysis, geospatial intelligence. The Java-based platform makes it easy to use existing libraries in client applications. In addition, ZVTM features several extension modules that enable, e.g., the layout of large networks, the visualization of treemaps, native high-quality PDF rendering, FITS astronomy image display, interactive navigation in OpenStreetMap, from world overview down to street level. Future work will focus on improving the Java2D/OpenGL rendering pipeline by optimizing the stream of instructions. The implementation of a higher-level communication protocol, based on HID definitions on top of OSC, will improve dynamic input device registration and configuration. jBricks will be made available under an open-source software license (`http://insitu.lri.fr/JBricks`).

ACKNOWLEDGEMENTS

We wish to thank Caroline Appert and Olivier Chapuis for helpful comments on early drafts of this paper. This work is supported by a Région Île-de- France / Digiteo grant.

REFERENCES

1. C. Appert and M. Beaudouin-Lafon. SwingStates: Adding state machines to Java and the Swing toolkit. *SP&E*, 38(11):1149 – 1182, 2008.
2. C. Appert, S. Huot, P. Dragicevic, and M. Beaudouin-Lafon. FlowStates: Prototypage d'applications interactives avec des flots de données et des machines à états. In *Proc. IHM '09*, 119–128. ACM, 2009.
3. R. Ballagas, M. Ringel, M. Stone, and J. Borchers. istuff: a physical user interface toolkit for ubiquitous computing environments. In *Proc. CHI '03*, 537–544. ACM, 2003.
4. B. Bederson and J. Meyer. Implementing a zooming user interface: experience building pad++. *SP&E*, 28:1101–1135, August 1998.
5. B. B. Bederson, J. Grosjean, and J. Meyer. Toolkit Design for Interactive Structured Graphics. *IEEE Trans. Software Eng.*, 30(8):535–546, 2004.
6. A. Bierbaum, C. Just, P. Hartling, K. Meinert, A. Baker, and C. Cruz-Neira. VR Juggler: A Virtual Platform for Virtual Reality Application Development. In *Proc. VR '01*, 89. IEEE, 2001.
7. P. Dragicevic and J.-D. Fekete. Support for input adaptability in the icon toolkit. In *Proc. ICMI*, 212–219. ACM, 2004.
8. S. Eilemann, M. Makhinya, and R. Pajarola. Equalizer: A Scalable Parallel Rendering Framework. *IEEE TVCG*, 15(3):436–452, 2009.
9. G. Humphreys, M. Houston, R. Ng, R. Frank, S. Ahern, P. D. Kirchner, and J. T. Klosowski. Chromium: a stream-processing framework for interactive rendering on clusters. *ACM Trans. Graph.*, 21(3):693–702, 2002.
10. S. Huot, C. Dumas, P. Dragicevic, J.-D. Fekete, and G. Hégron. The MaggLite post-WIMP toolkit: draw it, connect it and run it. In *Proc. UIST '04*, 257–266. ACM, 2004.
11. B. Jeong, L. Renambot, R. Jagodic, R. Singh, J. Aguilera, A. Johnson, and J. Leigh. High-performance dynamic graphics streaming for scalable adaptive graphics environment. In *Proc. SuperComputing*. ACM, 2006.
12. W. König, R. Rädle, and H. Reiterer. Interactive design of multimodal user interfaces. *J Multimod. UI*, 3:197–213, 2010.
13. M. Lorenz, G. Brunnett, and M. Heinz. Driving tiled displays with an extended chromium system based on stream cached multicast communication. *Parallel Comput.*, 33(6):438–466, 2007.
14. M. Nancel, J. Wagner, E. Pietriga, O. Chapuis, and W. Mackay. Mid-air pan-and-zoom on wall-sized displays. In *Proc. CHI '11*. ACM, 2011. In press.
15. T. Ni, G. S. Schmidt, O. G. Staadt, M. A. Livingston, R. Ball, and R. May. A Survey of Large High-Resolution Display Technologies, Techniques, and Applications. In *Proc. VR '06*, 223–236. IEEE, 2006.
16. E. Pietriga. A Toolkit for Addressing HCI Issues in Visual Language Environments. In *Proc. VL/HCC'05*, 145–152. IEEE, 2005.

SCIVA - Designing Applications for Surface Computers

Tobias Hesselmann
OFFIS Institute for IT
Oldenburg, Germany
tobias.hesselmann@offis.de

Susanne Boll
University of Oldenburg
Oldenburg, Germany
susanne.boll@uni-oldenburg.de

Wilko Heuten
OFFIS Institute for IT
Oldenburg, Germany
wilko.heuten@offis.de

ABSTRACT

The usability of surface computing applications largely depends on a thorough consideration of the specific characteristics and constraints of surface computers during development. Nevertheless, established user interface design processes do not sufficiently consider these aspects. Thus, Developers designing applications for Interactive Tabletops and Surfaces often need to rely on best practices and intuition rather than a systematic development process based on facts and specifications. We address this problem by presenting SCIVA, an iterative process for designing gesture-based, visual interfaces for interactive surfaces. We identify challenges in the design of applications for surface computers, describe necessary steps to address them and suggest user-centric methods that can be applied to the respective steps.

Author Keywords

Design Processes, Reference Models, Interactive Tabletops and Surfaces, Multi-Touch, Surface Computing

ACM Classification Keywords

H5.2. User Interfaces: Style Guides; Evaluation/ methodology

General Terms

Design

INTRODUCTION

Interactive Tabletops and Surfaces (ITS) mostly share the same notion: They are highly visual systems, which are usually controlled by touches and gestures performed on the surface of the system, enabling users to directly interact with visualized objects using their hands. These systems have experienced a strong proliferation in the recent years. Consequently, demand for specific surface computing applications has increased likewise. In research and the industry, we can observe surface computing (SC) applications appearing in many domains, including information visualization and visual analytics [1], education [2], public exhibitions [3], and many more.

EICS'11, June 13–16, 2011, Pisa, Italy.

With more and more ITS applications being built, more and more problems and challenges in ITS development become aware. Most notably, the specific characteristics of surface computers regarding affordance, form, size, and used interaction concepts, largely differ from the characteristics of ordinary Desktop PCs. Consequently, developers need to consider these factors appropriately during the design of ITS applications, and failing to do so can negatively impact the user experience in final applications.

Thus, developers are confronted with the question which guidelines and processes they should apply during ITS application development to build systems with a sufficient user experience. On the one hand, general user interface design processes, such as the broadly accepted Human Centered Design process (HCD) [4], provide rough guidelines for developing user interfaces in a user-centered, iterative way. Nevertheless, these processes are device-agnostic and consequently do not consider the specifics of Surface Computers. On the other hand, specific guidelines exist that explicitly target development for Surface Computers, such as design patterns for ITS [8], sets of guidelines and best practices compiled by the industry [5], or user-centric methods for the definition of gestures for ITS applications [14]. Nevertheless, these guidelines focus fairly different levels of detail in ITS development, leaving developers without clear guidance about when and where to apply the corresponding methods. Between these two extremes, currently no integrated design process exists that (1) structures the development process in a way that it can easily be followed by UI engineers and (2) specifically considers the essential characteristics of ITS.

We address this challenge by proposing a user centered and iterative design process for ITS application development, aiming to facilitate the creation of highly usable applications for developers: SCIVA (Surface Computing for Interactive Visual Applications) puts a strong emphasis on the visual and gestural affordance of ITS and proposes user-centric methods for each step in the process.

We make the following contributions:

- We systematically identify problems and challenges occurring in surface computer development
- We propose necessary steps to address these problems
- We suggest appropriate development methods that can be applied to the individual steps

RELATED WORK

The challenges in designing ITS applications are recognized more and more in the scientific community, as well as in the industry. In particular, we can identify the following related work.

Design Processes and Guidelines for ITS

Most established design processes for user interface design, such as the well accepted Human Centered design process [4], are device agnostic, i.e., they do not explicitly consider device specific characteristics and constraints. While providing valuable guidelines for the development of software and user interfaces, they naturally do not consider device specific interaction paradigms, such as gestural interactions with a system.

The industry has recognized this problem, and provides device specific UI guidelines taking these aspects into account, such as user interface guidelines for the Microsoft Surface [5] or Apple iOS devices [6]. Nevertheless, these guidelines are optimized towards a particular product and brand. Accordingly, the advice provided by such guidelines can often not be transferred to other platforms and devices without adaptation.

Bachl et al. identify eight challenges in the design of ITS systems, as well as some guidelines for approaching them, including visual cues to increase the affordance of touchscreens, and visual or auditory feedback mechanisms to compensate the missing haptic feedback of touchscreens [6]. We consider these challenges in our process design, adding issues identified in own previous works.

Design Patterns for ITS

In software engineering, the application of *design patterns* has become a standard procedure to address commonly recurring problems in application development and to increase the overall quality of products. As a next step, Borchers has transferred this concept to the design of interactive applications in general [8], and Remy et al. have further devised this approach for ITS, presenting a set of design patterns supporting ITS development [9]. The presented patterns provide valuable guidelines for common features of applications, yet naturally do not structure the development process itself. To achieve this, we propose a design process that is based upon the challenges presented in the following.

CHALLENGES IN ITS DEVELOPMENT

The vast majority of established tools and application development processes is focusing on the development for traditional Desktop PCs. Nevertheless, standard procedures used in classical UI design cannot be transferred to surface computers without adaption. As a result, ITS designers often need to rely on best practices and intuition rather than on a systematic development process based on facts and specifications, which bears the risk that critical issues are overlooked during development, resulting in usability issues occurring in final applications.

For example, Desktop PCs are typically designed for single user operation, are operated with mice and keyboards and rely on the user sitting in front of a screen in a fixed position. On the UI level, most applications rely on the established WIMP paradigm: Contents are presented in windows, icons and menus are used to trigger functions, and a pointing device (typically a mouse) is used for interaction with the system. Furthermore, interactions with the system are decoupled from the visualization: Applications are visualized on a distinct device (the display), while interactions are carried out with another device (mouse and keyboard). WIMP has become the de-facto standard in application development over the last decades, and the vast majority of applications developed today follows this standard.

On the contrary, Interactive Tabletops and Surfaces are typically operated by finger touches or styli. They are often used for collaborative tasks in multi-user environments. In addition, they often can be accessed from different positions, e.g., opposing sides of an interactive tabletop. Furthermore, users can orientate themselves towards the screen in different ways, raising issues regarding proper readability and reachability in applications (see Figure 1).

Figure 1. Interactive Multi-Touch Tabletop being accessed by multiple users

An appropriate design for ITS should address these issues in typical development tasks. To consider them, the design process presented in this paper is based on an extensive analysis of related work, as well as experiences gathered from own previous work, including TaP, a system for the visual analysis of multidimensional data on interactive tabletops [1], "Stacked Half-Pie Menus", a specific menu design for launching functions and selecting data in ITS applications [10], and an annotation system for presentations, where the audience could collaboratively annotate slides of ongoing talks.

The described systems have been built iteratively following the HCD process, involving context of use analyses, requirements definitions, and design phases. After each development cycle, we evaluated the applications qualitatively employing a think aloud protocol. Between 3 and 12 participants took part in the individual evaluations. All in all, we could identify 23 distinct design flaws, which can be classified into the following categories:

- *General problems*, such as problems understanding the purpose of the application.
- Problems caused by the *appearance and configuration of the hardware*, such as a too weak system performance, and
- Issues related to the *application behavior*, such as unexpected animations triggered by certain application functions

While these factors clearly influence the user experience in final systems, they occur in a broad range of applications and are not specific to surface computing applications. Nevertheless, we could also identify issues that were specific to the field of surface computing. The first set of issues was related to the *visualization level*. In particular, participants pointed out that

- Text was too small to read on the display
- Objects were not orientated towards them, resulting a bad visibility and readability
- They could not identify what areas and objects they could interact with
- Parts of the screen containing information were occluded by their fingers, hands or arms
- Objects were too far away from their current position to properly perceive or read them

Other SC specific issues can be identified in the *gestural interaction* with the system. Participants pointed out that

- Objects were too far away to interact with them
- Gestures imposed too much physical strain, leading to muscular fatigue
- They could not intuitively find gestures to trigger functions in the system
- They expected a different gesture to trigger a function
- Objects were too small to properly interact with

Analysing these issues, it becomes clear that despite applying the HCD process during development, several problems occurred frequently in final evaluations, which could not be eliminated by the application of HCD alone. While the evaluation phase of the HCD process is a valuable means to increase the overall usability and quality of the system, the goal remains to reveal and eliminate design flaws as early as possible in the development lifecycle in order to avoid costly changes in the later stages of development: According to Bias and Mayhew [11], the cost of changes made to an application increases exponentially, while the number of possible design alternatives decrease exponentially during the course of a typical software lifecycle.

We therefore used the results gathered in our evaluations and the related work to develop a process model considering the presented issues already in the *design phase*, which is described in the following.

THE SCIVA DESIGN PROCESS

SCIVA [ʃi:va] is an iterative process for the design of gesture-controlled, visual interfaces for surface computers (see Figure 2). Its structure is based upon the suggestions of "ISO 9241-210: Human-centred design for interactive systems" [4], which makes clear demands on the characteristics of design processes: According to these guidelines, design processes should be "iterative", include "explicit understanding of users, tasks and environments" and "involve users throughout design and development". Designs should be "driven and refined by user-centred evaluation" and "address the whole user experience". In addition, the design team should include "multidisciplinary skills and perspectives".

The key idea of SCIVA is to formalize the steps needed to build user interfaces for SC and to instantiate each step with methods involving strong user involvement. SCIVA aims to (1) act as a guideline for developers to structure the development of ITS applications and (2) separate the definition of visualizations, functions and gestures in SC development to make possible changes to the system more lightweight.

It should be noted that different methods can be used to instantiate each step of the process. The methods provided in this article can be considered as recommendations based on the current state of the art, but they can be substituted when required. Note that the process is usually iterated after the fifth step (evaluation) at latest, but iterations are also possible in the individual steps, as necessary. Of course, it is also possible to skip individual steps if necessary and meaningful. SCIVA consists of five distinct steps, which are illustrated in Figure 2 and which are described in the following.

Step 1: Task Analysis

In SCIVA - corresponding to traditional HCD - the first steps in the development process are dedicated to gaining a thorough understanding of necessary tasks of final users, their needs, and their context of use. In contrast to HCD, we put more emphasis on the design phase of development in SCIVA, and thus summarize these aspects within in a single step, the *task analysis*. We propose the following approach:

Definition of high level goals

First, we suggest to formulate *high-level tasks and goals* which developers can refer to during the design process. An example might be "The system should allow emergency call centers to collaboratively plan rescue operations". Note that these goals do not go down to the functional level and make no statement about the look and feel of a system yet. A similar approach is used in extreme programming, where a development "metaphor" is used to describe the overall goal of a system. Note that the number of goals should be kept down to a minimum. They should act as a guideline for shaping the development, but they should not confuse developers by providing a too high level of detail.

Understanding the context of use of final users.

Following classical HCD, it is necessary to gain an understanding of the *context of use* of final users. Developers need to understand *who* will use their software, *what* tasks users will need to carry out, and *where* the software will be deployed. Typical methods covering this step are stakeholder analyses, interviews with final users or field studies.

Requirements definition

During or after the context of use analysis, *requirements* are defined based upon the needs of final users. These are typically more concrete than the high level tasks defined before, and provide clear suggestions regarding functionality of the final application. As this step corresponds to the second phase in classical HCD and the concept of defining requirements is well known, it will not be recited here. Typical methods include the definition of use cases, personas, or story cards, regularly involving users in the definition process.

Definition of Constraints

In addition, technical constraints should be identified, which limit the space of possibilities during development. This might include hardware limitations, such as specific surface computer platforms the application will be deployed on. Also, software constraints are identified, e.g., the necessity to support specific touch detection APIs, such as the Windows 7 Touch API.

The following three steps - Visualizations, Functions, and Gestures - can be seen as concretizations of the HCD design phase, which are strictly orientated towards Interactive Tabletops and Surfaces.

Step 2: Visualizations

Due to the tight coupling between input (in terms of touch and gestures) and output (in terms of visualized objects on the screen), choosing the right visualizations is particularly important for the overall usability of ITS applications. To select appropriate visualizations, we propose the following approach:

Select technically suitable data representations

The visualizations used in applications typically differ significantly, particularly in SC applications, which often do not conform to established interaction and visualizations standards. As a starting point, we propose to select suitable representations for the data that will be visualized in the final system. When choosing appropriate visualizations, it should be considered that visualizations based on the direct manipulation metaphor might facilitate touch-based interaction with the application, depending on the tasks.

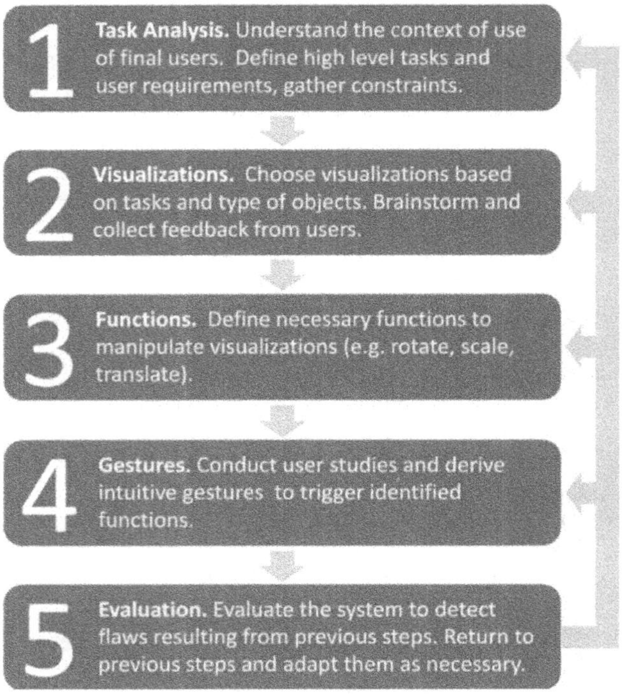

Figure 2. The SCIVA Design Process

Brainstorm and gather feedback from final users

Users should be included in the definition of appropriate visualizations as early as possible. Brainstorming sessions with users can help either to broaden the space of possible visualizations by letting users envision visualizations, or narrowing the space of possibilities by letting users assess visualizations previously envisioned by a development team. It can be helpful to provide prototypic samples of visualizations as a basis for discussions, but it should be kept in mind that concrete examples of visualizations will also bias the feedback gathered from users. Multiple iterations of visualization prototypes might be necessary before reaching consensus regarding visualizations with final users.

Optimize visualizations according to the characteristics of ITS

After a general agreement between developers and users has been established, the chosen visualizations need to be adapted and optimized for usage on surface computers, primarily considering the following aspects, which are derived from the challenges identified before.

Occlusions. Other than traditional desktop PCs, surface computers are typically controlled by direct interactions (using fingers, tangibles or styli) with the surface of the system. In consequence, parts of the screen and visualized objects might be occluded by fingers, hands, or arms. As proposed in [10], one method to circumvent this problem is to selectively or statically move items in occluded areas of the screen to visible areas. Another approach is to increase the size of touchable items, so that they cannot be completely occluded by fingers anymore.

Position and Orientation. With ITS, the *location* and *orientation* of users operating the system is often not fixed. This particularly applies to horizontal surfaces, such as interactive tabletops. Such devices are often accessed by users from different sides, and they may orientate themselves towards the SC in different directions. Often, it is technically impossible to automatically detect the position and orientation of users at the system. Thus, developers should consider these aspects in the visualization design. "Orientation agnostic" visualizations can be used for optimal readability independent of the current orientation of users at the screen, as proposed by Allalah et al. [12]. Alternatively, the visualization can be orientated towards a user on demand, e.g. by placing visualizations on rotatable canvases. Similarly, different positions of users should be supported accordingly, e.g., by introducing movable canvases that users can pull towards their current position on demand.

Distance. An aspect closely related to position and orientation is the *distance* between visualized objects and users, which primarily influences the *visibility* and *reachability* of such objects. If objects are too far away from the position of the user, texts become hardly readable and smaller objects become harder to recognize. In addition, users might be unable to reach distant objects. For example, using a large interactive wall, smaller people or children might not be able to interact with higher parts of the display. Additionally, physical fatigue can negatively influence the user experience if users need to reach out for distant objects. Developers should consider these aspects by either bridging larger distances between user and objects by appropriate interaction methods or by avoiding them, e.g., by placing interactive objects near users' hands to minimize motoric movements, as proposed in [10].

Affordance. First time users often find it particularly hard to identify objects and areas they can interact with in surface computing applications. Bachl et al. propose approaches to circumvent these problems [7], including the provision of visual cues, such as written text or buttons. Whenever possible, we suggest the usage of subtle hints to indicate affordances of interactive elements. For example, in [10] we deliberately showed only half of the required information in a rotatable area in order to indicate that the area was interactive and could be rotated using a dialing gesture.

Step 3: Functions

In the context of ITS, visualizations are usually not static, but subject to change when manipulated by gestural interactions. For example, in a geographical information system, it might be necessary to increase the level of detail on a map by enlarging it. In this step, these changes are formalized as *functions* performed on visualized objects. The necessary functions can be derived by analyzing the user requirements defined in the first step.

Typically, defined functions are more detailed than requirements. For example, a requirement might be to "enhance the level of detail on a map". In this step, it will be exactly defined what the visualization will look like before and after applying that function. Thus, this step will not only result in a list of necessary functions, but also in a list of prototypic images showing the visualization before and after the application of a function. The compiled information should be used to gather feedback from users regarding the defined visualizations and functions. In addition, it will serve as the base for the definition of appropriate gestures in the next step.

Step 4: Gestures

When using an interactive surface as input/output device, application functions are typically triggered by gestures, including touches, on the surface of the system. Thus, appropriate gestures need to be defined to trigger the functions defined before.

Several methods for defining gestures have been proposed by the scientific community and the industry. A straightforward approach is to refer to defined sets of gestures provided by the industry, e.g. [5]. Unfortunately, these sets are often proprietary and inconsistent across different platforms and applications. This can cause usability issues and a lack of intuitiveness, which negatively impacts the user experience particularly for first-time users. Alternatively, cross-platform gesture libraries can be used as a basis for application development, such as the Open Exhibits Gesture Library [13]. Nevertheless, research on the usability and applicability of these methods in different contexts is still rather scarce.

In contrast to these approaches, user centric-methods have been proposed by the scientific community. A generic technique, which has become the de facto standard to define intuitive gestures for surface computers is presented by Wobbrock et al. [14]. In this approach, users are presented an animation showing a specific system behavior and are then asked which gesture they envision to trigger the respective behavior. The same article provides a set of empirically derived gestures, which can serve as a foundation for triggering common functions, such as moving or selecting objects in an application.

To derive appropriate gestures, we propose to employ an approach similar to [14], but present the user the before and after images compiled in the function definition step of SCIVA. Users can then be asked to envision gestures to reach one state from the other. The advantage of using images instead of animations is that this approach makes a less strong statement about the system behavior, resulting in less biased comments by participants. Combined with a think aloud protocol, users can be asked to describe the behavior they expect from the system after launching a function. Developers can accordingly consider these statements when design the system behavior.

An important aspect at this point, which is often not considered appropriately, is the tradeoff between efficiency and intuitiveness of a gesture set. While nearly all existing approaches target *intuitiveness* as the main aspect to consider when defining gestures, the long-term *efficiency* of a gesture set, as well as other factors such as the *cognitive, temporal and physical demand* of gestures also play an important role for the user experience of SC applications. When designing for occasional and first-time users, the intuitiveness of gestures plays a larger role than efficiency, while the opposite is important for frequent and expert users. Thus, users can also be consulted to rate gestures regarding parameters such as physical demand, in order to take these measures into account for the definition of a gesture set.

Step 5: Evaluation.

Following classical HCD again, an iteration of the process usually is concluded by a complete system evaluation to (1) find and eliminate functional errors in the application and (2) reveal design flaws negatively impacting the user experience. Qualitative feedback should be gathered, possibly employing standard methods, such as think aloud evaluations and usability questionnaires. The feedback gained can be used to improve the overall usability and quality of the system in follow-up iterations.

Depending on the results of the evaluation, some or all of the previous steps may need to be repeated iteratively. For example, if critical tasks have been overlooked, the task analysis is repeated and the following steps are checked for necessary adjustments. Likewise, if the used visualizations, gestures or functions turn out to be insufficient, the corresponding steps are repeated and the subsequent steps are adjusted appropriately. This process is repeated until a satisfactory result has been reached in the evaluation.

CONCLUSION

In this paper, we have presented SCIVA, a user-centric design process considering the specific characteristics and affordances of ITS, particularly emphasizing the visual and gestural aspects of such systems. Designers of ITS systems can apply the process during developments to appropriately consider necessary steps in ITS development, aiming for an overall increase the usability of their applications.

While we are aware that the proposed process is only one of many possible means to increase the overall quality of SC applications, we have designed SCIVA to meet typical demands and challenges occurring in SC application development. It can be particularly helpful for developers new to the domain of surface computing, but it can also aid experienced SC developers, as it structures the development process and aims for the optimization of applications to surface computers for final users.

While the formal evaluation of the proposed process is left for future work, we derived the process based upon an extensive analysis of own previous work and related work from the field. To evaluate the applicability of SCIVA empirically, we are applying the process in three ongoing case studies involving teams of 1-10 developers, observing advantages and challenges occurring during development. While this is still ongoing work, we received positive initial feedback from developers, indicating that the overall quality and usability of final applications is expected to improve compared to previous developments.

REFERENCES

1. S. Flöring, and T. Hesselmann. TaP: Towards Visual Analytics on Interactive Surfaces. In Proc. *COVIS 2009*.
2. Kharrufa, A., Leat, D., Olivier, P. Digital Mysteries: Designing for Learning at the Tabletop. In *Proc. ITS 2010*.
3. Correia, N., Mota, T., Nóbrega, N., Silva, L., Almeida, A. A Multi-touch Tabletop for Robust Multimedia Interaction in Museums. In *Proc. ITS 2010*.
4. International Organization for Standardization. ISO 9241-210: Human-centred design for interactive systems. http://www.iso.org, 2010.
5. Microsoft Corporation. Microsoft Surface User Experience Guidelines. Available on MSDNAA. 2009.
6. Apple Corp. iOS Human Interface Guidelines. http://developer.apple.com/library/ios/#documentation/UserExperience/Conceptual/MobileHIG. Date of Access: 04/03/2011
7. Bachl, S., Tomitsch, M., Wimmer, C. Grechenig, T. Challenges for Designing the User Experience of Multi-touch interfaces. Workshop on Engineering Patterns for Multi-Touch Interfaces, 2010.
8. Borchers, J. A Pattern Approach to Interaction Design. John Wiley & Sons, ISBN 0471498289, 2001.
9. Christian Remy, Malte Weiss, Martina Ziefle and Jan Borchers. A Pattern Language for Interactive Tabletops in Collaborative Workspaces. In *Proc. EuroPLoP 2010*.
10. T. Hesselmann, S. Flöring and M. Schmitt. Stacked Half-Pie Menus – Navigating Nested Menus on Interactive Tabletops. In *Proc. ITS 2009*.
11. Bias, R.G. and Mayhew, D.J. Cost-justifying usability, Morgan Kaufmann, ISBN 0120958104, 1994
12. Alallah, F, Jin, D., Irani, P. OA-Graphs: Orientation Agnostic Graphs for Improving the Legibility of Charts on Horizontal Displays. In *Proc. ITS 2010*.
13. GestureWorks. Open Source Gesture Library. http://openexhibits.org/gesturelibrary. Date of access: 2011/02/07
14. Wobbrock, J. O., Ringel Morris, M., Wilson, A. D. User-Defined Gestures for Surface Computing. In *Proc. CHI 2009*, pp. 1083-1092.

End-User Development of Service-based Interactive Web Applications at the Presentation Layer

Tobias Nestler
SAP Research Center
Dresden, Germany
tobias.nestler@sap.com

Abdallah Namoun
Centre for Service Research
University of Manchester
abdallah.namoune@mbs.ac.uk

Alexander Schill
Computer Networks Group
Technische Universität
Dresden
alexander.schill@tu-dresden.de

ABSTRACT
Lightweight service composition approaches are gaining a fast momentum in the integration landscape, among which is the *integration/composition at the presentation layer* where software components are integrated using their frontends, rather than application logic or data. This paper presents a new approach for composing web services through their user interfaces (UI) to form composite web applications in a purely graphical manner without the necessity to write any programming code. Unlike existing approaches, our service composition approach is shaped by a set of iterative user based evaluations to ensure no modeling or programming skills are required for web application development. Indeed our approach is tailored towards non-programmers. This paper provides an in-depth description of the general concepts and fundamental principles of our UI-centric design time approach, a brief description of our prototype, namely the ServFace Builder which serves as a proof of concept, and evaluation results.

ACM Classification Keywords
D.2.2 Design Tools and Techniques: User interfaces

General Terms
Design, Human Factors, Languages

INTRODUCTION
In recent years, end users have demonstrated a keen interest in developing the web through different online software applications, such as wikis, and social-networking sites. Customizable web-portals, such as iGoogle, are also gaining popularity as they empower users to create personalized web pages containing information feeds and gadgets. Although easy to use, these portals do not support the creation of advanced web applications because software services and data resources cannot be combined with each other. Typical users of Web 2.0 technologies are usually ordinary end users with no significant computing knowledge or experience. Therefore it is imperative to design powerful development tools that suit their skills and characteristics to ensure user continuity in the development of the web.

Although the composition of services via business processes are covered by existing tools and solutions, concepts for lightweight service composition by end users are still in a preliminary phase. The development of UIs for web services is still carried out manually by software developers for every new service, which is an expensive and error-prone process. The developer has to define parameter bindings to input and output control fields, has to write the code to invoke the web service operation and has to handle UI events (e.g. list selection). Currently many of these steps cannot be performed automatically due to missing tool support. Since the development of UIs is a time consuming task, the reuse of software components including their UI is a promising approach to simplify the development of composite applications, especially for non-programmers [15]. The complexity of SOA technologies and standards prevents ordinary users to capitalize on the benefits of web services and their functionalities. However, in a recent study [9], including 64 participants, end users expressed high interest in the composition of services due to various reasons: tailorability to one's needs, saving time, ability to perform tasks more efficiently, reusability of components. Such findings motivate more user research to empower non-technical people to develop service-based web applications through appropriate tools.

Approach and Contributions. The challenge to service and HCI research lays in finding new methods to open up service composition to a larger population by supplying non-technical users with an intuitive service development environment. We faced this challenge in the EU-funded projects ServFace[1] and Omelette[2]. Over the last three years we have developed a WYSIWYG (What You See Is What You Get) composition approach to empower skilled web users to develop service-based web applications. Thereby, users define all design time

[1] http://www.servface.eu
[2] http://www.ict-omelette.eu/

aspects of a composite application via the direct manipulation of UI elements without writing any code. This includes the definition of data- and control flows as well as the application layout and UI design. During the composition process, each web service operation is visualized by a corresponding UI, called service frontend.

We followed an iterative user-centric design approach, which depends primarily on involving representative end users in the development of interactive products. Their skills, needs and feedback are taken into consideration throughout the whole design process. This is a clear distinction from other projects which usually involve end users at the very end. As the ServFace project has just ended (Oct 2010), we would like to summarize and share our key findings and report on the latest changes to the research community. Whilst our former publications focused on the technical realization of the composition approach in the form of the ServFace Builder tool (e.g. model-driven development methodology, runtime generation of ServFace annotations), this paper presents, for the first time, a complete overview of the underlying conceptual framework. Our contributions fall along these points:

- We define the fundamental principles including the central modeling elements of our UI-centric composition approach independently from a specific implementation or technical realization.
- We discuss the visualization and composition of service frontends in order to define data and control flows.
- We specify composition patterns that ensure the typical interaction behavior for all frontend composition constellation.
- We report on selected evaluation results of our user studies in the form of conceptual issues and service design recommendations.

RELATED WORK

Historically, composition on the web has mainly focused on the problem of web service composition, e. g., in terms of BPEL[3], the composition standard by OASIS. Service composition is still a complex, time consuming, and error prone process requiring strong modeling skills and a deep knowledge of existing standards (WS* protocol) and composition languages. The need for situational applications (i.e. applications solving some immediate business problems) to address individual and heterogeneous needs as well as the shift to more flexible and dynamic business environments motivate the idea of lightweight composition and mashups.

Commonly a *mashup* is defined as a web application that integrates data, application logic, and pieces of UIs [3]. The ad-hoc composition style leads to numerous mashup applications being developed, e.g., see ProgrammableWeb[4] (5198 Mashups; Sept'10). While the majority of mashups are still hand-coded, graphical *mashup platforms* aiming for a simplified web development for less skilled programmers emerged. The graphical composition style of platforms like Yahoo Pipes[5] constitutes a step towards a user centric design and end-user programming [6] of web applications. With these platforms, users can define relationships between modules by dragging and linking them together within a visual editor. However most platforms primarily focus on the aggregation of data sources rather than the creation of an application (views and control-flow are typically not considered). Except projects like Marmite [14] or Vegemite [7] most approaches still lack concepts to support end users [12, 16]. While simplified visual design metaphors and end-user friendliness are important criteria for a good mashup platform, most of the existing platforms can be seen as visual programming platforms still requiring computing skills and good understanding of programming concepts such as message passing. Tools like Serena Mashup Composer[6] or LiquidApps[7] claim to be platforms for mashup development but became more and more powerful development instruments for experienced developers and lost their benefit to non-programmers.

The traditional design of web applications covers various modeling levels (content, hypertext, presentation) and aspects (structure, behavior) [13]. Methods like *UML-based Web Engineering*[8] (UWE) or *Web Modeling Language* [9] (WebML) are considered as mature and sophisticated development instruments to create web applications using established modeling techniques (e.g., UML, Task Models) and process models (e.g., RUP). As these approaches (overview provided by [13]) focus on the professional developer, it is unlikely they can be used by ordinary web users. The high expressiveness and variety of different models and views to describe an application from diverse perspectives by different roles (separation of concerns) prevent users without any background in computer science to capitalize on the benefits. Therefore, our approach reduces this common muli-level perspective and restricts all modeling activities to the presentation level or completely hides them from the user.

The creation of composite applications from reusable parts has been a research subject over a long time, but it is traditionally restricted to the integration on lower application layers, namely the data and the application layer. Therefore, the need for similar concepts at the presentation layer has become evident. The concept of

[3] http://docs.oasis-open.org/wsbpel/2.0/OS/wsbpel-v2.0-OS.html

[4] http://www.programmableweb.com/

[5] http://pipes.yahoo.com

[6] http://www.serena.com/products/mashup-composer/

[7] http://www.liquidappsworld.com/index.php

[8] http://uwe.pst.ifi.lmu.de/

[9] http://www.webml.org/

integration at the presentation layer was introduced by Daniel et al. [3], who concluded that there are no real UI composition approaches readily available, neither in existing desktop UI component technologies (e.g. .NET CAB[10]) nor in common portal technologies (e.g. Java portlets [11]). Related to these findings is the work of Yu [15], which presented the first mature concept to overcome this gap. Our work assigns the concept of UI integration to the composition of web services.

The research projects MashArt and CRUISe build upon the fundamentals of UI integration and follow a philosophy centered around the idea of event-based UI components. MashArt focuses on a *hosted universal composition* and aims to devise models, languages, paradigms, and development instruments that abstract from low-level implementation details, and to compose components that are characterized by heterogeneous technologies, ranging from simple feeds to complex web services and UI components, within one development environment. The central idea of CRUISe is the extension of the service-oriented paradigm to the presentation layer to support a universal composition of context-aware applications. This is accomplished by providing reusable UI components in a distributed, service-oriented fashion, and their context-aware, dynamic invocation and integration with other mashup components. The three main differentiations of our work to both projects can be seen in (1) the clear restriction to the presentation layer, (2) the direct interaction with UI elements during the design time in order to define all composition tasks on the UI level and (3) the focus on non-programmers as our main target end user group (3). An in-depth comparison of our composition approach and the concepts of CRUISe and MashArt is reported in [11].

END-USER REQUIREMENTS

As our UI-centric composition approach focuses on end-users we have to distinguish between the user who creates the application - i.e. the application developer - and the user who consumes the produced application. Within the paper we refer to only the first user role (i.e. application developer). The success of our approach, which endeavors to support active web users in the development of simple service-based applications, is highly-reliant on the correct definition of user requirements. Eliciting such requirements alongside the proper knowledge of their perceptions and skills are key elements to developing easy to use and effective development environments. End users of our composition approach fit into any of the following descriptions:

- *Domain experts* who are familiar with the semantics of their individual application domains and understand the meaning of the provided service functionality.
- *Information workers* who are office workers trained to work with office software such as Microsoft Office Suite (e.g. non-technical business users).
- *Everyday web users* who have practical experience working with blogs, wikis or social-networking web sites. These users are usually self-motivated to develop the web and generate content (*digital natives*).

Target end users of the above three categories are non-programmers since their primary job functions do not involve application modeling, program code writing, or understanding of technical concepts such as service operation, parameters, data types, etc. In our user-centered approach we have developed several personas [2] and user stories [1] to firstly envisage these potential users alongside their characteristics and secondly describe the true interaction between these users and the platform we developed (i.e. ServFace Builder). Both methods facilitated communication amongst developers and guided the design of the lightweight composition platform according to user needs.

In all user studies we conducted over the last three years, we involved people whose characteristics match the above criteria. The first part of each user study included a pre-test questionnaire aiming to capture participants' background knowledge in regard to web technologies and web development experience. Key results about our users' profiles are summarized in table 1. For each question we indicate the ratio of answers (yes, no, no answer (n.a.)) in relation to the total number of people we interviewed. Most of the participants have already heard of the term web service. However, all of them provided very basic and vague definitions (e.g. online services consumed by users on the Internet) that do neither reflect the true complexity of technical web services nor their inner workings. Unsuprisingly, some participants have already worked with tools to create blogs or web pages. In case of building personal web pages participants mentioned the use of WYSIWYG-Editors like MS Frontpage (7x) or Adobe Dreamweaver (3x). Finally, terms like mashup or widget are unknown to most of the participants. Through this pre-test questionnaire we ensured that our selected participants are true representatives of actual web users. In summary, the participants had a rather weak mental model of web services and service composition, as well as a very limited technical expertise with web development.

Initial analysis of our target user group and their skills enabled us to identify several requirements for the composition of service frontends and their potential interaction with a prospective composition tool:

- Hide programming code and technical details from the users, i.e. end-users should not be expected to write any programming code owing to their non-IT background.
- Use abstraction layers, visual representations [5], and metaphors to facilitate and realize the WYSIWYG

[10] http://msdn.microsoft.com/en-us/library/aa480450.aspx
[11] http://jcp.org/aboutJava/communityprocess/final/jsr168/

Question	Yes (in %)	No (in %)	No answer (n.a) (in %)	Number of interviewees
Do you know what a web service is?	60	30	10	30
Do you know what a web applications is?	66	34	0	32
Have you ever used a tool to create a blog?	25	71	4	52
Have you ever used a tool to create a web site?	31	69	0	52
Have you ever worked with Microsoft Frontpage?	29	71	0	38
Have you ever used technical tools for programming applications?	39	58	3	38
Do you know what mashups are?	5	92	3	42
Do you know what widgets are?	17	83	0	24

Table 1. Users background knowledge about web development and its technologies

approach. This requirement is motivated by the fact that end-users are proactive about developing the web and accustomed to interacting with widgets such as those of iGoogle.

- Represent services using their UI to effectively communicate their purpose and functionality to the user.
- Concentrate on the most important aspects that require knowledge or input from the user when modeling the logic of the desired application [5]. Therefore, frequently used algorithms, tasks, or processes should be provided to the user in the form of templates and patterns, or automated by the system.
- Implement common UI guidelines (e.g. Apple Human Interface Guidelines) to produce service-based applications of high usability. This is important since our end-users are not user interface designers, thus guidance to design the final UI of their application is a necessity.
- Provide proactive system help and sufficient documentations to the users. Most end-users are novice application developers, thus it is expected that they would require sufficient support from the system to avoid mistakes but also in case they make mistakes.

CONCEPTUAL FRAMEWORK

This section describes the main principles and core components of our design-time composition approach: *Service Composition at the Presentation Layer.* It can be considered as a conceptual framework for end-user service composition. It will be presented independently from a specific implementation and can be technically realized in various ways.

Reduction to the UI Level

The UI builds the part of an application which most people are familiar with. Thus, all composition tasks within our approach are performed at the presentation level, which means that the user interacts with only these visual representations to model all relevant aspects of the application. The user, in his role as an application developer, creates the desired composite web application following the "'What You See Is What You Get"'- paradigm (WYSIWYG) known from web page builders like Adobe Dreamweaver. As a result the work with various abstraction layers for the data management or process modeling can be avoided and the application can be modeled and structured in a graphical manner without writing any code.

Service Frontend as the Central Component

Yu et al. [15] proposes the usage of reusable UI components that bundle functionality and application logic behind a UI (e.g., widgets or portlets). The availability of such components builds the foundation for a UI integration and promises to expedite the development process. The transfer of this idea to web services provides another concept for our composition approach. More precisely, each operation of a SOAP-based web service is regarded as a reusable part and is therefore supplemented with a corresponding UI component referred to as *Service Frontend.* A service frontend provides the functionality and business logic of the desired application and is the main component of the design time.

An Application as a Set of Pages

In general, the structure of a composite web application is defined as a set of pages connected through navigational links. A *Page* represents a dialog of the final application, which could be, for instance, the complete screen of a web application or a pop-up window. If a page represents a whole application screen it consists of two main areas, a navigation area and a frontend area. The former includes navigation links (e.g., button) to other pages while the latter serves as a container for the service frontends, which can be integrated and arranged within the frontend area. Thus, the overall application design and layout is defined by the integrated frontends and simple page customizations (e.g., change background color, add image, position navigation area).

Focus on Central Composition Tasks

To simplify the composition tasks and lower the entry barrier for the end user, we reduced the expressiveness of the composition process to the usage of the two mentioned basic elements (page and service frontend). To reduce the steps a user has to accomplish, each element offers only one corresponding linkage mechanism that defines a relationship to another element. A connection between pages is called *transition* and defines the page-flow and therewith the navigation path of the final application. This linkage principle follows the hyperlink concept of connecting web pages. Each transition manifests itself automatically as a navigation link within the navigation area. A connection between frontends is called *frontend relation* and specifies a data-flow in order to reuse data that has been entered by the user or data that is given in the form of a service call result.

Limitations of the Graphical Composition

To support non-technical people in the development of service-based web applications the major goals are to hide the technical complexity and focus user efforts on the important tasks of the composition process. Indeed, this reduction in expressiveness and complexity has an impact on the resulting applications. The goal of our approach is not to present an alternative way for professional web development with task models or sophisticated web modeling languages like WebML or UWE with various abstraction layers addressing different kinds of specialists. Instead we endeavour to provide a solution that encourages non-programmers to participate in the development of web applications without the necessity to learn programming or modeling languages, since they do not have the time or the knowledge. Furthermore, we concentrate on web services that require interaction with the user and therefore need a user interface. Even though simple workflows based on the page-flow can be supported with our approach, processes beyond the data or control flow including time constraints or other conditions as well as hidden service composition behind a composite UI cannot be realized. Finally, the user has to rely primarily only on the functionality offered by the available web services and is unable to add new business logic to his application.

Summary

The following list summarizes the fundamentals of the conceptual framework:

1. *Service Composition at the Presentation Layer* is a design-time approach for the development of lightweight composite web applications.
2. The target end users are non-programmers.
3. The approach applies the WYSIWYG paradigm to web service composition.
4. SOAP-based Web Services build the foundation of the composition and constitute the single source of business logic.
5. The basic elements of the composition approach are service frontends, pages, frontend relations, and transitions.
6. Each web service operation is represented via a corresponding UI – the *service frontend*.
7. A *frontend relation* is defined as a data-flow between UI elements of service frontends.
8. A *page* acts as a container of frontends and represents a dialog visible on the screen.
9. An application is defined as a set of pages.
10. A *transition* represents a relationship between pages.
11. The creation of code for executable applications is done in the background without any user involvement.

THE SERVICE FRONTENDS

The central component of our composition approach is called *service frontend*. A frontend visualizes a single operation of a SOAP web service via a form-based UI (see Fig. 1). Since most end users are familiar with form-based applications, the frontend can clearly communicate the structure and purpose of the underlying service operation to the user. Following our presentation-oriented composition approach the visualized frontend builds the only interface to the underlying technical web service for the user. It can be placed and arranged within a page to give the user even during design time an impression of how the service operation will appear in the final application.

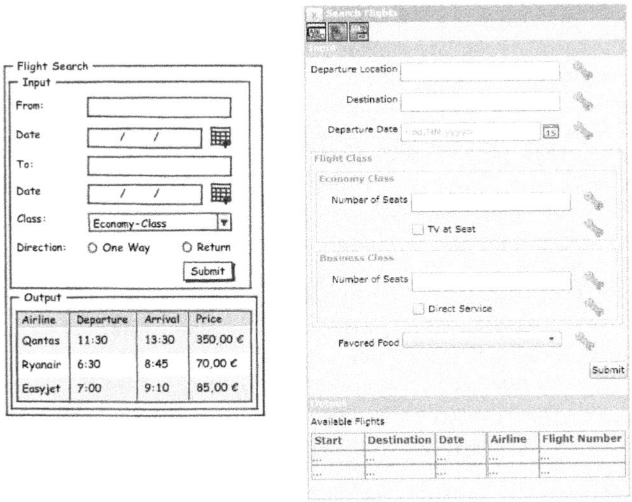

Figure 1. Concept and realization of a service frontend

Figure 1 depicts a service frontend containing an input and output part. The input part visualizes single UI-elements like text fields or combo boxes that are bound to the corresponding service operation parameters. They are required to be filled out in by the end user of the final application or automatically filled out in with data via a defined *frontend relation*. The *Submit* button belongs to the input part of a frontend and triggers the service call during runtime. Furthermore, the frontend presents the structure and data of the expected return value in the output part. Typically both parts are united within one service frontend, but can alternatively be separated on two pages. If a web service operation has no input parameter, the frontend will only contain the *Submit* button and the output part.

The visualization of a proper UI element within the input part prevents users from entering wrong input data and avoids service failures. The selection of the corresponding UI element depend on the class of the underlying parameter (e.g. input or output), the basic data type (according to the XML-Schema-Definition (XSD)), the data type configuration (e.g. enhancements, restrictions), and the cardinality (occurrence). In case the parameter is a simple data type, it can be represented by a UI element within the input section of a service frontend. Examples are the textbox for the String type, a calendar widget for the Date type or radio buttons for a Boolean data type. Complex data types need special consideration because they can be arbitrarily nested or can contain recursions. To ensure a presentation-oriented composition every simple child element of a complex type must be visualized by a corresponding UI element. A complex data type is presented by a table or a list as the standard output format. However, for complex types with a deeply nested structure the output can become more complex than a simple table and need to be visualized as special widgets.

DIMENSIONS OF THE FRONTEND COMPOSITION

The composition of service frontends constitutes the central step in the development of a composite application. The single frontends provide the basic logic and functionality of the underlying web service. A connection between these frontends specifies the transmission of data from a source- to a target-frontend and therewith a main part of the overall application logic. The following four dimensions specify all facets that have to be taken into account while composing frontends.

1. Frontend Relation. In order to define a relation between two frontends, the user has to indicate the source and the target UI-element of both involved frontends. Therewith, he specifies the data flow between the underlying service operations. The following three options are generally possible:

- **Input to Input:** An input field of the source frontend is connected with an input field of the target frontend (I $\rightarrow$ I). This connection leads to a synchronization of both input fields during runtime and avoids repetitive filling of fields by the end user of the created application. To ensure data consistency the strongest restriction of the connected data types applies for both input fields and might lead to an adaption of the UI element.
- **Output to Input:** An output field of the source frontend is connected with an input field of the target frontend (O $\rightarrow$ I). Therefore, results of a service call can directly be reused as input for the target frontend.
- **Input to Output:** A frontend can be separated into its input and output part and both parts can be placed on different pages (I $\rightarrow$ O). The connection between input and output is set automatically.

2. Type of Output. In case of an (O $\rightarrow$ I) relation, the type of the return value of the source service operation influences the way how it can be connected with another frontend:

- **Single:** The return value is a simple data type that can be displayed as a deactivated UI element or as plain text. A concrete connection of a source element that fills the input field of another frontend can be specified.
- **List:** The return value is a set of simple data types or one complex data type with simple child elements. These structures can be displayed as a list of disabled UI elements or plain text. Each of these source elements can be connected with a input field of another frontend to specify a data-flow.
- **Table:** A return value in form of a set of complex data types with simple child elements can be displayed as a table. Each column can be selected as the source that fills the input field of another frontend. Because of the multiple instances, the concrete value must be specified during runtime by the end user via selecting a table row.
- **Nested Table:** The return value is a nested complex data type or a set of complex data types. These structures are displayed in a nested form showing all instances including all dissolved simple types. Each UI element can be selected as source element that fills the input field of another frontend. Because of the multiple instances, the concrete value must be specified during runtime by the end user.

3. Frontend Distribution. Since an application is defined as a set of pages, there are two possible constellations of connected frontends:

- **Intra-Page:** The connected frontends are placed on the same page.
- **Inter-Page:** The connected frontends are distributed on different pages.

4. Frontend Dependency. Dependencies within a frontend relation occur depending on the number of involved frontends.

- **1:1:** The data is passed from one source frontend to one target frontend.
- **1:n:** The data of one source frontend is passed to several target frontends.
- **n:1:** The data of several source frontends are passed to one target frontend.

Figure 2 shows an example of a frontend relation. One service frontend can be used to search for available lights according to some filter criteria. As the output only provides basic data about each flight an additional service can be used to actually book one. He requires as one mandetory input parameter the flight number to accommblish the transaction. To establish a data flow between both services the user simply has to select one column of the table (e.g. Flight Number) and the source element in the second frontend (e.g. Flight Number as well). Thereby, he defines implicitly all dimensions of the frontend composition. In this case its clearly an $O \rightarrow I$ relation passing data from a table to a single UI element (Type of Output: Table). Both frontends (Frontend Dependency: 1:1) are placed on one page (Frontend Distribution: Intra-Page).

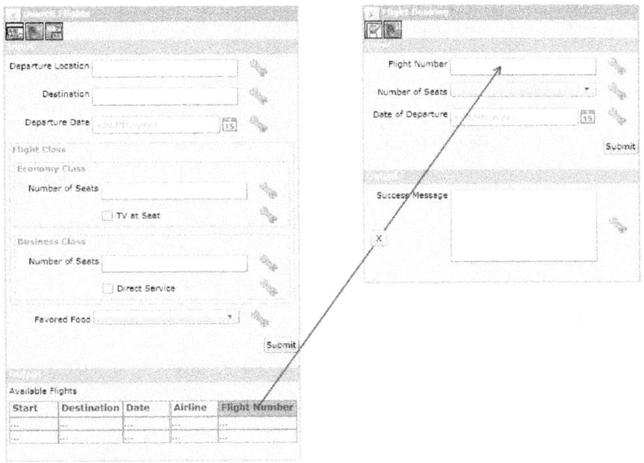

Figure 2. Example of a frontend relation

RUNTIME BEHAVIOR

Taking all dimensions into account, obviously several combinations for the composition of frontends are possible. Each combination describes the frontend composition only from a high level perspective without specifying the impact on the application structure and behavior during runtime. Indeed, this high level composition is required because the semantic relationship between frontends or pages depends on the desired purpose of the application and the actual content of a frontend or page. However, to cover the whole development process further technical aspects have to be considered. We summarize these aspects into three categories that cover the specification of events to trigger the data flows, transitions and the invocation of the underlying web service.

Each frontend relation specifies a data flow between fronteds. Therefore it has to be specified when the transmission from the source to the target frontend has to happen. We distinguish between three options that can trigger a data flow:

- **Synchronized:** Once the data is available at the source frontend it will be passed to the target frontend. In case of a $I \rightarrow I$ relation, the connection is bidirectional.
- **Click:** In case user has to select a specific instance (e.g. row click in a table) during runtime, this selection triggers the passing of data to the dedicated target frontend.
- **Transition:** The data will be passed to the target frontend after a page transition.

Page transitions define the navigation flow of various pages within the application. A transition can be triggered in various ways:

- **Navigation Button:** A button within the navigation menu triggers a page transition from the source page to the target page. It will be automatically created after a manual definition of transitions between pages or an "'Inter-Page"' frontend relation.
- **Condition:** In case a "'Single"' frontend output is from type Boolean, a condition can be attached to trigger a page transition based on the value (true or false).
- **Data flow:** The transition is triggered in coherence of a data flow. This is only valid for 1:1 relations.

As the service frontend is supposed to provide the actual functionality, the invocation of the underlying web service is required. A service can be invoked via three options:

- **Submit:** The invocation will be activated by pressing the "'Submit"' button.
- **Transition:** The service will be invoked after reaching the page where it is placed.
- **Auto-Trigger:** In case all input fields of a target frontend are filled by one source frontend, the invocation of the source frontend activates the invocation of the target frontend as well.

COMPOSITIONS PATTERNS

One of our requirements states that we want our end users to concentrate on the most important composition steps during the development process. In terms of frontend composition this means defining the general frontend relation by selecting source and target UI element, which implicitly specifies the previously described dimensions.

Due to this application context one of the presented runtime events has to be associated. The goal is to ensure a natural application behavior, which means that the final application behaves in a way an application consumer would expect it. As this task would require advanced modeling skills and understanding of interaction design, we combined dimensions and runtime events in predefined patterns that cover common composition constellations. Table 2 summarizes the identified composition patterns. A pattern consists of instances of each dimension and runtime events. If one category does not apply, we marked this with a "'n.a."'.

	Frontend Relation	Frontend Distribution	Frontend Dependency	Frontend Output	Trigger Dataflow	Trigger Transition	Service Invocation
1	I → I	Intra-Page	1:1, 1:n, n:1	n.a.	Synchronize	n.a.	Submit
2	I → I	Inter-Page	1:1, 1:n, n:1	n.a.	Transition	Navigation Button	n.a.
3	O → I	Intra-Page	1:1, 1:n, n:1	Single, List	Synchronize	n.a.	Submit
4	O → I	Intra-Page	1:1, 1:n, n:1	Table, Nested Table	Click	n.a.	Submit
5	O → I	Inter-Page	1:1, 1:n, n:1	Single, List	Transition	Navigation Button	Submit
6	O → I	Inter-Page	1:1, 1:n, n:1	Table, Nested Table	Click	Navigation Button	Submit
7	O → I	Inter-Page	n.a.	Single	n.a.	Condition	n.a.

Table 2. Composition Pattern

The patterns provide a framework for supporting end users during the composition process. The application of the pattern will reduce the single steps required to realize frontend connections and ensure the modeling of a typical interaction behavior and therewith lead to a better usability of the resulting application. However, this process is not fully automated. For specific constellations the user will be involved in the definition of the runtime behavior or is at least able to change the predefined setting. Therefore, the application of the pattern has to follow certain rules:

Trigger Data Flow: The options of this category will be set automatically without user involvement.

Trigger Transition: The options of this category will be set automatically without user involvement for pattern 1 to 6. Pattern 7 requires user input to define the condition. For pattern 5 to 6 the user is able to change the option "'Navigation Button"' to "'Data flow"'. Thereby, he defines that the transition to the target page will be executed immediately (Pattern 5) or after the selection of a concrete value (Pattern 6).

Service Invocation: The options of this category will be set automatically without user involvement. In case all input fields of a target frontend are filled by one source frontend, the option can be changed from "'Submit"' to "'Auto-Trigger"'. This leads to a more dynamic behavior of the application as every time the service of the source frontend is triggered, the data is passed to the target frontend and the underlying service will be invoked automatically. Since this option can be critical for non-read-only services, the user has to be involved in the decision.

To better illustrate the application of a pattern we consider a constellation of frontends, where a column of a table (output) is connected with the text field (input) of another frontend within one page (e.g., Fig. 2). Following the pattern that matches exactly this constellation ("'O → I"' frontend relation, Intra-Page, 1:1, "'Table"' output), the interaction behavior during runtime can be set automatically. In this case the pattern number 4 defines that the user of the created application has to click in a row of the table to trigger the data flow to the input field ("'Click"' data flow event). The data will be shown within the text input field and can be reused within the target frontend ("'Submit"' service invocation event).

THE SERVFACE BUILDER

The *ServFace Builder* (Fig. 3), our proof of concept, is a web-based authoring tool that aims to support non-programmers in the development of composite applications. It realizes the presented concept of *service composition at the presentation layer* and implements the composition of service frontends as described in the previous sections. As most of the tool's aspects have been already published, we will briefly describe the main features and point to the corresponding publications.

Essentially, the ServFace Builder follows a model-driven development approach. The underlying *Composite Application Model* (CAM) defines the application structure and describes the integrated services, the data flows as well as the navigation flow of the entire application. All aspects defined in the previous sections can be expressed in the CAM. Every user action (e.g., add frontend) is synchronized with the CAM instance to ensure a valid model representation of the application at any time of the design process. The model is used as serialization format and serves as the only input for the fully automated generation process of a deployable web application. The CAM is elaborated in [4].

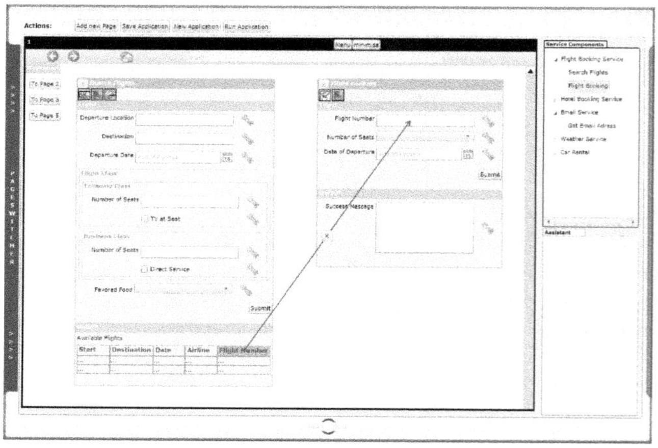

Figure 3. The ServFace Builder

Evaluation	No. of Participants	Type	Main Composition Problems
Study 1	15 non-IT university students with no modeling skills or programming experience	Contextual interview, formative evaluation	Weak understanding of web services and service composition, Difficulty understanding technical terms such as: service operations, parameters, data types, etc
Study 2	12 non-IT students with no modeling skills or programming experience	Contextual interview, formative evaluation	Difficulty getting started, Lack of guidance throughout the composition process, Weak understanding of data and control flow concepts
Study 3	12 non-IT staff and students with no modeling skills or programming experience	User testing, summative evaluation	Difficulty connecting service frontends and pages, Difficulty understanding the resulting connections, Difficulty differentiating between design time and runtime

Table 3. User based evaluations of the Service Composition at the Presentation Layer

The main area represents the current page in which the user can add service operations in the form of service frontends (Fig. 3). To visualize the service frontends during design time the tool infers the UI from the corresponding WSDL description of the underlying web service and generates UI elements for each service element that needs to be displayed within this service frontend. The frontend generation process is described in [10]. The visualized frontend can be modified by changing existing labels or hiding single UI elements.

The user can model data flow between frontends by simply selecting the UI element of the source frontend and UI element of the target frontend that should be filled in with data. The composition patterns define the corresponding interaction behavior automatically or ask the user in case more than one option is possible. Furthermore, the ServFace Builder contains an assistant tool which suggests suitable frontends for a data flow. Based on schema matching algorithms the tool analyses the WSDL part of the corresponding service operation and compares it with others in a repository. It is our aim to guide the user as much as possible.

The ServFace Builder provides a graph-like overview to specify page transitions. In addition, pre-defined navigation modes are offered. One example is the "'Guided Procedure"' mode, where pages can be connected only in a sequential order to create, for instance, a wizard-like application. Depending on the selected mode, the navigation area of the pages can change position and appearance. Furthermore, the creation of transition depends on the chosen mode of navigation. Considering again the "'Guided Procedure"' mode, it would not be possible to create alternative paths within a wizard.

USER-BASED EVALUATION

We adopted an iterative user-centred approach to design and evaluate the presented composition approach. Therefore two formative studies to shape the requirements for service composition at the presentation layer and one summative study to evaluate the approach were conducted. A succinct overview of the three user based evaluations and main composition problems are summarised in table 3. In between the three user studies, expert-based reviews were carried out to discover usability problems by comparing the ServFace Builder against a set of well-established usability guidelines. The results were used to continuously improve the ServFace Builder to achieve the user-centred design. It is worthwhile to note that this paper reports on mainly the findings related to the composition approach whilst more detailed analysis and findings focusing on the procedure, prototype and methodology are reported in [8].

The initial user study was conducted in order to explore users' mental models about services and service composition, and investigate their perspectives in regard to potential design issues that could arise from service composition. 15 participants viewed a set of low-fidelity prototypes demonstrating frontend composition and interacted with an early interactive prototype of the ServFace Builder. The evaluation took the form of contextual interviews, wherein the experimenter asks elaborating questions about the behavior whilst observing and listening to the user as she does her job. Participants demonstrated a high likeability towards the idea of building service-based applications that are tailored to their needs with the help of authoring tools. They argued that this will allow them to perform complex tasks more easily and rapidly. Participants recommended to include a clear guidance and tool-support through the development process. Other immediate recommendations from this study were to avoid technical terms like web services, functions or data flow and replace them with more general and user friendly terms.

A second formative evaluation was conducted using a fully functional ServFace Builder prototype and aimed to assess users' understanding of the main concepts, vocational time required to learn using the tool, and various usability aspects of the tool. In the explanatory part of the study the participants explored the tool without tasks but were allowed to ask clarifying questions. Most of the participants rated the tool as clearly structured and the functionality as self-explanatory. However, they encountered problems when they attempted to start the composition process. In the second part (i.e task-based part) the participants were instructed to build a simple travel-organizer application based on a given user scenario. Most participants stated that the design process of a multi-page application is straightforward and where able to handle the composition process quite well after a little time of familiarization, but they criticized the lack of guidance provided by the tool. Furthermore, only a few participants asked for the possibility to influence the order of the created pages or to define alternative flows and just added new pages and integrated service frontends in the linear order they had created the pages before. The immediate recommendation is to hide these aspects from users and automate them whenever possible.

In the third evaluation, a total of 12 university staff and students were instructed to build a student registration application using the latest version of the ServFace Builder that had all recommendations from user study one and two implemented. The usability testing started with a 10 minute training in which users viewed a comprehensive video tutorial elaborating various aspects of the tool and concepts of service composition using the frontends. Following this, users performed 12 development tasks ranging from adding frontends to the design space, customizing input and output parameters, adding pages to the application, and connecting service frontends and pages to specify the application logic using arrows. The main finding revealed that users had still some difficulty connecting frontends and pages and thereby understanding the resulting connections. As a consequence, we integrated system support which facilitates the creation of such connections. Users also highlighted the need to seamlessly switch between runtime and design time, which has been incorporated into the ServFace Builder too.

CONCLUSION

The paper presents the approach of service composition at the presentation layer for non-programmers. Thereby, service frontends are composed during design time in order to create composite web application in effective way and without writing programming code. The paper details the main elements and fundamental concepts to implement a WYSIWYG approach for service composition. It presents the ServFace Builder - a running implementation that realizes the discussed concepts - which constantly involved representative end users into its design fulfilling a truly user-centered approach.

Acknowledgment

This work is supported by the EU research projects ServFace and Omelette.

REFERENCES

1. D. Benyon, P. Turner, and S. Benyon. *Designing Interactive Systems: People, Activities, Contexts, Technologies.* Addison Wesley, 2005.
2. A. Cooper. *The Inmates Are Running the Asylum.* Macmillan Publishing Co., 1999.
3. F. Daniel, J. Yu, B. Benatallah, F. Casati, M. Matera, and R. Saint-Paul. Understanding UI Integration: A Survey of Problems, Technologies, and Opportunities. *IEEE Internet Computing*, 2007.
4. M. Feldmann, T. Nestler, U. Jugel, K. Muthmann, G. Huebsch, and A. Schill. Overview of an End User enabled Model-driven Development Approach for Interactive Applications based on Annotated Services. In *Proceedings of WEWST*, 2009.
5. A. J. Ko and B. A. Myers. Human Factors Affecting Dependability in End-User Programming. In *Proceedings of 1st Workshop on End-User Software Engineering*, 2005.
6. H. Liebermann, F. Paterno, M. Klann, and V. Wulf. *End-User Development.* Springer, 2006.
7. J. Lin, J. Wong, J. Nichols, A. Cypher, and T. A. Lau. End-User Programming of Mashups with Vegemite. In *Proceedings of IUI*, 2009.
8. A. Namoun, T. Nestler, and A. D. Angeli. Service Composition for Non-Programmers: Prospects, Problems, and Design Recommendations. In *Proceedings of ECOWS*, 2010.
9. A. Namoun, U. Wajid, and N. Mehandjiev. A Comparative Study: Service-based Application Development by Ordinary End Users and IT Professionals. In *Proc. of Service Wave*, 2010.
10. T. Nestler, L. Dannecker, and A. Pursche:. User-centric Composition of Service Front-ends at the Presentation Layer. In *Proceedings of ICSOC/ServiceWave Workshops*, 2009.
11. S. Pietschmann, T. Nestler, and F. Daniel. Application Composition at the Presentation Layer: Alternatives and Open Issues. In *Proceedings of iiWAS*, 2010.
12. A. Ro, L. S.-Y. Xia, H.-Y. Paik, and C. H. Chon. Bill Organiser Portal: A Case Study on End-User Composition. In *Proceedings of WISE*, 2008.
13. W. Schwinger and N. Koch. Modeling web applications. *Web Engineering: Systematic Development of Web Applications*, 2006.
14. J. Wong and J. I. Hong. Making Mashups with Marmite: Towards End-User Programming for the Web. In *Proceedings of CHI*, 2007.
15. J. Yu, B. Benatallah, R. Saint-Paul, F. Casati, F. Daniel, and M. Matera. A framework for rapid integration of presentation components. In *Proceedings of WWW*, 2007.
16. N. Zang and M. B. Rosson. Web-Active Users Working with Data. In *Proceedings of CHI*, 2009.

When the Functional Composition Drives the User Interfaces Composition: Process and Formalization

Cédric Joffroy, Benjamin Caramel, Anne–Marie Dery–Pinna, Michel Riveill
Laboratoire I3S (Université de Nice–Sophia Antipolis – CNRS)
Bâtiment Polytech'Sophia, Site des Templiers – 930 route des Colles – BP 145
F-06903 Sophia Antipolis Cedex, France
{joffroy,caramel,pinna,riveill}@i3s.unice.fr

ABSTRACT
The emergence of mashups made the reuse of applications easier by providing a simple solution to juxtapose applications. However, the resulting composite applications do not allow sharing data or create complex workflows. The only current way to do so is by composing applications at the functional level to create new services. Furthermore, user interfaces must be redesigned and regenerated in order to provide an interaction between user and this new service.

This paper proposes a solution to this problem. The implemented approach enables to reuse user interfaces while composing services. This composition relies on a process that first abstracts the applications to be composed and the functional composition. Then, it achieves to a composition at the abstract level regenerating a concrete user interface in a target language. Also, thanks to a mixed-initiative composition framework, the several identified composition conflicts are then solved, either automatically or by a developer.

Author Keywords
Functional composition, User interfaces composition, formalization, conflicts detection

ACM Classification Keywords
H.5.2 Information Interfaces and Presentation: User Interfaces; F.4.1 Mathematical Logic and Formal Languages: Mathematical Logic

General Terms
Algorithms, Theory

INTRODUCTION
The supply of Web services and off-the-shelf components has grown in recent years. The promising "Mashup effect" [10] opens the possibility of using many interactive services simultaneously. However, if the juxtaposition of interactive services is becoming easier, the creation of a new interactive service from two existing ones still remains difficult. Using Web services orchestration at the application's functional level provides a way to create a new Web service. In such a case, the user interface (UI) of the new service must be redesigned and regenerated.

In this paper, we introduce a process which attempts to compose n applications and obtain a new one. This composition is driven by functional composition. Taking advantage of the existing tools for functional composition (Web services orchestration, creation of composite components, etc.), our approach enables developers to reuse existing UIs from original applications and compose them. Such a composition remains consistent with the functional needs. In summary, the main advantages of our process are: (i) code reusing and process factoring and (ii) assistance to perform the UI composition. We provide a formalization to specify these aspects. Finally, in order to help developers in the composition process, we propose a framework which provides several tools that automate this process, detect conflicts (if any) and suggests several solutions if such conflicts cannot be automatically resolved. The framework provides a resulting user interface in a target language.

We demonstrate our approach with two Web services that allows to obtain information about (i) a health-insured person and (ii) an employee. These Web services are used in the following scenario: Sandra is a phone operator working in a hospital emergency ward. For each emergency call, she has to find as fast as possible, all personal and professional information concerning people calling for assistance. She uses two different Web applications from the same provider. But she often wonders: "Why does the developer never combine these two applications?"
Paul is concerned by this problem. He works as a developer in the company who develop both web applications. He clearly recognize the advantages offered by the composition of the two applications, especially in terms of code reusing and process factoring. The current applications being service-based, can be easily composed at the functional level. However Paul does not know how to compose the UIs accordingly, and sadly considers rewriting it entirely.

The remainder of this paper is organized as follows: first, we present approaches related to applications composition. Then, we introduce our contribution oriented to propose a new composition process. We also provide a formalization

EICS'11, June 13–16, 2011, Pisa, Italy.
Copyright 2011 ACM 978-1-4503-0670-6/11/06...$10.00.

for each part of this process. Next, we present some validation points and finally we present our conclusions and future work.

RELATED WORK

In this section we describe several approaches focused on applications composition. In the first part, we present some approaches dealing with compositions driven by UI composition. In the second part, we detail other approaches concerning compositions driven by functional composition.

Application composition that is driven by UI composition can be done by a developer as well as an end-user. Existing approaches used for this type of composition are: (i) the *Mashups*, (ii) the use of planning and (iii) the use of Web service annotations to generate associated UIs [7]. The approaches using *Mashups* enable end-users to create their own application by juxtaposing different applications in the same workspace. *iGoogle* or *Netvibes* propose such an approach. *Yahoo!Pipes* extends it and provides an environment to draw a *workflow*. This *workflow* aggregates information from multiple sources. Nevertheless, there are two major problems: UIs remains independent and users do not have any control on the UI produced by the *workflow* description.

The approaches using planning enable end-users to directly describe their need in a natural language [5]. User needs are transformed into tasks, which are then transformed into a planning problem. An inverse transformation (planning to task to UI) is then used to produce the final result. In this kind of approach, the user obtains multiple results and has to choose which ones satisfy the best her need. A weak point of this approach is the independency of functional elements which are not composed.

Another approach is to use Web service annotations: Nestler *et al.* [11] and Feldmann *et al.* [4]. Nestler *et al.* enable users (either developers or end-users) to graphically compose UI elements which are produced according to the annotations. Feldmann *et al.* work at the tasks level. The system tasks correspond to the operations of Web services and the interactive tasks are those derived from annotations. Thus, the composition is described through the use of system tasks. Also, UI elements can be removed by using a union operator as defined in `ComposiXML` [8]. However, they do not propose to reuse existing applications, only Web services and they do not allow to express interactor merging.

Unlike those approaches driven by the UI composition, our approach enables to determine the required interactors in a composite application. As a result, consistency is preserved during the functional composition. We do not have to realize a specific development to use our approach, we only need to respect a separation of concerns.

Next to the application composition driven by UI composition, there are also two approaches that are driven by the functional composition. The first one proposes to integrate UIs inside `SOA` by considering UIs as services [14]. UIs can then take advantage of all the properties of services: publication, discovery, composition. It is necessary to follow a development methodology to create the UIs: the authors add information about the UI *workflow* (based on sequence diagram), the UI category, the data profile and the interactors profile. The composition uses an application model similar to an activity diagram with UI compositions points in addition to application functionalities. Such composition points determine the place to insert UIs. However, compositions done at the UI level do not enable the merging of UI elements; any advantages given by the orchestration of Web services are thus lost.

The second one uses aspect oriented programming to compose volatile functionalities [6]. The goal of this approach is to always keep the main functionality and weave temporary functionalities. However, the result (at the UI level) only corresponds to additions of UI elements within the main UI without any merging possibilities. This composition is also dedicated to a specific technology (here `jsp`) and requires the specification of an `xslt` file describing the composition.

The composition approaches previously described use the functional composition to drive the composition of the UIs. However, compositions performed at the UI level only propose to aggregate UIs without merging elements. These approaches require a particular development for the UIs and for specifying `xslt` transformations. Finally, they do not use all the possibilities offered by the functional composition.

COMPOSITION PROCESS AND FORMALIZATION

The composition process is a sequential process divided into four steps: (1) abstraction of the applications to compose, (2) abstraction of the functional composition, (3) composition of the UIs at the abstract level, and (4) transformation of the resulting abstract interfaces into concrete interfaces. Figure 1 illustrates these steps which are detailed in the following subsections.

Step 1: Abstraction of applications to compose

The applications to compose can be developed in different languages, each one of them includes technological constraints at different levels (interaction, message protocol...). Hence, in order to reuse and compose these applications, two issues must first be answered: (i) the heterogeneity between the applications descriptions and (ii) the technological constraints related to the application descriptions. In order to get a homogeneous language-independent description of each application, we propose to work on an abstract description (see definition 1).

The abstract description focuses on UI elements that are directly linked to the functional core. In fact, we extract from the existing applications three kinds of information: (i) the description of the functional part, (ii) the description of the UIs and (iii) the description of the interaction between the functional part and the UIs (data exchange and events). Architectural patterns like MVC [13], PAC [3] or Arch [1] promote this separation. In the case of Web application, UI and interactions are coupled.

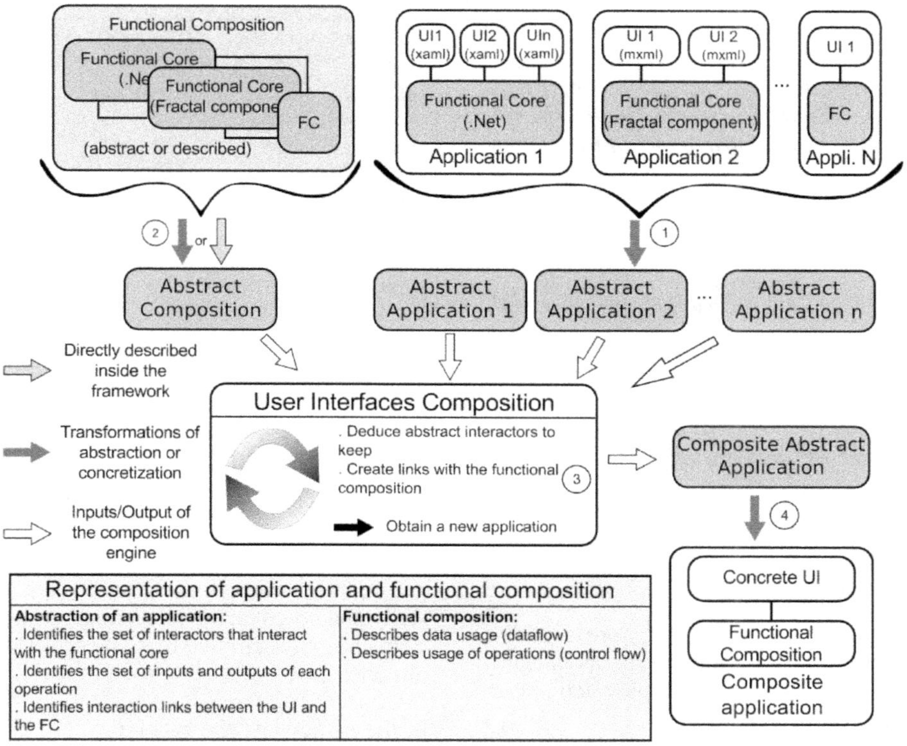

Figure 1. Overview of the applications composition process

In our approach, we describe the functional part and the user interface by using components. Such components are different from components described in Fractal [12] or SCA [9]. In fact, the description that we propose is more precise than others. We not only want to recognize the interface as a prototype of operation, but also we want to distinguish data from events and within data input from output. This gives the possibility to keep the relation between the UI and the parameters of the functional part.

DEFINITION 1 (ABSTRACTAPPLICATION). *An abstract application (appli) is defined by:*

- *id, an unique identifier of an application used inside a composition,*
- *cfc, the functional core component (FC component) of the application. It corresponds to the functional part of the application and it is an abstraction of a functional component or a Web service. It is denoted $cfc(appli)$ (see definition 2),*
- *$caui$, the UI component associated to the functional core. It corresponds to the graphical part of the application and it is an abstraction of the final user interface. Is is denoted $caui(appli)$ (see definition 3),*
- *Links correspond to interaction between the functional core component and the UI component that describe data exchange and trigger of events :*
  - *$DataLinkII$, links between two inputs that bind a graphical element of the $caui$ allowing the user to type information with an input of the cfc,*
  - *$DataLinkOO$, links between two outputs that bind an output of the cfc with a graphical element of the $caui$ displaying a result of the cfc,*
  - *$EventLink$, links between a graphical element of the $caui$ emiting an event triggering an action of the cfc.*

As hypotheses of the case study related to the scenario aforementioned, we consider that the functional part is described as a Web service (SOAP/WSDL) and the UIs/interactions are developed in Flex (MXML and Action Script).

Abstraction of the functional part

The functional part is represented by a FC component (see definition 2) having two kinds of ports: (i) data ports describing input parameters of an operation together with resulting parameters and (ii) action ports describing operations within the functional part (linked to data ports).

DEFINITION 2 (COMPONENTFC). *A FC component $cfc = cfc(appli)$ is defined by:*

- *a unique id identifying the FC component*
- *a set of action. The set of action is given by the function $action(cfc)$. Each action is defined by:*
  - *a unique id (obtained by $id(action)$),*

- *a* $name$ *corresponding to the operation's name (obtained by* $name(action)$*),*
- *a set of* $inputs$ *(obtained by* $inputs(action)$*) and* $outputs$ *(obtained by* $outputs(action)$*) corresponding to the input and output parameters of the operation.*

- *two functions giving the inputs and outputs of the FC component:*

$$input(cfc) = \left\{ \begin{array}{l} i \mid i \in inputs(action), \\ \forall action \in action(cfc) \end{array} \right\} \quad (1)$$

$$output(cfc) = \left\{ \begin{array}{l} o \mid o \in outputs(action), \\ \forall action \in action(cfc) \end{array} \right\} \quad (2)$$

Inputs and outputs have the same characteristics:

- a unique id (obtained by $id(in)$ or $id(out)$),
- a $name$ (obtained by $name(in)$ or $name(out)$) corresponding to the parameter name,
- a $type$ (obtained by $type(in)$ or $type(out)$) provided by the Web service description (a primitive type as integer, float, string, etc. or a complex type previously defined in the Web service description),
- an $arity$ (obtained by $arity(in)$ or $arity(out)$) provided by the data schema associated to the Web service description.

Each element described in the data schema can have two characteristics: *minOccurs* and *maxOccurs*. *minOccurs* specifies whether the element is optional or not and can take two values: 0 (optional) or 1 (required). *maxOccurs* specifies whether the element corresponds to a list or not and can take two values: 1 (a unique value) or $unbounded$ (a list of value). These two characteristics are grouped in a single one, $arity$, which is a couple of values. Possible couples are: $[0,1], [0,n], [1,1], [1,n]$.

A FC component may be a composite component. In such a case it is connected to subcomponents via links and respects some properties described in 5 on top of the previous ones.

In order to illustrate such abstraction on our scenario, we first need to get the WSDL interface and the XSD schema from the Web service. Listings 1 and 2 show extracts of these data.

```
<message name="getBusinessInfo">
  <part name="parameters"
        element="tns:getBusinessInfo"/>
</message>
<message name="getBusinessInfoResponse">
  <part name="parameters"
        element="tns:getBusinessInfoResponse"/>
</message>
...
<operation name="getBusinessInfo">
  <input message="tns:getBusinessInfo"></input>
  <output message="tns:getBusinessInfoResponse"></output>
</operation>
```

Listing 1. Extract of the Web service interface (wsdl)

```
<xs:element name="getAddresses" type="tns:getAddresses"/>
<xs:element name="getAddressesResponse"
            type="tns:getAddressesResponse"/>
<xs:complexType name="getAddresses">
  <xs:sequence>
    <xs:element name="fullName" type="xs:string"
                minOccurs="0" />
  </xs:sequence>
</xs:complexType>

<xs:complexType name="getAddressesResponse">
  <xs:sequence>
    <xs:element name="return" type="xs:string"
                nillable="true"
                minOccurs="0" maxOccurs="unbounded" />
  </xs:sequence>
</xs:complexType>
```

Listing 2. Extract of the data schema (xsd)

Then we only keep the operation prototypes provided by the Web service. Operation prototypes are the only useful data in our composition process. For each operation we want to get input parameters and resulting parameters. In our case study and based on the formalization, we get one action port: `getAddresses`, one input port: `fullName` and one output port: `return`.

In the same way, the second Web service dealing with the personal information of the callers is abstracted. It provides the operation `getByCard` with one input port `cardID` and three output ports: `personalAddress`, `contractNumber` and `fullName`.

Abstraction of the user interface

The abstraction of the UI considers just the interactors which are connected to the functional part. The resulting Abstract User Interface (AUI) is represented by a UI component (see definition 3) similar to the FC component and corresponds to an AUI as defined in the Cameleon Reference Framework [2]. The abstraction aims at extracting and categorizing the interactors into three types: input (if connected to an input parameter), output (if connected to an output parameter) and event (if triggering an operation call). The abstract interactors are represented by AUI ports: inputs and outputs are represented by data ports, and events by event ports.

DEFINITION 3 (COMPONENTAUI). *A UI component* $caui = caui(appli)$ *is defined by:*

- *a unique* id *identifying the component*
- *a set of event. The set of event is given by the function* $event(caui)$*. Each event is defined by:*
  - *a unique id (obtained by* $id(event)$*),*
  - *a* $name$ *corresponding to the operation's event name (obtained by* $name(event)$*)*
  - *a set of* $inputs$ *(obtained by* $inputs(event)$*) and* $outputs$ *(obtained by* $outputs(event)$*) corresponding to the input and output parameters of this event.*

- *two functions giving the inputs and outputs of the UI component:*

$$input(caui) = \left\{ \begin{array}{l} i \mid i \in inputs(event), \\ \forall event \in event(caui) \end{array} \right\} \quad (3)$$

$$output(caui) = \left\{ \begin{array}{l} o \mid o \in outputs(event), \\ \forall event \in event(caui) \end{array} \right\} \quad (4)$$

Inputs and outputs associated to an $event$ are different from those associated to a FC component. An $input$ (respectively an $output$) is characterized by:

- a unique id obtained by $id(in)$ (respectively $id(out)$),
- a $name$ obtained by $name(in)$ (respectively $name(out)$) corresponding to the associated label which names the interactor,
- a $uitype$ obtained by $uitype(in)$ (respectively $uitype(out)$). It is a subset of primitive types which can be found in the functional core. Possible values are: $number$, $string$, $date$ or $boolean$. They correspond to the main types available in an interactor.
- an $arity$ obtained by $arity(in)$ (respectively $arity(out)$). The $arity$ specifies whether the entered (respectively displayed) value is single or multiple. $arity$ can be equal to 1 or n. $arity = 1$ means that the described interactor takes (respectively displays) only one value. $arity = n$ means that the described interactor takes (respectively displays) a set of values.
- (For inputs with $arity = n$ only) a $selection$ item (obtained by $selection(in)$) associated to an interactor containing a set of value. The $selection$ item describes the type of selection the interactor can provide. Possible values are: $none$, $single$ or $multiple$.

This information is obtained by abstraction of the user interface. For example, a set of checkboxes corresponds to a $uitype$ equals to $string$, an $arity$ equals to n and a $selection$ equals to $multiple$. In the same way, this information influences the transformation to the concrete user interface.

Figure 2 illustrates the UI associated to the operation *getAddresses*. From the abstraction of this UI we get one input "`FullName`", one output "`Address`" and one event "`getAddresses`".

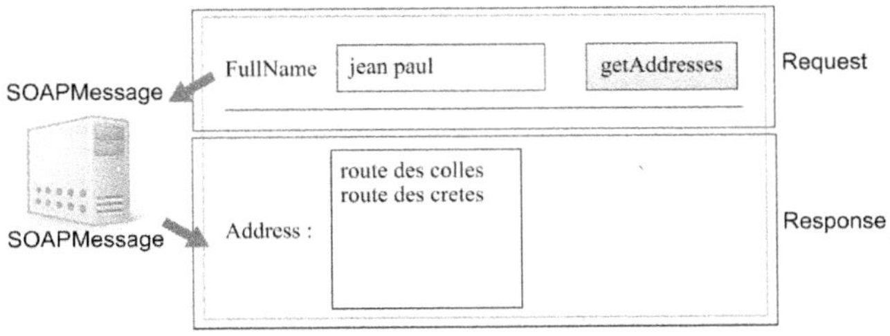

Figure 2. User interface associated to the *getAddresses* operation

Abstraction of the interaction between the functional part and the user interface

Three functions (see definition 4) define interaction links. These links describe data exchange and events sent by a UI component ($caui$) to trigger an action of the FC component (cfc).

DEFINITION 4 (INTERACTION LINKS). *The links are defined as:*

- $DataLinkII : CAUI \times CFC \rightarrow input(caui) \times input(cfc)$
  $DatalinkII(caui, cfc) = \{(i1, i2)) \mid i1$ *is the data input representation of the data input* $i2\}$
- $DataLinkOO : CAUI \times CFC \rightarrow output(caui) \times output(cfc)$
  $DatalinkOO(caui, cfc) = \{(o1, o2)) \mid o2$ *is represented by* $o1\}$
- $EventLink : CAUI \times CFC \rightarrow (event(caui) \times action(cfc)$
  $Eventlink(caui, cfc) = \{(ev, act)) \mid ev$ *triggers* $act\}$

Due to these links, the function $cfc(appli)$ has the following properties:

$$input(cfc(appli)) = \left\{ i \mid \begin{array}{l} \exists i1 \in input(caui(appli)) \wedge \\ (i1, i) \in DataLinkII(\\ caui(appli), cfc(appli)) \end{array} \right\} \quad (5)$$

$$output(cfc(appli)) = \left\{ o \mid \begin{array}{l} \exists o1 \in output(caui(appli)) \wedge \\ (o, o1) \in DataLinkOO(\\ cfc(appli), caui(appli)) \end{array} \right\} \quad (6)$$

$$action(cfc(appli)) = \left\{ a \mid \begin{array}{l} \exists e \in event(caui(appli)) \wedge \\ (e, a) \in EventLink(\\ caui(appli), cfc(appli)) \end{array} \right\} \quad (7)$$

From the interaction part of the fig. 2, we obtain two data links and one event link.

Step 2: Abstraction of the functional composition description

The functional composition provides information about the data that will be asked to the user and the data that will be provided to the user. More precisely, the functional composition describes the use of data through the dataflow (which specifies data exchanges) and the use of operations through the control flow (which specifies operations' execution). Hence it is possible to deduce what AUI ports will be required in the resulting composite application. Moreover, the abstraction of the functional composition results in a representation similar to the one describing the functional parts of an application (step1, definition 2). This leads to an homogeneous environment allowing composition.

The functional composition corresponds to the description of either a services orchestration or a components assembly. It is described by the function $ComposeFC$ given by the definition 5. Based on a set of applications, a functional composition results in a new composite functional component, links binding its subcomponents together and links binding the composite component to its subcomponents. There are two kinds of links: data links describe the dataflow and action links describe the control flow.

DEFINITION 5 (COMPOSEFC). *The functional composition is defined by the function :*

$$ComposeFC : APPLI^{+} \rightarrow CFC \quad (8)$$
$$composeFc(\cup_{i=0}^{n} appli_i) = cfc \quad (9)$$

- $APPLI^{+}$ *: the set of of application involved in the functional composition and more specifically the* $cfc(appli_i)$ *corresponding to the FC component of the application i,*
- cfc *: the composite component obtained by the function of composition* $ComposeFC(APPLI^{+})$*. This component is given by the function* $composeFC(\cup_{i=1}^{n} appli_i)$.

A side effect of this function of composition is the creation of links between subcomponents that describe data exchange between an output and an input and control flow linking two actions (see definition 6).

DEFINITION 6 (LINKS BETWEEN SUBCOMPONENTS). $SCALink$ *describes links between two subcomponent actions and*
$SCDLinkOI$ *describes links between one subcomponent output and one subcomponent input.*

- $SCALink : CFC \times CFC \rightarrow ACTION \times ACTION \mid \exists cfc_1, \exists cfc_2 \in \cup_{i=1}^{n} cfc(appli_i) \wedge SCALink(cfc_1, cfc_2) = \{(action_1, action_2) \mid action_1 \in action(cfc_1) \wedge action_2 \in action(cfc_2)\}$ *describes action links corresponding to the control flow between two subcomponent actions (*$action_1$ *and* $action_2$*),*
- $SCDLinkOI : CFC \times CFC \rightarrow OUT \times IN \mid \exists cfc_1, \exists cfc_2 \in \cup_{i=1}^{n} cfc(appli_i) \wedge SCDLinkOI(cfc_1, cfc_2) = \{(o_1, i_1) \mid o_1 \in output(cfc_1) \wedge i_1 \in input(cfc_2)\}$ *describes that an output parameter* o_1 *from a FC component* cfc_1 *is an input parameter* i_1 *of another FC component* cfc_2.

We also define links that bind port of the composite component cfc to its subcomponents (see definition 7). These links are present in the definition of an FC component and are described by: three distinct links: $TOSCALink$, $TOSCDLinkII$ and $TOSCDLinkOO$.

DEFINITION 7 (FC COMPONENT LINKS). *The following functions defines the links that bind ports of the composite component* cfc *to its subcomponents. Here,* cfc *corresponds to the composite component which is the result of the function of FC composition* $ComposeFC$*. According to definition 5,* $cfc = composeFC(\cup_{i=1}^{n} appli_i)$

- $TOSCALink : CFC \times CFC \rightarrow ACTION \times ACTION \mid cfc_2 \in \cup_{i=1}^{n} cfc(appli_i) \wedge TOSCALink(cfc, cfc_2) = \{(action_1, action_2) \mid action_1 \in action(cfc) \wedge action_2 \in action(cfc_2)\}$
- $TOSCDLinkII : CFC \times CFC \rightarrow INPUT \times INPUT \mid cfc_2 \in \cup_{i=1}^{n} cfc(appli_i) \wedge TOSCDLinkII(cfc, cfc_2) = \{(input_1, input_2) \mid input_1 \in input(cfc) \wedge input_2 \in input(cfc_2)\}$
- $TOSCDLinkOO : CFC \times CFC \rightarrow OUTPUT \times OUTPUT \mid cfc_1 \in \cup_{i=1}^{n} cfc(appli_i) \wedge TOSCDLinkOO(cfc_1, cfc) = \{(output_1, output_2) \mid output_1 \in output(cfc_1) \wedge output_2 \in output(cfc)\}$

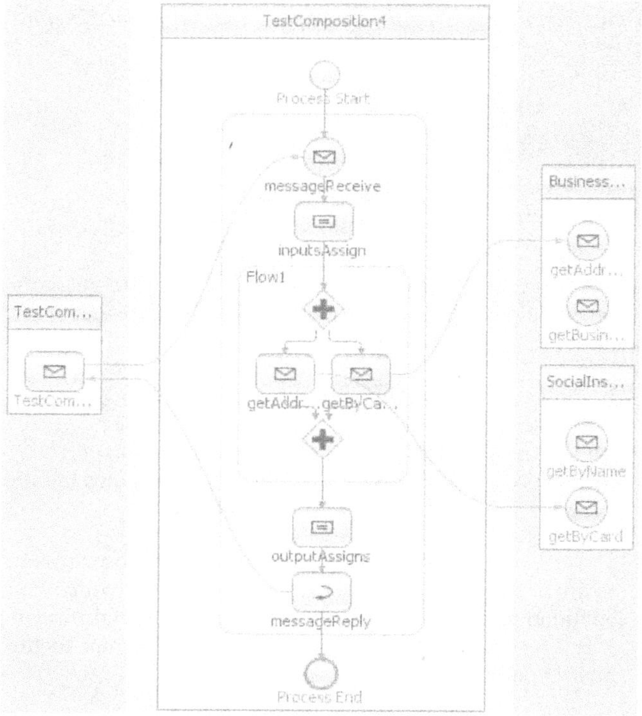

Figure 3. Functional composition workflow of the two Web services used in the scenario

In the scenario, Paul defines a functional composition that uses two operations from the different applications. This composition aims at merging professional and personal addresses to obtain a single list of addresses: Paul creates a workflow calling the two operations in parallel. Figure 3 illustrates this workflow.

Next, he specifies that he needs two parameters in input of the composite component to call the two operations. He thus keeps input parameters of both operations. As a consequence, a cardID and a fullName must be provided (Figure 4). Finally, he merges the addresses returned by both operations to get a single output (Figure 5).

The resulting abstraction of the functional composition is one action: `getAllAddresses`, with two inputs: `fullName` and `cardID` and one output `Addresses`. There are also four data links: two links binding the input parameters of the composite component's operation to the input parameters of the subcomponents' operations and two others to merge the output parameters in one output. Moreover, two event links are created to bind the functional composition operation to the two subcomponents' operations.

Step 3: Composition of the existing user interfaces

Based on the abstract descriptions of both the applications and the functional composition, we can now compose the existing interfaces. Function to compose (see definition 8) UIs requires input: one functional composition and a set of abstract applications. Some extra optional information can

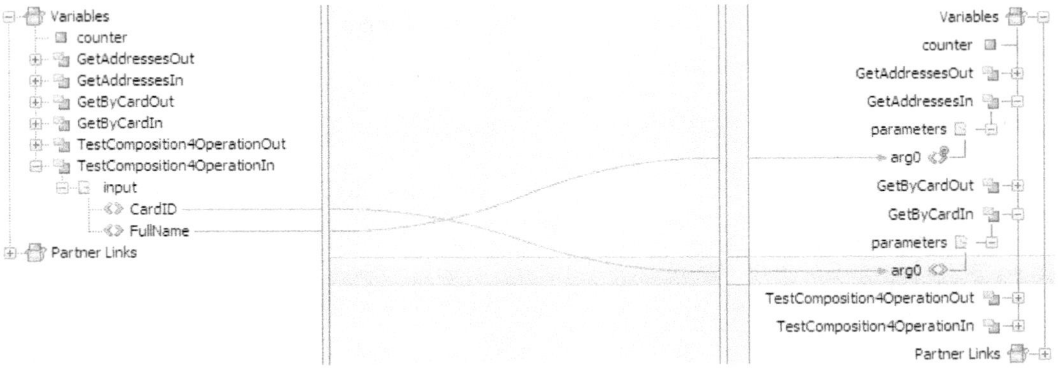

Figure 4. Inputs assignment for the two operations (using NetBeans IDE)

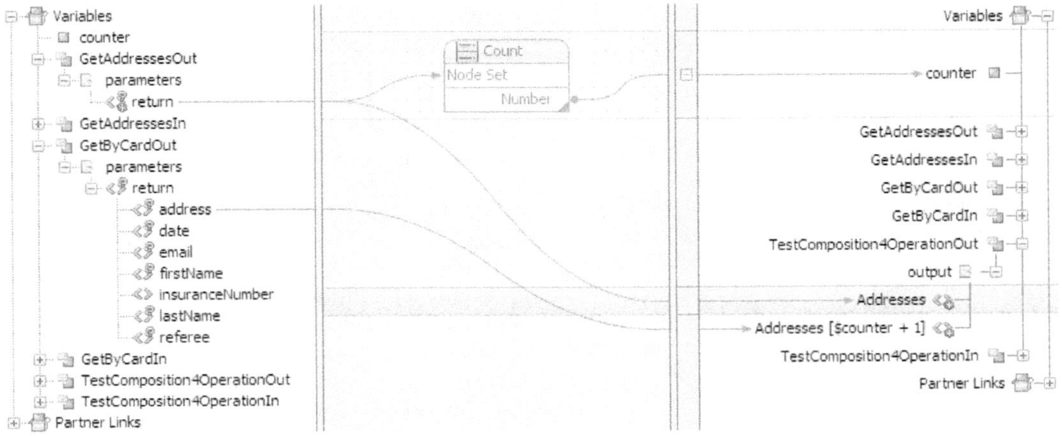

Figure 5. Merge of outputs of the two operations (using NetBeans IDE)

be added to automatically resolve conflicts. This function is divided into four steps:

1. AUI ports identification. For each port of the composite FC component, we determine associated AUI ports and link them to the port.

2. Detection of conflics. For each merging point (when an input of the composite FC component is shared between multiple inputs of the composite FC component's subcomponents or multiple outputs of the subcomponents are merged to obtain a single one), we check whether ports are identical or not.

3. Conflicts resolution. The developer manually choose one possibility among: (i) selecting one port from n different AUI ports, (ii) keeping every AUI ports or (iii) creating a new AUI port (by reusing information from conflicting AUI ports or directly by filling new information).

4. Finalization of the composition and creation of all the required UI components and links between the resulting UI components and the composite FC component.

DEFINITION 8 (COMPOSEUI). *The UI composition is given by the following function:*

$$ComposeUI : APPLI^{+} \times ComposeFC \rightarrow APPLI \quad (10)$$

$$composeUI\left(\begin{array}{c} \cup_{i=1}^{n} appli_i, \\ composeFC(\cup_{i=1}^{n} appli_i) \end{array}\right) = appli_{composed} \quad (11)$$

with in input:

- $composeFC(\cup_{i=1}^{n} appli_i)$ *is the functional composition which triggers the UI composition (see definition 5),*

- $\cup_{i=1}^{n} appli_i$ *is the set of applications involved in the functional composition (see definition 1). These applications are necessary to deduce AUI ports to keep.*

Step a: Determine AUI ports

In this step, the goal is to determine the AUI ports that must be present inside the resulting UI component at the end of the composition process (see definition 9). These ports are determined by using the functional composition cfc (result of the function $composeFC(\cup_{i=1}^{n} appli_i)$) and all the applications involved in the UI composition. From this and from definitions 4 and 7, all the inputs, outputs and actions of the composite FC component must be associated to the resulting UI component.

DEFINITION 9 (PORTS OF THE RESULTING UI). *The following functions concern ports of the UI component which is the result of the function of UI composition. We call here* $caui$ *the UI component obtained by the function* $caui(appli_{composed})$ *and* cfc *the composite FC component which is the result of the function* $cfc(appli_{composed})$. *Function* $copy\_of$ *creates a copy the selected element.*

$$input(caui) = \left\{ \begin{array}{l} i = copy\_of(i_3) \mid \forall i_1 \in input(cfc), \exists i_2 \\ \mid (i_1, i_2) \in TOSCDLinkII(cfc, cfc_1) \wedge \\ (i_3, i_2) \in DataLinkII(caui_1, cfc_1) \\ \Rightarrow DataLinkII(caui, cfc) = \\ DataLinkII(caui, cfc) \cup \{(i, i_1)\} \end{array} \right\} \quad (12)$$

$$output(caui) = \left\{ \begin{array}{l} o = copy\_of(o_3) \mid \forall o_1 \in output(cfc), \exists o_2 \\ \mid (o_2, o_1) \in TOSCDLinkOO(cfc_1, cfc) \wedge \\ (o_3, o_2) \in DataLinkOO(caui_1, cfc_1) \\ \Rightarrow DataLinkOO(caui, cfc) \\ = DataLinkOO(caui, cfc) \cup \{(o, o_1)\} \end{array} \right\} \quad (13)$$

$$event(caui) = \left\{ \begin{array}{l} e = copy\_of(e_3) \mid \forall a_1 \in action(cfc), \exists a_2 \\ \mid (a_1, a_2) \in TOSCALink(cfc, cfc_1) \wedge \\ (e_1, a_2) \in EventLink(caui_1, cfc_1) \\ \Rightarrow EventLink(caui, cfc) = \\ EventLink(caui, cfc) \cup \{(e, a_1)\} \end{array} \right\} \quad (14)$$

In the example, Paul uses the composition tool we developed to compose the applications. This tool provides him six interactors. Two interactors to provide the cardID and the fullName. Two other ones for the same functional composition output to display addresses. Finally, two interactors to trigger the call of the operation provided by the functional composition.

Step b: Detect conflicts

We can detect four kinds of conflicts: (i) conflict of name when the label associated is different (*e.g.* address and addresses), (ii) conflict of type when two different types are associated (*e.g.* string and number), (iii) conflict of arity (*e.g.* one with an arity equals to 1, another equals to n) and finally (iv) conflict of selection (*e.g.* two different selections: single and multiple).

Definition 10 formalizes equality between two inputs (resp. outputs and events).

DEFINITION 10 (EQUALITY OF AUI PORTS). *The equality between AUI ports is defined by:*

$$in_1 = in_2 \Rightarrow \left\{ \begin{array}{rcl} name(in_1) & = & name(in_2) \wedge \\ uitype(in_1) & = & uitype(in_2) \wedge \\ arity(in_1) & = & arity(in_2) \wedge \\ selection(in_1) & = & selection(in_2) \end{array} \right. \quad (15)$$

$$out_1 = out_2 \Rightarrow \left\{ \begin{array}{rcl} name(out_1) & = & name(out_2) \wedge \\ uitype(out_1) & = & uitype(out_2) \wedge \\ arity(out_1) & = & arity(out_2) \end{array} \right. \quad (16)$$

$$evt_1 = evt_2 \Rightarrow name(evt_1) = name(evt_2) \quad (17)$$

Definition 11 describes what is a conflict and the constraints associated to it.

DEFINITION 11 (CONFLICT). *AUI ports are in conflict when at least two AUI ports are not equal (see definition 10). We call* cfc *the composite FC component and* $caui$ *the UI component which is the result of the UI composition.*

- $in_{cfc} \in input(cfc), ConflictIn(caui, in_{cfc}) = \{in \mid (in, in_{cfc}) \in DataLinkII(caui, cfc)\} \Rightarrow card(ConflictIn(caui, in_{cfc})) \geq 2$
- $out_{cfc} \in output(cfc), ConflictOut(caui, out_{cfc}) = \{out \mid (out, out_{cfc}) \in DataLinkOO(caui, cfc)\} \Rightarrow card(ConflictOut(caui, out_{cfc})) \geq 2$
- $a \in action(cfc), ConflictEvent(caui, a) = \{evt \mid (evt, a) \in EventLink(caui, cfc)\} \Rightarrow card(ConflictEvent(caui, a)) \geq 2$

In the example, two conflicts are detected. The first one concerns AUI output ports. Two different AUI ports are able to display addresses, but one displays only one value whereas the other one can display multiple values: this is a conflict of arity. Furthermore, the displayed names are different ("*address*" for one "*addresses*" for the other): this is a conflict of name on the same AUI ports. The second conflict concerns AUI event ports that trigger the call of the composite FC component's action: the AUI ports' names are different (conflict of name): "*getAddresses*" and "*getByCard*".

We also provide the functionality to automatically remove conflicts on inconsistent AUI elements. It is only applied on the arity conflict. Inconsistent elements can appear when outputs with different arities are merged or when the port of the functional composition does not have the same arity than the connected ports of subcomponents. For example, if two ports with an arity $[0, 1]$ are merged and connected to a port with an arity $[0, n]$ or if two ports with different arities ($[0, 1]$ and $[0, n]$) are merged and connected to a port of the functional composition with arity $[0, n]$. The arity conflict can also occur when an input value is shared between different ports of subcomponents and their arity changes. For example, when, in the functional composition, it is only possible to set a single value (and not a set of values) and one of the connected port accepts to take a set of values. In this case, the corresponding AUI element must be checked to verify its adequacy. We use the table 1 to remove the AUI elements being not consistent with the functional composition.

	Arity of the functional port	Arity of the AUI ports
Input port	1	1 or n (if $selection = single$)
	n	1 or n
Output port	1	1 or n
	n	n

Table 1. Consistency table matching functional ports arities with AUI ports ones depending on the port's type

After applying the auto-remove operation, we obtain a new list of conflicts. In the example, one of the elements cannot display multiple values and the return parameter has an arity equals to n: the composition engine removes the conflicting element. At the end of this step, the developer has only one conflict to resolve.

Step c: Resolve conflicts

In this step, conflicts are resolved by the developer through the composition tool's front-end. Conflicts and possible solutions are displayed as illustrated in Figure 6, where Paul creates a new AUI port with the name *obtainAddresses*.

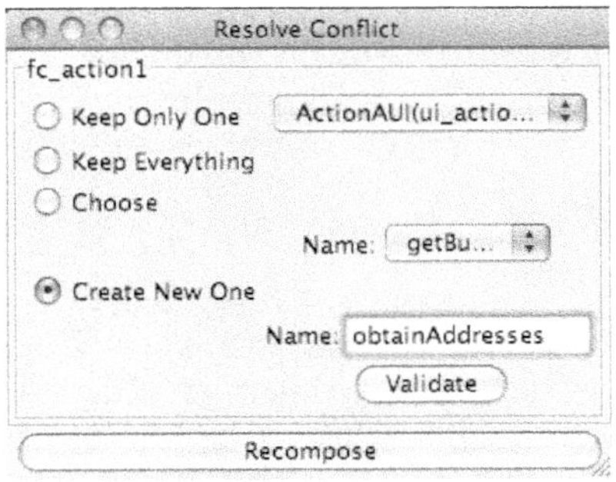

Figure 6. Solutions proposed to the developer to resolve the conflict (composition tool)

Creation of a new AUI ports removes all previous selected AUI ports associated to a port of the composite FC component. "Keep only one" functionality removes all other selected AUI ports.

Once all conflicts resolved, the creation of the composite application is finalized.

Step d: Finalize application creation

Based on the determined AUI ports and on information provided by the developer, it is possible to create the new application according to the following rule: a user interface is created for each action of the composite FC component. The final result is a set of new AUI components containing AUI ports from the original UI components or AUI ports created by the developer.

Step 4: Transformation into concrete user interface

This step offers a visual rendering of the resulting UIs. This visualization helps developers to check the composition and to know if it matches with their expectations. The abstract description of the UI is refined into a concrete UI in a target language such as MXML or Xaml. The result can be enhanced by the developer afterwards. Figure 7 displays a preview of the resulting UI in the case of our scenario. One can notice that the interface provides all the elements required for the interaction with the functional composition done by Paul.

VALIDATION

This section presents the composition tool and the evaluation realized to validate the composition process. The evaluation focuses on the conflict detection and the solutions to conflicts provided by the tool.

Composition tool

In order to validate our approach we developed a composition tool composed of an engine and a front-end. The engine

Figure 7. Preview of the resulting user interface (composition tool)

is developed in Prolog which provides several features such as unification and back-tracking. It realizes the composition process based on elements presented in the "Composition process and formalization" section. The front-end is developed in Java and is interfaced with the engine by using the JPL API [1] based on Swi-Prolog. It allows users to interact with the engine. The composition tool performs the whole composition process including conflicts detection and conflicts resolution. It takes as inputs the abstract descriptions of the applications and the functional composition.

Evaluation

We performed user tests to (i) confirm our four-steps process and (ii) check the relevance of both the detected conflicts and proposed solutions. Five expert developers used this tool individually to compose the applications presented in the aforementioned scenario, which was enhanced by other functional compositions. Following sections present the experiment and its results.

Experiment

The evaluation experiment followed three steps:

1. Users realized the composition on paper prototypes. Hence, they detected conflicts and provided a solution for each of them. They obtained a visual representation of the resulting composite application.
2. Users realized the same composition with our composition tool. Hence, they followed our composition process implemented in the tool and used its conflict detection and resolution functionalities.
3. A satisfaction sheet was given to the users. It included a 5-point Likert scale to assess the validity of the UI composition, the conflict detection reliability, the conflict resolution possibilities and the final result. A debriefing were then done to enable the users to express their opinion and to clarify the reasons of their choices.

Results

The results show that the final assembly (see Figure 8) corresponds to the users' expectations and to their prototype. Additionally, in this use case, one conflict is solved automatically. Users noticed that the automatic conflict resolution had reduced the number of conflicts they had to resolve. Conflict detection and resolution obtained good marks in the

[1]JPL: `http://www.swi-prolog.org/packages/jpl/prolog_api/overview.html`

satisfaction sheet. The results of the sheet also highlight the user assessment of our composition process, even if the debriefings with the users showed that usability flaws impacted their choice: one user scored 3/5, three users 4/5 , the last one 5/5.

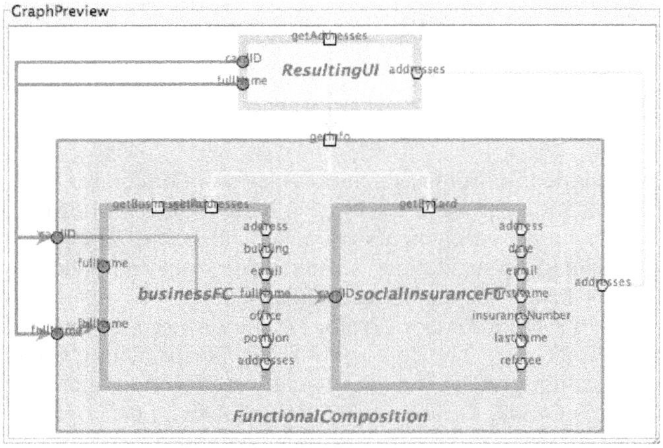

Figure 8. Resulting application assembly (composition tool)

CONCLUSION

This paper presented a composition process that reuses existing applications and takes advantage of functional compositions to achieve a full applications composition. The process starts by an abstraction of both the applications and the functional composition in order to provide a homogeneous environment for composition. The composition is then realized, mixing automatic composition with developer initiatives in order to resolve detected conflicts. Eventually, the resulting composite abstract user interfaces are transformed into concrete user interfaces taking advantage of the initial functional composition.

Based on this process, we developed a composition framework that helps developers to perform the composition, solve the conflicts that occur during the composition process, and display a preview of the resulting UIs. User tests assess the validity of the presented process, and also show lacks of usability in the composition tool. We now plan to reduce these lacks and enhance the concretization of the resulting UIs.

REFERENCES

1. L. J. Bass and J. Coutaz. A metamodel for the runtime architecture of an interactive system: the UIMS tool developers workshop. *SIGCHI Bull.*, 24(1):32–37, Jan. 1992.

2. G. Calvary, J. Coutaz, D. Thevenin, Q. Limbourg, L. Bouillon, and J. Vanderdonckt. A Unifying Reference Framework for multi-target user interfaces. *Interacting with Computers*, 15(3):289–308, June 2003.

3. J. Coutaz. PAC: an Object Oriented Model for Implementing User Interfaces. *SIGCHI Bull.*, 19(2):37–41, Oct. 1987.

4. M. Feldmann, G. Hubsch, T. Springer, and A. Schill. Improving task-driven software development approaches for creating service-based interactive applications by using annotated web services. In *Proceedings of the 2009 Fifth International Conference on Next Generation Web Services Practices*, NWESP'09, pages 94–97, Washington, DC, USA, 2009. IEEE Computer Society.

5. Y. Gabillon, G. Calvary, and H. Fiorino. Composing interactive systems by planning. In *Proceedings of the 4th French-speaking conference on Mobility and ubiquity computing*, UbiMob '08, pages 37–40, New York, NY, USA, May 2008. ACM.

6. J. Ginzburg, G. Rossi, M. Urbieta, and D. Distante. Transparent interface composition in web applications. In *Proceedings of the 7th international conference on Web engineering*, ICWE'07, pages 152–166, Berlin, Heidelberg, July 2007. Springer-Verlag.

7. P. Izquierdo, J. Janeiro, G. Hübsch, T. Springer, and A. Schill. An annotation tool for enhancing the user interface generation process for services. In *Proceedings of the 19th International Crimean Conference, Microwave & Telecommunication Technology*, CriMiCo 2009, pages 372–374, Sevastopol, Ukraine, Sept. 2009. IEEE.

8. S. Lepreux, A. Hariri, J. Rouillard, D. Tabary, J.-C. Tarby, and C. Kolski. Towards multimodal user interfaces composition based on UsiXML and MBD principles. In *Proceedings of the 12th international conference on Human-computer interaction: intelligent multimodal interaction environments*, HCI'07, pages 134–143, Beijing, China, July 2007. Springer-Verlag.

9. J. Marino and M. Rowley. *Understanding SCA (Service Component Architecture)*. Addison-Wesley Professional, 2009.

10. D. Merrill. Mashups: The new breed of Web app—An introduction to mashups. Technical report, IBM, Aug. 2006. `http://www.ibm.com/developerworks/xml/library/x-mashups.html`.

11. T. Nestler, M. Feldmann, A. Preuÿner, and A. Schill. Service Composition at the Presentation Layer using Web Service Annotations. In *First International Workshop on Lightweight Integration on the Web*, ComposableWeb'09, pages 63–68, June 2009.

12. Objectweb Consortium. The Fractal Component Model. `http://fractal.objectweb.org/`, 2008.

13. T. M. H. Reenskaug. MVC XEROX PARC 1978–1979. `http://heim.ifi.uio.no/~trygver/themes/mvc/mvc-index.html`, 1979.

14. W.-T. Tsai, Q. Huang, J. Elston, and Y. Chen. Service-oriented user interface modeling and composition. In *Proceedings of the IEEE International Conference on e-Business Engineering*, ICEBE '08, pages 21–28, Washington, DC, USA, Oct. 2008. IEEE Computer Society.

A Design Pattern Mining Method for Interaction Design

Claudia Iacob
University of Milan
Via Comelico, 39/41
Milan, Italy
iacob@dico.unimi.it

ABSTRACT

This paper reports on a design pattern mining method addressing pattern mining in interaction design. The method aims at identifying proven solutions to recurring design problems through design workshops and software application analysis. During a design workshop, a team of 3-5 designers is asked to design the GUI and the interaction process for an application in the domain of the mining process and the design issues they address are collected. Moreover, a set of software applications in the area of the mining process is analyzed in order to identify in what measure the design issues discussed during the workshops are considered in the implementation of existing applications. Candidates for being documented as design patterns are the most recurring design issues in both the workshops and the software analysis. The paper describes the method together with its application in mining for design patterns for the design of synchronous collaborative systems.

Author Keywords

Design patterns, design workshops, interaction design.

ACM Classification Keywords

D.2.10. Design: Methodologies.

General Terms

Design.

INTRODUCTION

The concept of design pattern was first introduced in the '70s by Alexander [2], who proposed a pattern language – defined as a collection of design patterns together with all the relationships existing between them - for architectural design. Later on, the concept was adopted in domains such as software engineering [11] and HCI [6, 23, 25]. In [14], a survey of 21 HCI pattern languages published between 1996 and 2007 shows that these collections target web user interface design, interactive exhibits, user interface related programming, hypermedia applications, or ubiquitous computing. Moreover, in the past few years, several collections of patterns have been proposed for the design of social interfaces [8], groupware technology [15], and cross-culture collaboration [20].

Often, design patterns are identified by experts in the field of application of the patterns [10] and the process these experts follow is seldom described. However, literature documents two types of methods for design pattern mining: a). inductive methods which start by observing the specifics of a context and move towards generalizations, and b). deductive methods which start from generalizations and move towards identifying the specifics of a context [4, 26].

Inductive methods include ad-hoc discussions among experts, structural analysis and play testing in fields such as game design, multi-disciplinary descriptions and validations [26], and systematic pattern development cycles targeting the design of e-learning systems. Such a cycle is proposed in [18], where a 4-phase pattern development process based on the reverse engineering of e-learning systems which embed good designs is described.

Deductive methods include drawing mind maps, describing metaphors, experts' experience, discussions held during the PLoP workshops, shepherding [26], open calls for patterns [21], and using ontologies as formal specifications of shared semantics [19]. Each of these methods is suited for specific domains of use; nonetheless, often times both inductive and deductive methods are used during pattern mining processes [19].

The aim of this work is to describe a structured method based on which design patterns for interaction design can be identified. The core idea of the method is inspired by the definition of a design pattern ("a proven solution to a recurring design problem" [6]) and consists in running a series of workshops during which teams of designers are asked to design the Graphical User Interface (GUI) and the interaction process of an application in the domain targeted by the pattern mining process.

The design process of each team follows a set of steps and uses several creative techniques such as scenario-based design [7], free associations, sketching, and mockup creation. Each team is observed by a facilitator and the designers are encouraged to externalize the design ideas, problems, concerns, solutions they might find useful, and any issue relevant to the design of the application. These

EICS'11, June 13–16, 2011, Pisa, Italy.

design issues form the basis of the pattern identification process. The most recurring design issues throughout the workshops point to potential candidates for design patterns in the field of the application under design.

To support the results of the workshops, a set of software applications in the area of the mining process are analyzed in order to identify in what measure the design issues discussed during the workshops are considered in the implementation of existing applications. Of interest to this work are the applications which support synchronous collaboration. The method was applied in mining for such patterns and 8 of the patterns identified are briefly described by the paper.

DESIGN WORKSHOPS FOR PATTERN MINING

A design workshop provides a team of 3-5 designers (the participants) with a set of problems. These problems are chosen from the area of interest for the design pattern mining process. For example, for identifying design patterns in the design of systems to support synchronous collaboration, the problems would address areas of synchronous collaboration such as collaborative sketching or collaborative text editing. Participants are asked to design the GUI and the interaction process for an application to tackle one of the problems proposed.

A design workshop brings together the team of designers and a facilitator. The role of the facilitator is to: a). describe the problems to the participants, b). walk the participants through each phase of the workshop, c). take notes of the participants' conversations and d). observe the participants throughout the workshop and support them if needed. Each workshop lasts for approximately 2 hours and has 3 phases, adapted from the definition of a creative process as proposed by Wallas [24].

During the first phase - the preparation phase - participants are encouraged to choose one problem from the set and to define as many scenarios as they can consider for software solutions (applications) to tackle the problem. In defining a scenario, they would consider answering the questions: a). who are the users?, b). what are they allowed to do through the application?, c). how could they achieve their goals using the application?, d). what is their motivation for using the application?, and e). when and where could the application be used?.

The second phase - the incubation phase - asks participants to choose another problem from the list and to find similarities and differences between the two problems (the one chosen during the first phase and the one chosen during the second phase). The purpose of this exercise is to identify commonalities and major differences between applications addressing different domains. Similarities would indicate the possibility of abstracting design details related to the two domains, while differences would suggest that similar design problems would require different design solutions for the two domains compared.

Lastly, during the illumination phase, participants are asked to design the GUI and the interaction process of the application related to the problem they initially chose during the first phase. For that, they are strongly encouraged to sketch their ideas, express all the design problems they encounter and, possibly, create a mock up of their overall design.

A PATTERN MINING METHOD FOR INTERACTION DESIGN

A first step in the design pattern mining process is running a set of design workshops as described in section 2. Throughout the design processes followed during the workshops, participants are encouraged to externalize any design problem, solution, or decision they consider relevant to their design process. In addition to that, the facilitator takes notes of their conversations. This leads to a list of design issues, a design issue being defined as any idea (problem, decision, solution, consequence, secondary effect) containing relevant information or concepts about the design of the application considered.

After each of the workshops conducted, all the design issues provided by the participants are collected. This sequence of steps (i.e. running a workshop and collecting the design issues discussed by the participants) is repeated until a fairly large number of different design issues are collected. A low number of such design issues (less than 150) would not constitute a large enough pool of data for the mining process.

Further on, for each of the design issues collected, its degree of recurrence (DoR) is computed as:

$$\mathrm{DoR(di)} = \frac{numberOfOccurrences(di)}{numberOfWorkshops} * 100$$

, where *numberOfOccurrences* represents the number of workshops during which the design issue *di* has been discussed and *numberOfWorkshops* is the total number of workshops conducted. The list of design issues is sorted based on the computed DoRs.

In order to support the design pattern mining, a set of existing software applications in the area of the mining process are analyzed. The analysis consists in walking through a scenario for each application and in collecting the design issues - relevant to the interaction affordances provided - considered in the application's implementation. The scenario should cover all the features provided by the application and should be tailored to each application in particular. For identifying the features provided, design documentation and/or requirements specification is used. Scenarios are written independently of the design workshops.

The goal of the software application analysis is identifying in what measure the design issues discussed during the workshops are considered in the implementation of existing applications. Moreover, the list of issues could be extended in the event that the analysis brings to light design issues not addressed throughout the workshops.

For each of the design issues, its degree of recurrence is computed with respect to the software analysis as:

$$\text{DoR(di)} = \frac{numberOfOccurrences(di)}{numberOfApplications} * 100$$

, where *numberOfOccurrences* represents the number of applications in whose implementations the design issue *di* was considered and *numberOfApplications* is the total number of applications analyzed.

Candidates for being documented as design patterns are those design issues with a higher DoR with respect to both the workshops' results and the software analysis.

THE METHOD APPLIED

The method has been applied for identifying design patterns for the design of software applications for synchronous collaboration. 13 teams participated in design workshops which addressed 5 problems subject to synchronous collaboration: drawing, text editing, database querying, puzzle solving, and crosswords solving.

The problem of collaborative drawing asked for the design of a software application which would allow the collaboratively creation of one diagrammatic representation. The problem of collaborative text editing required participants to design an application which would allow a group of users to create a summary of a written text in a synchronous collaborative fashion. The requirements for the collaborative querying application asked that several users would be able to create one query on a database containing information about movies. Lastly, the common requirement for both the puzzle solving and the crossword solving problems was that more users solve one game in the same time.

The total number of participants was 50, out of which 80% were male, and 20% female. 19 participants (38%) were Master students in a "Multimedia databases" class, so they were divided in five teams and worked on the collaborative database querying problem. 17 of the participants (34%) were Master students in a "Human Computer Interaction" class. They worked in 4 teams, each team working on one of the following problems: drawing, puzzle solving, text editing, and crosswords solving. 10 participants (20%) were undergraduate students in a course on "Technologies for Collaboration". They were divided into 3 teams, and they worked on the following problems: drawing, puzzle solving, and crosswords solving. Lastly, 4 of the participants (8%) were professional designers. They worked as a team in designing an application for collaborative drawing.

22% of the participants worked on the problem of collaborative drawing, 38% of the participants worked on the problem of collaborative database querying, and 8% of the participants chose the problem of collaborative text editing. Moreover, two teams comprising 14% of the participants worked on the problem of collaborative puzzle solving and two other teams (18% of the participants) chose the problem of collaborative crosswords solving.

The set of software applications analyzed included: one application for synchronous drawing [16], two applications for collaborative searching [3, 22], two applications for synchronous text editing [1, 12], and two collaborative games [5, 13].

Results

The design issues discussed by the teams were collected after each workshop. A list of these issues was created, and the DoR of each issue was computed.

Table 1 presents the design issues with the highest DoR, i.e. the mostly discussed issues throughout the workshops.

Design issue	DoR
Who is the coordinator in a real-time collaboration? How do collaborators coordinate themselves?	100
Support collaborators' communication; integrate instant messaging features in the application	76.92
Adapt application to several devices; make sure collaborators using different devices can work together in real time	69.23
Design the application for the web; web-based collaboration	69.23
Provide each user with the possibility of performing the activity supported by the application in a private area, individually	53.84
Support collaborators in providing feedback, comments, annotations, rankings	46.15
Visualize what the others are doing in real time	46.15
Allow each user to choose his/her collaborators	46.15
Support competition among various teams collaborating	38.46

Table 1 – List of the most recurring design issues during the conducted workshops

The analysis of the applications identified the top design issues described in Table 2.

Design issue	DoR
Who is the coordinator in a real-time collaboration? How do collaborators coordinate themselves?	85.71
Support the visualization of the history of the collaboration through log files and/or timelines	71.42
Support the tracking of each collaborator's individual contribution	71.42
Support collaborators' communication; integrate instant messaging features in the application	57.14
Visualize what others are doing in real time	57.14
Adapt application to several devices; make sure collaborators using different devices can work together in real time	42.85
Support collaborators in providing feedback, comments, annotations, rankings	42.85
Design the application for the web; web-based collaboration	42.85

Table 2 – List of the most considered design issues in the applications considered

As expected, most of the issues in the two tables are common. However, the software analysis points out two issues not addressed during the workshops, nonetheless relevant to the design process. The first one addresses the possibility of saving the history of the collaborative process, and the second one indicates allowing the tracking of each collaborator's individual contribution.

Identified Patterns

The design issues with a higher DoR were considered candidates for being documented as design patterns. Different authors proposed different templates for defining design patterns. These templates generally include the name of the design pattern, the description of the problem it addresses together with the forces (i.e. the consequences and secondary implications of the problem) that influence this problem, some examples of situations in which this problem can be met and a possible solution to tackle the problem [9]. The process of writing a design pattern starts with an identified recurring design issue and describes its implications, proven solutions and characteristics according to a pattern definition template [17].

This subsection briefly describes a subset of the design patterns identified in terms of the problem they address and the solution(s) proposed for the problem.

Who is the coordinator?

Problem. If more users work on the same resource in the same time, there needs to exist a coordination mechanism which: a). allows all collaborators to take part in the collaborations and b). maintains the resource in a consistent state at all times. The problem is how to determine who coordinates the collaborative process or what is the suited coordination mechanism for each concrete case.

Solution. Identify the context of the application and address the coordination issue according to the following considerations:

- ❖ If the application addresses a well formed community with unwritten rules, then link the application to the community and to the way the community as a whole coordinates itself.
- ❖ If the context requires one user to initiate the collaboration, then that user might be the coordinator of the whole process.
- ❖ Locking is a solution for coordination in cases in which time is not necessary an issue and where the common resource supports this operation.
- ❖ Timers support coordination by allowing each participant to the process to gain control of the resource for a limited time.
- ❖ Having separate blocks for each collaborator may also be a solution in cases in which the overall activity does not require to conform to some standards of definition.

Integrated chat

Problem. Collaborators should be able to exchange messages related to their collaboration, share knowledge based on each individual's expertise, and clarify any additional misunderstandings.

Solution. Integrate an instant messaging feature in the design of the application.

Eyes wide open

Problem. Each collaborator must be able to visualize what the others are contributing to the process at any time. In addition to that, each contribution should be made visible to all the collaborators in real-time in order to allow participants' coordination.

Solution. Update any changes on the commonly shared resource and notify (in real-time) all collaborators of these updates. The choice of notifications highly depends on the context of the application.

Choose your collaborators

Problem. Users should be provided with the option of getting together and collaborating with their own peers.

Solution. Allow each user to choose his/her collaborators as follows:

- Provide a list with all the users currently available.
- Allow a user to search for his/her peers in the list of available users.
- Allow users to invite each other to collaborate by creating a group.
- Allow each user to join a group already created after s/he logs in to the application.

Collaboration, always social

Problem. Collaboration is, more than anything else, a social process. Hence, supporting collaborators through social features can only enhance and improve their collaborative process.

Solution. Integrate mechanisms of tagging, ranking, annotating, and commenting in the application.

My contribution

Problem. Users should have available a straightforward and user friendly way to track their own contribution to the collaboration.

Solution. Support each collaborator in tracking down his/her contribution to the collaboration, as follows:

- For the cases where the shared resource is textual and where the group of collaborators is relatively small, assign a different color to each collaborator's contribution.
- The applications for which the shared resource is an image one's contribution may be highlighted by representing only those shapes added by a particular user.
- Show tooltips containing information on the author of that particular part when a user drags the mouse over parts of the shared resource.

Track history of collaboration

Problem. Synchronous collaborative processes are being held in real-time, so it could be the case that a lot of the information on the dynamics of the collaborative group and on the knowledge exchanged is lost.

Solution. Track the history of the collaboration and make it available either through repositories, log files or timelines.

With or without collaboration

Problem. Users might need, at times, to sketch their ideas before adding them to the area visible to all collaborators. Also, users might need to try out solutions without interfering with the others' actions or without blocking the collaborative process.

Solution. Provide users with an additional private area, not available to the other collaborators. Inside this area, each collaborator has total control and s/he is provided with tools specific to the context of the application.

CONCLUSION

The paper describes a design pattern mining method to be used in pattern mining processes in interaction design. The method follows the following steps:

1). A design workshop is run with 3-5 designers. They are asked to design the GUI and the interaction process of an application in the area of the pattern mining process.

2). All the design issues discussed by the designers are collected.

3). Step 1 and 2 are repeated until a fairly large number of design issues (at least 150) are being collected.

4). For each design issue (di) collected, its degree of recurrence (DoR) is computed as:

$$\mathrm{DoR(di)} = \frac{numberOfOccurrences(di)}{numberOfWorkshops} * 100$$

, where *numberOfOccurrences* represents the number of workshops during which the design issue *di* has been discussed and *numberOfWorkshops* is the total number of workshops conducted.

5). The design issues collected are sorted based on their DoRs.

In order to support the design patterns mining process, a set of existing software applications in the area of the mining process are analyzed for identifying in what measure the design issues discussed during the workshops are considered in the implementation of existing applications. Those design issues with a higher DoR are considered for being documented through design patterns.

The paper described the application of the method in a design pattern mining process aiming to identify design patterns in the design of systems for synchronous collaboration. 13 design workshops were conducted and 7 applications were analyzed, leading to the identification of 8 design patterns: *Who is the coordinator?*; *Integrated chat*; *Eyes wide open*; *Choose your collaborators*; *Collaboration, always social*; *My contribution; Track history of collaboration; With or without collaboration.*

ACKNOWLEDGMENTS

Special thanks to all the participants in the workshops for the inspiring ideas and great designs. This work was supported by the *Initial Training Network* "Marie Curie Actions", funded by the FP 7 – People Programme entitled "DESIRE: Creative Design for Innovation in Science and Technology".

REFERENCES

1. Adler, A., Nash, J. C., Noel, S. Evaluating and implementing a collaborative office document system. *Interact. Comput.* 18, 4 (2006), 665-682.
2. Alexander, C. *A pattern language: Towns, buildings, construction.* New York: Oxford University Press, 1977.
3. Amershi, S., Morris, M.R. CoSearch: a system for co-located collaborative web search. in *Proceeding of CHI '08* (Florence Italy, April 2008), ACM Press, 1647-1656.
4. Baggetun, R., Rusman, E., Poggi, C. Design patterns for collaborative learning: From practice to theory and back, in *Proceedings of International Conference on Educational Multimedia, Hypermedia and Telecommunications* (Lugano Switzerland, 2004), 2493-2498.
5. Battocchi, A., Pianesi, F., Tomasini, D., Zancanaro, M., Esposito, G., Venuti, P., Ben Sasson, A., Gal, E., Weiss, P.L. Collaborative Puzzle Game: a tabletop interactive game for fostering collaboration in children with Autism Spectrum Disorders. in *Proceedings of the International Conference on Interactive Tabletops and Surfaces* (2009). ACM Press, 197-204.
6. Borchers, J. *A Pattern Approach to Interaction Design.* John Wiley & Sons, Inc, 2001.
7. Carroll, J.M. *Scenario-Based Design: Envisioning Work and Technology in System Development.* John Wiley & Sons, Inc., New York, NY, USA, 1995.
8. Crumlish, C., Malone, E. *Designing Social Interfaces.* O'Reilly Media, Inc, 2009.
9. Díaz, P., Rosson, M. B., Aedo, I., Carroll, J. M. Web Design Patterns: Investigating User Goals and Browsing Strategies, in *Proceedings of the Symposium on End-User Development* (Siegen Germany, March 2009), 186-204.
10. Dong, J., Zhao, Y., Peng, T. A Review of Design Pattern Mining Techniques, *International Journal of Software Engineering and Knowledge Engineering* 19, 6 (September, 2009), pp. 823-855.
11. Gamma, E., R. Helm, R. Johnson, Vlissides, J. *Design Patterns: Elements of Reusable Object-Oriented Software.* Reading, MA: Addison-Wesley, 1995.
12. GoogleDocs http://www. *docs.google.com/*
13. Klopfer, E., Perry, J., Squire, K., Jan, M.F., Steinkuehler, C. Mystery at the museum: a collaborative game for museum education. in *Proceedings of the Conference on Computer Support for Collaborative learning* (2005), 316-320.
14. Kruschitz, C., Hitz, M. Analyzing the HCI Design Pattern Variety, in *Proceedings of AsianPLoP2010* (Tokyo Japan, March 2010), GRACE-TR-2010-01.
15. Lukosch, S., Schümmer, T. Communicating Design Knowledge with Groupware Technology Patterns: The Case of Shared Object Management. In *Proceedings of CRIWG 2004* (Costa Rica, 2004), 223-237.
16. Margaritis, M., Avouris, N., Kahrimanis, G. On Supporting Users' Reflection during Small Groups Synchronous Collaboration. in *Proceedings of 12th International Workshop on Groupware, CRIWG 2006* (Spain, 2006) LNCS 4154, Springer.
17. Meszaros, G., Doble, J. A pattern language for pattern writing. In *Proceedings of International Conference on Pattern languages of program design* (1997) Addison-Wesley Longman Publishing Co., Inc., Boston, MA, USA 529-574.
18. Retalis, S., Georgiakakis, P., Dimitriadis, Y. Eliciting design patterns for e-learning systems. *Computer Science Education* 16, 2 (2006), 105–118.
19. Schadewitz, N., Jachna, T. Comparing inductive and deductive methodologies for design patterns identification and articulation. *International Design Research Conference* 12, 15 (November, 2007).
20. Schadewitz, N. Design Patterns for Cross-cultural Collaboration. *International Journal of Design* 3, 3 (2009).
21. Schuler, D. A pattern language for living communication. in *Proceedings of PDC'02* (Malmö Sweden, June 2002).
22. Shah, C., Marchionini, G., Kelly, D. Learning design principles for a collaborative information seeking system. in *Proceedings of CHI '09* (Boston USA, April 2009). ACM Press, 3419-3424.
23. Tidwell, J. *Designing Interfaces: Patterns for Effective Interaction Design.* O'Reilly Media, 2005.
24. Wallas, G. *The Art of Thought*, Harcourt, Brace & World, New York, 1926.
25. Welie, M. Patterns in interaction design. Retrieved: June, 2[0th] 2010. Available at: http://www.welie.com
26. Winters, N., Mor, Y. Dealing with abstraction: Case study generalisation as a method for eliciting design patterns. *Computers in Human Behavior* 25, 5 (2009), 1079-1088.

Flippable User Interfaces for Internationalization

Iyad Khaddam and Jean Vanderdonckt
Université catholique de Louvain, Louvain School of Management
Louvain Interaction Laboratory, Place des Doyens, 1 – B-1348 Louvain-la-Neuve (Belgium)
{iyad.khaddam, jean.vanderdonckt}@uclouvain.be – Phone: +32 10 478525

ABSTRACT
The language reading direction is probably one of the most determinant factors influencing the successful internationalization of graphical user interfaces, beyond their mere translation. Western languages are read from left to right and top to bottom, while Arabic languages and Hebrew are read from right to left and top to bottom, and Oriental languages are read from top to bottom. In order to address this challenge, we introduce flippable user interfaces that enable the end user to change the reading direction of a graphical user interface by flipping it into the desired reading direction by direct manipulation. This operation automatically and dynamically changes the user interface layout based on a generalized concept of reading direction and translates it according to the end user's preferences.

Author Keywords
Adaptation, cultural background, internationalization, reading direction, user interface layout.

General Terms
Design, Experimentation, Human Factors, Verification.

ACM Classification Keywords
D2.2 [**Software Engineering**]: Design Tools and Techniques – *user interfaces*. D2.m [**Software Engineering**]: Miscellaneous – *Rapid Prototyping; reusable software*. H.5.1 [**Information interfaces and presentation**]: Multimedia Information Systems – *Animations*. H5.2 [**Information interfaces and presentation**]: User Interfaces – *Graphical User Interfaces (GUI); User-centered design, Windowing Systems*.

INTRODUCTION
Localization usually refers to the process of designing and developing a Graphical User Interface (GUI) that is adapted to a particular culture [6,13], continent [4], country [14] or region [18], or a set of them (based on [4]). The opposite process, called *globalization*, usually refers to the process of designing and developing a GUI that accommodates the common ground of the largest possible audience from different cultures, continents, countries, and regions (based on [4,18,21]. Making a UI *global* [21] therefore results into one single GUI, while making a UI *local* results into many different variations of the same initial GUI, but adapted to the different cultural backgrounds. These different variations are subject to a series of challenges: their design should be coordinated [4], culturally-aware [13], maintained simultaneously [18], and applicability of a change request depending on local settings. A single change request may indeed affect one or several variations of the same GUI. Many different factors could positively influence a successful localization [4,6,10,11,13,14,15,16,18,21]: color, format, metaphor, screen, layout, language, images, structure, density, ordering of information,….

Instead of producing several variations of the same initial GUI for the different localizations, it might be interesting to concentrate the adaptation logic into a single GUI that handles these variations depending on setting of the end user. A single GUI could be produced with adaptation, thus addressing the challenge of coordination and simultaneous maintenance, but leaving the challenges of culture awareness and dependability open in the adaptation logic.

One of the main critical factors of success is the adaptation of the GUI to the end user's language, which includes translation (e.g., by automated translation of all contents and resources [15]) and layout adaptation to the language reading direction [8]: this adaptation largely fosters the UI acceptance [8], other aspects, such as color, font, and size, are mostly lexical factors, and less critical, while high-level aspects, such as metaphors and organization are hard to predict in a systematic way [18] and their impact depends on many cultural parameters that are hard to reproduce [14].

This paper introduces the interaction technique of *flippable user interfaces* in order to support the adaptation to the end users' language, which subsumes translation, transformation of the layout to support a correct reading direction, mixing different directions, improving the visual properties of the layout (such as balance and symmetry [22]).

The remainder of this paper is structured as follows: the next section reports on some related work. Then, the design principles that underlie flippable user interfaces (i.e., based on a concept of generalized direction) are introduced, motivated, and exemplified. The software architecture supporting the implementation of flippable user interfaces as an adaptation interaction technique for addressing internationalization is discussed. Finally, a conclusion delivers the main points of this research and presents some future avenues, especially for the end user's acceptation.

EICS'11, June 13–16, 2011, Pisa, Italy.

RELATED WORK

This paper is aimed at developing an interaction technique (i.e., flippable user interface) as a support for internationalization (i.e., adaptation to end user's language) of GUIs with transition (i.e., animated transition between UI before and after adaptation). The following state of the art is structured with respect to these three main fields of research.

Adaptation to Cultural background

Three kinds of GUI adaptation are usually performed in order to localize a GUI: *technical adaptations* [18] that address the needs for making the GUI workable and displayable in the localized context of use (e.g., by use of appropriate alphabet, character set), *national adaptations* that address the needs of particularizing the information and their associated actions to a particular country (e.g., by adding information relevant to a country only, by removing unnecessary menu items for a particular task that does not require it in a specific country), and *cultural adaptations* that address the needs of cultural habitudes, conventions, and meanings [13,14]. While most of the adaptation operations are well documented in the literature, they are applied mostly on a case by case way. They are rarely applied systematically or encapsulated in an adaptation engine.

The main goals for adaptation towards localization are [8, 14,18]: communicate in the country's native language; support the natural writing symbols, punctuation, and so on; support native date, currency, weight scales, numbers and addresses; support natural work habits and the work environment, and communicate in an inoffensive manner. Again, while these principles are largely recognized and widely adopted, they are seldom translated into rules that automatically transform GUIs for a localized purpose.

In the market, we can find well-Arabized products and most of them are built on Microsoft Windows Operating System, as it was the pioneer in providing support for right-to-left (RTL) languages or on the web. ERP products were forced to provide RTL support due to market pressure.

Portenari & Amara explain the Arabic language characteristics and explain the challenges of the language in the context of providing OS support for Arabic. They discuss the issues related to encoding, character shaping and the "cursive" or "handwritten" style of writing in Arabic, vowels, numbers shapes and the mirroring effect on visual screens.

Rejmer *et al.* [18] discussed the internationalization of a web site that performs automated evaluation of W3C accessibility guidelines based on a set of design guidelines for supporting internationalization/localization. These guidelines only address Western languages (Latin alphabet), thus ignoring other reading directions, but identifying important GUI properties that are affected by internationalization.

XUL supports RTL UI [16] by providing the "dir" property at the UI element which is the base of all elements. The "dir" property can have one of two values: normal, reverse. The "normal" means: "position elements in the container according to their order in the xml file". The "reverse" value means: "position elements in the container according to their *reverse* order in the xml file". XUL does not directly address the RTL concept, but their concept of "reverse" fixes the orientation issue. On the other side, it does not address the control localization nor provide support to it. When the "dir" property is "reverse", this doesn't imply that the final control to be used is a control that supports RTL. XUL depends on the rendering framework to determine the final control (localized version). Therefore, it provides a localized version of Firefox for each language. The problem we note with XUL approach is that each localized version of the product will have a localized version of the design (the XUL file is copied for each language). This imposes a maintenance/update problem.

Quiroz *et al.* [16] implemented a genetic algorithm for automated generation of GUI layouts based on user fatigue based on the XUL language. By applying this algorithm, they demonstrate which layout causes the less fatigue, but again, the layout if only LTR since XUL itself is like that.XAML (www.xaml.net/) is a markup system that underlies user interface components of Microsoft's .NET Framework 3.0 and above. XAML supports RTL by adding a "FlowDirection" property to the containers and UI elements that takes one of the values: "LeftToRight", "RightToLeft". This causes the expected effect of RTL to be applied on the container and/or the element. Figure 4 gives an example.

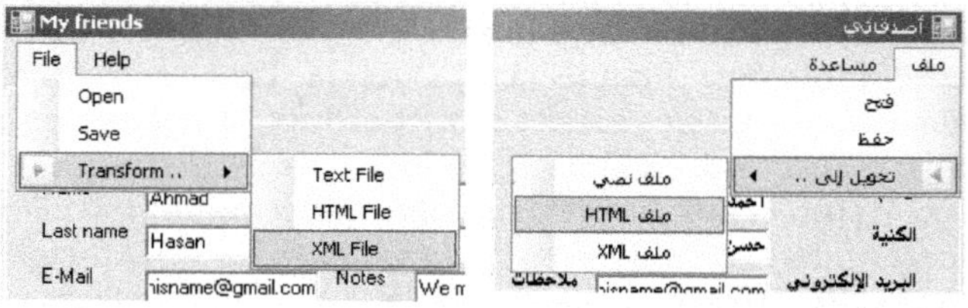

Figure 1. A sample LTR and the localized RTL version (in Arabic language).

Interaction techniques

Various interaction techniques have been investigated in Human-Computer Interaction (HCI) that are related to the *metaphor of flipping a page of a book*. This metaphor has been extensively used in hypermedia and hypertext applications since a long time (e.g., in HyperCard) and is still used today in multimedia presentations for the following reasons: (i) the flipping gesture is familiar with the activity of browsing a book, an album (e.g., *FlipAlbum* [7]), or a stack of pages or documents since a simple flip distinguishes forward from backward movement, (ii) the flipping gesture is natural and straightforward to produce, (iii) flip, drop, and turn, are basic operations of geometric symmetry [22] that respectively reflect an image around the y-axis, the x-axis, perform a 90° rotation to the right, and (iv) flipping a window could reveal additional information related to the window (e.g., as in Sun's Looking Glass 3D desktop). In other words, the flipping gesture indicates a direction, which is appropriate to denote the direction of reading. The flipping metaphor has however different interpretation: for Western countries where the page is flipped from right to left in order to support the reading direction from left to right and top to bottom. '*Fold and Drop*' [5] is an interaction technique enabling end users to drag an icon from a stack of overlapping windows and drop it onto a possibly hidden window by applying gestures on the windows, thus releasing the user to constantly switch from one window to another. *Orimado* [9] is a variant of this interaction technique for Oriental languages. While Fold & Drop and Orimado also rely on the metaphor of flipping, they are applied to window and maintain the direction from right to left without affecting the UI contents since this is not their goal.

The idea of rotated and peeling the windows (Figure 2), and snapped and zipped windows has already being introduced as an interaction technique recommended for manipulating multiple windows more efficiently [1]. Preliminary investigations [1,23] show that this interaction technique generates a high subjective satisfaction rate, not just because it is graphical or easy to use, but mainly for its metaphor that is pretty close to the real world.

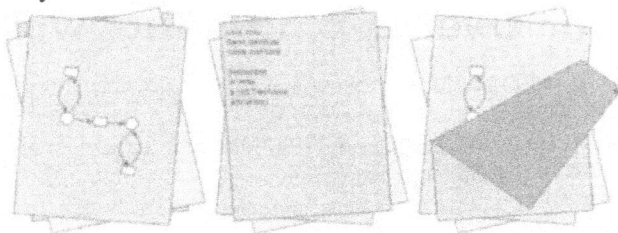

Figure 2. Example of the rotated and peeled-back metaphors.

Flip zooming [3] is an interaction technique that consists of splitting a screen into a sequence of objects (e.g., images, fragments of texts, or combinations of both types), putting the focus on of these objects, and letting the end user to flip through the sequence of objects from left to right, top to bottom to preserve the context. Zooming in/out is then used on any object of interest. The main drawback of this technique is a constant 'touch-and-go' between flipping (to navigate) and zooming in/out (to see the details).

Flying [12] is an interaction technique used for quickly browsing a large hypertext in order to gain some insight to features such as organization, size, depth, level of detail, and layout based on flipping. This technique is not intended to support reading the contents, but to provide a first idea of how it is structured, even in a non-linear order.

As we can see from existing work, it seems interesting to consider the concept of flippable UI that mimics paper-based operations in order to improve the end user's subjective satisfaction and naturalness of interaction. While different operations that mimic page flipping have been introduced, none of them really reproduce the flipping of a page in any direction. that results into an adaptation to the new state. This is why animated transitions are made for: convey the change of display.

Animated Transitions

It is well established [2,7,21,23] that it is generally considered easier for users to maintain a mental model of the data across smooth transitions and less time is spent comprehending the new data presentation. In other words, an animated transition between two states is appreciated because it supports a progressive transition from the initial state to the final state without any disruption between. Several visual techniques exist that could be applied to GUI design, whether it is for one localization [23] or for globalization of these GUIs [4,22], the two main dimensions of internationalization. Usability guidelines (e.g., [4,13,14,18]) also exist that reply on animated transition to change the state of a GUI depending on its culture [11].

DESIGN PRINCIPLES OF A FLIPPABLE USER INTERFACE FOR INTERNATIONALIZATION

In this section, we motivate, define, and discuss the design principles that led us to rely on flipping, an interaction technique augmented by an animated transition, as a way to support the change of cultural background (here, mainly Western vs. Eastern cultures, with various ways of reading).

Principle #1. Provide handles for direct flipping

In order to adhere to the principles of the direct manipulation, it is expected that the flipping interaction technique should be supported by handles (Figure 3) that indicate the direction where to flip: left to right (LTR), right to left (RTL), top to bottom (TTB) or bottom to top (BTT). Each flipping direction then indicates the reading order of the GUI, thus provoking its adaptation to the corresponding cultural background. In direct manipulation the objects should have a graphical representation, preferably one that is close to the real world if any, with an incremental interaction that is fast and reversible. For this purpose, horizontal handles (represented in red in Figure 3) control transformations along the X axis, while the vertical handles (represented in blue in Figure 3) control transformations along the Y axis. An arrow-shaped handle may convey a translation, a square-shaped handle may convey a change of scale, and a circle-shaped handle (represented in green in Figure 3) may convey a rotation. Similarly for a 3D object in space, these three handles could support respectively *nutation* (along X axis), *precession* (along the Y axis), and *rotation* (along the Z axis). For instance, The Card Stack had markers on front side and back side, so the user was able to flip it backward, and saw the backside of the 3D model. The central button, represented in grey in Figure 3, restores the transformation to its initial stage or identity. The ellipse and the lines depict the current status of transformation.

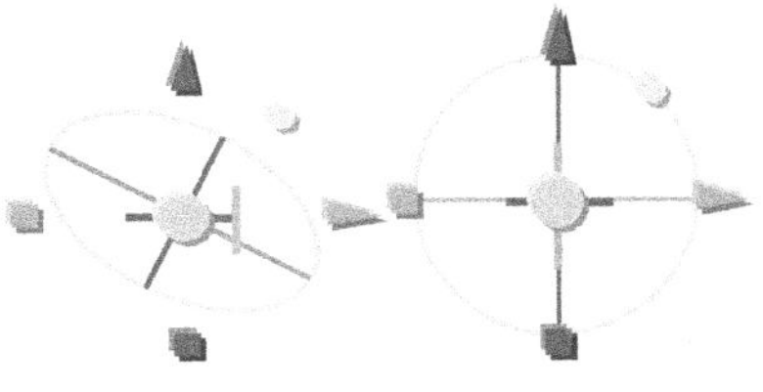

Figure 3. Handles for direct flipping.

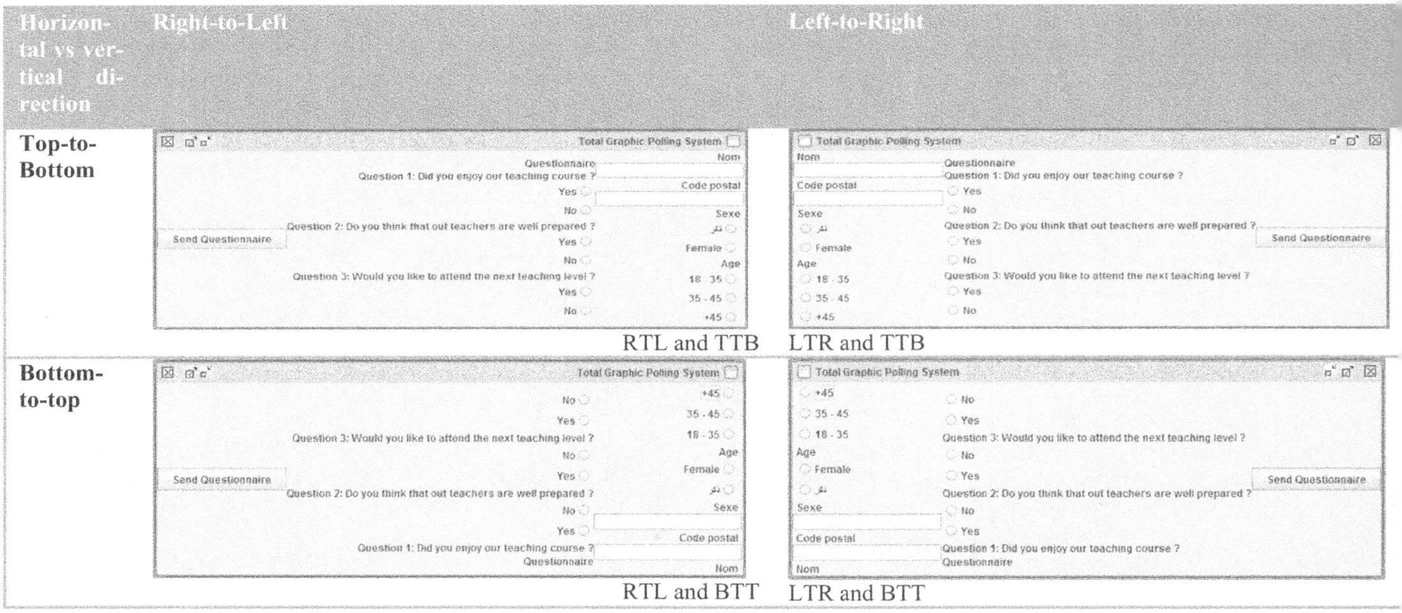
Horizontal vs vertical direction
Right-to-Left
Left-to-Right
Top-to-Bottom
Bottom-to-top
RTL and TTB
LTR and TTB
RTL and BTT
LTR and BTT

Figure 4. The four possible layouts depending on the generalized direction.

Principle #2. Perform adaptation according to flipping

From the aforementioned literature, we summarize the UI adaptation in basically two ways:

- The *orientation* (the mirroring): this consists of changing the reading direction of the contents depending on the end user's native language. Some languages are read LTR while some others are read RTL. In order to generalize this attribute, we also introduce the vertical dimension since some languages are read TTB or BTT. Therefore, each native language is assigned to a reading direction according to the horizontal dimension (LTR vs TRL) and the vertical dimension (TTB vs BTT), thus covering the four possible cases (Figure 4). The common direction in Western countries, e.g., LTR and TTB, is reproduced in the top right position of Figure 4. If the GUI is flipped to the left, it reverses the order from LTR to RTL; if the GUI is flipped to the bottom, it reverses the order from TTB to BTT. Figure 4 keeps the same contents and language in order to remain understandable. Automatic translation of the language [15] is a service that could be used for translating the labels, instructions, messages from one language to another, even at run-time. After changing the layout, several operations are required by the language change.
- The *localization*. The TRL localization has special characteristics that do not exist in Latin-alphabet languages, which makes the localization a challenge. We identify from the examples before the following characteristics for RTL localization:
  - *Text* localization:
    - Text localization: language encoding and character set (alphabet).
    - Direction switching: direction of text writing.
  - *Graphics* localization:
    - RTL sensitive graphics (non-horizontally symmetrical)
    - Images with text inside
    - Other localizable images (country flag…)
  - *Control* localization:
    - Control rendering: for instance, a label control should support writing from right to left.
    - Control behaviour: controls should be aware of special behaviour for special keys, like pressing "enter" key in a text area.

Principle #3. Ensure smooth transition for adaptation

To avoid startling and confusing users, we employ smooth slow-in and slow-out transitions [21,23] for every visual change occurred after the adaptation has been performed. This animated transition has the advantage to preserve most of the visual aspects of GUI widgets horizontally or vertically. Other animated transitions could be investigated depending on the adaptation operation that has been executed, thus opening a door for many different ways to ensure a smooth transition between the GUI before and after adaptation to a cultural background (here, localization). Animated transitions however suffer from the "lag" problem [21] that may cause end user frustration if the animated transition is too fast or too slow. Here, a flippable user interface does not suffer too much from the "lag" problem because the animated transition is performed at run-time while the end user is flipping the GUI. In the next section, we describe how this engineering technique has been implemented. Flipping at run-time is the target because a user may speak different languages and may want to switch from one language to another, because the "by default" language is not always right, even in an option menu, because a UI may contain various data simultaneously in different formats and languages and because manually developing different layouts for different languages requires extensive development efforts that are not required by our approach.

IMPLEMENTATION

This section describes how the three aforementioned design principles have been implemented together in order to make the concept of flippable user interface operational. The software architecture is structured as follows (Figure 5):

1. **The Widget Selector**: This component is responsible of mapping the nodes of a GUI specified in a User Interface Description Language (UIDL) to output components. It needs the mapping XML file. Each specific output type (swing, html) needs a specific map.xml, but the Widget Selector is the same for all maps. In our case, UsiXML (www.usixml.org) was used for testing, but other similar UIDLs could be used in the same way. A XML map is structured as follows: the root is usiMapModel. This contains sub elements "<cuiMap>" that determine how we will map UsiXML tags in the CuiModel section of the xml file. Element selection algorithms are simply saying: a set of conditions that determine the element selection. The control structure in the usiMapModel is the "<option>" tag. This tag has 2 sections: condition and action. The condition is a simple Boolean expression that can be written in groovy (a java like syntax, www.groovy.com) which is modeled with a "<condition>" tag in usiMapModel file. The actions are a set of commands that create the suitable widget and fine tune its properties. They are modeled using the "<maps>" tag. This tag contains an init attribute, and that is where we usually create the appropriate widget. The child node "<map>" is a statement to map a property from a Usi node to the mapped widget property.
2. **The CUI Tree Traversal:** This is simply a tree traversal algorithm. Currently, we implemented a Depth-First traversal algorithm for parsing the Concrete User Interface (CUI). If some type of rendering needs to consider Width-First traversal, then the Width-First class needs to be implemented and passed to the engine instead of the default traversal (Depth-First).
3. **The Merge Algorithm:** this is simply a component that merges the tree of components in a custom way suitable to the final output. In the case of Swing, the components are all of type *java.awt.Component*, and the merge algorithm will simply add Components to the Container (a sub class of Component) but calling the method add.
4. **The CuiRendering Engine:** The engine that orchestrates the messages among the above components. The engine calls the traversal to start traversing the UiModel, which will parse the UiModel tree looking for UsiXml nodes. For each node, it will notify the engine who will call the Widget Selector to resolve this node. If the map.xml file contains a mapping for this node, it will create the mapped component and return it to the engine, who in turn will store it a special storage called: UsiRuntime. The UsiRuntime contains a tree of rendered objects. The UsiRuntime allows us to retrieve the rendered component by using the "id" of the relative UsiXml element. This allows 2-ways mapping between original UsiXml element and the rendered element. When finished, the engine will call the Merge Algorithm to merge the resulting tree of components and returns the UsiRuntime object to the caller. The UsiRuntime now contains the roots components (if the UsiXml file contains 2 Window elements, UsiRuntime will contains 2 roots, and so on). The caller uses these roots for any purpose, e.g., display on screen, save.

Figure 6 shows how the control panel could be displayed for finely governing the layout of the GUI. By moving the handles according to the Principle #1, the end user is able to manipulate the geometry of the GUI in order to reverse its reading order, but also in order to accommodate constraints imposed by the screen resolution. This engineering technique therefore supports the concept of variable geometry layouts that could accommodate different physical constraints imposed by the target computing platform. A *user interface with variable geometry* is hereby defined as a GUI exhibiting the capability of altering its layout geometry by direct manipulation depending on the context of use, thus making it *plastic* to some extent.

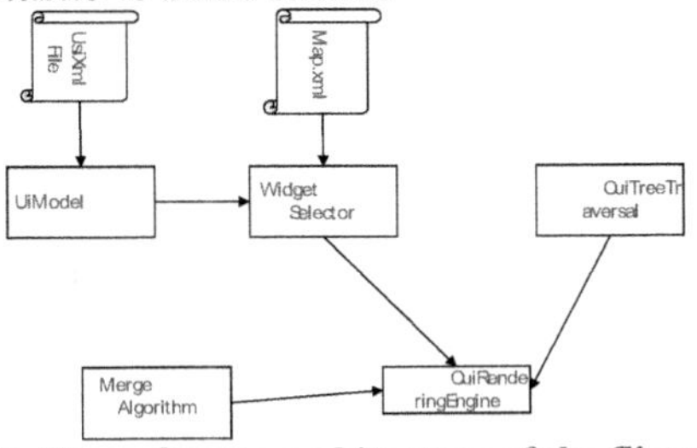

Figure 5. The software architecture of the flippable UI.

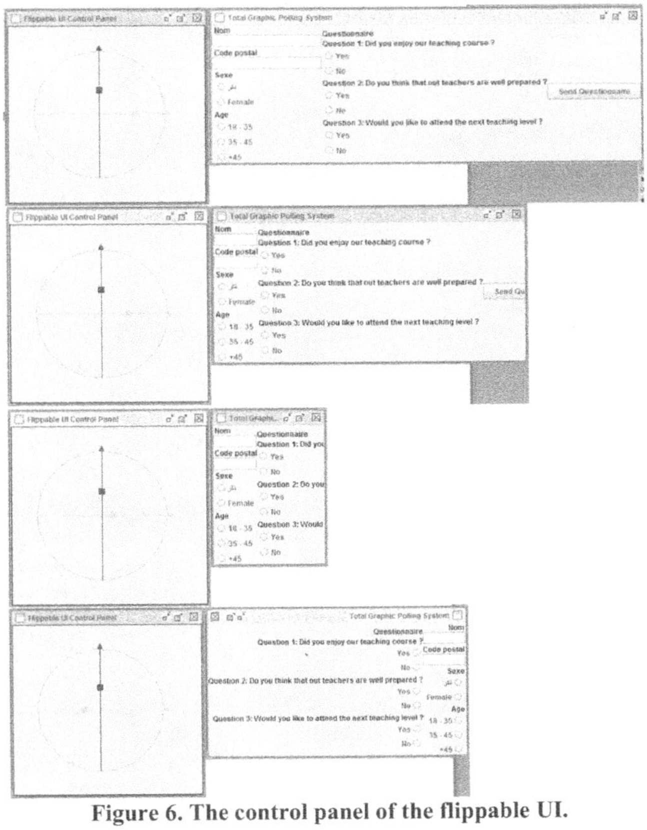

Figure 6. The control panel of the flippable UI.

When the end user does not want to finely manipulate the layout geometry, she could only flip the GUI in the desired direction, thus obtaining only the four possibilities depicted in Fig. 4, along with adaptation techniques executed as in Principle #2. Principle #3 preserves the continuity between the GUI before flipping and after flipping.

CONCLUSION

This paper presented the concept of flippable user interface as an interaction technique for supporting internationalization of graphical user interfaces. Traditionally, internationalization of a GUI is achieved by providing different sets of translated resources that are then incorporated in the executable code of the interactive application that is then responsible for switching to one layout to another. This method is largely *static* (all resources should be provided in resource files, translated and compiled) and *physically defined* (all layouts are done manually and embedded in the code). Instead, a flippable user interface introduces an engineering technique where the GUI definition is dynamically parsed, interpreted, and computed depending the default language and country settings of the end user. Switching from one cultural background to another, e.g., switching from English to Arabic is done performed dynamically by flipping the window by the end user in the desired reading order at runtime. Such a flippable UI could be flipped in any direction, vertical or horizontal. All other operations that are subsequent to a change of cultural background are then dynamically performed for all widgets, like localization of controls, text, messages, labels, etc. This approach is much more flexible both for the end user since there is no need to select parameters from a menu and for a designer/developer since all the variations are made flexible in the interpretation mechanism.

ACKNOWLEDGMENTS

The authors would like to acknowledge the support of the ITEA2-Call3-2008026 UsiXML (User Interface extensible Markup Language) European project and its support by Région Wallonne DGO6 as well as the FP7-ICT5-258030 Serenoa project supported by the European Commission.

REFERENCES

1. Beaudouin-Lafon, M. Novel Interaction Techniques for Overlapping Windows. In *Proc. of UIST'2001*. ACM Press, New York (2001), pp. 153–154.
2. Bederson, B.B. and Boltman, A. Does Animation Help Users Build Mental Maps of Spatial Information? In *Proc. of IEEE Symposium on Information Visualization InfoVis'99*. IEEE Computer Society Press, Los Alamitos (1999), pp. 28–35.
3. Björk, S., Holmquist, L.E., Redström, J., Bretan, I., Danielsson, R., Karlgren, J., and Franzén, K. WEST: A Web Browser for Small Terminals. In *Proc. of UIST'99* (Asheville, Nov. 7-10, 1999). ACM Press (1999), pp. 187–196.
4. DelGaldo, E.M. and Nielsen, J. *International User Interfaces*. John Wiley & Sons, New York (1996).
5. Dragicevic, P. Combining Crossing-Based and Paper-Based Interaction Paradigms for Dragging and Dropping Between Overlapping Windows. In *Proc. of UIST'2004* (Santa Fe, October 24-27, 2004). ACM Press, New York, pp. 193–196.
6. Evers, V. and Day, D. The role of culture in interface acceptance. In *Proc. of INTERACT'97* (Sydney, July 14-18, 1997). Chapman & Hall, London (1997), pp. 260–267.
7. FlipAlbum, http://www.flipalbum.com.
8. Halawani, S.M. The effect of language reading direction on user interface design. PhD thesis, 1996.
9. Inaba, K., Orimado (2010). http://www.kmonos.net/lib/orimado.en.html. Visited on: December 5th, 2010.
10. Ishida, R. Creating HTML Pages in Arabic, Hebrew and Other Right-to-left Scripts. W3 Consortium, Geneva (2002). http://www.w3.org/International/tutorials/bidi-xhtml/. Visited on December 5th, 2010.
11. Khaddam, I. and Vanderdonckt, J. Adapting UsiXML User Interfaces to Cultural Background. In *Proc. of 1st Int. Workshop on User Interface eXtensible Markup Language UsiXML'2010* (Berlin, 20 June 2010). Thales Research and Technology France, Paris (2010), pp. 163–170.
12. Lai, P. and Manber, U. Flying Through Hypertext. In *Proc. of 3rd ACM Conf. on Hypertext Hypertext'91* (San Antonio, Dec. 15-18, 1991). ACM Press, New York (1991), pp. 123–132.
13. Mahemoff, M. and Johnston, L. "Culturally-aware" requirements for internationalized software. In: *Proc. of 3rd Australian Conf. on Requirements Engineering ACRE'98* (Geelong, October 26-27, 1998). D. Fowler, L. Dawson (eds.), Deakin University, Geelong (1998), pp. 83–90.
14. Marcus, A. and West Gould, E. Cultural Dimensions and Global Web User-Interface Design. *Interactions* 7, 4 (July 2000), pp. 32–46.
15. Pérez-Quiñones, M.A., Padilla-Falto, O.I., and McDevitt, K. Automatic language translation for user interfaces. In: *Proc. of the Int. Conf. on Diversity in computing TAPIA'2005* (Albuquerque, October 19-22, 2005). ACM Press, pp. 60–63.
16. Portaneri, F. and Amara, F. Arabization of Graphical User Interfaces. In [2], pp. 127–150.
17. Quiroz, J.C., Louis, S.J., and Dascalu, S.M. Interactive evolution of XUL User Interfaces. In *Proc. of the 9th Annual Conf. on Genetic and evolutionary computation GECCO'2007*. ACM Press, New York (2007), pp. 2151-2158.
18. Rejmer, P., Cooper, M., and Vanderdonckt, J. Lessons Learned From Internationalizing a Web Site Accessibility Evaluator. In *Proc. of 3rd Int. Workshop on Internationalisation of Products and Systems IWIPS'2001 "Designing for global markets 3"* (Milton Keynes, July 11-14, 2001). Digital Printing Services, Milton Keynes (2001), pp. 61–79.
19. Sears, A. Layout Appropriateness: A Metric for Evaluating User Interface Widget Layout, *IEEE Transactions on Software Engineering 19*, 7 (July 1993), 707 - 719
20. Schlienger, C., Conversy, S., Chatty, S., Anquetil, M., and Mertz, Ch. Improving Users' Comprehension of Changes with Animation and Sound: An Empirical Assessment. In *Proc. of Interact'2007*. LNCS, Vol. 4662, Springer, pp. 207–220.
21. Stasko, J. Animation in User Interfaces: Principles and Techniques. In *Proc. of User Interface Software '93*, pp. 81–101.
22. Taylor, D. Global software: Developing applications for the international market. Springer-Verlag, Berlin (1992).
23. Vanderdonckt, J. and Gillo, X. Visual Techniques for Traditional and Multimedia Layouts. In: *Proc. of 2nd ACM Workshop on Advanced Visual Interfaces AVI'94* (Bari, 1-4 June 1994), ACM Press, New York (1994), pp. 95–104.

Engineering Interactive Ubiquitous Computing Systems

Albrecht Schmidt
Human Computer Interaction Group
Institut für Visualisierung und Interaktive Systeme (VIS)
Universität Stuttgart, Germany
http://www.vis.uni-stuttgart.de/
albrecht.schmidt@vis.uni-stuttgart.de

KEYNOTE

Over the last 20 years computer scientists and practitioner have made real progress in engineering interactive software for desktop computers. Development methods, prototyping and tools, components, framework, and standards have helped to improve the usability of many desktop and web applications. Looking back at user interfaces in the nineties and comparing them to current software we can see how much usability and user experience has improved.

As ubiquitous computing is becoming reality, making a phone call, operating household appliances, watching television, and driving a car have essentially become human-computer interaction tasks. Developing interactive applications for ubiquitous computing environments raises many new engineering challenges, and is motivated by Mark Weiser describing ubiquitous computing "*The most profound technologies are those that disappear. They weave themselves into the fabric of everyday life until they are indistinguishable from it*" [1]. Creating systems, devices, and software that become a part of people's lives and that can be operated (without noticing) as part of daily activities is a hard problem and the cost of failure is much higher than in traditional systems. With our vision of computing that extends our perception beyond the here and now, and where devices mediate our perception [2], these engineering challenges become even more severe.

When engineering interactive ubiquitous computing applications, we have to fundamentally re-think all steps in the design and development process – from requirements engineering, to concepts, to iterative design, prototyping, implementation, and deployment. The heterogeneity of technologies and users adds to the complexity and the creation of frameworks, components, and toolkits is more difficult than in traditional computing. Measuring the quality of solutions and evaluating the user experience is typically complicated by many external factors.

There are many trends, in technology as well as in society, that enable us to create ubiquitous interactive applications. Ingenuity and creativity of the developer are replacing processing power, memory, and network bandwidth as liming factors in the design of systems. A great variety of output technologies ranging from single bit notifications to large scale high-resolution displays, including visual, auditory, as well as haptic modalities, have become widely available. User input has been extended from pointing and text input to capture a richer picture. Technologies for 3D sensing, activity recognition, and physiological sensing are on the market and are used in games already. A great challenge arises from the fact, that technology by itself is often not enough to discriminate a product. A digital camera with 10 megapixel and a great user experience is probably easier to sell than a camera with 15 megapixel that is hard to use. Hence the expectations for engineering a great user experience are higher as they often impact directly on the value of a product on the market. At the same time there is real time feedback from customers and users via social software, like Facebook and Twitter, hence the reception of a product by users and their reaction can be observed in real time. For us it is an interesting question how this wealth of information from interaction in social networks can be exploited in the engineering process of interactive ubiquitous computing systems.

Over the last year we looked at how engineering interactive computing systems can be achieved and what problems will occur. Our experience is based on user interfaces in the domain of mobile systems, public display networks, and vehicles that we investigated over the last year. With upcoming modalities (3D sensing, physiological sensors, eye-gaze tracking) and means for harvesting ideas from the community of users we expect many interesting devices and applications coming out of research and development in interactive systems engineering over the next years.

ACM Classification Keywords
H.5.2: Evaluation/methodology

General Terms
Human Factors

REFERENCES

1. Mark Weiser. Computer of the 21st Century. *Scientific American*, 265(3) pp. 94-104. 1991.
2. Albrecht Schmidt, Marc Langheinrich, Kritian Kersting. Perception beyond the Here and Now. *IEEE Computer*, 44(2), pp. 86-88, 2011.

EICS'11, June 13–16, 2011, Pisa, Italy.
ACM 978-1-4503-0670-6/11/06.

An Extensible Digital Ink Segmentation and Classification Framework for Natural Notetaking

Adriana Ispas
Institute for Information Systems, ETH Zurich
8092 Zurich, Switzerland
ispas@inf.ethz.ch

Beat Signer
Vrije Universiteit Brussel
Pleinlaan 2
1050 Brussels, Belgium
bsigner@vub.ac.be

Moira C. Norrie
Institute for Information Systems, ETH Zurich
8092 Zurich, Switzerland
norrie@inf.ethz.ch

ABSTRACT
With the emergence of digital pen and paper technologies, we have witnessed an increasing number of enhanced paper-digital notetaking solutions. However, the natural notetaking process includes a variety of individual work practices that complicate the automatic processing of paper notes and require user intervention for the classification of digital ink data. We present an extensible digital ink processing framework that simplifies the classification of digital ink data in natural notetaking applications. Our solution deals with the manual as well as automatic ink data segmentation and classification based on Delaunay triangulation and a strongest link algorithm. We further highlight how our solution can be extended with new digital ink classifiers and describe a paper-digital reminder application that has been realised based on the presented digital ink processing framework.

Author Keywords
digital pen and paper, digital ink, natural notetaking, digital ink segmentation and classification framework

ACM Classification Keywords
H.5.m Information Interfaces and Presentation: Misc.

General Terms
Algorithms, Design

INTRODUCTION
Despite the availability of advanced digital information management tools, information workers often still rely on paper-based notetaking for recording information. Unfortunately, these paper-based work practices do not integrate well with digital applications dealing with recorded information in a post-capture phase [12, 19]. Recent technological innovations, such as Anoto's digital pen and paper technology, enable the digitalisation of handwritten paper notes into digital ink data without an intermediary transcription step. This creates opportunities for the integration of regular paper-based notetaking practices with information management tools and services. However, a number of studies have revealed that paper notebooks are an amalgam of notes destined for multiple tasks, activities and purposes [7, 25], parts of which might not be required in digital applications [6]. Even with remarkable advances in the digital ink parsing and processing domain [16, 3, 26], digital systems are still not able to classify different notes with the same accuracy that an information worker would achieve [15].

Most existing frameworks for developing digital pen and paper applications focus on the particular case where the identification of different paper notes as well as their integration with digital applications and services is achieved by introducing specific notetaking conventions and guidelines for this new type of interactive paper interface. Through specific pen and paper interactions, such as gesture-based marks or writing within special purpose capture areas, users have to indicate which digital ink data corresponds to particular paper notes. While this transformed pen and paper use may be suitable for specific information tasks, it does not integrate well with natural notetaking [4, 6]. There is a trade-off between providing comprehensive and accurate support for the digital integration of paper-captured information and the preservation of natural notetaking practices.

We have developed a digital ink segmentation and classification framework to address various requirements of digital pen and paper-based notetaking applications. In addition to user-driven approaches for segmenting and classifying digital ink data, our solution provides support for automatic and semi-automatic digital ink data processing. Digital ink data is separated into basic blocks of ink traces analogous to blocks visually perceivable to users such as paragraphs or bullet list structures. Moreover, heuristics for the high-level processing and classification of digital ink data can be implemented and incrementally added to the framework for further processing of these basic ink data blocks. The user-driven classification of digital ink data can be combined with an automatic separation and classification process, thus providing developers further options for dealing with specific limitations of both approaches, depending on specific needs of information workers and domain-specific applications.

We start by discussing limitations of existing tools for developing notetaking applications with respect to their support for natural notetaking. Further, we describe our approach

EICS'11, June 13–16, 2011, Pisa, Italy.

for separating digital ink data into blocks of ink data that reflect the visual representation of paper notes. After presenting our extensible framework for digital ink processing and classification, we highlight how the digital ink processing functionality has been integrated with an existing interactive paper application development framework, before providing some concluding remarks.

BACKGROUND

Various solutions have been proposed to offer information workers the advantages of both paper and digital media for notetaking. Early attempts range from paper notebooks with a predefined page configuration where the content can be extracted through an offline scanning process, such as introduced in the Paper PDA [5], to solutions that proposed the replacement of paper with pen-based computers, including PDAs [8] or Tablet PCs [24, 25]. Anoto's digital pen and paper technology enabled new types of notetaking solutions and these are commercially available for end users in the form of Livescribe's Desktop[1] application, Oxford's Easybook[2] or solutions integrated with Logitech's io Pen[3]. Information written on regular paper that is covered with a special Anoto dot pattern is captured by the digital pen's integrated infrared camera and transmitted to a computer via a Bluetooth connection or when the pen is connected to a computer via a docking station. Once transmitted to a computer, the pen stroke data that is represented as timestamped x and y coordinates can be further processed and integrated with digital applications.

Custom digital pen and paper solutions can be developed with the aid of a series of toolkits and SDKs, including the Anoto SDK for PC applications [1], Livescribe's Platform and Desktop SDKs [2], PaperToolkit[4] [28] and iPaper [14]. The focus of these solutions is on designing interactive paper applications based on active page areas that can be associated with digital callback functions to be executed while processing the pen data. Content written inside a predefined page area is interpreted by the application logic assigned to that particular part of the page. This approach is suitable for applications such as Anoto's form-based processing of information or the annotation of presentation slides based on printed handouts as realised in the PaperPoint [18] solution. However, the strict interaction conventions required by such approaches may result in discarding the digital pen and paper technology for more natural notetaking [6].

The use of dedicated page areas for semantic content identification can be replaced by the use of gesture-based content classification. PapierCraft [10] proposed a set of gestures for both the marking of excerpts of paper-captured information and the specification of how the corresponding digital ink data should be digitally processed. General gesture recognition solutions, such as the iGesture [17] framework, provide support for defining custom gesture sets and integrating gesture recognition functionality with digital pen and paper applications. The drawback of a gesture-based classification approach is that the digital ink processing step has to be able to distinguish between the ink data representing the content and the ink data to be interpreted as gestures. Since the most reliable solution is still to give control to the notetakers themselves by providing them with some content marking mechanism that they have to use, the process is currently limited by the degree of change in natural notetaking behaviour. For example, NiCEBook [4] uses dedicated page areas that have to be touched with a digital pen before performing the pen-based gestures to mark and classify specific handwritten notes. Furthermore, to support natural or quasi-natural notetaking, the set of gestures has to be designed in such a way that its use does not constrain the notetaking process [6]. In ButterflyNet [27], even a single simple gesture command used to mark specific paper content received negative feedback due to the increase in notetaking time.

Given the apparent correlation between the lack of interaction rules and the preference for paper-based notetaking, it seems obvious that an enhanced notetaking solution should employ automatic approaches for digital ink data processing as much as possible. A body of work has pointed out that even natural notes contain an implicit organisation based on spatial relations between pen strokes and systems have been proposed that exploit these implicit note structures for interactive whiteboard systems [13], "rough" document image editors [15] and interactive notetaking systems [9, 21]. While these solutions do not always provide a correct interpretation, the interactivity of these systems enables the user to immediately observe the resulting interpretation of their actions and to intervene in the case of misinterpretations.

Extensive work on automatic digital ink data processing exists. In particular, work on detecting lines of text and distinguishing between textual and graphical handwriting seems to be relevant for a potential notetaking solution that exploits implicit structures in paper notes [16, 3, 26]. However, to the best of our knowledge, there are no solutions based on digital pen and paper technology that integrate such automatic approaches for digital ink data processing. One of the reasons might be the fact that no direct feedback can be provided based on a paper interface. Possibilities for providing feedback about a user's actions include digital pen feedback [11] or feedback via various other external devices such as smart cameras as used in ButterflyNet [27]. Even if these approaches reach a certain maturity, the continuous feedback while taking notes might not be desirable. Solutions such as PapierCraft, Paper PDA or PaperProof [23] propose a graceful degradation approach where the interpretation of a user's actions is digitally reviewed in a post-processing phase.

It becomes apparent that a digital ink data processing solution for paper-based notetaking can neither rely solely on automatic processing nor on user-driven interpretation. We think that developers should be provided with framework support for both automatic and user-driven means of processing paper-based notes and have the possibility to switch between or combine the two approaches based on particular application requirements. We will present our proposal for

[1] http://www.livescribe.com
[2] http://www.oxfordeasybook.com
[3] http://www.logitech.com
[4] http://hci.stanford.edu/research/paper/

such an extensible digital ink processing framework, show how it has been integrated with an existing interactive paper solution and present a paper-based notetaking application that was implemented based on the presented framework.

DIGITAL INK DATA PROCESSING FRAMEWORK

Previous studies on natural notetaking have revealed that it is unlikely to be able to automatically identify different note categories and how they are meant to be used digitally unless some form of user intervention is involved [6]. At the same time, it was observed that notetakers are reluctant to adapt their notetaking behaviour to include user-generated metadata about how paper notes should be digitally processed. However, current framework support for developing digital pen and paper applications relies heavily on approaches for clustering and further processing digital ink data that introduce changes in the natural notetaking behaviour. Users are required to either write specific notes within designated page areas or mark them with pen-based gestures chosen by the developers based on certain observed notetaking patterns. All notes written in a predefined area or delimited in some way by one or more ink gestures will result in a digital ink cluster that is processed in a unitary manner defined by the developer in a digital callback function.

Works such as Ispas et al. [6], Wattenberg and Fisher [22] or Li et al. [9] have pointed out that handwritten notes represent a number of structured elements such as sketches or aggregations of text lines in the form of paragraphs or bullet lists. Such structured elements could potentially be automatically identified and extracted by clustering digital ink data based on spatial and temporal proximity. We propose that current software support for developing digital pen and paper-based applications should be extended to provide access to and means of manipulating such automatically extracted structures. For particular application domains, this could relax imposed notetaking conventions or even introduce an alternative to relying on multiple page areas or gestures and the assumption that users will use defined rules while taking notes. For example, a natural notetaking application that only requires access to note structures at the granularity level of paragraphs could rely on a paper-based interface with just one page area defined for each page. However, this approach requires more effort from developers since more sophisticated functionality able to identify and handle the structures within notes captured from a single page area needs to be provided inside associated callback functions. Certain automatic or semi-automatic approaches for the digital processing of handwritten information at the level of basic structures may be useful even for application domains that might require more refined access to the content of notes. Our goal is to provide means to combine user-driven approaches with automatically extracted structures to enable more flexible paper-based interfaces.

Figure 1 shows the paper-based user interface of a sample notetaking application. Except for a timeline positioned at the bottom, the page has the appearance of a regular notebook page with a writing area covering the remaining part. In the writing area, notetakers can take freehand notes. In addition, they can use the timeline to indicate that they want to be reminded by the digital notetaking application about particular notes within a certain period of time. The approach to mark handwritten notes implemented by the developer could for example consist of requiring notetakers to first mark the timeframe by touching the corresponding part of the timeline with the pen (1) and then select the notes by drawing a vertical line (2). As a result, all note structures located adjacent to the vertical pen stroke are combined into a higher level structure which is associated with the corresponding temporal metadata.

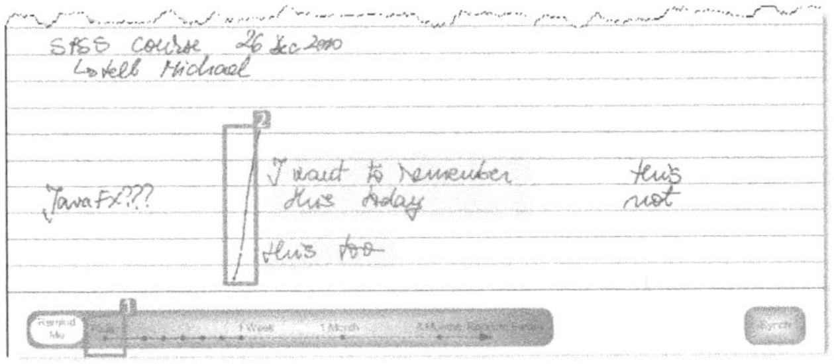

Figure 1. Notetaking application interface

Given that the support for extracting note structures is in place, developers may deal with handwritten notes at the level of the concepts shown in Figure 2. For a writing area represented by a `NotebookPage`, a developer can access its structural elements represented as `PageElement` instances. The `BasicElement` specialisation of the `PageElement` class represents the most basic entity that can be generated by a given digital ink data segmentation algorithm. Therefore, `BasicElement` instances aggregate low level ink data that has been assigned to single structures by the segmentation algorithm.

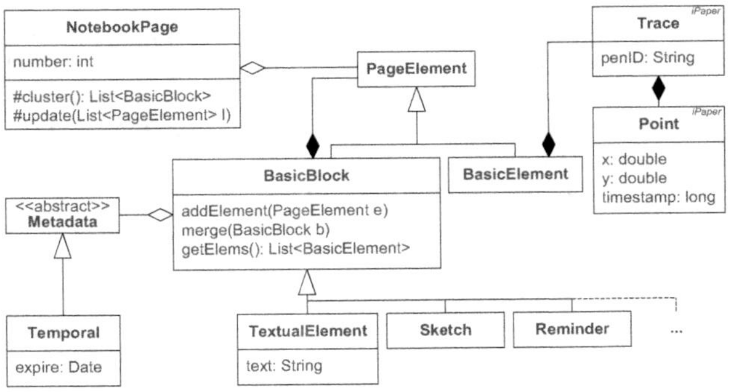

Figure 2. Notebook page class diagram

Typical representations for the digital ink data consist of providing a model for the handwritten strokes. We use here a representation based on `Traces` of timestamped `Points` which is the representation introduced by the iPaper framework [14]. The digital ink representations used by other digital pen and paper frameworks can easily be transformed to the iPaper format, for example, by using the InkML[5] representation as an intermediary format.

[5]http://www.w3.org/2002/mmi/ink

Multiple BasicElements positioned close to each other can be grouped forming BasicBlocks that represent collections of note elements. By default, page elements are grouped based on containment and intersection relationships between their bounding boxes. Custom heuristics for the grouping of note structures can furthermore be specified by overriding the protected cluster() method. For example, two BasicElements corresponding to two lines of handwritten notes could be grouped into a single block if the temporal gap between their last and respectively first digital ink data strokes fits into a certain interval identified as the time for a notetaker to switch to the next line. The method is invoked by default after the note segmentation step. A BasicBlock can be further specialised into various semantic structures such as the TextualElement, Sketch or Reminder classes. For this purpose, various heuristics for processing digital ink data at block level have to be implemented. For example, blocks that can be parsed into digital text can be classified as TextualElement. On the other hand, a BasicBlock consisting of one or several PageElements for which the handwriting recognition does not produce any accurate results might be classified as Sketch.

In addition to automatic approaches for detecting note structures, notetakers are also given the possibility to mark blocks of notes to be treated as a single semantic structure during the processing step as explained earlier when describing the paper interface in Figure 1. As opposed to automatically generated blocks of notes, user-specified blocks are associated with different Metadata classes such as the Temporal class in Figure 2 that could be used for our example to represent information about notes that users need to be reminded about at a specific time in the future.

Automatic Digital Ink Data Segmentation

In a previous study of notetaking practices [6], we identified three major types of note structures: paragraphs, bullet lists and sketches. For the first two types of structures, API support for manipulating individual lines of text may be useful and therefore we decided to take a bottom-up approach consisting of first extracting lines from the handwritten information and then grouping individual lines into blocks of notes according to their spatial relationships. As mentioned before, several approaches have been proposed for the clustering problem. Our implementation is based on the work of Ao et al. [3]. The authors present a technique for identifying textual lines based on the notion of a *link model*. Furthermore, they propose a solution for distinguishing between textual and graphical information. Inspired by their suggestions, we have chosen to identify sketch classes of note blocks based on the fact that the handwriting recognition engine does not return valid results.

According to the link model, a set of blocks composed of tightly connected pen strokes belong to the same textual line if their corresponding bounding boxes are located close to each other in a linear way and have comparable sizes. The three criteria are translated into measures applied to all segments formed between the centre points of all adjacent bounding boxes, called *links*. The links between the bounding boxes are identified by applying Delaunay triangulation.

In our digital ink data segmentation, we start with a set of note traces represented by the set of coordinates between successive pen down and pen up actions. As described in Ao et al., traces are first merged into blocks based on the timestamp information associated with each trace. Further, the minimum bounding boxes of the constructed blocks are computed. The minimum bounding box provides additional information about its associated trace such as the rotation with respect to the x-axis. Our computation of the minimum bounding boxes is based on rotating calipers [20] that are applied to the convex hull of a trace's points. For the Delaunay triangulation, we use the implementation of Paul Chew[6]. The three text line criteria μ_1, μ_2 and μ_3 for the closeness, linearity and similarity in size are implemented as follows:

Closeness

We consider that the measure μ_1 of the closeness of two bounding boxes is inversely proportional to the length l of the link between them:

$$\mu_1 = \frac{1}{l+1} \tag{1}$$

This results in $0 \leq \mu_1 \leq 1$. Note that we add 1 to the denominator to avoid division by zero in the situation where the two bounding boxes have the same centre point. In this case, we get the maximum value of 1 whereas a value of 0 results for $l \rightarrow \infty$.

Linearity

Given the two angles α_1 and α_2 representing the rotation of the two bounding boxes relative to their link, we define the linearity μ_2 of two bounding boxes as follows:

$$\mu_2 = \frac{1}{\mid \alpha_1 - \alpha_2 \mid +1} \tag{2}$$

For $\alpha_1 = \alpha_2$ the corresponding traces are positioned linearly.

Comparable sizes

To verify that two bounding boxes have similar sizes, we compute the value μ_3 based on their corresponding areas:

$$\mu_3 = \frac{1}{\mid A_1 - A_2 \mid +1} \tag{3}$$

The areas of the two bounding boxes are represented by A_1 and A_2, respectively.

[6]http://www.cs.cornell.edu/info/people/chew/Delaunay.html

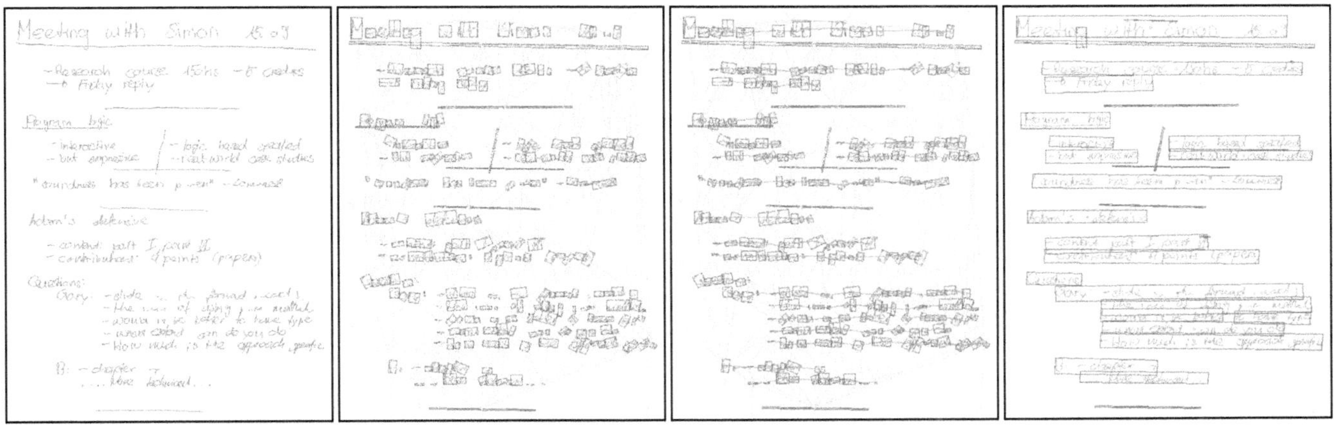

(a) Original notes (b) Delauney triangulation (c) Strongest links (d) Line segmentation

Figure 3. Successive line segmentation steps

Link strength

The link strength μ is computed based on the three criteria μ_1, μ_2 and μ_3 and is used in the detection of textual lines:

$$\mu = \mu_1 + \mu_2 + \mu_3 \qquad (4)$$

Given the original note page shown in Figure 3(a), the final result of the line segmentation is highlighted in Figure 3(d). In an intermediary step, we first apply Delaunay triangulation for the minimum bounding box computation shown in Figure 3(b) and then identify the strongest links shown in Figure 3(c).

The separation into basic page elements, which is equivalent to extracting lines in the case of the algorithm proposed by Ao et al., is provided by the `separate()` method of the `Separator` class shown in Figure 4. Every time some digital ink data is provided, for example by the iPaper framework in the form of a `Note` containing a number of traces in combination with information about the page number and the document and pen identifiers, this data is added to the `Separator` class. The invocation of the `separate()` method results in a list of `BasicElements` introduced earlier in Figure 1. The `cluster()` method that is invoked after the segmentation step generates a list of `BasicBlock` instances for each `NotebookPage`.

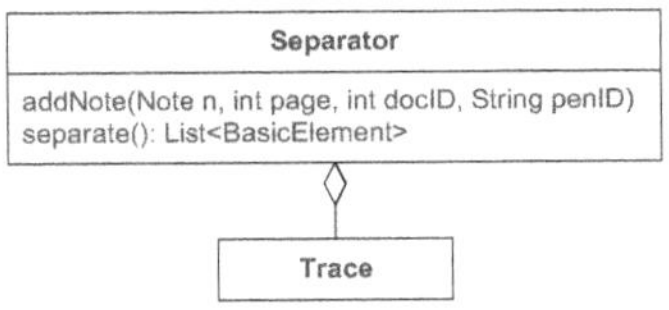

Figure 4. Class diagram for separation into basic elements

Listing 1 shows how the segmentation process was integrated with the iPaper framework for the sample notetaking application. iPaper provides support for defining active page areas and associating active components to be invoked when ink written within an area needs to be processed. The `DrawAreaStub` active component's `handleNote()` method contains the code to be invoked when processing notes captured from the main writing area of the application. When the user triggers the explicit synchronisation of their notes with the computer by touching the printed `Synch` button shown at the bottom right of Figure 1, the `SynchButtonStub` active component is instantiated. As illustrated in the listing, the `addNote()` method of the `Separator` class is invoked every time a new note has been captured. At synchronisation time, the `separate()` method of a `Separator` class is invoked. Existing `NotebookPage` instances are then refreshed via the `update()` method to reflect the new document structure after the last separation step.

Listing 1. iPaper active components for the sample application

```
public class DrawAreaStub extends CaptureNoteStub {
  public void handleNote(String docID, int page, Note n) {
    String penID = getDeviceAddress();
    Separator s = Separator.getInstance();
    s.addNote(n, page, docID, penID);
  }
}

public class SynchButtonStub extends SingleEventStub {
  public void finish() {
    Separator s = Separator.getInstance();
    // redo the separation and clustering for all pages
    List<BasicElement> basicElements = s.separate();
    List<BasicBlock> blocks = notebookPage.cluster();
    // add all blocks and basic elements into an update list
    List<PageElement> elements = ...
    notebookPage.update(elements);
  }
}
```

User-Driven Segmentation

In the case of the notetaking application interface described in Figure 1, we proposed an interaction model consisting of two successive pen-based interactions through which notetakers could provide guidelines for processing specific notes subsets. The first interaction step consists of pointing with the pen to a specific part of the printed timeline. This action is interpreted as an upper bound value for the lifetime of the reminder notes which are about to be selected in a second step. The system will interpret the selected notes as forming part of a single block structure containing one or several basic elements according to the length of the vertical line used to mark notes. The functionality is an example where traditional note processing support provided by a digital pen and paper application is used for manual user-driven segmentation and classification of a page's structural elements. For the classification, various metadata specified at the design time of the paper interface and associated with specific active page areas will generate the corresponding block metadata.

To support developers in designing paper-based interfaces with a user-driven classification of free-form notes, we propose a framework for the description of paper-based interaction models based on finite state machines (FSM). Figure 5 shows the class diagram of our solution for the specification of interaction models based on an FSM. The framework provides an extensible set of `States`, each of which has a unique name. Based on a given `Action` of type `GESTURE`, `TEXT`, `MESSAGE` or `TRACE`, the FSM gets into a new state via the `transition()` method. Each state can be configured with a method to be invoked and executed whenever the state is reached by using the `setInvokeMethod()` method. For each `Action`, an optional data value represented by the `data` field of a parametric type `T` can be configured. This allows the configuration of each action type with custom values such as the gesture class that has been recognised in combination with an action of type `GESTURE` or the text associated with an action of type `TEXT`.

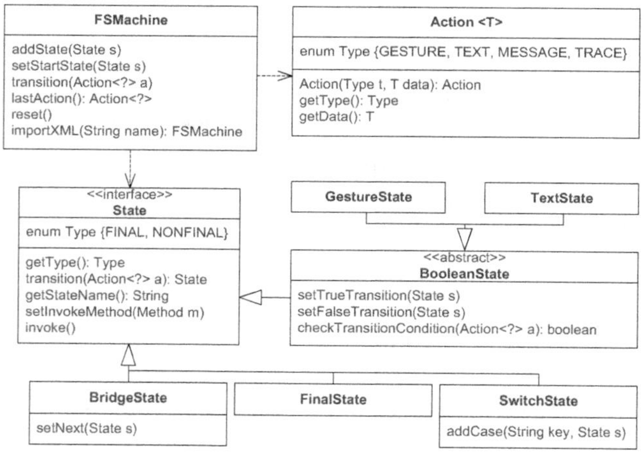

Figure 5. Class diagram for the finite state machine framework

Particular FSMs can be defined by a developer via an XML specification. Listing 2 shows the XML definition of a series of state types that are already provided by our framework.

Listing 2. XML representation of predefined state types

```
<machine>
  <state type="bridge" name="...">
    <next state="..." />
  </state>
  <state type="final" name="..." />
  <state type="gesture" name="..." />
    <condition className="..." />
    <true state="..." />
    <false state="..." />
  </state>
  <state type="text" name="..." />
    <condition text="..." />
    <true state="..." />
    <false state="..." />
  </state>
  <state type="switch" name="..." />
    <case key="default" state="..." />
    <case key="..." state="..." />
    ...
  </state>
</machine>
```

- *Bridge state*: From this type of node, the FSM will always transition to the state specified as `next`, regardless of the input action.

- *Final state*: When the FSM reaches a final node, it will continue its execution at the node that was marked as a start node as soon as the FSM receives a new input action.

- *Gesture state*: The FSM will transition from a gesture node to the state denoted by `true` when the `condition` is met. In all other cases, it will transition to the state denoted by `false`. The condition is met when the type of the input action is `GESTURE` and if the action's `data` field contains the value denoted by the `className` attribute.

- *Text state*: The text node is similar to a gesture node, with the difference that the input action type must be `TEXT`. In this case, the `data` field must contain the string value defined in the `text` attribute.

- *Switch state*: A switch state may have several possible outgoing transitions. It requires an input action of type `MESSAGE` and the `data` field must be assigned a value equal to one of the `key` attributes of the `case` elements. When none of the keys match the passed value, the transition marked by the default key is followed.

The FSM for our sample notetaking application is shown in Figure 6 and the corresponding XML code in Listing 3. The code for the iPaper active components presented previously has to be adapted to account for controlling the FSM as shown in Listing 4. Note that a third active component is associated with the different parts of the timeline. Every time the user touches the timeline with the pen, an instance of the active component will infer the temporal metadata value associated with the page area and create an `Action` of type `MESSAGE` configured with a "temporal" string value for its `data` field. Similarly, the `SynchButtonStub` active component creates an `Action` of type `MESSAGE`, but configured with a specific "synch" string value. No additional data is required in the `data` field of an `Action` of type `Trace`, an instance of which is created by the `DrawAreaStub` active component.

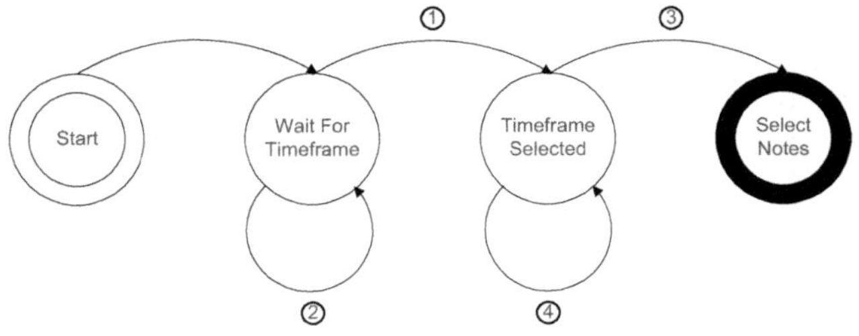

Figure 6. Finite state machine for sample notetaking application

In this case, the separation is managed through method calls specified in the XML description of the FSM. As long as a user takes notes in the main writing area, the FSM remains in the *Wait For Timeframe* state as shown by transition (2) and notes have to be added to the buffer maintained by the `Separator` class as shown by the `invoke` XML element. The `addNote()` method defined in a custom class, represented by the `Logic` class in Listing 3, is responsible for forwarding the call to the previously mentioned `addNote()` method of the `Separator` class. When the user selects a timeframe with the pen, transition (1) into the *Timeframe Selected* state is triggered. From this state, transition (3) is taken only if a user selects a group of notes by marking them with the digital pen. Otherwise, the FSM does not leave the state as indicated by transition (4). The `selectNotes()` method invoked after transition (3) is responsible for creating a new `BasicBlock` associated with the corresponding temporal metadata. Since new content has been added after the last segmentation, a new page separation into basic page elements is done before updating the block structure of the page. Further, `BasicElements` located next to the selecting vertical pen stroke (a single trace) will be grouped into a new block.

Listing 3. XML representation of a sample FSM

```
<machine>
  <state type="switch" name="WaitForTimeframe"
    start="true">
    <case key="default" state="WaitForTimeframe" />
    <case key="temporal" state="TimeframeSelected" />
    <invoke class="org.paperNotesManager.Logic"
      method="addNote" />
  </state>
  <state type="switch" name="TimeframeSelected">
    <case key="default" state="SelectNotes" />
    <case key="temporal" state="TimeframeSelected" />
    <invoke class="org.paperNotesManager.Logic"
      method="addNote" />
  </state>
  <state type="final" name="SelectNotes">
    <invoke class="org.paperNotesManager.Logic"
      method="selectNotes" />
  </state>
</machine>
```

In this particular case, the last pen stroke written in the main writing area will be used for the selection of the page elements that have to be associated with specific metadata, independently of their content or shape. Another possibility would be to perform the selection only if users draw a specific gesture or write a specific keyword immediately after defining the timeframe. For this purpose, a gesture or a text state could be introduced in the specified FSM after the *Timeframe Selected* state.

Listing 4. Adapted iPaper active components specification

```
public class DrawAreaStub extends CaptureNoteStub {
  public void handleNote(String docID, int page, Note n) {
    Action<String> action = new Action<String>(
      Action.Type.TRACE, null);
    Logic.getFSM().transistion(action);
  }
}

public class TemporalMarkerStub extends SingleEventStub {
  public void finish() {
    Date date = getTemporalMarker();
    Logic.addMetadata(new TemporalMetadata(date));
    Action<String> action = new Action<String>(
      Action.Type.MESSAGE, "temporal");
    Logic.getFSM().transistion(action);
  }
}

public class SynchButtonStub extends SingleEventStub {
  public void finish() {
    Action<String> action = new Action<String>(
      Action.Type.MESSAGE, "synch");
    Logic.getFSM().transistion(action);
  }
}
```

Custom Classification

The segmentation into basic page elements and the subsequent clustering into basic blocks reveals some details about the high-level structure of handwritten notes. However, this grouping into basic blocks only reflects spatial and temporal properties of the different notes and content is not taken into consideration. In this section, we therefore highlight how developers can further process the existing basic structures based on the classification components shown in Figure 7.

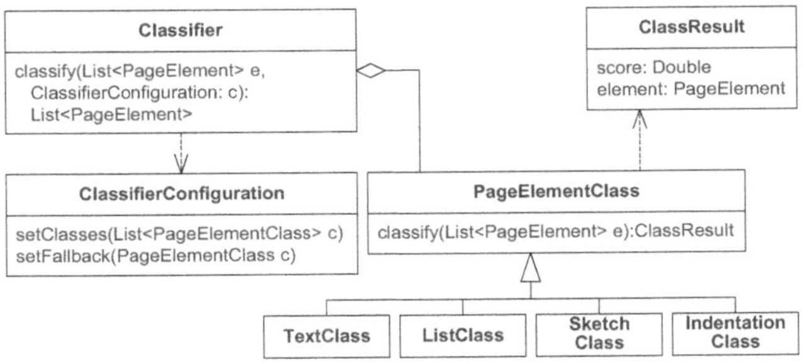

Figure 7. Classifier

Given a set of `PageElementClasses`, the `classify()` method defined in the `Classifier` class will analyse a collection of `PageElement` instances provided as input and create more specific `PageElement` subclasses. Each classification class returns a `ClassResult` instance consisting of a confidence score ($0 \leq score \leq 1$) for the membership of a given `PageElement` in a specific classification. The classifier generates this score for each of the classes configured in the `ClassifierConfiguration` and recommends the classification result with the highest score. The score has to be higher than a certain threshold, which in our implementation was set to 0.5. If there is no possible classification with a score higher than the threshold, the `Classifier` will return a fallback classification class as specified in a classifier's configuration. The basic configuration of a classifier is presented in Listing 5.

Listing 5. Basic configuration for the classification

```
List<PageElement> originalElements = ...

// set up the classes to be checked against
List<PageElementClass> classes =
   new LinkedList<PageElementClass>();
classes.add(new ExampleClass());

// set the fallback class to SketchClass
PageElementClass fallback = new SketchClass();
ClassifierConfiguration config =
   new ClassifierConfiguration(classes, fallback);

// classify the input elements
Classifier c = new Classifier();
List<PageElement> classifiedElements =
   c.classify(originalElements, config);
```

Our digital ink processing framework offers an implementation for some default classifiers:

Text Class

The `TextClass` is based on the output of a handwriting recognition algorithm and the score is directly related to the confidence value of the used handwriting recognition engine. In our implementation, we used the MyScript Intelligent Character Recognition from VisionObjects[7] for the handwriting recognition.

Sketch Class

The `SketchClass` is meant to be used as a fallback class with a classification score of 1. Typically, the classifier will generate a `Sketch` element if every other configured classification fails.

Indentation Class

The `IdentationClass` verifies whether a `BasicBlock` that contains several `PageElement` instances represents a multi-level bullet list structure. In a first step, the indentation level of each basic element contained within a block is determined. Page elements are sorted in ascending order based on the upper left corner of their bounding box. The ordering is done first for the x coordinate and then for the y coordinate. After the ordering, the corner points are iterated over and it is checked whether the difference to the previous anchor point is greater than some threshold. The threshold value is used to define what is to be interpreted as simple white space and what has to be considered list item indentation. Depending on the result of the comparison, an element's indentation level is set to the same value as the indentation level of the previous element or to a level increased by 1. Figure 8 shows the result of such a procedure. Finally, the score of the classification is set to a value equal to the average computed for the confidence levels returned by the handwriting recognition engine for each of the structural elements.

[7]http://www.visionobjects.com/

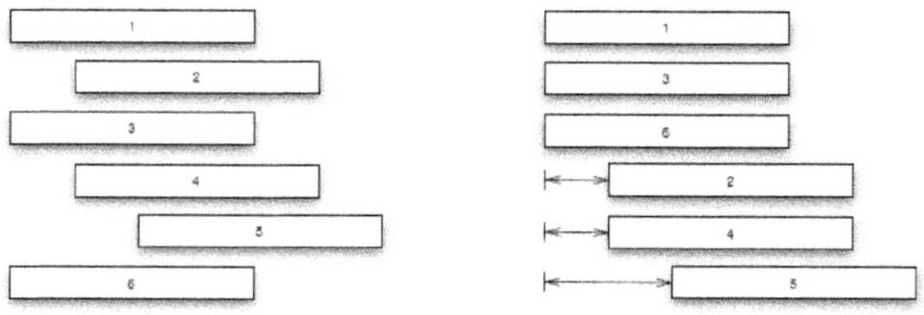

Figure 8. Determining the indentation of a set of lines

List Class

The `ListClass` can be seen as a specialisation of the indentation class where the subelements represent an item list on a single indentation level, each of them starting with a given token.

To give an idea about the effort required for implementing classification classes, we refer to Listing 6. Given a set of `PageElements`, the class creates a block classified as `Title` if all page elements can be parsed into text with a certain confidence and the element placed below all other elements is a straight line having a length comparable to or bigger than the length of all other elements placed above. An example of such a title element is shown at the top of the page in Figure 3(a). The score of the class can be computed, for example, by averaging the score of the handwriting recognition with the score from the straight line detector, the score of the straightness being given a higher importance.

Listing 6. Custom title classification

```
public class TitleClass implements PageElementClass {
  ...
  @override
  public ClassResult classify(List<PageElements> e) {
    double score = 0.0;
    // get the lowest element
    PageElement last = getLowestElement(e);

    // is the last element long?
    if (isStraightLineLong(e, last)) {
      // is the last element a straight line?
      score = scoreStraightLine(last);
    }

    // get text representation without the line
    e.remove(last);
    Result hwrResult = parseText(e);

    // construct the classification result
    ClassResult r = new ClassResult();
    r.score = (score*2 + hwrResult.getConfidence()) / 3.0;

    // create a new title page element
    e.add(last);
    r.element = new Title(e, hwrResult.getText());
    return r;
  }
}
```

It can be seen that developers are provided with the possibility of working at block level and simple computations such as determining relationships between the bounding boxes of the various elements already provide relatively powerful results. Furthermore, digital ink processing operations at page element level, as in the case of the list class presented earlier, can reveal further classification possibilities. However, the ink processing effort is restricted to parts of the notes.

Framework-based Application Development

Existing frameworks for digital pen and paper application development focus on the design of the paper-based interface of a particular solution in terms of active page areas and marking gestures. In addition to imposing changes on natural notetaking practices, this also leads to less flexibility in developing the digital counterpart of the solution since the latter becomes bound to the first. The structure of the paper interface determines the segmentation of the digital ink data and, subsequently, the level of granularity at which developers can access and handle digitally handwritten information. In the case that access at lower granularity levels is needed, developers are required to implement the segmentation of digital ink data. Furthermore, changing the paper interface leads to the necessity to also implement changes in the digital counterpart of the application.

Our framework provides access to basic note structures captured from a single page area and supports the further grouping of elementary structures based on custom heuristics. The basic or composed structures can be further classified based on an extensible set of heuristics. The benefits of our solution are twofold. First, the framework facilitates the handling of digital ink data, which reduces the amount of required low level digital ink processing by developers and enables them to focus on the GUI of an information management application and the rendering of digital ink data represented as `PageElements`. Second, rather than relying on complicated paper interfaces to enforce the digital ink data processing, parts of the processing can be shifted to the post-capture phase. In addition to improving the flexibility of the development process, applications may rely on less complicated paper interfaces, further relaxing changes imposed on natural notetaking.

Figure 9 highlights two applications that have been realised based on our digital ink processing framework and integrated with the paper interface described in Figure 1. Paragraphs and bullet lists of notes written in the main writing area of a page are extracted through an automatic segmentation process and integrated with a to-do list application or presented as post-it notes on the digital desktop. Notes can be presented in handwritten form or users can also switch to a version processed by a handwriting recognition engine. If some of the notes are associated with temporal metadata through user-driven segmentation, the corresponding post-its or to-do list items will have their due date automatically set based on the value selected by the user via the paper interface. Instead of having to deal with the low level processing of ink data, the main task of the developer of these applications was to implement the appropriate set of functionalities required

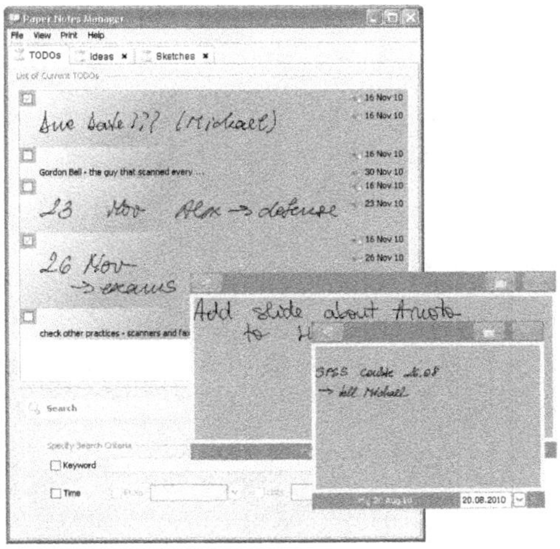

Figure 9. Paper notes as to-do list and post-it reminders

by the end user, such as support for updating the captured information or configuring user interface elements.

CONCLUSIONS

We have presented a digital ink segmentation and classification framework that significantly simplifies the development of digital pen and paper-based notetaking applications. The framework provides access to the main structural elements of handwritten notes made available after a segmentation process, support to further group such elementary structures and an extensible set of classification heuristics for digital ink data. This allows an application developer to focus on the aspects of presenting different classes of notes as part of digital applications rather than having to deal with the low level processing of digital ink data. In addition, we have presented a solution for the definition of paper-based interaction models based on finite state machines, simplifying the complex note processing and interactive paper interface definition. Last but not least, we have introduced two digital pen and paper-based notetaking solutions that have been realised based on the presented digital ink processing framework.

REFERENCES

1. Anoto SDK for PC Applications, June 2010. V 3.3.2.0.
2. Livescribe Desktop SDK, June 2010. V 0.7.0.
3. X. Ao, J. Li, X. Wang, and G. Dai. Structuralizing Digital Ink for Efficient Selection. In *Proc. of Conf. on Intelligent User Interfaces (IUI '06)*, Sydney, Australia, January 2006.
4. P. Brandl, C. Richter, and M. Haller. NiCEBook - Supporting Natural Note Taking. In *Proc. of Conf. on Human Factors in Computing Systems (CHI '10)*, Atlanta, USA, April 2010.
5. J. M. Heiner, S. E. Hudson, and K. Tanaka. Linking and Messaging from Real Paper in the Paper PDA. In *Proc. of Symposium on User Interface Software and Technology (UIST '99)*, Asheville, USA, November 1999.

6. A. Ispas, B. Signer, and M. C. Norrie. A Study and Design Implications for Incidental Notetaking with Digital Pen and Paper Technologies. In *Proc. of BCS Conf. on Human Computer Interaction (HCI '10)*, Dundee, Scotland, September 2010.

7. F. Khan. A Survey of Note-Taking Practices. Technical Report HPL-93-107, HP Laboratories Bristol, December 1993.

8. J. A. Landay and R. C. Davis. Making Sharing Pervasive: Ubiquitous Computing for Shared Note Taking. *IBM Systems Journal*, 38(4):531–550, 1999.

9. Y. Li, Z. Guan, H. Wang, G. Dai, and X. Ren. Structuralizing Freeform Notes by Implicit Sketch Understanding. In *AAAI Spring Symposium on Sketch Understanding SS-02-08*, Palo Alto, USA, March 2002.

10. C. Liao, F. Guimbretière, and K. Hinckley. PapierCraft: A Command System for Interactive Paper. In *Proc. of Symposium on User Interface Software and Technology (UIST '05)*, Seattle, USA, October 2005.

11. C. Liao, F. Guimbretière, and C. E. Loeckenhoff. Pen-top Feedback for Paper-based Interfaces. In *Proc. of Symposium on User Interface Software and Technology (UIST '06)*, Montreux, Switzerland, October 2006.

12. M. Lin, W. G. Lutters, and T. S. Kim. Understanding the Micronote Lifecycle: Improving Mobile Support for Informal Note Taking. In *Proc. of Conf. on Human Factors in Computing Systems (CHI '04)*, Vienna, Austria, April 2004.

13. T. P. Moran, P. Chiu, W. van Melle, and G. Kurtenbach. Implicit Structure for Pen-based Systems within a Freeform Interaction Paradigm. In *Proc. of Conf. on Human Factors in Computing Systems (CHI '95)*, Denver, USA, May 1995.

14. M. C. Norrie, B. Signer, and N. Weibel. General Framework for the Rapid Development of Interactive Paper Applications. In *Proc. of Workshop on Collaborating over Paper and Digital Documents (CoPADD '06)*, Banff, Canada, November 2006.

15. E. Saund, D. Fleet, D. Larner, and J. Mahoney. Perceptually-supported Image Editing of Text and Graphics. In *Proc. of Symposium on User Interface Software and Technology (UIST '03)*, Vancouver, Canada, November 2003.

16. M. Shilman, Z. Wei, S. Raghupathy, P. Simard, and D. Jones. Discerning Structure from Freeform Handwritten Notes. In *Proc. of Conf. on Document Analysis and Recognition (ICDAR '03)*, Edinburgh, Scotland, August 2003.

17. B. Signer, U. Kurmann, and M. C. Norrie. iGesture: A General Gesture Recognition Framework. In *Proc. of Conf. on Document Analysis and Recognition (ICDAR '07)*, Curitiba, Brazil, September 2007.

18. B. Signer and M. C. Norrie. PaperPoint: A Paper-based Presentation and Interactive Paper Prototyping Tool. In *Proc. of Conf. on Tangible, Embedded and Embodied Interaction (TEI '07)*, Baton Rouge, USA, February 2007.

19. A. Tabard, W. E. Mackay, and E. Eastmond. From Individual to Collaborative: The Evolution of Prism, a Hybrid Laboratory Notebook. In *Proc. of Conf. on Computer Supported Cooperative Work (CSCW '08)*, San Diego, USA, November 2008.

20. G. Toussaint. Solving Geometric Problems with the Rotating Calipers. In *Proc. of Mediterranean Electrotechnical Conf. (MELECON '83)*, Athens, Greece, May 1983.

21. T. Wang and B. Plimmer. SmartList: Exploring Intelligent Hand-written List Support. In *Proc. of Conf. of NZ ACM Special Interest Group on Human-Computer Interaction (CHINZ '09)*, Auckland, New Zealand, July 2009.

22. M. Wattenberg and D. Fisher. A Model of Multi-scale Perceptual Organization in Information Graphics. In *Proc. of Symposium on Information Visualization (INFOVIS '03)*, Seattle, USA, October 2003.

23. N. Weibel, A. Ispas, B. Signer, and M. C. Norrie. PaperProof: A Paper-digital Proof-editing System. In *Proc. of Conf on Human Factors in Computing Systems (Extended Abstracts) (CHI '08)*, Florence, Italy, April 2008.

24. S. Whittaker, P. Hyland, and M. Wiley. FILOCHAT: Handwritten Notes Provide Access to Recorded Conversations. In *Proc. of Conf. on Human Factors in Computing Systems (CHI '94)*, Boston, USA, April 1994.

25. L. D. Wilcox, B. N. Schilit, and N. Sawhney. Dynomite: A Dynamically Organized Ink and Audio Notebook. In *Proc. of Conf. on Human Factors in Computing Systems (CHI '97)*, Atlanta, USA, March 1997.

26. M. Ye, , P. Viola, S. Raghupathy, H. Sutanto, and C. Li. Learning to Group Text Lines and Regions in Freeform Handwritten Notes. In *Proc. of Conf. on Document Analysis and Recognition (ICDAR '07)*, Curitiba, Brazil, September 2007.

27. R. Yeh, C. Liao, S. Klemmer, F. Guimbretière, B. Lee, B. Kakaradov, J. Stamberger, and A. Paepcke. ButterflyNet: a Mobile Capture and Access System for Field Biology Research. In *Proc. of Conf. on Human Factors in Computing Systems (CHI '06)*, Montréal, Canada, April 2006.

28. R. B. Yeh, A. Paepcke, and S. R. Klemmer. Iterative Design and Evaluation of an Event Architecture for Pen-and-paper Interfaces. In *Proc. of Symposium on User Interface Software and Technology (UIST '08)*, Monterey, USA, October 2008.

Improving FTIR Based Multi-touch Sensors with IR Shadow Tracking

Samuel A. Iacolina [1]
samueliacolina@gmail.com

Alessandro Soro [1,2]
asoro@crs4.it

Riccardo Scateni [1]
riccardo@unica.it

[1] Department of Mathematics and Computer Science
University of Cagliari
Via Ospedale, 72 09124 - Cagliari, Italy

[2] CRS4 - Center for Advanced Studies, Research and Development in Sardinia
POLARIS Science Park - Ed. 1 - 09010 Pula - Italy

ABSTRACT

Frustrated Total Internal Reflection (FTIR) is a key technology for the design of multi-touch systems. With respect to other solutions, such as Diffused Illumination (DI) and Diffused Surface Illumination (DSI), FTIR based sensors suffer less from ambient IR noise, and is, thus, more robust to variable lighting conditions. However, FTIR does not provide (or is weak on) some desirable features, such as finger proximity and tracking quick gestures. This paper presents an improvement for FTIR based multi-touch sensing that partly addresses the above issues exploiting the shadows projected on the surface by the hands to improve the quality of the tracking system. The proposed solution exploits natural uncontrolled light to improve the tracking algorithm: it takes advantage of the natural IR noise to aid tracking, thus turning one of the main issues of MT sensors into a useful quality, making it possible to implement pre-contact feedback and enhance tracking precision.

Author Keywords

Multi-touch, FTIR, Tracking

ACM Classification Keywords

H.5.2 Information interfaces and presentation: User Interfaces. - Input Devices and Strategies

General Terms

Design

INTRODUCTION

Multi-touch displays represent an intriguing research field that, recently, has gained new attention. Following seminal work from, among others, Buxton [3], and up to the recent developments of Han [5, 6], multi-touch systems offer a suitable working environment for computer supported cooperative work, leveraging the exploration of new frontiers of social computing.

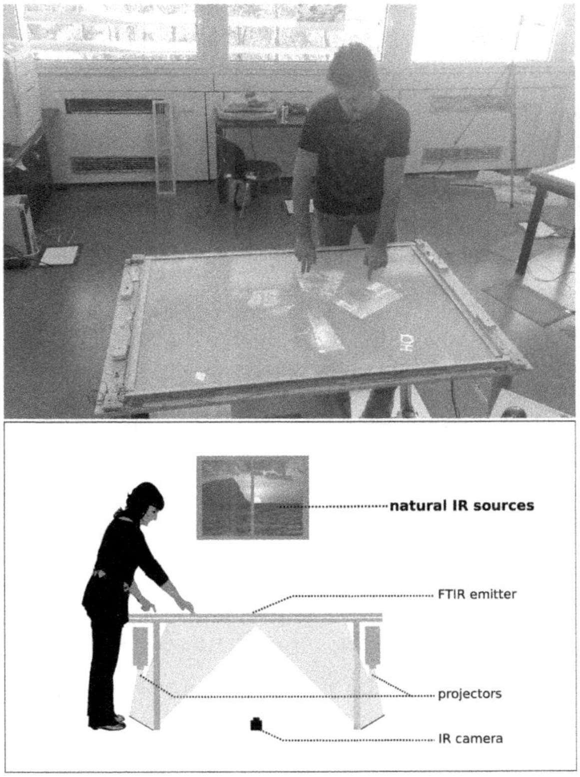

Figure 1. The top picture was captured while using the table, the bottom is a schema representing the overall setup of the table. Notice the operational conditions: strong direct lights and sharp variations of the luminosity.

A key technology for the design of multi-touch systems is Frustrated Total Internal Reflection (FTIR). Common FTIR

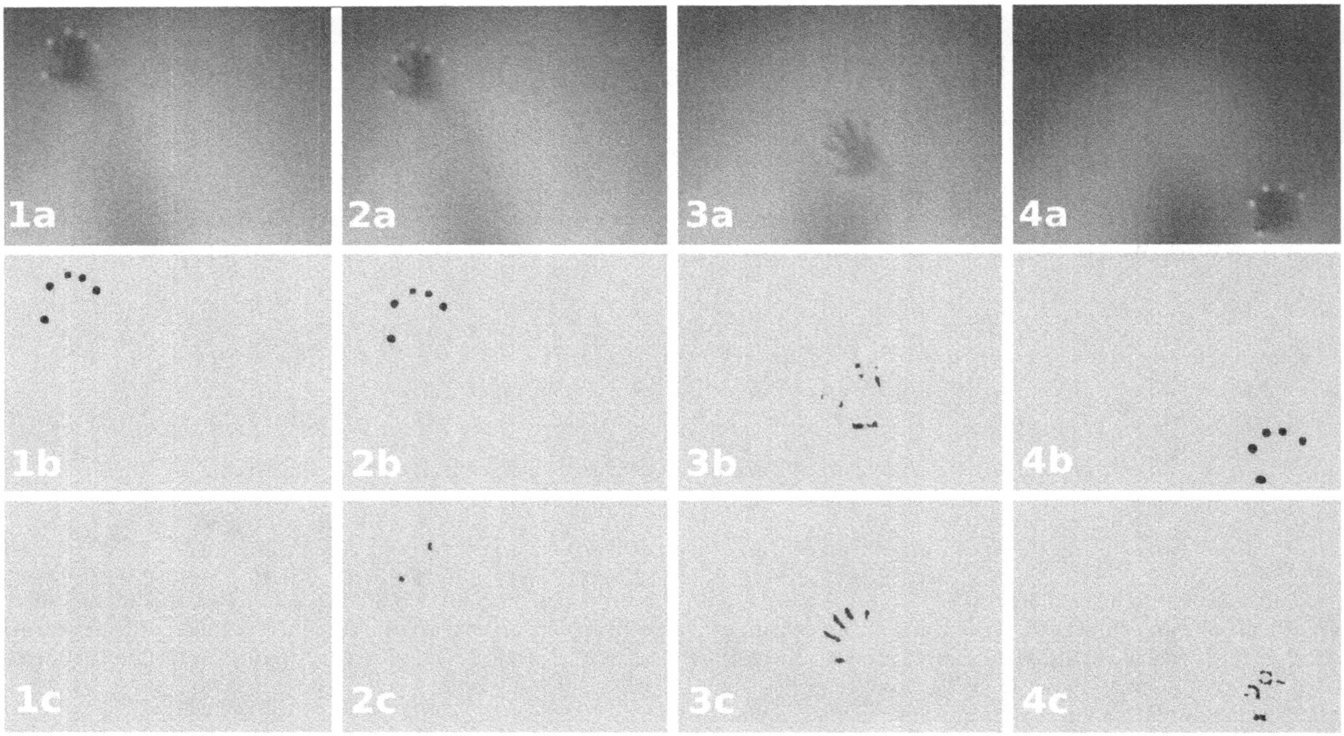

Figure 2. The result of tracking on IR light and IR shadow.

setups [5] have a transparent acrylic pane with a frame of LEDs around the side injecting infrared light. When the user touches the acrylic, the light escapes and is reflected at the finger's point of contact. The infrared sensitive camera at the back of the pane can clearly see these reflections. As the acrylic is transparent a projector can be located behind the surface (near to the camera) yielding a back-projected touch sensitive display. The software part consists in a basic set of computer vision algorithms applied to the camera image to determine the location of the contact point. An advantage of FTIR based sensors over competing solutions (such as DI, DSI [8]) is that this technology suffers less from ambient IR noise, and is thus more robust to changing lighting conditions. On the other hand, it is well known that FTIR has some disadvantages:

- it does not sense finger proximity, the user must touch the surface;
- it is difficult to track the fingers during movements;
- though more robust to changes in ambient light, it still relies on a control over lighting conditions.

To partly address such issues we propose to take advantage of the shadows that the hands of the user project on the interaction surface. Our experiments show that such solution allows to effectively sense user interaction in an uncontrolled environment, and without the need of screening the sides of the multi-touch table (see Figure 1). IR shadow tracking is described in depth in Section 2. In order to help other researchers and practitioners to duplicate our results the complete image processing pipeline is described in Section 3. References to related work and state of the art are given throughout the text where appropriate.

TRACKING IR SHADOWS

Tracking infrared shadows to improve the quality of multi-touch interaction has been studied before. Echtler and co-workers [4] describe a system to sense hovering on the surface, and thus provide pre-contact feedback in order to improve the precision of touch on the user's part. However the system they describe is based on a controlled IR lighting source above the table. In this sense their system exploits an additional artificial lighting source, increasing the dependence on the lighting conditions.

Our solution, as further described below, exploits natural uncontrolled light to improve the tracking algorithm. We take advantage of the natural IR noise to aid tracking, thus turning one of the main issues of MT sensors into a useful quality, making it possible to enhance tracking precision and implement pre-contact feedback.

The proposed technology exploits the shadows projected on the surface by the hands of the users to improve the quality of the tracking system. As said above, ambient light has a negative impact on the IR based sensors when the light coming from the IR LEDs is not bright enough to prevail on the background noise. However, the hands of the user project a shadow on the surface (that will appear as a dark area in the noisy background). Such dark area is easily tracked because it is almost completely free of noise.

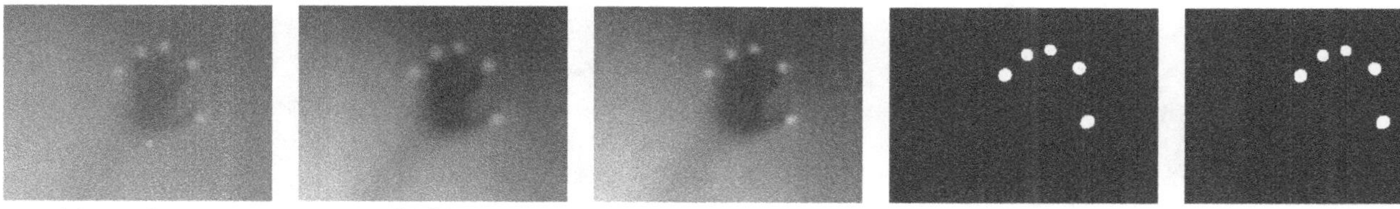

(a) raw image (b) blur (c) multiply (d) foreground (e) opening

Figure 3. Smoothing, enhancement and foreground segmentation on IR light blobs.

(a) raw image (b) blur (c) multiply (d) foreground (e) opening

Figure 4. Smoothing, enhancement and foreground segmentation on IR shadows.

Furthermore, fingertips correspond to the darker parts of the shadow, and can be recognized with good accuracy. Note that tracking the shadow is more and more effective as the ambient light increases (as opposite from IR blobs tracking), thus IR tracking and shadow tracking tend to complement each other, the former working better in full darkness, the latter in full daylight. A second useful feature, consists in the ability of the shadow tracking system to sense objects that are only close (i.e., don't actually touch) the surface, thus allowing the sensor to recognize a richer collection of gestures.

Finally, a well known problem of FTIR based systems is that blob brightness decreases as the user moves her hands fast. This problem is typically addressed covering the screen with compliant surface and silicon rubber. Shadow tracking does not suffer from this issue, and can thus be exploited to improve finger tracking during sharp movements. Such complementarities are key aspects of our work: it allows the system to work in less controlled environments, and to be more robust to changing lighting condition, as may easily happen in real world, off-lab installations. This latter is, as known, one of the major issues for computer vision based interactive systems.

Our implementation, based on OpenCV [7] for computer vision algorithms, shows significant improvements in the effectiveness of the sensor and, as a consequence, on the quality of interaction.

Figure 2 shows some frames from the image processing pipeline. Frames (1a-4a) are raw images as captured from the IR camera. The hand of the user is moving from top left to bottom right. Frames (1b-4b) are the output of the IR light tracking. Frames (1c-4c) are the output of IR shadow tracking. At (1a) the user has just touched the surface in an area relatively free of noise. The fingertips adhere well to the surface and the FTIR effect works perfectly as the result of IR tracking displayed in (1b) shows.

At (2a) the user is beginning to move her hand. As known, the IR light blobs tend to dim, but are still clear and trackable (2b). This is due to the fact that (i) the finger adhere less effectively to the surface while moving, and (ii) the hand is entering a noisy area. However the latter is partially counterbalanced by the IR shadow tracking (2c).

At (3a) the hand of the user is moving very fast and is within an area of high IR noise. The IR light blobs are invisible (3b), but the IR shadow appears clear and is easily tracked (3c).

Finally, at (4a) the user has completed the interaction phase and holds her hand still. Again the IR light blobs prevail on the noisy background and can be tracked with great precision (4b).

At this point, combining the two input sources (light blobs and infrared shadows) is a straightforward task; details are given in the next section (Tracking).

IMAGE PROCESSING PIPELINE

As known, the process of finger tracking for CV based multi-touch sensors is typically modeled as a pipeline consisting of several stages: from image acquisition to preprocessing, finger detection and tracking. All transformations are implemented by means of convolution matrices. The steps through which our implementation passes are as following.

Smoothing

A blur filter is applied to smooth the image removing the Gaussian noise, thus getting rid of pixel size spots (see Equation 1 and Figures 3b and 4b).

$$G(x,y) = e^{-\frac{x^2+y^2}{2\sigma^2}} \quad (1)$$

Enhancement

A rectification filter enhances the luminosity of each pixel (see Equation 2 and Figures 3c and 4c).

$$img(x,y) = \frac{(img(x,y))^2}{(max(img(x,y)))^2} \quad (2)$$

Background Removal Filter

The picture is filtered in order to find the areas of the screen on which an interaction is happening. To this purpose a 7×7 matrix with Gaussian distribution was empirically determined. The result is thresholded in order to select relevant areas. This operation in practice finds local maxima in the captured image. However the resulting image still presents some noise and must be further processed. Note that this same filter, applied to the negative image, is used in shadow tracking (see Figures 3d and 4d).

Opening

An opening filter erodes spots whose size is smaller than a given value, often referred to as *salt and pepper* noise (see Equation 3 and Figures 3e and 4e).

$$img \circ m = (img \ominus m) \oplus m \quad (3)$$

Lens Distortion Removal

The image is processed in order to compensate radial and tangential distortion due to the lens of the camera. Radial (Equation 4) and tangential (Equation 5) distortion correction require parameters p and k that can be computed by identifying distortions of images containing known regular patterns [2] (see Figure 5). Note that OpenCV provides black-box functions to this purpose.

$$\begin{aligned} x_{\text{corrected}} &= x(1 + k_1 r^2 + k_2 r^4 + k_3 r^6) \\ y_{\text{corrected}} &= y(1 + k_1 r^2 + k_2 r^4 + k_3 r^6) \end{aligned} \quad (4)$$

$$\begin{aligned} x_{\text{corrected}} &= x + [2p_1 y + p_2(r^2 + 2x^2)] \\ y_{\text{corrected}} &= y + [p_1(r^2 + 2y^2) + 2p_2 x] \end{aligned} \quad (5)$$

Perspective Distortion Correction

This last stage aims at transforming between capture coordinates and display coordinates and getting rid of perspective when (as often happens) the camera is not placed perfectly perpendicular against the plane of interaction. This operation requires four points on the screen to be matched against 4 points in the capture. Usually this is performed manually (during an initial *calibration* phase). Such transformation is efficiently computed as an inverse mapping between triangular meshes [1].

To do so, the position of a point to be mapped from camera space to display space can be expressed in baricentric coordinates: if A, B and C are the vertices of a triangle, a point P inside the triangle is uniquely identified by $P = \lambda_1 A + \lambda_2 B + \lambda_3 C$, where $\lambda_1 + \lambda_2 + \lambda_3 = 1$. Any deformation applied to the triangle does not change the baricentric coordinates of the point P, then since the coordinates of points A, B and C in the display are known from the calibration phase it's easy to compute the coordinates of point P on the display.

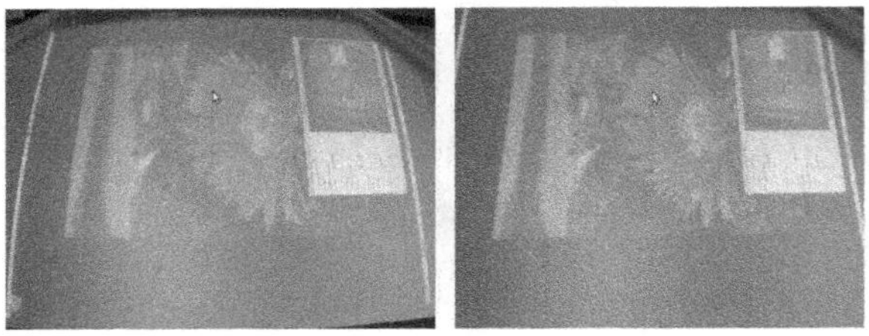

Figure 5. Lens distortion (pincushion and barrel) must be corrected.

The complete pipeline, both for IR blob light tracking and IR shadow tracking is depicted in Figures 3 and 4. See from left to right how the image is filtered to enhance meaningful features.

Tracking

Finally, tracking fingers that touch the screen is done as follows:

1. an improved Continuosly Adaptive Mean-shift algorithm (camshift) [7] is applied to determine a region of interest (ROI) surrounding the finger in each successive frame, in order to track the finger and reduce the region of calculation, the camshift algorithm constantly adjusts the size of the search window;
2. for each video frame, a matrix that represents the probability distribuition of the foreground image is analyzed to determine the centre of the ROI;
3. the current size and location of the tracked object are reported and used to set the size location of the search window in the next video image.
4. based on the previous items, the system searches for fingers both in the shadow and light foreground images so that the tracking will continue even in variable lighting conditions.

CONCLUSIONS AND FUTURE WORK

Summarizing, we have shown how the performances of FTIR based multi-touch sensors can be improved by tracking the shadows that user hands project on the screen. The value of such improvement becomes evident considering that the efficacy of shadows tracking is higher just in those condition that are more critical for IR blob tracking.

This allows to develop a sensor based on a combination of the two strategies, that is more robust to changing lighting conditions. Additional benefits include the ability of shadow tracking to sense proximity to the surface, where blob tracking is only sensitive to finger contact.

Further development will be aimed at exploiting shadows (tracing them back to the body of the person) to discriminate user action. The ability to associate the gestures sensed to the user that executes them is a key aspect in the development of multiuser collaborative (and even more for competitive) applications.

REFERENCES

1. Christopher J. Bradley. *The Algebra of Geometry: Cartesian, Areal and Projective Co-ordinates*. Highperception, 2007.

2. Duane C. Brown. Decentering distortion of lenses. *Photogrammetric Engineering*, 32(3):444–462, 1966.

3. William A. S. Buxton and Brad A. Myers. A study in two-handed input. *SIGCHI Bull.*, 17(4):321–326, 1986.

4. Florian Echtler, Manuel Huber, and Gudrun Klinker. Shadow tracking on multi-touch tables. In *AVI '08: Proceedings of the working conference on Advanced visual interfaces*, pages 388–391, New York, NY, USA, 2008. ACM.

5. Jefferson Y. Han. Low-cost multi-touch sensing through frustrated total internal reflection. In *UIST '05: Proceedings of the 18th annual ACM symposium on User interface software and technology*, pages 115–118, New York, NY, USA, 2005. ACM.

6. Jefferson Y. Han. Multi-touch interaction wall. In *SIGGRAPH '06: ACM SIGGRAPH 2006 Emerging technologies*, page 25, New York, NY, USA, 2006. ACM.

7. Intel Corporation. *Open Source Computer Vision Library - Reference Manual*, 2000.

8. Johannes Schöning, Peter Brandl, Florian Daiber, Florian Echtler, Otmar Hilliges, Jonathan Hook, Markus Löchtefeld, Nima Motamedi, Laurence Muller, Patrick Olivier, Tim Roth, and Ulrich von Zadow. Multi-touch surfaces: A technical guide. Technical Report TUM-I0833, University of Münster, 2008.

Towards Informed Metaphor Selection for TUIs

Stefan Oppl
Kepler University of Linz
Altenberger Strasse 69
4040 Linz, Austria
stefan.oppl@jku.at

Chris Stary
Kepler University of Linz
Altenberger Strasse 69
4040 Linz, Austria
christian.stary@jku.at

ABSTRACT
In TUI design the selection of metaphors influences user expectations and ease of use. Traditional TUI design processes have not addressed this issue explicitly so far. A reflection of existing approaches for metaphor classification in TUI design helps explaining why TUI metaphors not fitting could mislead users. Based upon these explanations, we could gain empirical insight into negative effects caused by selecting metaphors not fitting the situation of use. The results allow pursuing a metaphor-aware TUI specification process, as they address metaphor selection explicitly, and can be grounded in both, concept development, and empirical findings.

Author Keywords
Tangible User Interface, Metaphor, Specification, Study

ACM Classification Keywords
H5.2. Information interfaces and presentation (e.g., HCI): User Interfaces – Haptic I/O

ACM General Terms
Design, Human Factors

INTRODUCTION
Interaction based upon metaphors allows users selecting activities appropriate to their context of work and current task [1]. Selection of these metaphors is crucial for the comprehensibility, and thus usability (ease of use, conformance to user expectations, and learnability) of an interactive computer system [2]. In the field of Tangible User Interface (TUI) research, early works (e.g. by Ishii & Ullmer [3]) have already recognized the importance of metaphor. Recent publications [4][5][6] continue to consider this topic relevant.

Several authors [7][8][9] have systematically investigated metaphors for TUI (Tangible User Interface) design. However, they mainly focus on ex-post analytical classifications of TUI metaphors. Approaches targeting towards the specification of design tasks (e.g. the TAC paradigm as proposed by [10]) currently do not consider metaphor selection explicitly.

EICS'11, June 13–16, 2011, Pisa, Italy.

In this work, we describe the first steps towards a design process that fills this gap. In the first part of the paper, we review and summarize existing work on TUI metaphor classification and identify the design dimension to be considered when selecting metaphors for the elements of a TUI.

In the second part of the paper, we present empirical evidence of the effects of ill-chosen and well-chosen metaphors on TUI interactions. We then describe how the negative effects of ill-chosen metaphors could have been anticipated, once considering the conceptual framework in the course of design. In the final part of the paper we outline how the findings of this paper can be integrated with a structured specification process for TUIs.

METAPHOR SELECTION AS A (T)UI DESIGN TASK
In general, metaphors are pervasive in language and thought. They trigger actions [1] and are bound to human experience [13]. Since shaping also task accomplishment and interaction, they have to be considered by (T)UI designers.

Metaphors have been used to interpret and trigger actions at the computer side [14], and to facilitate human understanding when interacting with computers [15]. Antle et al. [16] show how embodied metaphors facilitate interaction in hybrid interaction spaces in the context of learning. According to their findings, several design goals when using metaphors can be set: (a) facilitate user (work) task accomplishment and (b) reduce cognitive workload of users when interacting with an artifact.

Metaphors emphasize the symbolic significance of particular elements in human(-computer) interaction, e.g., a box representing a relevant set of task items [17]. Even the most concrete and rational aspects of interaction - whether searching, arranging, replacing, or distribution of information - embody meanings, if not social constructions that are crucial for understanding what persons do [18].

Consequently, metaphor-based interaction spaces have to be considered as enacted domains. They are social enactments, as interactions are socially constructed. The persons who bring metaphors to life choose and structure internal and external relationships through a host of interpretive decisions that are extensions of individual properties and style.

Besides the addressed intertwined cognitive and social dimension of metaphor-based design, the virtual and concrete setting of an environment is affected through TUI design:

- Metaphor-based TUIs create and shape activities, hence influencing the way persons accomplish tasks, arrange information, or communicate ideas. Designers have to be aware that embodied metaphors have the capability to shape and guide organized action.
- Using multiple metaphors to organize work tasks and interactions tap different dimensions of a situation. Specific situations might lead to specific metaphors. Otherwise users will find themselves experiencing unanticipated interaction problems that hinder many developments, and lead to endless restructuring, re-inventing, or re-engineering interaction spaces.

Given the social enactment and shaping user behavior, metaphor-based TUI design enriches traditional development processes substantially [19]: Developers refrain from applying their formal authority, function, and role as a kind of protective input that insulates users and themselves from change. In the course of design they need to encounter human experience and develop shared understanding with users and domain experts.

TUIS AND METAPHORS

In an extensive review of existing literature on how to systematically describe (i.e. specify or assess) TUIs, we have identified several approaches, which explicitly consider "metaphor" as a dimension of TUI design or assessment. In the following sections, we briefly describe these approaches and point out how they reflect the findings described above.

Relevant Frameworks

Many authors have claimed the importance of metaphors when designing TUIs [4][5][6]. However, only few have explicitly addressed how to systematically approach the topic of metaphor-based design, how to classify different types of metaphors, and how these classes become manifest in existing systems.

Underkoffler & Ishii [7] have been the first to systematically approach the mapping between physical and digital world. They propose a continuum of object meanings to classify the elements of a tangible interface. Koleva et al. [8] propose a framework for TUIs in which they use the "degree of coherence" as the primary dimension for classifying TUI elements. The "degree of coherence" describes to which extent "linked physical and digital objects might be perceived as being the same thing". Finally, Fishkin [9] proposes a taxonomy for TUIs, in which "metaphor" is one of two dimensions. According to Fishkin, "metaphor" describes, whether the "system effect of a user action [is] analogous to the „real"-world effect of similar actions" [9].

None of the authors relate TUI design to their frameworks. They rather use them as means for ex-post classification and analysis. In the following, we examine the frameworks' potential to be applied in the course of designing a TUI.

Meanings of Tangible Objects

Underkoffler & Ishii [7] propose a continuum of object meanings that allows classifying the physical elements of TUIs. They restrict the scope of their classification to be applicable only to elements of "luminous tangible systems", a class of systems that now commonly is referred to as "interactive surfaces" [5].

In the center of their continuum they define the class "noun" to represent objects directly corresponding to their digital counterpart. Physical manipulations of these objects directly affect the representation of the manipulated property in the digital world. On either side of the continuum, either the physical properties of the object (i.e. what an object is), or the ways it can be manipulated (i.e. what an object does), is getting more and more irrelevant for the mapping to the digital world. Stripping away the manipulation of an object, classification becomes "attribute", where only parts of the physical properties of the object affect the digital representation. It finally leads to "pure object" where only the "being" of an object is represented in the digital world. On the other side of the continuum the physical properties of an object are not of interest. Classification here starts with "verb", where altering the digital representation is tied to some manipulation of a physical object, which, however, is not related to the object or phenomenon that is manipulated in the digital representation. Finally, the object becomes a "reconfigurable tool", where the object's physical appearance gives no hints at all of how it can be used and the object can be applied to trigger multiple manipulations in the digital world.

Degree of Coherence

Koleva et al. [8] classify TUIs along a continuum describing the "coherence" of the TUI elements. The "degree of coherence" describes the strength of coupling physical with digital objects, i.e. to which extent they are perceived "as being the same thing". Starting with strong coherence the initial classification is the "illusion of same objects". Users do not distinguish among physical and digital properties of an object here.

Stepping down the coherence scale the subsequent classifications are "projection" and "proxy". Both maintain a close coupling of physical objects with digital representations. However, they are still perceived as separate phenomena by the users. "Projections" are used whenever certain properties of a physical object directly map to the digital representation. The latter only exists, once the physical object is present. "Proxies" are still permanently coupled to certain digital representations. They allow for manipulation. The existence of the digital representation, however, is not necessarily bound to the presence of the physical token. "Identifiers" are objects representing only digital information while being physically present. However, they do not allow manipulating this information. "Specialized tools", in turn, do not have information assigned to permanently, but are used to perform specific manipulations using the digital representation. At the lower end of the coherence-scale "general-purpose tools" do neither represent specific information, nor indicate specific manipulations of the digital representation.

Taxonomy of Tangible Interfaces

Fishkin [9] proposes to use a two-dimensional taxonomy when classifying TUIs. The first dimension – "embodiment" – describes how "close" modalities of input are tied to output (with the scale ranging from "distant" of "environment" and "nearby" to "full", where e.g. "nearby" would be information projected onto a table surface just underneath a token that is used to manipulate or control this information). The second dimension – "metaphor" – describes to which extent user actions cause the same effects within the system as they would cause in the physical world.

A metaphor classification of "full" describes TUI objects not perceived differently from physical world objects in both, their appearance, and the way they can be manipulated. Digital information is integrated in a natural way, i.e. not disrupting the perception when interacting with a object from the physical world. TUI objects use a "Noun and Verb"-metaphor, in case both, the appearance of the TUI object ("noun"), and its usage "verb" resemble a corresponding physical world object and interaction. Users, however, still perceive the TUI and "plain" actual world objects to be in different contexts (i.e. a TUI object is not usable in the actual ("real") world and vice-versa). A metaphor of "verb" decouples actions from objects and shows analogies between TUI and "plain" actual world only on an interaction level. While the object used in the TUI does not have an actual world counterpart (as would be the case for a "generic" information-container token), the manipulations that can be performed on this object correspond to actual world interactions (i.e. hand over the token to give information to another person). Accordingly, an object with metaphor of "noun" shows analogies regarding its appearance, but cannot be manipulated or used as in the actual world. Finally, the metaphor classification "none" is used for objects having no correspondence in the actual world at all, neither regarding their appearance, nor their usage or manipulation.

Discussion

Each of the reviewed approaches aims to classify TUIs along the used metaphors. Although focusing on different aspects, the approaches share some concepts we are going to discuss.

None of the frameworks is applied to entire TUIs, but rather to objects they consist of. Thus, a TUI can be related to multiple classifications. Recognizing that the question arises, whether "consistency" (in terms of realizing metaphors in a way that all tangible objects can be assigned to a single specific class) is an issue here. While this aspect is beyond the scope of this paper, further research is required to examine the use of different metaphors within a specific TUI-based system.

The identified continua follow a similar approach when looking at the classes of metaphors. Figure 1 presents a mapping between the classifications found in the authors' descriptions. Fishkin [9] has provided a similar mapping between his approach and the Object Meanings of Underkoffler & Ishii. Our mapping deviates from his understanding in one detail:

We do not agree to Fishkin's mapping of Underkoffler & Ishii's "noun" class to the "noun"-class of his taxonomy. According to Underkoffler & Ishii, "noun" is a "maximally 'real-world' object reading", where objects are „fully literal, in the sense that they work in their luminous-tangible context very much the way objects 'operate' in the real world". This understanding would indicate a mapping to Fishkin's "Noun+Verb" or even "Full"-Class. We consider Fishkin's work inconsistent to that respect. He claims the building tokens of "Urp" to be an example for "Noun+Verb" in his taxonomy, where the main elements in "Urp" are mentioned as examples for "Noun"-meanings in Underkoffler & Ishii's work.

The mapping presented in Figure 1 points out the commonalities and differences in the classifications:

On the end of the continuum representing "stronger" metaphors, all approaches define a class of TUI objects that cannot be distinguished from actual world objects with respect to both, their appearance, and usage - digital information is integrated with the physical objects. On the other end of the continuum, representing "weaker" metaphors, all approaches describe TUI objects that do not resemble "real" objects, neither in appearance nor in usage.

Within the continuums, the authors differ with regard to

focus and granularity. Koleva et al. focus on "stronger metaphors" and define a more fine grain classification here. In turn, Underkoffler & Ishii provide more detail on "weaker" metaphors.

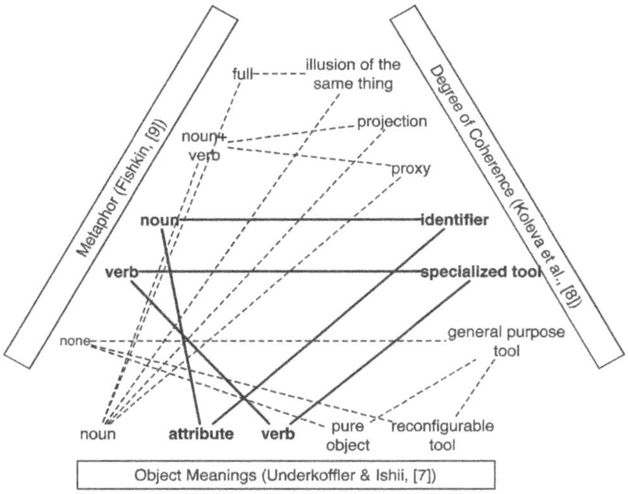

Figure 1: Mapping of frameworks for metaphor classification in TUIs

All three frameworks share the distinction between objects grounding their metaphor solely on their physical *appearance* (attribute [7] – identifier [8] – noun [9]) and objects grounding their metaphor solely to their *usage* (verb [7], specialized tool [8] – verb [9]).

Koleva et al. and Fishkin additionally share classifications that describe TUI objects, which use a metaphor based on both, physical appearance, and usage, but are still not equivalent to "real" world objects (i.e. are clearly perceived to be "different" by users).

The distinction between appearance-based and usage-based metaphors appears to be relevant for metaphor selection during TUI-design. Different contexts of use for TUI elements lead to different foci for the applied metaphor. Examples can be found in [9], e.g., when focusing on usage-based metaphors for elements that represent generic functionality like selecting another element. A similar distinction between "representation" (appearance) and "behavior" (usage) in the TAC-approach for TUI specification [10] provides a starting point for consideration of metaphors during TUI design.

EFFECTS OF METAPHOR SELECTION ON TUI USAGE

To validate the assumption that explicit consideration of metaphor types during TUI design has positive effects on the resulting interface, we have conducted a study on how metaphor selection affects the intelligibility of TUI elements. For this purpose we implemented a specific feature of a TUI using different types of metaphors and observed the user's reactions on both implementations.

The study is based on a system that has been developed in the context of supporting negotiation of meaning and development of a common understanding for groups by using concept maps [11]. The system is implemented using a tabletop interface with tangible building blocks that represent the concepts. Associations among the concepts are projected onto the table surface and can be set and removed by specific user interactions.

As part of a more extensive empirical evaluation, the interactions necessary for the removal of associations in a concept map have been examined with respect to the usage of different metaphors. A physical eraser represents the token used for removal. Hence, the *appearance* metaphor has been fixed. Two different forms of interaction have been implemented utilizing the eraser token. They differ in their *usage* metaphor.

In the first case presented here the eraser token was designed to be used to switch from the current to the "erase mode", by placing it somewhere on the surface. After the eraser had been put onto the table surface, the system switched to erase mode, and additional interaction was required to actually remove associations - no explicit usage dimension in the metaphor, functionality is tied to plain "being" [7] of the eraser.

Hence, the eraser tools have been built upon a purely appearance-based metaphor, ignoring the dimension of usage. Consequently, the eraser (physical appearance) switched to the connection-removal mode, but could not be used to actually erase connections (indicated interactive abilities).

In the second case, the erase interaction was altered to become stateless. It direct led to removal when placing the eraser on specific associations (usage metaphor: "erasing"). The interaction with the eraser token thus matched the metaphor suggested by its physical appearance (i.e. connections actually were erased). In Fishkin's metaphor the new version of the tool is classified as "Noun+Verb".

The following hypothesis was tested for both cases: *The metaphor the eraser token is based upon allows users in an intelligible way removing connections (H1).* H1 had to be rejected, in case users were unable to remove associations just by applying their assumptions about how the eraser token has to be applied.

Study Design & Methodology

Overall, 128 people (102 male, 25 female) participated in 57 mapping sessions (in groups of 2-3 people each). The participants were students of a curriculum in business information systems and had no prior experience in using the system. We recorded all sessions using video. The videos were the basis for transcribing problematic interactions between users or with the system (following the interaction analysis approach described by [18]).

Measures

To validate or falsify H1 two quantitative measures have been used alongside with qualitative findings from interaction analysis and user feedback in the questionnaires.

Misinterpretations (M) – measured by number of times the eraser has not been used in the way it was intended to be operated by the designer. The measure is represented as percentage of total eraser usage in the respective session. High values reveal various misinterpretations, and thus indicate problems applying the metaphor.

Number of times the eraser has been used for association removal in favor to other means of removal (ER) – measured by number of times the eraser has been used to remove an association in favor to alternative ways of removal (like "undo"). Alternative ways cause more interaction effort (take longer to be performed and/or have side effects on the remaining concept map). The measure is represented as percentage of total amount of removed associations. High values show intense usage of the eraser, and indicate an comprehensible metaphor.

Case 1: Noun-based metaphor

The first version of the eraser feature was tested in 36 mapping sessions with 91 participants (73 male, 18 female).

Across all sessions a total of 123 (successful and unsuccessful) removal activities occurred. In 19 cases users applied the eraser token, in the remainder of 104 cases users performed the removal using more complex ways. Thus, measure ER is 15,4%.

In 17 of the 19 situations in which the eraser token was used, connection removal was unsuccessful due to misconceptions of how to use the token. Thus, measure M is 89,5%.

Video recordings of these situations show how users acted confused and felt unsure on how to proceed after selection. Additionally, 60 of the 91 participants explicitly mentioned the eraser token as the most confusing feature when asked in an open question which aspect of the system they found least intuitive. Based upon these results, H1 has to be rejected for case 1.

Case 2: Noun+Verb-based Metaphor

37 participants (30 male, 7 female) tested the redesigned version the removal tool in 21 sessions (with 6 participants taking part in more than one session).

Across all sessions users performed a total of 130 (successful and unsuccessful) removal activities. In 103 cases the eraser token was used; the remainder of 27 cases was performed using one of the alternative ways for connection removal. Measure ER is 79,2%. ER is significantly higher for case 2 (usage of eraser codified with '1' and alternative ways with '0', one-sided Wilcoxon-test for unpaired samples: $W = 2895.5$, $p < 0.005$).

In none of the 103 situations the eraser token was used, connection removal was unsuccessful due to misconceptions of how to use the token. Hence, measure M is 0%. M is significantly lower for case 2 (misconception codified with '1' and no misconception with '0', one-sided Wilcoxon-test for unpaired samples: $W = 103$, $p < 0.005$).

In the written feedback following each session none of the participants mentioned the association removal feature or the eraser token feature, although being asked which aspect of the system they found least intuitive. Based upon these results, H1 can be accepted.

Discussion

The metaphor that has been used to implement the association removal feature was the eraser one. In the first case, however, this metaphor was only applied to the token itself, but not to the corresponding interaction. The eraser had led to state changes of the system, but had no immediately visible effects on the object to be manipulated (= the association to be removed). The intended form of interaction has not been transparent to the users of the system. They misinterpreted how to use the token or refused to use it at all (even after initial training of how to use the eraser token correctly).

In the second case, the eraser metaphor was applied to both, the token and the according interaction. The removal feature was triggered by the natural form of interaction with an eraser, namely rubbing it on the part of the surface where something should be removed. This version was used significantly more often, and also perceived significantly better than the first version.

Following the mapping between Koleva et al.'s and Fishkin's classification, these findings could have been anticipated already during design. "Noun"-based metaphors only should be used for "identifiers", not for "tools" (as it is the case for the first version of the eraser token). The implementation was changed in the second version to fit the "verb-based"-metaphor anticipated by users, thus making the token act as a tool. By considering "verb" and "noun" aspects of the chosen metaphor, higher coherence [8] could be reached.

The eraser token uses a strong appearance-based metaphor (using a physical eraser as a TUI object) that imposes certain affordances [27] (using the object as a tool, like a physical eraser, i.e. to rub on the drawings to be erased), which were not met by the noun-based implementation of the removal tool. The users intuitively extended the appearance-based metaphor with a usage-based metaphor. Hence, they upgraded the TUI object to a more "coherent" classification than it actually provided.

Consequently, it seems to be of importance not only to select a suitable metaphor for a feature to be implemented using a TUI. It is necessary to consistently apply the metaphor to both, the physical object embodying the tangible token, and the usage of the token effecting the digital representation.

CONCLUSIONS

Using a mapping between three existing classification schemes we have examined the role of metaphors in the design space for TUIs. Based on an empirical study we could illustrate the problems arising once metaphors are not well reflected for TUI design.

The classifications of Underkoffler and Ishii [7], Koleva et al. [8] and Fishkin [9] and their mapping provide starting points of how metaphors can be selected during TUI design. The distinction between appearance-based and usage-based metaphors appears to be a suitable approach to explicitly consider metaphor selection during TUI specification using the TAC-scheme [10]. The TAC-scheme enforces the definition of both, the (physical and digital) representation of a TUI element and its behavior. Depending on the intended purpose of a TUI element [8][9], such as the "removal *tool*" in the case of the eraser token, specification might either focus on metaphor selection for behavior (usage) or representation (appearance), while still considering the other dimension to ensure the metaphor's intelligibility.

In future work we will focus on the development of a metaphor-aware TUI specification process based upon the reviewed metaphor classification approaches and the TAC-scheme. The proposed specification process needs further empirical work for justification in "real" world scenarios.

REFERENCES

1. Genter, D., Bowdle, B.F., Wolff, Ph., Boronat, C. Metaphor is like Analogy, *The analogical mind: Perspectives from cognitive science*, eds: Gentner, D.; Holyonk, K.J., Kokinov, B.N., pp. 199-253, MIT Press, Cambridge, MA, 2003.
2. Alty, J., Knott, R., Anderson, B., and Smyth, M. A framework for engineering metaphor at the user interface. *Interacting with computers 13*, 2 (2000).
3. Ishii, H., and Ullmer, B. Tangible bits: towards seamless interfaces between people, bits and atoms. In *Proceedings of CHI '97* (1997), ACM, pp. 234–241.
4. Hornecker, E. Getting a grip on tangible interaction: a framework on physical space and social interaction. In *Proceedings of CHI '06* (2006), ACM, pp. 437–446.
5. Ishii, H. Tangible bits: beyond pixels. In *Proceedings of TEI '08*, ACM.
6. Jacob, R. J., Girouard, A., Hirshfield, L. M., Horn, M. S., Shaer, O., Solovey, E. T., and Zigelbaum, J. Reality-based interaction: a framework for post-wimp interfaces. In *Proceeding of CHI '08* (2008), ACM.
7. Underkoffler, J., and Ishii, H. Urp: A luminous-tangible workbench for urban planning and design. In *Proceedings of CHI '99* (1999), ACM, pp. 386–393.
8. Koleva, B., Benford, S., Ng, K., and Rodden, T. A Framework for Tangible User Interfaces. In Workshop-Proceedings on Real World User Interfaces, *Mobile HCI Conference 03* (2003), pp. 257–264.
9. Fishkin, K. P. A taxonomy for and analysis of tangible interfaces. *Personal and Ubiquitous Computing* 8, 5 (2004), 347–358.
10. Shaer, O., Leland, N., Calvillo-Gamez, E., and Jacob, R. The TAC paradigm: specifying tangible user interfaces. *Personal and Ubiquitous Computing* 8, 5 (2004).
11. Novak, J., and Cañas, A. J. The theory underlying concept maps and how to construct them. Technical Report IHMC CmapTools 2006-01, Florida Institute for Human and Machine Cognition, 2006.
12. Hornecker, E. *Tangible User Interfaces als* kooperationsunterstützendes *Medium*. Phd-Thesis, University of Bremen. Dept. of Computing, July 2004.
13. Boroditsky, L. Metaphoric structuring: understanding time through spatial metaphors, *Cognition*, Vol. 75, pp. 1-28, 2000.
14. Snoek, C.G.M, Worring, M., Geusebroek, J.-M., Koelma, D.C., Seinstra, F.J., Smeulders, A.W.M. The Semantic Pathfinder: Using an authoring metaphor for generic multimedia indexing, *IEEE Transactions on Pattern Analysis and Machine Intelligence*, Vol. 28, No. 10, pp. 1678-1689, October 2006.
15. Pirhonen, A., Brewster, St., Holguin, Ch. Gestural and audio metaphors as a means of control for mobile devices, *Proceedings CHI'02*, ACM 2002.
16. Antle, A.N., Corness, G., Droumeva, M. What the body does: Exploring the benefits of embodied metaphors in hybrid physical environments, *Interacting with Computers*, 21, pp. 66-75, 2009.
17. Glucksberg, S. Understanding metaphors, *Directions in Psychological Science*, 7, 39-43, 1998.
18. Moran, Th.P., Zhai, Sh. Beyond the Desktop Metaphor in Seven Dimensions, *Designing Integrated Digital Work Environments. Beyond the Desktop Metaphor*, eds: Kaptelinin, V., Czerwiniki, M., MIT Press, Cambridge, MA, pp. 335-354, 2007.
19. Wilson, D., Carston, R. Metaphor, relevance, and the 'emergent property' issue, *Mind and Language*, 21(4), pp. 404-433, 2006.
20. Norman, D. *The design of everyday things*. Doubleday/Currency, 1990.

Estimating Scale Using Depth from Focus for Mobile Augmented Reality

Klen Čopič Pucihar
School of Computing and Communications
InfoLab21, Lancaster University
Lancaster LA1 4WA UK
+44 1524 510393
k.copicpucihar@lancaster.as.uk

Paul Coulton
School of Computing and Communications
InfoLab21, Lancaster University
Lancaster LA1 4WA UK
+44 1524 510393
p.coulton@lancaster.ac.uk

ABSTRACT
Whilst there has been a considerable progress in augmented reality (AR) over recent years, it has principally been related to either marker based or apriori mapped systems, which limits its opportunity for wide scale deployment. Recent advances in marker-less systems that have no apriori information, using techniques borrowed from robotic vision, are now finding their way into mobile augmented reality and are producing exciting results. However, unlike marker based and apriori tracking systems these techniques are independent of scale which is a vital component in ensuring that augmented objects are contextually sensitive to the environment they are projected upon. In this paper we address the problem of scale by adapting a Depth From Focus (DFF) technique, which has previously been limited to high-end cameras to a commercial mobile phone. The results clearly show that the technique is viable and adds considerably to the enhancement of mobile augmented reality. As the solution only requires an auto-focusing camera, it is also applicable to other AR platforms.

Authors Keywords
Mobile, scale, metric scale, camera, DFF.

ACM Classification Keywords
H5.1. Information interfaces and presentation (e.g., HCI): *Artificial, augmented, and virtual realities.*

General Terms
Algorithms, Design, Experimentation, Performance.

INTRODUCTION
One of the main challenges of Augmented Reality (AR) systems is camera tracking, which can be implemented using fiducial markers or natural-features. In fiducial-based systems the scale ambiguity is not present as it can be easily derived by using markers of a known size, whereas in the natural feature based systems it is only possible if the system is of the informed type where the apriori knowledge of the view being studied is available, i.e. a database of landmarks forming the map is created offline and the map creation process introduces metric scale. In the case of natural feature tracking, where the 3D map is created online from natural features alone, the scale is unknown because it is impossible to determine the scale of the scene based on a sequence of images alone [5].

While scale ambiguity is not a problem in fiducial marker and apriori feature tracking systems, such systems offer a limited prospect of large scale deployment, as they require either wide scale augmentation of our physical space with fiducial markers or wide scale 3D mapping of our physical environment. The alternative options are marker-less AR systems that use online tracking approaches without apriori information where the method of map creation and camera pose estimation can vary from model-based to move-matching approaches.

In the case of online model-based approach, the camera pose is always estimated by comparing the initial frame with the current camera frame. The initial frame is an image taken directly from above the plane, or one that is synthetically un-projected from additional sensor information, by which perspective distortions of camera projections are removed and the extracted landmarks can be used as an object model of the plane in the scene. As the same initial frame is always taken for pose estimation, such system is not incremental and does not have problems with drift or loop closures [1]. However, such systems are limited to planar scenes, as landmarks not lying on a plane cannot be initialized from only one observation, thus making extraction of the depth information using stereovision impossible. Furthermore, as the initial frame is always used for the camera pose estimation, all newly added features need to be referenced to the initial frame, which, in practice, means long term maps where features are tracked over a long period of time.

AR systems that use model-based approach, but differ in the sense that their maps are created offline are [10, 13], however, there is no reason why such systems could not be modified to act as uninformed tracking systems, which would improve their use flexibility, but simultaneously introduce the scale ambiguity. One example of such a

EICS'11, June 13–16, 2011, Pisa, Italy.

system running on a mobile phone is Nestor [4], in which curves of planar shapes are used for tracking and shape-identification. The shapes are added to the database of known shapes by the method described above, and are then used as natural features for camera pose extraction, as well as to select 3D objects for augmentation. The drawback of this system is that it is also ambiguous up to scale.

In the later case of move-matching techniques, the camera pose is updated based on the frame-to-frame movement of tracked features. Such system [12] is incremental, as, after each frame is acquired, the camera pose update from the previous frame is added. This approach does not require long-term feature tracking and, with it, the requirement to maintain long-term maps, which makes it more flexible and faster, as computationally expensive bundle adjustment of the map is not required. However, as the method is incremental, it is hard to avoid drift, which also introduces the problem of loop closures [1]. In case of non-planar surfaces, one of the main problems is system initialization where the camera pose and the map environment are unknown. This problem can be solved by the move-matching technique known as Simultaneous Localization and Mapping (SLAM), developed in the field of robotic exploration and later adopted by hand-held AR systems.

Two such SLAM algorithms optimized for hand-held cameras are MonoSLAM [1] and Scalable Monocular Slam [3]. In these systems, the map is initialized by a fiducial marker through which the scale of the map becomes available. After initialization, the map is expended by natural features alone. However, in case of Eade and Drummond SLAM implementation [3], the map can also be initialized without the necessity of a marker, but in this case, the scale again becomes unknown.

Further developments in single hand-held camera tracking were achieved using the Parallel Tracking and Mapping algorithm (PTAM) [6], which differentiates from others by separating the mapping and tracking tasks. In PTAM bundle adjustment is used as an alternative to incremental mapping, in which long-term maps are created and features are frequently revisited. The map initialization is done with five-point stereo algorithm, or, in the later versions, by homography decomposition. In both cases, the metric scale is unknown if no additional information is available.

Currently, the only presented alternative for estimating scale is performed during the process of stereo map initialization as demonstrated in PTAM [6], whereby users were asked to provide first two keyframes of the map by moving the camera sideways for approximately 10 cm, from which the metric scale of the map could be estimated as additional information was introduced to the captured video stream. However, according to Klein and Murray, this map initialisation method proved to be problematic, as users tended to use pure rotation rather than lateral movement, thus the correct map initialization is heavily dependent on users' understanding of the stereo baseline requirements [7]. Further, the introduction of scale in this manner is subjective, as the user camera movement is approximate and subjectively assessed.

To date a highly modified variation of PTAM for the iPhone is the only implementation of six degrees of freedom camera tracking SLAM on a mobile phone where, according to Klein and Murray, stereo initialization was deemed inadequate not only because of the introduction of the user error previously defined, but also due to the limitations of the mobile phone platform, in particular the limited computational power and narrow camera field of view [7]. In the alternative map initialization, Klein and Murray ask the user to provide only the first key-frame, therefore, the previously defined additional information is lost. This means that, currently, there are no marker-less mobile AR systems that provide an estimate of scale.

Implementing scale is a vital component in ensuring that augmented objects are contextually sensitive to the environment they are projected upon. For example, if we wish to illustrate the footprints of extinct species on the ground next to a human footprint, it would be much more meaningful if the footprints of extinct species appeared scaled relative to the human footprint. Our research presents a solution to this problem, which has been missing in uninformed marker-less AR systems, or was only available through user-cooperation, whereby they subjectively and manually define the scale. The proposed solution utilizes the Depth From Focus (DFF) technique in order to, objectively, introduce scale to AR workspaces with no additional user requirements.

In the following section the theoretical background of the method is presented followed by the design patterns section for generic implementation. The proposed solution is then analysed through an empirical study of a specific implementation on a commercially available mobile phone, Nokia N900, followed by a demo application. Finally, conclusions with suggestions for future work are drawn.

THEORETICAL FRAMEWORK

Digital cameras are generally auto-focused by searching for the lens position that gives the 'best' focused image, thus the lens position is dependent on the distance to the object as shown in Figure 1. If the focused lens position and the focal distance of the lens are known, the thin Gaussian lens equation (1) can be used to calculate DFF i.e. the distance to the object u.

$$1/f = 1/u + 1/v \qquad (1)$$

This method has been mainly used in the domain of robotic vision as an alternative to stereo depth recovery. One of the main choices with this method is which focus measure to use in order to identify the best lens position [14]. An ideal focus measure is described as unimodal and monotonic in that it should have only one maximum at the point where the image is in focus [9]. However, in practice any focal measure has many local maximums, therefore, the global peak of the focal measure is not easy to find. Furthermore, as it has been observed by [9, 14], not only the texture and contrast of the scene but also the depth of field (DOF) influence the maximums of focus measure function. It is preferable to have good texture with high contrast as well as the smallest possible DOF, which can be achieved by using the maximum focal distance of the camera as well as maximum aperture. With bigger focal distance, the lens movements become bigger, which is expected to increases the resolution and precision of the lens positioning system.

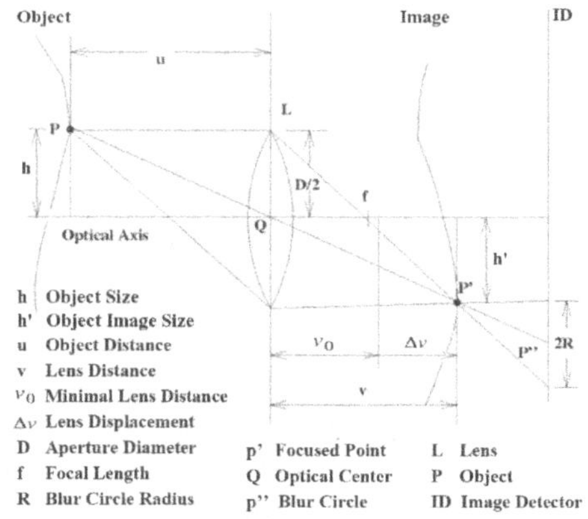

Figure 1: Image formation in a convex lens

In order to calculate the scale unit s of the scene, one needs to know the distance to the object plane u, the vertical or horizontal cameras field of view α and picture height or width in pixels $2h'$. The calculation of scale unit s is then based on simple trigonometry as shown in equation (2). In case of the augmented reality application, the user would need to focus on the plane, where at least two map points are present. After defining the scale between two map points, the scale of the whole map is known.

$$h = u\tan(\alpha/2) \quad \Rightarrow \quad s = h[mm]/h'[px] \qquad (2)$$

The measurable depth of DFF system is theoretically limited by the hyperfocal distance, which is defined as a minimal object distance at which we need to focus in order to consider the points at infinity to be in focus. However, as DOF needs to be as small as possible, in order to achieve reliable and accurate results, such distance lies much closer. In case of an AR application with the ability to expand maps, the scale estimation only imposes the limitation of close up map initialization. As maps can be expanded to desirable proportions, the size of the AR workspace is not limited by the close-up map initialization.

The above suggests that the scale could be introduced to offline marker-less AR system using DFF. In the following section the generic implementation will be designed.

DESIGN PATTERNS FOR GENERIC IMPLMENTATION

The motor count captured from the camera driver is assumed to represent the relative distance of the lens in the motor step domain. In order to use motor count with the Gaussian lens equation (1), the conversion to absolute distance in metric space (on Figure 1 shown as v) is required. An alternative is to capture measurements across the whole focusing range and define an approximation function that will define the transformation from motor count to object distance. This research analyzes both cases, as it has some significant implications for the user interaction requirements as well as system flexibility.

In the first mode of operation, the camera system is assumed to be unknown. In order to convert the motor count to object distance, the lens equation (1) can be used, however, as already indicated, the lens movement interval is usually unknown. The only information available about the lens position is its motor count, which needs to be converted to lens distance v in metric space.

The proposed solution is to focus the camera at the object, at two different, but known distances. The first measurement should be taken close to the minimal focusable object distance, and the second at approximately one tenth of the hyperfocal distance. The range is chosen in the close-up region of the camera, as the accuracy of DFF system is expected to decline with object distance, and it is important to ensure that the calibration of the motor step values is made in a way to best fit the lens equation in the close up region. As the distances to the object are known, the theoretical lens position can be calculated using the equation (1), by which the motor step *unit* is defined. The difference between the current motor count value m and the minimum motor count value m_0 make the conversion of motor step count to metric space possible by equation (3).

$$v = v_0 + \Delta m \cdot unit \qquad \Delta m = m - m_0 \qquad (3)$$

In the second mode of operation, an assumption of a known camera model is made, which enables the use of an approximation function to transform the motor count step to object distance. No user calibration is required, however the applicability is limited to known camera models, for which the approximation curve has to be predefined.

In the following section, the proposed solutions will be analysed through an empirical study of a specific implementation on the mobile phone Nokia N900.

EMPERICAL STUDY OF SCALE ESTIMATION

The data presented in this section was captured with four phones, where auto-focusing was performed by two focusing algorithms: namely, the native camera application algorithm and the 'gstreamer' library. The phone camera used is a 5-mega pixels camera with Carl Zeiss optics with a focal length of 5.2 millimetres, aperture f/2.8 and a horizontal field of view of 56 degrees.

In all measurements, the same colour poster, mounted on a wall, with good contrast, and texture was used. The phone was mounted on a stand, whose distance to the wall was measured with a ruler. The plane of the camera image and the poster were always parallel. The focusing was repeated 20 times at each given distance. In case of 'gstreamer' library, the phone was incrementally moved from 7 to 80

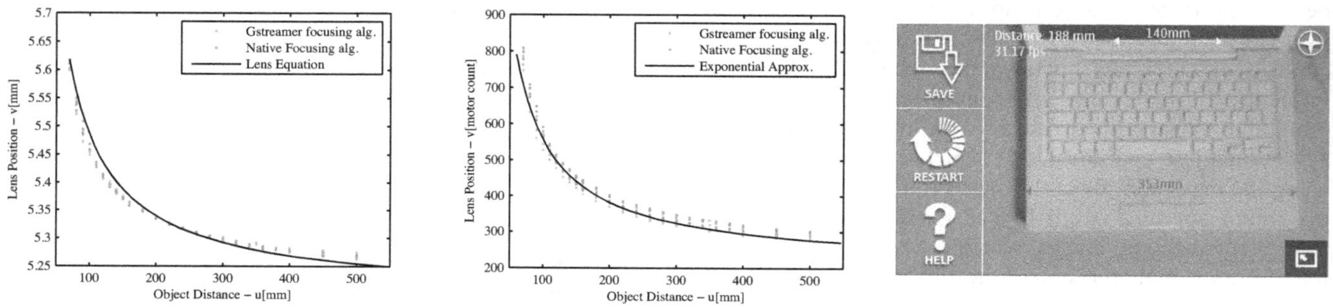

(a) (b) (c)

Figure 2: (a) The average lens position of four phones in relation to object distance (mode one operation) and the predicted lens position by the Gaussian lens equation (1); (b) The average lens position of four phones in motor step space in relation to object distance (mode two operation) and exponential approximation function (4); (c) The screen shot of the demo application Metre;

centimetres. Before capturing the measurement at each increment, the phone was focused at an object at random distance. In the case of native application, the measurements were taken in a sequence, starting at minimum object distance. The motor count value was assumed to be represented by the 'V4L2_CID_ FOCUS_ABSOLUTE' variable of the Video4Linux2 camera driver.

The analysis showed that the results captured at distances above 50 centimetres were deemed too unreliable, therefore only the data between 7 and 50 centimetres is presented. It has been found that the standard deviation of the estimated distance of any phone never exceeds 3 per cent, which is much smaller compared to the maximal standard deviation of 10.5 per cent experienced in the whole data set. Thus, the decision was made to not aggregate the data captured by each phone, but rather present the data individually. For clarity the graphs on Figure 3 only show the results of phones that performed best and worst for native and "gstreamer" focusing algorithms.

DFF Accuracy Using Gaussian Lens Equation (Mode 1)

In order to analyse how well the Gaussian lens equation (1) fits the captured data, the average values of measured lens displacements of each phone were plotted alongside the theoretical values obtained, using the lens equation function, and are shown in Figure 2a. The camera was calibrated at object distances of 7 and 25 centimetres. Although the shape of the theoretical curve runs relatively close to the captured data set, it is still considerably different. As expected, the dataset is best described close to the value of v_0, which is the lens position of the far point used in the calibration procedure of mode one operation. It can also be observed that the two focusing algorithms produce similar results and that the deviation between different phones is small. The results prove that the assumptions made are correct and that the captured value from the camera driver is interpreted correctly.

The accuracy of depth measurement can be best described with the average relative depth error (Figure 3a), which is also the relative error of the scale introduced to the AR system, because the only variable in scale calculation of equation (2) is the object distance. The maximum error at distances below 30 centimetres ranges from 9.4 up to 15.8 per cent, which is compared to results acquired with precise camera systems (0.098% acquired at 1.2 meters) very high [14]. However, it should be taken into the account that the focal length, lens mechanics, and quality of such high precision camera systems limit the comparability to the mobile phone camera. These limitations could also be seen as one of the reasons for deviation of the dataset from the theoretical lens equation. Furthermore, as discussed in the method section, some of these parameters have significant effect on the focus measure that is a crucial component of the auto-focusing accuracy.

DFF Accuracy Using Approximation (Mode 2)

In order to improve the accuracy of the system and to remove the need for user calibration, the mode two solution proposed the use of the approximation function for mapping the transformation from motor count space to object distance. The exponential approximation curve (4) was determined from the average data set of all measurements taken by the 'gstreamer' focusing algorithm. To make the function fit data best at a close range, only measurements up to 40 centimetres were considered.

$$v(u) = a / u + b \qquad (4)$$

Figure 2b shows that this new curve better represents the measurements, especially in the close-up region. The average relative depth error from mode two can be seen on Figure 3b, and it shows that the error does not drop, but stays at comparable levels to mode one operation. However it is clear that the approximation function describes the data far more consistently as in the case of lens equation because the graph on Figure 3b does not show the distinctive minimum at the calibration value v_0 that can be observed on Figure 3a, where results from mode one operation are presented. It can also be seen that the deviation between different phones seems to have grown compared to mode one operation. This is due to the fact that motor count values have not been normalized as in the case of mode one operation.

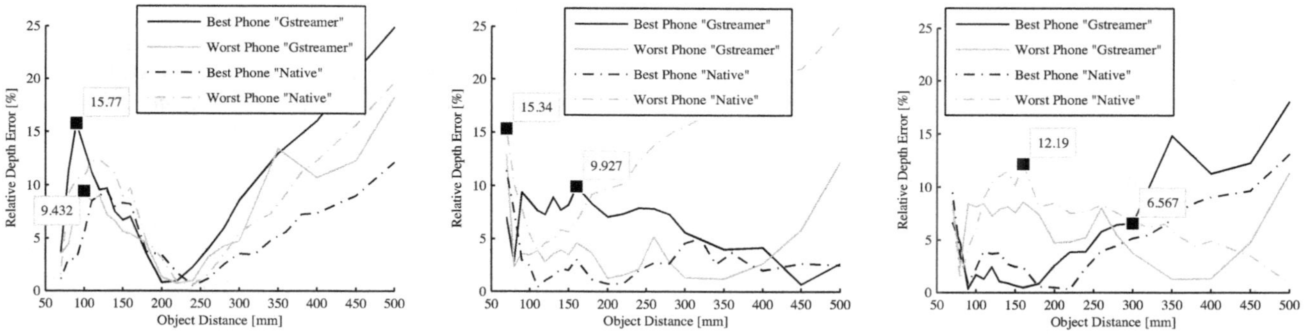

(a) mode one operation **(b) mode two operation** **(c) mode two with callibration**

Figure 3: Graphs show Average Relative Depth Error of DFF measuring for different operation modes and focusing algorithms. For clarity only results of the best and the worst phones for both algorithms are plotted. Each line represents a single phone data.

To explore the full potential of the system, a decision was made to analyse behaviour of the system where a simple one step user calibration was added to the mode two operation. As it is easier for the user to calibrate the device at the close up region, the user is asked to calibrate their phone close to the minimum focusable distance, in our case at 7 centimetres. The exponential approximation curve needs to be recalculated for the measurements, which are normalized at the maximum motor count captured by user calibration. Again only the measurements captured with 'gstreamer' focusing algorithm in the region up to 40 centimetres were used. In operation, each time the new motor count value is captured, it is subtracted from the user calibrated maximum motor count value, and converted to distance using the new fitting function. By doing this, the maximum average relative depth error shown on Figure 3c has dropped to a range between 6.6 to 12.2 per cent.

If the two different focusing algorithms are compared, their performance does not differ significantly in the close up region; this, however, is not the case in the regions further away from the camera. The accuracy of the native camera-focusing algorithm in distant regions is better then what would be expected. The possible reason for this could be the difference in the procedure of how the two experiments were executed. Contrary to the 'gstreamer' measurement, the native camera was not refocused at a randomly distant object before capturing each measurement, but was rather capturing the measurements in a sequence.

It is important to note that the captured measurements were taken under the controlled environment in good lighting conditions, with good focusing surface, with no user factor error, therefore, the accuracy in real world scenario could be expected to decrease. Further, as incremental SLAM techniques continuously update the map and camera pose with increments, the overall scale could be affected by accruing the local scale errors [2]. This would, however, not be the case in SLAM approaches, where batch methods are used to maintain long term maps. Furthermore, accruing of scale error would also not be present in the marker-less model-based tracking systems as those systems are not incremental and drift is not a problem.

To sum up, this data analysis shows that the proposed solution is valid and can produce reasonable scale estimation with maximum average relative error raging from 6.6 to 12.2 per cent for distances up to 30 centimetres.

APPLICATION SPECIFIC IMPLEMENTATION

Due to the time constraints, a demo application of a fully functional AR application was not possible. However, there are also other applications that can benefit from the proposed scale initialization. One such area would be in the domain of navigation system on mobile phones, which attempts to utilize public 'You are Here' maps to create a navigation system. One of the barriers is that this is only possible if the map contains a marker of a known size, or if the user introduces two geo-location reference points to the map [11]. Providing the first geo-location reference point is easy, as this point is usually already marked on the map, however, providing the second reference point is problematic, and could be avoided by the solution presented in this paper.

Another potential area for innovation are measuring applications. To highlight the use case of the presented solution, one such application called Metre (Figure 2c) was implemented. The application enables users to measure objects visible in the picture, where the metric scale was initialized by the designed DFF solution. The application was implemented on Nokia N900 phone, where the tracking part of the application was implemented, using the OpenCV library, the video capturing and auto-focusing, where implementation using "gstreamer" library and the scale was initialized by the previously presented mode two solution. In order to increase the maximum size of the objects and to improve accuracy of the measurement, the application enables users to introduce scale close to the object they want to measure and then move back to take a picture where the whole object is visible. In the scale initialization process, two natural features are chosen. As the distance between the two points is known, the scale is known as long as both features are successfully tracked.

CONCLUSION AND FUTURE WORK

The results show that auto-focusing capability of the camera phone can be used to effectively introduce scale estimate into the marker-less AR workspace without apriori information. However, currently the method is limited to the close up initialization (in our case, distances up to 30 centimetres), as in this region the maximum average relative scale error is in range of 6.6 to 12.2 per cent.

The limitation in range and accuracy is mainly due to the small focal length (5.2 millimetres) of a camera phone, which results in short hyperfocal distance and therefore a small DFF range. It was discovered that the region up to one tenth of the hyperfocal distance was sufficiently accurate. It is important to note that marker-less AR systems which create 3D maps online have the potential to dynamically expand these maps. This means the requirement of a close up scale initialization is only necessary at the start of the mapping process after which the map can be expanded to desired proportions. Further, range capability limitations are likely to be overcome by the next generation camera phones, in which the focal distance is expected to raise by the introduction of optical zoom lenses.

However, it is important to identify that the ideal AR platform would use a camera with a wide field of view, which, in practice, means even smaller focal distances than the ones used in this study. Further, most camera pose tracking systems use a camera projection model, where the intrinsic parameters are assumed to be known and fixed [8]. As zooming changes the intrinsic parameters of the camera, it is not permitted. However, this problem could be overcome by moving the zoom back to the original position after initializing for scale.

In the future, a fully featured uninformed marker-less augmented reality application with the proposed scale estimation will be implemented in order to explore novel user interaction possibilities of the newly added scale information. As the proposed scale estimation is device and platform independent, a more detailed feasibility study implementing the system on other AR platforms should be preformed. Finally, the accuracy of the system was only tested by focusing at vertical surfaces, which should be expended to horizontal surfaces, as well as to cases where camera image plan and the scene plane, we are focusing upon, are not parallel.

To conclude, the proposed solution is device and platform independent and can be used to introduce scale into marker less AR systems without the requirement of apriori knowledge of the workspace. However, such scale estimation is on a mobile phone limited to the close-up range. Because AR systems have the potential to dynamically expand their maps, the close up initialization does not limit the size of their workspace. Further, by introducing better lens optics and optical zoom lenses to mobile devices, the accuracy and range will inevitably improve.

ACKNOWLEDGMENTS
The authors would like to thank Nokia for the provision of software and hardware to the Mobile Radicals group.

REFERENCES

1. Davison, A.J., Reid, I.D., Molton, N.D. and Stasse, O. MonoSLAM: Real-Time Single Camera SLAM. *Pattern Analysis and Machine Intelligence, IEEE Transactions on, 29* (6). 1052-1067.
2. Eade, E. and Drummond, T. Presentation of paper: Scalable Monocular SLAM, 2006.
3. Eade, E. and Drummond, T., Scalable Monocular SLAM. in *Computer Vision and Pattern Recognition, 2006 IEEE Computer Society Conference on*, (2006).
4. Hagbi, N., Bergig, O., El-Sana, J. and Billinghurst, M. Shape recognition and pose estimation for mobile augmented reality *Proceedings of the 2009 8th IEEE International Symposium on Mixed and Augmented Reality*, IEEE Computer Society, 2009, 65-71.
5. Hartley, R.I. and Zisserman, A. *Multiple View Geometry in Computer Vision*. Cambridge University Press, ISBN: 0521540518, 2004.
6. Klein, G. and Murray, D. Parallel Tracking and Mapping for Small AR Workspaces *Proc. Sixth IEEE and ACM International Symposium on Mixed and Augmented Reality (ISMAR'07)*, Nara, Japan, 2007.
7. Klein, G. and Murray, D. Parallel Tracking and Mapping on a Camera Phone *Proc. Eigth IEEE and ACM International Symposium on Mixed and Augmented Reality (ISMAR'09)*, Orlando, 2009.
8. Lepetit, V. and Fua, P. Monocular model-based 3D tracking of rigid objects. *Found. Trends. Comput. Graph. Vis., 1* (1). 1-89.
9. Nayar, S.K. and Nakagawa, Y. Shape from focus: an effective approach for rough surfaces. *Robotics and Automation, 1990. Proceedings., 1990 IEEE International Conference on*. 218-225 vol.212.
10. Prince, S.J.D., Xu, K. and Cheok, A.D. Augmented reality camera tracking with homographies. *Ieee Computer Graphics and Applications, 22* (6). 39-45.
11. Schoning, J., Kruger, A., Cheverst, K., Rohs, M., Lochtefeld, M. and Taher, F. PhotoMap: using spontaneously taken images of public maps for pedestrian navigation tasks on mobile devices *Proceedings of the 11th International Conference on Human-Computer Interaction with Mobile Devices and Services*, ACM, Bonn, Germany, 2009, 1-10.
12. Simon, G., Fitzgibbon, A.W. and Zisserman, A. Markerless tracking using planar structures in the scene *Augmented Reality, 2000. (ISAR 2000). Proceedings. IEEE and ACM International Symposium on*, 2000.
13. Wagner, D., Reitmayr, G., Mulloni, A., Drummond, T. and Schmalstieg, D. Pose tracking from natural features on mobile phones *ISMAR '08: Proceedings of the 7th IEEE/ACM International Symposium on Mixed and Augmented Reality*, IEEE Computer Society, Washington, DC, USA, 2008, 125-134.
14. Xiong, Y. and Shafer, S.A. Depth from focusing and defocusing. *Computer Vision and Pattern Recognition, 1993. Proceedings CVPR '93., 1993 IEEE Computer Society Conference on*. 68-73.

BiLL – An Experimental Environment for Visual Analytics

Jan Wojdziak, Dietrich Kammer, Ingmar Steffen Franke, Rainer Groh
Institute of Software and Multimedia Technology, Technische Universität Dresden
Dresden, Germany
{jan.wojdziak | dietrich.kammer | ingmar.franke | rainer.groh}@tu-dresden.de

ABSTRACT
The field of Visual Analytics attempts to identify phenomena, guidelines, and algorithms to generate images suitable to communicate information efficiently and effectively. The benefit of using information visualizations is that the represented data can be quickly perceived and comprehended by the viewer. Research of novel visualization and interaction techniques in the context of three-dimensional computer graphics requires interactive computer systems. To this end, a component-oriented software framework is presented in this contribution. Bildsprache LiveLab (BiLL) allows independent implementation and combination of different components. Each component is responsible for various tasks in the context of investigating images of three-dimensional scenes. Two case studies covering *multiperspective* and *color perspective* illustrate the application of BiLL and its potential as an experimental environment for visualizing user-centered projections of three-dimensional scenes.

Author Keywords
Experimental environment, component-oriented, three-dimensional computer graphics, visual analytics, non-photorealistic rendering

ACM Classification Keywords
H.5.2 User Interfaces (D.2.2, H.1.2, I.3.6): User-centered design; Graphical user interfaces (GUI) I.3.7 Three-Dimensional Graphics and Realism: Virtual reality

General Terms
Design, Experimentation, Human Factors

INTRODUCTION
As more and more different technologies are combined to provide a rich user input and presentation of data, the role of visualization in the process of human cognition becomes a crucial aspect [9]. Visual Analytics is a research area, which investigates the way visualization and interaction techniques as well as findings from cognitive psychology can be used to create images. Visualizations should be capable to communicate information to facilitate analytical reasoning [38]. For the scope of this paper, visual analytics is considered in the context of interfaces that assist users in perceiving spatial information as effectively and efficiently as possible [22]. With advances in real-time computer graphics and three-dimensional rendering, phenomena, rules, and algorithms can be explored and investigated in order to design interactive interfaces of virtual environments. An essential requirement to achieve this aim is a user-centered projection of three-dimensional scenes. This contribution discusses related work and the capabilities of computer graphics to enhance interfaces based on human visual perception. An experimental environment is mandatory to investigate visualization and interaction methods to create effective and efficient interfaces. To this end, the engineering process of Bildsprache LiveLab (BiLL) is presented and its applicability as interactive visualization system is shown. BiLL is a component-oriented framework focused on three-dimensional computer graphics, which enables the combination of components that implement different algorithms to enhance, modify, and influence visualization and interaction techniques. The use of the component-oriented experimental platform is illustrated by two case studies from the field of visual analytics.

EICS'11, June 13–16, 2011, Pisa, Italy.

RELATED WORK
Visual Analytics originates from information visualization and scientific visualization [38]. In [36], Ware presents key principles for the creation of information visualizations including cognitive principles and a guide to human visual perception. Based on the visualization pipeline by Card et al. [12], Shneiderman describes essential guidelines for creating information visualizations with his Visual Information Seeking Mantra [31]. For instance, these methods and guidelines are used in [30] to explain complicated facts and relationships in two-dimensional visualizations. Three-dimensional visualizations should use these guidelines and methods as well. An experimental environment, as presented in this contribution, can facilitate the integration and manipulation of techniques to enable investigations and studies in the context of visual analytics.

Paintings of the Middle Ages and of the Renaissance also provide a number of techniques which could be useful for improving computer-generated images. Analyzing Renaissance paintings reveals that artists were faced with the same challenges as practitioners of current computer graphics: to map a three-dimensional scene realistically onto a two-dimensional plane [21]. A computer system calculates an image according to geometrical rules of projection. In contrast, artists integrate the so-called "human factor" into these rules because they construct paintings based on their own (human) visual impression [39]. With the advent of non-photorealistic rendering techniques, new opportunities to create images and interfaces based on methods and techniques of Renaissance paintings can be used in three-dimensional computer graphics [37]. Non-photorealistic rendering (NPR) is an essential discipline in the context of three-dimensional visualizations [33]. This technique typically produces images of three-dimensional scenes that have been modified from the original input to convey an artistic style. In interactive environments, NPR techniques can be used to visualize information in virtual environments. This can be achieved by manipulating the standard camera model of computer graphics [4,32,40], the image plane [13,41], and the object geometry [18].

The field of interactive computer systems reaches beyond the presentation of images on the screen. User input and the system's response are fundamental in this field of research. The research field explores a variety of input and output technologies, ranging from multi-touch systems [11,20], and 3D gesture interaction [8,26] to augmented reality [7,23]. The aims are to increase the accessibility and reach of interactive procedures and technologies in order to achieve user satisfaction. The presented experimental environment enables the implementation of the described visualization and interaction techniques. Moreover, the implementation of novel and unprecedented techniques is feasible.

BILDSPRACHE LIVELAB (BILL)

Our research is focused on the fields of Visual Analytics and NPR and applies the theory and methodology of designing interactive systems. This includes conceptual aspects of application, construction, and composition of visual forms to provide optimal communication and interaction between humans and technical systems. The goal is a user-centered data visualization to address the problem that visualization systems and applications exist, yet effective synergies of hardware and software considering user behavior are lacking [37].

Requirements

The following requirements for the core functionality were set to realize an experimental environment for the investigation of computer graphics, interaction, and cognitive science.

Functional requirements

- Loading and displaying of 3D scene data (modeling is covered by other tools)
- Free exploration of the 3D scene
- Selection and manipulation of objects in the scene
- Dynamic extensibility of functionality at runtime

Non-functional requirements

- Speed
- Efficiency
- Real-time capabilities
- User-friendly and ergonomic interface

Requirements for analysis and studies

- Discretely or continuously adjusting of object normals
- Object transformations (e.g. translation, rotation)
- Additional hierarchical near and far clipping planes and Level of Detail
- Projection techniques (e.g. multiperspective, camera weighting)
- Models of coloring, lighting, and texturing
- Semantic depth of field (cp. [24])

Technologies

The goal is to implement BiLL as an interactive computer system that is adaptable and extensible to realize high flexibility in implementing research relevant aspects. Rather than implementing all of the functionality needed for the framework from scratch, standard solutions were investigated and combined to create a flexible, efficient, and extensible system. Thus, the following considerations apply and reflect a best practice approach. For investigations of three-dimensional computer graphics, the image generation and manipulation of the image synthesis are essential. To visualize three-dimensional computer graphics in interactive computer systems, a graphics toolkit is needed. For the field of real-time computer graphics, the organization of data as a scene graph has proved most effective [10]. The scene graph is responsible for a number of tasks that otherwise programmers would have to care about. It is an abstraction of the actual underlying graphics hardware, simplifying and optimizing the use of available resources. For the rendering backend, OpenGL is often used to achieve cross-platform compatibility. Various implementations of scene graphs exist in C++. Two popular and recent efforts are OpenSG [29] and OpenSceneGraph (OSG) [25]. While the former has been subject to a lot of academic work, the latter enjoys an active developer community and a very good support through online forums and mailing lists. This was one of the main reasons to employ OSG within BiLL. The experimental environment is utilized in education of students, which is supported by OSG's documentation, Quick Start Guide [27], or the highly responsive mailing list. In addition, OSG comes with a clean API and regular updates.

Software components should work as independent units of deployment, subject to composition by third parties [35]. It is apparent that a component-oriented approach meets the extensibility requirement established before. Various implementations of component standards exist, for example Toolbus [14], CORBA [1], and OSGi [6]. The concepts of

OSGi met our requirements for an experimental platform best. There are a number of commercial and freely available Java implementations of OSGi. However, because of the performance in real-time computer graphics, C++ as the programming language was set to realize the non-functional requirements [5,15]. Complete C++ implementations of the OSGi standard are impossible due to the nature of the specification. In some parts, it explicitly exploits features of the Java programming language, which are unavailable to other languages. A subset of the original OSGi standard has already been implemented by the Service Oriented Framework [2] and the Open Service Platform (OSP) [28]. The latter is a commercial implementation which is by now the most complete OSGi framework available in C++. It is based on the open source POCO C++ libraries [3], a cross-platform standard library for C++, inspired by the standard libraries of Java and .NET. By exploiting the POCO Open Service Platform, the benefits of a standardized approach from Java are joined with those of keeping a very close connection to the hardware through C++ and OpenGL.

Another concern is a toolkit for the graphical user interface (GUI). Since there is no standard toolkit available for C++ like AWT or Swing for Java, there are numerous libraries to choose from. The inventor of C++, Bjarne Stroustrup lists 25 available toolkits in his report [34]. Qt, wxWidgets or Fast Light Toolkit (FLTK) are commonly used. Since the latter is a rather lightweight and unobtrusive framework, it is appropriate for BiLL as a framework focused on the visualization of three-dimensional scenes.

In summary, the following technologies are used in BiLL:

- Programming Language - C++
- Service-Oriented Framework - POCO OSP
- Graphics Toolkit - OpenSceneGraph
- GUI Toolkit - FastLightToolkit

Realization

The implementation of BiLL is described in this section. BiLL is realized as an application, which provides an editor window and a viewer window. The editor window visualizes the scene graph in a tree view, as shown in Figure 3. It is possible to obtain information from and apply basic modifications to selected nodes and the camera model of the scene. The editor allows modifications to the visualization algorithms and interaction techniques. Thus, the user can interactively engage in the visualization process. The viewer window in Figure 2 is responsible for the actual visualization of the 3D scene. As shown in Figure 1, the BiLL framework is constituted by a set of standard components. There are three layers, each divided by the dependencies between them. The basic layer provides joint access to the Fast Light Toolkit and the OpenSceneGraph framework. The BiLL service layer provides standard functionality to components of the BiLL bundle layer that exploits the full functionality of the BiLL framework. The BiLL service layer contains a component that instantiates

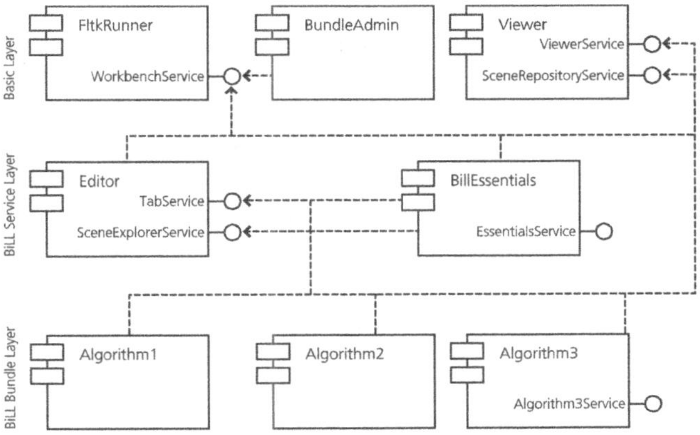

Figure 1: Layered architecture of the BiLL framework as a component diagram.

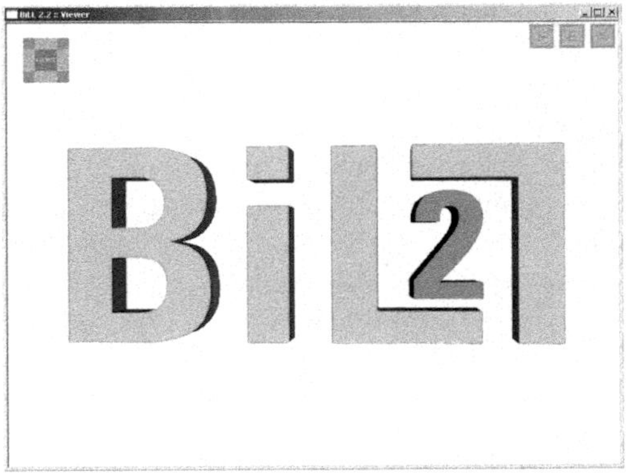

Figure 2: The viewer window of Bildsprache LiveLab shows a virtual scene and interactive interface widgets

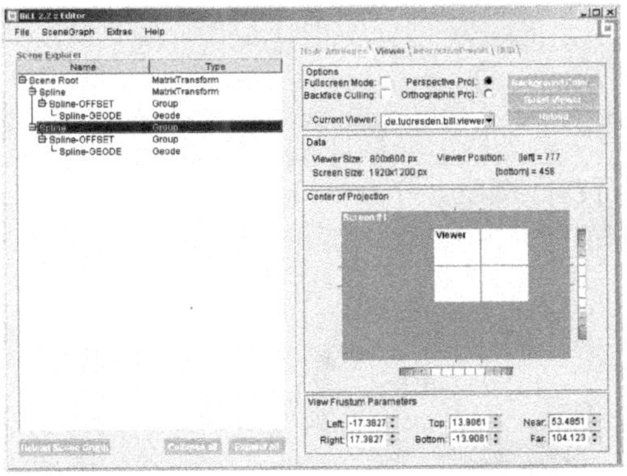

Figure 3: The editor window of Bildsprache LiveLab

the editor window and a component responsible to create a standard viewer window. However, other components (or *bundles* in the OSGi specification) can create new viewer windows as well as access the ones already registered with the viewer bundle. With these bundles, BiLL is dynamically extensible and visualization and interaction procedures are exploitable. Within the bundle layer, visualization methods and interaction techniques are implemented as separate components (bundles). With integrated services, bundles can communicate and provide reciprocal functionality.

CASE STUDIES

The previous section covered the software design and realization of Bildsprache LiveLab. This section illustrates the application of BiLL in two different contexts. Each of the case studies is focused on providing procedures that assist users in perceiving spatial information. Applications of techniques in computer graphics are illustrated in the following cases of multiperspective and color perspective.

Multiperspective

Computer rendering of three-dimensional scenes exhibits perceivable distortions. Obeying the rules of perspective projection is responsible for these effects. An indication is the elliptic appearance of spherical objects located far off the central line of projection (cp. Figure 4). In studies like [17,39] such distortion problems are addressed.

Computer graphics and user interfaces in general can be improved by using the concept of multiperspective, e.g. by means of NPR techniques. One approach using NPR to generate multiperspective images is the manipulation of the image plane. This is realized by the usage of several cameras combined according to predefined rules. The procedure creates a camera-framework consisting of a system camera and several object cameras. An object camera renders a defined object or part of the three-dimensional scene. The system camera renders the whole three-dimensional scene excluding objects which are attached to an object camera. The final image is a composition of the rendered frames of each camera ordered by the scene depth of the corresponding objects. For that, the image of the object camera is placed on the final image plane at the position it would have on the image plane of the system camera. Another approach presented in [18] reduces perceived geometric distortions as well. The idea is to directly modify the geometry of particular objects within a scene to compensate their distortion during the rendering process [18]. This approach results in computer generated images without distortions of scene objects as well.

Figure 4: Geometric arrangement rendered with the standard camera model of computer graphics using the algorithm to reduce distortion applied to the red-green spheres on the right wall. In comparison, the yellow-blue spheres on the left wall are distorted by perspective projection.

The responsible bundles in BiLL correct perspective distortion by using different algorithms to provide user-centered interfaces for a coherent communication of spatial information [37]. The resulting images have a multiperspective character without distortions. While user interaction, the correction of perspective distortions is adjusted to the modified camera position. This illustrates the potential of possible manipulations regarding the standard camera model of computer graphics in BiLL.

Color Perspective

Color in applications is an important part of design. Paintings of the Middle Ages and of the Renaissance exhibit different approaches to work with color. Techniques of classical painting can be used in addition to perspective projection to intensify three-dimensionality and to support spatial depth in computer generated images. Color-perspective is based on real world aerial perspective. This is a physical effect on the appearance of objects by the atmosphere. If the distance between object and viewer increases, the contrast between the object and its background decreases. As a result, the coloring of the object becomes less saturated and shifts towards the background color, which is usually blue. Aerial perspective is an important criterion to estimate distance [19].

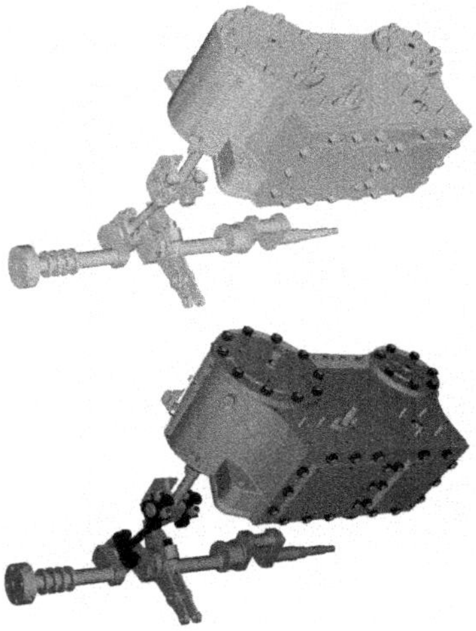

Figure 5: Shader-based color perspective to an interactive machine for an improved depth perception

Based on the principles of painting, it is conceivable to enhance computer generated images. The use of color in design in relation to pictorial concepts of color order and color perspective and its benefits regarding depth perception is a topic in [16]. Innovative methods and tools to improve depth perception by means of coloring and use of color, particularly for the interface development, can be considered. Potential benefits are in the fields of coloring, which supports interaction; searching, choosing, acting, and organization in interfaces (cp. [16]). Evaluations are feasible by using our experimental environment. Our vision is to improve communication of information with interactive images, which is explicitly supported by color. Current implementations of color perspective are either shader-based or exploit post processing. Figure 5 shows the use of color perspective. With the help of BiLL, it is possible to change colors and scene lighting depending on user interaction in real-time. The perception of spatial information and the color-assisted interaction in three-dimensional scenes can be investigated.

CONCLUSION

In this contribution, the engineering process of an interactive real-time system for three-dimensional computer graphics is presented. The component-oriented framework Bildsprache LiveLab (BiLL) is developed using standard components: OpenSceneGraph, FastLightToolkit and the POCO Open Service Platform. The software is adaptable and extensible based on scientific and technological developments. It allows exploration and investigation of aspects of interface design in the context of visual analytics and human-computer interaction. The component-based design enables development of dedicated components, which are focused on specific aspects of the stated research fields and can be realized independently. However, with this framework, procedures and algorithms can be investigated not only in isolation, but also in combination. Components can be loaded at runtime due to the flexible foundation. Furthermore, the development of component-based extensions was presented by introducing research topics in the area of information visualization and non-photorealistic rendering. The combination of components such as *multiperspective* and *color perspective* has already been realized. In summary, BiLL meets the requirements of an interactive real-time application to investigate interface design in the context of three-dimensional computer graphics.

FUTURE WORK

With the BiLL framework as an interactive computer system, open research questions about the effective and efficient perception of information can be pursued with great ease. A total of 22 research bundles has been developed or is currently under development by research assistants and students. In the future, tracking technologies will enable a wider range of user input, including speech, gestures, and whole body interaction. All of these technologies can be investigated with BiLL, both by users and developers. This offers possibilities to broaden the range of human-computer interaction in order to explore interaction with applications such as CAD-systems beyond mouse and keyboard. The experimental environment can also be used for formal user studies. For instance, multiperspective results in images and interfaces, which verifiably better reflect and support human perception and viewing behavior (cp. [17,39]). The starting point of our current experiments is the combination of BiLL with an eye-tracking system. This is achieved by using standard components as described in this contribution. Within the bundle layer, methods and techniques for multiperspective and eye-tracking communication are implemented as separate components (bundles). With the integrated services, these bundles can communicate and provide reciprocal functionality. In our experiment, human eye movement is detected by the eye tracking system and the data is transferred directly to the bundle responsible for multiperspective. The bundle corrects perspective distortions in computer generated images using own algorithms [37], which could not be tested in 3D real-time environments before the development of BiLL. Test persons were presented interactive visualizations of abstract three-dimensional scenes in the viewer window of BiLL. The investigator controlled the activity in the experiment by using the editor window. He decided which scenes and which scene configurations were visualized in the viewer window. The minimization of the perspective distortions is performed within the subject's saccades (rapid eye movements between fixations). Due to the change blindness associated with saccades, the changes in the image are not perceived by the test person. First results of this experiment indicate that perspective corrected images are perceived as more harmonious than uncorrected images. In addition, it was found that a saccade-dependent correction is not noticed and the viewing behavior is unaffected.

Further discussions with experts in the field of software engineering and visual analytics should evaluate the prospects of going open source with BiLL.

ACKNOWLEDGMENTS

Jan Wojdziak thanks European Social Fund (ESF), the European Union and the Free State of Saxony. Rainer Groh and Ingmar S. Franke thank Deutsche Forschungsgemeinschaft (DFG) (WaRP, DFG-GZ:GR 3417/1-1.).

REFERENCES

1. Object Management Group, Catalog of OMG corba/iiop specifications. http://www.omg.org/technology/documents/spec_catalog.htm.
2. SOF Service Oriented Framework. http://sof.tiddlyspot.com/.
3. Applied Informatics Software Engineering GmbH and Contributors, POCO C++ Libraries. http://pocoproject.org/.
4. Agrawala, M., Zorin, D., and Munzner, T. Artistic Multiprojection Rendering. *Proceedings of the Eurographics Workshop on Rendering Techniques 2000*, Springer (2000), 125-136.
5. Ahuja, S.P., Eggen, R., and Daucher, C. Performance Evaluation of Java And C++ Distributed Applications In A CORBA Environment. *Proceedings of the International Symposium on Performance Evalnation of Computer and Telecommunication Systems (SPECTS 2002), San Diego, CA*, (2002).
6. Alliance, O.S.G. OSGi Service Platform, Core Specification, Release 4, Version 4.1. *OSGi Specification*, (2007).
7. Azuma, R.T., others. A survey of augmented reality. *Presence-Teleoperators and Virtual Environments 6*, 4 (1997), 355–385.
8. Balakrishnan, R. and Kurtenbach, G. Exploring

bimanual camera control and object manipulation in 3D graphics interfaces. *Proceedings of the SIGCHI conference on Human factors in computing systems: the CHI is the limit*, ACM (1999), 56–62.
9. Bertoline, G.R. Visual science: an emerging discipline. *Journal for Geometry and Graphics 2*, 2 (1998), 181–187.
10. Bethel, W., Bass, C., Clay, S.R., et al. Scene graph APIs: wired or tired. *ACM SIGGRAPH*, 136–138.
11. Buxton, B. Two-Handed Input in Human-Computer Interaction. In *Haptic Input*. .
12. Card, S.K., Mackinlay, J.D., and Shneiderman, B. *Readings in information visualization: using vision to think*. Morgan Kaufmann, 1999.
13. Carroll, R., Agrawala, M., and Agarwala, A. Optimizing content-preserving projections for wide-angle images. *SIGGRAPH \uc0\u8217{}09: ACM SIGGRAPH 2009 papers*, ACM (2009), 1–9.
14. De Jong, H. and Klint, P. Toolbus: The next generation. *Formal Methods for Components and Objects*, (2003), 220–241.
15. Flores, A.P., Nacul, A., Silva, L., Netto, J., Pereira, C.E., and Bacellar, L. Quantitative evaluation of distributed object-oriented programming environments for real-time applications. *2nd IEEE International Symposium on Object-Oriented Real-Time Distributed Computing, 1999. (ISORC \uc0\u8217{}99) Proceedings*, (1999), 133-138.
16. Franke, I.S. and Groh, R. Colour Perspective in context of Navigation through Virtual Worlds an article on theoretical basics of interface design. *Proceedings of The Virtual 2006 - Designing Digital Experience*, (2006).
17. Franke, I.S., Pannasch, S., Helmert, J.R., Rieger, R., Groh, R., and Velichkovsky, B.M. Towards attention-centered interfaces. *ACM Transactions on Multimedia Computing, Communications, and Applications 4*, 3 (2008), 1-13.
18. Franke, I.S., Zavesky, M., and Dachselt, R. Learning from Painting: Perspective-dependent Geometry Deformation for Perceptual Realism. *Proceedings of the 13th Eurographics Symposium on Virtual Environments*, (2007).
19. Goldstein, E.B. *Cognitive psychology: Connecting mind, research, and everyday experience*. Wadsworth Pub Co, 2007.
20. Han, J.Y. Multi-touch interaction wall. *ACM SIGGRAPH 2006 Emerging technologies*, ACM (2006).
21. Hockney, D. *Secret Knowledge: Rediscovering the Lost Techniques of the Old Masters*. Thames & Hudson, 2006.
22. Jokela, T., Iivari, N., Matero, J., and Karukka, M. The standard of user-centered design and the standard definition of usability: analyzing ISO 13407 against ISO 9241-11. *Proceedings of the Latin American conference on Human-computer interaction*, (2003), 53–60.
23. Kato, H. and Billinghurst, M. Marker tracking and hmd calibration for a video-based augmented reality conferencing system. *iwar*, (1999), 85.
24. Kosara, R., Miksch, S., and Hauser, H. Semantic Depth of Field. *IEEE Symposium on Information Visualization (InfoVis)*, (2001), 97--104.
25. Kuehne, B., Martz. *OpenSceneGraph reference manual v2.2.* .
26. Lee, J.C. Hacking the Nintendo Wii Remote. *Pervasive Computing, IEEE 7*, 3 (2008), 39-45.
27. Martz, P. OpenSceneGraph quick start guide. *PMARTZ Computer Graphics Systems*, (2007).
28. Obiltschnig, G. The POCO Open Service Platform. http://www.appinf.com/en/products/osp.html.
29. Reiners, D., Voss, G., and Behr, J. OpenSG: basic concepts. *Proc. of OpenSG Symposium 2002*, (2002).
30. Roberts, J.C. State of the Art: Coordinated & Multiple Views in Exploratory Visualization. *Fifth International Conference on Coordinated and Multiple Views in Exploratory Visualization (CMV 2007)*, (2007), 61-71.
31. Shneiderman, B. The eyes have it: a task by data type taxonomy for information visualizations. *Proceedings of IEEE Symposium on Visual Languages*, (1996), 336-343.
32. Singh, K. A Fresh Perspective. *Proceedings of Graphics Interface 2002*, May 2002, 17-24.
33. Strothotte, T. and Schlechtweg, S. *Non-photorealistic computer graphics: modeling, rendering, and animation*. Morgan Kaufmann Pub, 2002.
34. Stroustrup, B. Evolving a language in and for the real world: C++ 1991-2006. *Proceedings of the third ACM SIGPLAN conference on History of programming languages*, (2007), 4.
35. Szyperski, C., Bosch, J., and Weck, W. Component-oriented programming. *Object-Oriented Technology ECOOP'99 Workshop Reader*, (1999), 795–795.
36. Ware, C. *Information visualization: perception for design*. Morgan Kaufmann, 2004.
37. Wojdziak, J., Zavesky, M., Kusch, K., Wuttig, D., Franke, I.S., and Groh, R. Figure out perspectives: perceptually realistic avatar visualization. *Proceedings of the IASTED Conference on Computer Graphics and Imaging (CGIM '11)*, (2011).
38. Wong, P.C. and Thomas, J. Visual Analytics. *Computer Graphics and Applications, IEEE 24*, 5 (2004), 20-21.
39. Yankova, A. and Franke, I. Angle of view vs. perspective distortion: a psychological evaluation of perspective projection for achieving perceptual realism in computer graphics. *Proceedings of the 5th symposium on Applied perception in graphics and visualization*, (2008), 204.
40. Yu, J. and McMillan, L. A framework for multiperspective rendering. *Rendering Techniques*, (2004), 61–68.
41. Zelnik-Manor, L., Peters, G., and Perona, P. Squaring the Circles in Panoramas. *Tenth IEEE International Conference on Computer Vision (ICCV'05) Volume 1*, 1292-1299.

QUIMERA: A Quality Metamodel to Improve Design Rationale

Alfonso García Frey, Eric Céret, Sophie Dupuy-Chessa and Gaëlle Calvary
University of Grenoble, Grenoble INP, CNRS, LIG
385, avenue de la Bibliothèque, 38400, Saint-Martin d'Hères, France
{Alfonso.Garcia-Frey, Eric.Céret, Sophie.Dupuy, Gaelle.Calvary}@imag.fr

ABSTRACT
With the increasing complexity of User Interfaces (UI) it is more and more necessary to make users understand the UI. We promote a Model-Driven approach to improve the perceived quality through an explicit and observable design rationale. The design rationale is the logical reasons given to justify a designed artifact. The design decisions are not taken arbitrarily, but following some criteria. We propose a Quality Metamodel to justify these decisions along a Model-Driven Engineering approach.

Author Keywords
User Interfaces, Perceived quality, Quality Metamodel, Design Rationale, QOC, Self-Explanation, Model-Driven Engineering.

ACM Classification Keywords
H.5.2 User Interfaces: Theory and method.

General Terms
Design, Human Factors.

INTRODUCTION
User Interfaces (UIs) must deal with new features such as the capacity of adaptation to the context of use (<user, platform, environment>). As designers cannot anticipate all the contexts of use at design time, UIs are generated dynamically giving rise to lacks of quality. This lack can be overcome through explanations. Self-Explanatory UIs (SE-UIs) aim at answering end-user questions about the UI. One of the SE-UIs approaches [16] is based on Model-Driven Engineering (MDE): explanations are generated from design models such as the Task and Domain Models used for UI generation. Good explanations about the UI need additional crucial information such as justification of design decisions or quality measures of the UI. Thus, we need an argumentation model to convey this information. This paper proposes a solution for explaining design decisions through quality models in the context of SE-UIs. The proposition is illustrated on a Seats Booking System.

EICS'11, June 13–16, 2011, Pisa, Italy.

The paper is fourfold. In the first section, it provides a short vision of related works about Quality and Design Rationale. Then, the Quality Metamodel is introduced and depicted through an example. Third part deals with design rationale. Finally, the fourth part is devoted to the case study that combines all the necessary pieces for self-explanation: a quality model, a design rationale, and a UI through a MDE approach.

RELATED WORKS
As we need quality models to explain design decisions, we relate existing quality models in the first section. Then, we review some design rationale representations explaining which one we use and why.

Quality Models
Different quality models have been proposed in the literature. McCall's hierarchical quality model [12] focuses on product quality, organizing it in two views: the external view for end-users and the internal view for developers. Boehm's model [13] adds a third level named *primitive characteristics* to deal with metrics and evaluation. The ISO/IEC 9126 standard series divides metrics into internal, external and quality-in-use.

This quality-in-use, also called usability or perceived quality, has been the main focus of the HCI community. Usability has evolved through standards such as the ISO 9241-110 [9], ISO/IEC 9126-1 [10] and ISO/IEC 25010 [11] among others. As a synthesis, Seffah encompasses most of the usability works in QUIM [14].

However Software Engineering quality models are more than usability. They deal with other important aspects of general quality in the whole System Development Life Cycle. ISO standards deal also with these aspects. To cover them, different quality metamodels have been proposed such as [18] for data quality, [19] as a quality metamodel for MDE, or [20] that defines a five step process for building product-specific quality models.

However, whilst several quality models exist in Software Engineering, most of them are oriented to evaluating source code or final products and not models or modeling activities. Other models don't deal with evaluation aspects

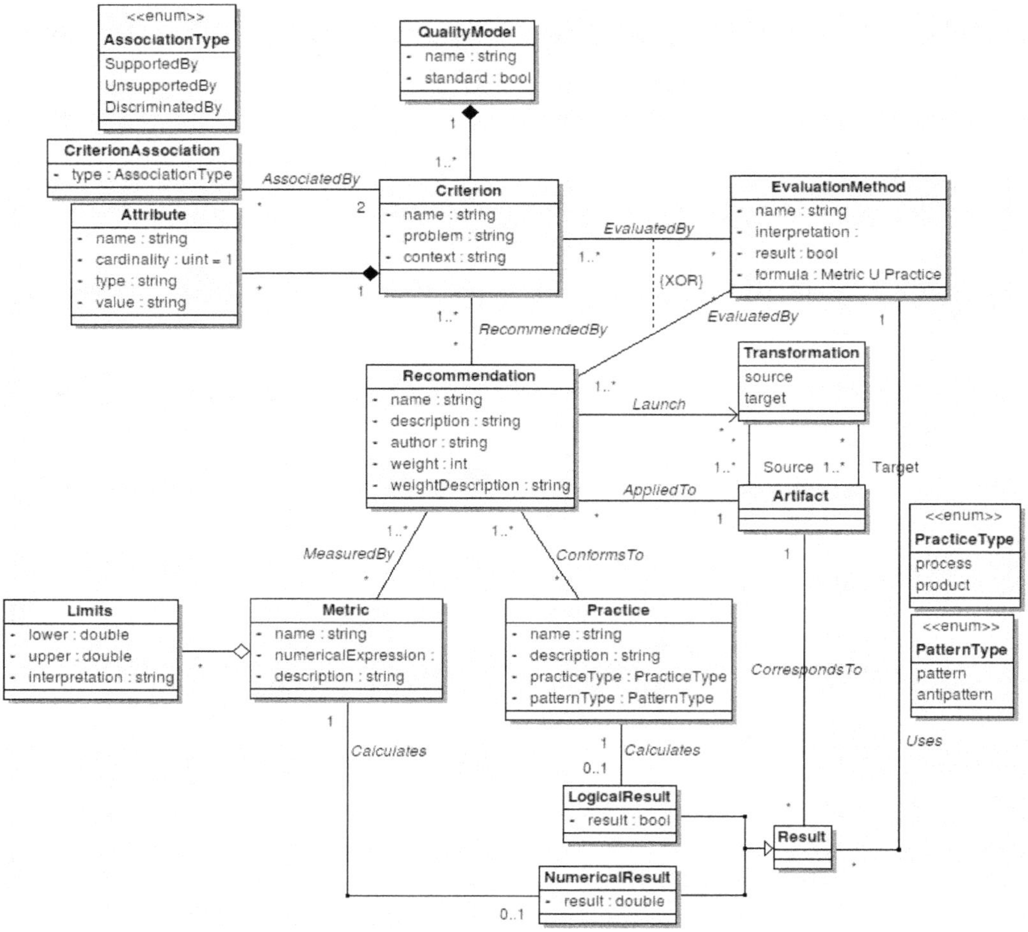

Figure 1: The Quality Metamodel

(evaluation methods, results...) or they just miss the different quality perspectives, as elicited in section two.

We propose QUIMERA, a quality metamodel, to take benefit from both HCI and Software Engineering while covering their requirements as well as our needs for UI quality. QUIMERA will be used to support design rational.

Design Rationale

Design Rationale is defined in [3] as: "An explanation of why a designed artifact (or some feature of an artifact) is the way it is."

Design rationale approaches like PHI [5] or QOC [6] (for Questions, Options and Criteria) are metamodel based. Non metamodel based approaches exist such as PDR [8]. For our purposes, we reuse QOC because it is the more expressive design rationale representation to work with different alternatives at the same time. QOC focuses directly on the discussion between those alternatives as shown in figure 4.

QUIMERA: THE QUALITY METAMODEL

In order to use a quality model to justify design decisions, we introduce a Quality Metamodel from which a quality model can be instantiated. QUIMERA stands for "QUality metamodel to IMprove the dEsign RAtionale". The first section shows the relations between QUIMERA and the system under study (SUS). The second section explains QUIMERA in detail. The final section shows an instantiation of QUIMERA that is put in practice later in the case study.

Quality Perspectives

QUIMERA (figures 1 and 2) has been designed to cover the needs of both Software Engineering and HCI. Quality can be expressed regarding four different perspectives [1]:

Expected Quality, or the quality the client needs. It is defined through the specification of the SUS.

Wished Quality is the degree of quality that the quality expert wants to achieve for the final version of the SUS. It is derived from the Expected Quality.

Achieved Quality is the quality obtained for a given implementation of the SUS. Ideally, it must satisfy the Wished Quality.

Perceived Quality is the perception of the results by the client, once the SUS has been delivered.

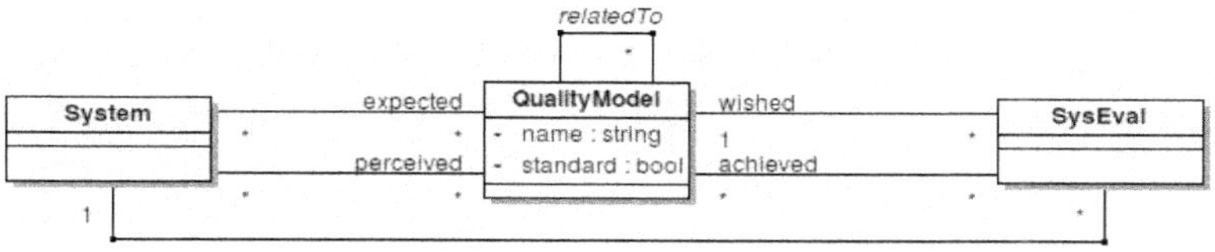

Figure 2: Quality perspectives in the Quality Metamodel

As stated in [2], these four perspectives can be related to the Systems Development Life Cycle by three dimensions. These dimensions are the Specification (related to the Expected and Wished Qualities), Implementation (related to the Achieved Quality) and Use (related to the Perceived Quality).

QUIMERA deals with these four perspectives as shown in figure 2. Here, the *System* entity represents the product to consider. *SysEval* represents a specific evaluation for that product. The four quality perspectives are four different uses of the same quality model. The attribute *standard* means that, when true, the quality model is not linked to *System* and *SysEval* as it only represents a quality standard such as ISO9241-110 or QUIM. In other words, the quality of these standards is not defined in terms of a product. Some internal parts of QUIMERA are not necessarily defined when *standard* is true.

Once the standard has been set, QUIMERA can be extended with the classes that are needed for each quality perspective, as we will see in the next section.

The Metamodel

Figure 1 shows QUIMERA in detail. A quality model is composed of criteria, that can be recursively decomposed into subcriteria through the class *CriterionAssociation*. Different recommendations can be specified for each criterion. A *Recommendation* is a positive assessment that characterizes Criteria. We can specify a weight for each recommendation to define which of them are more important than others for the considered system. Evaluations can be performed through *EvaluationMethods* that are specified by *Metrics* and/or *Practices*. In the first case, the measure is given by a *NumericalResult* that can be comprised between some *Limits* when defined. In the case of *Practices*, the result is a logical value, true or false, indicating if the *Practice* has been followed or not. Note that a *Practice* can be either a *pattern* or an *anti-pattern*, applied at the *process* level, or on a *product*. *Metrics* and *Practices* are directly evaluated on *Artifacts* through *Recommendations*. An *Artifact* can be no matter what element of the Software Development Life Cycle, such as code, classes of a model or the model itself.

Once a quality standard has been defined through *Criteria*, the metamodel can be reused with the association *relatedTo*, and extended with several classes such as *EvaluationMethods*, *Transformations* or *Artifacts,* to represent the four quality perspectives. For instance, *Metrics* can be defined in order to obtain some desired values (*Wished Quality*). The importance of every *Recommendation* can be customized using *Weights*. This allows designers to adjust the global quality precisely. Then, evaluations of the current quality of the SUS can be performed. When a *Result* of the evaluation (*Numerical* from *Metrics* or *Logical* from *Practices*) does not satisfy the expectations of the quality expert, this is, the *Achieved Quality* does not satisfy the *Wished Quality* (for instance, the value for a metric is not within the desired *Limits)*, the designer will need to increase the quality. This can be done by setting a *Transformation* or a set of *Transformations*. These *Transformations* are performed on the related *Artifacts* on which the *Result* has been previously calculated. Iterations can be done until the desired values defined by the quality expert (*Wished Quality*) are reached.

A Quality Model for the Ergonomic Criteria of UIs

Figure 3 shows a quality model representing Ergonomic Criteria in HCI [9]. For the sake of brevity, we explain only the three of them that are used later in the example:

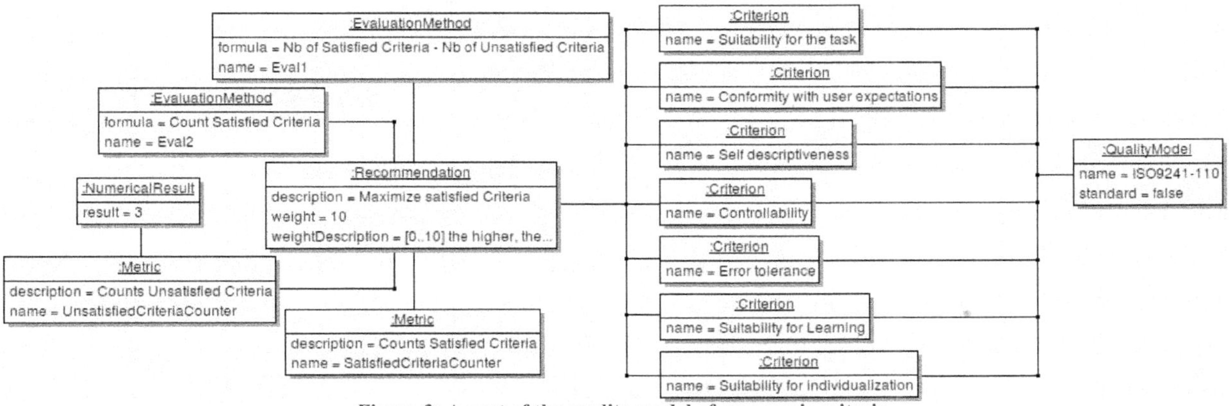

Figure 3: A part of the quality model of ergonomic criteria

Suitability for the task: A dialog is suitable for the task if the dialog helps the user to complete her/his task in an effective and efficient manner.

Self descriptiveness: A dialog is self descriptive if every single dialog step can immediately be understood by the user based on the information displayed by the system.

Error tolerance: A dialog is fault tolerant if a task can be completed without erroneous inputs with minimal overhead for corrections by the human user.

A *Recommendation* is a positive assessment that corresponds to one or more criteria. Figure 3 shows how different metrics are used for the same recommendation. For instance, in figure 3, the recommendation says that good quality can be achieved by maximizing the number of criteria that are satisfied by the UI. To evaluate Criteria, two different *EvaluationMethods* are defined. A detailed explanation about the left part of figure 3 including the *Recommendation*, the *Metrics*, the *EvaluationMethods* and the *Result*, is given later in the case study.

DESIGN RATIONALE

The main objective of QOC is the discussion of alternatives on specific artifact features. For our purposes, we consider only the following QOC elements:

Options that are artifact features under discussion.

Questions that are means of organizing the various Options, since every artifact feature responds to a specific design issue that can be framed as a Question.

Criteria that are used to determine the choice between Options. Equivalently, they can be seen as requirements or goals that have to be accomplished.

Assessments are links between Options and Criteria. If they satisfy a Criterion then the link is represented with a normal line. If not, a dotted line is used.

Figure 4 shows an example of QOC in which designers propose several interactors to let the user enter a date. The first interactor is composed of three input fields for the day, month and year respectively, and a label indicating format notations. The second interactor is a calendar. As shown in figure 4, the first interactor does satisfy the three criteria whilst the first interactor does not. This

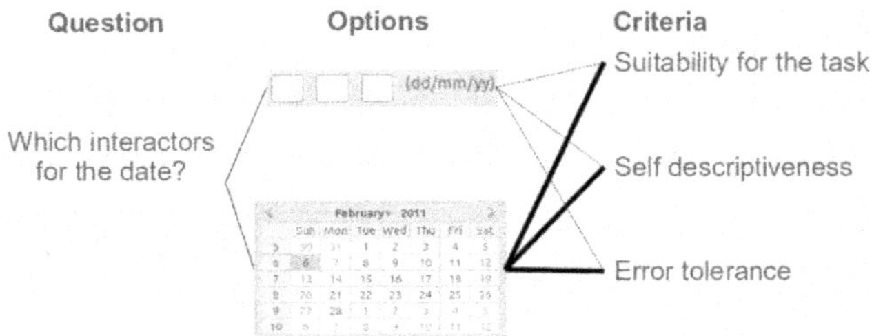

Figure 4: QOC notation for the example of the date

example is taken from the case study depicted in the next section.

PUTTING THE PIECES TOGETHER: A CASE STUDY

Figure 5 shows a booking system dialog inspired from [17]. With this UI, the end-user can book seats for a cinema session by entering the name, address, date of the session, time of the session (morning or evening) and the desired number of seats. The dialog has been derived in a MDE process from the task model shown in the same figure. The connection of various artifacts such as prototypes and tasks has also been proposed by previous authors [4,7]. The information provided in this UI is not clear enough. Some of its main problems are:

1. The prompting is insufficient. For instance, the label *Name* stands for First and Last names. (*Self descriptiveness*)
2. The guidance is ambiguous. Should the user type a ',' between names? (*Self descriptiveness*)
3. There is no prevention against errors. Users can enter any value because the verification is done in a later step. (*Error tolerance*)

This particular design has also two negative implications:

1. In case there is no seat available, the end-user has entered useless information.
2. If the end-user needs to book several seats at different times, for instance one in the morning and one in the evening, then the end-user needs to enter the same data several times.

A good design should ask for the information related to the seats first, and only if there are enough seats available, ask the end-user to provide the personal information.

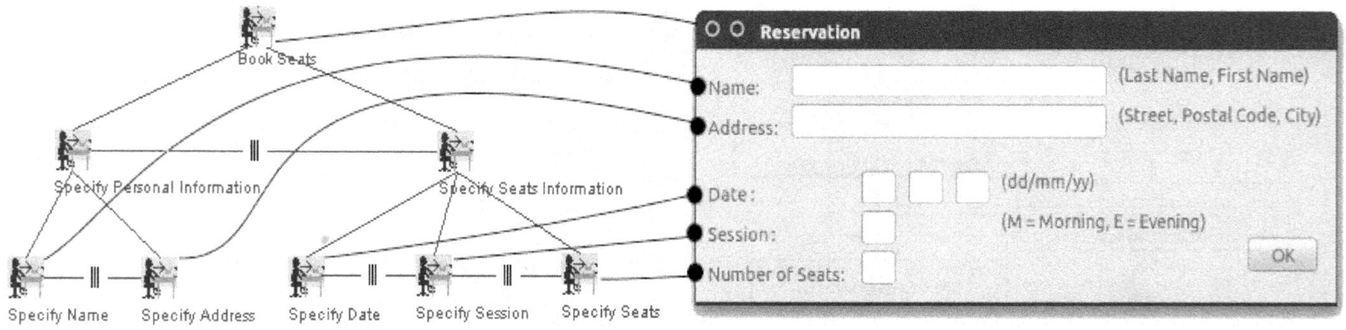

Figure 5: The UI of a Seats Booking System is obtained from a Task Model through a MDE process

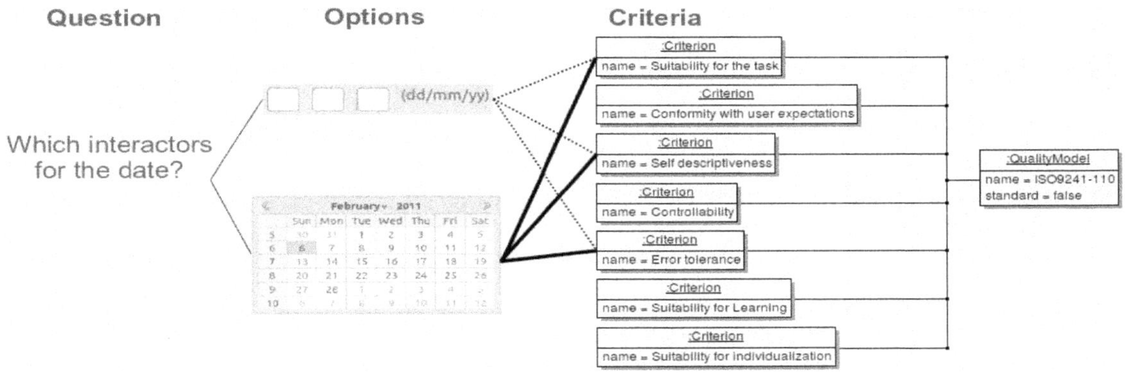

Figure 6: The quality model is used as the Criteria of QOC

In order to explain design decisions through quality models, designers use our approach as follows. First, the designers define a quality model based on QUIMERA. For this case study, we consider the quality model of ergonomic criteria of figure 3. Once the quality model is set, designers can keep trace of the design rationale through QOC. They need to describe the design rationale through questions, options and criteria. Designers write down the necessary questions to cover all the precedent problems that they have identified on the UI in figure 5, in the same way as it has been done in figure 4 for the question *Which interactor for the date?*

Our proposition is to use the quality model as the Criteria when describing the design rationale with QOC. Figure 6 shows this principle. With this approach, the three problems listed before about *Self descriptiveness* and *Error tolerance* are directly related to quality through the quality model. Note that the quality model is not a merely representation of the ergonomic criteria from [9], as it has been shown in other works like [15,21]. Ergonomic criteria play different roles becoming active for each quality perspective. For instance, the UI in figure 7 is better than UI in figure 5. The comparison between both UIs is based on *EvaluationMethods* depicted in the left part of figure 3. These methods use the specific formulas: "Satisfied Criteria minus Unsatisfied Criteria" for Eval1, and "Number of Satisfied Criteria" for Eval2". For Eval1 and regarding figure 6, we have Eval1(Calendar) = 3 - 0 = 3 and Eval1(Text-Fields) = 3 - 3 = 0, showing that the Calendar is better (3>0). The same conclusion is obtained for Eval2.

Advantages

The main advantages of this approach are:

1. Quality in design decisions becomes measurable.
2. Design decisions can be explained directly through quality models.
3. As a design rationale can be directly evaluated, two different solutions can be compared.
4. The quality model can be used not only for evaluation purposes, but as an active agent of the design rationale and the MDE process. As QUIMERA can launch transformations if the desired quality is not achieved, the MDE process for generating UIs can take benefit of it regarding how a transformation increases or decreases the achieved quality. For instance, figure 7 shows an improved version of the Seats Booking System. In this figure, two UIs have been generated to avoid the problem of typing personal information when there are no seats available. Here, the Task Model has been transformed (operator >>) and two UIs are generated now, maximizing the criterion *Suitability for the task.* Note that in figure 7, the task *Specify Name* is transformed into two sets of

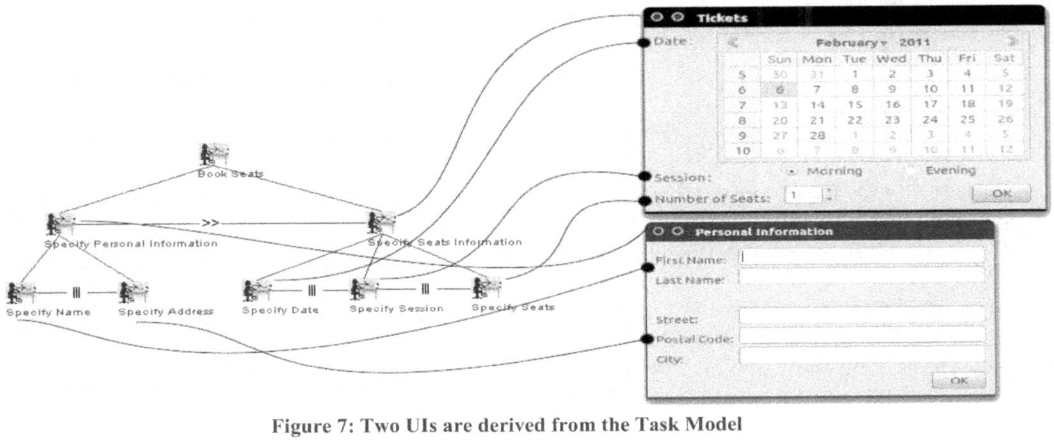

Figure 7: Two UIs are derived from the Task Model

Label + Text-Fields based on the two concepts (First name, Last name) that are manipulated in the task.

5. As a consequence of the previous point, adaptation of UIs can be quality driven.

Following this approach, designers can easily quantify design decisions regarding quality, and quality standards become active agents of the design process.

CONCLUSION AND FUTURE WORK

This paper presents QUIMERA, a quality metamodel that unifies quality aspects from HCI and Software Engineering, setting the bases for a quality driven adaption of UIs through quality models. Although QUIMERA is used to explain design decisions through quality models, it is domain independent, i.e. not only devoted to HCI.

We have detailed our approach through a case study, in which the metamodel is instantiated first, and used later as an active agent of the design rationale. The main advantages of this approach have been listed.

Future work will focus on implementing the proposed approach for evaluation purposes.

ACKNOWLEDGMENTS

The work is funded by the european ITEA UsiXML project (2009-2012).

REFERENCES

1.Carlier A. Management de la qualité pour la maîtrise du SI, Paris, Hermès, p. 28, 2006.

2.Si-Saïd Cherfi S., Akoka J., Comyn-Wattiau I. Conceptual Modeling Quality - From EER to UML Schemas Evaluation, Lecture Notes in Computer Science, Vol. 2503, p 414-428, January 2002.

3.Moran, T. P. and Carroll, J. M. Overview of design rationale. In Design Rationale: Concepts, Techniques, and Use, T. P. Moran and J. M. Carroll, Eds. LEA computers, cognition, and work series. Lawrence Erlbaum Associates, Inc., Mahwah, NJ, p 1–19, 1996.

4.Palanque P. and Lacaze, X. DREAM-TEAM: A Tool and a Notation Supporting Exploration of Options and Traceability of Choices for Safety Critical Interactive Systems. In Proceedings of INTERACT 2007, Rio, Brazil, Lecture Notes in Computer Science, Springer Verlag, September 2007.

5.McCall, R. J. PHI: A conceptual foundation for design hypermedia. Des. Stud. 12, 1, p 30 – 41, 1991.

6.MacLean, A., Young, R. M., Bellotti, V. M. E., and Moran, T. P. Questions, options, and criteria: Elements of design space analysis. Human-Comput. Interact. 6, 3-4, p 201–250, 1991.

7.Bramwell, C. Formal Development Methods for Interactive System: Combining Interactors and Design Ratio- nale. Ph.D. Thesis. University of York. 1995.

8.Carroll, J. M. and Rosson, M. B. Getting around the task-artifact cycle: How to make claims and design by scenario. ACM Trans. Inf. Syst. 10, 2 (Apr.), p 181–212, 1991.

9.ISO 9241-110:Ergonomics of human-system interaction - Part 110: Dialogue principles. ISO, 2006.

10. ISO/IEC 9126-1: Software engineering. Product quality - Part 1: Quality model. ISO, 2001.

11. ISO/IEC CD 25010.3: Systems and software engineering - Software product Quality Requirements and Evaluation (SQuaRE) - Software product quality and system quality in use models. ISO, 2009.

12. McCall, J. A., Richards, P. K., and Walters, G. F. Factors in Software Quality, Nat'l Tech. Information Service, no. Vol. 1, 2 and 3, 1977.

13. Boehm, B. W., Brown, J. R., Kaspar, H., Lipow, M., McLeod, G., and Merritt, M. Characteristics of Software Quality, North Holland, 1978.

14. Seffah, A., Donyaee, M., Kline, R. and Padda, H. Usability measurement and metrics: A consolidated model. Software Quality Journal, 14(2), p 159–178, June 2006.

15. Lacaze, X., Palanque, P., Barboni, E., Bastide, R., Navarre, D. From DREAM to Realitiy: Specificities of Interactive Systems Development with respect to Rationale Management. In: Dutoit, A.H., McCall, R., Mistrik, I., Paech, B. (eds.) Rationale Management in Software Engineering, pp. 155–172. Springer, Heidelberg, 2006.

16. García Frey, A. Self-explanatory user interfaces by model-driven engineering. In Proceedings of the 2nd ACM SIGCHI symposium on Engineering interactive computing systems (EICS '10). ACM, New York, NY, USA, p 341-344, 2010.

17. Nogier, J.F. De l'ergonomie du logiciel au design des sites Web, Third edition, Dunod 2005.

18. Kashif M, Si-Saïd Cherfi S., Comyn-Wattiau I. Data Quality Through Conceptual Model Quality-Reconciling Researchers and Practitioners Through a Customizable Quality Model. In International Conference on Information Quality (ICIQ), 2009.

19. Mohagheghi, P. and Dehlen, V. A Metamodel for Specifying Quality Models in Model-Driven Engineering. Nordic Workshop on Model Driven Engineering NW-MoDE '08, Reykjavik Iceland, p 20-22, August 2008.

20. Dromey, R.G. Concerning the Chimera. IEEE Software 13 (1), p 33- 43, 1996.

21. Martinie De Almeida, C., Ladry, J.F., Navarre D., Palanque P., Winckler, M. A. Embedding Requirements in Design Rationale to Deal Explicitly with User eXperience and Usability in an "intensive" Model-Based Development Approach (regular paper). In: Workshop on Model Driven Development of Advanced User Interfaces (MDDAUI 2010), Atlanta Georgia USA, Vol. 617, (Eds.), CEUR Workshop Proceedings, p. 29-32, 2010.

A Resource-Based Framework for Interactive Composition of Multimedia Documents

Paolo Bottoni
Dep. of Comp. Sc. – Sapienza Univ. of Rome
Via Salaria 113 – 00176 Roma, Italy
bottoni@di.uniroma1.it

Riccardo Genzone
Dep. of Comp. Sc. – Sapienza Univ. of Rome
Via Salaria 113 – 00176 Roma, Italy
riccardo.genzone@gmail.com

ABSTRACT
Interactive document composition requires users to launch complex programs, interleaving editing, integration, and formatting activities. Moreover, access to the document fragments may require specialised programs, possibly using proprietary formats. We propose a light-weight interaction framework for document composition, based on a notion of resource, where document construction amounts to selecting fragments, possibly generated via simple in-place editors or extracted from existing rich format documents. Actual document generation uses style sheets to produce different renderings for the same content.

Author Keywords
Resources, document composition.

ACM Classification Keywords
D.2.10 [Software Engineering]: Design – Methodologies.

General Terms
Design.

INTRODUCTION
Multimedia resources maintain information on concrete supports, residing at some physical location, reachable at a specific address and accessible through some protocol. An image, a text fragment or a video interval, are all examples of resources that a user may integrate into a document to be printed on paper or published on the web, thus requiring different rendering choices. While users are interested in resources as such to generate their documents, each resource may require specific software for its processing, visualisation, and integration in the document to be created.

In general, the associated applications are ridden with features not relevant to the current interaction and present an unnecessary level of complexity for the most common uses of the resources of interest. In particular, this is the case when the user is only interested in assembling existing content, available at different sources, with very few, or none at all, modifications of the content itself. As an example, consider the updating of a personal curriculum or of a company profile, where different parts might evolve independently, or different versions might be produced for different audiences. An academician might indeed choose to have a version of the curriculum in Italian and one in English, while drawing references to publications from a common list, and a company might offer different profiles to prospective business partners, employees, or the general public, exploiting a common base of pictures or graphics.

Moreover, different physical supports might be involved, e.g. HTML pages for the company Web presence, printed brochures or simple leaflets, derived from different selections or arrangements of available resources. While content management systems can help generate documents from multiple sources, they are still too complex for occasional users. We report here on the development of the Universal Resource Engine (URE), a visual tool for document composition, trough manipulation of (descriptors of) multimedia resources, without the need to access to their physical support. This is achieved by associating physical resources with virtual counterparts which are structured ensembles of metadata, and exploiting a logical model of document as aggregation of resources, to be exported towards open formats, according to information provided by style sheets, or invoking suitable renderers.

Paper organisation. We present a scenario and discuss related work. We then introduce the formal resource model, the composition process, and document generation from resource descriptions, before concluding the paper.

SCENARIO
Bob Bobbies' curriculum is structured in sections for personal data (further structured into immutable birth information and current address), education, professional activities (divided into past and current ones), and publications. Each piece of information is identified by a simple resource, e.g. *birth information*, *workplace* or *email*, while composite resources provide forms of aggregation.

Bob is simultaneously preparing two applications: one for a new position in a different company, and one for entering a Ph.D. program. He does not want to disclose information about the current workplace for the work application, and also decides not to send the list of publications, which instead he wants to present for the Ph.D. application.

EICS'11, June 13–16, 2011, Pisa, Italy.
Copyright 2011 ACM 978-1-4503-0670-6/11/06...$10.00.

Rather than creating two versions of the curriculum using a word processor application, he uses the URE environment, exploiting the available descriptions of relevant resources in his resource pool. Hence, he first retrieves the composite resource for the curriculum and creates a copy of it, from which he removes the simple resource referring to current workplace and the composite resource listing his publications. Finally, he saves the resource as a new one and activates an Apache FOP (Formatting Objects Processor) formatter[1] for creating a printed version of the curriculum based on an XSLT specification.

To prepare the Ph.D. application, he explores the composite resource for his list of publications and realizes that he has not yet inserted updated it with his paper in EICS 2010. He downloads the `bibtex` info from DBLP and saves it to a resource that he adds to the internal pool. Now, he can add reference to this info in the composite publication resource. He creates a new version of the curriculum where he includes the resource for the current job position and the list, saves the modified version of the composite resource for the curriculum and activates the FOP formatter.

The scenario illustrates requirements and issues for light-weight document composition. First, a user has to be aware of available resources, but need not organise them into inflexible structures, e.g. tables in a database or file system folders. Second, suitable representations are needed to give indications on a document fragment nature and content, without having to physically access it. Representations must support direct manipulation activities aimed at defining the logical composition of documents. Finally, resources must be composable: a same content can appear in a number of documents, without having to physically transfer it. The rest of the paper presents the URE approach to these issues.

RELATED WORK

The issue of relieving users from the need for several tools for document composition has been addressed at the industrial level by several companies (e.g. StreamServe, IsisPapyrus, PrintSoft[2]), based on corporate templates and complete management of the document life-cycle. The Alfresco Enterprise document management system[3] allows access to metadata, while retaining the original format of documents. Solutions based on XML for content storage, description and manipulation, e.g. Thunderhead[4], are gaining momentum. Zotero[5] offers an integrated way to collect information from different sources and annotate them while browsing the Web. However, Zotero is mostly oriented to the construction of reference libraries, rather than the organisation of personal information.

Wiki-based technologies allow rapid integration of content, but not a direct trace to its origin. RDF-based technologies manage content through tagged descriptions; integrating Description Logic [2,5] and Document Composition Logic [4], or of other logics [1] can achieve significant results. While URE can be adapted to use different logics to support retrieval of documents, we place emphasis on recursive composition of complex resources, based on the notion of a multiset of resources, rather than a graph.

We base our modelling of resources on the (Object-Oriented Modeling of MultiMedia Applications) OMMMA metamodel [6], to which types of simple and complex resources can be mapped, providing a flexible definition of the type structure. Interesting relations can be drawn with the metamodel for content repurposing proposed in [7], allowing the description of several aspects related to features of specific media and of interaction processes.

THE UNIFORM RESOURCE ENGINE

A resource is any entity which can be uniquely identifiable and accessible within a computer-based system and whose availability is limited in time or space. Attributes referencing physical resources are used as metadata for the description of a universal resource. In principle, any number of universal resources can be generated having as origin the same physical resource and maintaining a reference to it. As an example, a text about William Shakespeare could contain some biographical note, a sonnet, the birth and death dates, some lists of his work arranged by type, period or subject. The whole text, as well as each excerpt from - or composition of - this information potentially gives rise to a universal resource.

With reference to the OMMMA meta-model, simple resources are related to instances of sub-types of `Media`, while the interactive composition process performed with URE defines subtypes of `ApplicationUnit`. Figure 1 presents the model for curriculum composition, as derivable from the interaction described in the scenario.

URE Architecture

The URE environment is based on a two-level architecture, where the OMMMA metamodel provides the types for user-side activities of resource selection, composition and manipulation, while a resource-oriented programming language allows the formal specification of these activities from the computational viewpoint. The *Composer* system consists of (see Figure 2): 1) An *Aggregation Support* (AS) environment with primitives for resource availability check and for generation, editing and deletion processes. 2) A *Universal Resource Engine* (URE) resolving references to simple and complex resources, imported or generated in a resource pool. 3) A *Composition Support* (CS) with tools to convert resource contents into a format read- able by a

[1] http://xmlgraphics.apache.org/fop/

[2] http://www.streamserve.com,http://www.isis-papyrus.com http://www.printsoft.com

[3] http://www.alfresco.com/

[4] http://www.thunderhead.com

[5] http://www.zotero.org/

suitable generator of documents. 4) A collection (URPs) of pools of currently available Universal Resources.

The architecture is complemented by three types of components: 1) **Document Generators**, software components transforming resource descriptions from a URP into physical documents. 2) **In-place Editors**, interactive lightweight tools for producing simple textual or graphical documents. 3) **Universal Resources Generators**, external applications which can export resources in the URE format, or software services for exploring repositories of resources and importing them into a URP. Through the URE GUI, users can specify the composition of the resources they are interested in, explore the structure of the documents they are composing, and activate dedicated viewers for them.

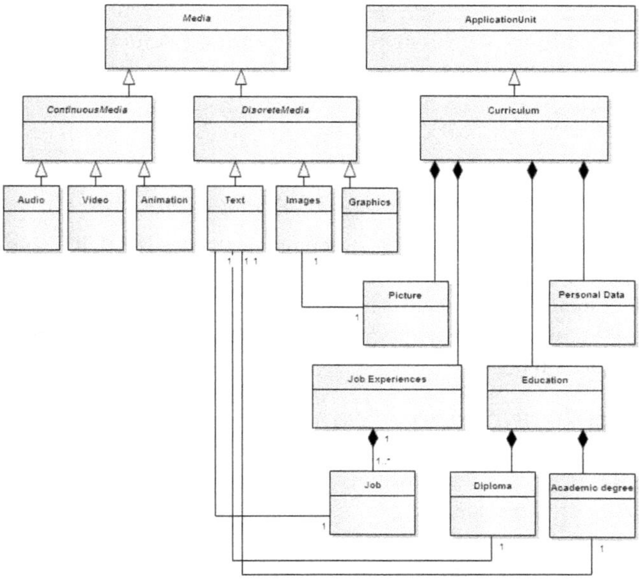

Figure 1: Derived OMMMA model for curricula.

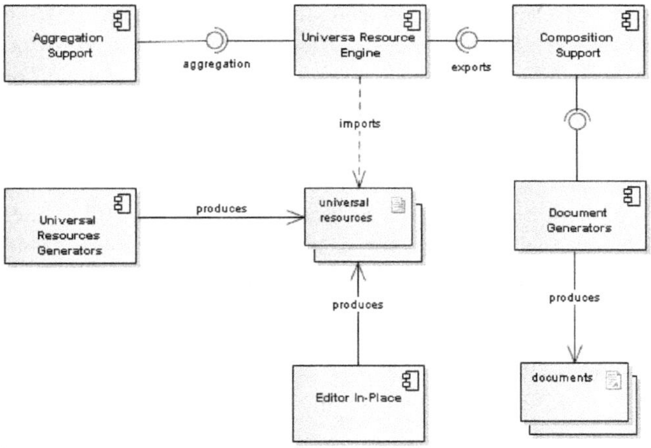

Figure 2: Overall architecture for URE.

The WIPPOG URE Machine

In the current URE implementation, the AS component is provided by the WIPPOG execution environment [3]. WIPPOG is a resource-aware rule-based programming language, with rules defined on collections of terms modelling resources. The term name gives the resource type; variables and constants are associated to attributes.

In particular, a rule can present six types of components, denoting: **WHEN**: a multiset of resources which must be present in the internal pool at rule application time; **GETS**: a multiset of externally produced resources which must be found in the input pool at rule application time; **IF**: a set of predicates on variables appearing in the **WHEN** or **GETS** components; **PROCESSES**: invocations of computational activities, e.g. assignments of attribute values for the created resources, possibly referring to variables introduced in the **WHEN** or **GETS** components; **PRODUCES**: a multiset of resources to be placed in the internal pool as a result of the transition; **OUTS**: a multiset of resources to be placed in the output pool and made externally available as a result of the transition. We have constructed *UREMachine*, a specific WIPPOG machine managing an internal pool and endowed with a suitable collection of rules.

The causal connection between the resources available to the *URE* and their representation in the *UREMachine* is based on the translation of resource descriptions into WIPPOG terms (with the name of the term corresponding to the *URE* type) and on the use of the WIPPOG *Input* and *Output* pools. In particular, user inputs from the *URE* GUI generate special request resources, which are inserted in the *Input* pool and matched to the **GETS** component of some rule triggering the corresponding transactional process in the *UREMachine*. Examples of requests are: creation of a new document, modification of its composition, document deletion, or modifications of its publication state in a distributed environment. Conversely, support resources placed in the *Output* pool as a result of some rule, and registered to the *URE-UREMachine* protocol, are used to provide feedback on the execution of the requests. To this end, the handling of the `outsPerformed` event during rule execution (i.e. the event generated when new resources are added to the output pool following specifications from the *OUTS* component) has been extended so that the produced resources are immediately exported to the *URE*.

To illustrate the communication between *URE* and *AS* (i.e. the WIPPOG *UREMachine*), Figure 3 presents the protocol for ensuring the causal connection for resource creation. When a resource needs to be created, a request of creation, is sent to WIPPOG, together with a coding of the description of the resource. WIPPOG processes the request activating the rules to create the resource and places the result in its output pool. *URE* can then import the created resource and make it available to its internal pool.

This two-way process is required as the logic for resource creation is in the AS. For example, there might be policies to restrict creation or access to sensitive or premium resources. A similar protocol has been defined for resource deletion: the *UREMachine* must process the consequences of deletion to maintain the environment consistent. The WIPPOG rule for deleting a simple resource is therefore:

WHEN: SimpleRsc(idRsc as idRsc1; type as type1)
GETS: idDelete(idRsc as idToDelete)
IF: idRsc1 = idtoDelete
OUTS: idDelete(idRsc as idToDelete)

If the resource identified by `idDelete` is not found in the internal pool, an exception is raised in the URE.

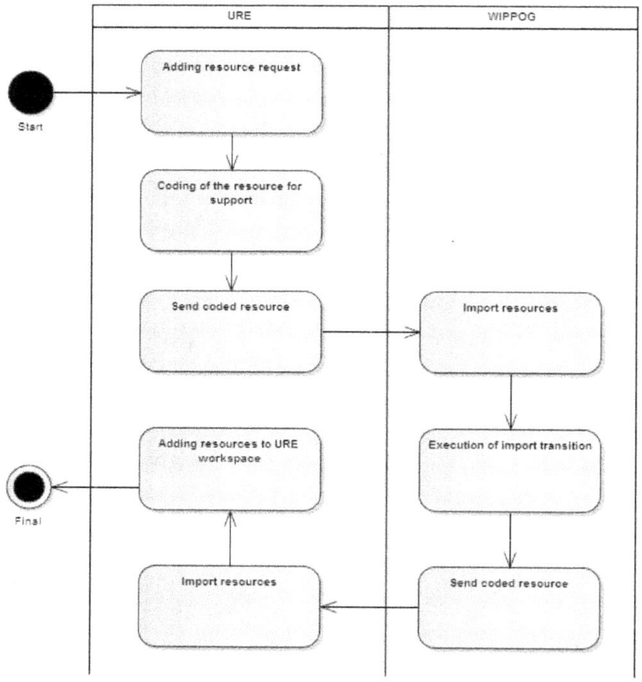

Figure 3: Protocol for resource creation.

Types of Resource

In URE, simple and composite resources are implemented as two corresponding Java classes. Both `SimpleResource` and `CompositeRsc` are specialisations of the abstract class `AUniversalResource`, which owns attributes to describe the features necessary to the description of any type of resource. In particular: `rscLabelField` maintains the user defined name of the resource; `topicField` gives the resource content; `keywordsField` stores descriptive keywords for indexing and retrieving ,purposes; `category` represents the family of resources (e.g. audio or text); and `type` has the name of the type of resource as value.

For simple resources, the values of `category` correspond to the `ContinuousMedia` and `DiscreteMedia` OMMMA subtypes, while composite ones are specialised to the types of categories entering the composition. For example, `TextAggregation` is for resources which only aggregate textual resources, `DiscreteMediaAggregation` for those including different categories from the `DiscreteMedia` superclass, and MixedMediaAggregation for heterogenous resources with categories from both `DiscreteMedia` and `ContinuousMedia`. The value of `type` establishes a correspondence with the Java class for its implementation, with each composite resource associated with an instance of the `CompositeRsc` class. A reflective mechanism can therefore be employed to create the needed resource instances based on their XML descriptions.

This structure can be used to create specific queries according to the category of resources to be retrieved. For example, Figures 4 and 5 show the different panels for query composition according to the `Text` and `Image` types.

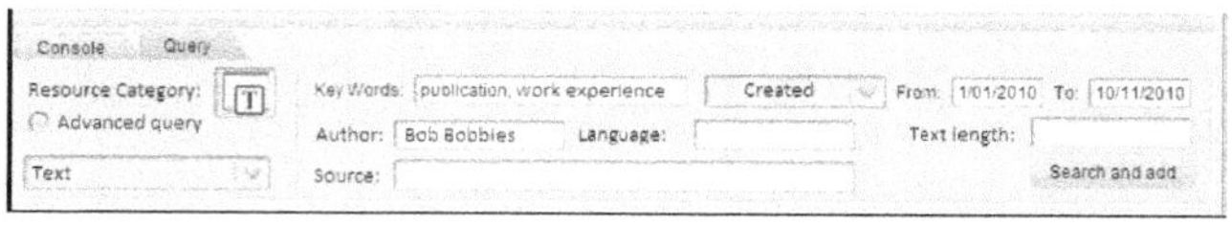

Figure 4: Query panel for textual resources.

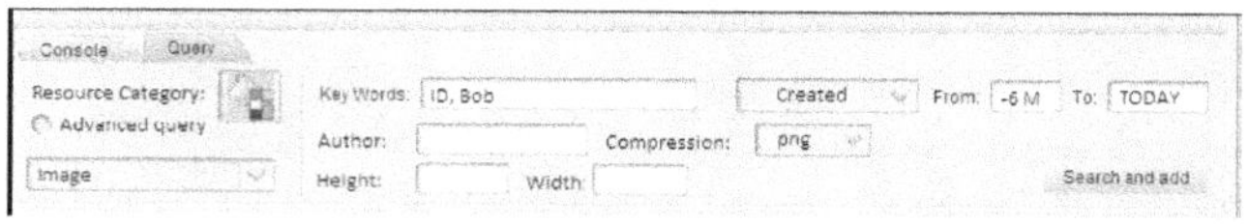

Figure 5: Query panel for image resources.

To ensure representation independence between URE and aggregation support, the `SupportFormat` interface declares methods to translate between URE internal format and that of the support. The current implementation provides the `WIPPOGSupport` implementation class.

DOCUMENT COMPOSITION

The interactive composition of a document specification in URE is obtained by formulating requests through the URE browser interface, which makes available a collection of viewers for: a) requesting the construction of composite resources by aggregating both specifically identified existing resources and resources to be retrieved based on some descriptor; b) exploring the composition of existing composite resources, possibly manipulating it via inclusion or removal activities; c) observing the actual content, or some thumbnail preview, of the existing simple resources.

Figure 6 shows the initial screen at the launch of the URE Browser. The top-left panel presents a tree-list view of the composition of the universal pool, while the top-right panel presents two tabs, one for accessing simple resources and one for composite ones. The bottom-left panel allows exploration of the content of simple resources selected in the tree list, while the bottom-right panel presents two tabs, one accessing a console for feedback messages and the other one for the interactive specification of queries.

Figure 7 shows a screenshot from the scenario discussed above. The universal pool contains a composite resource of type `TextAggregation`, named `personalData` with four simple `Text` resources. The user has selected this resource and the bottom-left panel shows its composition, also providing links to view resources in the proper textual format. The top-right panel presents a tab for each type of resource in the *Universal pool*, in which pairs label/icon are presented for each individual resource of that type.

As discussed before, the interactive query panel is specialised to the desired resource type. A generic panel is also usable, based on attributes common to any resource type. For example, in Figure 8 Bob wants to retrieve all resources tagged *Bob*, *Bobbies* and *publications*, created between 2000 and 2010, independent of their types. All the resources satisfying these criteria retrieved among those accessible to the browser are loaded in the universal resource pool and made available to user manipulation.

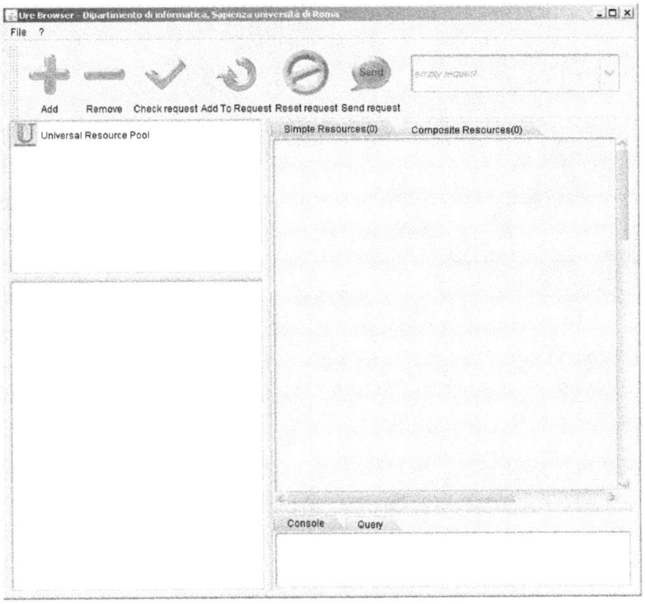

Figure 6: The URE Browser after its launch.

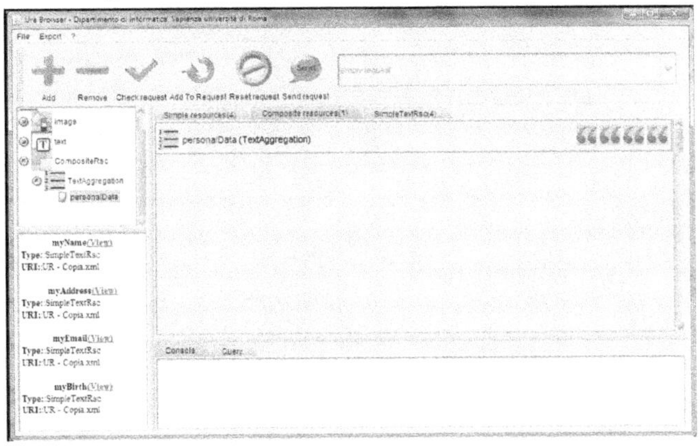

Figure 7: Visualising resource pool and resources.

Based on the available resources loaded in the internal pool (either as the result of a query or via direct manual addition) users can specify the composition of a resource they intend to create. Figure 9 shows the upper panels of the browser while the user is formulating a composition request. The user has selected a number of resources in the panel showing the universal pool, and has clicked on the `Add` button at the top, to import them in the URE working pool. The panel now presents a tab for each type of simple resource and one for composite resources, to provide some visual support for formulating a composition query.

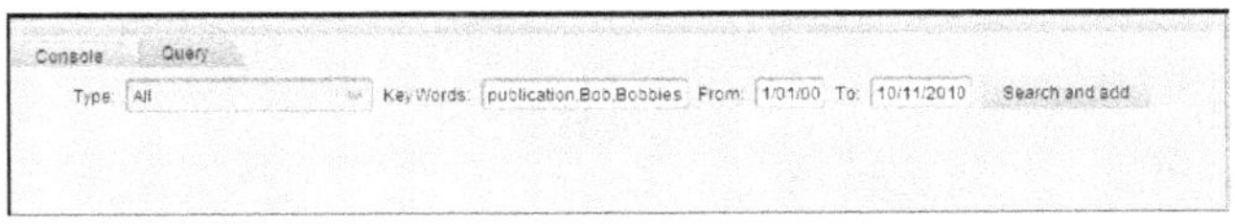

Figure 8: Composing a query to load information.

The composition of a new resource can be specified by requesting to include either some specific resource (click on the resource label to select its ID), or resources of a certain type (click on the type icon in a resource), among those available. The user can also check resource availability prior to issuing the request, by clicking on the `Check` button. In this case, only the availability of resources requested by type is checked, whereas the availability of identified resources is taken for granted.

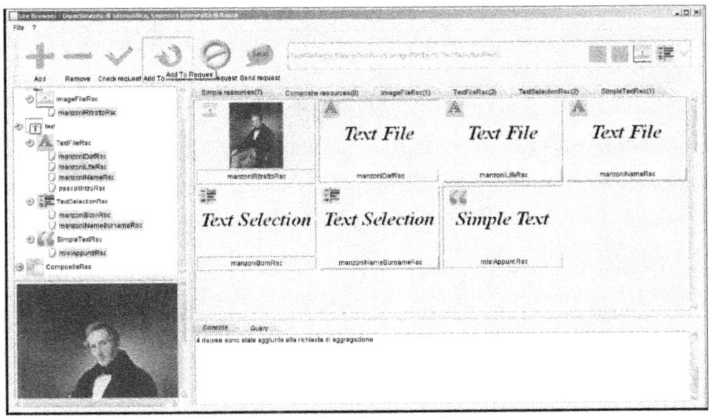

Figure 9: Interacting to request a composition.

A transactional process is started in the AS via a request resource of the form *CompositeRequest(idRsc: String; componentsTypes: String; componentsId: StringList)*, where the second argument contains a description of the needed types and the third one contains IDs of explicitly resources required. A type is inserted in *componentsTypes* as many times as the number of times a resource of that type is needed. The *idRsc* argument identifies the original request. The process presents four phases, with a WIPPOG rule for each one. A *Preliminary composition* rule transports the composition request resource from the input to the output pool and creates an empty `CompositeRsc`. In the *ID-based iteration* phase, a rule is iterated to retrieve all resources in the *componentsId* list and add them to the composite resource. A *Type-based iteration* retrieves and adds resources (not already included in the ID-based phase) according to the *componentsTypes* list. Finally, a *Completion* rule produces the resource, makes it available in the pool, and outputs its description to notify URE.

Document Generation

Different documents can be produced from a composite resource, exploiting specialised *Document Generators*. The

Apache FOP is a Java library for generating printable documents in several formats, both textual and graphical. For example, to use a `TextAggregation` textual resource to format a curriculum, the composition support prepares the resource description as an XML file and defines the rendering rules for its components. Figure 10 schematises a simple XSL specification organising a document in a number of sections. Each section is to be populated with resources extracted from a composite, and formatted according to the XLS-FO instructions in the XSL file.

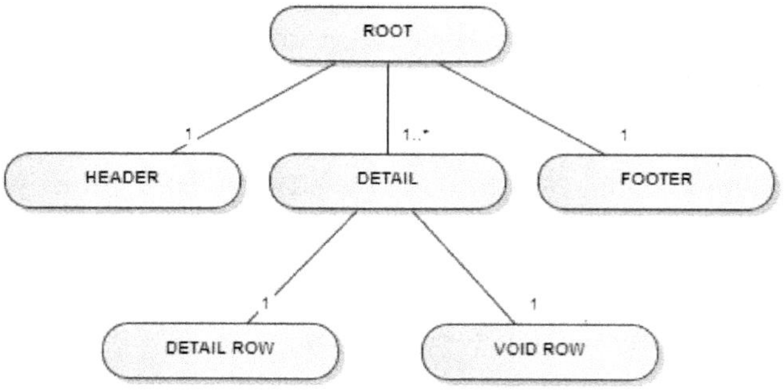

Figure 10: XLS Structure for document formatting.

Using such a file, Bob can format his curriculum as shown in Figure 11. The alternative version of the curriculum, derived from a different resource, can use the same formatting organisation, while a different outcome can be produced by changing translation rules or processing order.

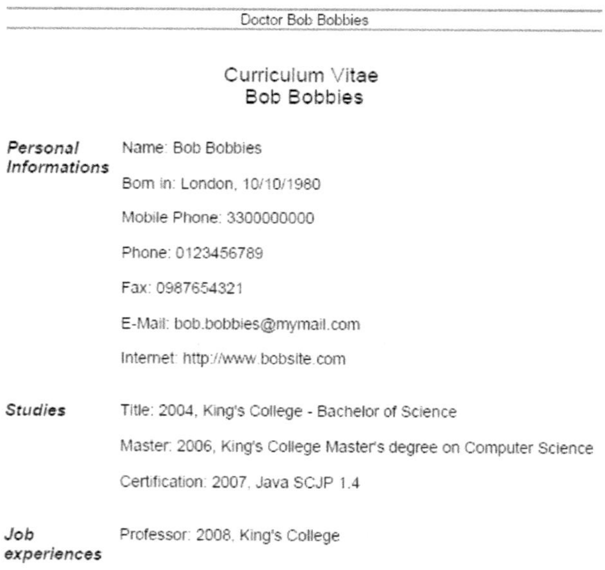
Doctor Bob Bobbies

Curriculum Vitae
Bob Bobbies

Personal Informations	Name: Bob Bobbies
	Born in: London, 10/10/1980
	Mobile Phone: 3300000000
	Phone: 0123456789
	Fax: 0987654321
	E-Mail: bob.bobbies@mymail.com
	Internet: http://www.bobsite.com
Studies	Title: 2004, King's College - Bachelor of Science
	Master: 2006, King's College Master's degree on Computer Science
	Certification: 2007, Java SCJP 1.4
Job experiences	Professor: 2008, King's College

Figure 11: A curriculum produced with FOP.

CONCLUSIONS

URE is a resource-oriented environment for visual interactive document composition. It supports resource retrieval and manipulation, and separates document production from composition through selection of sources. Resources, corresponding to document media fragments of heterogeneous nature, are treated in a uniform way through metadata descriptions, while still enabling users to exploit suitable viewers for exploring their content. URE allows the dynamic adaptation of a document components without having to create different versions of the whole document, while actual document generation is performed on demand.

The approach is also suitable to cooperative document composition through mechanisms which support import and export of resources among individual resource pools. In particular, the WIPPOG implementation already provides the possibility of exchanging such distributed resources.

The URE Browser allows interaction with familiar representations of the types of resources and supports both generic and type-specific queries without the need to learn specialised languages for resource manipulation, such as RDF or OWL. On the other hand, the approach is rapidly extendible to the transparent use of such languages, by incorporating aggregation supports for their processing and defining communication protocols with the URE core.

URE modularity can be exploited to integrate different types of document generator, and to provide immediate access to lightweight in-place resource. This would favour working styles interleaving document composition with generation or modification of text snippets or images.

REFERENCES

1. J.M.Almendros-Jiménez. RDF query language based on logic programming. *ENTCS*, 200(3):67-85, 2008.
2. F. Baader, D. Calvanese, D. L. McGuinness, D. Nardi, and P. F. Patel-Schneider. *The Description Logic Handbook: Theory, Implementation, Applications*. Cambridge University Press, 2003.
3. P. Bottoni, M. De Marsico, P. Di Tommaso, S. Levialdi, and D. Ventriglia. Definition of visual processes in a language for expressing transitions. *JVLC*,15(3):211-242, 2004.
4. S.-K. Chen, K.-L. Wu, and J.-S. Yih. Decoupled common annotations for reusing XML document composition logic. In *Proc. IASTED Conf. on Software Engineering and Applications*, pages 678-683, 2004.
5. D. Fensel, F. van Harmelen, I. Horrocks, D. L. McGuinness, and P. F. Patel-Schneider. OIL: An ontology infrastructure for the semantic Web. *IEEE Intelligent Systems*, 16(2):38-45, 2001.
6. S. Sauer and G. Engels. UML-based behaviour specification of interactive multimedia applications. In *Proc. HCC 2001*, pages 248-255. IEEE CS, 2001
7. Z. Obrenovic, D. Starcevic, and B. Selic. A model-driven approach to content repurposing. *IEEE Multimedia*, 11(1):62-71, 2004.

User Experience Quality in Multi-Touch Tasks

Ioannis Leftheriotis
Ionian University
Tsirigoti sq. 7, Corfu, Greece
midmandy@gmail.com

Konstantinos Chorianopoulos
Ionian University
Tsirigoti sq. 7, Corfu, Greece
choko@ionio.gr

ABSTRACT

In this paper, we present an updated set of experimental tasks and measures for large multi-touch (MT) input devices. In addition to a multi-user condition, we have employed an updated set of tasks, as well as subjective measures for user enjoyment. In the first experiment (a target acquisition task with two moving targets), the MT was more efficient than the mouse. Surprisingly, we found that the reduced accuracy of MT did not affect the perceived usability, or the enjoyment of the users. In the second experiment (a multiple shapes docking task), the MT was again more efficient and enjoying than the mouse. In the two-user condition, we found that performance and enjoyment was always higher than the single-user conditions, regardless of input device and task. Besides the quantitative results, we observed that users employed diverse interaction strategies in the MT condition, such as bi-manual input. The proposed tasks and the results support the use of MT in entertainment applications (multimedia and video-games), collaborative work, and scientific visualizations with complex data.

Author Keywords: Multi-touch, large screen, task, mouse, multi-user, input, user experience.

ACM Classification Keywords: H5.m. Information interfaces and presentation: Miscellaneous.

General Terms: Design, Experimentation

INTRODUCTION

Multi-touch (MT) applications are not considered to be traditional WIMP (Windows, Icons, Menus, Pointer) applications. MT applications rely on multiple fingers, gestures, and in general, more natural interaction techniques (Figure 1). Therefore MT is a completely different input device compared to traditional input devices of the past. According to Buxton, "One solution I see, is that we will start building new classes of computational devices that are not constrained by the legacy applications that were designed for a very different style of interaction." (cited in [13]).

Previous research has compared traditional indirect-mapping input devices such as mouse with MT devices. For example, Shanis et. al [14] tested MT against mouse and touchpad for speed, performance and wrist posture. They showed that cursor positioning was better with the mouse and that MT caused significantly less wrist extension than the touchpad, but was comparable to the mouse. Forlines et al. [2] have shown that MT is more efficient (i.e., less time) than mouse in target selection, but worse in shape matching. Wigdor et al measured accuracy of the Ripples MT system with traditional target selection tasks [6]. Overall, researchers have compared the MT to the mouse in the face of traditional computer tasks, such as single target acquisition and shape dragging.

Figure 1: The majority of current MT applications regard actions such as drag, resize and rotate of photos: a) Microsoft Surface Collage application, b) Jeff Han manipulating pictures with two finger gestures [3], c) multiplayer MT demo on PyMT[4], d) MT navigation application[4].

In this research, we have developed a set of experimental tasks that are more suitable for a MT surface than a mouse. Previous experiments mainly relied on traditional tests that have been designed for a single pointing device, such as the mouse. For example, target acquisition is an established task since the early studies on input devices by Card and colleagues at Xerox PARC [1]. In contrast, Kin et al [8] conducted a multi-target selection experiment. There were multiple targets on the screen and users were asked firstly to touch targets serially and finally touch as many targets as they could in parallel. Here, the established experimental tasks have been adapted to the characteristics of a MT screen. However, the scaling or rotation of objects was not used in our experiments because it has already been studied extensively in the past (e.g. [2]). In the following sections, we present two user experiments that feature multiples shapes, moving targets, and multiple users. In addition to the traditional usability measures (time, accuracy, preference), we have also employed flow and enjoyment user experience constructs, which have not yet been considered by previous research.

EXPERIMENT 1 – TARGET ACQUISITION

The first experiment was a target acquisition task. Although there have been multiple targets in previous experiments and the measure of "target acquisition time" has been studied before, there has not been any report on a task that considers multiple moving targets. We have designed a task with moving targets because there are several research and commercial MT applications (e.g. [9], games, advertising setups) that provide moving elements as part of the UI. In our task, users had to hit two moving targets (Figure 3).

During our initial exploratory experiments our MT display found to have tracking problems. As a consequence it was unable to track moving objects and thus mixed results were produced. In an effort to solve this issue the MT surface tracking system was improved. It became more accurate and thus allowed fast dragging of objects without losing the blobs at a rate of more than 95%.

Apparatus

The experimental set-up was based on FTIR technology [3], which is supplied by Nortd[1] labs (Figure 2). Community Core Vision[2] was employed to transform the video input from the camera to tracking data and events. We used the PyMT[4] toolkit to develop the MT applications.

Figure 2: Our installation: a 25 inch vertically placed FTIR MT surface, a Sony 1024x768 projector and a Unibrain infrared camera.

System Implementation

During the design and implementation of our experimental set-up we realized that this is a fragile installation. There are a number of devices that need to be precisely calibrated and moreover, there are factors such as ambient lighting, for example, that could influence the performance, accuracy and robustness of our installation. There are mapping issues between the projected image and the surface that the user touches, or even positioning or focusing the camera correctly. Nevertheless, we managed to establish a robust set-up (Figure 2) that did not affect the performance of the users.

Although the majority of MT systems are positioned in a horizontal axis we decided that we wanted to have a vertical MT surface. As it is shown in [10], vertical displays have the advantage of being able to accommodate larger groups of people. Our main motivation for a vertical installation is that we would like to use it in a classroom, where a teacher shows images or interacts with applications in order to improve the educational procedure. Thus, the MT surface was positioned vertically and users were asked to sit in a chair in front of the MT screen and interact in a natural way as comfortable as possible. Image was back-projected and there was no use of mirrors since the installation was vertical.

Both in MT and mouse condition the same screen was used. Subjects were sitting on a chair placed in front of the MT screen at about 1 meter distance. A mouse (with BlueTrack tracking technology – 1000 dpi) was used along with a mouse pad. Since the analysis of the screen was 1024x768 and the size of the screen that was used was 25 in, the mouse cursor was bigger than the size of a typical cursor on a Desktop pc with Mac OS X. However, since the distance between the users and the screen was relatively larger than the typical distance between a user and his desktop pc, there were no users complaining about locating the mouse cursor or about its size in general. The tracking speed of the mouse was placed in the middle of the scale (five out of ten) on the system preferences of the Mac OS X environment and users were asked whether the mouse sensitivity/tracking speed was satisfying.

Participants

Seven users took part in the study (five females, two males). They were recruited from the department of Informatics and given a bonus of half grade in HCI lesson for their time. The age ranged from 19 to 34 years with an average of 27.23 years (SD = 7.79). All participants, but one who was ambidextrous and used primarily his right hand, were right-handed. Three of them had used a large MT surface before. Four of them were familiar with MT technology as they held one or more MT mobile devices (iPhone, iPod etc.).

Task

At the beginning of each task, targets are still. Users are asked to touch/click on the targets being as accurate and fast as possible. To complete the target acquisition task users should have hit fifty targets. The system is automatically storing the number of efforts and the time needed to hit all fifty targets. That is the time saved is the interval between the first and the fiftieth hit and the number of efforts derives from the sum of the fifty successful hits of the targets along with the number of the unsuccessful ones. In the event of hitting all fifty targets, a green screen with a message "task completed" is being shown.

---

[1]Nortd labs, Website: http://labs.nortd.com/touchkit/

[2]NUI Group Community. Community Core Vision (CCV) software, Website: http://ccv.nuigroup.com/.

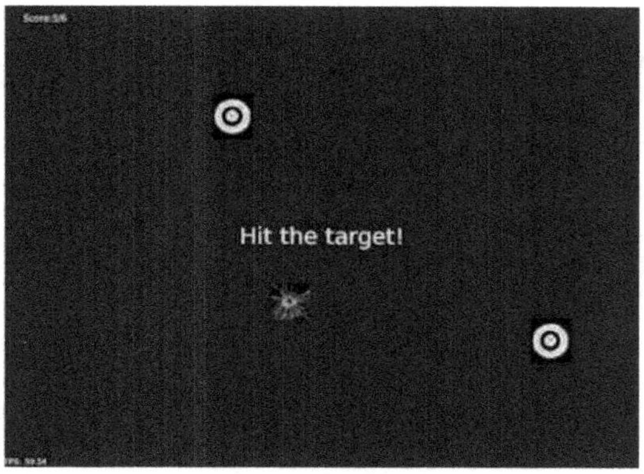

Figure 3: Target acquisition application: Users were asked to touch the two moving targets with their fingers on the first condition, or click on them with mouse on the second.

Targets on the screen are moving with constant speed (approximately 100 pixels or 5 cm per second) Targets appear in random places near one side of the screen (i.e. left part of the screen) and are moving to the opposite side (i.e. right part of the screen). Users have to touch the targets with their fingers or click on them with their mouse. Whenever a user touches a target, a counter that counts the succeeded efforts is increased, that target disappears and a new target is created near one side of the screen. Whenever user fail to touch a moving target an image of a broken piece of glass is shown as a negative feedback to the user (Figure 3) and the total efforts are increased too. The target is moving until the user touches it, or until it reaches the other side of the screen, where it stops moving. We chose the speed of moving targets, so that all users could hit them before they reached the end of the screen.

The task of selecting multiple moving targets is representative in MT surfaces. Moreover, this application could be used with one hand, with two hands, or with two users collaboratively.

Procedure

In the beginning of the experiment we screened users for previous experience with MT devices. Then, the application was presented to them. They were asked to interact with the MT screen for as long as they needed to feel comfortable. In the experiment there were targets that were 48x48 pixels (2.4x2.4 cm). But in order for user to feel familiar with the MT surface a variety of different sizes of targets were shown as a warm up procedure. The total number of targets that were hit prior to the main experiment for familiarizing purposes was 150 targets for each condition (mouse or MT) per user. We waited for users to feel comfortable with the task before the beginning of the experiment.

Four users started the experiment with the MT and the other three started with the mouse. Users were asked to be as accurate and as fast as possible during the experiment. The total number of targets that were used during the experiment was 50 targets for each condition (mouse or MT) per user. In the end of this task two users were asked to work together on the MT screen for hitting 50 more targets.

After each condition the subjective quality questionnaires were given to users. In particular, we employed the flow state scale [7], the PQ, and HQS questionnaire form [5]. All questions were rated on a 7-point scale, ranging from 1 (strongly disagree) to 7 (strongly agree). In the end of this experiment a preference questionnaire was given to users and they were asked to reply which condition they preferred, and in which condition they felt they were more accurate or faster.

Results

In agreement to other works [2,12], it seems that MT has better performance in target acquisition, even when there are two moving targets on the screen. As it is depicted in table 1 users needed 37.4 seconds (std = 2.7) to hit 50 targets with MT while they needed 50.4 (std = 7.8) seconds to click on the targets with the mouse. The quantitative results of the study are indicative of the performance differences between an indirect and a direct input device. Moreover, the qualitative results (user observation) indicate a preference to use an MT as a single touch direct input device. Nevertheless, the MT condition has been also evaluated in the two-user condition, which would not be possible without multiple touches.

Experiment 1: Target acquisition	Average Time	Standard Deviation
MT	37.40	7.8
Mouse	50.47	2.7
MT 2 users	24.50	4.3

Table 1: In the two moving targets acquisition task MT performs better.

The average mark for flow questionnaire was 5.29 out of seven (std=0.83) for mouse and 5.94 out of seven (std=0.58) for MT, for the two moving targets acquisition task. As far as the Hedonic Quality-Stimulation (HQS) rankings is concerned, MT obtained 5.1 while mouse obtained 2.8 out of seven. Finally, MT was rated with 5.7 on Pragmatic Quality (PQ) whether mouse was rated with 3.2 out of seven (Figure 4). All in all, MT not only performed better considering time but users were able to understand that they were performing better too.

Experiment 1: efforts	Average Efforts	Standard Deviation
MT	59.8	2.8
Mouse	53.4	1.3
MT 2 users	55.5	2.1

Table 2: In the two moving target acquisition task, considering selection errors MT proves to be less accurate than mouse.

There are some interesting results with regard to the accuracy and the multi-user condition. Most notably, the mouse proved to be more accurate. In order to hit 50 targets with MT, users had approximately 60 efforts, and thus a success rate of 83% while in mouse condition they needed only 53 efforts and thus their access rate was 94%. In addition, the two users' condition showed that two users outperform one user as it was expected. Two users prove to be more than two times faster (24.5 sec) than one user using mouse but not twice as fast as the condition with one user using MT (table 2). Additionally, as far as the number of efforts to hit all the targets, they are almost equal to one user MT condition. Therefore, increasing the number of users on an MT does not proportionally increase the efficiency, but it improves the accuracy per user. During the tasks users were not guided on how they should hit the targets. Almost all users, apart from two experts, used only their dominant hand to touch the targets.

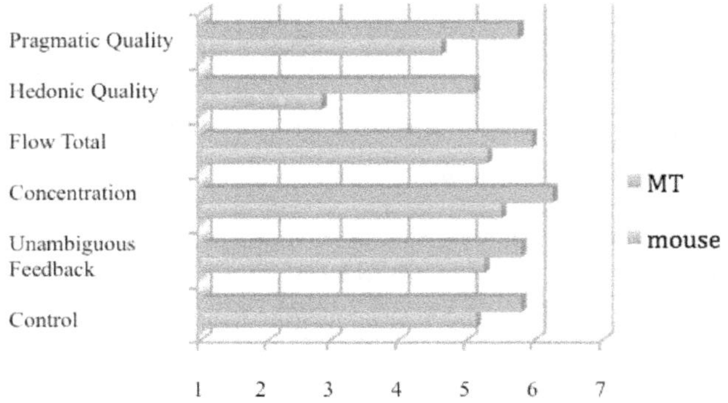

Figure 4. Target acquisition task: Questionnaires results.

Discussion

Although there have been previous studies comparing input devices showing that MT performs better in target acquisition, it is shown that even when there are two targets on the screen moving constantly the MT outperforms mouse significantly. Additionally, users seemed to enjoy the MT condition in target selection more than the mouse condition. Apparently, they could estimate correctly that they performed in less time with the MT. In addition, users felt that they were in-control with the MT surface. In the two-user condition, it was obvious that they enjoyed more due to their facial expressions and the fact that they were involved more by deploying strategies in order to improve their time while they were playing. Nevertheless, the two-user condition was not as efficient as expected. We observed that issues such occlusion or cluttering the display with multiple moving hands are responsible.

EXPERIMENT 2 – SHAPE DOCKING

Instead of using a simple docking task with one shape, repeatedly, as in [2], we considered that a MT screen offers more than one finger touches. Thus, there was more than one shape on the screen. This could increase the cognitive and motor load, but it could guide in interesting results as far as the multitasking (two users or two hands) is concerned on a MT surface. In our second experiment the setup of the first experiment was used. In order to conduct our experiment, six new (different from the first experiment) users were recruited from the local university. Their average age was 27 years old and they were all males with a previous experience in MT technology (mostly with MT mobile devices).

Task

At the beginning of each task, twenty-two shapes such as triangles or rectangles appear on the screen in random places. There are eleven colored and eleven white shapes. Note that the eleventh shape is the trigger to the counter of the task completion time. The time to dock ten shapes is finally measured. Each colored shape has its twin white shape. The main purpose is to match all the colored shapes with their corresponding white ones. Thus, users are asked to move each colored shape over its identical white one. Once this happens, these two shapes disappear. It is not necessary for the user to position precisely the colored shape above the white one that matches. There is a threshold of ten pixels (or 0.5 cm) (as in [11]) that allows the shapes to disappear when they come into proximity. Only colored shapes can be moved. In addition, users are able to move more than one shape simultaneously either with one or two hands. The system gives feedback for each touch. A small yellow circle appears (Figure 5) around the spot where the finger touches the screen for every touch.

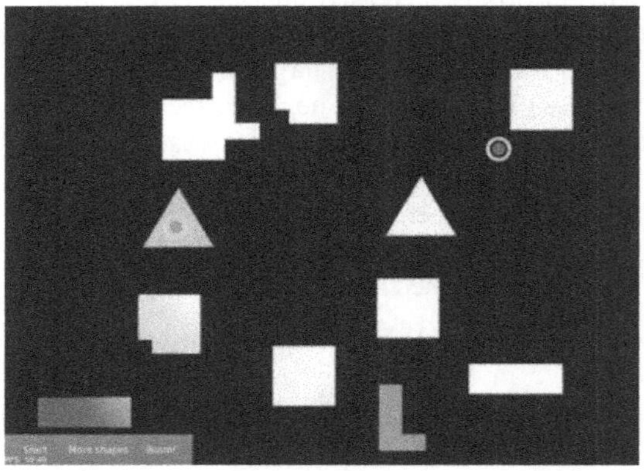

Figure 5. Object docking task: Users were asked to move the colored shapes to the white matching ones in order to dock and disappear.

Design and procedure

In this experiment users were asked to match the colored shapes with the white ones. The size of each shape was 50x50 pixels (or 2.5x2.5 cm apart from the blue bar shape which was sized 60*20 pixels or 3x1 cm).

The application was firstly presented to users. They were asked to interact with the MT screen for as long as they needed to feel comfortable in dragging subtasks. Additionally, larger sized shapes were used in order to make users feel familiar with the dragging subtask on the MT screen, which were followed by shapes the same size as the experiment. When users felt familiar with the dragging subtask (after matching plethora of shapes) we were ready to begin the experiment. It was a within group experiment with three conditions, MT, mouse, two users MT just as multiple target acquisition experiment. In order to minimize the learning effect, we have employed random assignment to the treatments: three users started firstly the experiment with the MT condition and the other three users started with the mouse. Users were informed that they should be as accurate and as fast as possible. In the task, there were eleven colored shapes to be matched with their corresponding white ones. The time needed to match all the shapes on the screen was measured. The time counter started when the first shape match occurred, measuring the time to match ten shapes.

After the experiment the flow and enjoyment questionnaire were given to the users just as in the target acquisition experiment. In the end of this experiment a preference questionnaire was given to users and they were asked to reply which condition they preferred, mouse or MT and in which condition they felt they were more accurate or faster.

Results

As it is shown in table 3, MT outperformed mouse in the shape-matching task, considering completion times. In order to dock 10 colored shapes to the 10 white ones users needed 17.94 seconds with MT and 22.19 with mouse.

Experiment 2: Shape Matching	Average Time	Standard Deviation
MT	17.94	0.36
Mouse	22.19	2.80
MT 2 users	10.16	0.44

Table 3. Shape matching task: MT proves to be faster than mouse. Two users on MT are almost two times faster than with the mouse.

According to the questionnaires, users preferred the MT instead of the mouse again (table 4). As it can be seen from Figure 6, the average mark from flow (derived from concentration, unambiguous feedback and control) questionnaire was 5.4 out of 7 for mouse and 6.3 for MT condition. As far as the HQS rankings is concerned, MT obtained 5.17 while mouse obtained 3.63 out of seven. On the other hand, MT was rated with 5.9 on PQ whether mouse was rated with 5.7 out of seven. Although those two ratings are very close with each other, we suppose that this happens due to the fact that Pragmatic Quality is based on user experience and we consider users much more experienced in the use of mouse.

Experiment 2: Shape Matching Questionnaire	Mouse	MT
Preferred	3.33	7.0
Fast	3.50	7.0
Entertaining	2.83	7.0
Effective	4.16	6.5

Table 4. Shape matching task: Users seem to prefer MT condition much more.

All in all, MT not only performed better considering time but users were able to understand that they were performing better too. But as we can see both from the table 4 and the HQS (Hedonic Quality) in Figure 6, the greatest difference between the input devices appears to be related to the entertainment factor.

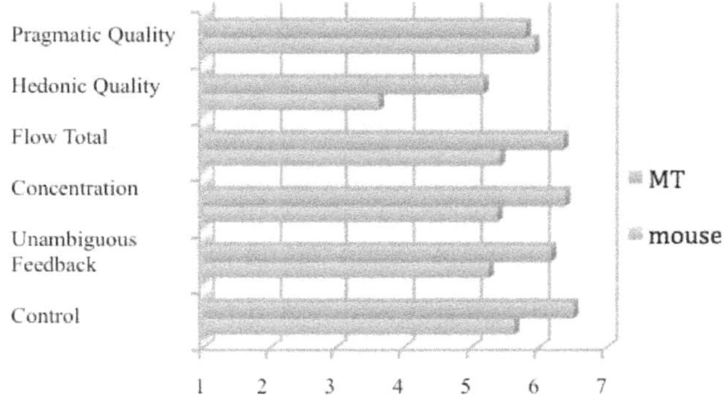

Figure 6. Object docking task: Questionnaires results

As in experiment one almost all users enjoyed more the two users condition. Two users MT condition (Figure 7.c) improved significantly the task completion time but again two users where not two times faster than one user with MT.

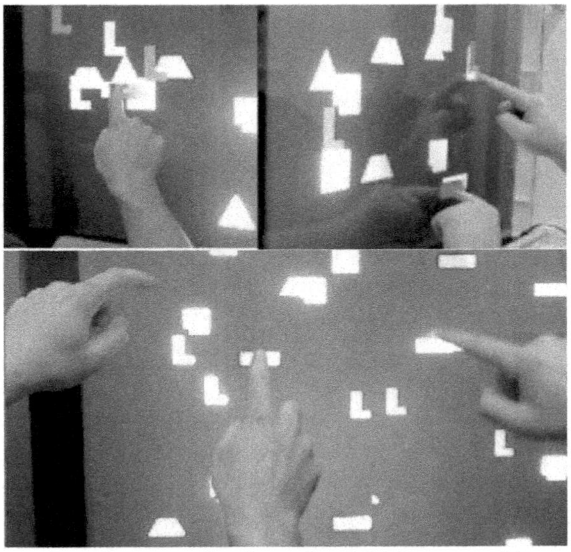

Figure 7. a) One user, dominant hand. b) One user, bimanual interaction, c) Two users, both using both their hands.

Discussion

In this experiment, most of the users used primarily their dominant hand (Figure 7.a) but sometimes users tried to use both hands. Moving shapes with both hands seems to be easy but trying to dock them with their white respective ones proved to be difficult (Figure 7.b). Although accuracy was not measured directly in log files due to the fact that there was a 10 pixels threshold (0.5 cm), users seemed to be accurate in matching shapes except from when they tried to do it simultaneously with both their hands.

MT surfaces not only proved to be faster in dragging task but produced feelings of enjoyment of interaction, improved control and in general an entertaining atmosphere.

CONCLUSION

In this research, we examined the potential of MT surfaces by conducting two laboratory experiments with a relatively small number of users. The results from more users would probably improve the reliability of the study, but we would not expect any significant difference in its validity because the measurements are focused on the differences between experts' pointing and dragging performance. Actually, the original mouse comparative study [1] had only four users and established that a small number of users are enough as long as there is sufficient training and multiple repeated tasks (i.e. expert users). Moreover, we extended established experimental tasks and measures for input device comparisons, in order to compare MT and multi-user conditions. In particular, we introduced user tasks that are suitable for MT applications, such as multiple moving target acquisition and multiple objects docking. The tasks might seem artificial when compared to real applications, but those tasks are atomic and unique for every MT user interface. Regardless of how advanced the UI is, the user has to reach for multiple screen elements and to move them around. Thus, the tasks were suitable for our experiment, because they stand for basic user actions. Moreover, additional measurements such as flow or enjoyment were employed to highlight the benefits of MT.

In those two experiments, we figured out that the MT surface and its tracking system plays the most important role when measuring enjoyment and effectiveness of the MT surface. The system must be as accurate as possible in detecting finger blobs because users' opinion is really influenced. Thus the improved tracking system we had in the experiments allowed having more valuable results.

Finally, we believe that since MT surfaces have some unique attributes, an updated set of measures such as engagement of the user, in-control feeling or flow should be applied. Correlations between traditional measures such as performance or accuracy and the updated set of measures proposed should be investigated in order to evaluate applications dedicated for MT surfaces. Finally, we argue that future MT and multiuser systems should be evaluated with respect to collaboration effectiveness.

ACKNOWLEDGMENTS

We would like to thank our pilot users, the NUI community and particularly the PyMT project team. This work has been partly supported by project CULT (http://cult.di.ionio.gr). CULT (MC-ERG-2008-2308940) is a Marie Curie project of the European Commission (EC) under the 7th Framework Program (FP7).

REFERENCES

1. Card, S. K., English, W. K., and Burr, B. J. Evaluation of mouse, rate-controlled isometric joystick, step keys, and text keys, for text selection on a CRT, *Ergonomics 21* (1978), 601-613.
2. Forlines, C., Wigdor, D., Shen, C., and Balakrishnan, R. Direct-touch vs. mouse input for tabletop displays. In *Proc. of the SIGCHI conference on Human factors in computing systems - CHI 2007*, ACM Press (2007), 647-656.
3. Han, J. Y., Low-cost multi-touch sensing through frustrated total internal reflection. In *Proc. of the 18th annual ACM symposium on User interface software and technology, UIST 2005*, ACM Press (2005), 115–118.
4. Hansen T., Denter C., Virbel M., Using the PyMT toolkit for HCI Research, Forum on Tactile and Gestural interaction, Lille(France), (2010).
5. Hassenzahl, M. The Interplay of Beauty, Goodness, and Usability in Interactive Products. *Human Computer Interaction*, *19*(4), (2004), 319-349.
6. ISO, 2002. Reference Number: ISO 9241-9:2000(E). Ergonomic requirements for office work with visual display terminals (VDTs)—Part 9—Requirements for non-keyboard input devices (ISO 9241-9), (2002).
7. Jackson, S. A., and Marsh, H. Development and validation of a scale to measure optimal experience: The Flow State Scale, *Journal of Sport & Exercise Psychology*, Vol. 18(1), (1996), 17-35.
8. Kin, K. and Derose, T. Determining the Benefits of Direct-Touch , Bimanual , and Multifinger Input on a Multitouch Workstation. *Graphics Interface Conference*, (2009).
9. Peltonen, P., Kurvinen, E., Salovaara, A., Jacucci, G., Ilmonen, T., Evans, J., Oulasvirta, A., and Saarikko, P. "It's mine, don't touch": Interactions at a large multitouch display in a city Center. In *Proc. of the SIGCHI conference on human factors in computing systems (CHI'08),* ACM Press, (2008), 1285-1294.
10. Rogers Y., Lindley S., Schwartz, Collaborating around vertical and horizontal large interactive displays: which way is best?, *Interacting with Computres*, 16, 2 (December 2004), 1133-1152.
11. Schmidt, D., Block F., and Gellersen, H. A comparison of Direct and Indirect Multi-touch Input for Large Surfaces, *Interact 2009*, 582-594.
12. Sears, A., and Shneiderman, B. High precision touchscreens: design strategies and comparisons with a mouse. *International Journal of Man-Machine Studies 34*, 4 (1991), 593-613.
13. Selker, T. Touching the future. *Communications of the ACM 51*, 12 (2008), 14.
14. Shanis, J. M., Hedge, A., Comparison of Mouse, Touchpad and Multitouch Input Technologies, In *Proc. of Human Factors and Ergonomics Society Annual*, Communications , pp. 746-750(5).

TREC: Platform-Neutral Input for Mobile Augmented Reality Applications

Jason Kurczak and T.C. Nicholas Graham
School of Computing, Queens University
Kingston, Canada K7L 3N6
{kurczak, graham}@cs.queensu.ca

ABSTRACT

Development of Augmented Reality (AR) applications can be time consuming due to the effort required in accessing sensors for location and orientation tracking data. In this paper, we introduce the TREC framework, designed to handle sensor input and make AR development easier. It does this in three ways. First, TREC generates a high-level abstraction of user location and orientation, so that low-level sensor data need not be seen directly. TREC also automatically uses the best available sensors and fusion algorithms so that complex configuration is unnecessary. Finally, TREC enables extensions of the framework to add support for new devices or customized sensor fusion algorithms.

Author Keywords

augmented reality, tracking sensors, input framework, sensor fusion

ACM Classification Keywords

H.5.1 Information Interfaces and Presentation: Artificial, augmented and virtual realities

General Terms

Design

INTRODUCTION

Mobile Augmented Reality (mobile AR) is rapidly making inroads in the consumer market, with applications such as Car Finder [1] and Layar [2] being released for mobile phone platforms. These applications use the phone's camera and screen to superimpose information on a video feed of the real world, and have served to demonstrate the potential of mobile AR to the general public.

Mobile AR applications use sensors such as GPS, compass, and inertial sensors to determine the physical location and orientation of the device. The problem for mobile AR developers is that such sensors may be unreliable and noisy. Applications often must fuse inputs from multiple sensors to

EICS'11, June 13–16, 2011, Pisa, Italy.

Figure 1. Using the tourist application

determine accurate values. Even when a framework is used to handle the input devices, it can require complex manual configuration and be hard to extend or modify. These problems require the developer to focus on low-level sensor programming rather than focusing on the functionality and usability of the application.

In this paper, we present an architecture for input frameworks designed to help address these issues, which is implemented in the TREC (TRacking using Extensible Components) framework. The advantages of this architecture are illustrated by its use in the Noisy Planet application described in the Motivating Example and Applying TREC sections.

The main advantages provided by TREC's architecture include giving programmers open access to a hierarchy of devices, transformative modules, and high-level abstracted interfaces; being able to dynamically select sensors and sensor fusion algorithms thanks to multiple levels of abstraction; and allowing modification and extension at every level.

MOTIVATING EXAMPLE: AN AR TOURIST APPLICATION

To provide context to our description of TREC, we introduce *Noisy Planet*, a mobile tourist guide. This application, shown in figures 1 and 2, has been implemented using TREC. Noisy Planet allows a tourist staying in an unfamiliar city to navigate to proximate destinations on foot while also allowing serendipitous exploration of the area.

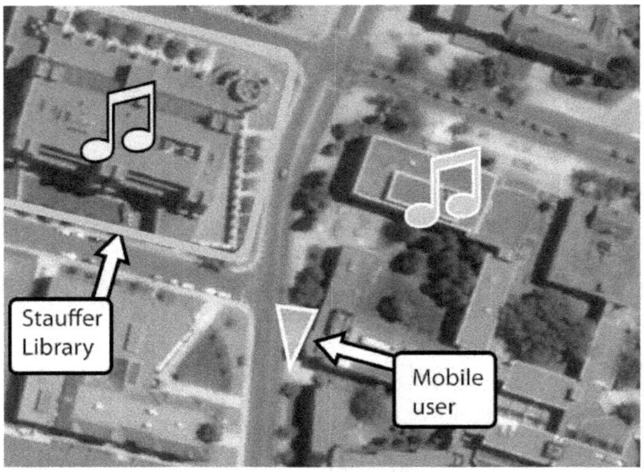

Figure 2. Overhead view

Noisy Planet uses 3D sound to convey to users the position and distance of nearby points of interest. For example, in figure 1, the user "hears" that the Stauffer Library is behind him and to his right. Each point of interest is represented by a subtle repeating tone – for example, the sound of riffling pages represents the library; clinking glasses represent a restaurant, and jingling coins represent a bank. The application overlays an aural landscape over the physical world. The sounds emanate from the correct location, even as the user walks or turns his head. Since the sounds are subtle and repeating, the tourist can easily choose to listen to them or tune them out.

The Noisy Planet implementation must track the user's location and head orientation so that sounds appear to emanate from the correct direction. It is challenging to accurately determine this information using off-the-shelf sensor equipment, and often multiple sensors are required to accurately estimate location and orientation. We currently use GPS, compass and gyroscope devices. Each device has its own data format, requiring programmers to write low low-level interfacing code. Each device type has limitations that cause it to deliver highly innacurate data under some circumstances. The programmer must therefore and must identify and code heuristics determining which device to use when they deliver conflicting information. As we shall see, our TREC framework helps with these difficulties.

INPUT HANDLING IN MOBILE AR APPLICATIONS

Before presenting the design of TREC, we first review current methods for obtaining input in mobile AR applications. We consider hardware support for location and orientation input, then review the state of the art in sensor fusion, and finally discuss existing input toolkits.

Hardware for Location and Pose Detection

A variety of off-the-shelf devices are available for estimating a user's location and pose in mobile contexts.

GPS devices triangulate their position using signals from orbiting satellites. Consumer devices have an accuracy of about 5-10m, depending on overhead visibility in outdoor environments [14].

Accelerometers can be used to track changes in position by calculating acceleration vectors based on the experienced forces, and integrating this data twice to obtain displacement [8]. Accelerometers provide faster updates and higher resolution updates than a GPS, but lack an absolute frame of reference and are subject to drift, therefore requiring periodic checks with some other absolute measure of position.

Other methods for tracking position include triangulation of signals from known locations, such as cellular tower signals, wifi signals or ultrasonic transmitter systems [6]. These approaches suffer from limited coverage.

Digital compasses (or magnetometers) detect orientation relative to magnetic north, but suffer serious drawbacks in accuracy. With the help of a 3-axis accelerometer to track the direction of earth's gravitational pull, a magnetometer can provide pitch, yaw, and roll data. Errors arise due to the lack of uniformity of the earth's magnetic field and its susceptibility to magnetic materials and artificial magnetic fields. In addition, outside forces (e.g., from walking) disturb the accelerometers' measurement of the gravitational vector and can cause large deviations in measured orientation when walking.

Gyroscopes measure angular displacement relative to some initial orientation, and so cannot indicate absolute direction on their own. However, unlike magnetometers, they are not affected by magnetic anomalies or by outside forces. Errors accumulated over time, however, will cause drift from the true direction. At high speeds of rotation (e.g., due to rapid head movement) some gyroscopes may exceed their upper limit of measurement and return wildly inaccurate results.

Sensor Fusion Techniques

Sensor fusion improves accuracy by combining data from multiple sensors [3]. A simple form of sensor fusion is to average the input of multiple sensors that are measuring the same property, in order to average out the noise from individual sensors (e.g. averaging the measurements of multiple anemometers to ascertain wind speed). More complex techniques take advantage of known properties of different sensor types. For example, a gyroscope, magnetometer, and accelerometer might be used in tandem, where the magnetometer is used to calibrate the gyroscope whenever the sensor is at rest.

Another approach is to use a Kalman filter [13], which takes multiple noisy sensor measurements, estimates the error in these measurements, and then estimates the actual state of the system being measured [4].

Programming fusion algorithms requires iterative tuning based on deep knowledge of the properties of the underlying sensors.

Frameworks

TREC is far from the first framework used to process input from tracking devices.

VRPN provides an interface between input hardware and Virtual Reality (VR) applications. VRPN allows VR hardware peripherals to be shared across many computers on the same network, and simplifies development by providing a standardized interface for peripherals with the same functionality [12]. VRPN standardizes the sensor data being delivered to applications so that their code is not dependent on the sensors being used. It does not, however, dynamically choose which of the attached devices to use; this must be specified by the application developer. In terms of extensibility, VRPN permits the creation of new devices and device types, while also supporting *layered devices* that let the developer program higher-level behaviour based on input from one or more sensors.

OpenTracker supports tracking hardware with a flexible and customizable architecture [10]. It uses dataflow graphs to manage data being passed from sensors to applications. Here, "device drivers" act as source nodes that bring data into the system; "filter nodes" transform, merge, or otherwise modify passed data from source nodes, and "sink nodes" output the data to an application. OpenTracker has a high level of configurability, using an XML schema to define the dataflow graph and supporting custom nodes. Like VRPN, however, OpenTracker does not offer automatic configuration and choice of devices, requiring the developer to provide a configuration file that describes the exact dataflow graph and devices to use.

Ubitrack, on the other hand, is designed for automatic configuration [9]. It is meant to support large networks of sensors to provide AR tracking using all available resources, with completely dynamic configuration of dataflow networks based on Spatial Relationship Graphs (SRGs) of the sensors in the network. There does not appear to be any way to modify or extend the algorithm used to configure the dataflow networks, or to override this algorithm to use specific devices or configurations.

The *OpenInterface Project* [11] has very interesting parallels in another area of HCI research. It is an open source platform for rapidly prototyping multimodal input interfaces for computer programs, with the benefit of a GUI interface. OpenInterface is designed to transform hardware input into a format suitable for the client application using modular transformation components, support a broad range of input devices, and be easily extensible. OpenInterface does not support the automatic selection of sensors and fusion algorithms, requiring explicit configurations by the developer like VRPN and OpenTracker.

All of these AR frameworks support abstraction of sensor data to standard interfaces. VRPN, OpenTracker, and OpenInterface are extensible, allowing new sensor types to be easily added. Ubitrack provides automatic sensor configuration. None of these toolkits addresses all three of these important goals. The TREC framework has been designed specifically to fill this gap.

THE TREC FRAMEWORK

TREC is a software framework for input handling in mobile AR applications. TREC's goals are to reduce the time required to develop interfaces for hardware sensors, and to reduce the difficulty of adapting AR apps to work with a particular collection of sensors. Specifically, TREC addresses the problems identified in the last section where: 1) writing low-level interfaces to sensors distracts developers from the core application design; 2) changing the set of available sensors may break applications, requiring extensive recoding; 3) combining the input from different sensors is tricky, requiring experimentation and iteration

First, in order to make the application programmer's job easier, TREC abstracts all sensor data into a high level representation of *location* and *orientation*. TREC provides the application programmer with simple interfaces for these two properties in its *abstract input layer*.

Second, TREC automatically configures the sensors by determining at runtime which of the connected sensors can be used to provide the best data to the application. Because the TREC layered architecture hides all differences between sensor hardware, it can provide the application plug-and-play compatibility with different sensors.

Finally, TREC uses sensor fusion algorithms automatically when a supported configuration is available, and the architecture makes it easy to extend the framework to support new algorithms. It uses a three-layer hierarchy (see figure 3) to abstract device details. This allows newly added sensors in the *device layer* to work automatically with existing applications, and fusion algorithms in the *abstract device layer* can take advantage of the abstracted devices automatically. The framework is open and allows access and modification at any level, meaning low-level sensor data can always be accessed directly if necessary.

In summary, the 3-layered architecture of TREC allows it to provide open access to high and low levels of abstraction, makes it easier to support automatic configuration based on a hierarchy of device types, allows sensor fusion algorithms to be dynamically chosen in the same way as devices, and makes new devices and algorithms easily interoperable with existing code.

The TREC Architecture

The framework is structured around a three-layer architecture: the Abstract Input Layer, the Abstract Device Layer, and the Device Layer.

The lowest layer, the device layer, contains objects that expose the data provided directly by device sensors. Devices must implement one one more abstract device interfaces (see below). For example, the OceanServer USB Compass provides both compass and accelerometer functionality. To add

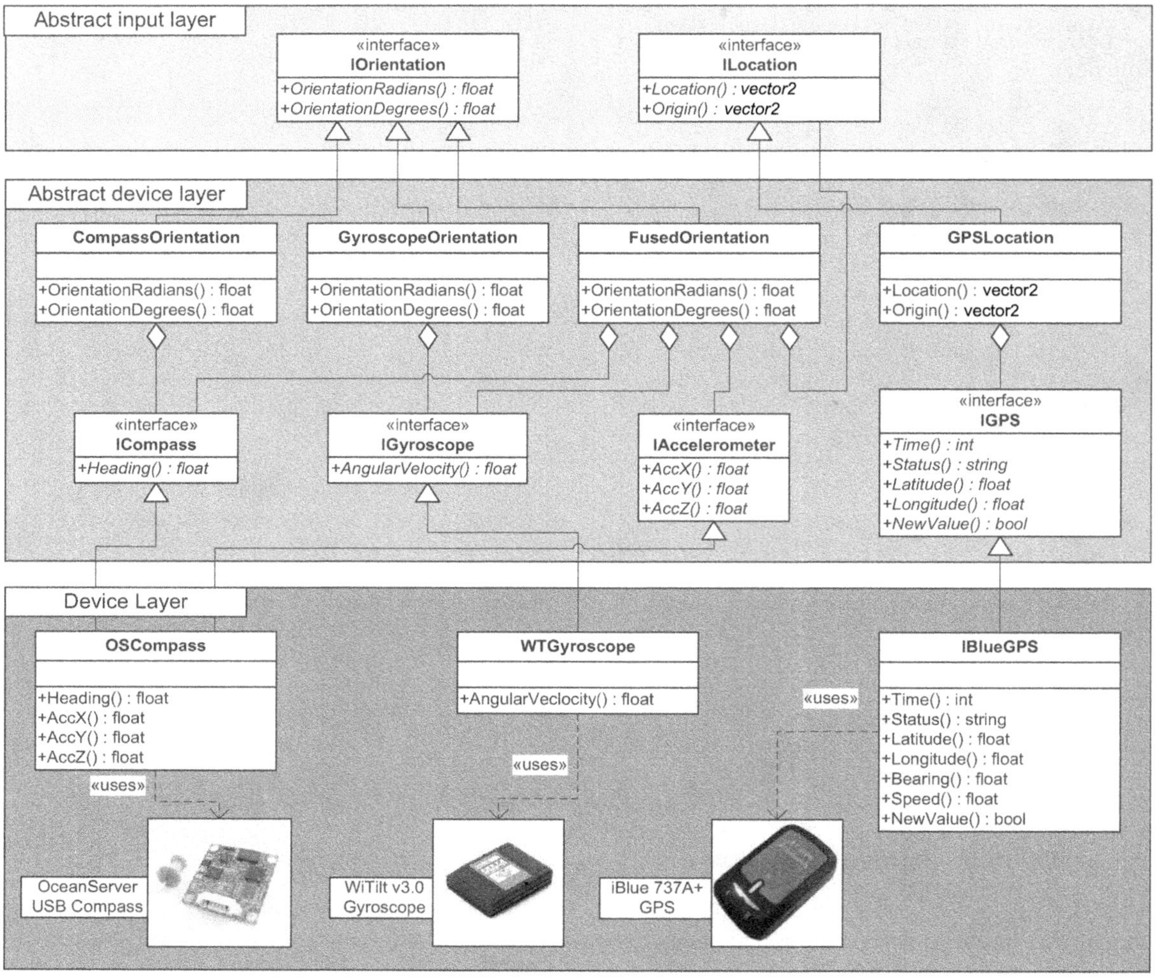

Figure 3. The TREC 3-layered architecture.

a new device to the framework, a developer needs to create a device-layer class for the device.

The abstract device layer groups standard types of sensor devices, and also provides virtual sensors by fusing the data from multiple concrete devices. For example, the *CompassOrientation* class provides orientation data from compass-like devices, such as OSCompass, while the *GyroscopeOrientation* class provides orientation data from gyroscope-like devices. Meanwhile, *FusedOrientation* provides orientation information by fusing data from a number of devices.

Finally, the abstract input layer provides interfaces for specific input data types. In the current version of the framework, two types of input are defined: *IOrientation* provides head orientation data and *ILocation* provides position information. To access input, an application queries the TREC device manager for one of these types of input, and receives an object in return implementing the appropriate abstract input type. In this way, the TREC framework shields applications from the details of individual devices or fusion algorithms, and simplifies the work of the developer by providing a simple and uniform way to access input information.

APPLYING TREC

We now show, by example, how TREC helps both application programmers creating a mobile AR system, and systems programmers adding new functionality to TREC itself.

The Application Programmer's Perspective

To illustrate how TREC helps in developing mobile AR applications, we examine the implementation of the Noisy Planet tourist application. Users of the application carry a mobile device containing a GPS, and wear a gyroscope and compass for head tracking. These sensors are hidden behind TREC's *IOrientation* and *ILocation* abstract input types.

To access the abstracted sensor data, the Noisy Planet code requests an appropriate data source from TREC's Device Manager. E.g., when an orientation data source is requested, the Device Manager provides an object that adheres to the *IOrientation* interface, with data coming from either the *OS-*

Compass or *WTGyroscope* device. The application cannot tell which device is supplying this data, and does not need to know since the incoming data is in a standardized format. This allows TREC to provide the best available sensor, and allows new devices to be added to TREC without impacting application code. If the programmer for some reason preferred a compass, he/she could choose to access the *CompassOrientation* object in the abstract device layer to guarantee the use of a compass, or even directly access the *OSCompass* in the device layer to choose that specific device.

In addition to automatically choosing from available sensors, TREC can automatically use sensor fusion algorithms when sufficient sensors are available. Noisy Planet could actually receive a *FusedOrientation* object (from the abstract device layer) after the earlier request for an orientation object. This happens without any changes or configuration on the application side. TREC decides which device or combination of devices to use based on an internal rating mechanism, which is currently a hard-coded list of the known devices.

For comparison, we implemented a version of Noisy Planet without access to TREC. This implementation required approximately 250-350 lines of code per sensor (GPS, compass, gyroscope) to handle serial input from these devices, in addition to another 80 lines to manage these sensors and perform the sensor fusion. The version using TREC requires just two method calls: one to get the current orientation, and another for the current location.

The Toolkit Developer's Perspective

TREC is an open framework, making it straightforward to add support for new devices. We now discuss our experience in adding a new hardware and a new virtual device to TREC.

Adding a New Hardware Device

The custom code that connects to and processes data from a sensor is contained within a class at the device layer. Based on the type of sensor, accessor methods need to be created that will adhere to the proper interface at the abstract device layer (e.g., the *IBlueGPS* in figure 3 must implement the *IGPS* interface in order to automatically work with TREC applications).

Adding a Simple Sensor Fusion Algorithm

TREC's layered architecture allows easy integration of sensor fusion algorithms into applications, and allows the fusion code itself to be shielded from the details of the underlying devices. Sensor fusion algorithms are written as abstract device modules that adhere to a standard interface. Therefore, any program taking advantage of TREC's abstract input modules (*IOrientation* and *ILocation*) can automatically use the new algorithm.

For example, to implement the *FusedOrientation* class of figure 3, a new abstract device class is created in the abstract device layer. This class implements the *IOrientation* interface, and therefore can be used whenever orientation information is requested by the application. Inside *FusedOrientation*, a gyroscope, compass and accelerometer are used (each of which are abstract devices), and some kind of location service is used (an abstract input.) Specifically, the gyroscope is used to determine orientation; the compass is used to calibrate the gyroscope from time to time, but not when the compass is moving (as determined via the accelerometer or from changes in location).

This example shows how the fusion algorithm leverages TREC's layered architecture. When necessary, the fusion algorithm knows the kind of device that it is using (gyroscope, compass, etc.), but does not need to know exactly which device is in use. Furthermore, when it is not necessary to know the kind of device (i.e., for the location service), the appropriate abstract input can be used.

DISCUSSION

We have shown how TREC helps developers by providing a single standardized view of sensor data, making sensor selection and sensor fusion automatic, and letting developers easily extend the framework to support new devices or custom fusion algorithms. We now discuss broader questions related to TREC's design.

Platform Standardization: Smartphone platforms are making sensors suitable for mobile AR applications broadly available. Exciting future work would involve customizing TREC around the sensor packages in common phones. The easy extensibility of TREC is important, as the sensors change between generations of phones, requiring updates to the framework. One limitation to this approach is that current phones do not provide sensors suitable for head-tracking.

Computer vision for tracking: Computer vision is widely used for pose detection in AR applications (e.g., using ARToolkit [7]), but we have not discussed its use in TREC. Vision is less immediately useful in mobile applications, due to the difficulty of placing fiduciary markers in the outside environment. However, there is no inherent reason why vision could not be included as a sensor type within the framework. This would integrate into the TREC hierarchy just as any other sensor does, though requiring a new abstract device interface to be defined for vision systems.

Extending to other kinds of AR: The framework as presented is heavily influenced by the ambient audio Noisy Planet application. In Noisy Planet, head tracking is important to overlay an audio soundscape onto the real world, and this head tracking need only be in a 2D plane. TREC can easily be extended to other forms of AR, however, simply by adding new device types.

For example, one common form of mobile AR involves tracking the position and orientation of a handheld device (e.g., a Smartphone), so that its display can provide visual overlays onto the real world. Here, positioning information is detected for the device, not the head, using the sensors in the device. TREC's *IOrientation* interface would need to be extended to provide 3D positions. This change would require additional programming, but does not represent a fundamental change to TREC's design.

Sensor management: Future work with TREC includes improving the sophistication of its sensor management capabilities. Currently, TREC's Device Manager determines which among the available set of sensors to use by traversing a ranked list of known devices. An improved device manager would automatically determine the best set of a sensors to use, and would dynamically reconfigure the sensor set (e.g., in response to failure of one of the sensors.) This issue of sensor management has been more thoroughly covered in the Ubitrack system [9] and in the hybrid tracking AR system of Hallaway et al. [5].

Sensor fusion: The layered architecture of TREC permits AR applications to use sensor fusion automatically. An example was shown in the last section of how a simple sensor fusion algorithm could be implemented as an abstract device. More investigation is required to assess the difficulty of implementing more general fusion algorithms, than the one presented in the example. The algorithm used there does not depend on specific devices and will work with any sensors of the same type. A Kalman filter, however, may require unique knowledge about each sensor to create a good model of the system. In future work, we hope to investigate whether TREC can support these advanced algorithms without restricting their use to predetermined hardware.

CONCLUSION

In this paper we have presented TREC, a new framework for handling sensor input in mobile augmented reality applications. TREC has been designed to provide high-level abstraction of the sensor data, automatic configuration, and ease of extension and manual configuration when desired. While there are many other frameworks addressing these issues comprehensively, none provide all of these features together in a cohesive package.

The key to TREC's success is its three-layer architecture. An abstract input layer provides high-level input types that completely abstract the underlying hardware. An abstract device layer collects classes of sensors (e.g., compass, accelerometer), as well as virtual devices implementing sensor fusion. Finally, a device layer provides interfaces to concrete devices. This architecture allows the abstraction of different hardware sensors into a uniform representation of location and orientation, and simplifies the automatic use of available sensors at runtime (including the automatic fusion of multiple devices). This hierarchy also makes the process of adding new devices straightforward, while providing compatibility with any applications already using TREC.

The next steps for the TREC framework include adding broader support for hardware sensors, investigating the implementation of complex sensor fusion algorithms using the abstract devices in TREC, and implementing a robust sensor-management algorithm to allow better dynamic configuration of the system.

ACKNOWLEDGEMENTS

This work was funded by NSERC Strategic Project #365040-08 and by the GRAND Network of Centres of Excellence. We would like to thank Claire Joly for her feedback on using TREC, and Jonathan Segel for his contributions to the design of Noisy Planet.

REFERENCES

1. Intridea Car Finder. http://carfinderapp.com/.
2. Layar Augmented Reality Browser. http://www.layar.com/.
3. B. Dasarathy. Sensor fusion potential exploitation-innovative architectures and illustrative applications. *Proceedings of the IEEE*, 85(1):24 –38, 1997.
4. E. Foxlin. Inertial head-tracker sensor fusion by a complementary separate-bias Kalman filter. In *IEEE VRAIS*, pages 185–194, 267, 1996.
5. D. Hallaway, S. Feiner, and T. Höllerer. Bridging the gaps: Hybrid tracking for adaptive mobile augmented reality. *Applied Artificial Intelligence*, 25:477–500, 2004.
6. J. Hightower and G. Borriello. Location systems for ubiquitous computing. *Computer*, 34(8):57–66, 2001.
7. H. Kato, M. Billinghurst, I. Poupyrev, K. Imamoto, and K. Tachibana. Virtual object manipulation on a table-top AR environment. In *ISAR*, pages 111–119, 2000.
8. P. Lang, A. Kusej, A. Pinz, and G. Brasseur. Inertial tracking for mobile augmented reality. In *IMTC*, volume 2, pages 1583–1587, 2002.
9. D. Pustka, M. Huber, C. Waechter, F. Echtler, P. Keitler, J. Newman, D. Schmalstieg, and G. Klinker. Ubitrack: Automatic configuration of pervasive sensor networks for augmented reality. *IEEE Pervasive Computing*, preprint, June 2010.
10. G. Reitmayr and D. Schmalstieg. Opentracker: A flexible software design for three-dimensional interaction. *Virtual Reality*, 9:79–92, 2005.
11. M. Serrano, L. Nigay, J.-Y. L. Lawson, A. Ramsay, R. Murray-Smith, and S. Denef. The OpenInterface framework: a tool for multimodal interaction. In *CHI extended abstracts on human factors in computing systems*, pages 3501–3506, 2008.
12. R. M. Taylor, II, T. C. Hudson, A. Seeger, H. Weber, J. Juliano, and A. T. Helser. VRPN: a device-independent, network-transparent VR peripheral system. In *VRST*, pages 55–61, 2001.
13. G. Welch and G. Bishop. An introduction to the Kalman filter. Technical Report TR 95-041, Department of Computer Science, University of North Carolina at Chapel Hill, 1995.
14. M. G. Wing. Consumer-grade global positioning system (GPS) accuracy and reliability. *Journal of Forestry*, 103:169–173, 2005.

Low-Fidelity Prototyping of Gesture-based Applications

Ali Hosseini-Khayat **Teddy Seyed** **Chris Burns** **Frank Maurer**

Computer Science Department
University of Calgary
Calgary, AB Canada
{hosseisa, aseyed, ccburns, fmauer}@ucalgary.ca

ABSTRACT
Touch-based devices are becoming increasingly common in the consumer electronics space. Support for prototyping touch-based interfaces is currently limited. In this paper, we present a tool we developed in order to bridge the gap between user interface prototyping and touch-based interfaces.

Author Keywords
User interface, Prototyping, Touch, Tabletops

ACM Classification Keywords
D.0 Software: General

General Terms
Design, Human Factors

INTRODUCTION
Prototyping serves an important role in detecting and addressing usability issues in a user interface. Usability testing of prototypes detects usability issues that can be fixed. This leads to both improved and more intuitive interfaces for the user.

Low fidelity prototyping is a fast and cost effective approach that fits well with short iterations typically found in agile software development processes. Low-fidelity prototypes are typically sketches with pen and paper but also include digital sketches. Tools such as Microsoft's SketchFlow, allow for teams and developers to rapidly create a digital low-fidelity prototype for a design and test it with a user and gather feedback. These tools address prototyping of applications that utilize the traditional input paradigm of the keyboard and mouse.

Recently however, multi-touch and surface computing environments have become increasingly common in several areas such as education, retail and medicine. The affordances these technologies provide is a critical reason for their success, as collaboration and data visualization can be better facilitated on a large surface or multi-touch display. Additionally, the gestures that multi-touch can provide opportunities for developers and designers to create intuitive and innovative interfaces.

Undoubtedly, these touch and gesture based technologies mark a shift in the input paradigm and consequently, creating tools that support the design of applications utilizing them is vital. Currently, toolsets for digital low fidelity prototyping are limited to the keyboard and mouse paradigm, with limited or no support for multi-touch or gesture-based applications.

In this paper, we present our work on a low-fidelity prototyping tool that addresses the aforementioned limitations and is particularly targeted towards gesture-based interactions.

RELATED WORK
Khandkar has done work in the area of gesture definitions and processing for touch-based interactions. His framework, Gesture Toolkit, provides a complete gesture recognition system along with a domain specific language (DSL) for defining gestures [1] [2] [3]. This system has several touch input providers supporting a large number of platforms including the SMART Table, Windows Touch devices and even the Nintendo Wii. Gesture Toolkit provides a strong basis for cross-platform touch detection and gesture recognition [4].

Derboven et al. performed a study comparing the use of low-fidelity versus high-fidelity prototyping for designing multi-user, multi-touch interfaces [5]. They report that low-fi prototypes can be a valuable tool for designing user interactions for multi-touch tabletops. Rick et al. performed a study of low-fi prototyping of tabletop applications for children and concluded that low-fi prototyping is a useful approach, although they recommend adapting desktop applications to digital surfaces [6]. We believe this approach results in less effective user interfaces for tabletops.

DTFlash [7], is an early attempt to develop a rapid prototyping tool for multitouch devices. Built for use with Multimedia Flash applications, the touch system is delivered using the DiamondTouch SDK. The system allows developers to rapidly create prototype applications using a graphics-oriented Flash authoring tool. This results in hi-fi prototype applications rather than low-fi

EICS'11, June 13–16, 2011, Pisa, Italy.

prototypes. Example applications created with the tool can be interacted with online via Flash-enabled browsers. A drawback to this system is its reliance on the DiamondTouch SDK.

Low-Fidelity Testing Tool Support

Tool support for interaction designers is somewhat limited. Some tools, such as Microsoft Expression Blend – SketchFlow [**8**], are explicitly developed for that purpose. Other tools, such as Microsoft Visio [**9**] and PowerPoint [**10**], are simply adapted for interaction design work and have a much more general function.

Most prototyping is done using pens and paper, which has the advantage of being low cost and requires no training to use. A prototype can be generated quickly and changed easily, simply erase part of the sketch and redraw it as desired. Since paper prototypes have no emotional attachment, as they are cheap and easy to create, they can be modified extensively even during a test session. The physical nature of paper sketches becomes a disadvantage, however, since they cannot be shared easily with users in distributed teams. Users also sometimes have difficulty viewing the paper sketches as the future application they are supposed to represent.

SketchFlow, a tool developed by Microsoft, allows users to create low-fi and medium-fi prototypes. It provides a suite of UI elements that have the appearance of being hand drawn. Designers can use button-clicks, dragging and dropping and other interactions to transition between states in a prototype, creating a flow that simulates a real application. As the prototype is developed the fidelity level can be increased and eventually even moved into production development. This particular emphasis on reuse of components is unique to SketchFlow. Using the SketchFlow player users can execute the prototype at a remote location.

WOzPro [**11**] captures freehand drawings rather than using defined widgets. It also supports templating, pages can be based off a single master page and updates to the master page will propagate out to all the template pages. It does not, however, provide any interaction support but rather displays the prototypes through a simple slideshow. Since it does not provide any interaction, its utility as a usability evaluation tool is limited.

Another set of design tools use widgets, dragged and dropped into a canvas, as a mechanism for prototype creation. SILK [**12**] [**13**], DENIM [**14**], Serena Prototype Composer [**15**], Visio [**9**] and Balsamiq Mockups [**16**] are all among this set. While these products support interaction by test users, they limit the designer to an existing set of widgets. Serena Prototype Composer provides a more hi-fi prototyping feature while there rest use widgets explicitly designed to appear hand drawn or rough.

Another tool, often used for prototyping interfaces, is Microsoft PowerPoint. Prototypes can be easily created as a package of slides and widely distributed because of PowerPoint's wide install base. However, designing interactive prototypes using PowerPoint can be a time consuming process given the intended use of the application.

Tools for prototyping mobile device interfaces have emerged recently, such as Briefs [**17**] which runs live on the iPhone and iPhone Mockup [**18**] which runs through a browser. These can execute functionality and accept interaction. Briefs allows users to defined prototypes using images and then host them for others to view via a "briefcast". iPhone Mockup relies on a web hosted solution rather than a native application. Mockups are created using a web application from a series of defined UI widgets and then distributed and hosted via the application. Both applications, however, are specifically targeted at developing iPhone applications and do not facilitate designing a more general prototype.

To the best of our knowledge, tool support for low-fidelity of prototyping touch-based user interfaces is non-existent at the time of writing.

ACTIVESTORY TOUCH

Touch-based devices and interactions are gaining increasing momentum in the consumer space, with touchscreen smartphones, tablets, and surfaces. However, prototyping and tool support for prototyping touch-based interfaces have not evolved at the same pace. In fact, existing tools lack support for touch-based interactions entirely. Given the importance of usability, particularly in the context of touch-based applications, we attempted to address this issue.

Motivation

Previously, ActiveStory Enhanced was developed to provide tool support for low-fidelity prototyping and usability testing [**19**]. The tool was built with standard desktop applications with mouse-based interactions in mind. Designers sketch pages of a prototype such that each page represents a state of the user interface. Once the various pages of the prototype are sketched, the designer adds interaction to the pages by clicking and dragging over areas of the page that should be hotspots. Upon creation of a hotspot, the designer specifies which page of the prototype the hotspot should navigate to when clicked by test users. After the prototype has been designed, it can be deployed to a web server where test users can interact with and attempt to complete tasks specified by the designer. Usability data, such as mouse movements, time spent on pages and comments, are automatically collected by the web testing tool as users interact with the prototype. Designers can then analyze the collected usability data through the web-based reports component.

The question of whether ActiveStory Enhanced would suffice for touch-based user interfaces gave rise to a pilot study that was conducted with two participants, with the main goal of evaluating the applicability of the tool to prototyping touch-based applications. One participant was a user experience (UX) professional and the other was a graduate student. The graduate student used the tool as part of an actual project and designed a prototype for the user interface of a tabletop media manager and player. An interview was conducted and feedback was elicited. The UX professional was asked to create a UI for a similar application and think aloud while doing so. This participant was asked to use the tool and design the prototype on a tabletop (a SMART table), in order to understand whether it makes sense to design a prototype for a tabletop application on a tabletop. This was a side-goal in addition to the main goal of the study. The researchers observed the participants' interaction with the tool and his attempt at creating a prototype for the application. This was followed-up by an interview regarding his experience prototyping a surface application with the tool.

Both participants indicated that they found it difficult to represent interactions such as dragging and dropping, scaling (pinch-to-zoom) and rotations. This was because hotspots always acted like buttons in the testing environment, i.e. once they were touched they would immediately navigate to the target page, regardless of the gesture used. The UX professional pointed out that prototyping on the tabletop with ActiveStory Enhanced was difficult at best. Some of the difficulties arose from the tablet-oriented nature of the tool, whereas other difficulties were caused by the hardware and the tabletop form factor. Difficulties with the tool included lack of support for specifying gestures other than a tap, the inability to run prototypes within the design environment (i.e. preview the prototype at design time) and the need to reach across the table to access the menus and palettes. Issues with the tabletop included lack of precision, washed-out colors and unresponsive touch input.

In an effort to bridge this gap, ActiveStory Enhanced [**19**] was extended to provide support for adding touch-based interaction and allowing test users to interact with the prototype on a touch device. The new tool, ActiveStory Touch, addresses some of the issues with prototyping touch-based interfaces that were discovered in ActiveStory Enhanced, mainly the lack of support for defining different gestures for prototype elements[1].

Usage Scenario

ActiveStory Touch allows UI designers to sketch prototypes using the designer portion of the tool and subsequently distributes them to test users for evaluation over the web. Prototypes can be sketched on a tablet, tabletop or desktop computer. The designer tool is shown in Figure 1 and the process workflow for ActiveStory Touch is presented in (Figure 5).

[1] Available at activestoryenhanced.codeplex.com

Once the various pages of the low-fidelity prototype have been sketched, the designer can specify which page to navigate to for a given gesture and a given part of a prototype page (Figure 2, Figure 3). For example, a designer can specify that page 2 should be navigated to when a UI element is tapped and page 3 should be navigated to when a user presses-and-holds.

Once the designer has completed sketching the prototype, it can be published in the form of a Silverlight web application, allowing test users to access it remotely (Figure 4). Test users can use a touch-based device to interact with the prototype as if it were an actual touch-based user interface for an application. In other words, a user with a touch device capable of running Silverlight can navigate to a web server where a prototype is hosted, view the prototype and perform gestures on it in the same way they would for a touch-enabled application on a touch-based device. Various usability data such as mouse movements, clicks and time spent on pages is automatically collected, however the usability data is not the focus of this paper. This rapid deployment and feedback loop allows designers to iterate through various designs quickly and determine how they would be used and whether they are usable. The tests with potential end-users allow identifying any usability flaws that may exist in the design.

Design

ActiveStory Touch prototypes consist of multiple pages. Pages consist of ink strokes, imported images and prototype elements. Each page corresponds to a page of a prototype as it would have been sketched on paper, i.e. a given state of the user interface.

Prototype elements are currently limited to hotspots, i.e. a given area that is specified by the designer and reacts to clicks or touch interaction. Elements may be extended in the future to include support for mixed-fidelity prototyping with text boxes, combo boxes and other common widgets. Each element is associated with a set of gestures and target behaviors in the form of a dictionary. In other words, each element can react to one or more gestures and perform a different behavior for each, for example navigating to different pages based on the type of gesture, where Navigation is the behavior. While the possible behaviors are currently limited to navigating to different pages in the prototype, future work includes adding support for animations and other behaviors on the same page of the prototype.

ActiveStory Touch prototype projects are serialized in XML to allow easy reuse of the data. The same project file is then used as input for the Silverlight-based testing tool, allowing it to render a given page of the prototype. Once the page is rendered, the prototype elements are created and their corresponding gesture events are registered with Gesture Toolkit. Behaviors are implemented by listening to the gesture

Figure 1. Designing a prototype using the ActiveStory Touch Designer Tool

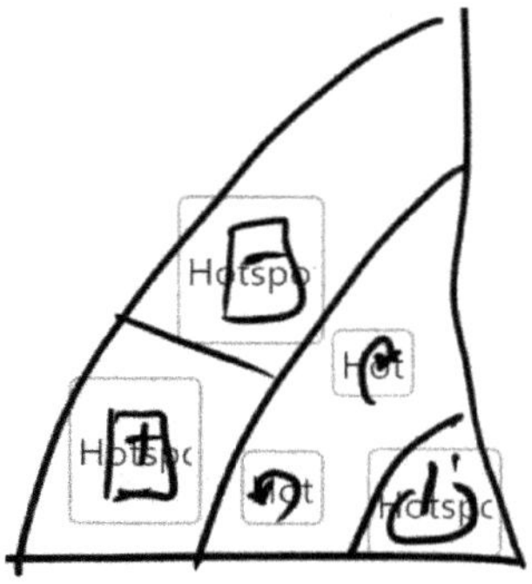

Figure 2. Adding hotspots to the sketch.

Figure 3. Specifying a gesture and behavior for hotspots.

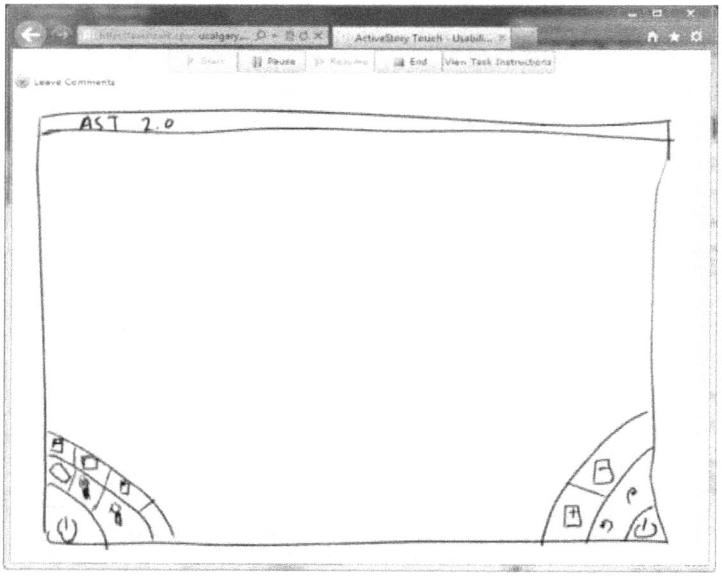

Figure 4. ActiveStory Touch Usability Testing tool, allows multi-touch input and gesture recognition.

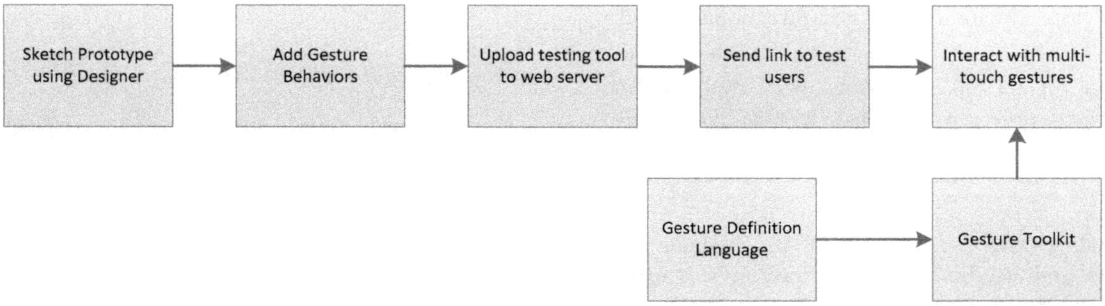

Figure 5. ActiveStory Touch prototype design and evaluation workflow.

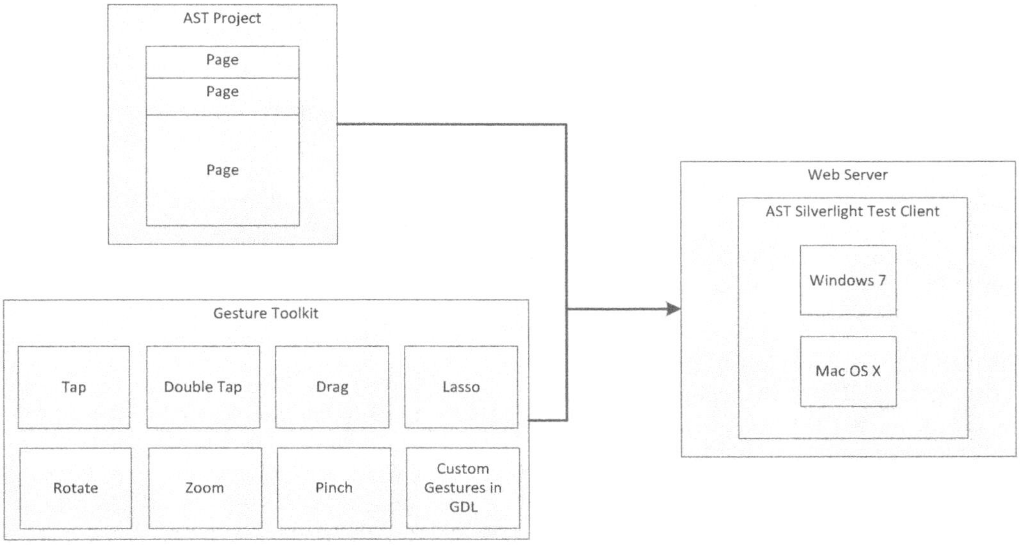

Figure 6. ActiveStory Touch Architecture

events and performing a common method, BehaviorInvoked. BehaviorInvoked is supplied with any parameters that are specific to the behavior, for example the target page for a Navigate behavior. This allows for a generic prototype player that can render any prototype created in the designer by simply changing the input XML project file.

System Implementation

ActiveStory Touch was developed in C# using the Microsoft Windows Presentation Foundation (WPF) for the desktop designer portion of the tool and Microsoft Silverlight for the web-based testing portion. Silverlight provides support for touch-based interactions through a web-browser across touch-enabled versions of Windows and Mac OS. In addition, Silverlight applications can be run out-of-browser, as if they are desktop applications. As a result, the usability testing component of ActiveStory Touch can be executed as if they were native multi-touch applications. Running a prototype in full screen mode, out-of-browser allows the designer to perform testing on a tabletop or wall-mounted surface. Gesture Toolkit [4] was used for gesture detection and handling in the testing tool. Using Gesture Toolkit, ActiveStory Touch provides support for detecting common gestures such as dragging, swiping, pinching, tapping, double-tapping and lassoing as well as being easily extensible through Gesture Toolkit to provide support for custom-defined gestures. For example, a designer could define a counter-clockwise circle gesture in Gesture Toolkit and subsequently specify, within ActiveStory Touch, that when a user performs that gesture the prototype player should show a state in which the "undo" action was performed. ActiveStory Touch's use of Gesture Toolkit also provides the advantage of being cross-compatible between WPF and Silverlight, allowing for future extension of ActiveStory Touch to allow for a more flexible environment for tablet and tabletop design, perhaps providing a tabletop-based user interface for designers. An overview of the architecture is presented in Figure 6.

FUTURE WORK

Further work on ActiveStory Touch involves adding support for the collection of real-time usability data, further enhancing the development process of an application with automated feedback from non-collocated users.

ActiveStory Touch will also be further extended to provide better support for collaborative prototyping on a digital tabletop, including a non-directional touch-conducive UI.

The support of cross- platforms and multi-surface interactions and prototypes is also an area we plan to extend ActiveStory Touch, particularly to support development in areas where multi-surface environments are necessary.

Finally, studies will be conducted to evaluate the effectiveness and usefulness of the tool in supporting prototyping of touch-based interfaces.

REFERENCES

1 Khandkar, Shahedul Huq. *A Domain-Specific Language for Multi-Touch Gestures*. University of Calgary, Department of Computer Science, Calgary, December 2010.

2 Khandkar, Shahedul Huq and Maurer, Frank. A Domain Specific Language to Define Gestures for Multi-Touch Applications. (Reno/Tahoe, Nevada 2010), The 10th SPLASH Workshop on Domain-Specific Modeling.

3 Khandkar, Shahedul Huq and Maurer, Frank. A Language to Define Multi-Touch Interactions. (Saarbrucken, Germany 2010), The ACM International Conference on Interactive Tabletops and Surfaces.

4 Khandkar, Shahedul Huq, Sohan, SM, Sillito, Jonathon, and Maurer, Frank. Tool Support for Testing Complex Multi-Touch Gestures. (Saarbrücken, Germany 2010), The ACM International Conference on Interactive Tabletops and Surfaces.

5 Derboven, Jan, Roeck, Dries De, Verstraete, Mathijs, Geerts, David, Schneider-Barnes, Jan, and Luyten, Kris. Comparing user interaction with low and high fidelity prototypes of tabletop surfaces. In *Proceedings of the 6th Nordic Conference on Human-Computer Interaction: Extending Boundaries (NordiCHI '10)* (New York, NY 2010).

6 Rick, Jochen, Francois, Phyllis, Fields, Bob, Fleck, Rowanne, Yuill, Nicola, and Carr, Amanda. Lo-fi prototyping to design interactive-tabletop applications for children. In *Proceedings of the 9th International Conference on Interaction Design and Children (IDC '10)* (New York, NY 2010), ACM.

7 Esenther, A. and Ryall, K. Fluid DTMouse: Better Mouse Support for Touch-Based Interactions. *Advanced Visual Interfaces (AVI)* (May 2006).

8 *Microsoft Expression Blend - SketchFlow - Product Overview*. http://www.microsoft.com/expression/products/SketchFlow_Overview.aspx.

9 *Microsoft Visio - Product Overview*. http://office.microsoft.com/en-us/visio/default.aspx.

10 *Microsoft PowerPoint - Product Overview*. http://office.microsoft.com/en-us/powerpoint/default.aspx.

11 *WoZ Pro Project Site*. http://www.eecs.wsu.edu/~veupl/soft/woz/.

12 Landay, James A. and Myers, Brad A. Sketching Storyboards to Illustrate Interface Behaviors. In *CHI '96 Conference Companion: Human Factors in Computing Systems, ACM* (New York, NY 1996), 193-194.

13 Landay, J.A. and Myers, B.A. Interactive Sketching for the Early Stages of User Interface Design. In *CHI, ACM Press* (Denver 1995), 43-50.

14 Lin, James, Newman, Mark W., Hong, Jason I., and Landay, James A. DENIM: An Informal Tool for Early Stage Web Site Design. In *Video poster in Extended Abstracts of Human Factors in Computing Systems: CHI 2001* (Seattle, WA March 31-April 5, 20), 205-206.

15 Site, Serena Protoype Composer Product. http://www.serena.com/products/prototype-composer/index.html.

16 *Balsamiq Mockups Product Site*. http://www.balsamiq.com/products/mockups.

17 *Breifs - A Cocoa Touch Framework for Live Wireframes*. http://giveabrief.com/.

18 *iPhone Mockup - Site*. http://iphonemockup.lkmc.ch/.

19 Hosseini-Khayat, Ali. *Distributed Wizard of Oz Usability Testing for Agile Teams*. University of Calgary, Calgary, 2010.

20 *ActiveStory Enhanced - CodePlex Project Site*. http://activestoryenhanced.codeplex.com/.

Specifying Concurrent Behavior to Evaluate Ubiquitous Computing Environments

René Zilz
University of Rostock
18059 Rostock, Germany
rene.zilz@uni-rostock.de

ABSTRACT
Usability evaluation in ubiquitous computing environments is a rapidly developing research area in human computer interaction because most of the traditional evaluation methods are difficult to apply for this purpose. The paper discusses the idea of using virtual environments to conduct evaluation. Until now, we can conduct real time scenarios in a 2D based virtual environment called ViSE. But there are a number of disadvantages when using real time scenario evaluation. For instance, we cannot specify concurrent user behavior in an acceptable way. For the specification of such a behavior a system is needed where the start and end times of every user action can be specified in the scenario definition. We introduce an approach that can improve existing approaches by associating time lines for users, devices and items belonging to the ubiquitous computing environment. As a result, the expert is able to evaluate concurrent interacting test cases which are crucial for collaborative systems.

Author Keywords
Usability Evaluation, Ubiquitous Computing

ACM Classification Keywords
H5.m. Information interfaces and presentation (e.g., HCI): Miscellaneous.

ACM General Terms
Design, Theory

INTRODUCTION
Ubiquitous computing environments are complex systems that are composed of different devices and each device might support a variety of different input modalities (e.g., voice, touch and keyboard/mouse input). Users can move freely in such an environment while interacting with devices, other users or further physical entities. Even though a huge number of usability evaluation methods for desktop applications have been developed, most of these traditional evaluation methods are difficult to apply in ubiquitous computing environments. That is because the expert encounters several problems while evaluating the usability of such a system. For instance, users in traditional desktop applications are interacting explicitly, users in smart environments can also interact implicitly (e.g., user enters the room and light turns on). Further problems that occur are an expensive development of prototypes and resource intensive user tests. Thus, experts have to rely on either low-fidelity techniques (such as paper prototypes and mental walkthroughs) or simply wait for a near full scale deployment [5]. Thus, an increasing number of evaluation environments exists that can be used to evaluate scenarios in a virtual ubiquitous computing environments. Using those evaluation environments, an expert is able to evaluate the system at early stages of development. However, it is difficult to specify concurrent behavior in such evaluation environments.

RELATED WORK
UbiWise [3], TATUS [1], USEd (User Scenario Editor) [2] and ViSE (Virtual Smart Environment) [7] are examples for evaluation environments as introduced in the introduction. These systems focus on a sophisticated visualization and animation of the ubiquitous computing environment and their components in terms of a virtual environment. In general, such applications can be exploited for evaluation in ubiquitous computing environments but because USEd and ViSE are especially developed for evaluation we focus on them in the following.

USEd [2] is a 3D-based scenario editor that allows an expert to record and validate user scenarios in ubiquitous computing environments. USEd provides two modes for creating scenarios: real-time data transformation and data editing. In the first mode, an expert can create scenarios based on a textual description or video data of scenarios. Thereby, users have to be moved manually by the expert according to the textual description or video data. In the data editing mode, the expert is able to add, remove, replace or modify the concrete movement paths of users involved in the scenario.

ViSE [7] can be used for expert evaluation in context of smart environments, such as the SmartLab [6] of the University of Rostock. The SmartLab is a smart environment that is composed of a dynamic, ad-hoc ensemble of heterogeneous devices.

ViSE conducts a model-based usability evaluation methodology and provides a 2D visualization of the SmartLab where the expert can specify scenarios in real time. Therefore performable user tasks are specified in terms of concur task trees (CTT). CTT is a graphical notation to model user activities and distinguishes between different kinds of tasks (e.g., abstract, user, interaction and application). Subsequently, tasks are hierarchically decomposed and linked with each other using temporal operators (e.g., enabling, concurrent etc.) in order to specify the relationships between them. Devices are specified in terms of state charts and the environment is specified in terms of a location model. While the expert performs a scenario, the models are evaluated via an interactive walk-through. As a result, the expert is able to analyze and interpret the developed models in terms of possible usability problems. Context awareness can be defined with the CTML (Collaborative Task Modelling Language) [6].

Figure 1 depicts the visualization of the SmartLab including different entities, such as users, devices (e.g., laptops, PDAs or smart phones) and certain other items (e.g., pens or sponges). ViSE allows the expert to associate devices or items with users in order to define interactions between those entities and to change the positions of them. In addition, ViSE is able to generate sensor data based on scenarios referring to users' positions and interaction between users and devices.

Furthermore, scenarios can be created and replayed on base of those sensor data or sensor data acquired in a real environment.

USABILITY EVALUATION

A variety of traditional evaluation methods are conducted empirically. In these evaluation methods a group of persons is observed while using an application that should be evaluated. As already described in the introduction, such an observation is hard to realize in ubiquitous computing environments, because multiple users have to be observed concurrently. Additionally, rough mistakes that possibly disturb users can be eliminated by the expert. Thus, it is necessary to conduct an expert evaluation in front of the user evaluation. Because in the most cases multiple users act concurrently in ubiquitous computing environments the expert needs to specify concurrent behavior.

Specifying Concurrent Behavior

In [2], two basic approaches for specifying collaborative scenarios and thus concurrent behavior are presented: one-by-one scenario recording and multiple person recording. The specification of concurrent behavior in ViSE is quite similar. In the following, both approaches are described briefly.

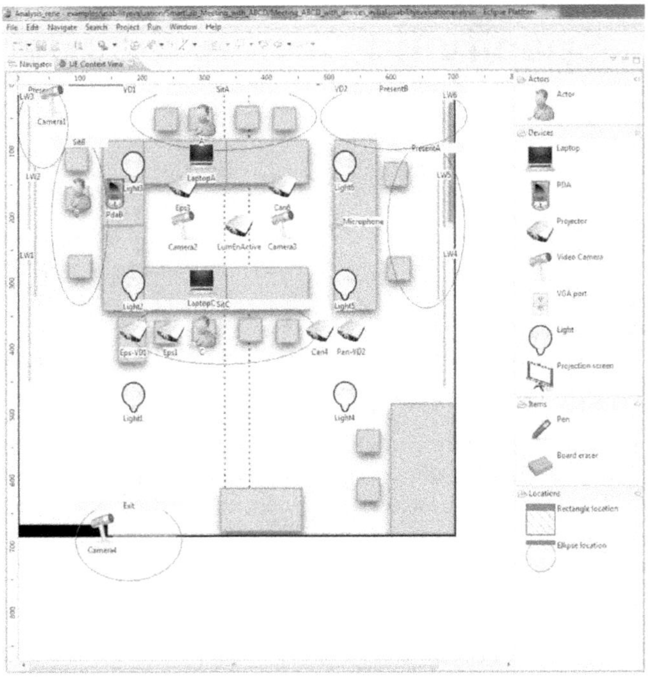

Figure 1. Virtual Smart Environment (ViSE)

One-by-one scenario recording – USEd as well as ViSE provide this scenario recording technique. One user or the users's behavior is recorded while other users that were already recorded are replayed to help with the synchronization of multiple users. However, the expert should know the kind and the timing of actions performed by the users that were recorded. If the synchronization fails the expert can either play backward to correct it or create a completely new recording. In addition to one-by-one scenario recording, USEd supports another approach called multiple person recording to specify concurrent behavior.

Multiple person recording – In this technique all users are recorded simultaneously. After that, the expert is using the edit mode and can shift the actions to appear concurrently.

Since one-by-one scenario recording as well as multiple person recording specify concurrent behavior only after scenario definition, they are very time-consuming. Additionally, a correct synchronization is heavy viable in case of multiple users. Especially in collaborative systems such as ubiquitous computing environments there are often numerous users that interact concurrently. Furthermore, many entities, such as users, devices or items, are involved in one scenario and therefore the number of feasible scenarios can be very high. That is why we think that the current approaches are not suitable to define concurrent behavior in ubiquitous systems.

Approach Requirements

With regards to the last section, we make the following demands to specify concurrent behaviors in one scenario.

- The expert should be able to change the scenario at any time.
- The expert should be able to define start and end time of every action at any time.
- Scenarios can be played backward and forward.
- Interactions should be defined as easy and realistic as possible.
- It should be possible to shift interactions in time.

Time Line Approach

Now we are presenting our approach to specify concurrent behavior in virtual ubiquitous computing environments. For this purpose, each entity is associated with a time line. Scenarios are recorded as following: If the expert conducts an action with entities, he can define start and end time. Thereby, it is possible to specify concurrent behavior during the scenario recording. Existing actions could be modified, shifted or removed as well. There are further advantages by combining those time lines with techniques such as key framing and movement paths. For instance, we can define and modify changes in person's position. If the expert tends to specify that a user needs ten seconds to move from one position to another, he only needs to create two key frames encoding the corresponding positions. As a result, the duration in time to transform a scenario is decreased substantially. The approach presented above is also applied in motion graphics and multimedia software such as Adobe Flash.

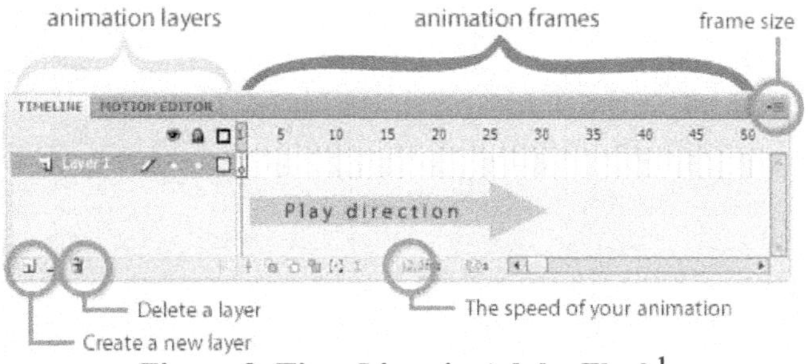

Figure 2. Time Lines in Adobe Flash[1]

For example, Figure 2 shows a timeline that is applied in Adobe Flash in order to enable web page animations. The timeline is used to control how different objects change over time. Thereby, the time line is divided into cells that represent one unit in time and are empty by default. The cells can be filled with normal frames or keyframes. Keyframes indicate that something will change in the animation whereby normal frames are used in order to maintain the animation.

[1]Source: http://www.bill-morrison.com/class/adobe-flash/1-graphics-animation/page-media/images/flash-cs4-timeline.gif

Improvements for the Scenario Specification

An expert can avoid useless time and effort consumption by using the time line approach introduced in the section above. Furthermore, the expert does not have to care about scenarios synchronization anymore. Additionally, for each entity the expert can specify the duration of actions and the exact time of occurrence. Context-depended conflicts, such as resource conflicts, can be visualized on the time line in order to support the expert in finding errors in the scenario specification. In case of similar scenarios there is no need to record multiple scenarios because an existing scenario can easily be adapted.

Improvements for the Usability Evaluation

Because the time line approach allows an easy specification of concurrent behavior, there is a further improvement for usability evaluation in general. User evaluation can be used for evaluating existing smart environments. It seems to be promising to define some kind of reference scenario defining sequences of actions that are performed by the users involved in the scenario. Multiple instances of the reference scenario can be recorded and used to determine arithmetic means of the individual actions defined in the reference scenario. On the basis of the calculated, arithmetic means significantly different scenarios can be identified quickly. Subsequently, a user inquiry can give some information about potential problems referring to the usability.

CONCLUSION

In this paper we have presented a possibility to specify concurrent user behavior in a virtual ubiquitous computing environment. Such a specification is particular of interest in collaborative systems where we need to evaluate concurrent interacting test cases. At first, we presented existing approaches for the specification of concurrent behavior and we shown advantages and disadvantages of them.

After that, we made demands for an improved approach and introduced such an approach using time lines for every entity. Finally, we listed some improvements for the specification and usability evaluation of such systems.

ACKNOWLEDGMENTS

This research is funded by the German Research Foundation (DFG) within the context of the project MuSAMA (Multimodal Smart Appliances Ensembles for Mobile Applications).

REFERENCES

1. E. O'Neill, M. Klepal, D. Lewis, T. O'Donnell, D. O'Sullivan, and D. Pesch. A testbed for evaluating human interaction with ubiquitous computing environments. In *First International Conference on Testbeds and Research Infrastructures for the*

Development of Networks and Communities, 2005. Tridentcom 2005, pages 60–69, 2005.

2. Ivo Maly, Jan Curin, Jan Kleindienst, and Pavel Slavik. Creation and visualization of user behavior in ambient intelligent environment. *Information Visualisation, International Conference on*, 2008.
3. J. Barton and V. Vijayaraghavan. Ubiwise: A ubiquitous wireless infrastructure simulation environment. *HP Labs*, 2002.
4. M. Wurdel, D. Sinnig, and P. Forbrig. CTML: Domain and task modeling for collaborative environments, 2008.
5. P. Singh, H.N. Ha, P. Olivier, C. Kray, Z. Kuang, A.W. Guo, P. Blythe, and P. James. Rapid prototyping and evaluation of intelligent environments using immersive video. *MODIE*, page 36, 2006.
6. Smart Appliance Lab. http://mmis.informatik.uni-rostock.de/index.php?title=Smart_Appliance_Lab
7. Stefan Propp. Usability Evaluation in intelligenten Umgebungen. PhD thesis, University of Rostock, 2010.

Toward a Closer Integration of Usability in Software Development: A Study of Usability Inputs in a Model-Driven Engineering Process

Carine Lallemand
Centre de Recherche Public Henri Tudor
29, avenue John F. Kennedy
L-1855 Luxembourg, Luxembourg
carine.lallemand@tudor.lu

ABSTRACT

Even though the benefits of usability have widely been proven, it seems that development-oriented companies face many difficulties to introduce usability practices into their defined development processes. This paper describes the overall methodology deployed as an attempt to achieve a closer integration of usability practices in the software development process. Model-Driven Engineering (MDE) is used as a basis for this integration. Providing a precise framework composed of models and transformations, it allows to track usability problems and to highlight where exactly they occur in the development process. We will thus be able to link every step of the process to specific ergonomic inputs and to study their consequences on the usability of the generated system. Because MDE will only be used as a way among others to investigate some hypotheses on usability and User-Centered Design (UCD) in general, our results are expected to provide valuable and generic information on usability and UCD processes.

Author Keywords

Usability, User-Centered Design, Software Engineering, Model-Driven Engineering, Transformation Rules

ACM Classification Keywords

H.5.2 Information Interfaces and Presentation: User Interfaces: User-Centered Design; Evaluation/methodology

General Terms

Design, Human Factors, Measurement, Performance

INTRODUCTION

For more than twenty years, researchers and practitioners have been developing a theoretical background and practical tools in order to improve the usability of systems. It is easily understandable when considering the benefits related to more usable systems. Thus, several studies have shown that usable systems were associated with an increased productivity, reduced errors, reduced need for training and support, improved acceptance and enhanced reputation ([15], [18]).

But even though the benefits of usability have widely been proven, most software developers do not apply correctly any methodology related to usability. The main reasons explaining this fact are related to the time and costs associated with the integration of usability into software development. Following Seffah et al. [21], we also speculate that another reason for this phenomenon could be the lack of reference framework for usability practices that indicates where and how in the software process usability inputs need to be provided [9].

It makes sense, therefore, to try to fill the gap between Software Engineering (SE) and usability practices by studying how we could reach a closer integration of both fields. To address this problem, we decided to focus on Model-Driven Engineering (MDE), a software development methodology, which specifies an automated process for developing interactive applications from high-level models to code generation. The very formal separation of every stage of the development process in MDE constitutes an ideal basis for our study. In this framework, we propose a 3-step methodology, which aims at understanding the relationships between software development stages and usability aspects.

1.1. Usability: a concept with multiple definitions and models

The most common definition of usability is given by the standard ISO 9241-11 [13], which defines it as the "extend to which a product can be used by specified users to achieve specified goals with effectiveness, efficiency and satisfaction in a specified context of use".

Originating from computer sciences, where it was perceived as a human factor in a quality system [24], usability has been also studied in social sciences [6]. Shackel [23] is probably one of the first to define and specify the components of usability that include effectiveness, learnability, flexibility and attitude. However, during the late 1980's and 1990's, several authors focused their attention on the definition of usability, each author relating this concept to different attributes [19]. Usability was also defined in several ways across international standards ([13], [14], [15]). We could also notice that not all authors use the term "usability attribute" to designate the entities, which to them make up the usability. These entities can also be called dimensions, components, scales, criteria or factors of usability [11]. Whatever the term used to identify these dimensions, usability criteria appear to be very numerous and diverse. For the time being, there is no consensus on the definition of usability and its related dimensions. Still, some authors have already tried to build consolidated models ([21], [25]) to go beyond the omissions and contradictions in current models and guidelines.

In the literature, the issue of usability is mostly addressed through the perspective of its evaluation. According to Hornbaek [12], the measures of usability help "make the general and somewhat vague term usability concrete and manageable". However, in his systematic review, the author insists on the fact that a lot of challenges still have to be resolved. The main shortcoming of usability evaluation methods is that they generally need an already developed system or prototype (and most of the time, real users) to produce recommendations ([11], [16]). That will lead to high cost and time and will not allow intervening at the earliest stage of the development process. Moreover, most of the usability criteria are difficult to translate into accurate metrics that can be implemented into the code. Therefore, it is hard for the developers to integrate usability at the early stage of the development process.

Finally, these findings lead us to several conclusions. On the one hand, it is obvious that the overarching conceptual framework of usability lacks consensus and there seem to be no models that deal with all the requirements. This lack of a consistent and consolidated framework for usability is probably one of the main reasons why usability is still not well integrated into SE practices. On the other hand, even if the tools provided by the field of usability are able to assess a system's degree of usability, they are still not really able to provide predictive guidelines which will ensure usability at the design level or even just guide developers by classifying the usability criteria into the different stages of their defined processes. Our project aims at investigating and, so far as possible, solving these issues. We will therefore look at how some studies attempt to integrate usability principles or practices in the software development process.

1.2. Integration of Usability in the Development Process

In the 1980's and 1990's, usability was seen by developers as an issue only related to the presentation of information, before they included system functionality in their concerns. As stated by Seffah et al. [22], this narrow view of usability was definitely not able to ensure the whole usability of a system. Fortunately, further works came to the conclusion that even non visible system features would impact the interaction between the user and the system [4]. Starting from this observation, researchers and practitioners have been concerned with the goal of achieving usability through software architecture ([3], [11]). Some authors provide architecture mechanisms or design patterns that directly relate to usability aspects ([3], [22]). Other studies try to define strategies to introduce HCI techniques and activities into mainstream software engineering practices [10]. In the same manner, the famous international standard ISO 13407 [15] proposes a framework for the integration of usability at all stages of a development process. Its wide concept of User-Centered Design (UCD) is described as an "approach to interactive system development that focuses specifically on making systems usable".

Even so, it seems that current usability engineering practices fail to drive design at all stages [11]. We make the assumption that some concepts or methods introduced by SE could be useful to answer the problems emerging from the field of usability and to reconcile closely SE and usability. We assume that Model-Driven Engineering could constitute a favorable framework to our project.

1.3. Model-Driven Engineering: a Way to Achieve Closer Integration of Usability into Software Development?

Model-Driven Engineering (MDE), and its variant Model-driven Architecture, have recently attracted the interest of both researchers and practitioners and are currently seen as key perspectives in the field of SE. MDE is a software development methodology which specifies an automated process for developing interactive applications, based initially on models of abstract description of the system, manually specified by the software developer (user model, task tree, etc.). These models are gradually transformed into transient models of description, more concrete, of the interactive system (Abstract User Interface and Concrete User Interface), resulting in the generation of executable source code, the basis of the Final User Interface. The Cameleon Reference Framework [5] is one of the most commonly used tools for MDE.

By separating the design tasks from the development ones and applying progressive model-to-model transformations, MDE allows the usability to be integrated into the whole user-system interaction process and not only at the graphical level of the user interface. As Juristo, Moreno and Sanchez-Segura [17] insist, user interface is only the visible part of the system but "interaction is a wider concept".

Some authors are already conducting studies linking MDE and usability ([1], [2], [7]). Abrahão, Iborra and Vanderdonckt [1] try to show how the usability of user interfaces that are generated by an MDA-compliant tool can be assessed. They introduce the idea of "usability by construction" and already imagine future trends: "It is our belief that model-driven development provides the basis for tight integration of usability evaluation in the MDA development process, allowing usability issues to be addressed as an integrated part of the system design and not just as an ad-hoc solution after most of the development has been completed". Our research goal is closely related to this work since the authors are investigating whether MDE methods improve software usability through model transformations. Fernandez, Insfran and Abrahão [8] provide a usability model to evaluate usability at several stages of a MDE-compliant development process. We could possibly adapt or extend this model to reach our research objectives and test our hypotheses.

Finally, it seems that MDE conveys new perspectives for the usability research field. It allows to track usability problems and to highlight where exactly they occur in the development process. The fact that it constitutes a precise framework composed of models and transformations, allows us to link every step of the process to specific ergonomic inputs and to study their consequences on the usability of the generated system, at a global or specific level. Thanks to these properties, MDE constitutes an ideal basis to reach our objectives. However, it emphasizes once again the need for operationalization of ergonomic rules. Thus, further research is needed to achieve true integration of usability into software development. We aim at going further than the existing studies by providing a whole integration of UCD into MDE. We will therefore focus on the transformational approach in MDE, as this methodology provides an ideal basis for the integration of usability at every stage of the development process.

2. RESEARCH OBJECTIVES

The overarching research question is formulated as follows: How and to what extent is it possible to provide a solid framework for User-Centered Design in order to reach a closer integration of usability in software development?

In terms of scientific contribution, our project will try to counter the limitations of the current usability models and guidelines. We will use MDE, a SE tool, in order to deepen the understanding of how usability inputs should be implemented within the development process. Because MDE will only be used as a way among others to investigate some hypotheses on usability and UCD in general, our results are expected to provide valuable and generic information on usability and UCD processes.

The research questions addressed by this study are numerous: (i) Based on the existing usability models, what usability model could be the most appropriate to improve the integration of usability in the software development lifecycle? (ii) How to structure the ergonomics inputs according to the different steps of a design process in order to build a shared framework for both usability specialists and software engineers? (iii) By studying the usability inputs into the software architecture, could it be possible to evaluate the usability of a system, based on the coverage (in number and quality) of each specific usability dimensions at the different stages of software development?

3. METHODOLOGY

Our methodology will be structured in 3 major steps.

In a first step, a systematic review of the literature on the usability concept will be performed to investigate the different definitions of usability and its related dimensions. Based on the existing usability models, we aim to find, adapt or define a consolidated usability model that would be appropriate to improve the integration of usability in the design process. The criteria for the definition of this model will encompass: the quality and orthogonality of the usability dimensions, the ability to be used for the design as well as for the evaluation of a system and the ability to be operationalized in a development process.

The second step aims at classifying the various dimensions of usability defined in step 1 according to the different stages of an MDE development process. At this stage, our purpose is to know where the different usability dimensions would play a role and, consequently, where they would have to be taken into account and implemented. We aim to create a table that establishes a classification of the usability dimensions identified in our consolidated model and the different stages of the development process.

The last step of the methodology encompasses: a stage of use cases design and a stage of usability analysis performed on these use cases. We plan to use at least 2 use cases. In collaboration with IT-engineers, we will develop three different interfaces for each use case. Following the Cameleon Reference Framework [5], our MDE design approach will cover 4 steps that consist of applying transformations rules in order to move progressively from Task and Domain Models to a Final User Interface. The difference between these 3 interfaces will lie in the operationalization of usability criteria into transformation rules. The number of transformation rules covering each criteria and the quality of the coverage will therefore vary and we will thus be able to compare the usability of each generated system. The usability of the generated systems will be assessed through 3 usability analyses: a heuristic evaluation performed on the transformation rules during the development, a heuristic evaluation performed on the final user interface and, finally, users tests performed in a usability laboratory.

In summary, the results obtained through this methodology will allow us first to evaluate the quality of the generated interfaces. Second, we will be able to investigate the possible links between the coverage of each specific usability dimension at the different stages of software development and the whole usability of the final interfaces. We also aim to formulate a set of propositions for the improvement of user-centered design and the integration of usability into the development lifecycle, both as a basis for further research work and for the attention of practitioners.

CONCLUSION

In this study, Model-Driven Engineering is used as a basis to achieve a closer integration of usability at the different stages of software development. The very formal aspect of this approach will allow us to take support on a precise and well-defined process to track usability problems at the different level of abstraction, which could represent the different levels of a development lifecycle. If possible, we would aim at generalizing our results to every development lifecycle, this way giving the practitioners a better understanding of the usability related issues. Usability specialists could derive benefits from our results, especially by being more integrated in the earliest stages of the development process. We also aim at providing them with relevant information on the link between transformation rules and usability dimensions.

ACKNOWLEDGMENTS

The author would like to thank her corporate and academic supervisors: Dr. Guillaume Gronier (CRP Henri Tudor), Dr. Vincent Koenig and Pr. Romain Martin (University of Luxembourg). She would like also to thank Pr. Jean Vanderdonckt for his valuable advices and support.

REFERENCES

1. Abrahão, S., Iborra, E., Vanderdonckt, J. Usability Evaluation of User Interfaces Generated with a Model-Driven Architecture Tool. In Law, E. & al. (Eds) *Maturing Usability: Quality in Software, Interaction and Value*, Springer (2008), 3-32
2. Aquino, N., Vanderdonckt, J., Condori-Fernández, N., Dieste, O., & Pastor, O. Usability evaluation of multi-device/platform user interfaces generated by model-driven engineering. *In Proc. ESEM'2010*, ACM Press (2010).
3. Bass, L, & John, B. E. Linking usability to software architecture patterns through general scenarios. *Journal of Systems and Software*, 66, 3 (2003), 187-197.
4. Bass, L., John, B. E., & Kates, J. *Achieving Usability through Software Architecture*, Carnegie Mellon University/Software Engineering Institute Technical Report No. CMU/SEI-TR-2001-005, 2001.
5. Calvary, G., Coutaz, J., Thevenin, D., Limbourg, Q., Bouillon, L., and Vanderdonckt, J. A Unifying reference framework for multi-target user interfaces. *Interacting with Computers*, 15, 3 (2003), 289-308.
6. Carroll, J. M. Human-computer interaction: psychology as a science of design. *Annual review of psychology*, 48 (1997), 61-83.
7. Fernandez, A., Abrahão, S. & Insfran, E. Towards to the Validation of a Usability Evaluation Method for Model-Driven Web Development, *In Proc. ESEM 2010*, ACM Press (2010).
8. Fernandez, A., Insfran, E., & Abrahão, S. Integrating a Usability Model into Model-Driven Web Development Processes. *In Proc WISE 2009*, Springer (2009)
9. Ferre, X., Juristo, N., & Moreno, A.M. Framework for integrating usability practices into the software process. *In Proc. PROFES'05,* Springer (2005).
10. Ferre, X., Juristo, N., & Moreno, A.M. Improving software engineering practice with HCI aspects. Software Engineering Research and Applications, Springer-Verlag, San Francisco, USA (2003), 349-363
11. Folmer, E., & Bosch, J. Architecting for usability: a survey. *Journal of Systems and Software*, 70, 1-2 (2004), 61-78.
12. Hornbaek, K. Current practice in measuring usability: Challenges to usability studies and research. *International Journal of Human-Computer Studies*, 64, 2 (2006), 79-102.
13. International Organization for Standardization. ISO 9241-11: Ergonomic requirements for office work with visual display terminals (VDTs) – Part 9: Guidance on usability, 1998.
14. International Organization for Standardization. ISO/IEC 9126-1:2001 Software engineering – Product quality – Part 1: Quality model, 2001.
15. International Organization for Standardization. ISO 13407: Human-centred design processes for interactive systems, 1999.
16. John, B., & Marks, S. Tracking the effectiveness of usability evaluation methods. *Behaviour & Information Technology*, 16, 4 (1997), 188-202.
17. Juristo, N., Moreno, A.M. & Sanchez-Segura, M. Analysing the impact of usability on software design. *The Journal of Systems and Software*, 80 (2007), 1506-1516
18. Maguire, M. Methods to support human-centred design. *International Journal of Human-Computer Studies*, 55, 4 (2001), 587-634.
19. Nielsen, J. *Usability Engineering*. San Diego, CA: Academic Press, 1993.
20. Scapin, D., & Bastien, J. M. C. Ergonomic criteria for evaluating the ergonomic quality of interactive systems. *Behaviour & Information Technology*, 16, 4 (1997), 220-231.
21. Seffah, A., Donyaee, M., Kline, R. B., & Padda, H. K. Usability measurement and metrics: A consolidated model. *Software Quality Journal*, 14, 2 (2006), 159-178.
22. Seffah, A., Mohamed, T., Habieb-Mammar, H., & Abran, A. Reconciling usability and interactive system architecture using patterns. *Journal of Systems and Software*, 81, 11 (2008), 1845-1852.
23. Shackel, B. Usability - context, framework, design and evaluation. In B. Shackel & S. Richardson (Eds.*), Human factors for informatics usability*. Cambridge: Cambridge University Press, 1991, 21-38.
24. Shneiderman, B. Improving the human factors aspect of database interactions. ACM Transactions on Database Systems, 3, 4 (1978), 417-439
25. Winter, S., Wagner, S., & Deissenboeck, F. A Comprehensive Model of Usability. *In Proc. EIS 2007*.

Sustainable Management of Usability Information

Ben Heuwing
University of Hildesheim
Hildesheim, Germany
+49 5121 883 872
ben.heuwing@uni-hildesheim.de

ABSTRACT

Information from usability engineering activities can be useful in different contexts beyond the scope of a specific development project. This dissertation project aims at developing a model of usability information in order to support corresponding information needs of usability engineers in organizations with a usability information system. Results of interviews with usability professionals are presented, indicating that usability related information is already put to use in practice and that access to this information can be improved.

Keywords

usability engineering, evaluation, information management

ACM Classification Keywords

H.5.2 User Interfaces---Evaluation/methodology; Benchmarking; User-centered design

General Terms

Design, Management

RESEARCH PROJECT

Different types of data and documentation are generated during user-centered software development projects. For example, use cases and personas are products of user research that are used as input for prototypes and other design artifacts, which in turn can be evaluated to produce descriptions of usability issues and possible improvements (see Figure 1). A considerable amount of time and resources is required to apply these methods in projects, especially to achieve conformance with standardized process models, for example ISO 9241-210 [7].

Although the deliverables and results produced during the process are intended for the current development project, this information could also be used during the development of succeeding versions and new products. However, the information often is not readily available within an organization. Therefore, making the information accessible in a sustainable and efficient way has the potential to optimize development processes, to reduce costs of user-centered development practices, and to improve the overall quality of software.

Research Questions

The underlying question of this project is the usefulness of the application of collected and aggregated usability information from past projects and to identify tasks that benefit from this information. A general model of heterogeneous types of usability information will be proposed, which provides a foundation for tools that help to organize and aggregate relevant information and make it accessible for the tasks identified. Additionally, this model has the potential to improve the understanding of the connections between different process stages and methods of user-centered design processes. The model should take into account information needs and constraints that characterize real projects, which is rarely done in existing approaches.

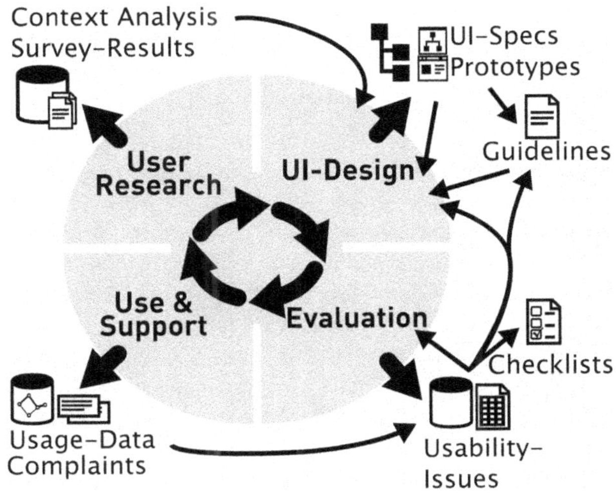

Figure 1: Information resources used in the usability engineering processes

Project plan

The dissertation project encompasses three stages:

1. User research: Interviews are conducted to identify information needs of usability professionals in order to construct valid scenarios of use. Additionally, current practices of the management of usability information within organizations are analyzed, and possible obstacles are identified.

2. Model generation: Based on the analysis of existing usability information and evaluation data, a model of usability information will be derived, taking into account existing international standards. The model will then be evaluated using feedback of usability professionals. The evaluation of conceptual models (in contrast to existing technology and prototypes) represents a methodological problem [11].

3. Prototype generation and evaluation: Based on the model a prototype will be generated that offers access to usability information in a specific context of use. This prototype will be evaluated by usability professionals regarding its usefulness and usability in the context of development projects.

Currently, the project is in the phase of user research. Early results of interviews with usability professionals about their application of information from past projects are described in the last chapter of this article.

CURRENT RESEARCH

Empirical research on the contents, structure, and management of usability information is still sparse. An analysis of the dissemination of usability related information within a large software development company revealed that different channels are used to discuss usability issues among usability researchers, project managers, and developers [2]. Informal meetings, web tools (such as wikis or blogs), instant messaging, and e-mail are commonly used, whereas bug-tracking systems and formal meetings are used to a lesser degree. Further research has been done regarding the contents and style of reports of usability evaluations, e.g. in [10].

Recently, there has been a growing interest in tools and methods to manage information in usability engineering processes. Various frameworks and systems have been proposed for the organization of usability information. Recently, a new ISO-Standard, ISO TR 25060, has been published describing the information produced in the activities of a user-centered development process [8]. ISO 25060 also suggests intended users and usages within a development project. This standard can serve as a high-level framework for the organization of usability information.

More specific approaches attempt to structure the results of particular usability activities. For example, usability issues (e.g. as results of usability tests) can be organized using the User Action Framework (UAF), based on a classification of the user action affected [1] and explored using the "Vizability"-Tool [12]. One of the goals of the UAF is to provide a foundation for integrated usability tools. Results of interface design can be managed using pattern-based approaches, see [5] for examples. More generally, an idea has been proposed to publish test results as interoperable information objects in a global, publicly accessible repository, and to link these objects to corresponding design guidelines and patterns [6]. This type of linkage between evaluation results and products of interface design is also an integral element of the knowledge management system for UI-Designers proposed in [4]. In order to make methods and templates more readily available and usable for software developers a recommender system for usability engineering methods and tools based on previous ratings and an analysis of the project context has been introduced [9].

Existing approaches and models offer viable solutions, but only for specific aspects of usability information management, while others take a more general, inter-organizational perspective. The approach presented in [9] offers a very pragmatic, project oriented solution, but is focused on automatic recommendations and does not allow for exploration and manual analysis of available resources.

RESULTS OF EXPLORATORY INTERVIEWS

Qualitative, semi-structured interviews have been conducted with eight in-house usability engineers and interaction designers working in German companies. Their everyday work practices involve tasks in one or more of the following areas: user research, user interface design, and evaluation of products and prototypes.

Participants were asked to recall an incident where they had consulted usability information from past projects. Participants had been selected according to their prior experience regarding this practice, so every participant was able to report on such an event. After this question, participants were presented with a number of tasks that had been identified in literature and in previous interviews and were asked about the occurrence of these tasks in their daily work life. At the end of the interview, they were asked about their opinion on systematically documenting and using information from past usability activities and about advantages and possible difficulties.

Scenarios of Use

Most descriptions indicate that information from past projects is already used as input for current design decision. In these cases, results and materials of field studies, surveys, or usability tests are consulted that are applicable to the current development context. As a consequence, fewer empirical studies have to be conducted and the impact of findings on the development process can be increased. Existing materials and descriptions of study settings are utilized to facilitate preparation of new studies.

Another typical task identified was to compare different products or versions of a product regarding their level of usability regarding specially designed benchmark-studies or to increase consistency. Furthermore, analysis revealed that existing generalized guidelines are derived from design specifications and evaluation results and that existing information can be a useful resource to support orientation for employees new to an application domain.

Information management

In most companies tools are used to support management of usability information, ranging from spreadsheet documents to document servers and wikis with adapted systems for categorization. Issue-tracking tools are used to document usability issues and non-conformance to style guides.

Possible Obstacles

Frequently, information from usability studies is made accessible company-wide. Some participants regard this as a problem and opted against it, while others perceived it as an opportunity to make their work visible within the organization. In one case, the publication of information about usability issues was considered a potential imminence by product management. The judgment of relevance and applicability of the results to different contexts was perceived as a highly demanding task, resulting in the possibility that this information might be transferred to inappropriate contexts and be used to support arbitrary arguments. Additionally, concerns with privacy issues regarding both internal business information and personal data were raised. Another important issue was the additional effort required for data acquisition and documentation, which should remain at a very low degree compared to established procedures.

OUTLOOK: PROTOTYPE DEVELOPMENT

This project will focus on the management of results from user studies, especially evaluations, which are a central element of the usability engineering process and a valuable asset for a company. A prototype which enables retrieval of relevant resources will be developed and evaluated in the context of a project in a software development company. Additional key features of the prototype will depend on the requirements of the project where it is put to use. For example, it is possible to include other resources such as use case descriptions, interface designs and prototypes.

The planned approach will give usability professionals access to existing resources using a retrieval interface which leverages metadata descriptions of resources for facetted search in order to facilitate exploration of the collection and ensure the completeness of result sets. Resources will be stored as information objects instead of documents. The information-model, from which the facets will be derived, focuses on aspects of the context of the result acquisition (e.g. method, user group, task-model, interface-model).

Key indicators will be displayed for result sets and sub-sets in addition to the number of results, to enhance the capability for exploratory search, to help to understand the existing collection and to discover previously unknown features [3]. For this, existing measures of usability can be used in conjunction with indicators of the applicability of results in a given context based on their classification.

The evaluation of this prototype will help to improve the proposed information model and to understand the process of retrieval and application of usability information.

SUMMARY

Most existing research approaches, which structure usability related information, do not specifically consider actual information needs that arise in companies. Preliminary results from interviews show that information from past projects is already applied by in-house usability professionals in various contexts and in an increasingly systematic way. Although this study does not claim to be representative, it indicates that there is potential for improvement.

The results will be used to derive a model and a prototypical information system. The evaluation of this prototype in a realistic context is expected to provide new insights into the process of retrieval and application of results from previous usability engineering efforts.

REFERENCES

1. Andre, T.S., Hartson, H.R., Belz, S.M., and McCreary, F.A. The user action framework: a reliable foundation for usability engineering support tools. *International Journal of Human Computer Studies 54*, 1 (2001), 107-136.
2. Bach, P.M., Hao, J., and Carroll, J.M. Sharing usability information in interactive system development. *Proc. of the 2008 international workshop on Cooperative and human aspects of software engineering*, ACM (2008), 9-12.
3. Ben-Yitzhak, O., Golbandi, N., Har'El, N., et al. Beyond basic faceted search. *Proc. of the international conference on Web search and web data mining*, (2008), 33–44.
4. Chevalier, A., Fouquereau, N., and Vanderdonckt, J. The influence of a knowledge-based system on designers' cognitive activities: a study involving professional web designers. *Behav. Inf. Technol. 28*, 1 (2009), 45-62.
5. Deng, J., Kemp, E., and Todd, E.G. Managing UI pattern collections. *Proc. of the 6th ACM SIGCHI New Zealand chapter's international conference on Computer-human interaction: making CHI natural*, ACM (2005), 31-38.
6. Douglas, I. Testing object management (TOM): a prototype for usability knowledge management in global software. In N. Aykin, ed., *Usability and Internationalization, Part I, HCII 2007*. Springer, Heidelberg, 2007, 297-305.
7. ISO. Human-centred design for interactive systems. Ergonomics of human system interaction Part 210 (ISO 9241-210). 2009.
8. ISO. Common Industry Format (CIF) for usability - General framework for usability-related information (ISO/IEC TR 25060). 2010.
9. Metzker, E. Adoption-Centric Usability Engineering -

Systematic Deployment, Evaluation and Improvement of Usability Engineering Methods in the Software Engineering Lifecycle. 2005.

10. Molich, R., Dumas, J., and Jeffries, R. Making Usability Recommendations Useful and Usable. *Journal of Usability Studies 2*, 4 (2007), 162-179.
11. Moody, D.L. Theoretical and practical issues in evaluating the quality of conceptual models: current state and future directions. *Data Knowl. Eng. 55*, 3 (2005), 243-276.
12. Pyla, P.S., Howarth, J.R., Catanzaro, C., and North, C. Vizability: a tool for usability engineering process improvement through the visualization of usability problem data. *Proc. of the 44th annual ACM Southeast regional conference*, ACM (2006), 620-625.

Toward a Flexible Design Method Sustaining UIs Plasticity

Eric Ceret
LIG Laboratory, University of Grenoble
385 rue de la Bibliothèque
38041 Grenoble Cedex 9 France
+33 (0)476 635 970
Eric.Ceret@imag.fr

ABSTRACT

More and more, plasticity is a main concern in User Interface (UI) design, and its complexity impulses the need for a sustaining design method or a guide to compose methods' fragments. But facing the quantity of methods makes it hard to choose which one is the most adapted one regarding to a project's context. In this paper, we propose a taxonomy that enables the designers to compare methods' process models, and so empowers them to make enlightened choices, and we describe our approach to create a new design method, empowering flexible conception of plastic UIs.

Authors Keywords

Process model, taxonomy, UI Design Method

ACM Classification Keywords:

I.0 GENERAL

General Terms:

Design, Reliability

INTRODUCTION

Thevenin and Coutaz [23] define the plasticity of a UI and its ability to adapt to the variations of the context of use, itself defined as the triplet <User, Platform, Environment>, while preserving usability and the value waited by the user. Added to the advent of ubiquitous computing, the increasing amount of platforms and devices and the need for sustaining adaptation, the development of software becomes more and more complex. Thus, the designer needs guidance to develop UIs, in particular multi-device, multi-user, multi-culturality, multi-organization, multi-context, multi-modality and multi-platform UIs.

Coutaz [7] enumerates many paths that have explored to achieve this question, starting from several points of view. According to her, some researches have tried to access plasticity at the toolkit level, others started from the infrastructure level or from task level modeling. Artificial Intelligence researchers are also involved in some part or another of this problem. For instance, Oikonomopoulos *et al.* [16] estimates that Artificial Intelligence can be a great help to evaluate human actions and to distinguish what is present in the scene, enabling someone to build an UI with "the naturalness of human-human interaction". In the last decade, Model-Driven Architecture has been sensed as an approach with a great potential [24].

So there is several methods that sustain UI design. In this profusion of sometimes partial or immature approaches, designer may feel it difficult to choose a well-adapted process. But making the right choices addresses only one part of the problem: the designer wants also to benefit of the strengths of each method, and of course, to avoid the points not so well adapted to his project. In one word he wants flexibility in the methods he is getting to use.

In this paper we present the study we are making to answer these two questions. Promote (**Pro**cess **Mo**dels' **T**axonomy for **E**nlightening choices) is the result of the state of art, made to study the needs and the possibilities in terms of methods. Concretely, it is a conceptual tool for classifying methods and thus better understand each of them and consequently make the right choices. To sustain flexibility, we are building a design method based on fragments and components composition.

After an overview of the related works, we describe our approach of these questions, and we present Promote, a multidimensional taxonomy. Then we describe the method we propose.

RELATED WORKS

Design methods in a nutshell

According to Harmsen [12], a method is "an integrated collection of procedures, techniques, product descriptions, and tools, for effective, efficient, and consistent support of the (Information System) engineering process". Booch [4] defines a method as "a disciplined process for generating a set of models that describe various aspects of a software system under development, using some well-defined notation". According to these two authors, we retain that a method is the association of a process model, a language and a collection of tools. Our work focuses on process models.

Strengths and limits of existing methods

Several approaches and tools have been presented over the time. Most of them represent major advances which largely sustained the conception of UIs.

But the propositions which gave rise to all the aspects of a method are rare.

For instance, User-Centered Design [15] is a paradigm defining 12 key principles [11] that places the user at a central place in the development process. According to Abras *et al.* [1], it is both a philosophy and a spectrum of ways in which users are involved in UCD, but the key point is that users are involved one way or another. So, in itself, UCD is neither sustaining plasticity nor proposing flexibility points in the development process.

UCD has inspired several methods like Web Site Design Method (WSDM) [9]. This method is certainly an advance for web designers, but it defines neither a language nor tools, and its process model enables no extension or adaptation.

ISO 13407 [14] promotes usability, a very important key point for UI design, but is recognized to be "neither a method nor a software process": it is a characterization of user-centered processes [10].

Value-Centered Design [6] explains how value is a major concern in UI design and should be focused on in the same time than system, user and context concerns. But however important can be the study of worth during the development process, it is one more concern and not a process model nor a method as we defined below.

OVID [20] is quite close to the definition of a method, for it is described as an "iterative development process", including the description of several activities, from the requirements analysis to the implementation. But it had a very small diffusion, and its process model defines no flexibility point.

Cameleon [2] proposes a framework for sustaining UIs adaptation to context, through a dynamic models' transformation process in which the context influences the results at each step. Coutaz [7] describes this process: "conventional UI generation operates by the way of top-down vertical transformations. Typically, an abstract UI (AUI) is derived from the domain-dependent concepts and task models. In turn, the AUI is transformed into a concrete UI, followed by the final executable UI". The reverse process infers abstract models from more concrete ones. This framework gives rise to plasticity. But it doesn't propose any way to adapt it to the specific needs of a project: there no flexibility in it.

None of these approaches answers our wish. Studying all these methods tempts to combine parts – the best parts, of course – of each one, so that to define a model embedding as many key points as possible. This is why we are working on a method's definition.

APPROACH

The study of several process models makes it obvious that defining a complete and flexible process model, able to sustain UI plasticity, is far from being easy. Thus, a first step is to better understand what a method is, and to be able to identify its characteristics, its strengths, and possibly its weaknesses. This identification relies on a classification of methods: Promote is the conceptual tool that supports this work.

PROMOTE, A TAXONOMY OF PROCESS MODELS

Taxonomy is the process of naming and classifying entities into groups within a larger system, according to their similarities and differences. This definition contains the approach we used: we identified the main similarities and differences between many process' models, and then abstract these concepts to define the categories of entities, categories that we are named to name axes and sub-axes within Promote.

A key point we want to focus on is the fact that we decided to classify what a process model actually says, and not what is usual to be done with it, nor what is just a general consideration of the method. For example, if a method says that its process is iterative and incremental, we retain these two characteristics only if the way to iterate and the way to increment are explicitly defined. If the method doesn't talk about iterations or increments, but design/development teams are used to apply it with iterations, we don't consider the method to be iterative.

Of course, this selection of characteristics and this evaluation of what is really said in a method are two subjective part of our survey that will need to be discussed and enriched.

At this time, we have defined nine main axes divided into 32 sub-axes. Process' *focus* relates the viewpoint of the process as described in [12]. The viewpoint is the path used by the process model to finally identify the activities that are to be done during the development process. It can be focused directly on *activities*: first, requirements analysis, then test plan and so on. The process model can *product* oriented and "represent the development process through the evolution of the product" [3]. Another orientation is to focus on *decisions*, where activities appear to be the consequences of the decisions that decide of the product evolution. The two last orientations are close to each other: context-oriented processes describe the combinations of observed situations with intentions [18], and *strategy*-oriented models propose to identify goals and the different possibilities to reach them [22].

The *cycle* identifies recommended iteration's granularity, lifecycle duration, increments, backlashes management, top-down or bottom-up approach. *Collaboration* categorizes the proposed forms of relationship between the design/development team's members, and between them and the other stakeholders; it lists the characteristics of user-centered and usage-centered approaches. *Artifacts* classify the proposal of making prototypes, executable or not, reusable or not, and the proposed formalism. Method's *recommended use* identifies all what the method can say about its own context of use, like best project and team sizes, required knowledge, requirements maturity, managed situations (UI plasticity, multi-core, cloud computing). *Diffusion* evaluates the actual user acceptance, and *vitality* measures how the method is 'alive', how it evolves and can support a designer. *Maturity* tries to measure how well the method has been reinforced by actual use in the course of time. And at last, *adaptability* measures the flexibility of the process model, for example if it includes possible choices or if it can be extended by its users.

TOWARD A DESIGN METHOD FOR UIs PLASTICITY

Promote helps us in understanding the concept of method, but by applying it to HCI method, it reveals a variety of practices that are difficult to gather into one method. Thus, to connect all this variety, our method should be opened and flexible. But it must also guide designers with appropriate practices when they need support. We propose to keep a process skeleton that would be based on the Cameleon reference framework. It will use the UsiXML models[1] as the spinal column of our method. Any other models could be used while they can be transformed into UsiXML's ones.

To face the needs of adaptation and flexibility in the design, the method engineering domain has promoted the notion of method fragments [19] [5] which can be reused, selected and combined to answer to specific project needs. The main problems of the approaches are the selection of the appropriate fragments and the fragments combination. To facilitate them, goals [21] have been added to fragments [8] [17]. However fragments combination remains an open question. To avoid this drawback, we will base our method on a spinal column where flexibility will be added by goals. Our method will provide a path where each step answers to one goal. Other activities could be proposed for each step if they answer to the same goal. For example, the goal "study the user interaction" is the global goal of several HCI activities such as organizing focus groups or card sorting. As these processes answer to the same goal, they can be considered as different *strategies* in the focus of the process.

[1] See http://www.usixml.org

CONCLUSION AND PERSPECTIVES

This paper presents our approach to propose a new design method sustaining UIs plasticity and the flexibility we think wished by designers.

At this time, we have finished the state of the art about the methods, and we have defined Promote, a taxonomy supporting the comparison of methods and thus enlightening of their relative strengths, weaknesses and originalities.

In a very close future, we want to classify more methods, in order to create a knowledge database about them, and thus validate the completeness of Promote's axes. We also want to pursue an evaluation in progress, where a very few users have confirmed our faith: using the classification helped them to discover a method, for it forced them to have a look at characteristics they would usually have ignored. They also concluded that it is a good tool to compare methods. Some axes have been declared hard to understand, and we are adapting our work them to make more easy to master.

We are now working on the definition of the method, which is going to sustain the development of demonstrators.

REFERENCES

1. Abras, C., Maloney-Krichmar, D., Preece, J. User-Centered Design. In Bainbridge, W. Encyclopedia of Human-Computer Interaction. Thousand Oaks: Sage Publications, 2004.
2. Balme, L., Demeure, A., Barralon, N., Coutaz, J., Calvary, G. CAMELEON-RT: a Software Architecture Reference Model for Distributed, Migratable, and Plastic User Interfaces. In EUSAI 2004, LNCS 3295, pp 291-302, 2004.
3. Benabdellatif, M. Process modelling analysis: comparison between activity-oriented models, product-oriented models and decision-oriented models. In Data Mining III, A Zanasi, CA Brebbia, NFF Ebecken & P Melli (Eds), WIT Press, 2002.
4. Booch, G. Object Oriented Analysis and Design with Application, Benjamin-Cummings, Publishing Co., Inc., Redwood City, California, 1991.
5. Brinkkemper S., Saeki M., Harmsen F., Assembly Techniques for Method Engineering. Proc. of the 10th Conf. on Advanced Information Systems Engineering, Pisa Italy, 1998.
6. Cockton, G. A development framework for value-centred design. In Proceedings of CHI'05 extended

abstracts on Human factors in computing systems, ACM New York, NY, USA, 2005

7. Coutaz, J. User Interface Plasticity: Model Driven Engineering to the Limit! In ACM, Engineering Interactive Computing Systems, pp 1-8, 2010.
8. Crescenzo P., Mirbel I.: Improving Collaborations in Neuroscientist Community, Web2Touch workshop in conjunction with International Conference on Web Intelligence, Milan, Italy, September 2009.
9. De Troyer, O.M.F., Leune, C.J. WSDM: A User Centered Design Method for Web. in Computer Networks and ISDN systems, Proceedings of the 7th International World Wide Web Conference, Elsevier, pp. 85-94, 1998.
10. Ferre, X., Juristo, N., Moreno, AM. Which, When and How Usability Techniques And Activities Should Be Integrated. A Seffah (eds), Human-Centered Software Engineering– Integrating Usability in the Development Process, pp 173-200, Springer, Berlin. 2005.
11. Gulliksen J. Göransson B., Boivie I., Blomkvist, S. Persson, J, Cajander, Å. Key principles for user-centred systems design. A Seffah (eds), Human-Centered Software Engineering – Integrating Usability in the Development Process, pp 17-36, Springer. 2005.
12. Harmsen, F. Situational Method Engineering. Thesis at Université de Twente, Nederland, Moret Ernst & Young Management Consultants, January 1997.
13. Hug, C., Front, A., Rieu, D. A Process Engineering Method based on a Process Domain Model and Patterns. MoDISE-EUS, CAiSE workshop, Montpellier - France, June 2008.
14. ISO 13407. Human-centered design processes for interactive system. Geneve, International Organization for Standardization, 1999.
15. Norman, D.A., Draper, S. W. (Eds). User-Centered System Design: New Perspectives on Human-Computer Interaction. Lawrence Earlbaum Associates, Hillsdale, NJ, 1986.
16. Oikonomopoulos, A., Patras, I., Pantic, M., Paragios, N. Trajectory-based Representation of Human Actions. Lecture Notes on Artificial Intelligence,. AI for Human Computing, 2007.
17. Perez-Medina, J.-L., Dupuy-Chessa, S., Rieu, D. A service-oriented approach for interactive system design, 8th International Workshop on TAsk Models and DIAgrams LNCS 5963, D. England et al. Eds, Springer Verlag, September 2009, Belgium, pp 44-57, 2010
18. Pohl K., Assenova, P., Dömges, R., Johannesson P., Maiden, N., Plihon, V., Schmitt, J.R., Spandoukakis, G. Applying AI Techniques to Requirements Engineering: The NATURE Prototype. In Proceedings ICSE-Workshop on Research Issues in the Intersection Between Software Engineering and Artificial Intelligence., 1994.
19. Ralyté J., Rolland C. An Assembly Process Model for Method Engineering. Proc. of the 13th Conf. on Advanced Information Systems Engineering (CAISE'01), Interlaken, Switzerland, June 2001. K. Dittrich, A. Geppert, M. Norrie (Eds.). LNCS 2068, Springer-Verlag, pp. 267-283, 2001.
20. Roberts, D., Berry, D., Isensee, S., Mullaly, J. Designing for the User with OVID: Bridging the Gap Between Software Engineering and User Interface Design. Macmillan Technical Publishing, 1998.
21. Rolland, C.: Capturing System Intentionality with Maps, Conceptual Modeling in Information Systems Engineering. pp. 141--158. Springer, Berlin, Germany, 2007.
22. Rolland, C., Prakash, N., Benjamen, A. A Multi-model View of Process Modelling. Requirements Engineering Journal, pp. 169-187, 1999.
23. Thevenin, D., Coutaz, J. Plasticity of User Interfaces: Framework and Research Agenda. In Edinburgh, A.S., Johnson, C. (eds.) Proc. Interact 1999, pp. 110–117. IFIP IOS Press Publ., Amsterdam, 1999.
24. Vanderdonckt, J., Calvary, G., Coutaz, J. Multimodality for Plastic User Interfaces: Models, Methods, and Principles. In Multimodal user interfaces: signals and communication technology, pp 61-84, D. Tzovaras (ed.), Lecture Notes in Electrical Engineering, Springer-Verlag, Berlin, 2007.

Distributed User Interfaces in Space and Time

Jérémie Melchior
Université catholique de Louvain, Louvain School of Management
Louvain Interaction Laboratory, Place des Doyens, 1 – B-1348 Louvain-la-Neuve (Belgium)
Jeremie.melchior@uclouvain.be

ABSTRACT

Distributed User Interfaces (DUIs) have been imagined in order to support end users in carrying out interactive tasks that could be distributed in space (e.g., some subtasks are carried out in different locations) and time (e.g., some subtasks are carried out during different time intervals, depending on who is contributing to the task. Classical interactive applications involving a single-user, single-context user interface are rarely developed in a way that distributing parts or whole of the user interface is made effective and efficient. In order to facilitate the deployment of such distributed user interfaces, this thesis provides the following contributions: a series of models capturing the various aspects of a DUI based on new concepts (i.e. distribution scene and scenario), an engineering method for specifying DUIs based on these concepts, and a supporting toolkit providing the developers with distribution primitives.

Author Keywords

Distributed User Interfaces, Mobility, Ubiquity, Design.

General Terms

Design, Experimentation, Human Factors, Verification.

ACM Classification Keywords

C.2.4 [**Computer-Communication Networks**]: Distributed systems – *Distributed applications.* D2.2 [**Software Engineering**]: Design Tools and Techniques – *Modules and interfaces; user interfaces.* H5.2 [**Information interfaces and presentation**]: User Interfaces – *graphical user interfaces, user interface management system (UIMS).*

INTRODUCTION

A *Distributed User Interface* (DUI) is hereby defined as any application User Interface (UI) whose components can be distributed across different displays of different computing platforms that are used by different users, whether they are working at the same place (co-located) or not (remote collaboration) [1,2,7,9]. Consequently, DUIs allow for the UI to be spread out over a set of displays/devices/platforms taking advantage of each display/device/platform's unique properties instead of residing on a single display/device/platform [1] with the interaction capabilities that are constrained on this display/device/platform. People use one or several computing devices every day. In order to improve applications, researchers try to provide usable *user interfaces* (UIs) for this purpose. But applications only run on one single platform. Now, there are concepts such as distributed applications and *distributed user interfaces* (DUI) [2,5,6,8,9,10]. While the first has become popular, the second is only used by some groups of researchers and are not ready to a public use.

Motivations

The main motivations can be described with two small examples from [8]. "A user of a tabletop surface may wish to grab and use a keyboard from a nearby PC". In this first example, we have a multi-device system that we would like to organize in another way. We would like to use the keyboard device with the computer as well as the tabletop surface. To generalize this small example, we would like to be able to choose the way devices are logically connected at running time of the system. "Or an application running on a Smartphone might discover that its battery is about to expire, and look for another device onto which it can migrate while offering minimal interruption to its user". The second example shows an example of smart application. We would like to have **independence between user interface and logical part of an application** [8]. In the Smartphone example, we notice that there are a strong coupling between the user interface and the devices on which it runs. The place where the application is displayed should not be dependent from where the application runs. Users and applications might organize the user interface across several devices without other constraints than physical ones. Due to the lack of a single and complete description of what an application should be, there are a lot of different ways to create applications. Depending on what aims the application, it will be created using a toolkit, a framework, an API, a software development kit which may be more specific to the domain of the application [7]. The diversity of ways to create interactive applications leads to different ways to realize the same application. A consequence of this wide choice is that it is not easy to choose the one which is the most appropriate for the application. The choice can reduce the functionalities because some improvements exists but with different solutions. A major problem in computing science is to use the powerful varieties of operating systems, interaction mechanisms and form factors to create a large and powerful world that could be widespread like in the same room or interactive space [9]. The objective of all the operating systems is to be the most effective platform as possible but there are still a lot of features that still need to appear. Almost all the applications are local and the only interaction mechanisms for which they are written are the basic keyboard and mouse. Multiplatform applications are very specifics and represent a few percent of all the applications. In order to get more powerful applications, there is a need for more development around multiplatform, multiuser and multimodal. Applications such as office automation and drawing application are developed for a single user and a single platform [7].

Starting concepts

The main concepts used in the thesis are:

- A *device* is a single physical unit such as a computer, a mobile phone or a complex interaction platform.
- A *user interface* is the set of graphical components of an application.
- A *user* is a concept of a human person interacting with the system.
- A *context of use* describes the environment and the material in which he is. A context of use C is composed by a platform P, a user U and an environment E.
- The *platform* is the software architecture (such as an operating system) provided to the user to interact with the device.

The *context of use* considered in the thesis may be more complex than one single platform, user and environment. Depending where and when the user is accomplishing the tasks, she is evolving in an *environment*. For example, he can be at work, at home or traveling. Even the easiest tasks can become difficult if the environment is not appropriate.

THESIS

Two dimensions: time and space. An important aspect of the distribution is the way users interact with the application. Users may be working at the same time in a competitive way or cooperating together to increase the effectiveness of the work. There can be different users working on the same application but at different time. Multiuser can be sequential or concurrent on a single computer or on several computers. While some users are working on the same computer, other users may interact with them from other computers wherever they are.

Concerns. we propose a description of the distribution domain, a toolkit for creating DUIs, a catalog of distribution primitives and concepts of distribution graphs and scenarios. It allows applications to be distributed across multiple devices, multiple screens and for multiple users. The concerns that this thesis try to address are [2,5,6,7,8,9]:

- *Concern #1. Development of distributed user interfaces:* the development of DUI is not supported by usual tools. Most of the time, developers have to manage the development in their own way. A lot of time is spent on the development of DUIs mostly the distributed aspects.
- *Concern #2. Support for distribution of user interfaces at running time:* existing DUIs are limited to predefined applications and domains of application which lead to little support for the various possibilities of distribution.
- *Concern #3. Support for multi-user collaboration:* multi-user applications are developed in different ways depending on the use and domain of application. The lack of a common base is slowing down the development.
- *Concern #4. Execution control in the distributed environment:* the control of the distribution is a real problem when managing DUI systems [4]. The limitations are high especially with a fixed level of granularity. Some systems can replicate windows while not being able to replicate widgets. Others can manipulate widgets one at a time but no group of widgets.
- *Concern #5. Network transparency:* The distribution of the UIs has to be network transparent in the sense that the user should not have to worry about network details such as IP address, user network and network settings.
- *Concern #6. Lack of description of the distributed domain and models:* The researches around multi-user applications and distributed user interfaces are very specifics to the needs of the developers and are almost never documented or badly documented.

Model-based Approach. The main contribution we bring to DUI is a model-based approach for designing distributed user interfaces (DUIs), i.e. graphical user interfaces that are distributed along one or many of the following dimensions: end user, display device, computing platform, and physical environment. The three pillars of this model-based approach are: (i) a Concrete User Interface model for DUIs incorporating the distribution dimensions and able to express in a XML-compliant format any DUI element until the granularity of an individual DUI element is reached, (ii) a specification language for DUI distribution primitives that have been defined in a user interface toolkit, and (iii), a step-wise method for modeling a DUI based several concepts we introduce in the thesis. The model-based approach for DUIs consists of conducting the following steps:

1. Build a cluster model of the platforms.
2. Build a CUI model for each platform.
3. Assemble models in the distribution scene.
4. Write a distribution scenario based on distribution primitives.
5. Develop the distribution scenario

Underlying models. The Concrete User Interface (CUI) model is independent of any computing platform and implementation language. A CUI model is hereby defined as recursive hierarchy of containers (e.g., windows, tabbed dialog boxes, group boxes) and individual widgets (e.g., check boxes, push buttons, list boxes, etc.). Widgets are laid out either horizontally or vertically. Each widget is defined as a vector $W=(P_i, V_i)$ where P_i denotes the ith property of the widget and V_i denotes the value of this property (e.g., the background color of a push button is grey). A selector consists of a selection of UI element types of a particular CUI model that satisfy a first-order predicate logical formula. In this way, a template is applied for a selector instead of a (potentially long) sequence of widgets as:

1. *Universal Selector*: applies the template to all UI elements belonging to a particular CUI, whatever they are.

2. *Element Type Selector*: applies the template to all UI elements belonging to a particular CUI which correspond to the selector's type (e.g., all containers).
3. *Class Selector*: applies the template to all UI elements belonging to a particular CUI.
4. *Identifier Selector*: applies the template to only one UI element belonging to a particular CUI: the one whose id property matches the string contained in the parameter.

We also introduce a platform model. The UI distribution concerns the repartition of one or many UI elements from one or many DUIs in order to support one or many users to carry out one or many tasks on one or many domains in one or many contexts of use, each context of use consisting of users, platforms, and environments. Therefore, the context of use is hereby considered as a cluster of individual components. In order to represent this cluster, we adopted the *Delivery Context Ontology* (DCO) standardized by W3C (www.w3.org/TR/dcontology), a subset of which in Fig. 1.

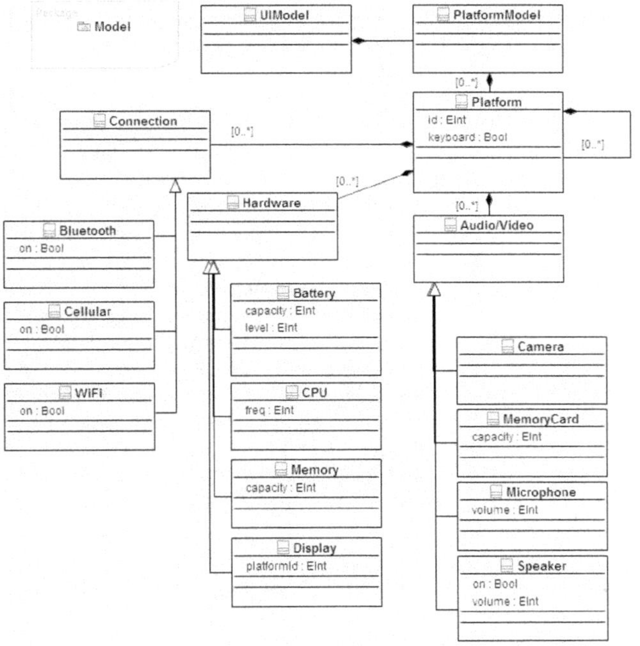

Figure 1. The platform model used for DUI.

According to DCO, a platform model is divided into one or many platforms. For example, a laptop itself consists of three platforms: the laptop, the display and the keyboard. Each platform has three main categories of components: a *connection* category representing the input and output connections to other devices or to the internet, the *hardware* category that defines the main components such as the CPU, the memory and if the platform has a display or not, and any component linked to the medias (e.g., audio and video). Based on this, a *cluster* is defined by a graph $G=(N_j,R_j)$ which is a set of nodes N_j connected together through R_j relationships. Each *node* consists of a DCO-compliant platform model representing any kind of device or components able to interact with the system (e.g., computers, displays, keyboards and mice are representative examples). Each relationship represents a communication channel (e.g., a Wi-Fi network or a Bluetooth connection) between nodes. Fig. 2a denotes a cluster composed of three platforms: a laptop connected to a flat monitor and a mobile phone. In order to properly express DUIs, to operate them and to reason on them, it is required to know at time what DUI is residing on which platform of the cluster. For this purpose, we hereby define a *distribution scene* as a cluster in which each node is associated to a CUI model, all CUI models connected to each other by a graph (Fig. 2b). Any cluster node contains a reference to a particular CUI model that could evolve over time. Consequently, a distribution scene holds a two-layer structure: (1) a cluster representing the physical setup of interaction elements and devices and (2) an associated graph of CUI models attached to any element in this cluster that supports some interaction. Not all platforms run a UI at any-time. To depict this, full circles in Fig. 2a represent that no DUI exist for those two platforms at some point (e.g., the starting time). The dashed circle around the laptop means that it holds a DUI. All models manipulated in this approach have their semantics defined in a UML V2.0 class diagram, a concrete syntax defined via a EBNF, and their stylistics defined.

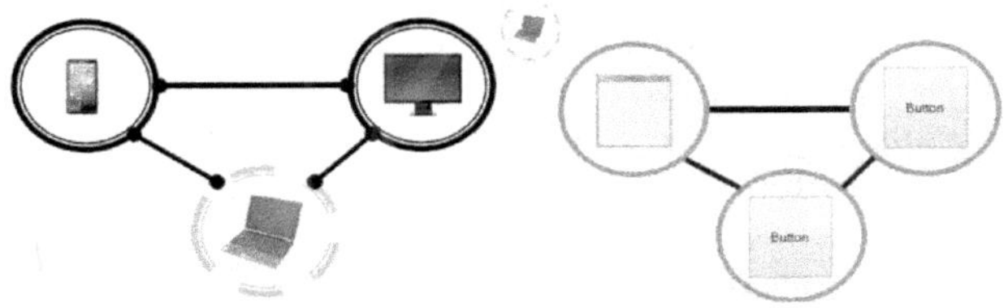

Figure 2. A distribution scene made up of: a cluster of three platforms (a) and an associated graph of CUI models (b).

Catalog of distribution primitives. A distribution primitive consists of a basic operation in order to support distribution of any element of the CUI model of the cluster with respect to multiple devices/displays. The syntax of these distribution primitives is defined through an Extended Backus Naur Form (EBNF) grammar. Instances of distribution primitives are called by *statements*. The definitions of an operation, a source, a target, a selector and some other ones are defined in Fig. 3 (excerpt only). For instance, COPY button_1 TO button_2 ON shared_display means that button_1 is copied on shared_display and identify it as button_2. In this example, button_2 inherits everything from button_1, both presentation and behavior. This may induce some prioritization aspects since two push buttons could trigger the same function for instance. We are now working on extending these primitives in order to transfer partial/total presentation and/or behavior. For instance, button_2 could inherit the presentation from button-1, but its behavior will be expanded in order to address multi-user aspects. Or vice versa: button_2 could inherit the behavior of button_1, but its presentation will be changed. Different types of behavior inheritances are under study depending on which interaction status should be preserved.

```
statement = operation , white_space , source , white_space , "TO" ,
white_space , target ;
operation = "SET" | "DISPLAY" | "UNDISPLAY" | "COPY" |
"MOVE" | "REPLACE" | "TRANSFORM" | "MERGE" |
"SWITCH" | "SEPARATE" | "DISTRIBUTE";
source = selector ;
target = displays | selector , white_space , "ON" ,
white_space , displays ;
displays = display_platform , { "," , display_platform}
display_platform = display , [ white_space , "OF" ,
white_space , platform] ; selector = identifier , { "," , identifier
} | universal ;
display = identifier ; platform = identifier ;
```

Figure 3. EBNF grammar for distribution primitives.

Toolkit for Distribution Primitives. A toolkit is being developed upon the aforementioned model-based approach in order to provide the developer with the distribution primitives of the catalog. It creates application with UI separated in two-parts: the proxy and the rendering. The proxy is represented as a separate part of the application than the rendering. The first keeps the state of the application and ensures the core functionalities, while the second displays the user interface. Application supporting DUI allows the rendering to be distributed on other platforms while the proxy stays where the application has been created. The toolkit works in an environment supported by Microsoft Windows XP and up, Apple Mac OS X, Linux and Android. We are currently working on Apple iOS. The applications created with this toolkit are multi-platform. Each graphical component is described as a record containing several keys and values. It ensures compatibility with XML because the keys/values become the name/value pairs of the XML.

Multiple meta-user interfaces. Any DUI based on the distribution primitives can be controlled by a meta-user interface [3] with the following interaction styles: command line interface, menu selection, drag and drop (partially), and programming language. Further investigation is needed in order to determine which interaction style is appropriate.

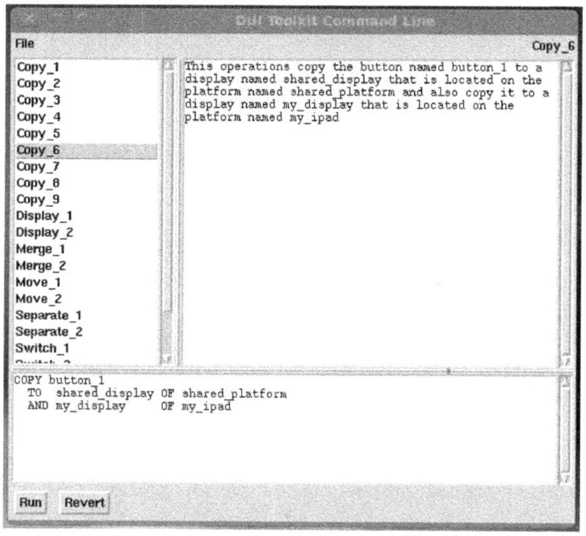

Figure 4. Command line and menu selection for distribution.

CONCLUSION AND FUTURE WORK

The very first step in order to come up with a full method for designing DUIs consists of investigating which models, languages, development approach, and supporting software could be defined and implemented. This is why distribution primitives have been defined prior to any other step. But it is not because a distribution primitive could be implemented in a more effective way than by hand that the resulting DUI is usable for the end user. Multiple interaction styles exist that could support the same distribution primitive. In order to become effective, a DUI resulting from the aforementioned model-based approach should be offered via different interaction styles that are appropriate for the end user and task. So far, the metaphors used to control the DUIs are limited to keyboard/mouse interactions. For this purpose, we are conducting an experiment that would determine what are the end user preferences for some interaction style for a distribution primitive. We would like to extend these interactions by adding touch and multi-touch gestures to enable the distribution primitives. We think that the more natural the DUIs will be presented to the public, the better it will be for users.

REFERENCES

1. Beale, R. and Edmonson, W. Multiple Carets, Multiple Screens and Multi-Tasking: New Behaviours with Multiple Computers. In *Proc. of HCI'2007*, British Computer Society.
2. Berglund, E. and Bång, M. Requirements for distributed user interface in ubiquitous computing networks. *In Proc. of Conf. on Mobile and Ubiquitous MultiMedia MUM'2002*
3. Coutaz, J. Meta-User Interfaces for Ambient Spaces. In *Proc. of TAMODIA '2006*. LNCS, Vol. 4385. Springer, pp. 1–15.
4. Coyette, A., Vanderdonckt, J. A Sketching Tool for Designing Anyuser, Anyplatform, Anywhere User Interfaces. In: Proc. of 10th IFIP TC 13 Int. Conf. on Human-Computer Interaction INTERACT'2005 (Rome, 12-16 September 2005). LNCS, Vol. 3585, Springer-Verlag, Berlin, 2005, pp. 550-564.
5. Luyten, K. and Coninx, K. Distributed User Interface Elements to support Smart Interaction Spaces. In *Proc. of the 7th IEEE Int. Symposium on Multimedia*, (2005), pp. 277-286.
6. Luyten, K., Van den Bergh, J., Vandervelpen, Ch., and Coninx, K. Designing distributed user interfaces for ambient intelligent environments using models and simulations. *Computer & Graphics. 30*, 5 (2006) 702-713.
7. Melchior, J., Grolaux, D., Vanderdonckt, J., and Van Roy, P. A toolkit for peer-to-peer distributed user interfaces: concepts, implementation, and applications. In: *Proc. of EICS'09* (Pittsburgh, July 15-17, 2009). ACM Press, NY (2009), pp. 69–78.
8. Qiu, X.F. and Graham, T.C.N. Flexible and efficient platform modeling for distributed interactive systems. In: (Pittsburgh, July 15-17, 2009). ACM Press, New York (2009) pp. 29-34.
9. Vandervelpen, Ch., Vanderhulst, G., Luyten, K., and Coninx, K. Light-Weight Distributed Web Interfaces: Preparing the Web for Heterogeneous Environments. In *Proc. of ICWE'2005*. Springer-Verlag, Berlin (2005), pp. 197-202.
10. Vanderdonckt, J. Distributed User Interfaces: How to Distribute User Interface Elements across Users, Platforms, and Environments. In: *Proc. of XIth Congreso Internacional de Interacción Persona-Ordenador Interacción'2010* (Valencia, 7-10 September 2010). AIPO, Valencia (2010), pp. 3–14.

A Computational Framework for Multi-Dimensional Context-aware Adaptation

Vivian Genaro Motti

Université catholique de Louvain, Louvain School of Management
Louvain Interaction Laboratory, Place des Doyens, 1 – B-1348 Louvain-la-Neuve (Belgium)
vivian.genaromotti@uclouvain.be

ABSTRACT

Most interactive applications often assume a pre-defined context of use of an able-bodied user, a desktop platform, in a stable environment. In contrast, users compose a heterogeneous group, interacting via different means and devices in varied environments; which requires, thus, context-aware adaptation. Adaptation has been largely investigated, but the studies are often constrained to one context dimension at a time: user or platform or environment. To address this issue and to bridge the gap between high-level adaptation goals and implementation of adaptation, this research aims at developing a computational framework for user interface adaptation based on distinct dimensions and contexts of use. This framework consists of four main contributions: a design space to characterize context-aware adaptation of user interface, a reference framework to classify adaptation techniques for distinct scenarios, an ontology of adaptation techniques based on a 3-level Adaptation Rules, and an interpreter of adaptation rules to address techniques defined in the design space and reference framework.

Author Keywords

Adaptation, context awareness

ACM Classification Keywords

D.2.2 [**Software Engineering**]: User interfaces. H.1.2 [**Information Systems**]: Human factors. H.5.1 [**Information Interfaces and Presentation**]: Multimedia Information Systems. H5.2 [**Information interfaces and presentation**]: User Interfaces – *User-centered design*.

General Terms

Human Factors, Design

INTRODUCTION

Adaptation transforms different aspects of the systems, regarding the needs, wishes and preferences of users [2]. An application can also be adapted concerning its context information, such as user profile, platform and environment [4]. The goal of adaptive applications is to improve the interaction providing users proper changes, according to their context. Context involves any information relevant to characterize an entity, typically related to user profiles, states, locations, and the technological resources [5].

EICS'11, June 13–16, 2011, Pisa, Italy.

Adaptation can be automatic, manual or combine approaches (mixed-initiative), but it must always take into account the context. Different dimensions in an application can be subject to adaptation, and also in different levels. Previous works grouped the dimensions in: navigation, presentation and content [13], and methods and techniques used in this domain were described [10]. Most studies of adaptation focuses in specific contexts, little attention is devoted to multi-dimensional context-aware adaptation in a unified and consistent way. Current applications rely on a pre-defined context, of an able-bodied user, in a stable environment, with a desktop PC. Actually, nowadays, users, not only compose a significantly heterogeneous group, but also interact via different means and using different devices. Adaptation started to be investigated in the 90's and since then new devices, technologies, applications and approaches arose, evolved and became more popular, e.g., idTVs, RIAs, AJAX and MDE. This thesis aims to develop a framework considering in a structured and systematic way both context information and adaptation dimensions. The main goal is to analyze current adaptation techniques to propose a framework that eases the development of adaptive applications. The specific goals include: a systematic review of the scientific literature to organize adaptation techniques, the definition of a taxonomy to describe context-information, a framework to support the development of adaptive applications, and the validation and evaluation of the developed methods with case studies.

In this paper, Section 2 presents the motivations, Section 3 describes related work, Section 4 explains the contributions of this research and Section 5 presents the final remarks.

MAIN MOTIVATIONS

Many applications domains benefit of context-aware adaptation, like: education (tele-teaching) [2], entertainment (museums) [13], geography (for map locations) [1], and electronic commerce [11]. This is a good motivation to advance the investigation of methodologies that support the implementation of adaptive and adaptable applications. Besides, the offer of new technologies increases, which makes a consistent methodology for user interface adaptation each day more necessary. Brusilovsky [3] stated that for the Future Internet users will be involved in multiple, dynamic and on-demand contexts of use, requiring high adaptation levels. These methodologies should be grounded on a conceptual modeling approach of the adaptation process of user interfaces leading to a computational framework based on these concerns.

RELATED WORK

This thesis aims to develop a computational framework for adaptation considering methods and techniques previously created; this Section summarizes efforts in this domain. As it is a result of an initial literature review, the coverage of related works is still limited. The execution of a Systematic Review, planned for the first phase of the project, intends to gather more information relevant in this domain.

Dieterich classified adaptation configurations and techniques according to four stages for adaptation [6]: *initiative*, *proposal*, *decision* and *execution*. This taxonomy does not cover the full adaptation life cycle (excluding, for instance, the feedback after adaptation) and it only considers that two entities can be responsible for the four stages, i.e. the user or the system (although a third party can be involved or any combination of these entities).

Brusilovsky [2,3] made an extensive effort to classify and structure adaptation techniques, but not explicitly based on context of use (e.g. supporting user, platform, and environment). The adaptation was analyzed concerning *what* (adaptation of what with respect to what), but the context of use was not fully exploited. Moreover, other dimensions of adaptation (e.g., when, how, with which constraints) were not extensively researched, thus raising the need for a multi-dimensional framework for adaptation.

W3C (http://www.w3.org/TR/di-atdi/) documented adaptation techniques, but mainly concerning the platform (device and web browser). This dimension is an important constraint for adaptation, but it is not the only one. The structure of the document of techniques types could be expanded with refined categories, and linked to current techniques.

The Project MyMobileWeb [12] focused also in the creation of an adaptation framework, but for the domain of mobile web applications to multiple handsets and web browsers. Other modalities and platforms were not considered.

The research conducted in context-aware adaptation is often restricted to one dimension. Although each dimension is important and has been investigated, different dimensions influence each other and must be considered integrally. There is a lack of general techniques, methods and tools for adaptation [11], thus the generated systems are inflexible and their adaptation knowledge is hard to reuse. This thesis aims to investigate context-aware adaptation globally, gathering and considering possible dimensions and levels in a unified and consistent way.

A COMPUTATIONAL FRAMEWORK

Shortcomings and Requirements

An initial analysis of the literature revealed shortcomings in the domain of context-aware adaptation. Some of them receive special attention in this thesis; they consist in limitations in current approaches:

1. The context information is usually constrained to one or two dimensions (either user or platform, for instance);
2. The technological space is limited;
3. The methodologies are not extensible or out of date;
4. Current approaches are not unified and consistent (e.g., different names were associated to the same technique);
5. Current approaches do not support the whole development life-cycle.

The concerns and shortcomings observed for context-aware adaptation delineate the problem space of this project. They lead to conclude requirements and improvements in this domain, which consider different dimensions and state that:

1. The information context must be considered broadly;
2. All possible technological spaces must be considered;
3. The methods must be extensible (allowing update);
4. The techniques must be consistent;
5. Methodologies must support adaptation in the entire life-cycle of development (considering, for instance, the feedback from the user to (re)adapt the application).

The methodology presented in the next subsection intends to fulfill these requirements and tackle the shortcomings.

Methodology

In a *first step*, literature is extensively reviewed to gather and analyze adaptation studies. The goal is to identify the state-of-the-art of context information, dimensions, methods and techniques for adaptation. A **Systematic Review** supports and formalizes these tasks. In this review, an initial question is defined, and then the answer is searched with a systematic analysis of documents that report related works. The goal is to gather the state-of-the-art in a specific topic, trends and gaps [8]. Systematic Reviews are time-consuming and require significant efforts to be conducted, however, it is apparently the most appropriate technique in this case, in which many documents need to be analyzed and consistently synthesized to obtain relevant information.

In a *second step* the context-aware adaptation framework will be created based on the results of the systematic review. It includes four methods: a Taxonomy, a Design Space, a Reference Framework, and an Ontology.

The **Taxonomy** lists context information relevant for adaptation concerning user, platform and environment, and organizes it in domains. Figure 1 illustrates a sample of context information of the user. The **Context-aware Design Space** (CADS) identifies design dimensions and levels relevant to accommodate different requirements and scenarios (Figure 2). The CADS supports the whole adaptation life cycle allowing each step being performed by the user, the system, a third party or any combination of them. The CADS addresses 3 virtues of such a design space: *descriptive* to consistently describe an adaptation dimension, *comparative* to identify similarities and differences between two or more applications, and *exploratory* to identify underexplored aspects. A **Context-Adaptation Reference Framework** (CARF) defines adaptation related to the context of use based on the Cameleon Reference Framework (CRF) [4], where the context of use is distributed into user, platform, and environment [16], which are in turn described through an individual model. Each model is based on traditional contextual properties and normative properties, e.g. from W3C Delivery Context Ontology (DCO).

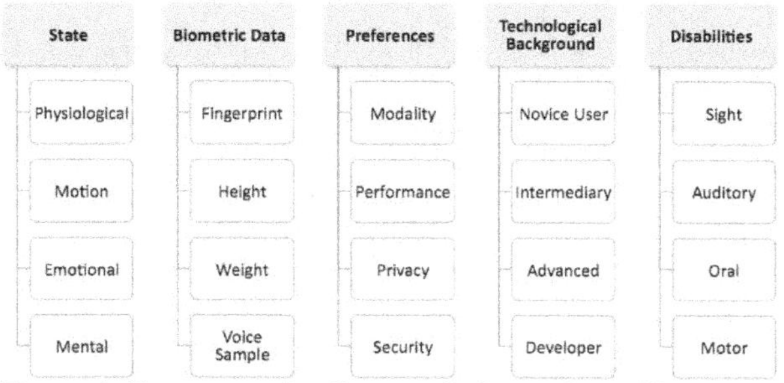

Figure 1. Taxonomy for Context-Information – User example.

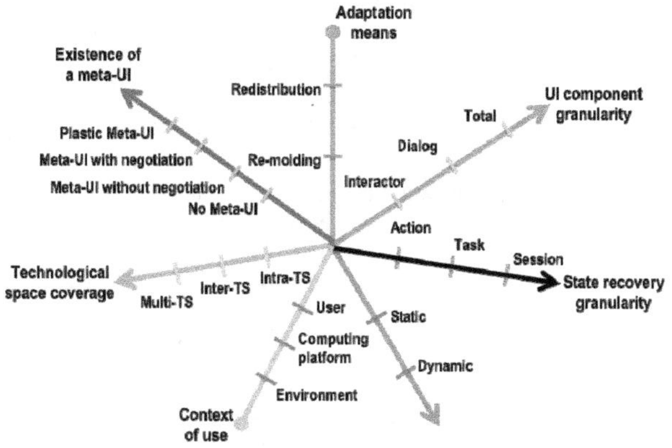

Figure 2. A Context-Aware Design Space composed by 7 dimensions of an application that are related to adaptation.

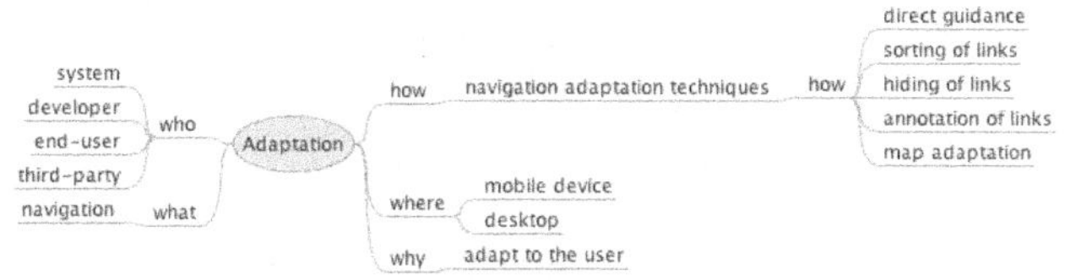

Figure 3. A Context-aware Reference Framework for navigation adaptation, techniques defined by Koch (2000).

Figure 3 exemplifies a CARF for navigation with 5 techniques. A website was created to organize techniques, systematically (with the use of a description template). This template contains 11 information fields, for each technique: the name, description, references, rationale, example, context, advantages, disadvantages, a code sample (e.g. an algorithm), a picture and additional comments. The template can be seen in **Table 1** that details the resizing of text content. The template is being filled for all the techniques gathered with the Systematic Review. The content will be iteratively refined to keep it consistent (e.g. identifying and associating alternative names for identical techniques). The adoption of a well-defined methodology permits constant updates (once new techniques may rise), assuring extensibility. An **Ontology** is a formal and explicit specification of shared concepts [7]. It provides semantic description, classification and relationships among different concerns involved in advanced adaptation logic. It will be the main formalism to support and represent adaptation knowledge.

The computational framework produced will be used during the *third step* to compose adaptation rules based in context information, adaptation dimensions, levels and adaptation techniques. User studies are planned to identify their preferences and to obtain their feedback. An adaptation rule can be considered as *first-order rule* (e.g., any rule for adapting a UI to its context of use such as R1="replace a radio box by a drop-down list if platform is mobile" or R2="replace a radio box with an edit field with codes if platform is mobile with limited entries"), *second-order rule* (e.g., a second-order adaptation rule is a rule that govern other first-order adaptation rules – such as "prefer R1, then R2"), or *third-order rule* (i.e., all adaptation strategies that promote or demote sets of second-order rules, such as "reverse the order of "prefer R1, then R2" if the user is expert") with different adaptation strategies depending on the context of use expressed in a more structured and intelligent way (e.g., by factoring out common parts). These rules can be examined by a parser to select rules proper for specific situations defined along the axes of the CADS. An evolution model to capture the dynamic aspects of context changes over time and space is also planned. The ultimate goal is a system that learns from the adaptations according to designers and end-users. Machine learning techniques, such as *Markov Chain Decision Process*, *Markov Models depending on Features*, *Bayesian Networks*, and *Cross-Entropy Methods* seemed at a first moment to support correctly the automatic and dynamic adaptation in user interfaces. Figure 4 illustrates the enlargement of the size of a push button when the cursor is hovering it in order to speed up the selection and to increase the legibility of the label based on animation techniques [15].

Name	Font Resize
Reference	http://www.w3schools.com/css/tryit.asp?filename=trycss_font-size_px
Description	Change the font size according to the context.
Rationale	Given a text content, an adaptation rule is applied in order to change the text size, increasing or decreasing it.
Example	A visually impaired user accesses a news portal but the font size is inappropriate for reading. The font size can be increased, allowing the user to read the text.
Context	User with visual impairments, small, far screens, content in small sizes.
Advantages	The readability of the text will become possible or it will be improved.
Disadvantag-es	The flow of the content may change, parts of the text may be hidden, scrolling may be required, the quality of the content may decrease (according to its resolution).
Sample (CSS)	`h1 {font-size:40px;}` `h2 {font-size:30px;}` `p {font-size:14px;}`
Picture	**This is heading 1** **This is heading 2** This is a paragraph.
Comments	The results of the adaptation must be evaluated once the information flow or content distribution may be affected.

Table 1. Template for Adaptation Techniques - Text resize example.

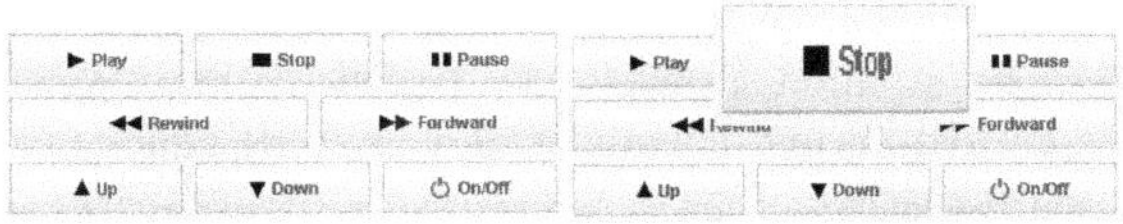

Figure 4. Enlarging the push buttons in a small screen.

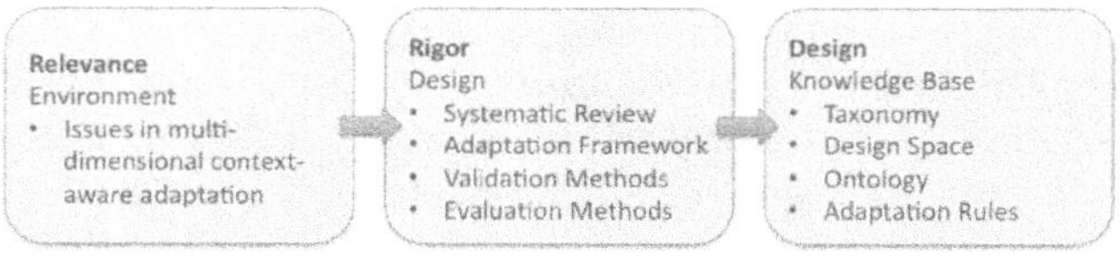

Figure 5. The environment defines the problem and research opportunities; the design artifact and process defines the methodology; and the knowledge base is the research result.

In a *fourth step* case studies for different use scenarios will be used to validate the proposal and evaluate its applicability. Proper evaluation methods will be defined and applied to identify usability issues according to end-users. Possible evaluation methods are *Cognitive Walkthrough*, *Heuristics*, *Questionnaires* and *Interviews*. The case studies will consider different scenarios e.g.: visually impaired users, mobile phones, noisy environments. Varied dimension levels will be combined, for: devices (a mobile phone, an extra-screen), user profiles (children, color-blind users) and environments (driving a car, watching television). Users will also be involved in early stages of the project, in order to obtain their feedback iteratively.

In this project, reference models and meta-models that define different abstraction layers for UI will be considered. Model-Driven Engineering (MDE) techniques may support the definition of transformation rules and the different models. The organization of the design phase in models may help to reduce the gap between the requirements and the implementation. Besides, it may help to coordinate the project efforts, by dividing it in models of different abstraction levels and by mapping the transformation of them [14].

Hevner [8] suggests the use of cycles for understanding, executing and evaluating IS research. In this sense, three activities cycles are considered (Figure 5): *relevance*, *rigor* and *design*. These cycles structure the methodology of the project in (i) *environment*, (ii) *design*, (iii) *knowledge base*.

FINAL REMARKS

It is a challenge to identify all context information relevant for multi-dimensional adaptation. For instance, optimizing adaptation with respect to one dimension may deteriorate the quality with respect to another dimension. Sometimes, the final result is not necessarily better than the initial user interface. Consequently, it is even more challenging to consider this information providing a high usability level and transparency. The excess of adaptation can confuse users, get them lost during the interaction and cause cognitive overloading [13]. During this thesis, iterative evaluations with end-users are planned to handle these issues. The adoption of a scientific and systematic methodology will aid the fulfillment of the requirements identified with the analysis of shortcomings in the domain of context-aware adaptation. Previous works are limited to specific adaptation dimensions. This proposal represents an attempt to unify in a solution all possible contexts of information, as well as adaptation dimensions and levels, by identifying techniques and applying adaptation for different scenarios.

REFERENCES

1. Arhippainen, L., Rantakokko, T. and Tahti, M. Navigation with an Adaptive Mobile Map-Application: User Experiences of Gesture- and Context-Sensitiveness. UCS. (2004), Tokyo, Japan.
2. Brusilovsky, P. Adaptive and Intelligent Technologies for Web-based Education. In: Special Issue on Intelligent Systems and Teleteaching, *Künstliche Intelligenz*, 4, (1999), 19–25.
3. Brusilovsky, P., Kobsa, A., and Nejdl, W. The Adaptive Web, Methods and Strategies of Web Personalization. Springer
4. Calvary, G., Coutaz, J., Thevenin, D., Limbourg, Q., Bouillon, L., Vanderdonckt, J., A Unifying Reference Framework for Multi-Target User Interfaces. *Interacting with Computers*, 15, 3 (2003), 289–308.
5. Dey, A. K. and Abowd, G. D. CybreMinder: A Context-Aware System for Supporting Reminders. In *Proc. of HUC'1999*. Lecture Notes in Computer Science, Vol. 1707, Springer-Verlag, Berlin (1999), pp. 172–186.
6. Dieterich, H., Malinowski, U., Kuhme, T., and Schneider-Hufschmidt, M. State of the art in adaptive user interfaces. In: Schneider-Hufschmidt, M., Kuhme, T., Malinowski, U. (Eds.), *Adaptive User Interfaces Principles and Practice*. Elsevier Science Publishers B.V., Amsterdam (1993), pp. 13–48.
7. Gruber, T. A Translation Approach to Portable Ontology Specifications. *Knowledge Acquisition*, 5, 199–220.
8. Hevner, A.R., A Three Cycle View of Design Science Research. *Scandinavian Journal of Information Systems* 19, 2, Article 4 (2007)
9. Kitchenham, B. Procedures for performing systematic reviews. Technical Report, Keele University and NICTA. (2004)
10. Koch, N. P. Software Engineering for Adaptive Hypermedia Systems: Reference Model, Modeling Techniques and Development Process. PhD thesis. Ludwig Maximilians University, Munich (2000)
11. López-Jaquero, V., Vanderdonckt, J., Montero, F. and González, P., Towards an Extended Model of User Interface Adaptation: the ISATINE framework, In *Proc. of Engineering Interactive Systems EIS'2007*. Lecture Notes in Computer Science, Vol. 4940, Springer-Verlag, Berlin (2008), pp. 374-392.
12. MyMobileWeb, open source software platform that simplifies the development of top- quality mobile web applications and portals, providing an advanced content & application adaptation environment. http://mymobileweb.morfeo-project.org/
13. Paterno, F.; Mancini, C. Designing Web Interfaces Adaptable to Different Types of Use. In *Proc. Workshop Museums and the Web*.
14. Vanderdonckt, J., A MDA-Compliant Environment for Developing User Interfaces of Information Systems, In *Proc of CAiSE'05*, LNCS, Vol. 3520, Springer-Verlag (2005), 16–31.
15. Vanderdonckt, J. and Gillo, X. Visual Techniques for Traditional and Multimedia Layouts. In *Proc. of 2nd ACM Workshop on Advanced Visual Interfaces AVI'94* (Bari, 1-4 June 1994), ACM Press, New York (1994), pp. 95–104.
16. Vanderdonckt, J. Distributed User Interfaces: How to Distribute User Interface Elements across Users, Platforms, and Environments. In: *Proc. of XIth Congreso Internacional de Interacción Persona-Ordenador Interacción'2010* (Valencia, 7-10 September 2010). AIPO, Valencia (2010), pp. 3–14.

Modeling Animations for Dependable Interactive Applications

Thomas Mirlacher
IRIT-ICS, Université Paul Sabatier
118, avenue de Narbonne, 31062 Toulouse Cedex 9, France
thomas.mirlacher@irit.fr

ABSTRACT

While today most parts of a graphical user interface are static, animations are increasingly used. This increase of use can be attributed to the fact that CPU resources remain available after the system's main functions are performed. Additionally, animations have been demonstrated useful to support users in their understanding of the user interface's behavior and evolution. However, adding animation significantly increases specification and implementation complexity.

This paper elaborates on a model-based approach to describe animations in a complete and unambiguous way, while keeping the complexity low. Such models can then be exploited to predict the impact of an animation on system performance, users' performance and experience.

Author Keywords

User interfaces, Animation, Model

ACM Classifications

H1.2 Models and Principals: User/Machine Systems

General Terms

Design, Reliabilty, Verification

INTRODUCTION

Animations are increasingly applied in graphical user interfaces (GUI) for different purposes. The increase of use can be attributed to the fact that CPU resources remain available after the system's main functions are performed. Purposes of use can be: education [5,22], representation of life-like behavior on simulated objects such as avatar faces [17] or clothes [12], to support understanding of dynamic systems (e.g. programs) [10,20] and for GUIs [1].

Using animations can decrease cognitive load [6,8], as it visually supports understanding the system's evolution from the current state to the next one. With animations, the user does not have to remember a state of the system and find the difference to the new state. Additionally, with animations, changes are illustrated in a natural, fluid, step-by-step way.

While animations might increase usability, they also increase the complexity of the software and therefore the probability of occurrence of faulty or undesired behavior. The time-based nature of animations makes them hard to specify and hard to assess their detailed behavior prior to implementation. In addition, their close relationship with cognitive and perceptive processes of the users makes them hard to design [19] and evaluate [5]. While this is a known issue in various fields of interactive systems, it raises severe concerns if such animations are to be designed and deployed in the context of safety critical interactive systems such as interactive aircraft cockpits.

This doctoral consortium submission describes a PhD subject and its current development, describing animations in a complete and unambiguous way. We propose the use and the extension of a formal description technique in order to cope with animations in a systematic way. Furthermore, we present how this contribution can support other aspects such as analysis of animations, prediction of behavior and performance prior to implementation.

THE PROBLEM

GUIs today are mostly based on a series of static frames changing the display to a different state when specific events are received. Usually, these events are produced via physical actions of the users through an input device or internal state changes of a system. At the output level, these changes appear abrupt and often unexpected, surprising the user and forcing her to mentally step away from the task in order to grasp what is happening in the interface itself. An example is the opening of a new window on a screen following the double click on an application icon. The user might be confused if the window appears at an unexpected place on the screen or far away from the icon position (Figure 1).

Figure 1 A new window is opened, supported by an animation. After the user double-clicks on an icon, the window is animated, so it seems it appears from the icon.

When a user is not able to visually track the progress of changes in a user interface, the causality between the previous and new state is not immediately clear, and the mental load - to figure out what just happened - increases.

Animations might help (if well designed and implemented) to visually track changes, by providing a natural, smooth transition to a new state. They also provide answers for the following problems and questions, which usually arise when interacting with a GUI:

- How do the current objects on the screen relate to the objects, which were displayed just a moment ago?
- Do these objects represent the same objects, or have they been replaced by completely different ones?
- What changes are related to the event triggered by the user's actions and which changes are incidental [3]?

To support the user in the interpretation on what has happened when the screen changes state, the system needs to prepare the user with an expectation for the changes to come. For non-animated interfaces, this expectation can only come with experience, because the interface itself is not conveying information and hints what will happen, what is happening, or what has happened.

Chang and Ungar [6] as well as Thomas and Calder [18] build the case for GUIs using animation effects to prepare the user for coming transitions, as well as to use these effects for accenting what has happened. They argue that animations used in user interfaces can support the user in understanding and preparing for a transition between two different states.

What is Animation?

Animation is the illusion of movement created by displaying a series of changing pictures, or frames in rapid sequence [18]. This optical illusion of motion is caused by the phenomenon of persistence of vision. Each frame contains a small change, and if the frames are produced in a high enough frequency, the human visual system fills in the details and the illusion is complete.

At software level, the foundation of animation is to display multiple related graphical elements within a given period of time and at a given frequency. For computer animations, each frame is usually displayed for no longer than 24ms. Each frame displays a change in the user interface, one step at a time. This gradually changing display supports the user to grasp the changes more easily and naturally than a sudden change of the whole screen.

Today, tools for defining animations for GUIs are scarce. Aside from the tools mainly applied for web application development (e.g. flash), animations are defined in a programmatic way. Not every animation designer can write code, define specifications or build a model, so using a ruler and stopwatch to gather information from a designed animation by the developer for the final implementation is not an uncommon approach.

Constraints for designing animations

There are additional properties to be taken into account in order to make it possible to embed animations in dependable interactive systems:

- Analyze how interactive applications designers currently design animations. Presently, mockups are practical but they only convey a small amount of the complexity of animations [7], leaving a huge portion of the design to the implementation level.
- Provide a way to describe animation at a higher abstraction level making it possible to describe states and state changes as well as rendering of these states and states changes on the GUI.
- Describe animation independently from the implementation language, so that peculiarities don't jeopardize the migration to different exploitation platforms. This is very important for our PhD as we target both home entertainment systems (such as iTV [4,13]) but also command and control systems (such as Unmanned Aerial Vehicles workstations).
- Deal explicitly with quantitative temporal aspects as, even though usually triggered by users, they then evolve according to time.
- Handle performance aspects by providing alternatives. Indeed, even if everything would be specified correctly, things might go wrong. A system might reach the limit of its available processing power or available memory, ... thus loosing (due to contingency issues) the benefit of the animation. Therefore, a description of animations has to be designed for default operation as well as for a system exhibiting performance degradation.
- Analyze the animation description. Indeed, there is a need to verify properties (on the animation and on the interactive system as a whole), to be able to conduct performance evaluations and possibly to execute the description itself, in order to avoid implementation errors while going from the description to the actual code. This is particularly important when building applications for critical interactive systems.

Contributions from a model-based approach

Model-based approaches [21], and for some aspects formal description techniques would provide means for handling animations and related constraints (as listed above). Transforming and describing an animation with the help of a model allows one to precisely capture its requirements and describe all behavioral aspects including the connection to the rendering on the UI. An example of such approach can be found in [7].

Some modeling techniques allow the prediction of the performance required in terms of time, CPU cycles, and presentation. It also helps to build more reliable interactions, with respect to: graceful degradation when performance limits are reached and switching models when required (for instance through reconfigurations [14]).

If an adequate formal description technique is used, specifying, simulating and verifying an animation will allow one to produce dependable implementations of animated user interfaces, and will provide a tool for handling the added complexity in a systematic way (with respect to interactive software without animations).

One of the few notations able to handle concurrency, large state space and quantitative time are Petri nets. In addition to properties verification [9] they also allow designers to utilize performance evaluations on the models [11].

A specific dialect of Petri nets called ICOs [15] has already been proposed to describe the behavior of interactive systems. Our proposal is to build upon that formal description technique and extend it to additionally handle animations.

PHD PROGRAMME

For being able to define a complete model to describe animations in user interfaces, the following steps are planned:

Analyze common animations, so they can be broken down in several building blocks.

Translate those building blocks into the ICO notation. During this process, the notation needs to be extended to be powerful enough to express all the building blocks needed to model an animation.

Verify that we can capture user interface animation with the model, by describing example problems.

Optimize to ensure real-time execution of the model – so we can simulate and prototype the final system by using the model itself. Again, these would be extensions to the current runtime platform offered by PetShop [2]

Demonstrate the power of modeling through a description of an already existing GUI prototype for the iTV domain.

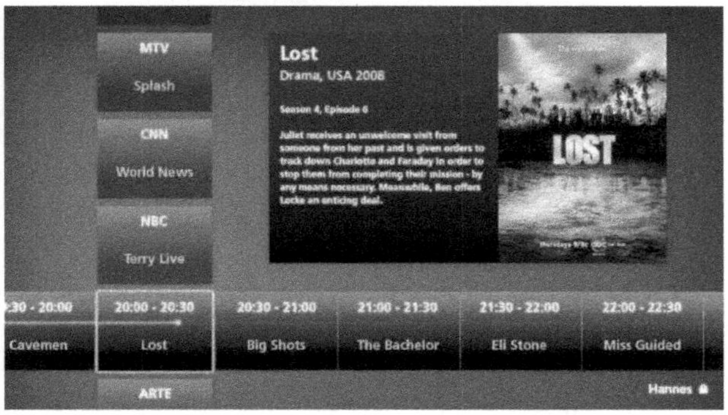

Figure 2 Animation in real-life user interfaces. In this case this screenshot is taken from a iTV prototype application.

Vocomedia (**Figure** 2) is a GUI developed for set-top boxes in the iTV domain. This means that in this domain certain restrictions in terms of processing power and graphics power apply. The vocomedia user interface prototype relies - amongst other things - on animations to support the user in the interaction in an environment prone with interruptions and distractions [16]. Upon display of the main menu, the vertical bar (**Figure** 2) is faded in, to gradually prepare the user for the new menu. After this vertical bar is fully shown, the horizontal bar moves in, to hint the user she can interact with this bar and move in a horizontal direction. Animations like this can be found throughout the whole GUI.

While we have developed the vocomedia application in a user-centered design approach, iterated with the support of usability testing, it became apparent that one of the constraints for a flexible design was the lack of a formal, implementation independent and easy to change definition of animations.

PROGRESS

Currently, based on deep insight into the vocomedia prototype GUI [13], we are analyzing the animations required for presenting a GUI in the iTV domain. Furthermore, we have identified possible underlying notations that will form the groundwork for developing a model defining animations.

We have also started to represent animations with the current ICO notation in order to identify obstacles that are either impossible or cumbersome to describe. This will end up is a set of requirements for either extension of the modeling power or inclusion of modeling primitives supporting the effective and efficient modeling of animations.

CONCLUSION

We decided to start with a notation based on Petri nets as this is one of the very few formalisms able to deal both with quantitative time as well as true concurrency and these two characteristics are required for describing animations. However, we might face usability and understandability issues with the notation, especially if used by designers with limited knowledge in state-based notations. The acceptability of the notation will be carefully studied and issues might be addressed by encapsulating the formalism within specific tools, allowing designers to build models in an indirect way.

Developing animated GUIs is the result of a multi-disciplinary team, and interaction designers need to be more embedded in this approach. The designer has to be trained on a more technical level and has to have a strong developer background.

We pursue the goal of defining a model-based approach for the defining interactive systems featuring animation. Indeed, modeling animations allows to automatically verify the animation and side effects on the performance of the whole system. It allows for graceful degradation in case the system performance is not enough, to sustain a default animation. Furthermore, modeling supports the definition of an animation independent of its final implementation.

ACKNOWLEDGEMENTS

This doctoral research is supervised by Prof. Philippe Palanque and Dr. Regina Bernhaupt.

REFERENCES

1. Baecker, R.M., Small, I., and Mander, R. Bringing icons to life. *Proceedings of the SIGCHI conference on Human factors in computing systems Reaching through technology - CHI '91*, Myers (1991), 1-6.
2. Bastide, R., Navarre, D., and Palanque, P. A model-based tool for interactive prototyping of highly interactive applications. *CHI 2002: Extended abstracts on Human factors in computing systems*, (2002), 516.
3. Baudisch, P., Cutrell, E., Robbins, D., et al. Drag-and-Pop and Drag-and-Pick: techniques for accessing remote screen content on touch- and pen-operated systems. *Interact 2003: Human-Computer Interaction*, (2003), 57-64.
4. Bernhaupt, R., Wilfinger, D., and Mirlacher, T. Individualizing the TV Experience: vocomedia - a Case Study from interactive TV. In *Mass Customization for Personalized Communication Environments: Integrating Human Factors*. IGI Global, 2009.
5. Byrne, M. Evaluating animations as student aids in learning computer algorithms. *Computers & Education 33*, 4 (1999), 253-278.
6. Chang, B.-W. and Ungar, D. Animation: from cartoons to the user interface. *Sun Microsystems, Inc. Mountain View, CA, USA*, March (1995), 1-18.
7. Chatty, S. Defining the Dynamic Behaviour of Animated Interfaces. *Proceedings of the IFIP conference on Engineering Human-Computer Interfaces (EHCI '92)*, (1992), 95.
8. Heer, J. and Robertson, G. Animated transitions in statistical data graphics. *IEEE transactions on visualization and computer graphics 13*, 6 (2007), 1240-7.
9. Jensen, K. *Coloured Petri Nets - Modelling and Validation of Concurrent Systems*. Springer, 2009.
10. Karavirta, V., Korhonen, A., Malmi, L., and Naps, T. A comprehensive taxonomy of algorithm animation languages. *Journal of Visual Languages & Computing 21*, 1 (2010), 1-22.
11. Marsan, M.A., Bobbio, A., and Donatelli, S. Petri Nets in Performance Analysis: an Introduction. In G. Rozenberg and W. Reisig, eds., *Lectures on Petri Nets I: Basic Models*. Springer Verlag, Berlin, 1998.
12. Meyer, M., Debunne, G., Desbrun, M., and Barr, A.H. Interactive animation of cloth-like objects in virtual reality. *The Journal of Visualization and Computer Animation 12*, 1 (2001), 1-12.
13. Mirlacher, T., Pirker, M., Bernhaupt, R., et al. Interactive Simplicity for iTV: Minimizing Keys for Navigating Content. *euroITV 2010*, (2010).
14. Navarre, D., Palanque, P., and Basnyat, S. A formal approach for user interaction reconfiguration of safety critical interactive systems. *Safety, Reliability, and Security*, (2008), 373-386.
15. Navarre, D., Palanque, P., Ladry, J.-F., and Barboni, E. ICOs: A Model-Based User Interface Description Technique dedicated to Interactive Systems Addressing Usability, Reliability and Scalability. *ACM Transactions on Computer-Human Interaction 16*, 4 (2009), 1-56.
16. Palanque, P., Winckler, M., Ladry, J.-F., Beek, M.H. ter, Faconti, G., and Massink, M. A formal approach supporting the comparative predictive assessment of the interruption-tolerance of interactive systems. *EICS 2009: Proceedings of the 1st ACM SIGCHI symposium on Engineering interactive computing systems*, ACM Press (2009), 211.
17. Radovan, M. and Pretorius, L. Facial Animation in a Nutshell : Past , Present and Future. *Proceedings of the 2006 annual research conference of the South African institute of computer scientists and information technologists on IT research in developing countries (SAICSIT '06)*, (2010), 71 -79.
18. Thomas, B.H. and Calder, P. Applying cartoon animation techniques to graphical user interfaces. *ACM Transactions on Computer-Human Interaction (TOCHI) 8*, 3 (2001), 198-222.
19. Thomas, B.H. and Calder, P. Supporting cartoon animation techniques in direct manipulation graphical user interfaces. *Information and Software Technology 47*, 5 (2005), 339-355.
20. Urquiza-Fuentes, J., Angel, J., Azquez-Iturbide, V.E.L., Rey, U., and Carlos, J. A Survey of Successful Evaluations of Program Visualization and Algorithm Animation Systems. *Computing 9*, 2 (2009), 1-21.
21. Vodislav, D. A visual programming model for user interface animation. *Proceedings. 1997 IEEE Symposium on Visual Languages (Cat. No.97TB100180)*, (1997), 344-351.
22. Wang, P.-Y. The Impact of Animation Interactivity on Novices ' Learning of Introductory Statistics. *Design*, 2010.

Identifying, Relating, and Evaluating Design Patterns for the Design of Software for Synchronous Collaboration

Claudia Iacob
University of Milan
Via Comelico, 39/41
Milan, Italy
iacob@dico.unimi.it

ABSTRACT

Many working environments require that geographically-distributed or co-located work group members work together - supported by software - in developing and refining one commonly shared resource in the same time. Hence, synchronous collaboration is common to various contexts and domains, examples being drawing, searching, text editing, and game solving. However, little work has been done in identifying design patterns for the design of systems for such collaboration. This line of research aims at identifying, relating and evaluating such design patterns for providing: a). a better understanding of the design processes of synchronous collaborative software, and b). a repository of knowledge comprising best practices in such design processes for practitioners.

Author Keywords

Design patterns, synchronous collaboration.

ACM Classification Keywords

D.2.10. Design: Methodologies.

General Terms

Design.

PROBLEM AND MOTIVATION

Many working environments require that geographically-distributed or co-located work group members work together in developing and refining one commonly shared resource in the same time. Several such examples are depicted in the literature. Based on interviews with teachers, librarians, and researchers, it is concluded in [3] that there are many situations in which "groups of people gather around a single computer to jointly search for information online". Synchronous collaborative drawing is common mainly to architectural design, graphic design, or education [14]. Moreover, the editing of documents, drawings, presentations and spreadsheets is often a collaborative activity [1]. Technology has simplified this type of collaboration, several developments being carried on today in the area of software which supports synchronous collaboration, targeting common activities such as searching, drawing, and text editing [1, 3, 14, 17].

Even so, little work has been done in identifying and documenting best practices and commonly met design considerations in the design of systems which support such collaboration. Design patterns provide a way of capturing and sharing knowledge related to design problems, being defined as proven solutions to recurring design problems [5]. In this sense, design patterns prove to be useful and valuable tools for documenting and sharing design experiences and decisions. Different authors proposed different templates for defining design patterns. These templates generally include the name of the design pattern, the description of the problem it addresses together with the forces (i.e. the consequences and secondary implications of the problem) that influence this problem, some examples of situations in which this problem can be met and a possible solution to tackle the problem [8].

In design, problems are not isolated: they refer to each other, smaller problems arising in the context of larger ones. Therefore, patterns are not isolated, but linked according to the relationships among the problems whose solution they document. These links relate design patterns together to form a pattern language [2], a shared repository of a finite number of problem-solution specifications.

This work aims to identify, relate, and evaluate a set of design patterns for the design of software systems which support people in performing collaboratively and synchronously activities such as drawing, text editing, searching, and game solving.

BACKGROUND AND RELATED WORK

The concept of design pattern was first introduced in the '70s by Alexander [2], who proposed a pattern language - defined as a collection of design patterns together with all the relationships that exist among them - for architectural design. Alexander conceived design patterns as multimedia documents to be used by architects: a) as knowledge and wisdom repositories about the solutions of often recurring urban design problems, b) as means of communication of the solutions among the architect communities and, c) as

EICS'11, June 13–16, 2011, Pisa, Italy.

communication means between architects and their clients in the design of urban spaces.

Alexander's approach had a wide impact in several domains, including software engineering [9] and Human-Computer Interaction (HCI) [5]. Software engineering applied design patterns for expressing Object-Oriented software design experience. Software engineering patterns address mainly professional programmers and are not intended for a general audience. Moreover, the collection of design patterns and the relationships among them are not complete enough to form a pattern language in the Alexandrian sense.

HCI designers adopted the design patterns and the design pattern language approach to document and describe "the reasons for design decisions and the experience from past projects, to create a corporate memory of design knowledge" [5].

In [12], a survey of 21 HCI pattern languages published between 1996 and 2007 shows that these collections target web user interface design, interactive exhibits, user interface related programming, hypermedia applications, or ubiquitous computing. A collection of patterns targeting the design of social interfaces is introduced in [7]. The focus of these patterns is on the design of systems which support social activities like: broadcasting and publishing, collecting data, rating, or collaborative editing. Moreover, several collections of patterns have been proposed for the design of groupware technology [13], and cross-culture collaboration [15].

Although the situations in which work group members work together being supported by software systems are common to various domains, little work has been done in identifying best practices in designing collaborative software applications. Examples are scarce: a collection of patterns for building communities in collaborative systems is introduced in [16], while [13] describes a set of patterns for shared object management.

RESEARCH GOALS AND METHOD

There are three research questions addressed by this work.

i). What design patterns can be identified in the design of software systems which support synchronous collaboration?

To answer this first question, I applied the design pattern mining method described in [10], following two phases. During the first phase, I conducted a series of design workshops in order to identify the recurring design issues designers would consider in the design of software applications for synchronous collaboration. 13 teams, consisting of professional designers (8%), graduate students in Computer Science (72%), and undergraduate students in Computer Science (20%), participated in such workshops. Each team was presented with a list of problems (all addressing synchronous collaboration and described below) and was encouraged to choose one problem. Having done that, they were asked to design the GUI and the interaction process for a software application to tackle the problem.

The design process of each team followed a set of steps and used several creative techniques such as scenario-based design [6], free associations, sketching, and mockup creation. Each team was observed by a facilitator and the participants were encouraged to externalize the design ideas, problems, concerns, solutions they might find useful, and any issue relevant to the design of the application. All the design issues discussed by the teams were collected, and for each issue its degree of recurrence was computed as the percentage in which the issue has been discussed throughout the workshops.

During the second phase, I analyzed a set of 20 software applications which support synchronous collaboration in order to identify those design issues considered in the implementation of concrete cases of applications and their degree of recurrence in the implementations analyzed. The analysis consisted in walking through a scenario for each application. The scenario covered all the features provided by the application and was tailored to each application in particular.

The design pattern mining method considers the design issues with the highest degree of recurrence in both the workshops' results and the software analysis results as candidates for being documented through design patterns. Both the design workshops and the software analysis targeted 4 domains for synchronous collaboration.

Collaborative drawing

The problem of collaborative drawing asked for the design of a software application which would allow the collaborative creation of one diagrammatic representation in real-time. Three teams (22% of the participants) worked on this problem during the workshops, and five software applications to support collaborative synchronous [14] drawing were analyzed.

Collaborative querying

The application for the collaborative querying had a concrete context of application: movie database querying. The requirements for this application asked that several users would be able to create through visual virtual tools a query on a database containing information about movies. The query would be run only after all the users who edit it would agree on it and each participant is free to edit his/her contribution to the query at any time (before the query is run). Five teams (38% of the participants) worked on the problem of collaborative querying and 7 such applications [3, 17] were analyzed.

Collaborative text editing

The problem of collaborative text editing required participants to design an application which would allow a group of users to create a summary of a written text in a synchronous collaborative fashion. One team (8% of the participants) chose to work on this problem, and 4 such applications [1] were analyzed, independently of the workshops.

Collaborative games

The set of games considered for collaborative solving consisted of puzzles and crosswords. Separate teams worked on these problems, each team focusing on one of the problems. The common requirement for both was that more users solve one game in the same time. Two teams (14% of the participants) worked on the problem of collaborative puzzle solving, while two other teams (18% of the participants) chose the problem of collaborative crossword solving. The number of analyzed collaborative games [4, 11] was four.

ii). What relationships exist between the design patterns identified?

In order to identify the relationships between the design patterns, I defined an ontology for representing the design issues collected through both the workshops and the software analysis. The questions the knowledge base based on the defined ontology answer are: 1). Given a design pattern, what are the patterns related to it and how are they related?, 2). Given 2 design patterns, what relationship exists between them (if any)?, 3). What are the design patterns between which there is a given relationship R?, 4). Given 2 design patterns, what are their common keywords (if any)?, 5). Given a set of keywords, what are the patterns related to them? To support designers' querying the knowledge base, I developed a prototype able to answer all the questions above.

iii). What is the impact of using these patterns by teams of software designers?

For answering this third question, I am planning the evaluation of the design patterns identified. For that, I will conduct a series of workshops with both novice and professional software designers. They will work in teams and they will be asked to first get familiar with the patterns and then, to make use of them during the design of synchronous applications. Data collected during these workshops will include: a). the number of times the designers search for a problem, b). the number of times they apply a solution, c). the number of times they browse the collection of patterns, d). the number of times they use the patterns for explaining concepts related to the design space of the application. Moreover, the processes followed by the designers will be recorded and observed in order to study comparatively the strategies developed by novice and professional designers in making use of the patterns.

PARTIAL RESULTS

This section briefly describes some of the design patterns identified.

Who is the coordinator? addresses the problem of providing a coordination mechanism which: a). allows all collaborators to take part in the collaborations and b). maintains the resource in a consistent state at all times.

Integrated chat addresses the problem of supporting the communication among collaborators, suggesting the integration of an instant messaging feature in the design of the application.

Eyes wide open addresses the problem of allowing each collaborator to be notified about and visualize what the others are contributing to the process at any time.

Choose your collaborators suggests allowing each user to be able to choose the people s/he wants to work with during the collaboration.

Collaboration, always social suggests integrating mechanisms of tagging, ranking, annotating, and commenting in the application in order to support the collaborators in forming a community.

With or without collaboration addresses the issue of providing users with an additional private area, not available to the other collaborators, where each collaborator has total control and where s/he is provided with tools specific to the context of the application.

My contribution addresses the problem of supporting the identification of each individual's contribution to the collaborative process.

Track history of collaboration suggests saving the history of the collaborative process and making it available through repositories, log files, or timelines.

Adapt application to device suggests supporting the materialization of the application on various devices so that users are allowed to collaborate even if they use different devices for that.

Annotate suggests allowing users to enhance the shared resource with textual, audio, or video notes on the misunderstandings, additional explanations, or inquiries they might have. Any annotation is in itself a thread-like entity, allowing the collaborators to answer back through text, audio, or video material.

Support versioning indicates enhancing the application with a versioning mechanism able to support the collaborators in viewing and editing older versions of the document they are working on.

Support reverting changes suggests supporting the users in undoing changes performed on the shared document, maintaining the resource consistent.

Customize collaboration points to providing the collaborators with the possibility of customizing the parameters of their collaborative process. These parameters could be simple visualization or editing options, or more complex options such as assigning roles and rights among the collaborators.

Shared summary suggests providing the collaborators with an automatic way to create summaries of their collaborative processes. These summaries could include intermediary results of their process, statistical data, or simplified versions of the shared resource.

Resume collaboration suggests allowing the collaborators to pause their collaborative process, store its state, and restore it later without affecting any collaborator's contribution.

CONTRIBUTIONS

This work provides a better understanding of the design issues to be faced during the design of synchronous collaborative systems. The output of my work consists in a pattern language for the design of synchronous collaborative systems developed through the on-the-go experience of teams of software designers, literature review and software application analysis. Thus far, I have identified a set of design patterns for the design of software systems to support synchronous collaboration together with the relationships between them. Also, I have implemented a prototype application able to answer queries on the knowledge base representing the patterns. Further on, I am evaluating the impact of using the patterns by teams of both novice and professional software designers.

ACKNOWLEDGMENTS

This work was supported by the *Initial Training Network* "Marie Curie Actions", funded by the FP 7 – People Programme entitled "DESIRE: Creative Design for Innovation in Science and Technology".

REFERENCES

1. Adler, A., Nash, J. C., Noel, S. Evaluating and implementing a collaborative office document system. *Interact. Comput.* 18, 4 (2006), 665-682.
2. Alexander, C. *A pattern language: Towns, buildings, construction*. New York: Oxford University Press, 1977.
3. Amershi, S., Morris, M.R. CoSearch: a system for co-located collaborative web search. in *Proceeding of CHI '08* (Florence Italy, April 2008), ACM Press, 1647-1656.
4. Battocchi, A., Pianesi, F., Tomasini, D., Zancanaro, M., Esposito, G., Venuti, P., Ben Sasson, A., Gal, E., Weiss, P.L. Collaborative Puzzle Game: a tabletop interactive game for fostering collaboration in children with Autism Spectrum Disorders. in *Proceedings of the International Conference on Interactive Tabletops and Surfaces* (2009). ACM Press, 197-204.
5. Borchers, J. *A Pattern Approach to Interaction Design*. John Wiley & Sons, Inc, 2001.
6. Carroll, J.M. *Scenario-Based Design: Envisioning Work and Technology in System Development*. John Wiley & Sons, Inc., New York, NY, USA, 1995.
7. Crumlish, C., Malone, E. *Designing Social Interfaces*. O'Reilly Media, Inc, 2009.
8. Díaz, P., Rosson, M. B., Aedo, I., Carroll, J. M. Web Design Patterns: Investigating User Goals and Browsing Strategies, in *Proceedings of the Symposium on End-User Development* (Siegen Germany, March 2009), 186-204.
9. Gamma, E., R. Helm, R. Johnson, Vlissides, J. *Design Patterns: Elements of Reusable Object-Oriented Software*. Reading, MA: Addison-Wesley, 1995.
10. Iacob, C. A Design Pattern Mining Method for Interaction Design, in *Proceedings of the 3rd Symposium on Engineering Interactive Computing Systems 2011* (Pisa Italy, June 2011).
11. Klopfer, E., Perry, J., Squire, K., Jan, M.F., Steinkuehler, C. Mystery at the museum: a collaborative game for museum education. in *Proceedings of the Conference on Computer Support for Collaborative learning* (2005), 316-320.
12. Kruschitz, C., Hitz, M. Analyzing the HCI Design Pattern Variety, in *Proceedings of AsianPLoP2010* (Tokyo Japan, March 2010), GRACE-TR-2010-01.
13. Lukosch, S., Schümmer, T. Communicating Design Knowledge with Groupware Technology Patterns: The Case of Shared Object Management. In *Proceedings of CRIWG 2004* (Costa Rica, 2004), 223-237.
14. Margaritis, M., Avouris, N., Kahrimanis, G. On Supporting Users' Reflection during Small Groups Synchronous Collaboration. in *Proceedings of 12th International Workshop on Groupware, CRIWG 2006* (Spain, 2006) LNCS 4154, Springer.
15. Schadewitz, N. Design Patterns for Cross-cultural Collaboration. *International Journal of Design* 3, 3 (2009).
16. Schümmer, T., 2004. Patterns for building communities in collaborative systems. in Proceedings of the European Conference on Pattern Languages of Programs (EuroPLoP'04). UVK, Konstanz, Germany, Irsee, Germany, pp. 379-440.
17. Shah, C., Marchionini, G., Kelly, D. Learning design principles for a collaborative information seeking system. in *Proceedings of CHI '09* (Boston USA, April 2009). ACM Press, 3419-3424.

A Model-Based Approach for Gesture Interfaces

Lucio Davide Spano
ISTI-CNR
Via G. Moruzzi 1, 56124, Pisa, Italy
lucio.davide.spano@isti.cnr.it

ABSTRACT
The interaction technologies had substantial enhancements in later years, with the introduction of devices whose capabilities changed the way people interact with games and mobile devices. However, this change did not really affected desktop systems. Indeed, few applications are able to exploit such new interaction modalities in an effective manner.

This work envisions the application of model-based approaches for the engineering of gesture user interfaces, in order to provide the designer with a comprehensive theoretical framework for usage-centred application design. The differences between existing gesture-enabling devices will be tackled applying more general solutions for multi-device user interfaces.

Author Keywords
HCI Models, Gestures, multi-touch, natural interaction

ACM Classification Keywords
H.5.2 Information interfaces and presentation (e.g., HCI): User Interfaces.

General Terms
Design, Human Factors, Languages.

INTRODUCTION
Gesture-based videogames opened the electronic entertainment market to a wider set of users and they are currently available on all major game consoles. However, the employment of this modality on different kinds of applications is still at a research stage, even in those areas where they have already demonstrated to be useful (e.g. collaborative environments, educational and museum scenarios, etc.). The main problem is the difficulty in creating such interactive applications. In order to build a gesture system, the engineers should create their hardware and software configuration for both recognizing and managing movements. The recognition system choice is usually made before the interaction design, with a really high probability of an overall poor usability of the final application.

The objective of this work will be the application of model-based approaches for user interfaces (UIs) to the gesture modality. This will provide a theoretical background to designers that want to create effective and usable gesture interfaces, first defining the interaction that should be supported and then choosing the right recognition technology. The exploitation problem of really different recognition devices can be addressed with the more general solutions for multi-device user interfaces. In particular, in this paper will be described some preliminary results for the definition of a gesture description model, which tries to provide a new abstraction for designers that overcomes the traditional event model limitations in gesture modelling.

BACKGROUND
Gestures in natural interaction consist of movements of hands, face or other body parts that are used for communication between people, replacing or enhancing speech. Gesture interfaces emulate such kind of communication, recognizing a set of gestures an exploiting them as input for computers. Many tracking and sensing technologies have been employed in order to recognize gestures. In [4] it is possible to find a survey of the different approaches.

The release of the *Nintendo Wii*[1] in 2006 marked the leverage of gesture based interaction from research studies to the market. This game console introduced an innovative controller called *Wii Remote*. Its hardware configuration allowed the development of games that break the standard and static game pad interaction, in which the player has to stay motionless and control actions pressing buttons. The user can indeed control avatars through the remote, performing the movements that should be done by their virtual counterparts. *Sony PlayStation 3* adopted a similar controller in 2010 with the *PlayStation Move*[2].

Another option for gesture recognition is the usage of motion tracking techniques in order to recognize human movements. An example of this approach is *CamSpace*[3], a software tool that exploits webcams for turning any object into a controller. This generic approach comes at the price of loosing possible haptic feedback coming from a dedicated

[1] http://www.nintendo.com/wii
[2] http://us.playstation.com/ps3/playstation-move/
[3] http://www.camspace.com

device: the object is only tracked and cannot be used to send interaction outputs to the user. Another great change in the way people interact with games has been produced with the launch of *Microsoft Kinect*[4], designed for the *XBox 360* game console, which was released in November 2010.

Still in game environments, it is possible to find another device type enabling for full body movement interaction, the so-called *Dance pads*. Introduced by *Konami* with *Dance Dance Revolution*[5], they are essentially huge directional pads with big arrow-shaped buttons that can be pressed with feet. This configuration allows the player to move following the music and the button sequence displayed on screen. Another kind of floor device is the *Wii balance board*, that is a rectangular feet panel that is equipped with two pressure sensors. It is mainly used in snowboard emulation games and also in aerobic and yoga activities.

GESTURE CONCRETE USER INTERFACE

In order to tackle with the existence of all these different devices and recognition capabilities, we propose to place the gesture UI modelling in the broader scope of model-based approaches for user interfaces. The gesture modality will be integrated as a *platform* into the MARIA XML [6] modelling language. A platform is a hardware and software configuration that allows the interaction with a system. The approach followed in MARIA XML is the definition of a multi-device user interface through the following levels of abstraction: the *Concepts and Tasks level*, the *Abstract User Interface* (AUI), the *Concrete User Interface* (CUI), and the *Final User Interface* (FUI). The Concepts and Tasks level contains the description of the concepts managed by the application together with the tasks that should be supported. The AUI contains a user interface description independent with respect to the device and the interaction modality. The CUI contains a user interface description abstract with respect to the technology used for the implementation. The FUI contains the final implementation of the user interface, expressed in source code.

Considering these abstraction levels, it will be defined a CUI meta-model, exploiting the concepts provided by CTT [5] for tasks and the current MARIA XML *Abstract User Interface* meta-models. More precisely, the gestures will be categorized under the *Selection*, *Control* and *Edit* interaction semantics categories. The *Only Output* interactor description will be described reusing the graphical desktop model already contained in MARIA XML. It is assumed that the screen is the main output device, together with the audio modality. Differently from the existing MARIA XML CUIs, the gesture CUI will also take into account the haptic feedback, which is a peculiar characteristic of some gesture enabling devices. The gesture CUI meta-model will be constructed using the following building blocks:

- *Gesture description model.*
- *Gesture effect model.*
- *Presentation model.*
- *Dialog model.*

The *Gesture description model* will contain the description of the gestures that can be performed for interacting with the application. The description will define only how human beings can execute a gesture, without associate any meaning to it. It will be defined a taxonomy of basic body gestures. A starting point can be the *HamNoSys*[7] notation, using the *SiGML* [2] syntax. Furthermore we need also to define the gesture composition operators, in order to allow the design of complex gestures starting from basic ones. For instance it is possible to describe the usual head movement for saying "no" with a sequence of four basic movements, starting from the head rest position: left rotation, return to the rest position, right rotation, return to the rest position.

From the human communication theory, we know that the gesture execution can be described using three categories [3, p. 86]: *static* (gesture that does not take movements into account), *dynamic* (hand trajectories or change of posture over time) and *spatio-temporal* (a subset of the dynamic gestures that move through the workspace over time). Thus the gesture description taxonomy should not only consider a sequence of body positions, but also the timing and the space used in order to perform the gesture, which can be exploited by the designer as arguments. For instance, in a golf game, the swing speed can be associated to the power of the simulated strike. The classical event model that supports the *point and click* interaction is not suitable for describing such gestures. Events are usually atomic notification of changes in some observed variables, which should be handled without assuming any temporal relation between them. Currently, gestures are modelled with single atomic events, which notify their occurrence. The problem with this notification mechanism is the lack of feedback during the performance, which is really often needed (gestures have a higher time duration compared with clicks). The solution is typically the access to the low level signals coming from input devices, with the consequent loss of an high-level event view for the considered gesture.

With the envisioned gesture description model it will be possible to manage the gesture as a whole, but there will be also the possibility to access to its components, in order to provide intermediate feedback once some basic gestures have been recognized. Moreover, it should be also possible to study the creation of an ergonomic measurement function. Indeed, once identified the basic gestures, each one can be assigned to a fatigue value. After that it can be investigated how the composition operators have influence in the perceived fatigue, with the possibility of estimating the physical cost of a complex gesture. This fatigue model should also consider the impact of the spatio and temporal characteristic of the described gesture. The gesture taxonomy and the composition operators identified can drive the creation of gesture recognizers: complex gesture recognizer can be built using a composition of basic recognizer implemented with a device-dependent library. Designers have not to reinvent the wheel for each UI, so it should be available a set frequently-

[4]http://www.xbox.com/en-US/kinect
[5]http://www.konami.com/ddr/

used complex gestures. Their definition should be ready out of the box, and they should be classified under the MARIA XML AUI interactor categories (*Select, Control, Edit*).

The *Gesture effect model* will contain the definition of the effects that the gesture interaction produces on the current UI state, together with user feedback for the gesture recognition (including also the haptic modality). This part will reuse the existing constructs contained into MARIA XML, introducing some refinements if needed.

The gesture modality usually cooperates with other ones, especially graphical and audio, because it is rarely able to provide complex feedback. For this reason, it has also to be included a *Presentation model*, which will define the graphical presentations of system output, together with audio and video media. The constructs for modelling such presentations are already defined into MARIA XML graphical CUI. If the current vocabulary is not expressive enough, such constructs will be refined. In particular, it will be considered the introduction of an explicit expression of the well-known *CARE*[1] properties for multimodal interfaces. Assigning such properties not only to graphical UI parts, but also to the gesture definitions can enable the automatized derivation of different versions of the same gesture CUI, in order to support different recognizing technologies, and also for defining different gestures with the same effect. For instance, the aforementioned head rotation gesture can be performed either starting from the right or from the left. From a descriptive point of view these gestures are different, but from the interaction point of view they can be defined as *equivalent*. These gestures can be commonly complemented with a forefinger oscillation, in this case we have the *redundancy*.

The *Dialog model* will contain the constructs for defining the complex gesture availability according to the different UI states. It will define which gestures can be used in a given state and their temporal relations (which ones should be performed in sequence, which ones can be performed in parallel etc.), the assignment of gestures to effects and the definition of the state transitions. The temporal relations between gestures can be defined using CTT [5] operators.

The depicted CUI meta-model should be able to describe gesture interfaces taking into account an abstract technology that has all the recognizing capabilities currently available. However, as should be clear from the discussion in the Background section, different technologies with different recognizing capabilities exist. Unfortunately, the differences between these devices cannot be reduced to a simple change of vocabulary between different implementation technologies (e.g. two different widget tookits for the graphical desktop platform). This means that aside the gesture CUI meta-model, it is necessary also to describe in a coherent manner the recognizing capabilities of a given set of devices. The distinction that can be currently made is between *remote based, motion-tracking based* and *floor device based*. It is also possible to add to these categories the *glove based*, due to the experiments that can be found in literature. These sub-platforms should be described with a *Gesture recognizer model* that should list the set of basic gestures that the sub-platform is able to recognize and the composition operators supported.

PRELIMINARY RESULTS

The work for the gesture CUI definition has started with the application of the ideas described in the previous section to multitouch, which can be considered the simplest gesture interaction example. The proposed gesture description meta-model consists of three main entities: *Sample, Block* and *Gesture*.

Each *Sample* contains an identifier, a point, a type (start, move, end) and a flag representing its state (consumed if its data has been exploited or not consumed otherwise). It models the information provided by the device about the on-screen touches.

A *Block* represents an atomic gesture that can be recognized from samples and performs updates on gesture state. The blocks defined for multi-touch gestures are *TouchStart, TouchMove* and *TouchEnd*, which recognize respectively new touches, the location change of an existing touch, and the end of an existing touch (finger lifted from the screen). Each block reads the information contained in samples and optionally updates its internal state and/or the gesture-global state. When reading the information from a sample, a block can switch to a *completed* state if the recognition finished correctly or to an *error* state, if the recognition was not successful. Blocks can share a sample identifier in order to consume only samples having the same id and ignore the others (without producing errors). This mechanism links together blocks that deal with the same touch during the described gesture sequence.

A *Gesture* contains a set B of *Blocks* and their connections. $S \subset B$ contains the blocks that represent the initial gesture state (that is the atomic action to be recognized), $C \subset B$ contains the current state and $F \subset B$ contains the final states. When the recognition starts $C \equiv S$ and the gesture is considered recognized if a block $b \in F \cap C$ is completed (the atomic action that represents has been recognized). When an intermediate block completes, the gesture-defined block connections are exploited in order to add elements to C. Instead, if a block in C do not recognize its atomic action, the gesture is reset to its initial state. The gesture state contains also the data related to the current touches, which is updated by its inner blocks. When the device raises a touch-related event, the gesture forwards it only to blocks in C. When the block consumes a sample, it raises an event. This model allows the definition of gestures in four simple steps:

1. Define the set of blocks needed, marking the initial and final ones.
2. Define block connections. This specifies the gesture sequencing.
3. Define block shared identifiers, in order to assign the same touch to different blocks.
4. Define sample consumed event handlers for blocks.

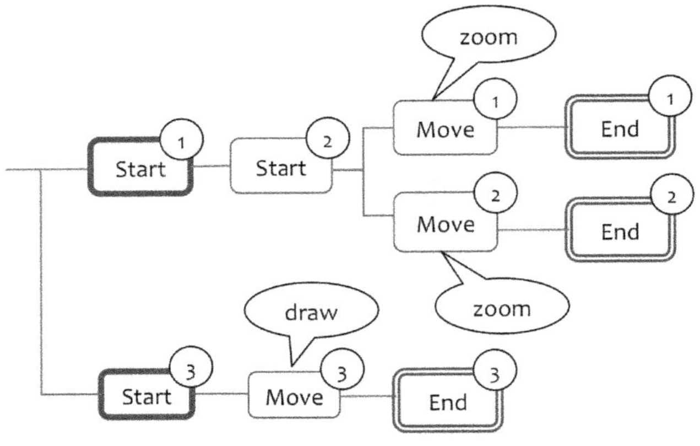

Figure 1. Prototype gesture description model

The first three steps are simply the gesture sequencing declaration, which identifies how many touches are considered and how the user will perform the interaction. Step 4 defines the interaction effect on the application data.

Figure 1 shows the multitouch gesture description modelled for the implementation of a zoomable finger-drawing canvas for the iPhone. The application recognizes two gestures, allowing the user to draw lines on a canvas with his/her finger, and to zoom the view with the classical pinch gesture. In Figure 1, rounded rectangles represent blocks. Starting ones have a bolder line while double lines represent final. The circle-enclosed numbers are touch identifiers, while balloons represent event handlers for consumed samples, attached to blocks. Lines between blocks define connections. The drawing gesture is a simple pan (Figure 1, lower part), represented by a pipe of a *TouchStart*, a *TouchMove* and a *TouchEnd* block. Each block shares the same sample identifier. It is worth pointing out that the identifiers are not related to touch ordering: having the identifier number 3 does not mean that the touch has to come after the number 1 and 2, but simply that it is different from them. The move block has a sample consumed event handler that draws a line corresponding to touch point Δx and Δy.

The pinch has been modelled as a two-finger gesture (Figure 1, higher part), which starts with the first finger touch, continues with a second finger touch. After that there is a parallel moving of the first and the second finger, and finally the end of one of the two touches. The event handler is the same for both move blocks: it evaluates the distance between the touch number 1 and 2 and updates the view zoom accordingly.

While the interaction described is not really new, there are some characteristics that should be pointed out. First of all, the interaction is completely defined by the designer composing building blocks. This means that it is possible to define custom gestures, without reimplementing the touch tracking. The designer has no more a single recognition event, but it can enhance the gesture description with handlers that provide intermediate feedback to the user, improving the interface usability. For instance, the designer can decide to draw two arrows corresponding to touches while performing the pinch gesture. These arrows converge for the zoom in or diverge for the zoom out. This is typically not possible with the high-level pinch zoom event: the application receives the notification only when the gesture is performed, without intermediate steps. Currently, the only solution is to track low level touch events. Last but not least, it is possible to express parallel gesture interaction in a straightforward manner, which is simply declaring that the two gestures work on different touches. Using the aforementioned configuration of the touch identifiers, it is possible with the prototype to draw lines while zooming the view and vice versa.

CONCLUSIONS AND FUTURE WORK

This work proposed the application of model based approaches for user interfaces to gesture interaction, in order to overcome two main problems that currently affect such modality. The first one is the existence of different recognition device with different capabilities that currently drive the interaction design. The second one is the lack of a suitable gesture definition meta-model, able to overcome the limitation of handling atomic events related to high-level gestures. A description model has been defined for multi-touch interaction, which will be enhanced in the future for body gestures and included as a platform for the MARIA XML language.

REFERENCES

1. J. Coutaz, L. Nigay, D. Salber, A. Blandford, J. May, and R. Young. Four easy pieces for assessing the usability of multimodal interaction: the CARE properties. In *Proceedings of INTERACT*, volume 95, pages 115–120, 1995.
2. R. Kennaway. Experience with and requirements for a gesture description language for synthetic animation. *Gesture-Based Communication in Human-Computer Interaction*, 2915:449–450, 2004.
3. P. Kortum. *HCI Beyond the GUI: Design for Haptic, Speech, Olfactory, and Other Nontraditional Interfaces (Interactive Technologies)*. Morgan Kaufmann Publishers Inc. San Francisco, CA, USA, 2008.
4. S. Mitra and T. Acharya. Gesture recognition: A survey. *IEEE Transactions on Systems, Man and Cybernetics - PART C*, 37(3):311–324, 2007.
5. F. Paternò. *Model-based design and evaluation of interactive applications*. Applied computing. Springer, 2000.
6. F. Paternò, C. Santoro, and L. D. Spano. Maria: A universal, declarative, multiple abstraction-level language for service-oriented applications in ubiquitous environments. *ACM Transaction in Computer-Human Interaction*, 16:19:1–19:30, November 2009.
7. S. Prillwitz, R. Leven, H. Zienert, T. Hanke, and J. Henning. *HamNoSys: Hamburg Notation System for Sign Languages: an Introductory Guide*. Signum Press, 1989.

Designing Visual User Interfaces for Mobile Applications

Luca Chittaro
Human-Computer Interaction Lab
University of Udine
Via delle Scienze 206, 33100 Udine, Italy
http://hcilab.uniud.it

ABSTRACT
People want to do more with their mobile phones and every day new mobile applications are launched in a increasingly wide number of domains. However, traditional UI knowledge is not sufficient to design effective interfaces for mobile applications because the mobility context presents developers with several peculiarities and new challenges. This tutorial will introduce participants to the design of visual interfaces for mobile applications. In particular, it will: (i) illustrate the peculiar aspects of mobile interaction that make it more difficult to build effective user interfaces for mobile users, (ii) show how the powerful graphics capabilities of today's mobile devices can be exploited to create interfaces that help users on the move do more with their phones, requiring less time and attention,. (iii) look at recent developments in the engineering of mobile UIs such as tool support for mobile interface development, including mobile end-user programming.

Author Keywords
Mobile devices, mobile phones, user interface design, visual interfaces, multimodal interfaces, design constraints

ACM Classification Keywords
H.5.2 User Interfaces: Graphical user interfaces (GUI), H.5.2 User Interfaces: Evaluation/methodology, D.2.2. Design Tools and Techniques: User interfaces.

General Terms
Design, Human Factors

INTRODUCTION
People want to do more with their mobile phones and every day new mobile applications are launched in a increasingly wide number of domains ranging from games to personal productivity, from navigation systems to health and fitness. Moreover, some mobile applications exploit the in-built sensors of recent phones to enrich the interaction with features such as context-awareness and augmented reality.

Unfortunately, traditional UI knowledge is not sufficient to design effective interfaces for mobile applications because the mobility context presents developers with several peculiarities and new challenges. This invited tutorial introduces participants to mobile UI design, focusing especially on visual interfaces, because sight is the dominant sense exploited by most mobile interfaces. More specifically, the tutorial will reach its goal by analyzing the topic from three points of views: (i) understanding the peculiar aspects of mobile interaction that distinguish it from interaction with desktop systems and make it difficult to build effective user interfaces for mobile users, (ii) facing the design constraints and issues that affect visual mobile UIs, also examining the different techniques proposed to this purpose in the literature, (iii) looking at recent developments in the engineering of mobile UIs such as tool support for UI development, including mobile end-user programming.

EICS'11, June 13–16, 2011, Pisa, Italy.
ACM 978-1-4503-0670-6/11/06.

Distinctive aspects of mobile HCI
A first set of aspects that distinguishes mobile from desktop interfaces is device-related. For example, while recent years have seen significant increases in the size of the displays we use in the office or at home, allowing us to organize our tasks better and carry out more complex task with less effort, nothing similar has happened on mobile phones: their screens remain small and the size and resolution gaps with respect to desktop screens is widening.

A second set of aspects concerns the context of use. For example, mobile applications must take into account that people can devote only a very limited attention to the device while they are on the move. Unlike office environments, when we are in a street or at the airport or in a bar, we have to attend to a constant flow of events and stimuli that come from the environment, and respond to those events with proper actions. Some of these events can affect the accomplishment of out goals (e.g., hearing a gate change announcement concerning our flight), others our social relations (e.g., properly listening and responding to what people who are with us are saying), others even our personal safety (e.g., noticing and avoiding potential dangers while we are in a street). This makes using the mobile device a secondary rather than a primary task.

The tutorial will consider all distinctive aspects related to the device, its hardware, software and programming, as well as those related to the context, which comprise perceptual, motor, cognitive and social aspects [10].

Designing mobile GUIs and mobile visualizations
The tutorial will illustrate how a proper design of mobile GUIs can help people do more with their mobile phones,

requiring them less time and attention. The availability of devices with increasingly powerful graphics capabilities is indeed making it possible to develop novel interfaces, based on interactive 2D (or even 3D) graphics, to help mobile users in dealing more quickly and easily with larger amounts of information. Moreover, to address issues of limited cognitive resources and safety of mobile users, mobile graphics can be effectively exploited to provide information at-a-glance that is understood with less cognitive resources and distracts less the user from her surrounding environment.

Mobile visual interfaces become even more interesting and provide functionalities that were unavailable on desktop systems when they exploit various sensors (e.g., GPS, NFC, accelerometers, physiological sensors,...) that allow one to adapt the behavior of the application to position in space (location-awareness) and other parameters (context-awareness). This way, the mobile UI becomes able to automatically choose what to show and how to show it on the display based on what is happening to the user as well as the surrounding environment. Besides further contributing to decrease user's cognitive load, this supports the creation of new kinds of interactive applications, e.g. personal trainers [6] and persuasive fitness games [7].

Several advanced techniques have been tested in mobile HCI to improve the effectiveness of mobile GUIs, e.g. visual dynamic queries [3], new navigation widgets [1], 3D visual instructions [11], zoomable user interfaces [5], visual references to off-screen content [4]. The tutorial will examine these techniques and also several other techniques proposed by various authors, concentrating especially on the design issues which are harder to face on mobile devices, such as the presentation problem [9].

Engineering mobile visual (and multimodal) interfaces

Finally, the tutorial will consider relations between the visual modality and other modalities in the wider context of engineering mobile multimodal interfaces. A useful class of tools concentrates on rapid development of mobile UIs, even based on end-user programming methodologies. This also supports an easy exploration of different modalities and their combinations as well as on-the-fly tuning of the parameters of each modality. Tools for rapid development of multimodal mobile interfaces will allow the designer to make changes to the interface in the field without requiring much time or having to go back and forth from the lab as it often happens today. From this perspective, these tools should also consider content besides interaction, e.g. making quick in-the-field changes to the database of points of interests or the maps of a location-based application.

Engineering visual (and multimodal) mobile UIs would also benefit from new tools that could help to understand better how mobile users exploit or respond to different modalities. For example, automatically logged usage data concerning the various modalities could be analyzed by tools that present the designer with informative visualizations of that data at different levels of detail. The collected data can include actions on the phone touchscreen [2], user's position in the environment [8], physiological parameters [12], studied using detailed (e.g., VCR-like replay) or abstract (e.g., heat maps) visual analytics techniques.

REFERENCES

1. Burigat S., Chittaro L., Gabrielli S. Navigation Techniques for Small-screen Devices: an Evaluation on Maps and Web pages. *International Journal of Human-Computer Studies 66*, 2 (2008), 78-97.
2. Burigat S., Chittaro L., Ieronutti L. Mobrex: Visualizing Users' Mobile Browsing Behaviors. *IEEE Computer Graphics and Applications 28*, 1 (2008), 24-32.
3. Burigat S., Chittaro L. Interactive Visual Analysis of Geographic Data on Mobile Devices based on Dynamic Queries. *Journal of Visual Languages and Computing 19*, 1 (2008), 99-122.
4. Burigat S., Chittaro L. Visualizing References to Off-Screen Content on Mobile Devices: a Comparison of Arrows, Wedge, and Overview+Detail. *Interacting with Computers 23*, 2 (2011), 156-166.
5. Burigat S., Chittaro L., Parlato E. Map, Diagram, and Web Page Navigation on Mobile Devices: the Effectiveness of Zoomable User Interfaces with Overviews, *Proc. MOBILE HCI 2008*, ACM Press (2008), 147-156.
6. Buttussi F., Chittaro L. MOPET: A Context-Aware and User-Adaptive Wearable System for Fitness Training. *Artificial Intelligence In Medicine 42*, 2 (2008), 153-163.
7. Buttussi F., Chittaro L. Smarter Phones for Healthier Lifestyles: An Adaptive Fitness Game. *IEEE Pervasive Computing 9*, 4 (2010), 51-57.
8. Chittaro L., Ranon R., Ieronutti L. VU-Flow: A Visualization Tool for Analyzing Navigation in Virtual Environments. *IEEE Transactions on Visualization and Computer Graphics 12*, 6 (2006), 1475-1485.
9. Chittaro L. Visualizing Information on Mobile Devices. *IEEE Computer 39*, 3 (2006), 34-39.
10. Chittaro L. Distinctive aspects of mobile interaction and their implications for the design of multimodal interfaces. *Journal on Multimodal User Interfaces 3*, 3 (2010), 157-165.
11. Chittaro L., Nadalutti D. Presenting Evacuation Instructions on Mobile Devices by means of Location-Aware 3D Virtual Environments. *Proc. MOBILE HCI 2008*, ACM Press (2008), 395-398.
12. Nadalutti, D., Chittaro, L. Visual Analysis of Users' Performance Data in Fitness Activities. *Computers & Graphics 31*, 3 (2007), 429-439.

Enhancing Interaction with Supplementary Supportive User Interfaces (UIs): Meta-UIs, Mega-UIs, Extra-UIs, Supra-UIs ...

Alexandre Demeure
University of Grenoble, LIG
INRIA, 655 av. de l'Europe, 38334
St Ismier Cedex, France
First.Last@inrialpes.fr

Grzegorz Lehmann
DAI-Labor, TU-Berlin
Ernst-Reuter-Platz 7
10587 Berlin, Germany
First.Last@dai-labor.de

Mathieu Petit, Gaëlle Calvary
University of Grenoble, CNRS, LIG
385, av. de la bibliothèque
38400 St Martin d'Hères, France
First.Last@imag.fr

ABSTRACT
In order to improve the interaction control and intelligibility, end-user applications are supplemented with Supportive User Interfaces (SUI), like meta-UIs, mega-UIs, helping or configuration wizards. These additional UIs support the users by providing them with information about the available functionalities, the context of use, or the performed adaptations. Such UIs allow the user to supervise and modify an application interactive behavior according to her/his needs.

Given the rising complexity of interactive systems, supportive UIs are highly desirable features. However, there is currently no common understanding of types and roles of supportive UIs. Enabling concepts and definitions underlying the engineering of such UIs are also missing. In order to fill this gap, the workshop seeks a discussion with a broad audience of researchers, who have experience with the design and development of supportive UIs.

Author Keywords: Supportive User Interfaces, UIs quality, explanative UIs, help systems, awareness of the context of use, meta-UI, mega-UI, supra UI.

ACM Classification Keywords
H.5.2 [User Interfaces]: Ergonomics, Graphical user interfaces (GUI), Prototyping, User-centered design, Evaluation/methodology. D.2.2 [Software Engineering]: Design Tools and Techniques, User Interfaces.

General Terms: Design, Human factors, Algorithms.

INTRODUCTION
Enabling technologies make it possible to create more and more complex systems in terms of functional core, new interaction techniques and context-of-use dynamics. Coming along with systems complexity, the users require a better understanding and control of their applications.

In the aftermath of "pervasive intelligibility" researches [5], this workshop focuses on human-computer interaction and more specifically on the engineering of user interfaces to foster intelligibility and control. User interface intelligibility has been approached from different perspectives. The concept of "Meta-UI" has been introduced as a metaphorical UI to *control and evaluate the state of interactive ambient spaces* [1]. Other works focus on self-explanatory user interfaces, and make it possible for the end-user to *understand the design of the user interface* [4]. The Crystal tabletop prototype has been developed to handle a complex platform composed of components like TVs, robots, picture frames, etc. [3]. Crystal provides the users with intelligible UIs to *control the media distribution and the component discovery.*

Such research projects exemplify the notion of **supportive UI**. In a broader context this workshop aims to identify and classify the supportive UIs that may enhance the interaction (e.g., by rendering the workflow in e-government applications or making it possible to the end-user to see the available platforms in the surrounding and redistribute the UIs him/herself). These include Meta-UIs [1], Mega-UIs [2], self-explanatory UI, Supra-UIs and others. The goals of the workshop are to:

- Define the concept of supportive UI,
- Elicit the dimensions of supportive UIs through a taxonomy that would cover both the abstraction and presentation of supportive UIs,
- Discuss the properties supportive UIs should convey,
- Explore how to integrate supportive UIs into development processes and Model-based UI development,
- Identify the key research stakeholders for further research.

To that end, examples of points of discussion could be:

- What is the added-value for the users? Which one is the border between UI and supportive UI? Do UIs for help, personalization or end-user programming belong to supportive UIs?
- Are supportive UIs parts of the original UI? Are they generic or do they require application-specific features or rendering?
- How to take benefit from model-based approaches to integrate supportive UIs by design?

EICS'11, June 13–16, 2011, Pisa, Italy.
ACM 978-1-4503-0670-6/11/06.

- How to evaluate supportive UIs?

The relevance of the workshop is two-fold: first, to improve the quality of UIs, and to reconcile research areas (e.g., model-based approaches, end-user programming).

ORGANIZATION

Alexandre Demeure is assistant professor at the University of Grenoble. His main research interests include plasticity of UIs, software architecture for HCI, multitouch interaction and creativity support. **Grzegorz Lehmann** is a PhD student at the Technische Universität Berlin. His research focuses on the utilization of runtime and executable models for developing ubiquitous UIs**. Mathieu Petit** is a post doctoral fellow at the University of Grenoble. His current research focuses on model description and automated transformation to design plastic UIs. **Gaëlle Calvary** is professor at the University of Grenoble. Her research area is about UI plasticity to ensure UI quality along the variations of the context of use. She mostly explores model-driven engineering.

FORMAT

We propose a one-day workshop with six working hours, excluding the breaks. Our goal is to facilitate a combination of presentations, demonstrations, discussions and community building.

Candidate participants must submit a short paper or a position statement. The short paper describes experiences, ongoing work or results related to the workshop's topic. We encourage submissions including video demonstrations. A position statement describes requirements or issues the participant encounters when designing and/or implementing supportive UIs, as well as desirable solutions from the author's point of view.

In order to focus the discussion on supportive UIs concepts and design, the organizers will select the most prominent themes relative to the workshop topic from the set of accepted papers. The authors will be asked to mainly focus their presentations on these relevant themes.

At first, the participants will introduce themselves. Each introduction should include a short statement about the favorite problem to tackle during the workshop. After the introductions, Jeremy Melchior, from Université Catholique de Louvain (Belgium) will give an introduction speech about quality properties for intelligent UIs. The workshop will then focus on reviews and discussions of topics emerged from the position papers. The selected papers will be presented in two one-hour slots.

After the lunch break, participants will be split into groups structured around the core topics provided in the papers and statements. Afterwards, the groups will report back to the plenary forum. The following is a tentative schedule for the workshop, time given in working hours, excluding breaks:

0:00-0:15	Introduction by the organizers
0:15-45	Brief introduction talk by each participant, using predefined template (e.g., background, experience, favorite problem)
0:45-1:15	Invited talk : "Quality properties of intelligent interfaces" by Jeremy Melchior
1:15-2:15	Selected paper presentations
2:15	Break
2:15-3:15	Selected paper presentations
3:15-3:30	Summary and presentation of afternoon works
3:30	Lunch
3:30-5:00	Breakout groups – initiation
5:00-6:30	Plenary discussion on group results, future agenda and follow-up activities

PROGRAM COMMITTEE

- Jean Vanderdonckt
- Gerrit Meixner
- Joëlle Coutaz
- Kris Luyten
- Peter Forbrig
- Marco Blumendorf
- Melanie Hartmann
- Natalie Aquino
- Oscar Pastor
- Victor Lopez
- Dominique Scapin
- Philippe Palanque
- Marco Winckler
- Audrey Serna
- Dirk Roscher

WEBSITE AND CONTACT

http://www.supportiveui.org/ ; chairs@supportiveui.org

REFERENCES

[1] Coutaz, J. **Meta-User Interfaces for Ambient Spaces**. *In Proc. of the 5th Int. Ws. on Task Models and Diagrams for Users Interface Design: TAMODIA 2006*, pp 1-15, Coninx, K., Luyten, K. and Schneider, K. A. (eds.), Springer LNCS 4385. Hasselt, Belgium, October 23-24, 2006.

[2] Sottet, J-S., Calvary, G., Favre, J-M. and Coutaz, J. **Megamodeling and Metamodel-Driven Engineering for Plastic User Interfaces: MEGA-UI**. *In Human-Centered Software Engineering*, pp 173-200, Seffah, A., Vanderdonckt, J. and Desmarais, M. C. (eds.), Springer Human-Computer Interaction Series. 2009.

[3] Seifried, T., Haller, M., Scott, S. D., Perteneder, F. Rendl, C., Sakamoto, D. and Inami, M. **CRISTAL. Design and implementation of a remote control system based on multi-touch system**. In *Proc. of the 4th Int. Conf. on Interactive Tabletops and Surfaces: Tabletops 2009*. ACM. Banff, Canada, November 23-25, 2009.

[4] Garcia Frey, A., Calvary, G. and Dupuy-Chessa, S. **Xplain: an editor for building self-explanatory user interfaces by model-driven engineering**. In *Proc. of the 2nd Int. Symp. on Engineering Interactive Computing Systems: EICS 2010*, pp 41-46, ACM. Berlin, Germany, June 19-23, 2010.

[5] Vermeulen, J., Lim, B. Y. and Kawsar, F. **Proc. of the Int. Ws. on Intelligibility and Control in Pervasive Computing**. *Held in conjunction with the 9th Int. Conf. on Pervasive Computing : Pervasive 2011*. St Francisco, CA, USA, June 12-15, 201.

Second Workshop on Engineering Patterns for Multi-Touch Interfaces

Kris Luyten, Davy Vanacken
Expertise Centre for Digital Media
Hasselt University – tUL – IBBT
{firstname.lastname}@uhasselt.be

Malte Weiss, Jan Borchers
RWTH Aachen University
{weiss, borchers}
@cs.rwth-aachen.de

Miguel Nacenta
iLab, University of Calgary
miguel.nacenta@ucalgary.ca

ABSTRACT
Multi-touch gained a lot of interest in the last couple of years and the increased availability of multi-touch enabled hardware boosted its development. However, the current diversity of hardware, toolkits, and tools for creating multi-touch interfaces has its downsides: there is only little reusable material and no generally accepted body of knowledge when it comes to the development of multi-touch interfaces. This workshop is the second workshop on this topic and the workshop goal remains unchanged: to seek a consensus on methods, approaches, toolkits, and tools that aid in the engineering of multi-touch interfaces and transcend the differences in available platforms. The patterns mentioned in the title indicate that we are aiming to create a reusable body of knowledge.

Author Keywords
Multi-touch, Engineering Patterns.

ACM Classification Keywords
H5.m. Information interfaces and presentation (e.g., HCI): Miscellaneous.

General Terms
Design, Human Factors

THEME, GOALS, AND RELEVANCE
The theme of this workshop series is "engineering multi-touch interfaces", with the main focus on methods, approaches, toolkits, and tools for developing actual multi-touch interfaces. The current body of work is mainly tailored toward a specific hardware platform, or relies on platform specific toolkits. In contrast with engineering WIMP (or single touch) interfaces, there is no established work on transcending the diversity in hardware and software platforms. To name a few challenges posed by multi-touch that remain relevant:

- Different hardware platforms often provide different ways to specify the touch data, using different levels of detail (e.g. a set of 2D coordinates, a set of ovals, the actual touch shape, pressure, etc.).
- The form factor and orientation of multi-touch devices strongly influence the user experience. Horizontal tabletops, for instance, afford collaborative work and support annotation tasks, whereas vertical displays are more appropriate for reading and presentation purposes. Mobile multi-touch devices require a completely different user interface.
- Each tracking technology (FTIR, DI, capacitive sensing, etc.) comes with its own advantages and drawbacks, and strongly influences the enabled interaction styles. For example, while capacitive sensing allows the use of thin displays, detecting markers of tangible interfaces is a hard task.
- Text input on multi-touch devices is still an open problem.

The main goal of this workshop is to reach a consensus on methods, approaches, toolkits, and tools that aid in the engineering of multi-touch interfaces and transcend the differences in available platforms.

A secondary goal is to establish a series of re-occurring workshops covering this theme. As the user base and available software for multi-touch platforms is still increasing and reaches for maturity, this workshop series can provide regular updates on the current state of the art for engineering multi-touch interfaces, as well as foster a community working on this topic.

FORMAT
Specialists from the field that are involved in the development of multi-touch interfaces are invited for the workshop, including software developers, interface designers, tool(kit) builders, hardware manufacturers and researchers. Our goal is to facilitate a combination of presentations, demonstrations, discussions and community building.

Candidate participants submit a short paper or a position statement. The short paper describes experiences, ongoing work or results related to the workshop's topic. Video demonstrations are encouraged. A position statement describes requirements or issues the participant encounters

EICS'11, June 13–16, 2011, Pisa, Italy.
ACM 978-1-4503-0670-6/11/06.

when engineering multi-touch interfaces, as well as desirable solutions from the author's point of view.

The workshop will start with brief introductory talks from each participant, followed by a review and discussion of topics emerged from position papers. If possible, we would like to start with a set of experience reports, describing engineering issues with current multi-touch platforms. Next, participants will be split in discussion groups structured around the core topics provided in the papers and statements. Afterwards, the groups will report back to the plenary forum.

ORGANIZATION

Kris Luyten is a professor at Hasselt University, affiliated with the Expertise Centre for Digital Media (EDM). His main research interests are context-aware user interfaces, user interface description languages, model-based and user-centered interface development, multi-touch interaction, mobile guides, ubiquitous computing, and social and collaborative software.

Davy Vanacken is a research assistant and PhD student at Hasselt University, affiliated with the HCI group of the Expertise Centre for Digital Media (EDM). His main research interests include modeling interaction, collaborative systems, and multi-touch user interfaces.

Malte Weiss is a research assistant and PhD student at RWTH Aachen University. His research focuses on haptic feedback and tangible user interfaces on tabletops.

Jan Borchers is a full professor of computer science and head of the Media Computing Group at RWTH Aachen University. With his research group, he explores the field of human-computer interaction, with a particular interest in new post-desktop user interfaces for smart environments, ubiquitous computing, interactive exhibits, and time-based media such as audio and video.

Miguel Nacenta is currently a post-doctoral fellow at the iLab, University of Calgary. His research is focused on new form factors for interaction such as tabletops, large displays, and mobile devices and on how to combine them together to create useful multi-display environments.

PARTICIPANTS

We aim for participants with various backgrounds, though our main goal is to gather participants who are involved in the different stages of the design, creation, realization, and deployment of multi-touch interfaces. We expect most participants to have a design or engineering (technical) background.

WORKSHOP CONTENTS

This year, the workshop program consists of seven contributions. These contributions cover a wide variety of issues typically encountered when engineering multi-touch interfaces. The presented research ranges from different hardware platforms (from iPhone interaction to large surfaces) over support for multi-user configurations and situations to interaction techniques and reusable frameworks:

- Konstantinos Chorianopoulos, Ioannis Leftheriotis, and Panagiotis Pandis. *Design of Scalable Collaborative Multi-touch Screens.*
- Tobias Hesselmann, Susanne Boll, and Wilko Heuten. *Towards an Integrated Process for Interactive Surface Application Development.*
- Dietrich Kammer, Dana Henkens, Jan Wojdziak, and Georg Freitag. *Formalization and Combination of Touch and Point Interaction.*
- Michele Marchesoni and Cristina Costa. *Augmenting natural interaction in projective capacitive displays with tangible interfaces.*
- Paolo Olivo, Damien Marchal, and Nicolas Roussel. *Software requirements for a (more) manageable multi-touch ecosystem.*
- Fabio Paternò, Carmen Santoro, Lucio Davide Spano, and Flavio Zaccaro. *Modelling Multi-Touch UIs in Mobile Devices with MARIA.*
- Chenjun Wu, Yongqiang Qin, Yue Suo, and Yuanchun Shi. *uTableSDK - Enabling Rapid Prototyping of Window-based Applications on Interactive Tabletop.*

Model-based Interactive Ubiquitous Systems

Thomas Schlegel
Technische Universität Dresden
01062 Dresden
thomas.schlegel@tu-dresden.de

Stefan Pietschmann
Technische Universität Dresden
01062 Dresden
stefan.pietschmann@tu-dresden.de

ABSTRACT
Ubiquitous systems are introducing a new quality of interaction both into our lives and into software engineering. Software becomes increasingly dynamic making frequent changes to system structures, distribution, and behavior necessary. Also, adaptation to user needs and contexts as well as different modalities and communication channels make these systems differ strongly from what has been standard over the last decades.

Model-driven engineering forms a promising approach for coping with the dynamics and uncertainties inherent to interactive ubiquitous systems (IUS). This workshop discusses models and model-driven architectures addressing the challenges of interaction with and engineering of IUS with regard to the design and runtime.

Author Keywords: models, MDA, ubiquitous systems, software engineering, ubiquitous interaction, multimodal interfaces, context-awareness, self-adaptation, EICS workshop

ACM Classification Keywords
D.2.2 Design Tools and Techniques: Modules and interfaces; user interfaces. D.2.11 Software Architectures: Patterns. D.2.13 Reusable Software: Domain engineering; reuse models. H.5.2 User Interfaces: Interaction styles; standardization

General Terms: Design, Human Factors

THEME, GOALS, AND RELEVANCE
Model-based interactive ubiquitous systems form a new promising yet challenging domain within the scope of engineering of interactive computing systems. This workshop is intended to discuss these challenges and possible solutions of the EICS community to design and runtime aspects of interactive ubiquitous systems with a focus on model-based approaches.

The related problem space becomes clear when looking at typical future scenarios: users will not only carry their data but also their applications and profiles with them. This may mean switching from planning a project on a desktop system to a collaborative setting in a meeting and further to a mobile or public display setting where a mobile device is used for creating sketches for the first steps in the project. Consequently, applications will evolve from device-oriented to emergent cyber-physical and ubiquitous software in a broad sense, forming interactive and socio-technical systems. This opens manifold possibilities, but also a number of research problems regarding both the development process and the execution environment for those kinds of applications.

The MODIQUITOUS workshop is intended to provide a basis for discussion the adequate solution space. Therefore, it aims to bring together researchers and practitioners focused on different challenges of IUS, including:

- Model-driven architecture (MDA) in the context of IUS
- Advantages and potential problems of using MDA in the IUS domain
- Meta models for IUS, specifically for IUS-related aspects like interaction, different modalities, dynamic distribution, context-awareness, etc.
- Domain-specific models for IUS
- Model-driven generation of (intelligent) IUS
- Model-to-model and model-to-code transformations for IUS development
- Model-driven development and execution architectures, i.e., runtime systems for IUS
- Tools and frameworks for supporting the model-driven development of IUS
- Concepts for context-awareness and self-adaptation of IUS on model and runtime
- Software Engineering aspects of IUS
- Human Computer Interaction aspects of IUS

All these topics are of high relevance to a big part of the EICS community as their use is not restricted to ubiquitous systems and will show new ways for many kinds of new systems like mobile device settings, pervasive computing and social software.

FORMAT
This half-day workshop aims to provide a forum for discussing new ideas, issues and solutions in model-driven design of IUS. To this end, we invite participants with different academic or industrial backgrounds, ranging from interaction design, ubiquitous computing, model-driven engineering and context-aware systems. Apart from their scientific contributions, MODIQUITOUS shall cater the community building.

The workshop will include introductory statements, presentations of workshop contributions from participants, demonstrations and discussions regarding the contributions

EICS'11, June 13–16, 2011, Pisa, Italy.
ACM 978-1-4503-0670-6/11/06.

and selected topics from the field of IUS. Candidate submissions include research and position papers as well as demonstrations to achieve an interactive workshop atmosphere and discuss challenges in a real-life setting.

The goal is to create a workshop result in the form of a poster or paper, which can serve as an initial research agenda for the field of model-based approaches for interactive ubiquitous environments.

ORGANIZATION

Co-Organizers

Thomas Schlegel is Junior Professor for Software Engineering of Ubiquitous Systems at the Institute of Software and Multimedia Technology at the Technical University of Dresden. At Fraunhofer IAO from 2002 on, he has organized different seminars, workshops and conferences as well as different scientific events in the frame of the European Network of Excellence I*PROMS as a research cluster leader, member of the executive board and research project leader in diverse international research projects. He serves also as reviewer and member of the program committee in diverse international conferences.

Stefan Pietschmann is research associate and Ph.D. student at the Institute of Software and Multimedia Technology of the Technical University of Dresden. He has been actively involved in several research projects in the field of collaborative and context-aware web applications. In the project CRUISe he specifically addresses the model-driven development of adaptive interactive applications based on the idea of a universal service composition.

Programme Committee

- Uwe Aßmann
  Technical University of Dresden, Germany
- Jan van den Bergh
  Hasselt University, Belgium
- Birgit Bomsdorf
  Fulda University of Applied Sciences, Germany
- Raimund Dachselt
  Otto v. Guericke University Magdeburg, Germany
- Florian Daniel
  University of Trento, Italy
- Alfonso Garcia-Frey
  University of Grenoble, France
- Geert-Jan Houben
  Technical University of Delft, Netherlands
- Heinrich Hussmann
  Ludwig-Maximilian University Munich, Germany
- Sevan Kavaldjian
  Vienna University of Technology, Austria
- Gerrit Meixner
  DFKI, Germany
- Philippe Palanque
  University of Toulouse, France
- Fabiò Paterno
  CNR-ISTI, Italy
- Michael Raschke
  University of Stuttgart, Germany
- Dirk Roscher
  Technical University Berlin, Germany
- Enrico Rukzio
  University Duisburg-Essen, German)
- Stefan Sauer
  University of Paderborn, Germany
- Thomas Springer
  Technical University of Dresden, Germany
- Gerhard Weber
  Technical University of Dresden, Germany
- Anette Weisbecker
  Fraunhofer IAO Stuttgart, Germany
- Jürgen Ziegler
  University Duisburg-Essen, Germany

PARTICIPANTS

The workshop aims to bring together researchers and practitioners working on different aspects of IUS or related areas, such as: model-driven design of interactive applications; interaction design; models for interaction and dynamic distribution; models and systems for self-adaptive interactive applications, software engineering of ubiquitous systems, etc.

WORKSHOP CONTENTS

Candidate submissions cover a wide range of aspects, which are discussed in the context of existing works and addressed with adequate models or model-based systems.

The workshop will include papers targeting the development cycle of ubiquitous systems, giving an overview on existing models their relation to the individual phases of development. New models and methodologies are presented, such as privacy models for ubiquitous systems and how they can actively support requirements engineering. Also, reusable models for representing context features for context-aware appliances are discussed.

Papers addressing model-driven architectures and model usage include approaches for model-based testing of ubiquitous systems, model-based generation concepts for interactive, service-enabled appliances, and platform-independent multi-touch technologies integrating with pervasive sensor and communication components.

Finally, highlighting the interaction aspect, new user interface and interaction concepts are presented, taking into consideration interaction models, current and future modalities as well as requirements from sensors and backend systems.

AFTER THE CONFERENCE

The community benefits from a wide distribution and availability of the papers presented at the workshop. Contributions and workshop results will be available in a as proceedings on the workshop website.

Pattern-Driven Engineering of Interactive Computing Systems (PEICS)

Marc Seissler
University of Kaiserslautern
67663 Kaiserslautern, Germany
Marc.Seissler@mv.uni-kl.de

Kai Breiner
University of Kaiserslautern
67663 Kaiserslautern, Germany
Breiner@cs.uni-kl.de

Gerrit Meixner
German Research Center for Artificial Intelligence (DFKI)
67663 Kaiserslautern, Germany
Gerrit.Meixner@dfki.de

Peter Forbrig
University of Rostock
18051 Rostock, Germany
Peter.Forbrig@uni-rostock.de

Ahmed Seffah
Troyes University of Technology
10000, Troyes, Aube France
Ahmed.Seffah@utt.fr

Kerstin Kloeckner
Fraunhofer Institute for Experimental Software Engineering (IESE)
67663 Kaiserslautern, Germany
Kerstin.Kloeckner@iese.fraunhofer.de

ABSTRACT

Since almost one decade HCI pattern languages are one popular form of design knowledge representations which can be used to facilitate the exchange of best practices, knowledge and design experience between the interdisciplinary team members and allow the formalization of different user interface aspects. Since patterns usually describe the rational in which context they should be applied (when), why a certain pattern should be used in a specific use context (why) and how to implement the solution part (how) they are suitable to describe different user interface aspects in a constructive way.

But despite intense research activities in the last years, HCI pattern languages still lack in a *lingua franca*, a common language for the standardized description and organization of the pattern. This makes it difficult to design suitable tools that support the developers in applying HCI patterns in model-based user interface development (MBUID) processes. To enable the constructive use of HCI patterns in the model-based development process the informal textual, or graphical notation of HCI patterns has to be overcome.

Besides that, evaluating the effectiveness of a pattern, i.e. when is a pattern a "good" pattern is an important issue that has to be tackled to fully benefit from HCI patterns and to improve their applicability in future design processes.

Author Keywords: HCI Pattern, UX Pattern, Model-Based Development, Pattern Formalization.

EICS'11, June 13–16, 2011, Pisa, Italy.
ACM 978-1-4503-0670-6/11/06.

ACM Classification Keywords

D.2.2 **[Software Engineering]**: Design Tools and Techniques – evolutionary prototyping, user interfaces. D.3.3 **[Programming Language]**: Language Constructs and Features – Patterns.

H.5.2 **[Information Interfaces and Presentation]**: User interfaces - Standardization, Ergonomics, Theory and methods.

General Terms

Documentation, Design, Experimentation, Human Factors, Standardization, Languages.

THEME, GOALS, AND RELEVANCE

Goals of the workshop:

- Pattern organization which allows the use of patterns within the different development-phases of a model-based user interface development process (task/concept, AUI, CUI, FUI).
- Formal description of the solution-part which overcomes the textual representation of patterns and enables the instantiation of patterns.
- Pattern Languages as formalization of designers knowledge
- How to measure effectiveness of a pattern
- Empirical evaluation of patterns
- How to insert quality factors into pattern language
- How to design an interactive computing system from one or more pattern languages

Potential outcome of the workshop:

- A specification of different abstraction levels for patterns
- A concept for an improved pattern retrieval

- A concept for instantiation of pattern solutions and integration into models
- A concept for the multi-platform-use of patterns
- A methodology how patterns can be integrated into runtime-adaptive user interfaces
- A concept how to guide developers in the design of usable user interfaces
- A concept to formalize user interface aspects in a constructive, reusable way
- A common language for designers, engineers and ergonomic experts that allows the communication and reuse of good design solutions.

ORGANIZATION

Marc Seissler received his diploma in computer science (2009) from the University of Kaiserslautern. Since July 2009 he is working as a researcher and PhD candidate at the center for human machine interaction (ZMMI) at the University of Kaiserslautern.

Kai Breiner holds a diploma degree in Computer Science of the University of Kaiserslautern. Since August 2006, he has been working as a scientist at the Software Engineering Research Group at the computer science department of the University of Kaiserslautern as well as at the Fraunhofer-Institute for Experimental Software Engineering (IESE).

Gerrit Meixner got his diploma and his master degree in Computer Science from the University of Applied Sciences Trier and a doctoral degree in Mechanical Engineering from the University of Kaiserslautern. Currently he is a senior researcher and group supervisor for Human-Machine-Interaction at the German Research Center for Artificial Intelligence (DFKI) in Kaiserslautern, Germany.

Peter Forbrig is a full professor of software engineering at the University of Rostock in Germany. He got his PhD in compiler construction and his habilitation in software engineering methods.

Ahmed Seffah is currently a professor at UTT Troyes France and adjunct associate professor and the Research chair on Human-Centered Software Engineering at Concordia University. He got his Ph.D and habilitation from Ecole Centrale de Lyon (France).

Kerstin Kloeckner has a diploma degree in Computational Linguistics. Currently, she is a project leader at the Fraunhofer Institute for Experimental Software Engineering (IESE) in the Information System Development (ISD) department.

FORMAT

During workshop

After a brief introduction to the workshop, there will be a keynote presentation held by an invited speaker giving an introduction into the field of HCI patterns. In a short "madness" presentation each of the participants will have to summarize the addressed problem, their solution idea, (expected) benefit as well as the action taken. Since the slides have to be made available to the organizers in advance, these presentations will already be clustered with respect to affinity. According to the presented major topics, there will be several discussion groups preparing their contribution towards a general roadmap (ideally comprising all the actions out of the madness presentations) which we will then create during a final presentation of the workshop outcome followed by a plenary discussion.

After workshop

We consider publishing the presented papers in form of CEUR proceedings within a reasonable time after the workshop. Furthermore, the results of the discussion groups are intended to be included as short papers as part of these proceedings. The participants of the group discussion will be the authors of these short papers.

DATE

The workshop is planned as a half-day workshop starting at 14:00 (after lunch) and finishing at 17:30 (3.5 hours including short breaks).

PARTICIPANTS

The workshop is planned to be organized at EICS, and therefore it will focus on the engineering of interactive systems based on HCI patterns integrated e.g. in model-driven development processes. Our deliberate intention is to attract a heterogeneous audience bringing together software engineers, designers and especially user experience specialists that may bring in their expertise with respect to the evaluation and classification of the usefulness of patterns. We hope to attract at least 7 up to 10 participants to get lively discussions in heterogeneous working groups.

PREVIOUS WORKSHOPS

This workshop will be the second workshop focusing on pattern-driven engineering of interactive computing systems. The first PEICS workshop has been conducted at the EICS 2010.

Also, this workshop is a spin-off of our very successful Model- Driven Development of Advanced User Interfaces (MDDAUI)-workshop series. The increasing demand for HCI pattern integration in model-driven user interface development processes was the key reason for establishing this spin-off workshop.

PLAN FOR ADVERTISEMENT

One of the organizers will act as publicity chair and will distribute the CfP at different mailing lists (ACM SIGCHI, British HCI news, Planet MDE, SEWorld etc.), trough different groups and associations (ACM, UPA, GI, IFIP HFES etc.) and through personal contacts of the program committee. Since the aim is to establish an active community all the previous authors will of course be contacted.

PAPER PUBLICATION

It is planned that the accepted workshop papers will be published as CEUR workshop proceedings.

COPYRIGHT

The authors of the published workshop papers will be the copyright holder of their paper. The organizer of the workshop will be the copyright holder of the complete proceedings.

Engineering Interactive Computer Systems for Medicine and Healthcare (EICS4Med)

Ann Blandford
UCLIC
University College London
London WC1E 6BT
United Kingdom
a.blandford@ucl.ac.uk

Giuseppe De Pietro & Luigi Gallo
ICAR-CNR
Via Pietro Castellino 111
80131 Naples, Italy
{giuseppe.depietro, luigi.gallo}@na.icar.cnr.it

Andy Gimblett, Patrick Oladimeji & Harold Thimbleby
FIT Lab
Swansea University
Swansea, Wales, SA2 8PP
{a.m.gimblett, p.oladimeji, h.thimbleby}@swansea.ac.uk

ABSTRACT

This workshop brings together and develops the community of researchers and practitioners concerned with the design and evaluation of interactive medical devices (infusion pumps, etc) and systems (electronic patient records, etc), to deliver a roadmap for future research in this area. The workshop involves researchers and practitioners designing and evaluating dependable systems in a variety of contexts, and those developing innovative interactive computer systems for healthcare. These pose particular challenges because of the inherent variability — of patients, system configurations, and so on. Participants will represent a range of perspectives, including safety engineering and innovative design.

The **focus** is: ***engineering safe and acceptable interactive healthcare systems***.

The **aim** is: ***develop a roadmap for future research on interactive healthcare systems***.

Author Keywords

Medical devices; healthcare; HCI; interaction technologies; handheld devices; advanced user interfaces; mobile computing; modeling; formal methods; safety.

ACM Classification Keywords

H5.m. Information interfaces and presentation (e.g. HCI): Miscellaneous.

General Term

Human Factors.

THEME, GOALS, AND RELEVANCE

Modern healthcare is relying increasingly on a variety of devices, both in hospitals and by patients or their carers at home. It is vital that they are both reliable and easy to use: that they are well-engineered dependable systems that inter-operate with many other systems in the context of use. Yet healthcare systems are increasingly characterized by the diversity of devices and use contexts. Systems exploit evolving technologies such as mobile devices, location and tracking tools, as well as wearable, portable, and implantable medical sensors. Furthermore, healthcare systems are increasingly characterized by the diversity of their users. Designing highly interactive computing systems to take advantage of the potential of such a variety of devices and contexts to deliver reliable solutions to real problems is a major challenge. Estimates of the number of preventable adverse events in healthcare vary, but are generally agreed to be around 10% of patients in most advanced healthcare systems. Many of these events involve errors with interactive medical systems. Some of these systems are used by people without extensive training; if nurses, doctors or patients misread the systems or, for example, make slips when setting up drug doses then this can result in incorrect treatment, and may even kill.

The design requirements of interactive medical systems are different to the main thrust of interaction design, which is often more concerned with user experience and efficiency. Instead, dependability is essential: trustworthiness of a computing system that allows a user to rely on the service it delivers and on the data that is provided; this includes predictability (for the user), rigor (for the developer), and appropriate integration between the two: solid engineering that results in interactive systems consistent with their documentation and requirements of use.

Healthcare is certainly complex. Designs are regulated and (most) systems certified by national and international organisations. Typically, systems are procured by hospitals in large quantities, and consistency, compatibility and interoperability between systems is a serious issue. Features appear to make devices more useful, yet increasing numbers of features increases risks of feature selection errors during use. Manufacturers are businesses, and commercial pressures do not yet significantly drive dependability, particularly in areas of user error identified after a system design is certified, since certification implies that the design is "right" and that any resultant harm is the responsibility of the medical practitioners.

The purpose of this workshop, then, is to build a community of researchers developing complementary but

EICS'11, June 13–16, 2011, Pisa, Italy.
ACM 978-1-4503-0670-6/11/06.

interconnected approaches to engineering dependable and innovative interactive medical systems.

The EICS community is centrally concerned with rigorous approaches to the design and evaluation of interactive computer systems, across a range of domains. Medical systems (by which we mean configurations of medical devices and information systems, together with professionals and lay people working to improve the health of a patient) are particularly challenging examples of such systems, being safety-critical, highly reconfigurable, and diverse. These systems therefore "stress" the disciplinary approaches being explored within the EICS community by presenting particularly challenging examples for modeling, especially with highly-complex non-computerised contexts.

This workshop will bring together members of the EICS community, and others working in related fields, to exchange insights into approaches to designing, engineering, representing and reasoning about interactive medical systems to ensure their dependability. This will result in fertile knowledge exchange, the identification of synergies between approaches, and the development of a roadmap for future research in this area.

FORMAT

The workshop will be all day, with a (self-pay) meal in the evening. Participants will present their position papers briefly as a form of introduction and to set the context. Most of the workshop will be devoted to breakout group activities, focusing on approaches to ensuring dependability, complementarity between approaches, gaps in the research agenda, and to specify future directions. The later afternoon session will draw threads together and develop a roadmap of future research agenda, including a consideration of future events to develop this community. A web report of the workshop will be made available after the event, summarizing key points from the discussions and activities.

ORGANIZATION

Ann Blandford is Professor of Human–Computer Interaction and Director of UCL Interaction Centre, and is Deputy Chair of IFIP WG2.7/13.4. She leads major EPSRC research projects on interaction design for medical devices.

Giuseppe De Pietro is a Senior Researcher at the ICAR-CNR and a grant professor of Information Systems at the Second University of Naples. His research interests cover pervasive computing and Virtual Reality environments.

Luigi Gallo is a Research Fellow at the ICAR-CNR. His current research is focused on human interface aspects of medical visualization. He is a member of ACM and a featured member of KES Intelligent Systems Society.

Andy Gimblett is a Research Assistant in Swansea University's Future Interaction Technology Lab. His current research is focused on linguistic approaches to user interface design and analysis.

Patrick Oladimeji is a Research Assistant in Swansea University's Future Interaction Technology Lab. His research interests include safety-critical interaction design and interactive information visualisation.

Harold Thimbleby is Professor of Computer Science in Swansea University's FIT Lab. He is the author or editor of a number of books, including *Press On* (2007) and *User Interface Design* (1990), and nearly 400 other publications.

WORKSHOP CONTENT

Contributors to the workshop have submitted the following position statements and papers. This gives an indication of the breadth of interest and topics the workshop addresses.

1. Blandford, A., Cauchi, A., Curzon, P., Eslambolchilar, P., Furniss, D., Gimblett, A., Harrison, M., Huang, H., Lee, P., Li, Y., Masci, P., Oladimeji, P., Rajkomar, A., Rukšenas, R. and Thimbleby, H. Comparing actual practice and user manuals: a case study based on programmable infusion pumps
2. Cabitza, F., Corna, S., Gesso, I. and Simone, C. WOAD, a platform to deploy flexible EPRs in full control of end-users
3. Carbone, M., Condino, S., Ferrari, V., Ferrari, M. and Mosca, F. Surgical simulators integrating virtual and physical anatomies
4. Catarci, T., D'Addario, M., Felli, P., Franceschetti, L., Lembo, D., Mecella, M., Pipan, T., Russo, A., Vestri, A. and Villari, P. User-centered design for citizens' empowerment through the portal of the italian ministry of health
5. Cauchi, A., Curzon, P., Eslambolchilar, P., Gimblett, A., Harrison, M., Huang, H., Lee, P., Li, Y., Masci, P., Oladimeji, P., Ruksenas, R. and Thimbleby, H. Towards dependable number entry for medical devices
6. Chehri, A.: Survivable and scalable wireless solution for e-health and e-emergency applications
7. De Mauro, A. Virtual reality based rehabilitation and game technology
8. De Paolis, L.T. and Aloisio G. Visualization and interaction system of virtual organs for surgical planning
9. Dittmar, A., Kuhn, R. and Forbrig, P. Coordination in perioperative systems – a tacit view
10. Ferrari, V., Ferrari, M. and Mosca, F. Video see-through in the clinical practice
11. Forsslund, J., Pysander, E-L.S. and Palmerius K-J.L. Design of perceptualization applications in medicine
12. Furniss, D., Blandford, A., Rajkomar, A., Vincent, C. and Mayer, A. The visible and the invisible: distributed cognition for medical devices
13. Mentler, T. and Kindsmüller, M.C. Care & prepare – usability engineering for mass casualty incidents
14. Wicht, A., Meixner, G. and Klein, U. Design and prototypical development of a web based decision support system for early detection of sepsis in hematology

Author Index

www.ingramcontent.com/pod-product-compliance
Lightning Source LLC
Chambersburg PA
CBHW080907220326
41598CB00034B/5504
9781450313865